QBasic

Fundamentals & Style

Second Edition
with an Introduction
to Microsoft® Visual Basic®

James S. Quasney
John Maniotes
Roy O. Foreman

Purdue University Calumet

COURSE TECHNOLOGY
ONE MAIN STREET
CAMBRIDGE MA 02142

Thomson Learning™

Australia • Canada • Denmark • Japan • Mexico • New Zealand • Philippines
Puerto Rico • Singapore • South Africa • Spain • United Kingdom • United States

Asia (excluding Japan)
Thomson Learning
60 Albert Street, #15-01
Albert Complex
Singapore 189969

Japan
Thomson Learning
Palaceside Building 5F
1-1-1 Hitotsubashi, Chiyoda-ku
Tokyo 100 0003 Japan

Australia/New Zealand
Nelson/Thomson Learning
102 Dodds Street
South Melbourne, Victoria 3205
Australia

Latin America
Thomson Learning
Seneca, 53
Colonia Polanco
11560 Mexico D.F. Mexico

South Africa
Thomson Learning
Zonnebloem Building,
Constantia Square
526 Sixteenth Road
P.O. Box 2459
Halfway House, 1685
South Africa

Canada
Nelson/Thomson Learning
1120 Birchmount Road
Scarborough, Ontario
Canada M1K 5G4

UK/Europe/Middle East
Thomson Learning
Berkshire House
168-173 High Holborn
London, WC1V 7AA United Kingdom

Spain
Thomson Learning
Calle Magallanes, 25
28015-MADRID
ESPANA

ISBN 0-619-01625-6

5 6 7 8 9 10   BC   04 03

C O N T E N T S

Preface	viii
Notes to the Student	xv
List of Programming Case Studies	xvi

Chapter 1   Computers and Problem Solving: An Introduction

1.1 WHAT IS A COMPUTER?	1
Advantages of a Computer	1
Disadvantages of a Computer	1
1.2 COMPUTER HARDWARE	2
Input	3
Output	3
Main Memory	3
Auxiliary Storage	3
Central Processing Unit (CPU)	3
1.3 THE PC FAMILY	4
Keyboard	5
Monitor	5
CPU and Main Memory Unit	6
Auxiliary Storage	7
Network System	8
1.4 THE STORED PROGRAM CONCEPT	8
1.5 COMPUTER SOFTWARE	8
The Internet	10
The Operating System	10
The Graphical User Interface	11
The Compiler and the Interpreter	12
1.6 PROBLEM SOLVING AND PROGRAM DEVELOPMENT	12
Flowcharts	13
Pseudocode	14
1.7 ADDITIONAL INFORMATION ON PERSONAL COMPUTERS	16
1.8 WHAT YOU SHOULD KNOW	16
1.9 TEST YOUR QBASIC SKILLS	17
1.10 PC HANDS-ON EXERCISES	19

Chapter 2   QBasic: An Introduction

2.1 CREATING A QBASIC PROGRAM	21
General Characteristics of a QBasic Program	21
Keywords	22
Variable Names and Constants	22
Arithmetic Operators	23
The PRINT Statement	23
The END Statement	23
Some Relationships between Statements	23
2.2 THE INPUT STATEMENT	24
Input Prompt Message	26
2.3 THE PRINT AND CLS STATEMENTS	28
Clearing the Screen — The CLS Statement	29

2.4 CODING AND DOCUMENTING	29
Coding Techniques	29
Documenting a Program — The REM Statement	30
Program Flowcharts	32
Multiple Statements per Line	32
2.5 GETTING ACQUAINTED WITH THE QB OPERATING ENVIRONMENT	32
Starting a QBasic Session	32
The QBasic Screen	33
Dialog Boxes	35
Terminating a QBasic Session	35
2.6 EDITING QBASIC PROGRAMS	35
2.7 EXECUTING PROGRAMS AND HARD COPY OUTPUT	37
Executing the Current Program	37
Listing Program Lines on the Printer	38
Listing a Portion of the Program on the Printer	39
Printing the Results on the Output Screen	39
2.8 SAVING, LOADING, AND ERASING PROGRAMS	40
File Specifications	40
Saving the Current Program to Disk	40
Loading a Program from Disk	41
Starting a New Program	42
2.9 THE QB SURVIVAL GUIDE ONLINE HELP SYSTEM	42
2.10 A GUIDE TO WRITING YOUR FIRST PROGRAM	43
2.11 WHAT YOU SHOULD KNOW	46
2.12 TEST YOUR QBASIC SKILLS	48
2.13 QBASIC PROGRAMMING PROBLEMS	50

Chapter 3   Calculations, Strings, and an Introduction to the Top-Down Approach

3.1 INTRODUCTION	55
3.2 CONSTANTS	56
Numeric Constants	56
Numeric Constants in Exponential Form	57
Type and Range of Numeric Constants	58
String Constants	59
3.3 VARIABLES	60
Selection of Variable Names	61
Declaring Variable Types	62
3.4 THE LET STATEMENT	62
3.5 EXPRESSIONS	65
Formation of Numeric Expressions	65
Evaluation of Numeric Expressions	66
The Effect of Parentheses in the Evaluation of Numeric Expressions	67
Construction of Error-Free Numeric Expressions	69
Numeric Functions	70
Rounding and Truncation	70
Developing a Rounding and Truncation Procedure	70

String Expressions 71
Use of LEFT$, LEN, MID$, and RIGHT$
String Functions 72

3.6 THE TOP-DOWN (MODULAR) APPROACH AND THE GOSUB AND RETURN STATEMENTS 73
Top-Down Design 74
High-Level Design 74
Detailed Design 76
Implementing a Top-Down Design Using Subroutines (Modules) 76
The GOSUB and RETURN Statements 77
Recommended Style and Tips When Using the Top-Down Approach 79
More about Subroutines 79
Flowchart Representation of GOSUB, RETURN, and Referenced Subroutine 79
Nested Subroutines 80
Stubs 82

3.7 WHAT YOU SHOULD KNOW 82
3.8 TEST YOUR QBASIC SKILLS 84
3.9 QBASIC PROGRAMMING PROBLEMS 88

Chapter 4 Looping and Input/Output

4.1 INTRODUCTION 95
Testing for the End-of-File 99
4.2 THE DO AND LOOP STATEMENTS 100
Selecting the Proper Do Loop for a Program 101
Conditions 101
4.3 THE READ, DATA, AND RESTORE STATEMENTS 103
The DATA Statement 103
The READ Statement 104
The RESTORE Statement 106
4.4 THE PRINT STATEMENT 107
Print Zones and Print Positions 108
Representation of Numeric Output 108
Representation of String Output 108
Use of the Comma Separator 108
Use of the Semicolon Separator 109
Creating Blank Lines 109
Use of the TAB Function 109
Displaying Spaces — The SPC Function 110
Calculations within the PRINT Statement 110
Using the Immediate Window 111
The LPRINT Statement 111
4.5 THE PRINT USING STATEMENT FOR FORMATTED OUTPUT 112
Declaring the Format of the Output 113
Format Symbols 113
The Number Sign Symbol 113
The Decimal Point (Period) Symbol 116
The Comma Symbol 116
The Plus and Minus Sign Symbols 117
The Dollar Sign Symbol 118
The Asterisk Symbol 118
Formatted Character String Output 119
The LPRINT USING Statement 121
4.6 THE LOCATE STATEMENT 126

4.7 WHAT YOU SHOULD KNOW 131
4.8 TEST YOUR QBASIC SKILLS 132
4.9 QBASIC PROGRAMMING PROBLEMS 136

Chapter 5 Structured Programming and Menu-Driven Programs

5.1 STRUCTURED PROGRAMMING 143
Control Structures 144
Combining Conditions 145
Top-Down versus Structured 145
5.2 THE IF STATEMENT 145
Comparing Numeric Expressions 147
Comparing String Expressions 147
Values of Conditions 148
5.3 ACCUMULATORS 149
Counters 149
Running Totals 149
Programming Styles 154
5.4 IMPLEMENTING THE DO-WHILE AND DO-UNTIL STRUCTURES 155
The WHILE and WEND Statements 156
5.5 IMPLEMENTING THE IF-THEN-ELSE STRUCTURE 156
Simple Forms of the If-Then-Else Structure 156
Nested Forms of the If-Then-Else Structure 158
5.6 LOGICAL OPERATORS 160
The NOT Logical Operator 160
The AND Logical Operator 161
The OR Logical Operator 162
The XOR, EQV, and IMP Logical Operators 163
Truth Tables 164
Combining Logical Operators 164
The Effect of Parentheses in the Evaluation of Compound Conditions 165
5.7 DATA-VALIDATION TECHNIQUES 166
The BEEP Statement 166
The Reasonableness Check 167
The Range Check 167
The Value or Code Check 168
The Digit Check 168
5.8 THE SELECT CASE STATEMENT AND MENU-DRIVEN PROGRAMS 169
Valid Match Expressions 172
5.9 WHAT YOU SHOULD KNOW 181
5.10 TEST YOUR QBASIC SKILLS 182
5.11 QBASIC PROGRAMMING PROBLEMS 188

Chapter 6 Sequential Files, Paging Reports, and Control-Break Processing

6.1 INTRODUCTION 197
6.2 DATA FILES 197
File Organization 199
6.3 SEQUENTIAL FILE PROCESSING 199
Opening Sequential Files 199
Closing Sequential Files 201
Writing Reports to a Sequential File 202

Flowchart of the **OPEN** and **CLOSE** Statements 206
Writing Data to a Sequential File 206
The **INPUT #n** Statement 211
The **EOF** Function 212
6.4 PAGING A REPORT 213
Paging Output on the Screen 218
6.5 CONTROL-BREAK PROCESSING 219
6.6 WHAT YOU SHOULD KNOW 230
6.7 TEST YOUR QBASIC SKILLS 231
6.8 QBASIC PROGRAMMING PROBLEMS 233

Argument-Organized Tables 276
Serial Search 277
Ordering the Table Arguments
for a Serial Search 280
Binary Search 281
Combining Table-Access Methods 284
Some Formulae for Searching 284
7.9 WHAT YOU SHOULD KNOW 285
7.10 TEST YOUR QBASIC SKILLS 287
7.11 QBASIC PROGRAMMING PROBLEMS 292

Chapter 7 FOR Loops, Arrays, Sorting, and Table Processing

7.1 INTRODUCTION 241
7.2 THE FOR AND NEXT STATEMENTS 242
The Do-While Loop versus the For Loop 242
The Execution of a For Loop 242
Flowchart Representation of a For Loop 244
Valid Values in the **FOR** Statement 244
Stepping by 1 245
Stepping by a Value Other than 1 246
Initializing the Loop Variable to a Value
Other than 1 246
Decimal Fraction Values in a **FOR** Statement 246
Negative Values in a **FOR** Statement 246
Variables in a **FOR** Statement 246
Expressions as Values in a **FOR** Statement 247
Initial Entry into a For Loop 247
Redefining For Loop Values 247
Exiting a For Loop Prematurely —
the **EXIT** Statement 248
Iterations in a For Loop 249
Another Look at the For Loop 250
Nested For Loops 250
Valid Nesting of For Loops 252
7.3 ARRAYS VERSUS SIMPLE VARIABLES 253
7.4 DECLARING ARRAYS 254
The **DIM** Statement 254
The **OPTION BASE** Statement 256
Dynamic Allocation of Arrays 256
7.5 MANIPULATING ARRAYS 257
Subscripts 257
Summing the Elements of an Array 258
7.6 MULTIDIMENSIONAL ARRAYS 264
Manipulating Two-Dimensional Arrays 264
Initializing Arrays 265
Arrays with More than Two Dimensions 265
Determining the Lower- and Upper-Bound
Subscript Values of an Array 266
7.7 SORTING 267
The Bubble Sort 268
The **SWAP** Statement 269
Implementing the Bubble Sort 269
The Shell Sort 272
7.8 TABLE PROCESSING 274
Table Organization 274
Positionally-Organized Tables 274

Chapter 8 More on Strings and Functions

8.1 INTRODUCTION 299
8.2 STRING FUNCTIONS AND STATEMENTS 299
Concatenation, Substrings, and Character
Counting Revisited — **+, LEN, LEFT$,
RIGHT$,** and **MID$** Functions 300
Substring Searching and Replacement —
INSTR Function and **MID$** Statement 303
Converting Character Codes — **ASC**
and **CHR$** Functions 305
Changing Case — **LCASE$**
and **UCASE$** Functions 306
Modifying Data Types — **STR$**
and **VAL** Functions 308
Duplicating Strings — **SPACE$**
and **STRING$** Functions 309
Trimming Blank Characters — **LTRIM$**
and **RTRIM$** Functions 309
Accessing the System Time and Date —
DATE$** and **TIME$ Functions 310
Setting the Time and Date — **DATE$**
and **TIME$** Statements 314
Accepting String Data — **LINE INPUT**
Statement, **INKEY$** and **INPUT$** Functions 314
8.3 NUMERIC FUNCTIONS 316
Arithmetic Functions — **ABS, FIX, INT,
CINT,** and **SGN** 317
Generalized Procedures for Rounding
and Truncation 318
Exponential Functions — **SQR, EXP,** and **LOG** 318
Trigonometric Functions — **SIN, COS, TAN,**
and **ATN** 322
Utility Functions — **POS, CSRLIN,** and **SCREEN** 322
Performance Testing — **TIMER** Function 323
Random Number Function
and the **RANDOMIZE** Statement 324
8.4 USER-DEFINED FUNCTIONS 329
The **DEF FN** Statement 329
Referencing User-Defined Functions 331
8.5 TRAPPING EVENTS 335
8.6 WHAT YOU SHOULD KNOW 337
8.7 TEST YOUR QBASIC SKILLS 337
8.8 QBASIC PROGRAMMING PROBLEMS 341

Chapter 9   File Maintenance, Random File Processing, and Simulated-Indexed Files

9.1 INTRODUCTION   349
   Random Files   349
   Indexed Files   349
9.2 FILE MAINTENANCE   350
9.3 RANDOM FILE PROCESSING   364
   Opening and Closing Random Files   364
   Creating the Record Structure
      for a Random File — The TYPE Statement   365
   The GET and PUT Statements   367
   The LOC and LOF Functions   368
9.4 SIMULATED-INDEXED FILES   375
   Part 1 Tasks: Build Index File   376
   Part 2: Displaying and Updating Records
      in the Simulated-Indexed File   379
9.5 WHAT YOU SHOULD KNOW   389
9.6 TEST YOUR QBASIC SKILLS   390
9.7 QBASIC PROGRAMMING PROBLEMS   391

Chapter 10   Computer Graphics and Sound

10.1 INTRODUCTION   397
   PC Graphics Modes   399
   The SCREEN and WIDTH Statements   401
   The WIDTH Statement   402
10.2 TEXT-MODE GRAPHICS   403
   The COLOR Statement for Text Mode   411
   Suspending Execution of a Program   414
10.3 MEDIUM-RESOLUTION AND
      HIGH-RESOLUTION GRAPHICS   418
   The COLOR Statement for
      Medium-Resolution Graphics Mode   419
   The PSET and PRESET Statements   420
   The LINE Statement   421
   The CIRCLE Statement   423
   The PAINT Statement   425
   Tiling   426
   The DRAW Statement   428
   The WINDOW Statement   431
   The PMAP and POINT Functions   432
   The VIEW Statement   434
   The GET and PUT Statements for Graphics   435
10.4 SOUND AND MUSIC   437
   The SOUND Statement   438
   The PLAY Statement   439
10.5 WHAT YOU SHOULD KNOW   440
10.6 TEST YOUR QBASIC SKILLS   442
10.7 QBASIC PROGRAMMING PROBLEMS   447

Chapter 11   Subprograms, Functions, and Chaining

11.1 INTRODUCTION   453
11.2 SUBPROGRAMS   453
   Subroutines versus Subprograms   453
   Types of Subprograms   455
   Parameters and Arguments   455
   Passing No Values to a Subprogram   456
   Passing Constants and Expressions   456
   Passing Variables and Individual Array Elements   458
   Passing an Entire Array   459
   Passing Values between Subprograms   460
   Sharing Variables with Individual Subprograms   460
   Sharing Variables with All Associated
      Subprograms   462
11.3 USING THE QBASIC EDITOR
      TO ENTER SUBPROGRAMS   463
   Editing Subprograms   465
   Splitting the View Window   467
   Saving, Loading, and Executing the Main
      Program and Associated Subprograms   468
   Printing the Main Program
      and Associated Subprograms   468
11.4 FUNCTIONS   469
   An Example of a Recursive Function   471
   Using the QBasic Editor to Enter Functions   473
11.5 CHAINING   477
11.6 WHAT YOU SHOULD KNOW   479
11.7 TEST YOUR QBASIC SKILLS   480
11.8 QBASIC PROGRAMMING PROBLEMS   482

Chapter 12   An Introduction to Visual Basic

12.1 WHAT IS VISUAL BASIC?   483
12.2 THE THREE-STEP APPROACH TO BUILDING
      APPLICATIONS WITH VISUAL BASIC   484
   Create the Interface   484
   Set Properties   485
   Write Code   486
   Methods   488
   Functions   489
12.3 THE VISUAL BASIC ENVIRONMENT   489
12.4 BUILDING A CURRENCY CONVERSION
      APPLICATION   491
12.5 CREATING THE INTERFACE FOR THE
      CURRENCY APPLICATION   491
   Setting the Size of a Form   492
   Positioning a Form   493
   Adding and Removing Controls   493
   Changing the Location and Size of Controls   496
12.6 SETTING PROPERTIES FOR THE
      CURRENCY APPLICATION   496
   The Caption Property   496
   The Text Property   497
   The BorderStyle Property   498
   The Name Property   498

12.7 WRITING CODE FOR THE CURRENCY CONVERSION APPLICATION 500
12.8 SAVING A VISUAL BASIC PROJECT 501
12.9 STARTING, OPENING, AND RUNNING PROJECTS 502
Starting a New Project 503
Opening a Project 503
Running an Application 504
12.10 EXITING VISUAL BASIC 504
12.11 WHAT YOU SHOULD KNOW 504
12.12 VISUAL BASIC APPLICATION PROBLEMS 505

Appendix A Program Design Tools — Flowcharts, Pseudocode, Nassi-Schneiderman Charts, and Warnier-Orr diagrams

A.1 PROGRAM FLOWCHARTING 507
Purpose of Flowcharting 507
Flowchart Notation 507
A.2 GUIDELINES FOR PREPARATION OF FLOWCHARTS 510
Straight-Line Flowcharts 510
Flowcharts with Looping 510
A.3 CONTROL STRUCTURES 512
A.4 PROPER PROGRAMS 514
A.5 FLOWCHARTING TIPS 514
A.6 PSEUDOCODE 516
A.7 NASSI-SCHNEIDERMAN CHARTS 518
A.8 WARNIER-ORR DIAGRAMS 519
A.9 TEST YOUR QBASIC SKILLS 521

Appendix B Menu Commands and Windows

B.1 SELECTION COMMANDS 525
B.2 THE QBASIC MENU BAR 526
The File Menu 526
The Edit Menu 527
The View Menu 527
The Search Menu 528
The Run Menu 529
The Debug Menu 529
The Options Menu 530
The Help Menu 531
B.3 USING WINDOWS TO YOUR ADVANTAGE 532
Changing the Active Window 532
Changing the Window Size 532
Scrolling in the Active Window 532

Appendix C QBasic Debugging Techniques and Programming Tips

C.1 DEBUGGING TECHNIQUES 533
Examining Values through the Immediate Window 533
Executing One Statement At a Time 534
Setting Breakpoints 534
Tracing 535
Set Next Statement 535

C.2 TRAPPING USER ERRORS (ON ERROR GOTO AND RESUME) 535
C.3 PROGRAMMING TIPS 539
C.4 PROGRAM STYLE TIPS 541

Appendix D ASCII Character Set and Personal Computer Literature and Web Sites

D.1 ASCII CHARACTER CODES 543
D.2 PERSONAL COMPUTER MAGAZINES, NEWSPAPERS, AND URLS 543
Personal Computer Magazines 545
Personal Computer Newspapers 545
URLs 545

Appendix E Answers to the Even-Numbered Test Your QBasic Skills Exercises 547

INDEX 565

QBASIC REFERENCE CARD R.1

P R E F A C E

OBJECTIVES OF THIS BOOK

This book was developed specifically for an introductory computer programming course that utilizes QBasic or the commercial version of Microsoft QuickBASIC. The objectives of this book are as follows:

- To acquaint the reader with the proper and correct way to design and write high quality programs.
- To emphasize the top-down approach, structured programming, and modern programming practices early and consistently throughout the book.
- To teach the fundamentals of the QBasic programming language.
- To teach good problem-solving techniques that can be used in advanced computing and information-processing courses.
- To emphasize interactive applications and menu-driven programs, the most popular type of programming in today's world.
- To develop an exercise-oriented approach that allows the reader to learn by example.
- To use practical problems to illustrate the applications of computers.
- To encourage independent study and help those who are working alone on their own personal computer systems in a distance education or e-education environment.

LEVEL OF INSTRUCTION

No previous experience with a computer is assumed, and no mathematics beyond the high school freshman level is required. The book is written specifically for the student with average ability, for whom continuity, simplicity, and practicality are characteristics we consider essential. Numerous insights, based on the authors' one-hundred cumulative years of experience in teaching and consulting in the field of computer information systems, are implicit throughout the book. For the past thirty-five years, one of us has taught an introductory programming course.

FUNDAMENTAL TOPICS ARE PRESENTED IN DETAIL

In addition to introducing students to the correct way to design and write programs by means of structured and top-down techniques, this book presents fundamental topics concerning computers and programming that should be covered in any introductory programming class. These include the stored program concept; getting acquainted with the computer; editing programs; input/output operations; variables and constants; simple and complex computations; the use of functions, subroutines, and subprograms; decision making; the use of counters and running totals; rounding and truncation; looping and end-of-file tests; counter-controlled loops; the use of relational and logical operators; string manipulation; and graphics and sound. Other essential topics include data validation; control breaks; paging reports; table processing; sequence checking; selection; searching; matching; merging; sorting; file processing; the differences between batch and interactive applications; and an introduction to event-driven programming through the use of Microsoft Visual Basic for Windows. Every one of these topics is covered in detail in this book.

CHAPTER ON MICROSOFT VISUAL BASIC

This text includes a section (Chapter 12) on Microsoft Visual Basic, which introduces the student to event-driven programming. Topics include starting Visual Basic; designing a form and adding labels, text boxes, and command buttons; changing the properties of controls; specifying an event procedure; running and saving applications; and accessing information about Visual Basic through the Help facility.

Students are introduced to the three-step process of building Windows applications:

1. Create the user interface
2. Set properties
3. Write code

Microsoft Visual Basic uses the same programming statements and functions as QBasic. Thus, once the student is able to write programs in QBasic, he or she has the experience to accomplish the third step in creating a Windows application.

HOW TO OBTAIN FREE COPIES OF QBASIC AND BUNDLE THE WORKING MODEL EDITION OF MICROSOFT VISUAL BASIC

QBasic comes free with MS-DOS version 5 and higher. It is also available on the Windows CD-ROM in the folder other/oldmsdos. Microsoft also has available an educational version of Visual Basic called the **Working Model Edition**. The Working Model Edition can be bundled with this textbook for a minimal charge. The major limitation of the Working Model Edition is the inability to convert Visual Basic programs to executable files that run outside of Visual Basic. The Working Model Edition, however, contains all the basic features and functionality necessary to achieve an introductory understanding of Visual Basic.

DISTINGUISHING FEATURES

The distinguishing features of QBasic Fundamentals and Style 2nd Edition include the following:

A Proven Book

This book has evolved over the past thirty years and is based on the authors' ten prior books on BASIC programming. Many instructors and students who have used our books have shared with us their comments and suggestions for improvement as new programming techniques have been developed. They have done much to shape the contents of this book, which reflects modern programming practices.

Early Presentation of the Top-Down (Modular) Approach and the Structured Programming Approach

Students are introduced to the top-down approach early, before they learn about looping and decision making. By the time they get to the larger and more complex programs, they are solving problems top-down by habit.

To implement the top-down approach, this book consistently uses subroutines (GOSUB and RETURN statements), which are easier for beginning students to understand than subprograms (CALL and RETURN statements). In Chapter 3, the student is also introduced to important design concepts, including high-level design, detailed design, and the use of stubs. These design concepts are then used throughout the book. Hence, the student is introduced early to the proper and correct way to design and code a program top down.

Particular attention is given to designing proper programs by means of the three logic structures of structured programming: Sequence; Selection (If-Then-Else and Case); and Repetition (Do-While and Do-Until). A disciplined method for implementing the structured design is adhered to throughout the book.

Early and Complete Coverage of File Processing

Complete coverage of sequential, random, and simulated-indexed files provides the reader with knowledge that is central to a real programming environment. Topics include creating all three types of files; file maintenance (matching and merging operations); and an information retrieval system that features simulated-indexed files. Sequential file processing is covered immediately following the presentation of the top-down approach and structured programming.

Data Disk

The Data Disk includes all the executable programs and data files presented in the text. The Data Disk files can be obtained either from your instructor or electronically from the Course Technology website by connecting to course.com, and then searching for this book title. Students can use the program and data files for the following:

- To step through the **PC Hands-On Exercises** at the end of each chapter
- To select a program similar to their solution for a programming assignment (this will save keying time)
- To experiment on their own with developing alternative solutions to the programming case studies presented in the text
- To access data files required in the programming assignments
- To store their solutions to programming assignments

Program file names are in the form of PRGc-n, where c represents the chapter number and n represents the program number. For example, PRG2-8 refers to the eighth program presented in Chapter 2. Data file names correspond to the names used in the text.

BASIC Programming Problems with Sample Input and Output

Over 60 challenging, field-tested BASIC Programming Problems are included at the end of the chapters. Each of the problems includes a statement of purpose, a problem statement, sample input data, and the corresponding output results. Solutions to these problems are given on the Instructor's Resource Kit (ISBN 0-619-01626-4).

Interactive Applications (Menu-Driven Programs)

Although examples of batch processing are presented, the primary emphasis is on interactive processing. The reader is introduced to the INPUT, PRINT, and CLS (Clear Screen) statements early in Chapter 2. The LOCATE statement is presented in Chapter 4 and thereafter is used extensively to build screens. Several menu-driven programs are illustrated to familiarize the reader with the type of programming that is prevalent today.

Emphasis on the Program Development Life Cycle

The program development life cycle is presented early in Chapter 1 and is used throughout the book. Good design habits are reinforced, and special attention is given to testing the design before attempting to implement the logic in a program.

Emphasis on Fundamentals and Style

Heavy emphasis is placed on the fundamentals of producing well-written and readable programs. A disciplined style is used consistently in all program examples. Thorough documentation and indention standards illuminate the implementation of the Selection and Repetition logic structures. The programming and style tips recommended throughout the book are summarized in Appendix C.

Summary of the QBasic Language on a Reference Card

A summary of the statements, functions, special keys, operators, and reserved words can be found on a reference card at the back of the book. This summary is invaluable to the beginning student as a quick reference tool.

Presentation of Programming Case Studies

This book contains 25 completely solved and annotated case studies, illuminating the use of QBasic and computer programming in the real world. Emphasis is placed on problem analysis, program design, and an in-depth discussion of the program solution. The program solutions to these programming case studies, as well as all other programs found throughout the book, are on the accompanying Data Disk.

Program Design Aids

The authors recognize top-down charts and flowcharting as excellent pedagogical aids and as the tools of an analyst or programmer. Hence, many of the programming case studies include both top-down charts and program flowcharts to demonstrate programming style, design, and documentation.

Debugging Techniques and Programming Tips

A characteristic of a good programmer is that he or she has confidence that a program will work the first time it is executed. This confidence implies that careful attention has been given to the design and that the design has been fully tested. Still, errors do occur; and when they do, they must be corrected. Throughout this book, especially in Appendix C, efficient methods for locating and correcting errors are introduced using the QBasic debugger. Tracing, as well as other debugging techniques, is discussed in detail. The sections in Appendix C that deal with programming tips and style tips serve as excellent references, facilitating the writing of efficient, readable code.

Applications-Oriented Approach

More than 150 QBasic programs, illustrating a wide range of practical applications, along with many partial programs, are used to introduce specific statements and the proper and correct way to write programs.

Emphasis on Data Validation

The reliability of a thoroughly tested program cannot be guaranteed once it is turned over to a user. Most abnormal terminations in a production environment are due to user errors rather than programmer errors. This is especially true for programs that interact with the user or are executed on personal computers. Good programmers will attempt to trap as many user errors as possible. This book pays particular attention to the illustration of various data validation methods for ensuring that incoming data is reasonable or within limits.

What You Should Know

Each chapter contains a succinct, list-formatted review titled, What You Should Know, which reinforces key concepts and computer information system terminology.

Test Your QBasic Skills

A set of short-answer exercises identified as Test Your QBasic Skills appears at the end of each chapter. More than 200 problems, many of which are complete programs, are included for practice. Through the use of these exercises, the student can master the concepts presented, and instructors are afforded a valuable diagnostic tool. Answers for the even-numbered Test Your QBasic Skills exercises are available to the students in Appendix E. Answers to the odd numbered exercises can be found in the Electronic Instructor's Manual described below.

Graphics and Sound

Chapter 10 covers all the graphics statements and functions in QBasic that are central to understanding what can be done with graphics on the PC. The topics provide the student with knowledge of how to create, change, display, and store graphic designs and animation sequences. Furthermore, the necessary sound and music statements are discussed and are applied to various applications.

Additional PC Information

In addition to a general introduction to personal computers in Chapter 1, Appendix D includes a list of popular magazines, newspapers, and Web sites to help keep the student abreast of the new developments in the computer field.

The Internet

The authors recognize the use of the Internet as an excellent source of information. Hence, various chapters include Uniform Resource Locators (URLs) so that the student may select from the Web timely information on such topics as QBasic, programming languages, applications software, and manufacturers of PCs, chips, peripheral equipment, etc.

Instructor's Resource Kit

A comprehensive Instructor's Resource Kit (IRK) accompanies this textbook in the form of a CD-ROM. The CD-ROM includes an Electronic Instructor's Manual and teaching and testing aids. The CD-ROM (ISBN 0-619-01626-4) is available through your Course Technology representative or by calling one of the following telephone numbers: Colleges and Universities, 1-800-648-7450; High Schools, 1-800-824-5179; and Career Colleges, 1-800-477-3692; Canada, 1-800-268-2222; and Corporations and Government Agencies, 1-800-340-7450. The contents of the CD-ROM are listed as follows.

Electronic Instructor's Manual   The Electronic Instructor's Manual consists of Microsoft Word files. The files include lecture notes, solutions to laboratory assignments, and a large test bank. The files allow you to modify the lecture notes or generate quizzes and exams from the test bank using your own word processor. Where appropriate, solutions to laboratory assignments are embedded as icons in the files. When an icon appears, double-click it and the application will start and the solution will display on the screen. The Electronic Instructor's Manual includes the following for each chapter: chapter objectives; chapter overview; detailed lesson plans with page number references; teacher notes and activities; answers to the odd-numbered end-of-chapter exercises; large test bank of true/false, multiple-choice, and fill-in-the-blank questions with page number references; and transparency references. The transparencies are available through the Figures on CD-ROM described below. The test bank questions are numbered the same as in Course Test Manager. Thus, you can print a copy of the chapter test bank and use the printout to select your questions in Course Test Manager.

Course Test Manager   Course Test Manager is a powerful testing and assessment package that enables instructors to create and print tests from our large test bank. In addition, instructors with access to a networked computer lab (LAN) can administer, grade, and track tests online. Students also can take online practice tests, which generate customized study guides that indicate where in the textbook students can find more information for each question.

Instructor's Solutions   Solutions and required files for all the QBasic Programming Problems at the end of each chapter.

Student Files   All the executable programs and data files presented in the text are included.

ACKNOWLEDGMENTS

We would like to thank and express our appreciation to the many fine and talented individuals who have contributed to the success of this book. We were fortunate to have a group of reviewers whose critical evaluations of our first ten BASIC books; Standard BASIC Programming, BASIC Fundamentals and Style, Complete BASIC for the Short Course, Applesoft BASIC Fundamentals and Style, Structured BASIC Fundamentals and Style for the IBM PC and Compatibles, Structured Microsoft BASIC Essentials for Business, QBasic Fundamentals and Style, QBasic Using Subprograms, QBasic Fundamentals and Style with an Introduction to Microsoft Visual Basic, and QBasic Using Subprograms 2nd Edition, were of great value during the preparation of these books. Special thanks again go to the following individuals:

Dory Lyn Anderson, Saint Cloud Community College
William Bailey, Casper College
Chester Bogosta, Saint Leo College
David Bradbard, Auburn University
John J. Couture, San Diego City College
Louise Darcey, Texas A&M University
I. Englander, Bentley College
James E. Evans, Tulsa Jr. College SE
Deborah L. Fansler, Davenport College
George Fowler, Texas A&M University
John T. Gorgone, Bentley College
James N. Haag, University of San Francisco
Juan A. Henriques, Grantham College

Linda Kosteba, Purdue University Calumet
Riki Kucheck, Orange Coast College
Jerry Lameiro, Colorado State University
John Monroe, Roberts Wesleyan College
Donald L. Muench, St. John Fisher College
Leroy Robbins, Bee County College
John Ross, Indiana University at Kokomo
R. Waldo Roth, Taylor University
Al Schroeder, Richland College
Syed Shahabuddin, Central Michigan University
Sumit Sircar, University of Texas at Arlington
Dave Talsky, University of Wisconsin-Milwaukee
David Van Over, University of Idaho
V. Diane Vaught, National Business College
Michael Walton, Miami-Dade Community College North
Mick Watterson, Drake University
Charles M. Williams, Georgia State University

The instructional staff of the Information Systems and Computer Programming Department of Purdue University Calumet provided many helpful comments and suggestions, and to them we extend our sincere thanks. Special thanks to Sam A. Maniotes for enhancing Chapter 10 and for his contributions to the problem statements and their solutions of Basic Programming Problems 10.6 to 10.9 and Exercises 10.15 to 10.19 involving graphics, animation, and music.

No book is possible without the motivation and support of an editorial staff. Therefore, our final acknowledgment and greatest appreciation are reserved for the following individuals at Course Technology: Kristen Duerr, Publisher, for the opportunity to write this book; Becky Herrington, Director of Production, whose creative talents show up throughout this book; Jennifer Muroff, Senior Product Manager; Doug Cowley, Production Manager; Jeanne Black, Quark Expert; Cristina Haley, Indexer; and Cherilyn King, Proofreader.

Hammond, Indiana
July 2000

James S. Quasney
John Maniotes
Roy O. Foreman

NOTES TO THE STUDENT

A few things to help you get going:

1. The first occurrence of a computer or programming term in this book is printed in **bold**. Its definition can be found in the same or the next sentence.

2. The line numbers that appear to the left of program lines throughout this book are not part of the programs. QBasic does not require line numbers. Their appearance is strictly for reference purposes during the discussion of the program. Beginning in Chapter 4, these line numbers also appear near symbols in top-down charts and program flow-charts in order to show their relationship to the corresponding program.

3. Each chapter ends with an important, useful review section called What You Should Know.

4. The answers to all the even-numbered Test Your QBasic Skills questions are in Appendix E.

5. A convenient, fully detailed language reference for QBasic is never farther away than your F1 key or right mouse button. Use these context-sensitive help keys whenever you have a question or want to learn more about the item nearest your cursor. This works for keywords, menu commands, error messages, dialog boxes, and just about anything else you can point to.

6. All the executable programs in the text are on the Data Disk. The Data Disk is available from your instructor or you can download it from the Course Technology website by connecting to course.com. The programs on the Data Disk that correspond to those in the text begin with the prefix PRG, followed by the chapter and program numbers. For example, PRG2-8 refers to the eighth executable program in Chapter 2.

   Each chapter-ending Test Your QBasic Skills section includes several PC Hands-On Exercises that utilize the programs on the Data Disk. Follow the directions and load, modify, and execute the programs. These short exercises will help you understand the significance of various QBasic statements and how slight modifications to a program can affect the results.

   You will also find the programs on the Data Disk helpful when you are solving assigned programming problems. These programs can be retrieved from the disk, and statements can be added, modified, or deleted to arrive at a solution. Most of the programming exercises in this book suggest which program should be loaded from the Data Disk and modified to develop a solution.

7. An easy-to-use Reference Card at the back of this book contains a summary of the QBasic statements, functions, special keys, operators, limits, and reserved words.

LIST OF PROGRAMMING CASE STUDIES

NO.	CASE	PAGE
1	Computing an Average	11
2	Determining a Salesperson's Commission	22
3	Tailor's Calculations	55
4A	Determining the Single Discount Rate	63
4B	Determining the Single Discount Rate with a Fixed Screen Format and an End-of-File Test	126
4C	Finding the Single Discount Rate Using Subprograms and Functions	473
5	Determining the Sale Price	95
6	Determining the Accounts Receivable Balance	121
7A	Weekly Payroll and Summary Report	149
7B	Writing the Weekly Payroll and Summary Report to Auxiliary Storage	204
8	A Menu-Driven Program	173
9	Creating a Sequential File	207
10	Processing a Sequential Data File and Paging a Report	214
11A	Sales Analysis Report — Single-Level Control Break	221
11B	Sales Analysis Report — Two Levels of Control Breaks	226
12	Analysis of Monthly Sales	259
13	Deciphering a Coded Message	306
14	Validating Payment Dates	310
15	Determining the Time to Double an Investment	319
16	Guess a Number between 1 and 100	327
17	Computer Simulation — Beat the House Roller	332
18	File Maintenance I — Adding Records by Merging Files	350
19	File Maintenance II — Deleting and Changing Records by Matching Records	358
20	Creating a Random File	369
21	Accessing Records in a Random File	372
22	Using a Simulated-Indexed File for Inventory Retrieval and Update	375
23	Logo for the Bow-Wow Dog Food Company	404
24	Horizontal Bar Graph of Monthly Sales	407
25	Animating an Inchworm Creeping across the Screen	415

CHAPTER 1

Computers and Problem Solving: An Introduction

1.1 WHAT IS A COMPUTER?

A **computer** is a machine that can accept data, process the data at high speeds, and give the results of these processes in an acceptable form. A more formal definition of a computer is given by the American National Standards Institute (ANSI), which defines a computer as a device that can perform substantial computations, including numerous arithmetic and logic operations, without intervention by a human operator.

Computers can handle tedious and time-consuming work and large amounts of data without ever tiring, which makes them indispensable for most businesses. In fact, computers have been among the most important forces in the modernization of business, industry, schools, and society since World War II. Keep in mind, however, that with all their capabilities, computers are merely tools and are not built to think or reason. They extend our intellect, but they do not replace thinking.

Advantages of a Computer

The major advantages of a computer are its speed and accuracy, as well as its capability to store and have ready for immediate recall vast amounts of data. Today's computers can also accept data from anywhere via telephone lines, cable, or satellite communications. They can generate usable output, such as reports, paychecks, and invoices, at several thousand lines per minute. Furthermore, they can display and distribute color graphics, images, sound, music, and video animation.

Disadvantages of a Computer

Some of the disadvantages of a computer concern obsolescence and ongoing costs for training and maintenance. Currently, computer models become technologically obsolete in a matter of a few years. Furthermore, in order for an organization's staff to derive its maximum benefits from a computer, the organization must continually invest in training and maintenance.

1.2 COMPUTER HARDWARE

Computer hardware is the physical equipment of a computer system. The equipment may consist of mechanical, magnetic, optical, electrical or electronic devices. Although many computers have been built in different sizes, speeds, and costs, and with different internal operations, most of them have the same basic five subsystems, as shown in Figures 1.1 and 1.2.

▌FIGURE 1.1

Basic structure of a digital computer, where the arrows represent the flow of data.

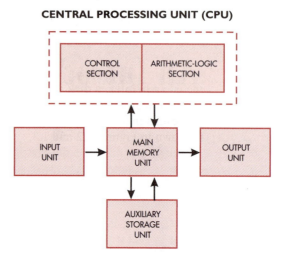

CENTRAL PROCESSING UNIT (CPU)

CONTROL SECTION | ARITHMETIC-LOGIC SECTION

INPUT UNIT — MAIN MEMORY UNIT — OUTPUT UNIT

AUXILIARY STORAGE UNIT

▌FIGURE 1.2

A computer consists of (a) one or more input units, (b) the system unit, (c) one or more output units, and (d) one or more auxiliary storage units.

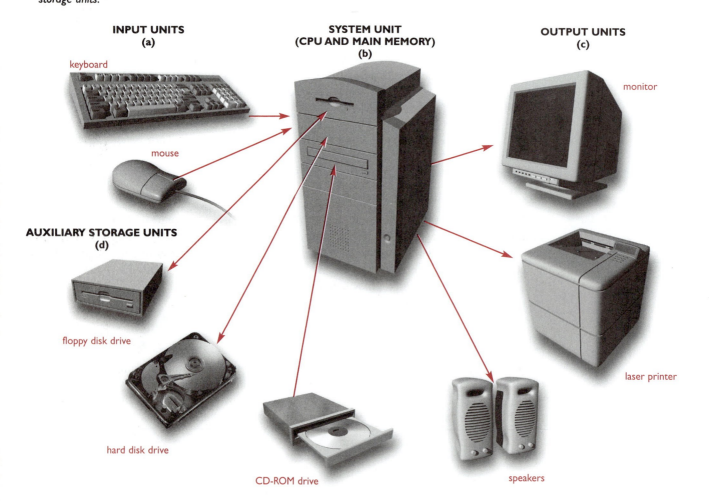

INPUT UNITS
(a)

keyboard

mouse

SYSTEM UNIT
(CPU AND MAIN MEMORY)
(b)

OUTPUT UNITS
(c)

monitor

AUXILIARY STORAGE UNITS
(d)

floppy disk drive

hard disk drive

CD-ROM drive

speakers

laser printer

Input

An **input unit** is a device that allows **programs**, instructions to the computer, and **data**, such as rate of pay, hours worked and number of dependents, to enter the computer system. This device converts the incoming data into electrical impulses, which are sent to the other units of the computer. A computer system usually has a **keyboard** and a **mouse** for input (Figures 1.2, 1.3 on the next page, and 1.4 on page 5). The disk drives, which are labeled as auxiliary storage in Figure 1.2, can serve as input devices or as output devices.

Output

When instructed by a program, the computer can communicate the results of a program to output units. A computer usually has a **monitor** for output. Other common output devices include a **printer**, a **disk unit**, and **stereo speakers**.

The monitor, also called a **video display device** or **screen**, can be used to display the output results in the form of words, numbers, graphs, images, or video animation. The monitor is shown in Figures 1.2 and 1.3.

The printer may be a dot-matrix printer, a laser printer, an inkjet printer, or a line printer. These devices can be used to print QBasic programs, reports, graphs, or drawings. Some of these printers are shown in Figures 1.2 and 1.3.

Main Memory

After the instructions and data have entered the computer through an input unit, they are stored in the computer's **main memory unit.** Because computers can process vast amounts of data in a short time and perform millions of calculations in just one second, the memory unit must be able to retain large amounts of data and make any single item rapidly available for processing.

Main memory in a computer is divided into storage locations, called **bytes,** each having a unique **address.** Each byte can store a character, such as the letter A or digit 9 or special characters. When instructions and data are entered, they are stored in various locations of main memory. The computer leaves data in a storage location until it is instructed to replace it with new data. While a data item is in memory, the computer can look it up as often as it is needed without altering that data item. Thus, when data is retrieved from a storage location, the stored contents remain unaltered. When you instruct the computer to put new data in that location, the old data is replaced.

Auxiliary Storage

The function of the **auxiliary storage unit** is to store data and programs that are to be used over and over again. Common auxiliary storage devices are magnetic tape drives, hard disk drives, floppy disk drives, and compact disc drives. Hard disk, floppy disk drives, and compact disc drives (CD-ROM or DVD) are shown in Figures 1.2 and 1.3.

These auxiliary storage devices can be used to store programs and data for as long as desired. A new program entering the system overwrites the previous program and data in main memory, but the previous program and data may be permanently stored on an auxiliary storage device for recall by the computer.

Central Processing Unit (CPU)

The **CPU** controls and supervises the entire computer system and performs the actual arithmetic and logic operations on data, as specified by the written program. The CPU is divided into the arithmetic-logic section and the control section, as shown in Figure 1.1.

The **arithmetic-logic section** performs such operations as addition, subtraction, multiplication, and division. Depending on the cost and storage capacity of the computer, the speed of the arithmetic unit will range from several million to many billions of operations per second.

The arithmetic-logic section also carries out the decision-making operations required to change the sequence of instruction execution. These operations include testing various conditions, for example, comparing two characters for equality. The result of these tests causes the computer to take one of two or more alternate paths through the program.

The **control section** directs and coordinates the entire computer system according to the program developed by the programmer and placed in main memory. The control section's primary function is to analyze and initiate the execution of instructions. This means that the control section has control over all other subsystems in the computer system.

1.3 THE PC FAMILY

In 1981, IBM introduced the IBM Personal Computer (PC), a fully assembled, easy-to-use computer, which has become the personal computer standard throughout the world.

Since that time, the original PC has undergone many enhancements, and additional models have been produced by IBM, as well as many other companies (Figure 1.3).

Millions of IBM PCs and compatibles have been manufactured since 1981. Currently, more than 100 manufacturers worldwide provide PC compatible systems and peripherals. Some of these manufacturers include such well-known names as Compaq, Dell, Gateway, Hewlett-Packard, Packard Bell, NEC, Toshiba, and Sony.

Many accessories and peripheral devices can be connected to the IBM PC and compatibles. This is possible because when IBM introduced the PC, it incorporated expansion slots so that users would be able to add enhancements at will (see Figure 1.6 on page 6). This *open architecture* has permitted many vendors to manufacture devices that enhance the performance of the PC.

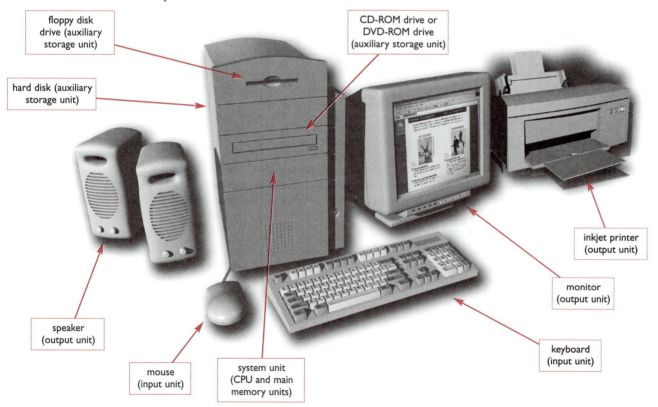

floppy disk drive (auxiliary storage unit)

hard disk (auxiliary storage unit)

CD-ROM drive or DVD-ROM drive (auxiliary storage unit)

inkjet printer (output unit)

monitor (output unit)

speaker (output unit)

keyboard (input unit)

mouse (input unit)

system unit (CPU and main memory units)

❙FIGURE 1.3   *An IBM PC compatible computer system.*

Keyboard

Figure 1.4(a) shows the enhanced IBM 101-key keyboard. The enhanced keyboard is similar to that of an ordinary typewriter keyboard, which is also referred to as the Qwerty keyboard. A **keyboard** is an input device used to enter programs and data into the main memory unit. Numeric, alphabetic, and special characters appear in standard typewriter format on the keyboard.

Note the layout of the function keys, the typewriter keys, and the numeric keypad. These keys will be explained in Chapter 2.

▌FIGURE 1.4(a)
The enhanced 101-key keyboard

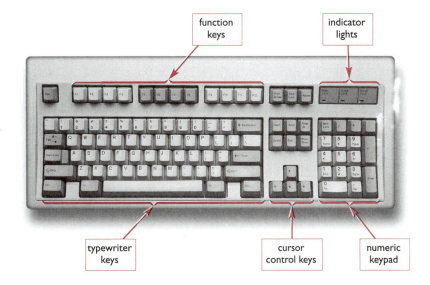

▌FIGURE 1.4(b)
The Microsoft ergonomic keyboard.

In order to reduce fatigue and repetitive stress injuries, many vendors have designed ergonomic keyboards. Figure 1.4(b) shows the Microsoft ergonomic keyboard where the keys used by the left and right hands are split and angled to make them easy to reach, resulting in less fatigue to the user.

Monitor

The standard size of monitors used for business applications is 15-, 17- or 19-inch, and those monitors used for scientific and engineering applications are 19-, 21-, or 24-inch in size.

Currently, several popular graphic standards and **pi**cture element (pixel) resolutions are associated with monitors. Some monitors have 640 pixels horizontally and 480 pixels vertically and are associated with the VGA standard.

Some monitors have 800 by 600 pixels and are associated with the Super VGA standard. Other monitors have 1,024 by 768 pixels and are associated with the XGA standard. Other high-resolution monitors have 1,280 by 1,024 pixels. Chapter 10 covers these and other graphic standards in greater detail.

CPU and Main Memory Unit

The original IBM PC was powered by a 16-bit Intel 8088 CPU, called a **microprocessor**, which was miniaturized on a **silicon chip** a fraction of an inch long (Figure 1.5). Over the years, Intel has developed a series of microprocessors, known as the x86 family, consisting of 8088/8086, 80286, 80386, 80486, Pentium, Pentium Pro, Pentium II, and Pentium III.

The Pentium III is a member of the x86 family and incorporates multimedia-enhancing (MMX) technology. The Pentium III CPU is shown in Figure 1.5.

FIGURE 1.5

The Intel Pentium III micro-processor crams 7.5 million transistors on a sliver of silicon and can execute at least twice as fast as its predecessor, the Pentium II.

Currently, most IBM PCs or IBM compatible systems use either the Intel x86 family of microprocessors or Intel compatible microprocessors manufactured by chip vendors such as Advanced Micro Devices and Cyrix.

The CPU and main memory unit are contained on the **mother board** (Figure 1.6) within the system unit. Main memory is sometimes called read/write memory, or **RAM** (random-access memory).

FIGURE 1.6

A top view of the mother board. The mother board is located within the system unit.

memory slots (RAM)

connectors for Pentium III chips

PCI expansion slots

ISA expansion slot

The original IBM PC was provided with 64 KB (65,536 bytes) of RAM expandable to a maximum of 640 KB (655,360 bytes) of RAM. Today's PC is more likely to have at least 32 MB (33,554,432 bytes) of RAM and could have more, practically without limit.

The letters **KB** (kilobyte) represent 1,024 bytes, the letters **MB** (megabyte) represent 1,048,576 bytes, and the letters **GB** (gigabyte) represent 1,073,741,824 bytes and are discussed further in the section dealing with auxiliary storage.

Read-only memory (**ROM**) is another form of storage. It is used to store the disc loader, patterns for graphics characters, and other essential instructions and data.

The term **megahertz** (**MHz**) – million cycles per second – is used as the most common measurement of a CPU's performance. Today's PCs range from 300 to 800 MHz in their CPU performance.

Auxiliary Storage

The IBM PC and compatibles currently use a 3½-inch floppy disk for storing and retrieving information (Figure 1.7).

Floppy disks are classified as double density, high density, and very high density. Very high-density floppy disks can store twice as much data as high-density floppy disks. High-density floppy disks can store twice as much data as double-density floppy disks. To store data in very high density, you need a very high-density floppy disk unit on your PC, as well as a very high-density floppy disk. Table 1.1 summarizes the storage capacity of the three densities of 3½-inch floppy disks.

FIGURE 1.7

The 3½-inch floppy disk is the most widely used portable storage medium. A single floppy disk typically stores 1.44 MB of data.

TABLE 1.1 – A Comparison of Densities for 3½-inch Floppy Disks			
FLOPPY DISK	**DENSITY**	**CAPACITY IN BYTES**	**NUMBER OF DOUBLE-SPACED TYPEWRITTEN 8½-BY-11-INCH PAGES**
3½-inch	Double	720 KB	250
3½-inch	High	1.44 MB	500
3½-inch	Very high	2.88 MB	1,000

A **floppy disk** is a thin, circular medium coated with a magnetic substance and comes in a permanent, protective plastic shell. The 3½-inch floppy disk has a protective slide that automatically opens and exposes the recording surface when the floppy disk is placed in the floppy disk unit (Figure 1.8). Once inside the floppy disk unit, the floppy disk is made to spin inside its protective plastic shell.

FIGURE 1.8

In a 3½-inch floppy disk, a flexible plastic disk is enclosed between two liners that clean any microscopic debris from the disk surface and help to disperse static electricity. The outside cover is made of a rigid plastic material, and the recording window is covered by a protective slide that slides to the side when the disk is inserted into the floppy disk drive.

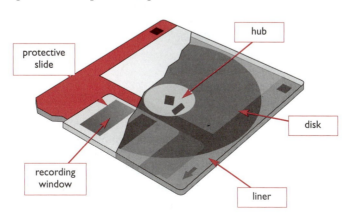

Floppy disks are delicate and should be handled and stored with care. Do not place floppy disks near heat, cold, or magnetic field sources such as magnets. Never touch the exposed recording surface; always hold the floppy disk by the protective plastic shell.

For additional auxiliary storage, a hard disk, containing anywhere from 4 GB to 20 GB (billion bytes) of storage, can be used with a PC. A 4 GB hard disk can store up to 2,200,000 double-spaced typewritten pages.

Network System

Many schools and businesses have opted to install a **network**, also called a **local area network (LAN)**. A network allows a printer, hard disk drive, other peripheral devices, software packages, and databases to be used by many interconnected personal computers. As shown in Figure 1.9, PCs in a network do not require their own individual printers.

With a network, many students operating PCs can be connected to an instructor-controlled PC. A network also allows students to access their programs and data files from the instructor's disk drives and use the printer. All processing of programs is done by the students on their assigned PC. When the students finish their work, they can store their updated programs and data files on their own floppy disk drives or on the instructor's hard disk drives.

Some of the leading manufacturers of LAN hardware and software systems are IBM, Compaq, Novell, 3 COM, and Cisco Systems.

FIGURE 1.9

A network of personal computers.

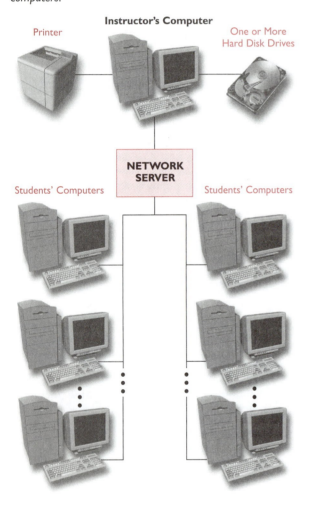

1.4 THE STORED PROGRAM CONCEPT

Before a computer can take action and produce a desired result, it must have a step-by-step description of the task to be accomplished. The step-by-step description is a series of precise instructions called a **program**. When these instructions are placed into the main memory unit of a computer, they are called the **stored program**. Main memory stores data along with the instructions, which tell the computer what to do with the data. The stored program gives computers a great deal of flexibility. Without it, the computer's capability to handle tasks would be reduced to that of a desk calculator.

After the program is stored, the first instruction is located and sent to the control section, where it is interpreted and executed. Then the next instruction is located, sent to the control section, interpreted and executed. This process continues automatically, instruction by instruction, until the program is completed or until the computer is instructed to halt.

For the computer to perform still another job, a new program must be stored in main memory. Hence, a computer can be easily used to process a large number of different jobs.

1.5 COMPUTER SOFTWARE

Computer software is a set of programming languages and programs concerned with the operation of a computer system. Some essential computer software comes with the purchase of a computer system. Additional software is either purchased or written by the user in a programming language the computer understands. Table 1.2 lists some popular software packages and their functions for business and schools. These packages do not require that you know how to write a program. They may be purchased at any computer store selling personal computer systems.

TABLE 1.2 - Popular Software Packages and Their Functions

SOFTWARE PACKAGE	FUNCTION
Microsoft Word or Corel WordPerfect	A **word processing program** used to write, revise, and edit letters, reports, and manuscripts with efficiency and economy.
Microsoft Excel or Lotus 1-2-3	An **electronic spreadsheet program** used to organize data that can be defined in terms of rows and columns. Formulas can be applied to current rows or columns to create new rows and columns of information. Graphic images can be produced on the basis of the data in the spreadsheet.
Microsoft Access or dBASE V or Paradox or Microsoft FoxPro	A **database system** used to organize data on an auxiliary storage device. It also allows for the generation of reports and for easy access to the data.
Microsoft PowerPoint or Harvard Presentation Graphics	A **graphics program** used to create line graphs, bar graphs, pie charts, and 3-D graphic images, for high-impact presentation purposes.
PageMaker or QuarkXPress	A **desktop publishing system** used to integrate words and pictures and generate typeset quality documents quickly and economically. Includes advanced typographic controls and improved text-handling features.
Netscape Navigator or Microsoft Internet Explorer	An **Internet browser program** used to access the World Wide Web and display information in the form of text, graphics, sound, music, video clips, and animation.

TABLE 1.3 - Popular High-Level Languages and Their Appropriate Areas of Use

LANGUAGE	AREA OF USEFULNESS
C and C++	These high-level languages provide easy access to many assembly language capabilities. C is useful for writing applications packages and systems software, like operating systems. C++ is useful for object-oriented programming where the objects are reusable software components from actual applications.
COBOL	The **CO**mmon **B**usiness **O**riented **L**anguage is an English-like language that is suitable for business data processing applications. It is especially useful for file and table handling and extensive input and output operations.
FORTRAN	**FOR**mula **TRAN**slation is a problem-solving language designed primarily for scientific data processing, engineering, and process-control applications.
Java	Java is an object-oriented programming language used to write general purpose applications, as well as interactive programs, for the Internet environment. Java programs can be written on one computer platform and run on any other computer platform without modifications.
Pascal	Pascal, named in honor of the French mathematician Blaise Pascal, is a programming language that allows for the formulations of solutions and data in a form that clearly exhibits their natural structure. It is used primarily for scientific applications and systems programming.
QBasic	**Q**uick **B**eginner's **A**ll-purpose **S**ymbolic **I**nstruction **C**ode is a very simple problem-solving language that is used with personal computers or with terminals in a time-sharing environment. QBasic is used for both business and scientific applications.
Visual Basic	This programming language is useful for writing Windows-based applications. Visual Basic code closely resembles QBasic code.

Programming languages are classified as **low-level languages,** such as machine language and assembly language, and **high-level languages,** such as QBasic, Visual Basic, C, C++, Java, Pascal, COBOL, and FORTRAN. Early generation computers required programmers to program in machine language, and this language was different for each computer manufacturer's system.

Currently, most applications for the PC are programmed in one of the many popular high-level languages listed in Table 1.3. A high-level language is generally machine or computer independent: this means that programs written in a high-level language like QBasic can easily be transferred from one computer system to another, with little or no change in the programs. The languages listed in Table 1.3 are available for personal computers.

The QBasic system for the PC was designed and developed by Microsoft Corporation, one of the largest microcomputer software companies in the world. The QBasic system includes the QBasic language, a fully integrated editor (Chapter 2 and Appendix B), a debugger (Appendix C), and pull-down menus.

The Internet

The Internet is one of the most popular and fastest growing areas. You can use the Internet to do research, access faraway libraries for information, conduct electronic commerce such as sales and other business transactions, obtain multimedia information, and participate in discussion groups with other people worldwide.

The Internet is a global collection of networks each of which is a collection of **inter**connected **net**works of computers. The collection of computers on the Internet is referred to as the World Wide Web, or WWW. Stored on these computers are documents called Web pages containing information in the form of text, graphs, sound, music, video clips, and animation.

Each Web page has a unique address called a Uniform Resource Locator (URL). For example, a popular Web page URL is:

www.yahoo.com

Figure 1.10 illustrates the web page that displays when you launch your browser and enter the URL, www.yahoo.com.

To access the Internet, you need a telephone, a modem, an Internet browser software, an Internet connection service provider, the telephone number of the provider, and a PC. Appendix D and PC Hands-On Exercise 3 at the end of this chapter provide URLs for some interesting World Wide Web sites.

FIGURE 1.10

The Yahoo Web page displays when you launch your browser and enter the URL, www.yahoo.com. The underlined words on the screen are hyperlinks to other Web pages.

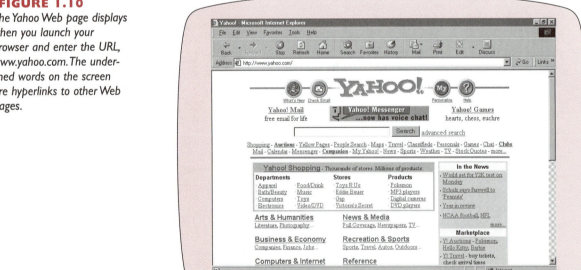

The Operating System

An operating system is a computer program that helps to act as an internal *traffic cop* in the PC by directing the flow of data into and out of the computer and the peripheral devices (see Figure 1.1 on page 2). For example, an operating system helps to load and execute programs, manage files, and accept commands from the keyboard.

The first operating system for the IBM PC was designed and developed by Microsoft and was called **PC-DOS** for the IBM PC and **MS-DOS** for the PC compatibles. MS-DOS stands for Microsoft Disk Operating System. PC-DOS and MS-DOS are essentially the same.

MS-DOS and PC-DOS, through a series of enhancements and new versions, have evolved to take advantage of the increased memory and computing power of the Intel x86 family of microprocessors. Over the years, Microsoft has developed a series of operating systems for the x86 family consisting of several versions of MS Windows.

Every PC comes with one of these operating systems, which is usually pre-loaded on the hard disk drive.

While MS-DOS is a single-user, single-task operating system, MS Windows, MS Windows 98, MS Windows NT Workstation, and MS Windows 2000 Professional are single-user, multitask operating systems for the PC. **Multitask** means that the computer can run multiple programs concurrently, but not simultaneously, because there is only one CPU.

The Graphical User Interface

A **Graphical User Interface** (**GUI**, pronounced as gooey) is the program interface between a user and the PC. A GUI is designed to increase the productivity of the user. An important design consideration for a GUI is that a user does not have to memorize or type commands into a PC, but can point to and select the function he or she needs to perform.

MS Windows has a GUI. A GUI uses windows, icons, and a mouse to accept commands primarily in the form of drop-down or pop-up menus, mouse movements, and mouse clicks. Each GUI is easy to use, is graphically oriented and icon driven, allows for the direct manipulation of objects on the screen, and has a consistent user interface across applications.

Furthermore, a GUI provides on the screen a visual **desktop** where a user can view **icons** (small graphical figures) representing documents, programs, and files. For example, to activate an application program, such as Excel or Word, a user points to its icon on the screen using a hand-held pointing device called a **mouse**.

Chapter 2 explains the QBasic environment. Although QBasic is not a GUI, it does use various windows, menu bars, scroll bars, dialog boxes, and many other features commonly found in a GUI environment.

PROGRAMMING CASE STUDY 1 – Computing an Average

Program 1.1 illustrates a program written in QBasic. It instructs the computer to compute the average of three numbers: 19, 25, and 40.

PROGRAM 1.1

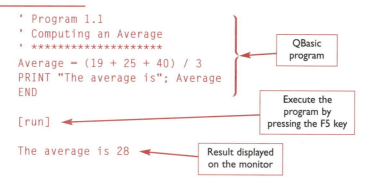

```
' Program 1.1
' Computing an Average
' ********************
Average = (19 + 25 + 40) / 3
PRINT "The average is"; Average
END
```
→ QBasic program

```
[run]
```
→ Execute the program by pressing the F5 key

```
The average is 28
```
→ Result displayed on the monitor

The displayed answer, found below [run], is 28. Although we are deferring detailed explanations about this program until the next chapter, Program 1.1 gives you some indication of instructing a computer to calculate a desired result using QBasic.

The Compiler and the Interpreter

Computers cannot directly execute programs, such as Program 1.1, written in a high-level language like QBasic. Computers must first translate the QBasic statements into equivalent machine language instructions that are understood by the computer.

Compilers and interpreters are two types of software programs that perform this translation, and these programs reside on the hard disk drive of a PC. The following paragraphs explain some of the differences between these two translation processes. Microsoft calls the compiler version QuickBASIC and the interpreter version QBasic.

Figure 1.11 illustrates the use of a compiler to translate programs written in QuickBASIC. The QuickBASIC **compiler** is a program which, when executed by the PC, will cause an entire QuickBASIC program to be translated into machine language *before* the actual execution of the program begins.

FIGURE 1.11

Compilation procedure for a program written in QuickBASIC.

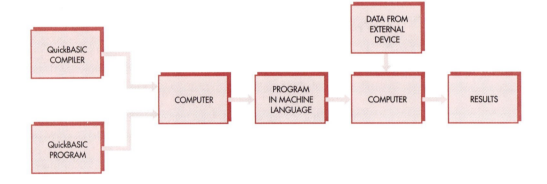

The compiler examines the entire QuickBASIC program, and if it is error free, the compiler generates the machine language instructions. Some PC systems can compile programs at speeds of more than 10,000 QuickBASIC statements per minute.

To produce results or answers, the machine language instructions, together with data from external sources, are then processed by the computer as shown in Figure 1.11.

Figure 1.12 illustrates the use of an interpreter to translate programs written in QBasic. An **interpreter** is a program, which when executed by a computer, will analyze each QBasic statement, translate it into equivalent machine language if the syntax is correct, and execute the machine language instructions to produce results, or answers, without the production of an intermediate machine language program.

FIGURE 1.12

Interpretation procedure for a program written in QBasic.

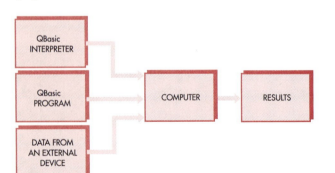

Depending on the content of a program, compiled QuickBASIC programs execute five to 10 times faster than interpreted QBasic programs. The interpreter version, QBasic, comes free with MS-DOS version 5 and higher. It is also available on the Windows 95 CD in the folder, other/oldmsdos, and the Windows 98 CD in the folder, tools/oldmsdos. You can use either QBasic or QuickBASIC with this book.

1.6 PROBLEM SOLVING AND PROGRAM DEVELOPMENT

Every action the PC is expected to make toward solving a problem must be spelled out in detail in the program. The step-by-step procedures listed in Table 1.4 will help you set up problems for the computer to solve. These procedures make up what is called the **program development life cycle**.

TABLE 1.4 - The Program Development Life Cycle

STEP	PROCEDURE	DESCRIPTION
1	Problem Analysis	Precisely define the problem to be solved, including the form of the input, the form of the output, and a description of the transformation of input to output.
2	Design the Program	Devise an **algorithm**, or a method of solution, for the computer to use. This method must be a complete procedure for solving the specified problem in a finite number of steps. There must be no ambiguity (no chance that something can be interpreted in more than one way).
		Develop a detailed logic plan or logic diagram, using **flowcharts**, **pseudocode**, or some other logic tool to describe each step that the PC must perform to arrive at the solution. As far as possible, the flowcharts or pseudocode must describe what job is to be done and how the job is to be done.
		Develop good **test data**. As best you can, select data that will test for erroneous input.
3	Test the Design	Step by step, go through the logic diagram, using the test data as if you were the PC. If the logic diagram does not work, repeat steps 1 through 3.
4	Code the Program	Code the program in a computer language, like QBasic (see Table 1.3 on page 9), according to the logic specified in the logic diagram. Include program documentation, such as comments and explanations, within the program.
5	Review the Code	Carefully review the code. Put yourself in the position of the PC and step through the entire program.
6	Enter the Program	Submit the program to the PC via a keyboard or other input device.
7	Test the Program	Test the program until it is error free and until it contains enough safeguards to ensure the desired result.
8	Formalize the Solution	Run the program, using the input data to generate the results. Review, and, if necessary, modify the documentation for the program.
9	Maintain the Program	Correct errors or add enhancements to the program. This step is usually initiated by users that have been running the program. After errors or enhancements are identified, the program development life cycle begins again at Step 1.

Flowcharts

A **program flowchart** is a popular logic tool used for showing an algorithm in graphic form. By depicting a procedure for arriving at a solution, a program flowchart also shows how the application or job is to be accomplished.

A programmer prepares a flowchart *before* he or she begins coding in QBasic. Eight basic symbols are used in program flowcharting. They are given in Table 1.5 on the next page with their respective names, meanings, and some of the QBasic statements they represent.

One rule that is basic to all flowcharts concerns direction. In constructing a flowchart, start at the top (or upper left corner) of a page. The flow should be top to bottom and left to right. If the flow takes any other course, arrowheads must be used. A plastic template can be obtained from most computer stores and bookstores. This template can be used to help you draw the flowchart symbols. Flowcharts also may be drawn using software packages such as Microsoft Word and Visio.

Figure 1.13 on page 15 shows a flowchart that illustrates the computations that are required to compute the average commission paid to a company's sales personnel and determine the number of male and female sales personnel. (For an in-depth discussion on flowcharts see Appendix A — especially, for this chapter, Sections A.1 through A.5.)

TABLE 1.5 - Flowchart Symbols and Their Meanings

SYMBOL	NAME	MEANING
	Process Symbol	Represents the process of executing a defined operation or group of operations that results in a change in value, form, or location of information. Examples: LET, DIM, RESTORE, DEF, and other processing statements. Also functions as the default symbol when no other symbol is available.
	Input/Output (I/O) Symbol	Represents an I/O function, which makes data available for processing (input) or for displaying (output) of processed information. Examples: READ, INPUT, and PRINT.
Left to Right / Right to Left / Top to Bottom / Bottom to Top	Flowline Symbol	Represents the sequence of available information and executable operations. The lines connect other symbols, and the arrowheads are mandatory only for right-to-left and bottom-to-top flow.
	Annotation Symbol	Represents the addition of descriptive information, comments, or explanatory notes as clarification. The vertical line and the broken line may be placed on the left, as shown, or on the right. Example: REM or '.
	Decision Symbol	Represents a decision that determines which of a number of alternative paths is to be followed. Examples: IF and SELECT CASE statements.
	Terminal Symbol	Represents the beginning, the end, or a point of interruption or delay in a program. Examples: STOP, RETURN, and END statements.
	Connector Symbol	Represents any entry from, or exit to, another part of the flowchart. Also serves as an off-page connector.
	Predefined Process Symbol	Represents a named process consisting of one or more operations or program steps that are specified elsewhere. Example: CALL.

Pseudocode

Pseudocode is an alternative to program flowcharts that uses natural English and resembles QBasic code. It allows for the logic of a program to be formulated without diagrams or charts. Figure 1.14 shows examples of specific operations in pseudocode.

Figure 1.15 on page 16 shows a pseudocode version of the flowchart solution presented in Figure 1.13. Although pseudocode has few formal rules, we have listed some commonly accepted rules, as well as several examples, in Section A.6 of Appendix A.

Appendix A also includes a discussion of Nassi-Schneiderman charts and Warnier-Orr diagrams. Nassi-Schneiderman charts and Warnier-Orr diagrams are alternative logic tools to flowcharts and pseudocode. Also, Chapter 3 presents top-down charts.

Each logic tool has its strengths and weaknesses. As you solve problems in the later chapters of this book, we suggest you try all of them, and then choose the tool that best suits you. Of course, your instructor may have specific requirements about the logic tool you use for the required assignments.

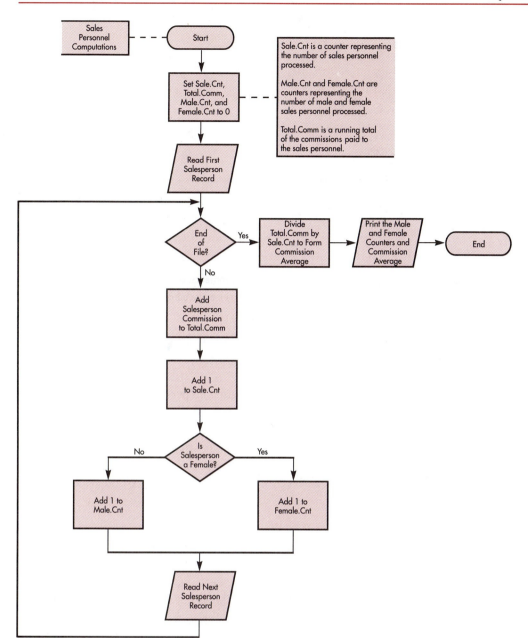

Sale.Cnt is a counter representing the number of sales personnel processed.

Male.Cnt and Female.Cnt are counters representing the number of male and female sales personnel processed.

Total.Comm is a running total of the commissions paid to the sales personnel.

▌FIGURE 1.14
Examples of operations in pseudocode.

```
Clear screen

Discount = rate × sale price

If male Then
    Add 1 to male counter
Else
    Add 1 to female counter
End-if
```

FIGURE 1.15

Pseudocode version of the sales personnel computation.

```
Program: Sales Personnel Computations
Set salesperson counter to 0
Set total commission to 0
Set male counter to 0
Set female counter to 0
Read first salesperson record
Do While not end-of-file
    Add salesperson commission to total commission
    Add 1 to salesperson counter
    If female Then
        Add 1 to female counter
    Else
        Add 1 to male counter
    End-if
    Read next salesperson record
End Do
Commission average = total commission / salesperson counter
Display male and female counters and commission average
End: Sales Personnel Computations
```

1.7 ADDITIONAL INFORMATION ON PERSONAL COMPUTERS

We encourage you to seek additional information on personal computers. To assist you in that search, Appendix D includes:

- A list of magazines and newspapers oriented to the PC (both provide current information on what is taking place with personal computers)
- A list of Uniform Resource Locators (URLs) of some interesting World Wide Web sites on the Internet

1.8 What You Should Know

To help you study this chapter, a summary of the topics covered in it is listed below. These statements apply to all computers, including the PC. This is not a test that includes true and false statements; all of the statements in this list are true.

1. A computer is a device that can perform substantial computations, including numerous arithmetic and logic operations, without intervention by a human operator.
2. The major advantages of a computer are its speed, accuracy, and capability to store and have ready for immediate recall vast amounts of data.
3. The major disadvantages of a computer are rapid obsolescence and the ongoing cost of training and maintenance.
4. However fast, computers are not built to think or reason. They extend our intellect, but they do not replace thinking.
5. Computer hardware is the physical equipment of a computer system.
6. A computer has five subsystems — input, output, main memory, auxiliary storage, and the central processing unit (CPU).
7. An input unit allows programs and data to enter the computer system.
8. Main memory is the computer's storage unit, where instructions and data are stored for processing purposes.
9. The central processing unit (CPU) controls and supervises the entire computer system and performs the actual arithmetic and logic operations on data, as specified by the written program. The CPU is made up of two sections — the arithmetic-logic section and the control section.

10. The arithmetic-logic section performs the arithmetic operations and carries out the decision-making operations required by a program.
11. The control section directs and coordinates the entire computer system.
12. The auxiliary storage unit stores data and programs that are to be used over and over again.
13. An output unit is used by the computer to communicate the results of a program.
14. A network is a group of interconnected personal computers that can share software programs and hardware, such as a printer, disk drive, and other peripheral devices. Networks are also called LANs (local-area networks).
15. A computer program is a series of instructions required to complete a procedure or task. When the program is loaded into the main memory unit of a computer, it becomes a stored program.
16. Computer software is a program or a set of programs written for a computer.
17. Software packages that do not require a person to know how to program are available for word processing, electronic spreadsheets, database management, desktop publishing, graphics, and Internet browsing.
18. Programming languages are classified as low-level languages, such as machine language and assembly language, and high-level languages such as QBasic, C, C++, Java, Pascal, COBOL, and FORTRAN.
19. Compilers and interpreters are two types of software programs that are used to translate the program statements into equivalent machine language instructions that are understood by the computer.
20. The program development life cycle is a set of step-by-step procedures for solving a problem.
21. In problem analysis, defining the problem is the first step in solving it.
22. Program design is made up of three steps — devising a method of solution, drawing logic diagrams, and selecting good test data.
23. A QBasic program should be coded only after the design is complete and has been carefully reviewed and tested.
24. A program flowchart is a popular logic tool used for showing an algorithm in graphic form.
25. Pseudocode is an alternative to program flowcharts and allows for the logic of a program to be formulated without diagrams or charts.

1.9 Test Your QBasic Skills (Even-numbered answers are in Appendix E)

1. State three major advantages that computers have over the manual computation of problems.

2. What are the basic subsystems of a computer system? Briefly describe the function of each subsystem.

3. Name the components of the CPU.

4. Name two devices that serve as both input and output devices.

5. Name five personal computer manufacturers.

6. What is meant by the term hardware? Software?

7. What do the following acronyms represent: CPU, KB, MB, GB, MHz, RAM, ROM?

8. List the different densities for 3½-inch floppy disks described in this chapter and their storage capacities.

9. Draw one flowchart that enables the Mechanical Man to accomplish efficiently the objectives in both phase 1 and 2, as illustrated in Figure 1.16 on the next page.

FIGURE 1.16

The two phases of the Mechanical Man.

PHASE 1

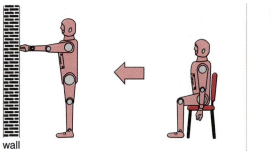

wall

PHASE 2

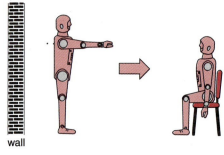

wall

The Mechanical Man is seated at an unknown integer number (0, 1, 2,...) of steps from the wall. He will stand up and walk forward until he touches the wall with his fingertips. When he is in a seated position with arms raised, his fingertips are aligned with the tips of his shoes.

After touching the wall, the Mechanical Man will return to his chair. Because the chair is too low for him to sense by touch, he can get to it only by going back exactly the number of steps as he came forward.

The Mechanical Man possesses the following properties:

- He is restricted to carrying out a limited set of instructions.
- He does *nothing* unless given a specific instruction.
- He must carry out any instructions he is given *one at a time*.
- He understands only the following instructions:

    a. Physical Movement:
      1. Stand up (into an erect position without moving feet).
      2. Sit down (into a sitting position without moving feet).
      3. Take one step (forward only, can be done only if he is standing, length of steps is always the same).
      4. Raise arms (into one fixed position, straight ahead).
      5. Lower arms (into one fixed position, straight down at his sides).
      6. Turn right (in place without taking a step, can be done only if he is standing, all right turns are 90-degree turns).

    b. Arithmetic:
      1. Add one (to a total that is being developed).
      2. Subtract one (from a total that is being developed).
      3. Record total (any number of totals can be remembered in this way).

    c. Logic: The Mechanical Man can decide what instruction he will carry out next on the basis of answers to the following questions:
      1. Arithmetic results
        a) Is the result positive? or negative? or zero?
        b) Is the result equal to a predetermined amount?
      2. Physical status
        a) Are the raised arms touching anything?

10. After reviewing the following three files with their specified records, answer the questions below:

File Number	Record Number	Salesperson Number	Salesperson Gender	Salesperson Commission
1	1	246	Male	$ 400
	2	501	Female	1,100
	3	876	Male	600
2	1	123	Male	$ 500
3		This file is empty; that is, there are no records.		

      a. According to Figure 1.13 on page 15, what is the value of Male.Cnt, Female.Cnt, Sale.Cnt, and Commission Average after File 1 is processed and the program terminates?

      b. Same as (a), but refer to File 2.

      c. Same as (a), but refer to File 3.

11. Same as question 9, but use pseudocode to develop the logic that enables the Mechanical Man to accomplish efficiently the objectives shown in Figure 1.16.

12. Explain the function of each of the following applications: word processing, spreadsheets, database, graphics, desktop publishing, and a browser. Identify a major software for each application.

13. **Payroll Problem I: Weekly Payroll**

    Problem: Construct a flowchart to calculate a weekly payroll using the following rules:

      a. Time and a half is paid for hours worked in excess of 40.

      b. $40.46 is allowed as nontaxable income for each dependent claimed.

      c. The withholding tax is 26 percent of the taxable income.

      d. Assume that end-of-file is defined as the condition in which the value for the number of hours worked is negative.

    Input Data: Each employee record includes the following data:

      a. Name

      b. Hourly rate of pay

      c. Number of hours worked

      d. Number of dependents

    Output Results: Display the following for each employee:

      a. Name

      b. Gross pay

      c. Net pay

      d. Income tax withheld

14. Identify the manufacturer, model number, operating system, and MHz of the computer system you will use to process your programs. Does the system include a QuickBASIC compiler or QBasic interpreter?

1.10 PC Hands-On Exercises

The following exercises are designed to acquaint you with your personal computer system. Consult with your instructor before running these exercises on your PC.

1. Identification of Keys on the Keyboard

Find the important keys on your keyboard listed in Table 1.6 on the next page. Make a check mark in the third column as you find each key.

2. Formatting a Floppy Disk

When you purchase a floppy disk, it is blank (that is, it has nothing recorded on the surface). For programs or data to be placed on a floppy disk, it must sometimes first be formatted.

    Obtain a blank floppy disk following the recommendation of your instructor and format it carefully following his or her instructions.

TABLE 1.6 - Special Keys on the Keyboard								
KEY	**SYMBOL**	**CHECK**	**KEY**	**SYMBOL**	**CHECK**	**KEY**	**SYMBOL**	**CHECK**
Enter	⏎		Print Screen	Print Screen		Home	Home	
Escape	Esc		Capital Lock	Caps Lock		End	End	
Tab	⇥		Numerical Lock	Num Lock		Insert Key	Ins	
Control	Ctrl		Scroll Lock	Scroll Lock		Function Key 1	F1	
Shift	⇧		Alternate	Alt		Delete	Del	
Backspace	←							

3. Surfing the Web

Using an Internet browser, display the Web pages of some of the PC hardware and software vendors mentioned in this chapter. Use the following Uniform Resource Locators (URLs):

www.compaq.com
www.gw2k.com
www.ibm.com
www.hp.com
www.intel.com
www.microsoft.com
www.netscape.com

Scroll down a given Web page and read the latest news and developments from the vendor. Click either underlined text or a graphical object and see what happens.

Use a Web search engine and search for an interesting topic on the Web. For example, use the following URL to access the AltaVista search engine:

www.altavista.com

When the AltaVista Web page displays, enter the keyword, `qbasic`, in the search box and watch the display of the numerous citations associated with QBasic. Click a citation and see what happens.

CHAPTER 2

QBasic:
An Introduction

2.1 CREATING A QBASIC PROGRAM

In this chapter we will concentrate on simple program illustrations, input/output operations, and the QBasic (QB) operating environment. The **QB operating environment** allows you to create, maintain, and execute QBasic programs on your PC. Upon successful completion of this chapter, you should be able to develop some elementary programs written in QBasic and enter them into your PC for execution.

General Characteristics of a QBasic Program

A QBasic program is composed of a sequence of lines. Each line may contain one or more statements, up to a maximum of 255 characters. Statements instruct the PC to carry out an action, such as assigning the value of an expression to a variable or displaying the value of a variable. In general, programmers type one statement per line and then start a new line by pressing the Enter key. The statements are placed in the program in the order they are to be executed, as illustrated by Figure 2.1.

FIGURE 2.1
The general form of a QBasic program.

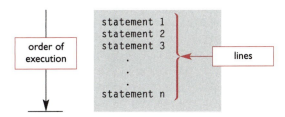

Programming Case Study 2 illustrates the composition of a QBasic program.

PROGRAMMING CASE STUDY 2 – Determining a Salesperson's Commission

Most salespeople work on a commission basis. Their earned commissions are often determined by multiplying their assigned commission rate by the amount of dollar sales. The dollar sales amount is computed by deducting any returned sales from the sum of their weekly sales. Given a biweekly period, the earned commission can be determined from the following formula:

Earned Commission = Rate × (Week 1 Sales + Week 2 Sales – Returns)

Let us assume that for the biweekly period, a salesperson's assigned commission rate is 18% and sales are $1,200 the first week, and $1,500 the second week. The returned sales are $75.

Program 2.1 instructs the PC to compute the earned amount and display it on the screen. The earned commission of 472.5 is just below [run]. When you see **[run]** in this book, it signals you to execute the program. To execute a program, click Run on the menu bar and then click Start, or click <F5=Run> on the status line.

PROGRAM 2.1

```
LET Commission = 0.18 * (1200 + 1500 - 75)          program
PRINT Commission
END


[run]                          displayed
                                result
  472.5
```

Keywords

This program contains three lines. The first line contains a LET statement. The LET **statement** consists of the keyword, LET, a variable name, Commission, an equal sign, four **constants** (0.18, 1200, 1500 and 75), and three **arithmetic operators** (*, +, and −). A **keyword** is a predefined word that has special meaning to QBasic. It indicates the type of action to be performed. In Program 2.1, three keywords are used: LET, PRINT and END. Keywords also are called **reserved words**. See page R6 on the Reference Card at the back of this book for a complete list of the QBasic keywords.

If a statement does not begin with a keyword and contains an equal sign, then QBasic assumes it is a LET statement. For example, the first statement in Program 2.1 may be written in the following form:

```
Commission = 0.18 * (1200 + 1500 - 75)
```

Although the statement does not contain the keyword, LET, it still is called a LET statement. It also may be referred to as an **assignment statement**. Except for Program 2.1, in this book all LET statements will be written without the keyword, LET.

Variable Names and Constants

In programming, a **variable** represents a location, or address, in your computer's memory, which can change values as the program is executed. In Program 2.1, the variable name, Commission, references the memory location assigned to it by QBasic. The first statement instructs the PC to complete the arithmetic operations and assign the resulting value of 472.5 to the memory location assigned to Commission. A **variable name** begins with a letter and may be followed by up to 39 letters, digits, and decimal points. Keywords, such as LET, PRINT, and END that have special meaning to QBasic, may not be used as variable names.

The **equal sign** in any LET statement means that the value of the variable to the left of the equal sign is to be replaced by the final value of the expression to the right of the equal sign.

Constants, such as 0.18, 1200, 1500, and 75, represent ordinary numbers that do not change during the execution of a program. Both constants and variables are covered in detail in Chapter 3.

Arithmetic Operators

The **plus sign** (+) in the LET statement in line 1 of Program 2.1 signifies addition between the two constants that represent the weekly sales. The **minus sign** (–) indicates subtraction of the returned sales from the sum of the weekly sales. The **asterisk** (*) indicates multiplication between the rate and the actual sales. The seven QBasic arithmetic operators are given in Table 2.1. As is the case in mathematics, the set of parentheses in line 1 of Program 2.1 is used to override the normal sequence of arithmetic operations.

TABLE 2.1 - The Seven Arithmetic Operators			
ARITHMETIC OPERATOR	**MEANING**	**EXAMPLES OF USAGE**	**MEANING OF THE EXAMPLES**
^	Exponentiation	2 ^ 3	Raise 2 to the third power, which in this example is 8.
*	Multiplication	6.1 * A1	Multiply the value of the variable A1 by 6.1.
/	Division	H / 10	Divide the value of the variable H by 10.
\	Integer Division	5 \ 3	The integer quotient of 5 divided by 3, which in this example is 1. (Operands are rounded to whole numbers.)
MOD	Modulo	5 MOD 3	The integer remainder of 5 divided by 3, which in this example is 2.
+	Addition	3.14 + 2.9	Add 3.14 and 2.9.
–	Subtraction	T - 35.4	Subtract 35.4 from the value of the variable T.

The PRINT Statement

The second statement in Program 2.1 is called a PRINT statement. A PRINT **statement** instructs the PC to bring a result out from main memory and display it on an output device, such as your monitor. The statement causes the PC to display 472.5, the value of Commission. The PRINT statement is covered in detail in Chapter 4.

The END Statement

The last line of Program 2.1 includes the END statement. When executed, the END **statement** instructs the PC to stop executing the program. Although the END statement is not required, it is recommended that you always include one.

Some Relationships between Statements

The PRINT statement in Program 2.1 would display a result of zero if earlier in the program we had failed to instruct the PC to assign a value to the variable Commission. That is, the PC cannot correctly display the value of Commission before it determines this value. Therefore, if Program 2.1 were incorrectly written, as below, the PC would *not* display the correct results unless, by chance, the earned commission was zero.

```
PRINT Commission
Commission = 0.18 * (1200 + 1500 - 75)          invalid
END                                             logic

[run]
```

0

The following program is incorrect for the same reason:

```
Pay = 0.18 * (1200 + 1500 - 75)
PRINT Commission
END
```
invalid logic

```
[run]

 0
```

When this program is executed, the PC calculates a value of 472.5 for the variable, Pay, but displays a result of zero. It displays zero because QBasic assigns all numeric variables a value of zero before executing the first statement in the program, and the value of Commission is not assigned any value in the program itself.

The correct program can be written as Program 2.1 or as Program 2.2.

PROGRAM 2.2

```
Pay = 0.18 * (1200 + 1500 - 75)
PRINT Pay
END

[run]

 472.5
```

Using the variable name, Pay, is no different from using the variable name, Commission, as long as the same name is used consistently. The relationship between output statements, such as the PRINT statement, and other statements in a program can be stated as follows:

OUTPUT RULE 1   *Every variable appearing in an output statement must have been previously defined within a previous statement in the program.*

Although the flexibility of the QBasic language permits certain statements to be placed anywhere in a program, logic, common sense, and style dictate where these statements are placed. Style is nothing more than disciplined, consistent programming. Discipline and consistency help programmers construct readable, reliable, and maintainable programs.

2.2 THE INPUT STATEMENT

One of the major tasks of any computer program is to integrate the data to be processed into the program. In Programming Case Study 2 on page 22, the data includes a rate of 18%, first week sales of $1,200, second week sales of $1,500, and return sales of $75. In Program 2.1, the data was included directly in the LET statement as constants. This technique has its limitations. For example, the LET statement must be modified each time a new salesperson is processed. An alternative method of integrating the data into the program is shown in Program 2.3.

PROGRAM 2.3

```
Rate = 0.18
Week1 = 1200
Week2 = 1500
Returns = 75
Commission = Rate * (Week1 + Week2 - Returns)
PRINT Commission
END

[run]

 472.5
```

data as constants

In this new program, data in the form of constants is assigned to the variables Rate, Week1, Week2, and Returns in the first four LET statements. The fifth LET statement, which calculates the earned commission, contains the variables that have been assigned the data. When it executes Program 2.3, the PC must be informed of the numeric values for Rate, Week1, Week2, and Returns before it can calculate a value for Commission. This can be generalized as follows:

ARITHMETIC RULE I *Every variable appearing to the right of the equal sign in a LET statement must be previously defined in the program.*

This second method of integrating the data into the program has the same limitations as Program 2.1. That is, the first four lines must be modified in order to process a new salesperson. The only advantage to Program 2.3 is that the LET statement that computes the commission in line 5 will work for any salesperson.

A third way to integrate data into the program is through the use of the INPUT statement. The INPUT **statement** provides for assignment of data to variables from a source outside the program during execution. The data is supplied during execution of the program.

Through the use of the INPUT statement, the solution to Programming Case Study 2 can be made more general for calculating the earned commission for any salesperson, no matter what his or her commission rate, weekly sales, or returned sales. One version of the rewritten program is shown as Program 2.4.

PROGRAM 2.4

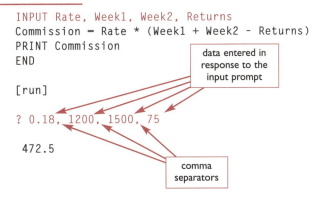

```
INPUT Rate, Week1, Week2, Returns
Commission = Rate * (Week1 + Week2 - Returns)
PRINT Commission
END

[run]

? 0.18, 1200, 1500, 75

 472.5
```

data entered in response to the input prompt

comma separators

The function of the INPUT statement in line 1 is to display an **input prompt** and suspend execution of the program until data has been supplied. QBasic displays a **question mark** (?) for the input prompt. It is then up to the user to supply the data. It is necessary that the user press the Enter key following entry of the last data item.

After the necessary data is supplied, the LET statement in line 2 determines the earned commission; line 3 prints the earned commission; and finally, line 4 terminates the program.

This third way of integrating data into a program, by means of the INPUT statement, is far more efficient than the other two ways, because we can process other sales personnel without modifying statements within the program. For example, to determine the earned commission for three salespeople, we can run the program three times, each time entering different data in response to the INPUT statements.

It is important that the variable names in the INPUT statement and the data supplied in response to the input prompt be separated by commas. A comma is used to establish a **list**, which is a set of distinct elements, each separated from the next by a comma. The comma must be used so that the PC can distinguish how many variables or data elements occur in each list. The order of the list of variables in the INPUT statement is also important. The INPUT statement in Program 2.4, INPUT Rate, Week1, Week2, Returns, may have been written as

```
INPUT Returns, Week2, Week1, Rate
```

If so, however, the data supplied for Salesperson 1 must be entered as

```
? 75, 1500, 1200, 0.18
```

It is also important that the user respond with numeric data. For example, if the value 6AB were entered as the returns, rather than 75, then the PC would respond with the following message:

```
Redo from start
```

This means that you must re-enter your data from the beginning. The same message will appear if too few data items are entered in response to the INPUT statement.

Input Prompt Message

To ensure that the data is entered in the proper sequence, QBasic allows for an **input prompt message** to be placed in the INPUT statement. When the PC executes an INPUT statement containing an input prompt message, the message, rather than the question mark, displays on the screen. Execution is suspended until the data is supplied. The following program requests one entry per INPUT statement:

PROGRAM 2.5

```
INPUT "Commission rate =====> ", Rate
INPUT "Week 1 sales ========> ", Week1
INPUT "Week 2 sales ========> ", Week2
INPUT "Return sales ========> ", Returns
Commission = Rate * (Week1 + Week2 - Returns)
PRINT Commission
END

[run]

Commission rate =====> 0.18
Week 1 sales ========> 1200
Week 2 sales ========> 1500
Return sales ========> 75
 472.5
```

When line 1 is executed in Program 2.5, the PC displays the input prompt message:

```
Commission rate =====>
```

After displaying the message requesting the commission rate, the PC suspends execution of the program until a response is entered. After typing 0.18, the user must press the Enter key.

If an acceptable response is entered, the PC displays the next input prompt message and suspends execution again. This process continues until the last INPUT statement has been executed.

After the last data item is entered for the INPUT statement in line 4, line 5 determines the earned commission. Then the PRINT statement in line 6 displays the earned commission, and finally, the END statement terminates the program.

The quotation marks (") surrounding the input prompt message and the comma (,) separating the message from the variable in the first four lines of Program 2.5 are required punctuation. If a semicolon (;) is used to separate the message from the variable, then a question mark (?) displays immediately after the input prompt message. For example, the following INPUT statement

```
INPUT "What is the commission rate"; Rate
```

displays the message followed by the question mark as shown here:

```
What is the commission rate?
```

Table 2.2 gives the general form of the INPUT statement. The INPUT statement consists of the keyword, INPUT, followed by an optional input prompt message, followed by a list of variables separated by mandatory commas. Here is the rule for determining the placement of the INPUT statement in a program:

INPUT RULE I
Every variable appearing in the program whose value is directly obtained through the keyboard must be listed in an INPUT statement before it is used elsewhere in the program.

TABLE 2.2 - The INPUT Statement	
General Form:	INPUT variable, ..., variable or INPUT "input prompt message", variable, ..., variable
Purpose:	Provides for the assignment of values to variables from an external device, like the keyboard.
Examples:	

INPUT Statements	**Data from the Keyboard**
INPUT A	23.5
INPUT X, Y, Z	2, 4, 6
INPUT A$, B	Gross, -2.73
INPUT "Please enter the sales tax: ", T	0.05
INPUT "What is your name"; N$	John
INPUT "Part number ====> ", P	1289

Note:	In the second general form, a question mark displays immediately after the input prompt message if a semicolon, rather than a comma, follows the message within quotation marks.

The INPUT statement allows the user complete interaction with the computer while the program executes. The main use of the INPUT statement is found in applications that involve one or all of the following:

1. Small amounts of data to be entered into a program
2. Data input that is dependent on the output or conditions of previous parts of a program
3. The processing of data as it occurs

This section on the INPUT statement has introduced you to one method of assigning values to variables in a program. Later, we will discuss two other methods that are used to process data, the READ and DATA statements (Chapter 4) and the use of data files (Chapters 6 and 9).

2.3 THE PRINT AND CLS STATEMENTS

One of the functions of the PRINT statement is to display the values of variables defined earlier in a program. You should understand by now that the following

```
X = 49
PRINT X
```

displays 49, the *value* of X, and not the letter X. The PRINT statement also can be used to display messages that identify a program result. This is shown by line 8 in Program 2.6. Line numbers have been added to the left of Program 2.6 so that you can easily follow the program discussion.

PROGRAM 2.6

```
1    CLS
2    INPUT "Commission rate =====> ", Rate
3    INPUT "Week 1 sales ========> ", Week1
4    INPUT "Week 2 sales ========> ", Week2
5    INPUT "Return sales ========> ", Returns
6    Commission = Rate * (Week1 + Week2 - Returns)
7    PRINT
8    PRINT "Earned commission ===>"; Commission
9    END

     [run]

     Commission rate =====> 0.18
     Week 1 sales ========> 1200
     Week 2 sales ========> 1500
     Return sales ========> 75

     Earned commission ===> 472.5
```

As with the INPUT statement, it is necessary in a PRINT statement to begin and end a message with quotation marks. The quotation marks in a PRINT statement inform QBasic that the item to be displayed is a message rather than a variable.

The semicolon following the message in line 8 instructs the PC to keep the cursor exactly where it is on the screen following the display of the message in quotation marks. The **cursor** is a movable, blinking marker on the screen that indicates where the next point of character entry, change or display will be. This means that the value of Commission will display immediately after the message.

QBasic displays a numeric value which consists of a sign, the decimal representation and a **trailing space**. Appearing immediately before the number, the sign is a **leading space** if the number is positive or zero and a **leading minus sign** if the number is negative. The space following the message displayed in line 8 in Program 2.6 represents the sign of the variable, Commission, as shown below:

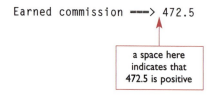

```
Earned commission ===> 472.5
```

a space here
indicates that
472.5 is positive

Clearing the Screen — The CLS Statement

One of the responsibilities of the programmer is to ensure that the prompt messages and results are meaningful and easy to read. A cluttered screen on a monitor can make it difficult for you to locate necessary information. QBasic includes the CLS **statement**, which erases the information on the output screen and places the cursor in the upper left corner. The **output screen** is the one that shows the results due to the execution of the current program. We will talk more about the output screen later in this chapter. The CLS statement usually is one of the first statements to be executed in a program. The general form of the CLS statement is found in Table 2.3.

TABLE 2.3 - The CLS Statement	
General Form:	CLS
Purpose:	Erases the information on the output screen.
Example:	CLS

Consider again Program 2.6. When the program is executed, the PC clears the output screen due to the CLS statement in line 1. Next, it displays the input prompt message

```
Commission rate =====>
```

as the first line of output. After obtaining a response through the keyboard, the PC displays the next input prompt message, and the rest of the program is executed. Line 7 in Program 2.6, which contains a PRINT statement without a list, shows how to instruct the PC to display a blank line in order to separate the input prompt messages from the results. A **null list** or **empty list** such as this causes the PRINT statement to display a blank line.

2.4 CODING AND DOCUMENTING

In the preceding programs, only one statement is written on each line, and the first letter in each statement is always written under the first letter of the statement above it. You will discover that this is an optional practice. However, a program written in such a form usually is easier to read and debug. **Debugging** is the process of removing errors from a program.

Coding Techniques

A QBasic program can be written on an ordinary sheet of paper. However, it is sometimes more convenient to write it on a specially printed sheet of paper called a **coding form**. Figure 2.2 on the next page shows Program 2.7 written on a coding form.

The coding form is divided into columns identified by the numbers near the top of the form. When constructing a QBasic statement, place the first letter in each statement, such as the P in PRINT, in column one.

The **space**, or **blank**, is also a character. It is obtained on a keyboard by pressing the Spacebar once for each blank character desired. The blank character may be used freely to improve the appearance and readability of the program. A useful rule of thumb for blank characters is this: leave spaces in a statement in the same places that you would leave spaces in an English sentence. If you do not, QBasic automatically inserts spaces around the equal sign, around any arithmetic operator, and after the comma and semicolon in a list. QBasic also will insert a semicolon followed by a space if no punctuation mark is placed between two items in a PRINT statement.

```
REM Program 2.7
REM Determining a Salesperson's Commission
REM J. S. Quasney, CIS 215, DIV. 01
REM September 30, 2002
REM ******************************
REM Clear Screen
CLS
REM Request Data from Operator
INPUT "Commission rate ======> ", Rate
INPUT "Week 1 sales ========> ", Week1
INPUT "Week 2 sales ========> ", Week2
INPUT "Return sales ========> ", Returns
REM Calculate the Earned Commission
Commission = Rate * (Week1 + Week2 - Returns)
REM Display the Earned Commission
PRINT
PRINT "Earned commission ===>"; Commission
END
```

FIGURE 2.2

Program 2.7 written on a coding form.

Capitalize the first letter of all variable names. Follow the first letter with lowercase letters. For example, use Commission, rather than COMMISSION or commission. All three of these variable names refer to the same storage location, but it is good practice to be consistent in the way you capitalize variable names.

Keywords are always capitalized. However, you may enter the keyword in lowercase. QBasic will immediately capitalize all the letters in the keyword when you press the Enter key. Finally, for purposes of readability, QBasic allows you to enter blank lines in a program. (For additional programming style tips, see Section C.4 in Appendix C.)

Documenting a Program — The REM Statement

Documentation is the readable description of what a program or procedure within a program is supposed to do. More often than not, programmers are asked to support the programs they write by means of internal comments. Documentation is used to identify programs and clarify parts of a program that would otherwise be difficult for others to understand.

The REM **statements** in Program 2.7, lines 1 through 6, 8, 13, and 15, are called **remarks** or **comments**. A remark consists of the keyword, REM, followed by a message or explanation intended solely for programmers. A REM statement can be located anywhere in a program.

REM statements are nonexecutable, which means they have no effect on the results of a QBasic program. However, REM statements do take up space in main memory. Program 2.7, which includes REM statements, and Program 2.6, which does not, both produce the same results. Again, line numbers are added to the left of Program 2.7 for the sake of clarity and are not part of the program.

PROGRAM 2.7

```
 1   REM Program 2.7
 2   REM Determining a Salesperson's Commission
 3   REM J. S. Quasney, CIS 215, Div. 01
 4   REM September 30, 2002
 5   REM ************************************
 6   REM Clear Screen
 7   CLS
 8   REM Request Data from Operator
 9   INPUT "Commission rate =====> ", Rate
10   INPUT "Week 1 sales ========> ", Week1
11   INPUT "Week 2 sales ========> ", Week2
12   INPUT "Return sales ========> ", Returns
13   REM Calculate the Earned Commission
14   Commission = Rate * (Week1 + Week2 - Returns)
15   REM Display the Earned Commission
16   PRINT
17   PRINT "Earned Commission ===>"; Commission
18   END


[run]

Commission rate =====> 0.18
Week 1 sales ========> 1200
Week 2 sales ========> 1500
Return sales ========> 75

Earned commission ===> 472.5
```

QBasic permits you to use an **apostrophe** (') as an abbreviation for the keyword REM. QBasic also permits the placement of a remark or comment on the right-hand side of a statement by requiring the insertion of an apostrophe before the comment. The following two lines are valid:

```
' Initialization Routine
CLS        ' Clear Screen
```

The general form for the REM statement is found in Table 2.4.

TABLE 2.4 - The REM Statement	
General Form:	REM comment or ' comment
Purpose:	To insert explanatory remarks or comments in a program for documentary purposes.
Examples:	REM Program 2.7 REM J. S. Quasney REM Determine the Balance Due ' ' *************************** ' Compute Gross Pay PRINT Answer ' Display result

Here are a few basic suggestions for including remarks or comments in a program.

1. Write and include your remarks as you code the program.
2. Write a narrative, including the program name, date, author and any other desirable remarks, at the beginning of each program. (See Section 2.13.)

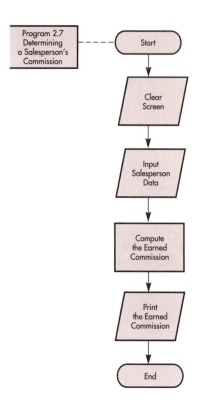

3. Remarks should come before each major procedure in a program.
4. Variable names should be explained when it is not apparent what they represent.
5. Use remarks only where the code is not self-explanatory. Do not insert remarks for their own sake. Insert them to make your program more readable.

Program Flowcharts

A general flowchart that corresponds to Program 2.7 is shown in Figure 2.3. A flowchart does not have to include a symbol for each statement in the program. For example, the four INPUT statements in Program 2.7 are represented by the single input/output (I/0) symbol, Input Salesperson Data, which follows the Clear Screen symbol in the flowchart in Figure 2.3. Furthermore, it is not necessary to include an annotation symbol in the flowchart for every REM statement.

Multiple Statements per Line

QBasic allows you to write multiple statements per line, up to a maximum of 255 characters. For example, Program 2.2 can be rewritten as the following:

```
' Program 2.2
Pay = 0.18 * (1200 + 1500 - 75) : PRINT Pay : END
```

The statements in the second line are separated by colons. The purpose of the colon is to inform QBasic that a statement has ended and that a new statement follows on the same line.

Do not precede any statement with a REM statement when using multiple statements per line. QBasic considers all characters following the keyword REM or the apostrophe (') to be a comment, including the colon. For the purpose of readability, it is recommended that you use multiple statements per line very sparingly.

2.5 GETTING ACQUAINTED WITH THE QB OPERATING ENVIRONMENT

To enter a program like Program 2.7 into the PC and execute it, you must familiarize yourself with the QB operating environment.

Starting a QBasic Session

Boot the PC and, after the PC is operational, start QBasic. Use Table 2.5 if QBasic is already on your computer's hard drive and you are starting QBasic from the DOS prompt or a DOS prompt window. Use Table 2.6 if there is a QBasic icon or shortcut on your Windows desktop.

TABLE 2.5 - Loading QBasic from the DOS Prompt
1. Place your Data Disk in the floppy disk drive.
2. At the DOS prompt, type QBASIC and press the Enter key.

TABLE 2.6 - Loading QBasic from an Icon or Shortcut
1. Place your Data Disk in the floppy disk drive.
2. Double-click the QBasic icon or shortcut.

Several seconds will elapse while the QBasic program is loaded from the hard drive into main memory. After QBasic is loaded into main memory, you are ready to create or load a program.

The first screen displayed by QBasic includes a Welcome message. In the Welcome message, QBasic directs you to press the Esc key to display the QBasic screen (Figure 2.4) to begin entering a program or press the Enter key to obtain help from the QB Survival Guide. The **QB Survival Guide** is an online help system that answers your questions about QBasic as fast as you can click the mouse or press the F1 key. The QB Survival Guide is discussed in more detail later in Section 2.9.

The QBasic Screen

The QBasic screen includes four main parts — the menu bar, the view window, the immediate window, and the status line, as shown in Figure 2.4.

FIGURE 2.4
The QBasic screen.

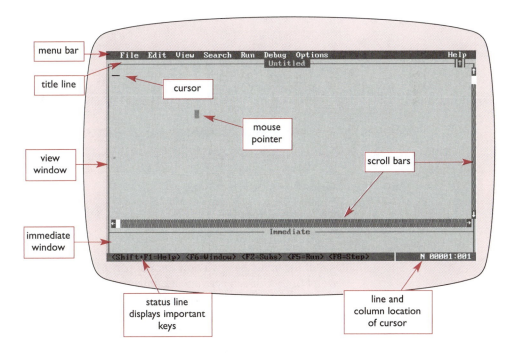

Menu Bar

The **menu bar**, the bar at the very top of the QBasic screen shown in Figure 2.4, displays a list of menu names. Each menu name has a corresponding menu of commands. These commands are useful when entering and modifying programs. In this chapter, we will discuss the most used commands. See Appendix B for a complete listing and description of QBasic commands.

To select a menu, click the name on the menu bar. QBasic immediately displays a *pull-down menu* that lists a series of commands. To select a command, click the command on the menu. Figure 2.5 shows the File menu superimposed over the display of Program 2.7. To deactivate the menu bar or any menu and activate the view window, click anywhere in the view window outside the menu bar or menu.

View Window

The **view window** is the largest part of the screen, and the one that contains the cursor as illustrated in Figure 2.4 on the previous page. In the view window, you can enter, modify, and display programs. When QBasic first starts, the view window is active; that is, if you start typing characters, they will appear on the first line of the view window. At the top of the view window is the title line. The **title line** displays the name of the current program. The program title is highlighted when the view window is active. The program is called, Untitled, until it is given a name. Program names will be discussed in another section.

Along the bottom and the right side of the view window are the scroll bars. With your mouse you can move the pointer along the scroll bars and move the window in any direction to see code that does not appear in the view window. See Appendix B for additional information on moving the view window in any direction.

FIGURE 2.5
The File menu.

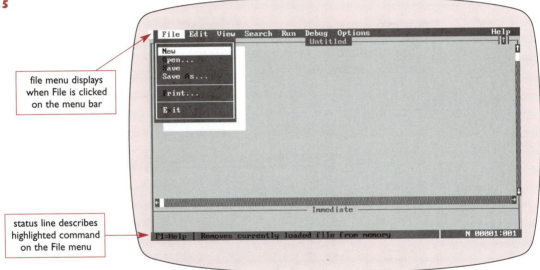

file menu displays when File is clicked on the menu bar

status line describes highlighted command on the File menu

Immediate Window

The narrow window below the view window is called the **immediate window**. The immediate window is used to execute statements as soon as they are entered. Statements entered in the immediate window are not part of the current program.

At any time, you can activate the immediate window by clicking anywhere within it. This moves the cursor from the view window to the immediate window. QBasic highlights the word, Immediate. Click anywhere in the view window and the cursor moves from the immediate window to the view window. Use of the immediate window as a calculator and debugging tool is discussed in Chapter 4, Section 4.4, and in Appendix C.

Status Line

The line at the very bottom of the QBasic screen is the **status line**. This line contains a list of the most used function keys and the line and column location of the cursor on the screen. Keyboard indicators, such as C for Caps Lock and N for Num Lock, display immediately to the left of the cursor line and column location counter when these keys are engaged.

If the menu bar is active and one of the menus is selected, then the status line displays the function of the highlighted command in the menu, as illustrated in Figure 2.5.

Dialog Boxes

QBasic uses **dialog boxes** to display messages and request information from you. For example, if you use a keyword for a variable name, such as PRINT LET instead of PRINT Bet, QBasic displays a dialog box when you move the cursor off the line containing the invalid variable name, LET. You move the cursor off the line by pressing the Enter key, clicking another line, or by pressing the Up or Down Arrow keys.

The dialog box shown in Figure 2.6 displays if you attempt to end the QBasic session without saving the latest changes made to the program in the view window. Dialog boxes list acceptable user responses in buttons and text boxes. **Buttons** are labeled to indicate what they represent. **Text boxes** are used to enter information, such as a file name.

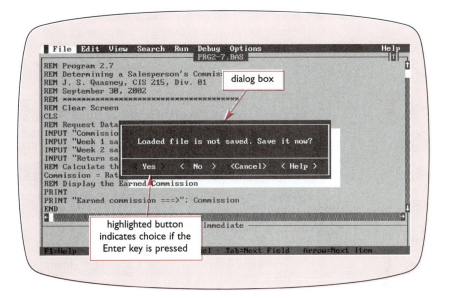

In response to the message in the dialog box in Figure 2.6, you can point to the desired button and then click.

Terminating a QBasic Session

To quit QBasic, click File on the menu bar and then click Exit on the File menu. If you did not save the latest version of the current program, the dialog box shown in Figure 2.6 displays. QBasic requests that you select one of the buttons before continuing.

2.6 EDITING QBASIC PROGRAMS

QBasic programs are entered one line at a time into the view window. The Enter key signals QBasic that a line is complete. During the process of entering a program, it is easy to make keyboard errors and grammatical errors because of your inexperience with the QBasic language. Logical errors also can occur in a program if you have not considered all the details associated with the problem.

Some errors can be eliminated if you use coding forms and logic tools, and if you carefully review your design and program before you enter it into the view window. Any remaining errors are resolved by editing the program. **Editing** is the process of entering and altering a program.

The remainder of this section describes the most common types of editing. You will find the editing features of QBasic to be both powerful and easy to use. For additional editing features, see Appendix B.

Deleting Previously Typed Characters

Use the arrow keys or the mouse to position the cursor. Press the **Delete key (DEL)** to delete the character under the cursor and the **Backspace key** to delete the character to the left of the cursor. See Figures 1.4(a) and 1.4(b) on page 5 for the location of these keys on the keyboard.

To delete a series of adjacent characters in a line, position the mouse pointer on the leftmost character to be deleted. Drag the mouse pointer until the characters to delete are highlighted. Press the Delete key or click Edit on the menu bar and then click Cut.

Changing or Replacing Previously Typed Lines

Move the mouse pointer to the character position where you wish to make a change and then click. Begin typing the new characters. QBasic is by default in the insert mode. In the **insert mode**, the cursor is a blinking underline and the character under the cursor and those to the right are pushed to the right as you enter new characters in the line. In the **overtype mode**, the cursor is a blinking box and the character under the cursor is replaced by the one you type. Use the **Insert key** to toggle between the insert and overtype modes.

Adding New Lines

Press the Enter key to add a new or blank line. To add a new line above the current line, click the first character in the line and then press the Enter key. To add a new line below the current line, click to the right of the last character and then press the Enter key.

The Enter key should only be pressed with the cursor at the beginning or end of a line. If you press the Enter key in the middle of a line, it is split. To join the split lines, press the Backspace key with the cursor on the first character of the second line.

Deleting a Series of Lines

To delete multiple lines, drag the mouse pointer from the first character to the last character in the series of lines. With the lines highlighted, press the Delete key or click Edit on the menu bar and then click Cut.

Moving Text

Moving text from one location to another in a program is called cut and paste. To **cut and paste** text, do the following:

1. Move the mouse pointer to the beginning of the text you wish to move.
2. Drag to select the text.
3. Click Edit on the menu bar and then click Cut. The deleted text is placed on the Clipboard. The **Clipboard** is a temporary storage area that contains the last text deleted using Cut.
4. Click on the new location. Click Edit on the menu bar and then click Paste.

Copying Lines

Copying text from one location to another in a program is called **pasting**. To paste text, do the following:

1. Move the mouse pointer to the beginning of the text you wish to paste.
2. Drag to select the text.
3. Click Edit on the menu bar and then click Copy. The copied text is placed on the Clipboard.
4. Click the new location. Click Edit on the menu bar and then click Paste.

2.7 EXECUTING PROGRAMS AND HARD COPY OUTPUT

The menu bar at the top of the screen contains seven menu names (Figure 2.4 on page 33). Each menu has a list of commands. As indicated earlier, you can select a menu by moving the pointer to the desired menu name and then clicking the mouse button. Perhaps the two most important menus are Run and File. The Run menu is used primarily to execute the current program. The File menu contains several important commands. One in particular, the Print command, is used to print all or part of the current program.

Executing the Current Program

You can execute, or run, the current program by clicking Run on the menu bar and then clicking Start (see Figure 2.7). The Start command can be selected in different ways, as described in Table 2.7.

FIGURE 2.7
The Run menu.

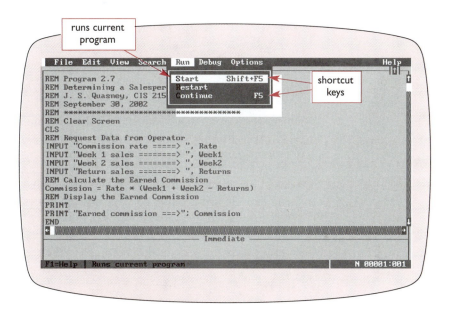

TABLE 2.7 - Executing the Current Program

METHOD	DESCRIPTION
Mouse	Click Run on the menu bar and then click Start.
Mouse	Click <F5=Run> on the status line.

When the program first executes, QBasic replaces the QBasic screen with the Output screen. The **Output screen** shows the results due to the execution of the current program. Figure 2.8 on the next page shows the Output screen for Program 2.7. After reading the output results, you can redisplay the QBasic screen by pressing any key (numeric, alphabetic, or special character) on the keyboard. This is indicated at the bottom of the Output screen. To redisplay the output results, click View on the menu bar and then click Output Screen.

The remaining commands on the Run menu are described in Appendix B.

FIGURE 2.8
The output screen.

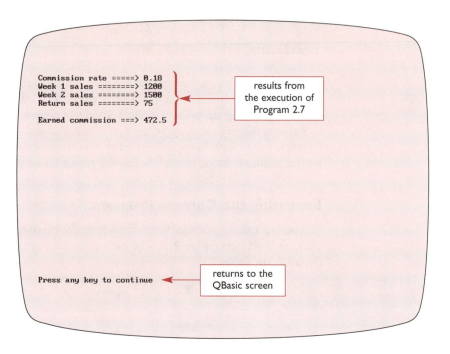

Commission rate =====> 0.18
Week 1 sales ========> 1200
Week 2 sales ========> 1500
Return sales ========> 75

Earned commission ===> 472.5

> results from the execution of Program 2.7

Press any key to continue

> returns to the QBasic screen

Listing Program Lines on the Printer

In many instances, it is desirable to list the program and the results on a printer. A listing of this type is called **hard copy output**.

You can list all or part of the current program on the printer by using the Print command on the File menu. With the printer in the Ready mode, click File on the menu bar (see Figure 2.9). Next, click Print to print the current program. The three periods following the Print command indicate that a dialog box will display requesting additional information. When the Print dialog box displays (see Figure 2.10), make sure the bullet is next to the option, Entire Program. Finally, click OK.

FIGURE 2.9
The File menu.

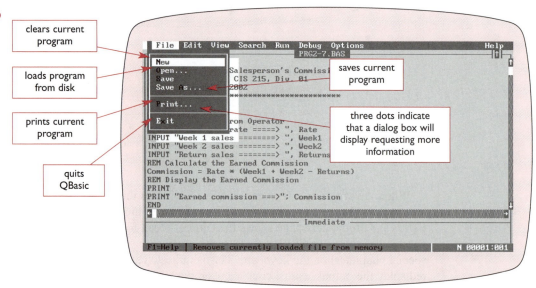

clears current program

loads program from disk

prints current program

quits QBasic

saves current program

three dots indicate that a dialog box will display requesting more information

```
File  Edit  View  Search  Run  Debug  Options                    Help
                              PRG2-7.BAS
New                           Salesperson's Commissi
Open...                         CIS 215, Div. 01
Save                          2002
Save As...                    *******************************
Print...
                              rom Operator
Exit                          rate ====> ", Rate
INPUT "Week 1 sales =======> ", Week1
INPUT "Week 2 sales =======> ", Week2
INPUT "Return sales =======> ", Returns
REM Calculate the Earned Commission
Commission = Rate * (Week1 + Week2 - Returns)
REM Display the Earned Commission
PRINT
PRINT "Earned commission ===>"; Commission
END

                              Immediate
F1=Help | Removes currently loaded file from memory        N 00001:001
```

FIGURE 2.10
Dialog box for the Print command.

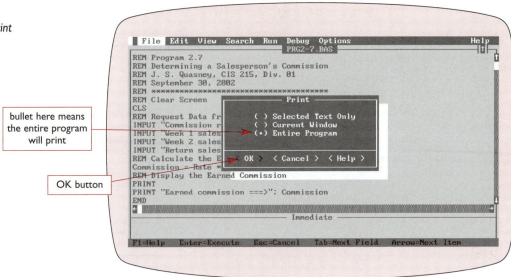

Listing a Portion of the Program on the Printer

To print a portion of the current program, use the mouse to highlight the lines in the program you wish to print. Next, follow the steps outlined in the previous paragraphs for printing the program. When the Print dialog box displays on the screen, the bullet should be in front of the Selected Text Only option (see Figure 2.10). QBasic automatically assigns the bullet to Selected Text Only when a series of lines is selected prior to issuing the Print command.

Printing the Results on the Output Screen

Depending on the operating environment you are using, the method of printing Output Screen results differs. Table 2.8 summarizes various techniques of printing Output Screen results. Later in Chapter 4, we will discuss the LPRINT statement as an alternative means to generating hard copy output.

TABLE 2.8 - Printing Output Screen Results	
ENVIRONMENT	**PROCEDURES**
DOS	Press the Print Screen key to print to your local printer. To retrieve your output, you may have to press the On Line button on your printer, press Form Feed, and then press On Line again.
Windows 3.1	Press the Print Screen key to copy the Output Screen results to the clipboard. Use Alt+Tab to return to Program Manager. Open the Accessories window and open the Notepad program. Click Edit on the menu bar and then click Paste. The output results should display. Click File on the menu bar and then click Print to print the results.
Windows 95/98	Click the Mark button on the Output Screen toolbar, drag through the Output Screen results to highlight them, and then click the Copy button on the Output Screen toolbar to copy the Output Screen results to the Clipboard. Click Start on the taskbar, point to Programs, point to Accessories, and then click Notepad. Click Edit on the Notepad menu bar and then click Paste. The output results should appear. Click File on the menu bar and click Print to print the results.

2.8 SAVING, LOADING, AND ERASING PROGRAMS

In addition to the Print and Exit commands, four additional commands on the File menu (see Figure 2.9 on page 38) are essential for your first session with QBasic — Save, Save As, Open, and New. The Save and Save As commands allow you to store the current program to disk. Later, use the Open command to load the program from disk into main memory to make it the current one. The New command removes the current program from main memory. It clears the view window and indicates the beginning of a new program. Before we discuss these four commands further, it is important that you understand the concept of a file specification.

File Specifications

A **file specification**, also called a **filespec**, is used to identify programs and data files placed in auxiliary storage. A filespec is made up of a device name, a file folder or path, a file name, and an extension.

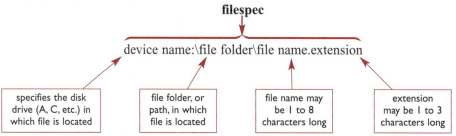

filespec

device name:\file folder\file name.extension

| specifies the disk drive (A, C, etc.) in which file is located | file folder, or path, in which file is located | file name may be 1 to 8 characters long | extension may be 1 to 3 characters long |

The device name refers to the disk drive. If no device is specified, then the filespec refers to the default disk drive of the PC. If a device name is included in the filespec, then it must be followed by a colon.

The file folder, or path, is the folder on the disk drive of the PC in which the desired file is located. If no file folder is specified, then the filespec refers to the current default file folder for the disk drive being accessed. A path may be composed of multiple file folders, but each file folder listed must be preceded by a backward slash (\) and the final file folder listed must be followed by one.

Because QBasic is a DOS environment program, file names are limited to one to eight characters in length. Valid characters are uppercase or lowercase A–Z, 0–9, and certain special characters ($ & # @ ! % " ( ) – { } _ / \). If an extension is used, then the file name must be followed by a period.

An extension that is up to three characters in length may be used to classify a file. Valid characters are the same as for a file name. With QBasic, the default extension is bas. That is, when you use a command that requires a filespec, QBasic will automatically append an extension of bas if one is not included.

Examples of valid filespecs include A:payroll, A:\programs\LAB2-1, PAYROLL.BAS, Accounts, and SA123. The first two examples reference files on drive A. The second example explicitly indicates the programs file folder. The latter three examples reference files on the default drive and in the default file folder.

Saving the Current Program to Disk

When you enter a program through the keyboard, it is stored in the computer's main memory, and it displays in the view window. When you quit QBasic or turn the computer off, the current program disappears from the screen and, more importantly, from main memory. To save a program to disk for later use, use the Save command or the Save As command in the File menu.

Use the Save command to save the program under the same name. Use the Save As command to save the program under a new name. Because this is the first time we are saving the program, we will use the Save As command.

To select the Save As command, click File on the menu bar and then click Save As. Here again, the three periods following the Save As command mean QBasic requires additional information. In this case, it needs to know the filespec.

When the Save As dialog box displays (see Figure 2.11), if necessary, click the proper drive and/or file folder, then type in the file name, and, finally, click OK. In Figure 2.11, we entered the file name prg2-7. QBasic stores the current program using the filespec a:prg2-7.bas. Note in Figure 2.11 that the default drive (A:\) is specified below the file name box.

FIGURE 2.11

Dialog box for the Save As command.

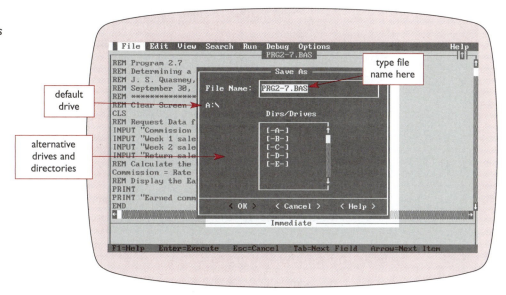

The **Dirs/Drives box** in the lower portion of the Save As dialog box includes a list of the disk drives and any file folders, or directories, that are part of the current default drive. You may use the mouse to activate this box and select a different default drive or file folder.

If you loaded the current program from disk or saved the program earlier, the file name will be in the file name box when you execute the Save As command. To save the program under the old file name, simply click OK. To change the file name, begin typing. The name you type replaces the old name. In this case, the old file remains in its present form, and a new file is created on disk.

Loading a Program from Disk

To load a program stored on disk into main memory, use the Open command on the File menu (see Figure 2.9 on page 38). This command causes the dialog box shown in Figure 2.12 to display. In the middle of the dialog box, QBasic displays the Files box. The **Files box** lists the file names on the default drive that have an extension of bas. The current default drive displays just above the Files box. To display any other file folder or directory on your PC, enter the disk drive, or path, in the File Name box or select one from the Dirs/Drives box and click OK. To display another file folder, you can also double-click an entry in the Dirs/Drives box.

FIGURE 2.12
Dialog box for the Open Program command.

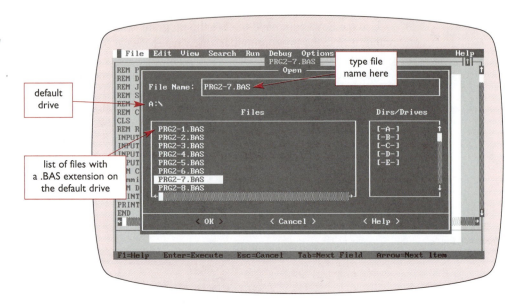

default drive

type file name here

list of files with a .BAS extension on the default drive

In the File Name box, enter the name of the program you want to load from auxiliary storage into main memory. In Figure 2.12, we entered the file name prg2-7. Enter the file name by typing it on the keyboard or use the mouse to select the file name from the Files box. To complete the command, click OK.

If you did not save the current program before attempting to load a new one, QBasic will give you the opportunity to save it before it loads the new program into main memory.

Starting a New Program

The New command on the File menu (see Figure 2.9 on page 38) instructs QBasic to erase the current program from main memory. This also clears the view window. Use this command when you are finished with the current program and wish to start a new one from scratch. Note that it is not necessary to clear the current program if you are loading a program from disk. The Open command clears main memory before it loads the new program.

TABLE 2.9 - QB Survival Guide Help

Device/Key	Action and Result
Mouse	Clicking Help on the menu bar pulls down the Help menu, which includes commands to link into the QB Survival Guide (see Figure 2.13).
Esc key	Exits the QB Survival Guide and activates the view window.
Right Button on Mouse	Displays **context-sensitive help** menus for the topic the mouse pointer is pointing at. For example, position the mouse pointer within a keyword, menu name, command in a pull-down menu, or any symbol and click the right button on the mouse. Figure 2.14 shows the context-sensitive Help screen for the LET statement.
Help Button	Click the Help button whenever a dialog box displays on the screen.
Mouse	Click Help on the menu bar and click Using Help to display the general Help screen shown in Figure 2.15.

2.9 THE QB SURVIVAL GUIDE ONLINE HELP SYSTEM

The QB Survival Guide is a fully integrated online help system with instant access to any QBasic question. You can request immediate help when you first enter QBasic by pressing the Enter key rather than the Esc key. Thereafter, at any time while you are using QBasic, you can interact with the QB Survival Guide and display help screens on any QBasic topic using the mouse or the keys described in Table 2.9. The QB Survival Guide is a complete reference manual at your fingertips.

The best way to familiarize yourself with the QB Survival Guide is to use it. Question 12 on page 50 in the Test Your QBasic Skills section of this chapter asks that you display and print several Help screens.

FIGURE 2.13
The Help menu.

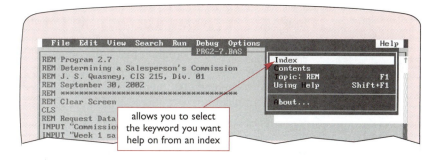

allows you to select the keyword you want help on from an index

FIGURE 2.14
The Help screen for the keyword LET.

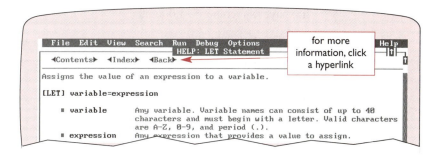

for more information, click a hyperlink

FIGURE 2.15
The initial Help screen when you click Help and then click Using Help.

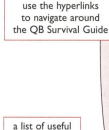

use the hyperlinks to navigate around the QB Survival Guide

a list of useful QB Survival Guide keys

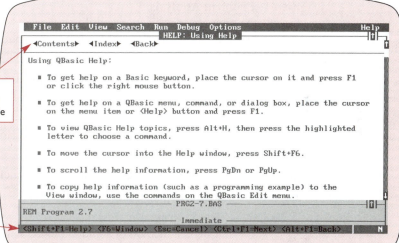

2.10 A GUIDE TO WRITING YOUR FIRST PROGRAM

Having read the first nine sections of this chapter, you should be ready to write your first program to use a computer for solving a problem. At the end of Chapter 2 you are given several QBasic Programming Problems. Each problem includes a short statement of the problem, suggested input data and the corresponding output results. Collectively, these items are the **program specifications**. Following the sample QBasic Programming Problem presented in the following paragraphs, we have suggested a step-by-step procedure for solving the problem. You will find this helpful when you begin solving problems on your own. You will also find it helpful to review Section 1.6 on pages 12 through 16.

Sample QBasic Programming Problem: Computation of State Tax

Problem: Construct a program that will compute the state tax owed by a taxpayer. The state determines the amount of tax by taking a person's yearly income, subtracting $800.00 for each dependent and then multiplying the result 3% to determine the tax due. Use the following formula:

Tax = 0.03 * (Income – 800 * Dependents)

Code the program so that it will request that the taxpayer's income and the number of dependents be entered through the keyboard.

Input Data: Use the following sample input data:

Taxpayer's income: $73,000.00

Number of dependents: 5

Output Results: The following results are displayed:

```
Taxpayer's income ========> 73000
Number of dependents =====> 5

State tax due ============> 2070
```

The following systematic approach to solving this exercise, as well as the other QBasic Programming Problems in this textbook, is recommended. In essence, this list is the same as the program development life cycle in Section 1.6 of Chapter 1.

Step 1: Problem Analysis

Review the program specifications until you thoroughly understand the problem to be solved. Ascertain the form of input, the form of output, and the type of processing that must be performed. For this problem, you should have determined the following:

Input Data: The program must allow for the user to supply the data through the use of INPUT statements. There are two data items: taxpayer's income and number of dependents.

Processing: The formula Tax = 0.03 * (Income – 800 * Dependents) will determine the state tax.

Output Results: The required results include the input prompt messages and the state tax due.

Step 2: Program Design

Develop a method of solution the PC will use. One way to do this is to list the program tasks sequentially. For this exercise, the **program tasks** are as follows:

1. Clear the screen.
2. Prompt the user for the necessary data.
3. Calculate the state tax.
4. Display the state tax.

After the program tasks have been determined, select the variable names you plan to use in the program solution. Three variable names are required. We will use the following:

1. Income — for Taxpayer's income
2. Dependents — for Number of dependents
3. Tax — for State Tax

Next, draw a program flowchart or write pseudocode that shows how the program will accomplish the program tasks. The flowchart for the sample programming exercise is shown in Figure 2.16.

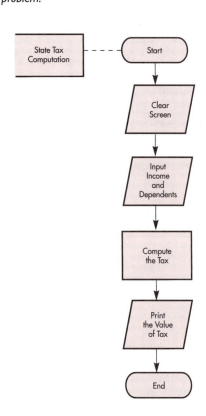

FIGURE 2.16

A general flowchart for the sample QBasic programming problem.

Step 3: Test the Design
Carefully review the design by stepping through the program flowchart or pseudocode to ensure that it is logically correct.

Step 4: Code the Program
Code the program, as shown in Figure 2.17, according to the program design.

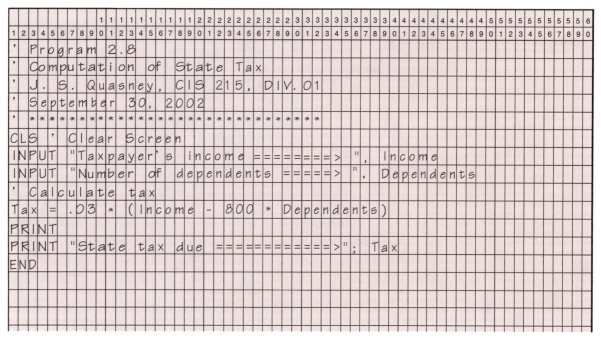

```
' Program 2.8
' Computation of State Tax
' J. S. Quasney, CIS 215, DIV. 01
' September 30, 2002
' ************************************
CLS ' Clear Screen
INPUT "Taxpayer's income ========> ", Income
INPUT "Number of dependents =====> ", Dependents
' Calculate tax
Tax = .03 * (Income - 800 * Dependents)
PRINT
PRINT "State tax due =============>"; Tax
END
```

Step 5: Review the Code
Carefully review the code. Put yourself in the position of the PC and step through the program. This is sometimes referred to as **desk checking** your code. Be sure the syntax of each instruction is correct. Check to be sure that the sequence of the instructions is logically correct so that the program will work the first time it is executed.

Step 6: Enter the Program
Enter the program into the PC, as shown in the upper screen of Figure 2.18. Before starting this step, you should be familiar with QBasic and the commands discussed in the previous sections.

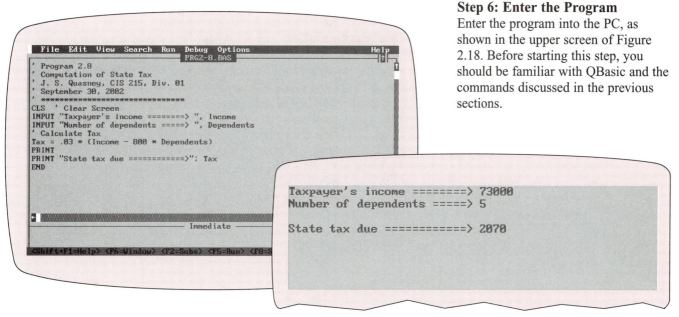

Program solution to the sample QBasic programming problem in the view window and the corresponding results displayed in the output screen.

Step 7: Test the Program

Test the program by executing it. Click Run on the menu bar and then click Start, or click <F5=Run> on the status line. The output results are shown in the lower screen in Figure 2.18 on the previous page. If the input data does not produce the expected results, the program must be reviewed and corrected.

Step 8: Formalize the Solution

Obtain a hard copy of the source program and the output results. If the program logic was modified in Steps 4 through 6, revise the documentation and redraw the program flowchart to include the changes.

Step 9: Maintain the Program

Correct errors or add enhancements to the program as per your instructor's request.

2.11 What You Should Know

The following list summarizes this chapter:

1. A QBasic program is composed of a sequence of lines. Each line may contain one or more statements, up to a maximum of 255 characters.
2. A keyword informs QBasic of the type of statement to be executed. LET, PRINT, and END are keywords. The keyword, LET, is optional in a LET statement.
3. Constants are ordinary numbers that do not change during the execution of a program.
4. A variable is a location in main memory whose value can change as the program is executed. Variables are referenced by their names.
5. A variable name begins with a letter and may be followed by up to 39 letters, digits, and decimal points. It is invalid to use a keyword as a variable name.
6. The equal sign in a LET statement means that the value of the variable to the left of the equal sign is to be replaced by the final value to the right of the equal sign.
7. As in mathematics, parentheses override the normal sequence of arithmetic operations.
8. The PRINT statement instructs the PC to bring a result out from memory and display it on the screen.
9. The line containing the END statement terminates the execution of the program.
10. Each program should contain an END statement.
11. Every variable appearing in an output statement should appear at least once earlier in the program in such a way that its value can be determined.
12. Although most QBasic statements can be placed anywhere in a given program, logic, common sense, and style dictate where these statements are placed.
13. Every variable appearing to the right of the equal sign in a LET statement should appear at least once earlier in the same program in such a way that its value can be determined.
14. The function of the INPUT statement is to display an input prompt and to suspend execution of the program until data has been supplied from a source outside the program, such as the keyboard. The input prompt must be followed by a comma or a semicolon separator. If a semicolon follows the input prompt, then a question mark displays following the input prompt when the INPUT statement is executed.
15. A comma is used to establish a list, which is a set of distinct elements. In a PRINT or INPUT statement, each element is separated from the next by a comma.
16. Every variable appearing in the program whose value is directly obtained through input must be listed in an INPUT statement before it is used elsewhere in the program.
17. In a PRINT statement, such as PRINT X, the PC displays the value of X and not the letter X.

18. The `PRINT` statement can be used to display messages as well as the values of variables.
19. In a `PRINT` statement, the semicolon separator instructs the system to maintain the current position of the cursor.
20. The `CLS` statement causes all the information on the output screen to be erased and places the cursor in the upper left corner of the screen.
21. A null list in a `PRINT` statement causes the PC to display a blank line.
22. A line in a program can contain more than one statement if colons are used to separate them.
23. Spaces should appear in a QBasic statement in the same places that spaces appear in an English sentence.
24. The `REM` statement, used to document a program, has no effect on the execution of the program. The apostrophe (') is an abbreviation for `REM`. It may also be used to insert a comment on the right-hand side of a QBasic statement.
25. Grammatical and syntactical errors can be corrected by editing the QBasic program. For example, you can correct errors while keying in a line. Lines can also be replaced, inserted, or deleted.
26. There are four main parts to the QBasic screen — the menu bar, the view window, the immediate window, and the status line.
27. The menu bar displays a list of menu names. Each menu name has a *pull-down menu* of commands. Select a menu name by clicking it.
28. In the view window, you can enter, modify, and display programs.
29. The immediate window is used to execute statements as soon as they are entered.
30. The status line displays important information, such as special keys, and the cursor line and column location on the screen.
31. Use the cursor movement keys or the mouse to move the cursor on the screen.
32. QBasic uses dialog boxes to display messages and request information.
33. To use the QB Survival Guide online help facility, click Help on the menu bar or right-click for context-sensitive help.
34. Editing is the process of entering and altering a program.
35. A file specification, also called a filespec, is used to identify programs and data files placed in auxiliary storage. A filespec is made up of a device name, a file folder or path, a file name and an extension.
36. To execute the current program, click Run on the menu bar and then click Start, or click <F5=Run> on the status line.
37. Select the Print command on the File menu to list all or part of the current program to the printer.
38. The output results of a program are displayed on the Output screen. Printing the Output screen will depend upon your environment.
39. Click the Save command on the File menu to save the current program to disk under the same file name.
40. Click the Save As command on the File menu to save the current program to disk under a new file name.
41. Click the Open command on the File menu to load a program from disk into main memory.
42. Click the New command on the File menu to remove the current program from main memory and begin a new program.
43. Click the Exit command on the File menu to quit QBasic and return control to your operating environment.

2.12 Test Your QBasic Skills (Even-numbered answers are in Appendix E)

1. Identify the eight major components of the QBasic screen shown in Figure 2.19.

FIGURE 2.19

The QBasic screen.

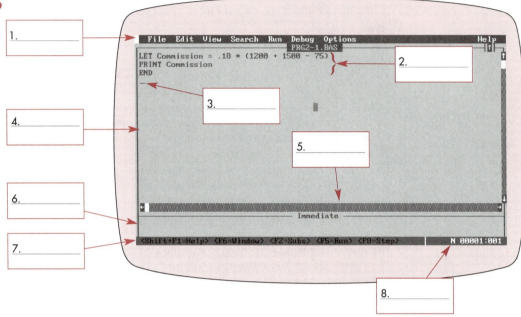

1. _____

2. _____

3. _____

4. _____

5. _____

6. _____

7. _____

8. _____

2. Put yourself in the place of the PC and record for each line the current values of A, B, and C. **Hint:** The value of a variable does not change until the program instructs the PC to change it.

1	A = 9
2	B = 2
3	C = 5
4	C = C + 3
5	A = C * B
6	PRINT A
7	B = B + 2
8	PRINT B
9	C = C - 4
10	PRINT C
11	A = A - 10
12	PRINT A
13	C = C / B
14	PRINT C
15	END

Line	A	B	C	Displayed
1				
2				
3				
4				
5				
6				
7				
8				
9				
10				
11				
12				
13				
14				
15				

3. For each program below, construct a table similar to the one in Exercise 2. Record for each line the current values of the variables and the results displayed by the PRINT statements.

a.
```
 1   A = 4
 2   B = 6
 3   PRINT A
 4   A = A + 2
 5   B = B - 2
 6   PRINT B
 7   A = A + 2
 8   B = B - 2
 9   PRINT A
10   END
```

b. A is assigned the value 6, and B is assigned the value 3 in line 3.
```
 1   C = 6
 2   PRINT C
 3   INPUT  A, B
 4   C = A \ B + C + 8 MOD 4
 5   A = A - 5
 6   B = C ^ A
 7   PRINT B
 8   END
```

c. A is assigned the value 8, B is assigned the value 5 in line 1.
```
 1   INPUT A, B
 2   C = A * A
 3   PRINT C
 4   D = A - B
 5   PRINT D
 6   E = 2
 7   PRINT E
 8   D = D - 2
 9   X = E / D
10   PRINT X
11   END
```

d. Principal is assigned the value 500 and Rate is assigned the value 12 in line 1.
```
 1   INPUT Principal, Rate
 2   Rate = Rate / 100
 3   Discount = Principal * Rate
 4   Rate = Rate * 100
 5   ' Display Results
 6   PRINT "Discount"; Rate
 7   PRINT "Price $"; Principal
 8   PRINT "Discount $"; Discount
 9   END
```

4. Write LET statements for each of the following:
   a. Assign T the value of 3.
   b. Assign X the value of T less 2.
   c. Assign P the product of T and X.
   d. Triple the value of T.
   e. Assign A the quotient of P divided by X.
   f. Increment X by 1.
   g. Cube the value of R.

5. What does the following program display when the value 14 is entered in response to the first INPUT statement and 8 in response to the second INPUT statement?

```
' Exercise 2.5
INPUT "What is the length"; Leng
INPUT "What is the width"; Wid
Area = Leng * Wid
PRINT "A rectangle with dimensions"; Leng; "and"; Wid
PRINT "has an area of"; Area; "."
END
```

6. Name three techniques presented in Chapter 2 for integrating data into a program.

7. In a QBasic program, how do you instruct the PC to display a blank line as part of the output results?

8. Explain in one sentence each the purpose of the following menu commands: Exit, New, Open, Print, Save As, and Start.

9. What is logically wrong with the following program?

```
' Exercise 2.9
INPUT D, E
D = E / F
PRINT "The answer is"; D
END
```

10. A program is needed that requests the user to input the hours worked and the rate of pay. The program determines the gross pay by multiplying the two values together and displays the calculated gross pay. Is the following program solution logically sound for the problem stated?

```
' Exercise 2.10
INPUT "Hours worked ===>", Hours
INPUT "Rate of pay ====>", Rate
PRINT "The gross pay is"; Pay
Pay = Rate * Hours
END
```

11. **PC Hands-On Exercise:** Load the QBasic program indicated below from your Data Disk and perform the indicated tasks. Download the Data Disk at course.com or see your instructor. With the QBasic screen on your monitor, do the following:
    a. Load Program 2.7 (PRG2-7.BAS) from the Data Disk.
    b. Print a hard copy of the program.
    c. Run the program and see what happens.
    d. Print a copy of the output screen.
    e. Quit QBasic and remove the Data Disk.

12. **PC Hands-On Exercise:** To gain experience with the QB Survival Guide, do the following:
    a. Start QBasic and click the message "Press Enter to see the Survival Guide" when the initial dialog box displays on the screen. Read the screen and click File, click Print, and then click OK to obtain a hard copy listing. Click <Esc=Cancel> on the status line to exit.
    b. Type the keyword INPUT. With the cursor in or near the keyword INPUT, click the right mouse button. When the Help screen appears, read it over and print a hard copy listing. Click anywhere in the Help window and then click <Esc=Cancel> on the status line to exit.
    c. Click Help and then click Using Help. When the Help screen displays, read the information and scroll downward. Scroll back up to the top and double-click the hyperlink, Contents. Navigate around the QB Survival Guide by double-clicking other hyperlinks.

2.13 QBasic Programming Problems

So that your computer programs will be documented properly, use the following identification format at the beginning of each QBasic program:

```
' Problem Number
' A Short Description of the Problem
' Your Name, Course Number, Course Division
' Today's Date
' ****************************************
```

In line 1, use the comment, Problem 2.1, to represent the first problem in Chapter 2. In line 2, use the title of the problem as the comment. (See Figure 2.18 on page 45.) Upon completion of each problem, turn in to your instructor the following:

1. A logic diagram in flowchart form or in pseudocode as required
2. A listing of the program
3. The listing of output results

(See Section 2.7 on how to obtain a hard copy of your program and output results.)

Use meaningful variable names in all programs. Each major section of the program should be documented with appropriate comment lines.

Be sure to save the program solutions to disk. Use file names of the form LABC-N, where C represents the chapter number and N represents the problem number.

NOTE: All programming problems in this book include partial or complete sample output results and, when applicable, sample input data. Learn to select good test data to evaluate the logic of your program. Check your design and program against the sample output and select your own data for additional testing purposes.

1. Computation of a Product

Purpose: To gain confidence in keying and executing your first QBasic program.

Problem: Key in and execute the following program, which determines the product of two numbers. Replace the verbiage in lines 3 and 4 with your name, course number, course division, and today's date as described earlier. After the program has displayed the proper output results, save the program as LAB2-1 and obtain a hard copy of the program and output results.

```
1    ' Problem 2.1
2    ' Computation of a Product
3    ' Your Name, Course Number, Course Division
4    ' Today's Date
5    ' ****************************************
6    CLS  ' Clear Screen
7    Product = 37.55 * 2.5
8    PRINT "The product is"; Product
9    END
```

Input Data: None.

Output Results: The following displays on the output screen:

```
The product is 93.875
```

2. Determining the Selling Price

Purpose: To become familiar with elementary uses of the INPUT, PRINT, and LET statements.

Problem: Merchants are in the retail business to buy goods from producers, manufacturers, and wholesalers, and to sell the merchandise to their customers. To make a profit, they must sell their merchandise for more than the cost plus the overhead (taxes, store rent, upkeep, salaries, and so forth). The margin is the sum of the overhead and profit. The selling price is the sum of the margin and cost.

Write a program, following the steps outlined in Section 2.10, that will determine the selling price of an item that costs $25.40 and has a margin of 20%. Develop your solution by loading and modifying PRG2-8 on the Data Disk. Download the Data Disk at course.com or see your instructor. You may also simply key in Program 2.8 as shown in Figure 2.18 on page 45. Save the program solution as LAB2-2.

Use the following formula:

$$\text{Selling Price} = \left(\dfrac{1}{1 - \dfrac{\text{Margin}}{100}} \right) \times \text{Cost}$$

Input Data: Use the following data in response to INPUT statements:

Cost: $25.40
Margin: 20%

Output Results: The output screen should display as illustrated by Figure 2.20.

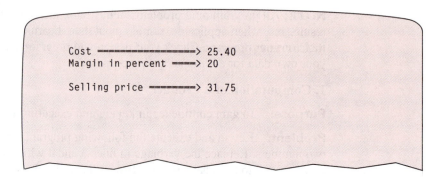

FIGURE 2.20
Output for Programming Problem 2.

```
Cost ==================> 25.40
Margin in percent ====> 20

Selling price =======> 31.75
```

3. The Optimal Investment

Purpose: To familiarize you with the use of the CLS, INPUT, PRINT, and LET statements and to perform multiple runs on the same program.

Problem: Three local banks have undertaken an advertising campaign to attract savings account customers. The specifics of their advertisements are shown in Table 2.10.

TABLE 2.10 – Interest Rates Charged by Three Local Banks		
BANK 1	**BANK 2**	**BANK 3**
Interest 6 7/8%	Interest 6 3/4%	Interest 6 5/8%
Compounded annually	Compounded semiannually	Compounded quarterly

Construct a single program, following the steps outlined in Section 2.10, that will be executed three times, once for each bank. The program is to compute and display the amount of a $750 investment for a period of one year. A comparison of the results will show the optimal investment. Develop your solution by loading and modifying PRG2-8 on the Data Disk. Download the Data Disk at course.com or see your instructor. Save the program solution as LAB2-3. Use the following formula:

Amount = Principal * (1 + Rate / T) ^ T

where T = number of times the investment is compounded per year (that is, the conversions).

Input Data: Enter the data found in Table 2.10 in response to INPUT statements. For example, for Bank 1 enter:

Bank: 1
Principal: $750
Rate: 6.875%
Conversions: 1

Output Results: The output screen for Bank 1 should display as illustrated in Figure 2.21.

FIGURE 2.21
Output for Programming Problem 3.

```
Please enter:

        Bank number ===============> 1
        Principal ================> 750
        Rate in decimal =========> 0.06875
        Number of conversions ===> 1

Amount of investment after one year for bank 1 ====> 801.5625
```

4. Currency Exchange

Purpose: To become familiar with elementary uses of the INPUT, PRINT, and LET statements.

Problem: Write a program that converts U.S.A. dollars to pesos, yen, euros, pounds, and Canadian dollars. The program should request the U.S.A. dollar amount via an INPUT statement, convert the U.S.A. dollar amount to the currencies listed in Table 2.11, and then print the results. Develop the required formulas using the information given in Table 2.11.

Develop your solution by loading and modifying PRG2-8 on the Data Disk. Download the Data Disk at course.com or see your instructor. Save the program solution as LAB2-4.

Input Data: Enter the following U.S.A. dollar amounts individually in response to an INPUT statement. Execute the program once for each of the following U.S.A. dollar amounts.

5
29
44

TABLE 2.11 - Exchange Rates	
Currency	Per U.S.A. Dollar
Peso	9.52
Yen	104.8
Euro	.95
Pound	.61
Canadian	1.47

Output Results: The results illustrated in Figure 2.22 display for 29 dollars.

FIGURE 2.22
Output for Programming Problem 4.

```
Currency Exchange:

        Dollars ===> 29

        Pesos =====> 218.08
        Yen =======> 3039.2
        Euro ======> 27.55
        Pounds ====> 17.69
        Canadian ==> 42.63

End of Report
```

5. Payroll Problem II — Gross Pay Computations

Purpose: To become familiar with some of the grammatical and logical rules of QBasic and to demonstrate some fundamental concepts of executing a QBasic program.

Problem: Construct a program following the steps outlined in Section 2.10 that will clear the screen, and then compute and display the gross pay for an employee working 80 hours during a biweekly pay period at an hourly rate of $13.75.

Version A: Insert the data, 80 and 13.75, directly into a LET statement that determines the gross pay. Save the program solution as LAB2-5A.

Version B: Assign the data, 80 and 13.75, to variables in LET statements and then compute the gross pay in a separate LET statement. Save the program solution as LAB2-5B.

Version C: Enter the data, 80 and 13.75, in response to INPUT statements. Save the program solution as LAB2-5C.

Output Results: The output illustrated in Figure 2.23 is displayed on the output screen for versions B and C of the program. For version A, display only the last line.

FIGURE 2.23

Output for Programming Problem 5.

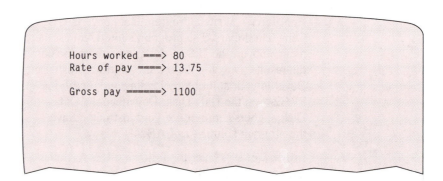

```
Hours worked ===> 80
Rate of pay ====> 13.75

Gross pay ======> 1100
```

Calculations, Strings, and an Introduction to the Top-Down Approach

3.1 INTRODUCTION

In Chapter 2 you were introduced to a few simple computer programs that demonstrated some of the grammatical rules of QBasic. Also presented were examples of programs that interact with the user through the use of the INPUT and PRINT statements. This chapter continues to develop straight-line programs with more complex computations and manipulation of data.

The focus of this chapter is on constants, variables, expressions, functions, rounding and truncation techniques, and the LET statement. This chapter also expands on the type of data that can be assigned to variables by introducing string values, examples of which include a word, a phrase, or a sentence.

Finally, this chapter presents the top-down, or modular, approach to solving problems. The top-down approach is a useful methodology for solving larger and more complex problems than those presented in Chapter 2. Included in the presentation are the GOSUB and RETURN statements.

Upon successful completion of this chapter, you will be able to write programs that manipulate string expressions and numeric expressions. You will also be able to solve problems by first breaking them into smaller and more manageable subprograms.

PROGRAMMING CASE STUDY 3 – Tailor's Calculations

Program 3.1 determines the average neck, hat, and shoe sizes of a male customer. The program uses the following formulas:

$$\text{Neck Size} = \frac{3 \times \text{Weight}}{\text{Waistline}} \qquad \text{Hat Size} = \frac{3 \times \text{Weight}}{2.125 \times \text{Waistline}} \qquad \text{Shoe Size} = \frac{50 \times \text{Waistline}}{\text{Weight}}$$

Program 3.1 on the next page computes the average neck size (15), hat size (7.058824) and shoe size (10) for Mike, who has a 35-inch waistline and weighs 175 pounds. Although it is not used in the computations, the customer name is requested in the program because it helps identify the measurements when more than one set of computations is involved.

PROGRAM 3.1

```
1    ' Program 3.1
2    ' Tailor's Calculations
3    ' Determine Neck Size, Hat Size, and Shoe Size
4    ' *********************************************
5    CLS   ' Clear Screen
6    INPUT "Customer's first name"; First.Name$
7    INPUT "Waistline"; Waist
8    INPUT "Weight"; Weight
9    Neck.Size = 3 * Weight / Waist
10   Hat.Size  = 3 * Weight / (2.125 * Waist)
11   Shoe.Size = 50 * Waist / Weight
12   PRINT
13   PRINT First.Name$; "'s neck size is"; Neck.Size
14   PRINT First.Name$; "'s hat size is"; Hat.Size
15   PRINT First.Name$; "'s shoe size is"; Shoe.Size
16   END


     [run]


     Customer's first name? Mike
     Waistline? 35
     Weight? 175


     Mike's neck size is 15
     Mike's hat size is 7.058824
     Mike's shoe size is 10
```

Program 3.1 contains a sequence of LET statements (lines 9 through 11) with expressions that are more complex than those encountered in Chapter 2. Furthermore, line 6 contains a variable, First.Name$, which is assigned a string of letters, Mike, rather than a numeric value. The value of First.Name$ displays along with the results because of the PRINT statements in lines 13 through 15. The following sections introduce some additional formal definitions and special rules for constructing constants, variables, and LET statements; and for manipulating strings.

3.2 CONSTANTS

Recall from Chapter 2 that constants are values that do not change during the execution of a program. Two different kinds of constants are valid for use in QBasic programs: numeric constants and string constants. **Numeric constants** represent ordinary numbers that can be used in computations. A **string constant** is a sequence of letters, digits, and special characters enclosed in quotation marks. String constants are used for such nonnumeric purposes as representing an employee name, Social Security number, an address, a telephone number, or an internet URL.

Numeric Constants

A numeric constant can have one of three forms in QBasic:

1. **Integer**: A positive or negative whole number with no decimal point, such as 174, 5903, 0, or –32768.
2. **Fixed Point**: A positive or negative real number with a decimal point, such as 713.1417, 0.0034, 0.0, –35.1, or 1923547.46.
3. **Exponential form**: A number written as an integer or fixed point constant, followed by the letter D or E and an integer. D or E stands for *times 10 to the power*. (An explanation of the difference between using D or E follows in Table 3.2 on page 58.) Examples include 793E19, 62E-23, 1E0, +12.34789D+7, and –2.3D–3.

Examples of numeric constants in Program 3.1 are 3, 2.125, and 50, found in lines 9, 10, and 11. Furthermore, the numeric data, 35 and 175, entered in response to the INPUT statements in lines 7 and 8 of Program 3. 1, must be entered in the form of numeric constants. This leads to the following rule:

INPUT RULE 2 *Numeric data assigned to numeric variables through the use of the* INPUT *statement must be entered in the form of numeric constants.*

Table 3.1 lists some ordinary numbers and shows how they may be expressed as valid numeric constants in QBasic. Examples 1, 2, and 3 in Table 3.1 show that special characters such as \$, ¢, and comma (,) are not allowed in numeric constants.

		TABLE 3.1 - Examples of Numeric Constants
EXAMPLE	ORDINARY NUMBERS	NUMERIC CONSTANTS IN QBASIC
1	\$3.14	3.14
2	+1,512.71	1512.71 or +1512.71 or 1.51271E3
3	4¢	4 or 4.0 or 4E0
4	-29.7822	-29.7822 or -2.97822E1
5	0	0 or 0.0 or 0E0 or 0D0
6	6.02257×10^{23}	6.02257E23 or +6.02257D+23

Examples 3 and 5 show that you may write an integer in any of the three forms. If a number is negative, as in example 4, the minus sign must precede the number. If a number is positive, as in example 2, the plus sign is optional.

Example 2 indicates that *commas must not be inserted into numeric constants.* Finally, spaces should not occur within numeric constants.

Numeric Constants in Exponential Form

Numeric constants may be written in **exponential form**. This form is similar to **scientific notation**. It is a shorthand way of representing very large and very small numbers in a QBasic program.

Using exponential form, a constant, regardless of its magnitude, is expressed as a value between 1 and 10 multiplied by a power of 10. For example, 1,500,000 can be expressed as 1.5×10^6 in scientific notation. The positive power of ten in 1.5×10^6 shows that the decimal point was previously moved 6 places to the left:

1.500000.

6 places to left

In order to write 1.5×10^6 as a QBasic constant in exponential form, the letter D or E, which stands for *times 10 to the power*, is substituted for the $\times$ *10*. Hence, the exponential form constant may be written as 1.5E6 or 1.5D6.

In the same way, a small number, such as 0.000000001234, can be expressed in scientific notation as 1.234×10^{-9} and in exponential form in QBasic as 1.234E-9 or 1.234D-9. The negative power of 10 in 1.234×10^{-9} represents the fact that the decimal point was previously moved nine places to the right, that is

0.000000001.234

9 places to right

Table 3.2 lists some ordinary numbers and shows how they may be expressed in scientific notation and as constants in exponential form in QBasic.

TABLE 3.2 - Examples of Scientific Notation and Exponential-Form Constants		
ORDINARY NUMBERS	SCIENTIFIC NOTATION	POSSIBLE EXPONENTIAL-FORM CONSTANTS
10,000,000	1×10^7	1E7 or 1.E+7 or 0.01E9
0.0000152	1.52×10^{-5}	1.52E-5 or +152D-7
0.001	1×10^{-3}	1E-3 or 0.001E0
−6000000000000	-6×10^{12}	-6E+12 or -6D12 or -0.6E13
−0.005892	-5.892×10^{-3}	-5.892E-3 or -5892E-6
186,000	1.86×10^5	1.86E+5 or 0.186D6

Type and Range of Numeric Constants

Numeric constants are stored in main memory in one of four forms: short integer, long integer, single precision, or double precision. The PC requires 2 bytes of main memory to store a short integer, 4 bytes to store a long integer, 4 bytes to store a single-precision constant, and 8 bytes to store a double-precision constant.

You instruct the PC how to store a numeric constant by the way you write it. For example, a numeric constant is stored in short integer form if it is between −32768 and +32767 and does not contain a decimal point or if it contains a trailing percent sign (%).

For the most part, you can let the PC decide how to store the numeric constants in your program; that is, *write the numeric constants the same way you would in algebra*. However, if desired, you can control the way a numeric constant is stored by appending a special character to it (see Table 3.3). Experienced programmers often use these special characters to improve the efficiency, accuracy, and speed of their programs.

TABLE 3.3 - Declaring the Type of Numeric Constant		
SPECIAL CHARACTER	TYPE	EXAMPLE
%	Short Integer	25%
&	Long Integer	343&
!	Single Precision	23!
#	Double Precision	87.3#
E	Single Precision (exponential form)	3.456E4
D	Double Precision (exponential form)	3.281937465746D-24

Table 3.4 summarizes the ranges of the different types of numeric constants and numeric variables in QBasic.

TABLE 3.4 - Range and Precision of Numeric Constants and Numeric Variables	
TYPE	RANGE AND PRECISION
Short Integer	-32,768 to +32,767
Long Integer	-2,147,483,648 to +2,147,483,647
Single Precision	-3.40E+38 to +3.40E+38 with up to 7 digits of significance
Double Precision	-1.8+308 to +1.79D+308 with up to 15 digits of significance

String Constants

A string constant has as its value the string of all characters between surrounding quotation marks. The length of a string constant may be from 0 to 32,767 characters. A string with a length of zero is a **null string** or **empty string**. The quotation marks indicate the beginning and end of the string constant and are not considered to be part of the value.

The messages that have been incorporated in INPUT statements to prompt for the required data and in PRINT statements to identify results are examples of string constants. For example, string constants appear in lines 6 and 13 of Program 3.1 on page 56 as shown below:

string constants

```
INPUT "Customer's first name"; First.Name$

PRINT First.Name$; "'s neck size is"; Neck.Size
```

Note that the apostrophe (') is different from quotation marks ("). While quotation marks have special meaning to QBasic, the apostrophe is just another character that you can include in a string constant.

String constants can be assigned to variables in a LET statement, as shown in Program 3.2.

PROGRAM 3.2

```
 1   ' Program 3.2
 2   ' Examples Of String Constants
 3   ' ***************************
 4   Model$ = "Q1937A"
 5   Part$  = "12AB34"
 6   Description$ = "Nylon, Disc"
 7   PRINT "Model number: "; Model$
 8   PRINT "Part number: "; Part$
 9   PRINT "Description: "; Description$
10   END


[run]


Model number: Q1937A
Part number: 12AB34
Description: Nylon, Disc
```

In line 4 of Program 3.2, the variable Model$ is assigned the value Q1937A. In line 5, Part$ is assigned the value 12AB34, and in line 6, Description$ is assigned the value Nylon, Disc.

String constants are used in a program to represent values that name or identify a person, place, or thing. They also are used to represent report and column headings and output messages. The capability to manipulate data of this type is important, especially in the field of business information systems. As you will see later in this chapter as well as in Chapter 8, QBasic also includes **string functions** for manipulating strings.

Table 3.5 lists sequences of letters, digits, and special characters and shows how they may be expressed as valid string constants.

EXAMPLE	STRING OF CHARACTERS	CORRESPONDING STRING CONSTANT IN QBASIC
1	555-2545 (telephone number)	"555-2545"
2	Nikole Rai	"Nikole Rai"
3	blank (space)	" "
4	EMPLOYEE FILE LIST	"EMPLOYEE FILE LIST"
5	310-38-6024 (Social Security number)	"310-38-6024"
6	She said, "No"	"She said, 'No'"
7	A null or empty string	""
8	calumet.purdue.edu (URL)	"calumet.purdue.edu"

TABLE 3.5 - Examples of String Constants

String data entered in response to the INPUT statement requires quotation marks only if one of the following is true of the string data item:

1. The string contains leading or trailing spaces
2. The string contains a comma or colon

The following rule summarizes the assignment of string data items through the use of the INPUT statement:

INPUT RULE 3   *String data that is assigned to string variables through the use of the INPUT statement may be entered with or without surrounding quotation marks, provided the string contains no leading or trailing spaces or embedded commas or colons. If the string contains leading or trailing spaces or embedded commas or colons, it must be surrounded with quotation marks.*

3.3 VARIABLES

In Chapter 2 you learned that a variable is a location in main memory whose value can change as the program is executed. In a program, the variable is referenced by a variable name. Variables are declared in a QBasic program by incorporating variable names in statements. For example, the following LET statements

```
Rank = 4
School$ = "Purdue"
```

instruct QBasic to set up independent storage areas for the variables Rank and School$, as well as the constants 4 and Purdue.

Although it may appear to you that Rank is being assigned the value 4 when you enter the statement through your keyboard, this does not occur until the program is executed.

Unlike a constant, a variable may be redefined; that is, its value may be changed during the execution of a program. However, its value may remain unchanged in a QBasic program, if you so desire. For example, if in the previous partial program a third line is added as shown:

```
Rank = 4
School$ = "Purdue"
Rank = 2
```

then the value of Rank changes from 4 to 2 when the third line is executed. QBasic recognizes that the two variable names are the same and during translation does not attempt to create an independent storage location for the second variable name, Rank. Only one variable in a program may be given the name Rank; however, it can be referenced and the value changed as often as needed.

Two categories of variables are valid for use in a QBasic program: simple variables and subscripted variables. **Simple variables** are used to store single values, while **subscripted variables** are used to store groups of values. Our discussion here concerns simple variables. Subscripted variables will be discussed in Chapter 7.

As with constants, there are two types of simple variables: numeric and string. A **numeric variable** may be assigned only a numeric value, and a **string variable** may be assigned only a string of characters.

When you execute a program, all numeric variables are assigned an initial value of zero, and all string variables are assigned a null value. The LET statement can be used to assign a variable a constant value or the result of a calculation. Variables also can be assigned values through INPUT statements.

Selection of Variable Names

A QBasic **variable name** can be up to 40 characters in length and must begin with a letter. The letter may be followed by up to 39 characters (letters, digits, or periods).

If a variable name ends with $, then QBasic establishes a location in main memory to receive a string value. If a variable name does not end with $, then QBasic establishes a location in main memory to receive a numeric value.

Keywords such as, LET, PRINT, and END, or any other keyword or **reserved word** that has special meaning to QBasic, may not be used as a variable name. See page R.6 of the Reference Card at the back of this book for a list of the QBasic reserved words.

QBasic is not **case-sensitive**. That is, the variable names COUNT, Count, count, and couNT all reference the same variable. In this book, all variable names are in lowercase with an initial capital letter, such as Employee$, Commission, and Rate. Variable names made up of more than one word contain a capital letter at the beginning of each word, and each word is separated by a period, such as Pay.Rate, Marital.Status$, and Cust.Num$.

Invalid and valid examples of numeric and string variable names are listed in Table 3.6 and Table 3.7.

TABLE 3.6 - Invalid Numeric Variables and Corresponding Valid Forms

INVALID NUMERIC VARIABLES	TYPE OF ERROR	VALID NUMERIC VARIABLES
3p	First character must be a letter.	Pay3 or Pay
Let	Let is a keyword.	Lit
Emp-Num	Special characters other than the period are invalid.	Emp.Num
Rate$	A numeric variable cannot end with $.	Rate

TABLE 3.7 - Invalid String Variables and Corresponding Valid Forms

INVALID STRING VARIABLES	TYPE OF ERROR	VALID STRING VARIABLES
Emp.Address	Appended dollar sign necessary.	Emp.Address$
Mid$	Mid$ is a keyword.	Middle$
Cust City$	Blank characters not permitted.	Cust.City$

When you compose variable names, make them as meaningful as possible. It is far easier for a person to read the various statements in a program if meaningful names are used. For example, assume the formula for gross pay is given by

Gross Pay = Rate × Hours

The following statement may represent the formula in a QBasic program:

```
A = B * C
```

However, it is more meaningful to write

```
G = R * H
```

It is even more meaningful to say

```
Gross = Rate * Hours
```

Some QBasic programmers use the period to separate words in the variable names or to group variable names as shown below:

Group name.Specific name

For example, if several variable names are needed to describe data in an employee record, then Emp may be used as the group name. That part of the variable name following the period differentiates the variable names beginning with the group name as shown here:

```
Emp.Number$
Emp.Name$
Emp.Address$
Emp.Salary
Emp.Code$
```

Develop a disciplined style for choosing meaningful variable names for a program. During the program design stage, establish guidelines for how variable names will be selected and rigorously follow these guidelines when coding the program. Of course, you must abide by the rules that may restrict or enhance the ways you make up variable names. For additional programming style tips, see Section C.4 in Appendix C.

Declaring Variable Types

The name of a variable determines whether it is string or numeric, and if numeric, what its precision is. If the dollar sign is absent at the end of the variable name, then the variable is declared to be numeric. As with numeric constants, numeric variables may be declared one of the following types by appending a special character to the variable name: short integer, long integer, single precision, or double precision. Table 3.8 summarizes the special characters used to define variable types.

If there is no trailing special character in a variable name, then QBasic defines it as single precision, as shown in Table 3.8. Variable names, such as Sum, Emp.Salary, and Product, are single-precision numeric variables. As with numeric constants, experienced programmers often append these special characters to numeric variables to improve the efficiency, accuracy, and speed of their programs.

An alternative to appending a special character to a variable name to declare its data type is to use the statements, DEFINT (integer), DEFLNG (long integer), DEFSNG (single precision), DEFDBL (double precision), and DEFSTR (string), at the beginning of a program. These statements are used to define the data type for a group of variables whose names begin with a letter in the specified range. For example, the statement

```
DEFINT S-U
```

declares all variables whose names begin with S through U as integer type. See Table 3.4 on page 58 for the range of values that can be assigned to the different numeric variable types and their precision.

TABLE 3.8 – Declaring the Type of Numeric Variable		
SPECIAL CHARACTER	TYPE	EXAMPLE
%	Short Integer	Count%
&	Long Integer	Count&
!	Single Precision	Count!
ƀ (Space)	Single Precision	Count
#	Double Precision	Count#

3.4 THE LET STATEMENT

As illustrated in Chapter 2, the LET statement in QBasic is used to assign a value to a variable. The general form of the LET statement is given in Table 3.9. Each LET statement consists of the optional keyword LET followed by a variable, followed by an equal sign, and then by an expression.

TABLE 3.9 - The LET Statement	
General Form:	LET numeric variable = numeric expression or LET string variable = string expression
Purpose:	Causes the evaluation of the expression, followed by the assignment of the resulting value to the variable to the left of the equal sign.

Examples:	```LET Perimeter = 2 * Side1 + 2 * Side2```
	```LET Q = (B + A) / 2 - Q + R```
	```Count = Count + 1```
	```Opposite = -Opposite```
	```Table(Y, 4) = 0```
	```Description$ = "Plier"```
	```Hypotenuse = (Base ^ 2 + Height ^ 2) ^ (1/2)```
	```P(I) = C(K) + P(J)```
	```E = M * C^2```
	```Number$ = Prefix$ + "0520"```

Note:	The keyword LET is optional.

The execution of the LET statement is not a one-step process for the PC. The execution of a LET statement requires two steps: evaluation of the expression, and assignment of the result to the variable to the left of the equal sign.

Although the equal sign is used in QBasic, it does not carry all the properties of the equal sign in mathematics. For example, the equal sign in QBasic does not allow for the symmetric relationship. That is,

```
LET A = B
```

cannot be written as

```
B = LET A
```

The equal sign in QBasic can best be thought of as meaning *is replaced by*. Therefore,

```
Interest = Principal * Rate * Time / 360
```

means that the old value of Interest is replaced by the value determined from the expression to the right of the equal sign.

PROGRAMMING CASE STUDY 4A – Determining the Single Discount Rate

Program 3.3 on the next page determines the single discount rate equal to the series of discount rates of 40%, 20%, and 10%, using the following formula:

$$\text{Rate} = 1 - (1 - \text{rate}_1)(1 - \text{rate}_2)(1 - \text{rate}_3) \ldots (1 - \text{rate}_n)$$

where Rate is the single discount rate, and rate_1, rate_2, . . . , rate_n is the series of discount rates. The number of factors of $(1 - \text{rate}_n)$ that is used to determine the single discount rate is dependent on the number of discounts. Program 3.3 is written to determine the single discount rate of a series of three discount rates.

PROGRAM 3.3

```
 1   ' Program 3.3
 2   ' Finding the Single Discount Rate
 3   ' ********************************
 4   CLS  ' Clear Screen
 5   PRINT "Enter in Decimal Form:"
 6   INPUT "          First Discount ======> ", Rate1
 7   INPUT "          Second Discount =====> ", Rate2
 8   INPUT "          Third Discount ======> ", Rate3
 9   Rate = 1 - (1 - Rate1) * (1 - Rate2) * (1 - Rate3)
10   PRINT
11   PRINT "Single Discount ================>"; Rate
12   END


     [run]

     Enter in Decimal Form:
              First Discount ======> 0.40
              Second Discount =====> 0.20
              Third Discount ======> 0.10

     Single Discount ================> .568
```

After the three discount rates are assigned decimal values in Program 3.3, line 9 determines the value of the single discount from the expression found to the right of the equal sign. Specifically, the expression is evaluated and the final value 0.568 is assigned to the variable, Rate. Line 11 displays the value for Rate before the program ends.

When dealing with rates that usually occur in percent form, it is often preferable to have the program accept the data and display the results in percent form. Program 3.4 shows you how to write a solution to Programming Case Study 4A that accomplishes this task.

PROGRAM 3.4

```
 1   ' Program 3.4
 2   ' Finding the Single Discount Rate
 3   ' ********************************
 4   CLS  ' Clear Screen
 5   PRINT "Enter in Percent Form:"
 6   INPUT "          First Discount ======> ", Rate1
 7   INPUT "          Second Discount =====> ", Rate2
 8   INPUT "          Third Discount ======> ", Rate3
 9   Rate1 = Rate1 / 100
10   Rate2 = Rate2 / 100
11   Rate3 = Rate3 / 100
12   Rate  = 1 - (1 - Rate1) * (1 - Rate2) * (1 - Rate3)
13   Rate  = 100 * Rate
14   PRINT
15   PRINT "Single Discount ================>"; Rate; "%"
16   END


     [run]

     Enter in Percent Form:
              First Discount ======> 40
              Second Discount =====> 20
              Third Discount ======> 10

     Single Discount ================> 56.8 %
```

In Program 3.4, the INPUT statements (lines 6 through 8) prompt the user to enter the discount rates in percent form. In lines 9 through 11, the rates are changed from percent form to decimal form by dividing Rate1, Rate2, and Rate3 by 100. The single discount is then determined by line 12. Line 13 replaces the assigned value of Rate (0.568) with 100 times Rate. That is, line 13 changes the value of Rate from decimal form to percent form. Line 15 then displays the value of Rate. The string constant % found at the end of line 15 helps identify the result as a percent value.

Program 3.4 includes two concepts that many beginning programmers have difficulty understanding. The first is that the same variable — Rate1, for example, in line 9 — can be found on both sides of the equal sign. The second concerns the reuse of a variable that had been assigned a value through computations in an earlier LET statement. In Program 3.4, Rate1, Rate2, and Rate3 are reused in line 12 after being assigned values in earlier LET statements. At the end of this chapter, several exercises can help you better understand these important concepts.

3.5 EXPRESSIONS

Expressions may be either numeric or string. **Numeric expressions** consist of one or more numeric constants, numeric variables, and numeric function references, all of which are separated from each other by parentheses and arithmetic operators.

The seven valid arithmetic operators and examples of their use are shown in Table 2.1 on page 23. They include exponentiation (^), multiplication (*), division (/), integer division (\), modulo (MOD), addition (+), and subtraction (–).

Recall that exponentiation is the raising of a number to a power. For example, 4 ^ 2 is equal to 16, and 3 ^ 4 is equal to 81. In programming, the asterisk (*) is used to indicate multiplication and the slash indicates division. Therefore, 8 * 4 is equal to 32, and 8 / 4 is equal to 2. For addition and subtraction, the traditional + and – symbols are used.

Two arithmetic operators that may be unfamiliar to you are the backslash (\) and MOD. Both are used to indicate division. The backslash instructs the PC first to round the dividend and the divisor to integers (whole numbers) and then truncate any decimal portion of the quotient. For example, 5 \ 3 is equal to 1, and 6.8 \ 3.2 is equal to 2.

The **modulo operator** returns the integer remainder of integer division. For example, 34 MOD 6 is equal to 4 because 34 divided by 6 is 5 with a remainder of 4. Also, 23 MOD 12 is equal to 11 because 23 divided by 12 is 1 with a remainder of 11.

String expressions consist of one or more string constants, string variables and string function references separated by the **concatenation operator** (+), which joins two strings into one. No other operators are available for string expressions.

A programmer must be concerned with both the formation and the evaluation of an expression. It is necessary to consider the purpose of the expression, as well as the rules for forming a valid expression, before it is possible to write valid QBasic statements with confidence.

Formation of Numeric Expressions

The definition of a numeric expression dictates the manner in which a numeric expression is to be validly formed. For example, it may be perfectly clear to you that the following invalid statement has been formed to assign A twice the value of B:

```
A = 2B ' Invalid Statement
```

However, the PC will reject the statement because a constant and a variable within the same expression must be separated by an arithmetic operator. The statement can be written validly as

```
A = 2 * B
```

It is also invalid to use a string variable or string constant in a numeric expression. The following are invalid numeric expressions:

```
6 + "DEBIT" / C
A$ / B + C$ - 19
```

invalid numeric expressions

Evaluation of Numeric Expressions

Formation of complex expressions involving several arithmetic operations sometimes can create problems. For example, consider the statement

```
A = 8 / 4 / 2
```

Does this assign a value of 1 or 4 to A? The answer depends on how the PC evaluates the expression. If the PC completes the operation, 8 / 4, first and only then 2 / 2, the expression yields the value 1. If the PC completes the second operation, 4 / 2, first and only then 8 / 2, it yields 4.

The PC follows the normal algebraic rules. Therefore, the expression 8 / 4 / 2 yields a value of 1.

The order in which the operations in an expression are evaluated is given by the following rule:

PRECEDENCE RULE 1 *Unless parentheses dictate otherwise, reading from left to right in a numeric expression, all exponentiations are performed first, then all multiplications and/or divisions, then all integer divisions, then all modulo arithmetic, and finally, all additions and/or subtractions.*

This order of operations is sometimes called the rules of precedence, or the hierarchy of operations. The meaning of these rules can be made clear with some examples.

For example, the expression 18 / 3 ^ 2 + 4 * 2 is evaluated as follows:

```
18 / 3 ^ 2 + 4 * 2 = 18 / 9 + 4 * 2
                   = 2     + 4 * 2
                   = 2     + 8
                   = 10
```

If you have trouble following the logic behind this evaluation, use the following technique. Whenever a numeric expression is to be evaluated, look or *scan* from left to right five different times meanwhile applying Precedence Rule 1. On the first scan, every time you encounter an ^ operator, you perform exponentiation. In this example, 3 is raised to the power of 2, yielding 9.

On the second scan, moving from left to right again, every time you encounter the operators, * and /, perform multiplication and division. Hence, 18 is divided by 9, yielding 2, and 4 and 2 are multiplied, yielding 8.

On the third scan, from left to right, perform all integer division. On the fourth scan, from left to right, perform all modulo arithmetic. In this example, there is no integer division or modulo arithmetic.

On the fifth scan, moving again from left to right, every time you detect the operators, + and −, perform addition and subtraction. In this example, 2 and 8 are added to form 10.

The following expression includes all seven arithmetic operators and yields a value of 2:

```
3 * 9 MOD 2 ^ 2 + 5 \ 4.8 / 2 - 3 = 3 * 9 MOD 4 + 5 \ 4.8 / 2 - 3      (at end of first scan)
                                  = 27 MOD 4 + 5 \ 2.4 - 3             (at end of second scan)
                                  = 27 MOD 4 + 2 - 3                   (at end of third scan)
                                  = 3 + 2 - 3                          (at end of fourth scan)
                                  = 2                                  (at end of fifth scan)
```

The expression below yields the value of –2.73, as follows:

```
2 - 3 * 4 / 5 ^ 2 + 5 / 4 * 3 - 2 ^ 3 = 2 - 3 * 4 / 25 + 5 / 4 * 3 - 8   ◄——(at end of first scan)
                                      = 2 - 0.48 + 3.75 - 8   ◄———————(at end of second scan)
                                      = -2.73   ◄—————————(at end of fifth scan)
```

The Effect of Parentheses in the Evaluation of Numeric Expressions

Parentheses may be used to change the order of operations. In QBasic, parentheses normally are used to avoid ambiguity and to group terms in a numeric expression; they do not imply multiplication. The order in which the operations in an expression containing parentheses are evaluated is given in the following rule:

PRECEDENCE RULE 2   *When parentheses are inserted into an expression, the part of the expression within the parentheses is evaluated first, and then the remaining expression is evaluated according to Precedence Rule 1.*

If the first example was rewritten with parentheses, as (18 / 3) ^ 2 + 4 * 2, then it would be evaluated in the following manner:

```
(18 / 3) ^ 2 + 4 * 2 = 6 ^ 2 + 4 * 2
                     = 36 + 4 * 2
                     = 36 + 8
                     = 44
```

The rule is as follows: *Make five scans from left to right within each pair of parentheses, and only after doing this make the standard five passes over the entire numeric expression.* The expression below yields the value of 1.41, as follows:

```
(2 - 3 * 4 / 5) ^ 2 + 5 / (4 * 3 - 2 ^ 3) = (2 - 3 * 4 / 5) ^ 2 + 5 / (4 * 3 - 8)
                                          = (2 - 2.4) ^ 2 + 5 / (12 - 8)
                                          = (-0.4) ^ 2 + 5 / 4
                                          = 0.16 + 5 / 4
                                          = 0.16 + 1.25
                                          = 1.41
```

Use parentheses freely when in doubt as to the formation and evaluation of a numeric expression. For example, if you wish to have the PC divide 8 * D by 3 ^ P, the expression may correctly be written as 8 * D / 3 ^ P, but you may also write it as

```
(8 * D) / (3 ^ P)
```

For more complex expressions, QBasic allows parentheses to be contained within other parentheses. When this occurs, the parentheses are said to be **nested**. In this case, QBasic evaluates the innermost parenthetical expression first, and then goes on to the outermost parenthetical expression. Thus, 18 / 3 ^ 2 + (3 * (2 + 5)) is broken down in the following manner:

```
18 / 3 ^ 2 + (3 * (2 + 5)) = 18 / 3 ^ 2 + (3 * 7)
                           = 18 / 3 ^ 2 + 21
                           = 18 / 9 + 21
                           = 2 + 21
                           = 23
```

Table 3.10 on the next page gives examples of the QBasic equivalent of some algebraic statements. Study each example carefully.

TABLE 3.10 - QBasic Equivalent Statements

ALGEBRAIC STATEMENTS	EQUIVALENT LET STATEMENTS
1 $H = \sqrt{X^2 + Y^2}$	`H = (X ^ 2 + Y ^ 2) ^ 0.5`
2 $S = AL^P K^{1-P}$	`S = A * L ^ P * K ^ (1 - P)`
3 $Q = \dfrac{-b + \sqrt{b^2 - 4ac}}{2a}$	`Q = (-B + (B ^ 2 - 4 * A * C) ^ 0.5) / (2 * A)`
4 $A = F\left[\dfrac{r}{(1+r)^n - 1}\right]$	`A = F * (R / (((1 + R) ^ N) - 1))`
5 $P = \sqrt[3]{(x-p)^2 + y^2}$	`P = ((X - P) ^ 2 + Y ^ 2) ^ (1 / 3)`
6 $Z = \dfrac{ab}{x + \sqrt{x^2 - a^2}}$	`Z = A * B / (X + (X ^ 2 - A ^ 2) ^ 0.5)`

Beginning programmers make two common errors. Often, beginning programmers surround the wrong part of an expression with parentheses and fail to balance the parentheses. Be sure that an expression has as many close parentheses as open parentheses. When operations of the same precedence are encountered, Precedence Rule 1 applies. For example,

```
A - B - C is interpreted as (A - B) - C
A / B / C is interpreted as (A / B) / C
A ^ B ^ C is interpreted as (A ^ B) ^ C
A \ B \ C is interpreted as (A \ B) \ C
A MOD B MOD C is interpreted as (A MOD B) MOD C
```

To illustrate the order of operations and the use of parentheses, Program 3.5 is yet a third solution to Programming Case Study 4A.

PROGRAM 3.5

```
1    ' Program 3.5
2    ' Finding the Single Discount Rate
3    ' ********************************
4    CLS  ' Clear Screen
5    PRINT "Enter in Percent Form:"
6    INPUT "            First Discount =====> ", Rate1
7    INPUT "            Second Discount =====> ", Rate2
8    INPUT "            Third Discount =====> ", Rate3
9    Rate = 1 - (1 - Rate1 / 100) * (1 - Rate2 / 100) * (1 - Rate3 / 100)
10   Rate = 100 * Rate
11   PRINT
12   PRINT "Single Discount ===============>"; Rate; "%"
13   END

[run]

Enter in Percent Form:
            First Discount =====> 40
            Second Discount =====> 20
            Third Discount =====> 10

Single Discount ===============> 56.8 %
```

Program 3.5 is similar to Program 3.4 in that both the data entered and the result displayed are in percent form. The major difference is that in this new solution all the computations have been incorporated into a single LET statement. Lines 9 through 12 in Program 3.4 on page 64 have been replaced by a new line 9 in Program 3.5.

The programmer's ability to control the sequence of operations with the use of parentheses is obvious in Program 3.5. If you have a mathematical background, you may find the method used in Program 3.5 to your liking. If you have less confidence in your mathematical ability, you may find it easier to use the technique of multiple LET statements, as shown in Program 3.4.

The following summarizes the arithmetic rules discussed in this section:

ARITHMETIC RULE 2   *A numeric expression may not contain string variables or string constants.*

ARITHMETIC RULE 3   *The formation and evaluation of numeric expressions follow the normal algebraic rules.*

Construction of Error-Free Numeric Expressions

After you have written a numeric expression observing the precedence rules, the PC is capable of translating it; no error messages will be generated. However, this is no guarantee the PC actually will be able to evaluate it. In other words, although a numeric expression may be formed in a valid fashion, your PC may not be able to evaluate it because of the numbers involved. In situations where error conditions arise during execution, QBasic will halt the program and display a dialog box informing you of the error. Applying the following rules to your program should help you avoid such hazards:

1. Do not attempt to divide by zero.
2. Do not attempt to determine the square root of a negative value.
3. Do not attempt to raise a negative value to a nonintegral value.
4. Do not attempt to compute a value that is greater than the largest permissible value or less than the smallest permissible nonzero value for your PC system.

By way of a dramatic summary, Figure 3.1 illustrates some of the combinations to be avoided in numeric expressions written in a QBasic program.

FIGURE 3.1

Examples of numeric expressions that cannot be evaluated.

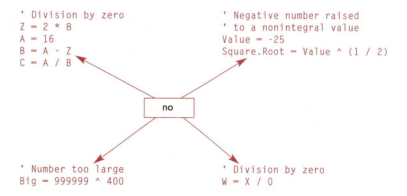

```
' Division by zero                    ' Negative number raised
Z = 2 * 8                             ' to a nonintegral value
A = 16                                Value = -25
B = A - Z                            Square.Root = Value ^ (1 / 2)
C = A / B



                        no



' Number too large                    ' Division by zero
Big = 999999 ^ 400                    W = X / 0
```

Numeric Functions

QBasic includes many **numeric functions** to handle common mathematical calculations. These numeric functions are discussed in detail in Chapter 8. Two of the most used numeric functions are the `INT` function and the `SQR` function. The `INT` **function** returns the largest integer not greater than the argument. The **argument** is a number or numeric expression surrounded by parentheses that immediately follows the word `INT`. Table 3.11 gives some examples of the `INT` function.

The `SQR` **function** returns the square root of the positive argument. Table 3.12 gives some examples of the `SQR` function.

TABLE 3.11 - The INT Function

VALUE OF VARIABLE	STATEMENT	RESULTS
R = 10.8	R = INT(R)	R = 10
X = 1.6543	X = INT(X + .5)	X = 2
Y = -3.45	W = INT(Y)	W = -4

TABLE 3.12 - The SQR Function

VALUE OF VARIABLE	STATEMENT	RESULTS
	Root = SQR(9)	Root = 3
X = 3, Y = 4	Hypo = SQR(X ^ 2 + Y ^ 2)	Hypo = 5
Cube = 625	Answ = SQR(SQR(Cube))	Answ = 5
Num = -25	Comp = SQR(Num)	Illegal Function Call

The following section illustrates the use of the `INT` function to round and truncate a value before it is displayed.

Rounding and Truncation

Many applications require that computation results be rounded or truncated before being displayed. Consider the result displayed for Mike's hat size in Program 3.1 on page 56:

```
Mike's hat size is 7.058824
```

Let us assume that it is desired to display the result 7.058824 to the nearest hundredths place — rounded to 7.06 or truncated to 7.05. There are various ways to round or truncate a result in QBasic. In this section, a generalized procedure for rounding and truncating positive numbers will be developed.

Developing a Rounding and Truncation Procedure

Recall from your mathematics classes that the rounding operation involves two steps. Assuming you are dealing with positive numbers, you first add five to the digit to the right of the digit to be retained. For example,

STEP 1. $7.058824 + 0.005 = 7.063824$

Second, you truncate, or drop, the digits to the right of the digit to be retained. For example,

STEP 2. $7.063824 = 7.06$

This second step of the rounding operation is the most complex part of the procedure for a beginning programmer to grasp. However, we can handle this in the following way:

STEP 2a. Multiply the value 7.063824 by 100 giving 706.3824

STEP 2b. Truncate the digits to the right of the decimal giving 706

STEP 2c. Divide the resultant value by 100 giving 7.06 (a rounded result)

Combining the steps, you may write the QBasic code in the following way:

```
Hat.Size = Hat.Size + .005
Hat.Size = Hat.Size * 100
Hat.Size = INT(Hat.Size)
Rounded.Hat.Size = Hat.Size / 100
```

step 1

step 2

With parentheses, these four lines of code can be rewritten as a single statement for rounding a value as follows:

```
Rounded.Hat.Size = INT((Hat.Size + .005) * 100) / 100
```

Recall from earlier discussions that the operations found in the innermost set of parentheses are completed first. Therefore, the number 0.005 is added to the value of Hat.Size first, and only then is the sum multiplied by 100. The INT function returns the largest integer not greater than the argument, which in turn, is divided by 100.

Similarly, the QBasic code can be written as a single statement for truncating a value:

```
Truncated.Hat.Size = INT(Hat.Size * 100) / 100
```

Program 3.6, which is similar to Program 3.1 on page 56 except that only the hat size is computed and displayed, illustrates the use of the procedures developed for rounding and truncating to the nearest hundredth before displaying them.

The rounding and truncation procedures developed here work only for positive numbers. Chapter 8 presents procedures that work for both positive and negative numbers.

PROGRAM 3.6

```
 1    ' Program 3.6
 2    ' Tailor's Calculations
 3    ' Determine Hat Size Rounded and Truncated
 4    ' ****************************************
 5    CLS  ' Clear Screen
 6    INPUT "Customer's first name"; First.Name$
 7    INPUT "Waistline"; Waist
 8    INPUT "Weight"; Weight
 9    Hat.Size = 3 * Weight / (2.125 * Waist)
10    Rounded.Hat.Size = INT((Hat.Size + .005) * 100) / 100
11    Truncated.Hat.Size = INT(Hat.Size * 100) / 100
12    PRINT
13    PRINT First.Name$; "'s hat size is"; Hat.Size
14    PRINT First.Name$; "'s hat size is"; Rounded.Hat.Size; "(Rounded)"
15    PRINT First.Name$; "'s hat size is"; Truncated.Hat.Size; "(Truncated)"
16    END

[run]

Customer's first name? Mike
Waistline? 35
Weight? 175

Mike's hat size is 7.058824
Mike's hat size is 7.06 (Rounded)
Mike's hat size is 7.05 (Truncated)
```

String Expressions

The capability to process strings of characters is an essential part of any programming language that is to be used for business applications. Letters, words, names, and a combination of letters and numbers all play important roles in generating readable reports and easing communication between nontechnical personnel and the computer.

In QBasic, string expressions include string constants, string variables, string function references, and a combination of the three separated by the concatenation operator (+).

Do not be confused by the dual function of the symbol + in QBasic. When dealing with numeric expressions, the + symbol represents the operation of addition. When dealing with strings, the + symbol represents the operation of concatenation; that is, the joining of two strings into one string. Consider the following program:

PROGRAM 3.7

```
 I   ' Program 3.7
 2   ' Examples of String Expressions
 3   ' ******************************
 4   CLS  ' Clear screen
 5   INPUT "Area code ===============> ", Area.Code$
 6   INPUT "Local number ============> ", Local.No$
 7   Comment$  = "Telephone number "
 8   Phone.No$ = Area.Code$ + "-" + Local.No$
 9   PRINT
10   PRINT Comment$; "=======> "; Phone.No$
11   END


     [run]

     Area code ===============> 219
     Local number ============> 555-0520

     Telephone number =======> 219-555-0520
```

Examples of string expressions in Program 3.7 include the string, Telephone number, in line 7, which is assigned to Comment$; and the string expression, Area.Code$ + "–" + Local.No$, in line 8, which is assigned to Phone.No$.

In line 8 the plus sign is the **concatenation operator** (+). When strings are concatenated, they are joined in the order they are found. The result is a single string. The value of Phone.No$, which displays by the PRINT statement in line 10, is illustrated in the output results of Program 3.7.

Use of LEFT$, LEN, MID$, and RIGHT$ String Functions

Although concatenation is the only valid string operation, QBasic includes functions that allow for additional string manipulation. The most often used string functions are presented in Table 3.13. Other string functions are presented in Chapter 8.

TABLE 3.13 - Common String Functions	
FUNCTION	**FUNCTION VALUE**
LEFT$(X$, N)	Returns the leftmost N characters of the string argument X$.
LEN(X$)	Returns the number of characters in the value associated with the string argument X$.
MID$(X$, P, N)	Returns N characters of the string argument X$ beginning at P.
RIGHT$(X$, N)	Returns the rightmost N characters of the string argument X$.
Where X$ is a string expression, and N and P are numeric expressions.	

Program 3.8 illustrates the use of the functions found in Table 3.13.

```
 1   ' Program 3.8
 2   ' Example of Referencing String Functions
 3   ' ****************************************
 4   CLS   ' Clear screen
 5   INPUT "Complete telephone number =====> ", Number$
 6   Area.Code$ = LEFT$(Number$, 3)
 7   Prefix$ = MID$(Number$, 5, 3)
 8   Local$ = RIGHT$(Number$, 4)
 9   Char.Cnt = LEN(Number$)
10   PRINT
11   PRINT "Area code ============> "; Area.Code$
12   PRINT "Prefix ===============> "; Prefix$
13   PRINT "Last four digits =====> "; Local$
14   PRINT "Character count in "; Number$; " =====>"; Char.Cnt
15   END

[run]

Complete telephone number =====> 219-555-2545

Area code ============> 219
Prefix ===============> 555
Last four digits =====> 2545
Character count in 219-555-2545 =====> 12
```

In Program 3.8, the function LEFT$ in line 6 assigns the three leftmost characters of Number$ to Area.Code$. Area.Code$ is assigned the string 219. In line 7, the MID$ function assigns three characters beginning with the fifth character 5 in Number$ to Prefix$. Prefix$ is assigned the string 555. In line 8, the function RIGHT$ assigns the last four characters of Number$ to Local$. Local$ is assigned the string, 2545. Finally, in line 9, the LEN function is used to assign the numeric variable Char.Cnt a value equal to the number of characters in Number$. Char.Cnt is assigned the numeric value 12. For a more detailed discussion on the operation of concatenation and the LEFT$, LEN, MID$, and RIGHT$ functions, see Chapter 8.

3.6 THE TOP-DOWN (MODULAR) APPROACH AND THE GOSUB AND RETURN STATEMENTS

This section presents the top-down, or modular, approach to solving problems. The top-down approach is a useful methodology for solving larger and more complex problems than those presented thus far. The objective of the **top-down approach** is to take the original problem and break it into smaller and more manageable subproblems, each of which is easier to solve than the original one. In other words, to solve a problem top-down, you divide and conquer.

The idea of solving a problem by dividing it into smaller subproblems is not new. In his *Discourse on Method,* written more than 300 years before the first computer was built, Rene Descartes made this same point. In essence, he says that the resolution of a problem can be achieved by doing the following: (1) divide each of the difficulties into as many parts as possible; and (2) think in an orderly fashion, beginning with those matters which are simplest and easiest to understand, and working toward those which are more complex.

At first the top-down approach may appear to be cumbersome, especially for the simple problems discussed so far. However with large, complex problems, it is the only logical way to develop programs. We are introducing this methodology early because most programmers find it difficult to change their plan of attack, that is, unlearn less sophisticated program development habits. By the time we get to the more sophisticated problems, we want to be sure that you are solving problems top-down by habit.

The top-down approach to problem solving involves four major steps: (1) problem analysis, (2) top-down design, (3) top-down programming, and (4) top-down testing and debugging. **Top-down design** is a strategy that breaks large, complex problems into smaller, less complex problems and then decomposes each of these into even smaller problems. **Top-down programming** is a strategy that codes high-level modules as soon as they are designed and generally *before* the low-level modules have been designed. **Top-down testing and debugging** is a strategy that tests and debugs the high-level modules of a system *before* the low-level modules have been coded and possibly before they have been designed.

The top-down approach to problem solving is a methodology recommended by most computer professionals. The claim is that a program developed from the top down is reliable, has simplicity of design, and is easy to read and maintain or modify. The steps in the program development life cycle described in Table 1.4 on page 13 should follow the top-down approach as shown in Figure 3.2.

FIGURE 3.2

The steps in the program development life cycle (Table 1.4) can be grouped to fit into the top-down approach to problem solving.

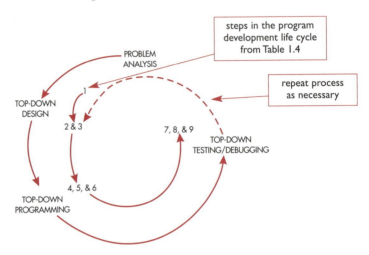

This chapter uses Programming Case Study 4A to illustrate the top-down approach to problem solving. Review the problem analysis for Programming Case Study 4A on page 63 before continuing.

Top-Down Design

Solutions to problems should be designed in a top-down fashion. The top-down design strategy is performed in two stages: (1) high-level design and (2) detailed design. High-level design identifies *what* tasks need to be performed, while detailed design addresses *how* the tasks should be performed.

High-Level Design

Top-down design takes a telescopic approach, beginning with the big picture and then zooming on the details. First, you identify the overall problem. Then, you identify the subproblems. Each subproblem may be further subdivided. This process continues until a level is reached where each problem identified is easily comprehended.

A graphical representation of the top-down design approach is a **top-down chart**, also called a **hierarchy chart** or **Visual Table of Contents — VTOC**. Figure 3.3 represents a top-down chart in which the problem or task presented in Programming Case Study 4A is broken down into subtasks. The overall task and each of the subtasks are represented by a process symbol with a short description written inside it. The top-down chart is read from top to bottom and, in general, from left to right.

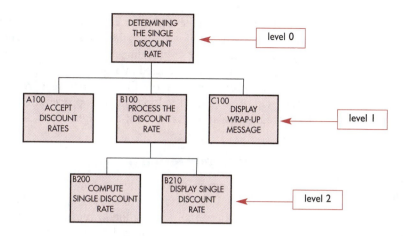

A top-down chart differs from a program flowchart, pseudocode, or other logic tools, in that it does not show decision-making logic or flow of control. A program flowchart, or pseudocode, shows *procedure*, but a top-down chart shows *organization* and *functionality*. A top-down chart allows you to concentrate on defining what needs to be done in the program before deciding *how* and *when* it is to be done, which is represented in a program flowchart, pseudocode, or other logic tools.

A top-down chart is similar to a company's organization chart; each subtask carries out a function for its superior. Think of the higher level subtasks as vice presidents of the organization who do the controlling functions of that organization. The top-down chart in Figure 3.3 resembles a small company with only two levels below the president. As a company grows and becomes more complex, additional levels are appended to the organizational chart to carry out the tasks for that organization. Likewise, as problems become larger and more complex, additional levels are added to the top-down chart.

As you design from top to bottom, or general to specific, the subtasks are connected to their superior tasks by vertical lines. Each subtask is subordinate to the one above it and superior to any that are below it.

Notice that each task in the top-down chart in Figure 3.3 is identified with a capital letter and a number; for example, A100 for ACCEPT DISCOUNT RATES. The letter identifies the branch of the top-down chart from left to right; the first digit of the number represents the level of the task within the branch. Collectively, the letter and the number are called a **level number**, which represents the placement of the task within the program. Subordinate tasks have the same letter as their superior with a higher number than their superior. In our example, level zero represents the highest task in the program; level one has three tasks; and level two, the lowest level, has two tasks.

In Figure 3.3, we adopted the technique of representing level one tasks as A100, B100, and C100. Because the two tasks in level two are subordinate to B100, task numbers are assigned in increments of ten; for example, B200 and B210 are subordinate to B100. If task C100 had three subordinate tasks at level two, they would be numbered as C200, C210, and C220. If task B200 had three subordinate tasks at level three, they would be numbered as B300, B310, and B320.

The same subtask may be subordinate to more than one superior task. Recurring subtasks are identified by darkening the upper right-hand corner of the process symbol as shown in Chapter 6, Figure 6.16 on page 222. At implementation, recurring subtasks are coded once and called as often as needed.

A top-down chart is not a program flowchart, nor does it replace the program flowchart or other logic tools in designing algorithms. A top-down chart is a tool that is used early in the design stage to decompose, in an orderly fashion, a large task into subtasks, and to some extent to show the flow of control among these subtasks. The result is a graphic view of what must be done to solve the overall problem. Therefore, creating top-down charts is referred to as **high-level design**.

The emphasis in the top-down approach is on careful analysis. The first top-down chart a programmer thinks of is seldom the one that is implemented. Typically, a top-down chart is reviewed and refined several times before it is considered acceptable. In many companies, top-down charts are submitted to a **peer review group**, composed of programmers and analysts, for further review and refinement before a programmer is allowed to proceed with the next step of program development. This process of review and refinement is sometimes referred to as a **structured walk-through**.

FIGURE 3.4

Program flowchart for level 0 task in Programming Case Study 4A.

Detailed Design

The next step is to design *how* the tasks in the top-down chart should be performed. In the top-down approach, the higher level tasks are designed, coded, and tested generally *before* the lower level tasks are even designed. This technique ensures correctness at each level before proceeding. Our next step, then, is to develop the logic for the level zero task in the top-down chart, Determining the Single Discount Rate. The logic is quite simple. As shown in the flowchart in Figure 3.4, the level 0 task performs no detail work; it only invokes (or *calls*) the lower level tasks.

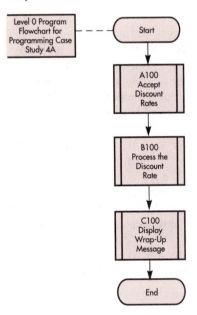

Implementing a Top-Down Design Using Subroutines (Modules)

After the flowchart for a higher level task has been designed, its solution should be coded and tested before the lower level tasks are designed. Each task in the top-down chart is called a **subroutine** or **module**. The highest level module in a program (level 0) is called the **Main module**. Our first programming step is to code the Main module as represented by the flowchart in Figure 3.4. Programming Case Study 4A, Determining the Single Discount Rate, calls three lower level modules: (1) A100 Accept Discount Rates, (2) B100 Process the Discount Rate, and (3) C100 Display Wrap-Up Message. For many practical problems, properly coded modules have one entry point, one exit point, no dead (unexecuted) code, and no infinite (endless) loops; however, exceptions exist. For additional information on properly coded modules, see Section A.4 in Appendix A.

A subroutine is a separate section of code intended to accomplish a specific task. A subroutine is executed only if referenced, or *called*, by an explicit instruction from some other part of the program, as illustrated in Figure 3.5. Following execution of the subroutine, control passes back to the statement that immediately follows the instruction that activated the subroutine. QBasic includes two sets of statements for implementing modules: (1) GOSUB and RETURN; and (2) CALL, SUB, and END SUB. We will use the GOSUB and RETURN statements to implement programs top down. (See Chapter 11 for a discussion on the CALL, SUB, and END SUB statements.)

FIGURE 3.5

A conceptual view of control transferring to a subroutine and eventually returning to the statement that immediately follows the instruction that activated the subroutine.

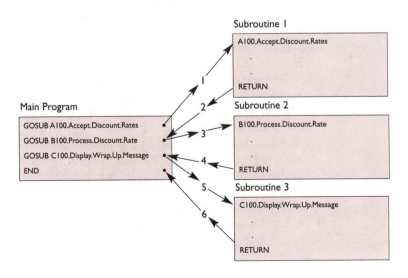

The GOSUB and RETURN Statements

The Main module may be implemented in a QBasic program as three GOSUB statements followed by an END statement. The GOSUB **statement** transfers control to a subroutine. The keyword GOSUB is followed immediately by the subroutine name to which control is transferred. The function of the first GOSUB is to invoke the A100 Accept Discount Rates module. At the completion of its prescribed task, the A100 Accept Discount Rates module returns control to the Main module. The second GOSUB invokes the B100 Process the Discount Rate module, which maintains control until the rate is processed. The final GOSUB in the Main module references the C100 Display Wrap-Up Message module. Upon completion of its task, the C100 Display Wrap-Up Message module returns control to the Main module and the program terminates. *Once coded*, the Main module is called the **Main Program**; that is, the term module refers to design and the terms program or subroutine refer to QBasic code.

A subroutine begins with a name or label, followed immediately by a colon (:), and ends with a RETURN statement. Like a variable name, a **subroutine name** can be up to 40 characters. As indicated above, the subroutine is called by a GOSUB statement. After control transfers, the instructions following the subroutine name are executed one after the other until the RETURN statement is executed. The RETURN **statement** returns control to the next executable statement following the corresponding GOSUB statement in the superior module. A subroutine, therefore, can exit only through a RETURN statement. The general forms for the GOSUB and RETURN statements are shown in Tables 3.14 and 3.15.

TABLE 3.14 – The GOSUB Statement	
General Form:	GOSUB label
	where **label** is a line label or line number that designates the beginning of a subroutine.
Purpose:	Causes control to transfer to the subroutine represented by label. Causes the location of the next executable statement following the GOSUB to be retained.
Examples:	GOSUB A100.Initialization GOSUB B100.Process.File GOSUB B200.Compute.Cost
Note:	In QBasic, if label is a line label, rather than a line number, then it must be followed immediately by a colon.

TABLE 3.15 – The RETURN Statement	
General Form:	RETURN
Purpose:	Causes control to transfer from the subroutine back to the first executable statement immediately following the GOSUB statement that referenced it.
Example:	RETURN
Note:	The RETURN statement may be followed by a label. This option is not used in this book.

Consider the following top-down approach to Programming Case Study 4A, Finding the Single Discount Rate, presented earlier in this chapter. The solution corresponds to the top-down chart in Figure 3.3 on page 75.

PROGRAM 3.9

```
 1     ' Program 3.9
 2     ' Determining the Single Discount Rate
 3     ' ***********************************
 4     ' *           Main Program          *
 5     ' ***********************************
 6     GOSUB A100.Accept.Discount.Rates
 7     GOSUB B100.Process.Discount.Rates
 8     GOSUB C100.Display.Wrapup.Message
 9     END
10
11     ' ***********************************
12     ' *        Accept Discount Rates       *
13     ' ***********************************
14     A100.Accept.Discount.Rates:
15         CLS  ' Clear Screen
16         PRINT "Enter in Percent Form:"
17         INPUT "         First Discount =======> ", Rate1
18         INPUT "         Second Discount =======> ", Rate2
19         INPUT "         Third Discount =======> ", Rate3
20     RETURN
21
22     ' ***********************************
23     ' *        Process Discount Rate       *
24     ' ***********************************
25     B100.Process.Discount.Rates:
26         GOSUB B200.Compute.Single.Rate
27         GOSUB B210.Display.Single.Rate
28     RETURN
29
30     ' ***********************************
31     ' *        Compute Single Rate         *
32     ' ***********************************
33     B200.Compute.Single.Rate:
34         Rate1 = Rate1 / 100
35         Rate2 = Rate2 / 100
36         Rate3 = Rate3 / 100
37         Rate = 1 - (1 - Rate1) * (1 - Rate2) * (1 - Rate3)
38         Rate = 100 * Rate
39     RETURN
40
41     ' ***********************************
42     ' *        Display Single Rate         *
43     ' ***********************************
44     B210.Display.Single.Rate:
45         PRINT
46         PRINT "Single Discount ================>"; Rate; "%"
47     RETURN
48
49     ' ***********************************
50     ' *       Display Wrap-Up Message      *
51     ' ***********************************
52     C100.Display.Wrapup.Message:
53         PRINT
54         PRINT "*********** End of Job ***********"
55     RETURN
56     ' ********** End of Program **********
```

```
[run]

Enter in Percent Form:
         First Discount =======> 40
         Second Discount =======> 20
         Third Discount =======> 10

Single Discount ================> 56.8 %

*********** End of Job ***********
```

When Program 3.9 is executed, the GOSUB statement in line 6 transfers control to the A100.Accept.Discount.Rates subroutine (line 14). This subroutine clears the screen and accepts the three discounts. The RETURN statement in line 20 returns control to line 7. Line 7 represents the next executable statement following the GOSUB in the Main Program which referenced the A100.Accept.Discount.Rates subroutine.

The GOSUB in line 7 calls the B100.Process.Discount.Rates subroutine which begins at line 25. The GOSUB on line 26 calls the B200.Compute.Single.Rate subroutine which begins at line 33. After the Single Discount Rate has been determined, the RETURN statement in line 39 returns control to line 27 in the B100.Process.Discount.Rates subroutine. The GOSUB in line 27 calls the B210.Display.Single.Rate subroutine that begins at line 44. The RETURN statement in line 47 returns control to line 28, another RETURN statement, which returns control to line 8 in the Main Program. Line 8, in turn, transfers control to the C100.Display.Wrapup Message subroutine (line 52). Following the display of the wrap-up message, the RETURN statement in line 55 returns control to line 9 of the Main Program.

The END statement in line 9 halts the execution of the program. Note that by placing the END statement in line 9, we prevent the A100.Accept.Rates subroutine from being executed again.

All programs previous to Program 3.9 use the END statement as the physical end of the program. In Program 3.9, the END statement in line 9 is used to indicate the *logical* end of the program, and line 56, a remark statement, is used to indicate the physical end of the program. It should be apparent now that QBasic does not require that the END statement be the last physical statement in the program.

Recommended Style and Tips When Using the Top-Down Approach

Consider the following tips when using the top-down approach:

1. Start each subroutine with a comment box. A **comment box** consists of three or more remark lines with asterisks surrounding a brief comment.
2. End each subroutine with a blank line.
3. Indent by three spaces the statements between the subroutine name and the RETURN statement.
4. So that lower-level subroutines can be located easily for debugging purposes, they should be placed below the subroutine which calls them and in the order in which they are numbered.

More about Subroutines

The last statement of a subroutine should always be the RETURN statement. Any attempt to execute a RETURN statement without executing an earlier corresponding GOSUB statement results in the display of a dialog box with the **diagnostic message**

```
RETURN without GOSUB
```

and the termination of the program. This can be summarized by the following rule:

RETURN RULE I   *A* GOSUB *statement must be executed before its corresponding* RETURN *statement can be executed.*

Flowchart Representation of GOSUB, RETURN, and Referenced Subroutine

The program flowchart representation of Program 3.9 including the GOSUB statements and the referenced subroutines, is shown in Figure 3.6 on the next page. Remember that a top-down chart, as shown in Figure 3.3 (page 75), is not a program flowchart. A top-down chart shows *what* must be done to solve a problem, and a program flowchart shows *how* to solve the problem.

The GOSUB statement, which calls the subroutine, is represented by the predefined process symbol, which was defined in Table 1.5 (page 14). The **predefined process symbol** consists of a set of vertical lines within the rectangle and indicates that the program steps of the subroutine are specified elsewhere. In Figure 3.6, the first subroutine, A100 Accept Discount Rates, is represented by the flowchart to the right of the Main module, and the RETURN statement is represented by the terminal symbol.

FIGURE 3.6

General flowcharts for the Main module and subroutines for Program 3.9

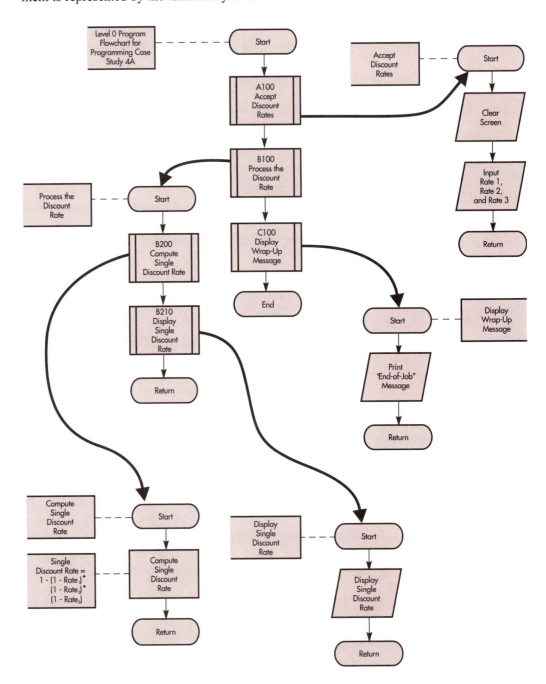

Nested Subroutines

As illustrated to some extent in Program 3.9 on page 78, one subroutine may call another subroutine, which may in turn call another, and so on. However, each subroutine must terminate with a RETURN statement. Program 3.10 illustrates the flow of control from the Main Program to the nested subroutines. The arrows and circled numbers represent the flow of control.

PROGRAM 3.10

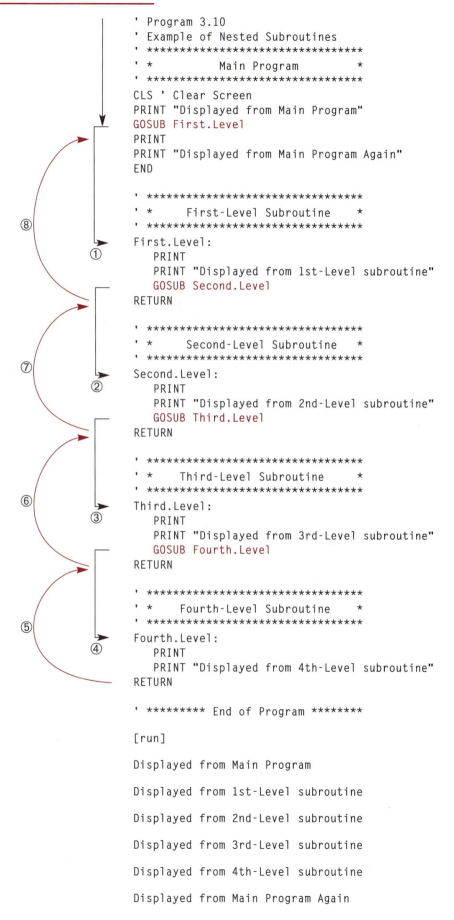

```
' Program 3.10
' Example of Nested Subroutines
' ********************************
' *           Main Program         *
' ********************************
CLS ' Clear Screen
PRINT "Displayed from Main Program"
GOSUB First.Level
PRINT
PRINT "Displayed from Main Program Again"
END

' ********************************
' *       First-Level Subroutine    *
' ********************************
First.Level:
    PRINT
    PRINT "Displayed from 1st-Level subroutine"
    GOSUB Second.Level
RETURN

' ********************************
' *      Second-Level Subroutine    *
' ********************************
Second.Level:
    PRINT
    PRINT "Displayed from 2nd-Level subroutine"
    GOSUB Third.Level
RETURN

' ********************************
' *      Third-Level Subroutine     *
' ********************************
Third.Level:
    PRINT
    PRINT "Displayed from 3rd-Level subroutine"
    GOSUB Fourth.Level
RETURN

' ********************************
' *      Fourth-Level Subroutine    *
' ********************************
Fourth.Level:
    PRINT
    PRINT "Displayed from 4th-Level subroutine"
RETURN

' ********* End of Program *******

[run]

Displayed from Main Program

Displayed from 1st-Level subroutine

Displayed from 2nd-Level subroutine

Displayed from 3rd-Level subroutine

Displayed from 4th-Level subroutine

Displayed from Main Program Again
```

To keep track of the proper place to return to in a program with nested subroutines, QBasic maintains a **control stack** of locations when RETURN statements are executed. Each time a GOSUB statement is executed, the location of the first executable statement following the GOSUB is placed onto the top of the control stack. When a RETURN statement is executed, the top statement location is removed from the control stack, and control is directed to that statement in the program.

Stubs

Program 3.10 on the previous page also illustrates subroutines that were not fully designed and coded. Because we have not yet designed the logic for the four lower-level subroutines in Program 3.10, we must implement these subroutines as stubs. A **stub** is a skeleton version of the final subroutine. It does not contain details or fulfill program tasks; it simply exists as the target of a GOSUB statement. Often programmers place one PRINT statement inside a stub. For example, a Process subroutine stub might be coded as shown below.

```
B100.Process:
    PRINT "You are now inside the B100.Process subroutine"
RETURN
```

Though the use of these *dummy* PRINT statements, stubs help demonstrate that a program flows as intended. With stubs, you can test and debug a program *as it is being built*. When the program is complete and functional, the *dummy* PRINT statements are removed.

3.7 What You Should Know

The following list summarizes this chapter:

1. Constants are values that do not change during the execution of a program.
2. The two types of constants are numeric constants and string constants.
3. Numeric constants represent ordinary numbers. A numeric constant may be written in one of three forms — integer, fixed point, or exponential form.
4. An integer constant is a positive or negative whole number with no decimal point.
5. A fixed point constant is one with a decimal point.
6. A numeric constant written in exponential form is one written as an integer or fixed point constant, followed by the letter D or E and an integer. D or E stands for *times 10 to the power*.
7. Depending on how it is written in a program, a numeric constant is stored as one of the following types: short integer, long integer, single precision, or double precision.
8. The only special characters allowed in a numeric constant are a leading sign (+ or - or blank), the decimal point and the letter D or E.
9. String constants represent strings of characters enclosed in quotation marks. A string constant can have from 0 to 32,767 characters.
10. In programming, a variable is a location in main memory that can be referenced by a variable name and whose value can change as the program is executed.
11. The two types of variables in QBasic are simple variables and subscripted variables. Simple variables are used to store single values. Subscripted variables are used to store groups of values. Either of the two can be defined as numeric or string.
12. A variable name can be up to 40 characters in length and it must begin with a letter. The letter can be followed by letters, digits, and periods.
13. You should develop a disciplined style for choosing meaningful variable names in a program.
14. A variable name that ends with a the dollar sign ($) declares that the variable will represent a string. If the last character is not a dollar sign, then the variable is numeric.

15. If a numeric variable name ends with an exclamation point (!) or no special character, then it is declared single precision. Other special characters appended to variable names are as follows: percent sign (%) declares it short integer, ampersand (&) declares it long integer, and number sign (#) declares it double precision. The statements DEFINT (integer), DEFLNG (long integer), DEFSNG (single precision), DEFDBL (double precision), and DEFSTR (string) may be used to declare the data types for groups of variables.

16. While short integer variables and constants take up 2 bytes of main memory, long integer and single-precision variables take up 4 bytes, and double-precision variables take up 8 bytes of main memory.

17. Numeric data assigned to numeric variables through the use of the INPUT statement must be entered in the form of numeric constants.

18. String data assigned to string variables through the use of the INPUT statement must be surrounded with quotation marks when the string contains leading or trailing blanks or embedded commas or colons.

19. The LET statement causes evaluation of the expression to the right of the equal sign, followed by assignment of the resulting value to the variable to the left of the equal sign.

20. The equal sign in QBasic can best be described as meaning *is replaced by*.

21. It is invalid to assign a string expression to a numeric variable or a numeric expression to a string variable.

22. A numeric expression is a sequence of one or more numeric constants, numeric variables and numeric function references, separated from each other by parentheses and arithmetic operators.

23. A string expression is a sequence of one or more string constants, string variables or string function references, separated by the concatenation operator (+).

24. The formation and evaluation of numeric expressions follow the normal algebraic rules.

25. Unless parentheses dictate otherwise, reading from left to right in a numeric expression, all exponentiations are performed first, then all multiplications and/or divisions, then all integer divisions, then all modulo arithmetic, and finally all additions and/or subtractions. This order is called the hierarchy of operations or the rules of precedence.

26. When parentheses are inserted into an expression, the part of the expression within the parentheses is evaluated first, and then the remaining expression is evaluated according to the rules of precedence.

27. No numeric expression can be evaluated if it requires a value that is not mathematically defined. For example, do not divide a number by zero in your program.

28. INT(N) returns the largest integer that is less than or equal to the argument N.

29. SQR(N) returns the square root of the positive argument N.

30. To round X to the nearest hundredths place, use the expression:

```
INT((X + 0.005) * 100) / 100
```

31. To truncate X to the nearest hundredths place, use the expression:

```
INT(X * 100) / 100
```

32. Concatenation generates a single string value, which is the result of combining the values of each of the terms in the order they are found in the expression.

33. The string functions LEFT$, LEN, MID$, and RIGHT$ are used to access and manipulate groups of characters, or substrings, within a string.

34. The top-down approach to problem solving is a popular method of solving large, complex problems. It involves four major steps: (1) problem analysis, (2) top-down design, (3) top-down programming, and (4) top-down testing and debugging.

35. Top-down design is a strategy that breaks large, complex problems into smaller, less complex problems and then decomposes each of these into even smaller problems. Top-down design is performed in two stages: (1) high-level design and (2) detailed design.

36. High-level design is implemented through a top-down chart, which is a graphical representation of the task broken down into subtasks. Top-down charts show organization and functionality.

37. Each task in a top-down chart should be assigned a level number, such as 100, which represents the placement of the task within the program.
38. In many organizations, top-down charts are submitted to a peer review group for further review and refinement before a programmer is allowed to proceed to detailed design. This process of review and refinement is sometimes referred to as a structured walk-through.
39. Detailed design is implemented through program flowcharts, pseudocode, or other logic tools, which show how the tasks in the top-down chart should be performed. The higher level tasks are designed, coded, and tested generally before the lower level tasks are designed.
40. Top-down programming is a strategy that codes high-level modules as soon as they are designed and generally *before* the low-level modules have been designed.
41. Top-down testing and debugging is a strategy that tests and debugs the high-level modules of a system *before* the low-level modules have been coded and possibly before they have been designed.
42. Each task in the top-down chart is called a module.
43. Properly coded modules have one entry point, one exit point, no dead code, and no infinite loops. Exceptions exist, however.
44. A subroutine, or module, is a group of statements within a QBasic program associated with a single programming task.
45. Subroutines are useful in solving large, complex problems because they allow a problem to be subdivided into smaller and more manageable subproblems, which can the be solved with appropriate subroutines.
46. A subroutine is referenced with a GOSUB statement. The keyword GOSUB is followed by a label that identifies the subroutine to which control will be transferred.
47. A subroutine begins with a subroutine name followed immediately by a colon (:). In selecting a subroutine name, follow the rules for a variable name.
48. The RETURN statement is always the last statement executed in a subroutine. Its function is to cause control to transfer from the subroutine back to the first executable statement following the corresponding GOSUB statement.

3.8 Test Your QBasic Skills (Even-numbered answers are in Appendix E)

1. Which of the following are valid numeric constants if each appeared exactly as written in a valid location in a QBasic statement?

    a. 1.2   b. 25$ c. +.216#   d. 0
    e. 4,200!   f. 313F2   g. 15%   h. $4.50

2. Write the number 43,600,000,000 in exponential form with one significant digit before the decimal point.

3. Which arithmetic operation is performed first in the following numeric expressions?

    a. 9 / 5 * 6   b. X - Y + A
    c. 3 * (A + 8)   d. (X * (2 / Y)) ^ 2 + Z ^ (2 ^ 2) - 6 MOD 3
    e. X / Y + Z   f. (B ^ 2 - 4 * A * C) / (2 * A)

4. Evaluate each of the following:

    a. 4 * 5 * 3 / 6 - 6 ^ 2 / 12   b. (2 ^ 4) + 5 * 2
    c. 12 * 6 / 2 + 7 MOD 3 + 3

5. Calculate the numeric value for each of the following valid numeric expressions if
   A = 3, B = 4, C = 5, W = 3, T = 3, X = 1, and Y = 2.

   a. (C - A * 3) + 8.1   b. (A / (C + 1) * 4 - 5) / 2 + (4 MOD 3 \ 3)
   c. 50 / (X * Y) ^ W   d. X + 2 * Y * W / 3 - 7 / (T - X / Y) + W ^ T
   e. SQR(C ^ 2 - B ^ 2)   f. INT((1012.346 + .005) * 100) / 100

6. Which of the following are invalid variable names in QBasic? Why?

   a. A   b. SaLe   c. Int   d. P.1#   e. 39
   f. Print   g. 7f   h. F-1   i. Q$ j. Q9%

7. Consider the valid programs below. What is displayed if each is executed?

   a. ' Exercise 3.7a
       CLS
       D = 3.2
       E = D ^ 2 / D - .5
       PRINT E
       E = 4 * D - (2 * D + 5)
       PRINT E
       D = -D
       PRINT D
       D = -D
       PRINT D
       END

   b. ' Exercise 3.7b
       CLS
       Total = 15
       GOSUB Increment.Total
       PRINT Total
       GOSUB Increment.Total
       PRINT Total
       GOSUB Increment.Total
       PRINT Total
       Total = Total / 2
       PRINT Total
       END
       ' ***Increment Total***
       Increment.Total:
           Total = Total + 1
       RETURN

   c. ' Exercise 3.7c
       X = 4
       Y = 1
       A = X + Y
       PRINT A
       B = Y - X
       PRINT B
       C = A + B - X
       PRINT C
       D = 2 * (A + B + C) / 4
       PRINT D
       END

   d. Assume 3 is entered for Seed.
       ' Exercise 3.7d
       INPUT "Enter seed number"; Seed
       Seed = Seed * (Seed + 1)
       PRINT Seed
       Seed = Seed * (Seed + 1)
       PRINT Seed
       Seed = Seed * (Seed + 1)
       PRINT Seed
       Seed = Seed + (Seed + 1)
       PRINT Seed
       END

8. Explain how you can declare a numeric variable to be of a special type type (such as short integer, long integer, etc.).

9. Can a validly formed numeric expression always be executed by a computer?

10. Calculate the numeric value for each of the following numeric expressions if
    X = 2, Y = 4, and Z = 8.

    a. X ^ 2 - Y
    b. Z * Y / X
    c. 5 * (Z - 1) + X + 2
    d. Z ^ Y ^ X
    e. X * Y + 2.5 * X + Z
    f. (X ^ (2 + Y)) ^ 2 + Z ^ (2 ^ 2)

11. Repeat Exercise 10 for the case of X = 4, Y = 2, and Z = 6.

12. Write a valid LET statement for each of the following algebraic statements:

a. $q = (d + e)^{1/3}$

b. $d = (A^2)^{3.2}$

c. $b = \left(\dfrac{20}{6 - S}\right)$

d. $Y = a_1 x + a_2 x^2 + a_3 x_3 + a_4 x^4$

e. $h = \sqrt{X} + \left(\dfrac{X}{X - Y}\right)$

f. $S = \sqrt{19.2 X^3}$

g. $v = 100 - (2/3)^{100 - B}$

h. $t = \sqrt{76{,}234/(2.37 + D)}$

i. $V = 0.12340005 M - \left[\dfrac{M^3}{M - N}\right]$

j. $Q = \dfrac{(F - 1000M)^{2B}}{4M} - \dfrac{1}{E}$

13. If necessary insert parentheses so that each numeric expression results in the value indicated on the right-hand side of the arrow.

a. 8 / 2 + 2 + 12 --> 14
b. 8 ^ 2 - 1 --> 8
c. 3 / 2 + 0.5 + 3 ^ 1 --> 5
d. 12 MOD 5 \ 2 + 1 ^ 2 + 1 * 2 * 3 / 4 - 3 / 2 --> 0.5
e. 12 - 2 - 3 - 1 - 4 --> 10
f. 7 * 3 + 4 ^ 2 - 3 / 13 --> 22
g. 3 * 2 - 3 * 4 * 2 + 3 --> -60
h. 3 * 6 - 3 + 2 + 6 * 4 - 4 / 2 ^ 1 --> 33

14. Which of the following are valid LET statements?

a. A = (50 / D + E * F)
b. x + 5 = B
c. 17 = X
d. P = 4 * 3 * 6
e. For.1 = SQR(16)
f. X = M * (1 + R) ^ 2 - N ^ 2
g. Get U = V ^ W + W - X
h. LET P = +4
i. G = 4(-2 + A)
j. X = X + 1

15. Consider the valid programs below What is displayed if each program is executed? Assume A is assigned the value 2 and B the value 3.

a.
```
' Exercise 3.15a
INPUT A, B
D = (A ^ 4 / A * B) - (8 * B / 4)
D = D + 1
PRINT D
END
```

b.
```
' Exercise 3.15b
INPUT A, B
B = 4
E1 = A * B
E1 = A ^ (16 / E1)
E2 = B * 8
E3 = 4 + 1
E2 = E2 / E3
A  = E1 + E2
PRINT A
END
```

16. Repeat Exercise 15 for the case where A is assigned the value 1 and B is assigned the value 2.

17. If the string David O. Osborne is entered in response to the INPUT statement, what is displayed by the following program?

```
' Exercise 3.17
CLS   ' Clear Screen
INPUT "Name ===> ", Name$
First.Name$  = LEFT$(Name$, 5)
Last.Name$   = RIGHT$(Name$, 7)
Mid.Initial$ = MID$(Name$, 7, 2)
Abbrev.Name$ = LEFT$(Name$, 1) + MID$(Name$, 8, 1)
Abbrev.Name$ = Abbrev.Name$ + MID$(Name$, 7, 2) + RIGHT$(Name$,7)
Char.Cnt = LEN(Name$)
PRINT Name$
PRINT First.Name$
PRINT Last.Name$
PRINT Mid.Initial$
PRINT Abbrev.Name$
PRINT Char.Cnt
END
```

18. Consider the valid program listed below. What is displayed when it is executed? Assume that Principal is assigned the value 3000 and Rate is assigned 12.

```
' Exercise 3.18
CLS   ' Clear Screen
INPUT "Principal ==> ", Principal
INPUT "Rate in % ==> ", Rate
Rate = Rate / 100
Amount = Principal + Rate * Principal
PRINT "Amount =====>"; Amount
END
```

19. What does the following program display?

```
' Exercise 3.19
CLS   ' Clear Screen
Average1 = 4 + 5 + 6 + 7 + 8 / 5
Average2 = (4 + 5 + 6 + 7 + 8) / 5
PRINT "Is the average of 4, 5, 6, 7, and 8 ";
PRINT "equal to "; Average1; "or"; Average2; "?"
END
```

20. Evaluate each of the following:

   a. INT(3.8)   b. INT(-3.8)
   c. SQR(400)   d. SQR(-400)

21. **PC Hands-On Exercise:** Load Program 3.1 (PRG3-1) from the Data Disk that is availabe for this book via the Internet. Download the Data Disk at course.com or see your instructor. Execute the program. Enter your name and measurements in place of Mike's. How close did Program 3.1 come in estimating your neck, hat, and shoe size?

22. **PC Hands-On Exercise:** Load Program 3.4 (PRG3-4) from the Data Disk that is available for this book via the internet. Download the Data Disk at course.com or see your instructor. In lines 9 through 11, rather than dividing the discounts by 100, multiply them by 0.01. Execute the program. Enter the same data used with Program 3.4. Are the results the same for the modified version of Program 3.4 as they were for the original?

3.9 QBasic Programming Problems

1. Sales Tax Computations

Purpose: To become familiar problem solving and with the use of constants, variables, and the INPUT, PRINT, and LET statements.

Problem: Design a program flowchart and write a straight-line program to determine the state sales tax. Use the formulas:

Sales Tax Amount = Sales Tax Rate times Sale Amount
Total Sale Amount = Sale Amount plus Sales Tax Amount

Input Data: Use 146.60 as the sale amount and 5% as the sales tax rate in response to the appropriate INPUT statements.

(**Hint**: The program solution must include a statement to change the sales tax rate from percent form to decimal form.)

Output Results: The output screen should appear as illustrated by Figure 3.7.

FIGURE 3.7
Output for Programming Problem 1.

```
Dollar amount of sale ====> 146.60
State sales tax in % =====> 5

The sales tax amount is ==> 7.33
The total sale amount is => 153.93
```

2. Maturity Value of an Investment Converted Quarterly

Purpose: To become familiar with the concepts associated with the top-down approach to problem solving, arithmetic operations with parentheses in expressions, and with the use of INPUT, LET, PRINT, GOSUB, and RETURN statements.

Problem: Design a program flowchart and write a top-down modular program to determine the maturity value of an investment of D dollars for Y years at P percent converted quarterly. Use the following formula:

$$S = D \left(1 + \frac{P}{M}\right)^{YM}$$

where S = maturity value
D = investment in dollars
P = nominal rate of interest
Y = time in years
M = number of conversions per year

(**Hint:** The program solution must include a statement to change the rate from percent form to decimal form.)

Use the top-down chart illustrated in Figure 3.8 as a design for your solution.

FIGURE 3.8
A top-down chart for the Maturity Value of an Investment problem.

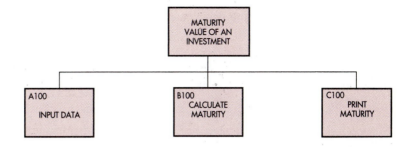

Input Data: Use the following sample data in response to the appropriate INPUT statements:

Investment: $5,000
Interest: 5.25%
Time: 2 years 3 months
Conversions: 4

Output Results: The output screen should appear as illustrated by Figure 3.9.

FIGURE 3.9
Output for Programming Problem 2.

```
Please enter the:
        Investment in $ -------> 5000
        Nominal rate in % ----> 5.25
        Time in years --------> 2.25
        No. of Conversions ---> 4

Maturity value ---------------> $ 5622.602
```

3. Determining the Monthly Payment on a Loan

Purpose: To become familiar the top-down approach to problem solving and with the hierarchy of operations in a LET statement; the use of the INPUT and PRINT statements; and the procedure for rounding a value.

Problem: Design a program flowchart and write a top-down modular program to determine the monthly payment for a loan where the annual interest rate (expressed in percent), the amount of the loan, and the number of years are entered via INPUT statements. The monthly payment for the loan is computed from the following relationship:

$$P = \left(\frac{r(1 + r)^n}{(1 + r)^n - 1} \right) \times L \qquad \text{where } \begin{aligned} P &= \text{payment} \\ L &= \text{amount of the loan} \\ r &= \text{monthly interest rate} \\ n &= \text{number of payments} \end{aligned}$$

Display the payment rounded to the nearest cent. Also determine the total interest paid by using the following formula:

Total Interest Paid $= nP - L$

(**Hint**: The annual interest rate must be divided by 1,200, and the time must be multiplied by 12.)

Use the top-down chart illustrated in Figure 3.10 as a design for your solution.

Input Data: Use the following sample data:

Loan: $15,000.00
Interest rate: 6.75%
Time: 5 years

Output Results: The output screen should appear as illustrated by Figure 3.11.

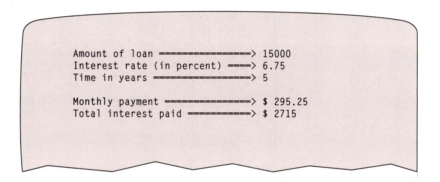

```
Amount of loan ═══════════════> 15000
Interest rate (in percent) ════> 6.75
Time in years ═════════════════> 5

Monthly payment ═══════════════> $ 295.25
Total interest paid ═══════════> $ 2715
```

4. Extracting Characters from a String

Purpose: To become familiar with the top-down approach to problem solving and string functions.

Problem: Design a program flowchart and write a top-down modular program that prompts the user to enter a word and assigns it to a string variable. Have the program print the word. Using the LEFT$ string function, extract the first letter of the word. Using the RIGHT$ string function, extract the last letter of the word. Using the LEN function, determine the number of characters in the word you entered. After the letters have been extracted, print the first letter and then print the last letter. Finally, print the number of characters in the word.

(**Hint**: See Program 3.8 on page 73.)

Use the top-down chart illustrated in Figure 3.12 as a design for your solution.

Input Data: Enter the word, Honest. Run the program a second time and enter a word, such as your last name.

Output Results: The output screen should appear as illustrated by Figure 3.13.

```
Enter a word ---> Honest

The word is:  Honest
The first letter of the word is:  H
The last letter of the word is:  t
The number of letters in the word is:   6
```

5. English to Metric Conversion

Purpose: To become familiar with the use of the top-down approach to problem solving, the INT function, declaring double-precision variables and constants to specify double-precision arithmetic, and a procedure for rounding.

Problem: Design a program flowchart and write a top-down modular program to convert an English measurement in miles, yards, feet, and inches, to a metric measurement in kilometers, meters, and centimeters. Use the following formula to change the English measurement to inches:

Total Inches = 63,360 * Miles + 36 * Yards + 12 * Feet + Inches

Use the following formula to determine the equivalent meters:

$$\text{Meters} = \left(\frac{\text{Total Inches}}{39.37} \right)$$

The variable used to represent the number of meters and the numeric constant 39.37 must be declared double precision — add a trailing number sign (#) to each. (This instructs the PC to carry out double-precision arithmetic.) Use the INT function to determine the number of kilometers, meters, and centimeters. Round the centimeters to two decimal places.

(**Hint**: After the number of meters has been determined, the maximum number of kilometers can be computed from: Kilometers = INT(Meters/1,000). Next, the remaining meters can be determined from: Remaining Meters = Meters – 1,000 * Kilometers. The number of integer meters in Remaining Meters can then be determined from: Integer Meters = INT(Remaining Meters). Continue with the same technique to compute the number of centimeters.)

Use the top-down chart illustrated in Figure 3.14 as a design for your solution.

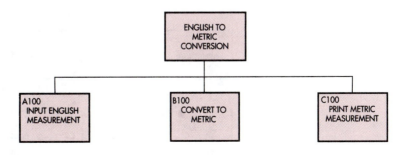

Input Data: Use the following sample data:

Miles: 2   Feet: 2
Yards: 5   Inches: 7

Output Results: The output screen should appear as illustrated by Figure 3.15.

FIGURE 3.15
Output for Programming Problem 5.

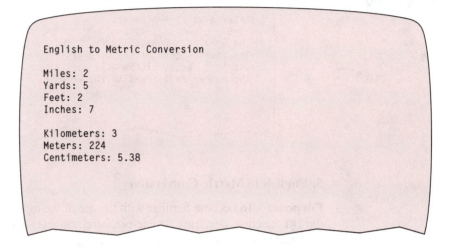

```
English to Metric Conversion

Miles: 2
Yards: 5
Feet: 2
Inches: 7

Kilometers: 3
Meters: 224
Centimeters: 5.38
```

6. Payroll Problem III: Federal Withholding Tax Computations

Purpose: To become familiar with the top-down approach to problem solving and the procedure for rounding a value.

Problem: Modify Payroll Problem II (Programming Problem 5 on page 5) in Chapter 2) to accept by means of INPUT statements an employee number, number of dependents, hourly rate of pay, and hours worked during a biweekly pay period. First design a program flow-chart and write the program using the top-down approach. Use the following formulas to compute the gross pay, federal withholding tax, and net pay:

1. Gross pay = hours worked x hourly rate of pay
2. Federal withholding tax = 0.26 × (gross pay – dependents × 40.46)
3. Net pay = gross pay – federal withholding tax

Round to the nearest cent the gross pay and federal withholding tax following their computation. Execute the program for each employee described under Input Data for this problem. Have the program clear the screen before accepting any data.

(**Hint**: See Program 3.6 on page 71.)

Use the top-down chart illustrated in Figure 3.16 as a design for your solution.

FIGURE 3.16
A top-down chart for Payroll Problem III.

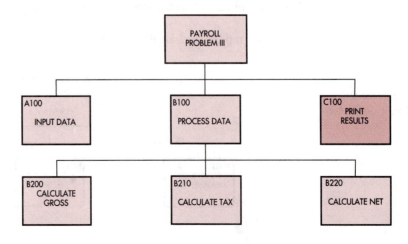

Input Data: Use the following sample data:

Employee Number	Number of Dependents	Hourly Rate of Pay	Hours Worked
123	2	$12.50	80
124	1	8.00	100
125	1	13.00	80
126	2	6.50	20

Output Results: The output screen should appear as illustrated by Figure 3.17 for employee 123.

FIGURE 3.17
Output for Programming Problem 6.

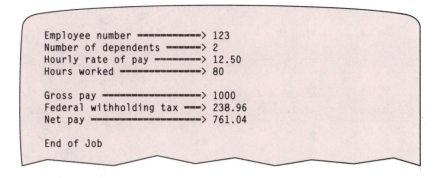

```
Employee number ============> 123
Number of dependents ======> 2
Hourly rate of pay ========> 12.50
Hours worked =============> 80

Gross pay ================> 1000
Federal withholding tax ==> 238.96
Net pay ==================> 761.04

End of Job
```

4

Looping and Input/Output

4.1 INTRODUCTION

The programs we have discussed so far are classified as **straight-line programs**. Up to this point, therefore, we have not yet utilized the complete power of the PC; essentially, we have used it as a high-speed calculator. However, the power of a PC is derived both from its speed and its capability to do repetitive tasks. One of the purposes of this chapter is to introduce you to the DO and LOOP statements. These statements allow you to instruct the PC to loop and repeat a task in a program.

The programs developed in Chapters 2 and 3 processed only small amounts of data. In this chapter we present a technique for integrating data into a program through the use of the READ and DATA statements. The READ and DATA statements usually are preferred over the INPUT statement when a program must process large amounts of data that are part of the program itself.

The third topic to be discussed in this chapter is the generation of tabular formatted reports. To write programs that can produce meaningful information in a form that is easy to read and understand, you need to know more about the PRINT statement. You also will learn about the PRINT USING and LOCATE statements. These statements give you even more control over the output than the PRINT statement does.

Upon successful completion of this chapter, you should be able to write programs that can process data that is part of the program itself, and you will be able to generate formatted reports. Furthermore, you will be able to write programs that can repeat the same task over and over.

PROGRAMMING CASE STUDY 5 – Determining the Sale Price

Program 4.1 computes the discount amount and sale price for each of a series of products. The discount amount is determined from the following formula:

$$\text{Discount Amount} = \frac{\text{Discount Rate}}{100} \times \text{Original Price}$$

The sale price is determined from the following formula:

Sale Price = Original Price – Discount Amount

The product data includes a product number, original price, and discount rate, as shown in Figure 4.1.

FIGURE 4.1

Product data for Programming Case Study 5.

Product Number	Original Price	Discount Rate in Percent
112841A	$125.00	14
213981B	110.00	16
332121A	98.00	13
586192X	88.00	12
714121Y	63.00	8
EOF	0	0 ← trailer record

The top-down chart that illustrates the organization of Program 4.1, the solution to Programming Case Study 5, is given in Figure 4.2. The flowchart for Program 4.1 is given in Figure 4.3. For your convenience in following the logic of the program, numbers have been placed on the top, left-hand corner of the symbols to illustrate the relationship between the chart and the program. Program 4.1 is presented in Figure 4.4 on page 98.

FIGURE 4.2

Top-down chart for the modules in Program 4.1.

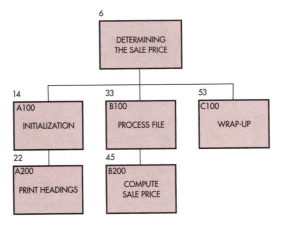

In Program 4.1 the Main Program includes three GOSUB statements. Each GOSUB invokes a subroutine that carries out a particular subtask. The GOSUB statement in line 6 invokes A100.Initialization beginning at line 14. A100.Initialization clears the screen and calls A200.Print.Headings, which begins at line 22. This nested subroutine displays the report and column headings before the RETURN statement in line 28 returns control to A100.Initialization. The RETURN statement in A100.Initialization (line 17), in turn, returns control to line 7 in the Main Program.

The PRINT statement in line 23 of A200.Print.Headings includes the TAB function that specifies the report heading is to begin exactly in column 21. The two PRINT statements in lines 25 and 26, and the one in line 37, contain a comma separator after each string constant or variable, which causes the PC to produce output that is automatically positioned in a tabular format. These concepts are described in detail in Section 4.4 (page 107).

The second GOSUB statement in the Main Program, line 7, calls B100.Process.File, which begins at line 33. Lines 34 and 38 contain READ statements that instruct the PC to assign values to Product$, Original.Price, and Rate from the sequence of data created from DATA statements that begin at line 59. Note that this data is part of Program 4.1 itself. The rules regarding the READ and DATA statements are presented in Section 4.3 (page 103).

FIGURE 4.3

Flowchart for the modules in Program 4.1.

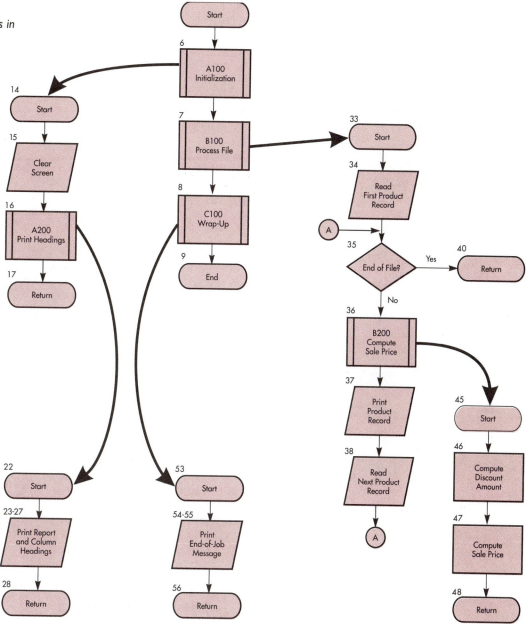

Following the first READ statement in line 34, lines 35 through 39 establish a Do loop. A **Do loop** begins with a DO statement and ends with a LOOP statement. The DO WHILE statement in line 35 (one form of the DO statement) and the LOOP statement in line 39 cause the range of statements between them to be executed repeatedly, as long as Product$ does not equal the string constant EOF. The expression, Product$ <> "EOF", following DO WHILE in line 35, is called a **condition**. A condition can be true or false. In the case of the DO WHILE statement, the statements within the loop are executed while the condition is true.

When Product$ does equal EOF, the condition in line 35 is false. Therefore, the PC skips the statements within the loop and continues execution at the first statement following the LOOP statement. The first statement following the LOOP statement is the RETURN statement in line 40. This statement transfers control to line 8 in the Main Program.

```
1    ' Program 4.1
2    ' Determining the Sale Price
3    ' ***********************************************
4    ' *                Main Program                 *
5    ' ***********************************************
6    GOSUB A100.Initialization
7    GOSUB B100.Process.File
8    GOSUB C100.Wrap.Up
9    END
10
11   ' ***********************************************
12   ' *               Initialization               *
13   ' ***********************************************
14   A100.Initialization:
15      CLS   ' Clear Screen
16      GOSUB A200.Print.Headings
17   RETURN
18
19   ' ***********************************************
20   ' *               Print Headings               *
21   ' ***********************************************
22   A200.Print.Headings:
23      PRINT TAB(21); "Determine the Sale Price"
24      PRINT
25      PRINT "Product", "Original", "Discount", "Discount", "Sale"
26      PRINT "Number", "Price", "Rate in %", "Amount", "Price"
27      PRINT
28   RETURN
29
30   ' ***********************************************
31   ' *               Process File                 *
32   ' ***********************************************
33   B100.Process.File:
34      READ Product$, Original.Price, Rate              ◄── reads first
35      DO WHILE Product$ <> "EOF"                           product record
36         GOSUB B200.Compute.Sale.Price
37         PRINT Product$, Original.Price, Rate, Discount, Sale.Price
38         READ Product$, Original.Price, Rate          ◄──
39      LOOP                                                 reads next
40   RETURN                                                  product record
41
42   ' ***********************************************
43   ' *            Compute Sale Price              *
44   ' ***********************************************
45   B200.Compute.Sale.Price:
46      Discount = Rate / 100 * Original.Price
47      Sale.Price = Original.Price - Discount
48   RETURN
49
50   ' ***********************************************
51   ' *                 Wrap-Up                    *
52   ' ***********************************************
53   C100.Wrap.Up:
54      PRINT
55      PRINT "End of Report"
56   RETURN
57
```

```
58   ' *************** Data Follows ******************
59   DATA 112841A, 125, 14
60   DATA 213981B, 110, 16
61   DATA 332121A,  98, 13
62   DATA 586192X,  88, 12
63   DATA 714121Y,  63,  8
64   DATA EOF,       0,  0  : ' This is the Trailer Record
65   ' *************** End of Program ******************
```

creates a sequence of data for use by the READ statements

```
[run]

                    Determine the Sale Price

      Product      Original      Discount      Discount      Sale
      Number       Price         Rate in %     Amount        Price

      112841A      125           14            17.5          107.5
      213981B      110           16            17.6          92.4
      332121A      98            13            12.74         85.26
      586192X      88            12            10.56         77.44
      714121Y      63            8             5.04          57.96

End of Report
```

One execution of a Do loop is called a **pass**. Note that the statements within the loop, lines 36 through 38, are indented by three spaces for the purpose of readability. Collectively, lines 36 through 38 are called the **range** of statements in the Do loop. B100.Process.File contains two READ statements located in lines 34 and 38. The first READ statement in line 34 is executed only once. This READ statement is called the **primary read** or **lead read**. The READ statement in line 38 is executed in each pass through the Do loop. Although many program styles exist, the programming style of using two READ statements and a Do loop will be used most often in this book.

Testing for the End-of-File

Lines 59 through 63 in Figure 4.4 contain data for only five products. The sixth product in line 64 is the **trailer record**. It represents the end-of-file and is used to determine when all the valid data has been processed. To incorporate an end-of-file test, a variable must be selected and a trailer record added to the data. In Program 4.1, we selected the product number as the test for end-of-file and the data value EOF. Because it guards against reading past end-of-file, the trailer record is also called the **sentinel record** and the value EOF is called the **sentinel value**. The value EOF is clearly distinguishable from all the rest of the data assigned to Product$. This sentinel value is the same as the string constant found in the condition in line 35.

After the READ statement in line 38 assigns Product$ the value EOF, the LOOP statement returns control to the DO WHILE statement. Because Product$ is equal to the value EOF, the DO WHILE statement causes the PC to pass control to line 40, which follows the corresponding LOOP statement.

The RETURN statement in line 40 returns control to the Main Program. Line 8 then calls C100.Wrap.Up, which displays the message, End of Report, and control is returned to the Main Program. Because the DATA statements are nonexecutable, lines 59 through 64 are ignored. Line 9 causes the PC to terminate execution of the program. Lines 53 through 56 also are referred to as an **end-of-file routine**.

Three other points are worthy to note about establishing a test for end-of-file in a Do loop:

1. It is important that the trailer record contain enough values for all the variables in the READ statement. In Program 4.1, if we only added the sentinel value EOF to line 64, there would not be enough data to fulfill the requirements of the three variables in the READ statement. We arbitrarily assigned zero values to each.

2. The Do loop requires the use of two READ statements. The first READ statement (line 34) reads the first product record, before the PC enters the Do loop. The second READ statement, found at the bottom of the Do loop (line 38), causes the PC to read the next data record. This READ statement reads the remaining data records, one at a time, until no more data records remain. Note that if the first record contains the product EOF, the DO WHILE statement will immediately transfer control to the statement below the corresponding LOOP statement.

3. Program 4.1 can process any number of products by simply placing each in a DATA statement prior to the trailer record.

4.2 THE DO AND LOOP STATEMENTS

By now the potential of the DO and LOOP statements should be apparent. As indicated earlier, the DO WHILE statement used in Program 4.1 to control the loop is just one form of the DO statement. This section describes the alternative forms of the DO statement and how to select one over the others when implementing a loop.

The general forms for the DO and LOOP statements are shown in Tables 4.1 and 4.2.

TABLE 4.1 - The DO Statement	
General Form:	DO
	or
	DO WHILE condition
	or
	DO UNTIL condition
	where **condition** is a relational expression.
Purpose:	Causes the statements between DO and LOOP to be executed repeatedly. The three general forms work in the following way:
	1. With the first general form, DO, the loop is controlled by a condition in the corresponding LOOP statement.
	2. DO WHILE causes the loop to be executed while the condition is true.
	3. DO UNTIL causes the loop to be executed until the condition becomes true.
	In the latter two cases, the condition is tested *before* the range of statements is executed. (See Figures 4.5(a) and 4.5(b).)
Examples:	DO
	DO WHILE Emp.Name$ <> "EOF"
	DO WHILE Side1 + Side2 < 5
	DO UNTIL Discount >= 500
	DO UNTIL Amount <= 125.25

TABLE 4.2 - The LOOP Statement	
General Form:	LOOP or LOOP WHILE condition or LOOP UNTIL condition where **condition** is a relational expression.
Purpose:	Identifies the end of a Do loop. The three general forms work in the following way: 1. If the condition is in the corresponding DO statement, then the LOOP statement automatically returns control to the DO statement. 2. LOOP WHILE causes the loop to be executed while the condition is true. 3. LOOP UNTIL causes the loop to be executed until the condition becomes true. In the latter two cases, the test to continue the loop is made *after* each pass. (See Figures 4.5(c) and 4.5(d).)
Examples:	LOOP LOOP WHILE Control$ = "Y" LOOP UNTIL Control$ = "Y"

Figure 4.5 on the next page illustrates the four ways you can formulate a Do loop. The DO or LOOP statement that contains the condition is represented in a flowchart by the diamond shape symbol. When you flowchart the branch to the top of the loop, you may want to use a connector symbol such as the circled A in Figure 4.3 on page 97, rather than flowlines shown in the flowcharts in Figure 4.5.

Selecting the Proper Do Loop for a Program

Your program flowchart should indicate the type of Do loop to use in your program. The type you choose is dependent on the following two points:

1. If the decision to terminate is at the top of the loop, use DO WHILE or DO UNTIL (see Figures 4.5(a) and 4.5(b)). If the decision to terminate is at the bottom of the loop, use LOOP WHILE or LOOP UNTIL (see Figures 4.5(c) and 4.5(d)).

2. Use the keyword WHILE if you want to continue execution of the loop *while* the condition is true. Use the keyword UNTIL if you want to continue execution of the loop *until* the condition is true.

In this book, we will use two of the four Do loops. When the decision to terminate is at the top of the loop, we will use the DO WHILE statement shown in Figure 4.5a. This form was used earlier in Program 4.1 on page 98. When the decision to terminate is at the bottom of the loop, we will use the LOOP UNTIL statement shown in Figure 4.5d. For an example of a program that uses the LOOP UNTIL statement, see Program 4.5 on page 128.

Conditions

In line 42 of Program 4.1, the DO WHILE statement contains the condition

```
Product$ <> "EOF"
```

The condition is made up of two expressions and a **relational operator**. The condition specifies a relationship between expressions that is either true or false. If the condition is true, execution continues with the line following the DO WHILE statement. If the condition is false, then control is transferred to the line following the corresponding LOOP statement.

The PC makes a comparison between the two operators based upon the relational operator. Table 4.3 on the next page lists the six valid relational operators.

FIGURE 4.5

The four ways to write a Do loop and their corresponding general flowcharts.

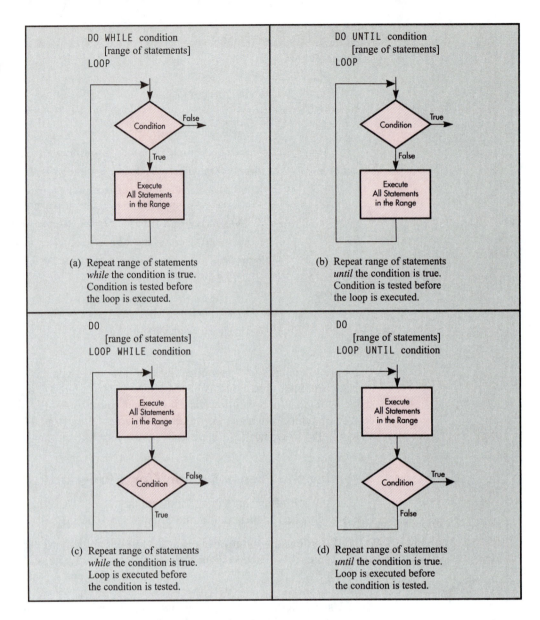

```
DO WHILE condition
   [range of statements]
LOOP
```

(a) Repeat range of statements *while* the condition is true. Condition is tested before the loop is executed.

```
DO UNTIL condition
   [range of statements]
LOOP
```

(b) Repeat range of statements *until* the condition is true. Condition is tested before the loop is executed.

```
DO
   [range of statements]
LOOP WHILE condition
```

(c) Repeat range of statements *while* the condition is true. Loop is executed before the condition is tested.

```
DO
   [range of statements]
LOOP UNTIL condition
```

(d) Repeat range of statements *until* the condition is true. Loop is executed before the condition is tested.

TABLE 4.3 - Relational Operators Used in Conditions

RELATIONS	MATH SYMBOL	QBASIC SYMBOL	EXAMPLES
Equal to	=	=	Code$ = "1"
Less than	<	<	Gross < 1000
Greater than	>	>	Rate > 0.05
Less than or equal to	≤	<= or =<	Tax <= 250
Greater than or equal to	≥	>= or =>	Count >= 10
Not equal to	≠	<> or ><	Same$ <> "End"

It is important to watch for several points in the application of conditions. For example, it is invalid to compare a string expression to a numeric expression. The following is invalid:

```
DO WHILE Dollars$ > 100    ' Invalid
```

Furthermore, the condition should ensure termination of the loop. If a logical error such as

```
DO WHILE 3 > 1  ←——      this condition
     [range of statements]    is always true
LOOP
```

is not detected, a never-ending loop develops. Only manual intervention can stop the endless program execution. Manual intervention includes pressing the Ctrl+Break keys on your PC keyboard. For additional examples of programs that include Do loops, see Programs 4.4 and 4.5 in this chapter, and Section 5.4 in Chapter 5 (page 154).

4.3 THE READ, DATA, AND RESTORE STATEMENTS

In Section 4.1 the READ and DATA statements were introduced briefly. These two statements are used in tandem to assign data items to variables such as INPUT statements. They differ from the INPUT statement in that you enter the data as part of the program rather than keying in the data after execution. The INPUT statement is the preferred form of input when processing small amounts of data, while the READ and DATA statements are preferred when processing large amounts of data that are part of the program itself.

This section illustrates the rules for use of the READ, DATA, and RESTORE statements and gives further examples of their use, as well as their limitations.

The DATA Statement

The DATA **statement** provides for the creation of a sequence of data items for use by the READ statement. The general form of the DATA statement and some examples are given in Table 4.4.

TABLE 4.4 - The DATA Statement	
General Form:	DATA data item,..., data item
	where each data item is either a numeric constant or a string constant.
Purpose:	Provides for the creation of a sequence of data items for use by the READ statement.
Examples (with READ statements):	
	DATA Jan, 3.14, 0.025, 95
	READ Month$, Discount, Commission, Returns
	DATA 0.24E33, 0, -2.5D-12, 1.23#, 2.46!, 5
	READ Dist, Fac, Adjust(J), X#, Y, Z%
	DATA 15, , ",", YES, "2 + 7 = ", NO, 2.2, ""
	READ H, A$, B$(3), C$, D$, E$, I, F$
Note:	In the last example, A$ and F$ are both assigned the null character.

The DATA statement consists of the keyword DATA followed by a list of data items separated by mandatory commas. The data items may be numeric or string and are formulated according to the following rules:

DATA RULE 1 *Numeric data items placed in a DATA statement must be formulated as numeric constants.*

DATA RULE 2

String data items placed in a DATA statement may be formulated with or without surrounding quotation marks, provided the string contains no trailing or leading blanks, or embedded commas or colons. A string that contains a trailing or leading blank or an embedded comma or colon must be surrounded with quotation marks.

FIGURE 4.6

The order of data items as represented in main memory from the sequence of DATA statements in Program 4.1, lines 59 to 64.

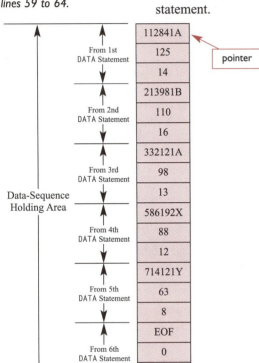

Data items from all DATA statements in a program are collected in main memory into a single **data-sequence holding area**. The order in which the data items appear in the DATA statements determines their order in the single data sequence (see Figure 4.6). In other words, the ordering of the data items is based on two considerations: the sequence of the DATA statements, and the order from left to right of the data items within each DATA statement.

The number of data items that can be represented in a DATA statement depends not only on the type of problem, but also on the programming style adopted by the programmer. Some programmers prefer to write one DATA statement for each data item, like this:

```
DATA 310386024
DATA JOE NIKOLE
DATA -3.85
DATA -1E-15
READ Soc.Sec$, Emp.Name$, Amt, Standard
```

Others prefer to write as many data items in a DATA statement as there are variables in the READ statement that refer to that DATA statement. For example, the previous DATA and READ statements can be rewritten in this way:

```
DATA 310386024, JOE NIKOLE, -3.85, -1E-15
READ Soc.Sec$, Emp.Name$, Amt, Standard
```

The DATA statement, like the REM statement, is a nonexecutable statement; that is, if the execution of a program reaches a line containing a DATA statement, it proceeds to the next line with no other effect. In this book, all DATA statements are placed at the end of the program, as shown in Program 4.1 (page 98).

The READ Statement

The READ **statement** provides for the assignment of values to variables from a sequence of data items created from DATA statements. The general form of the READ statement is given in Table 4.5. The READ statement consists of the keyword READ followed by a list of variables separated by mandatory commas. The variables may be numeric or string variables.

TABLE 4.5 - The READ Statement	
General Form:	READ variable, . . . , variable
	where each variable is either a numeric variable or a string variable.
Purpose:	Provides for the assignment of values to variables from a sequence of data items created from DATA statements.
Examples (with DATA statements):	See Table 4.4.

The READ statement causes the variables in its list to be assigned specific values, in order, from the data sequence formed by all of the DATA statements. In order to visualize the relationship between the READ statement and its associated DATA statement, you may think of a **pointer** associated with the data-sequence holding area, as shown in Figure 4.6. When a program first is executed, this pointer points to the first data item in the data sequence. Each time a READ statement is executed, the variables in the list are assigned specific values from the data sequence beginning with the data item indicated by the pointer, and the pointer is advanced one value per variable, in a downward fashion, to point beyond the data used.

Figure 4.7 illustrates the data-sequence holding area and pointer for a program containing multiple READ and DATA statements. The pointer initially points to the location of 565.33 in the holding area. When line 4 is executed, the value of 565.33 is assigned to the variable Mon.Sal; the pointer is advanced to the location of the next value 356.45, which is assigned to the variable Tue.Sal; and the pointer is advanced to the location of the next value, 478.56. When line 5 is executed, the variable Wed.Sal is assigned the value of 478.56, Thur.Sal the value of 756.23, and Fri.Sal the value of 342.23.

As this assignment occurs, the pointer advances one value per variable to point to a location beyond the data used, which is recognized by the PC as the end of the data sequence holding area.

FIGURE 4.7

Partial program and the corresponding data-sequence holding area.

```
 1   ' Determining the Average Daily Sales
 2   ' with Multiple READ and Multiple DATA Statements
 3   ' **********************************************
 4   READ Mon.Sal, Tue.Sal
 5   READ Wed.Sal, Thur.Sal, Fri.Sal
 6   Average = (Mon.Sal + Tue.Sal + Wed.Sal + Thur.Sal + Fri.Sal) / 5
 7   PRINT Mon.Sal, Tue.Sal, Wed.Sal, Thur.Sal, Fri.Sal
 8   PRINT "The average is"; Average
 9   ' *************** Data Follows ****************
10   DATA 565.33, 356.45, 478.56
11   DATA 756.23, 342.23
```

```
[run]

565.33          356.45          478.56          756.23          342.23
The average is 499.76
```

Data-Sequence Holding Area

| 565.33 | 356.45 | 478.56 | 756.23 | 342.23 | Undefined |

pointer before the exectuion of line 4

pointer after the exectuion of line 4

pointer after the exectuion of line 5

In the partial program in Figure 4.7, the PC is unable to calculate Average correctly until it has the values of Mon.Sal, Tue.Sal, Wed.Sal, Thur.Sal, and Fri.Sal. The READ statement should occur somewhere before the LET statement in the program. This example can be generalized to give the following:

READ RULE 1

Every variable appearing in the program whose value is directly obtained by a READ statement should be listed in a READ statement before it is used elsewhere in the program.

Unlike the DATA statements, the placement of the READ statement is important. Furthermore, more than one DATA statement may be used to satisfy one READ statement, and more than one READ statement may be satisfied from one DATA statement.

READ RULE 2

A program containing a READ statement must also have at least one DATA statement.

If there are an insufficient number of data items to be assigned to the variables of a READ statement, a dialog box displays in the middle of the screen with the diagnostic message, Out of DATA. Excessive data items in a program are ignored.

Finally, the type of data item in the data sequence must correspond to the type of variable to which it is assigned. If they do not agree, a dialog box displays in the middle of the screen with the diagnostic message, Syntax error.

READ RULE 3	*Numeric variables in* READ *statements require numeric constants as data items in* DATA *statements, and string variables require quoted strings or unquoted strings as data.*

The RESTORE Statement

Usually data items from a DATA statement are processed by a READ statement only once. If you want the PC to read all or some of the same data items later, you must use the RESTORE statement to restore the data.

The RESTORE **statement** allows the data in a given program to be reread as often as necessary by other READ statements. The general form of the RESTORE statement is given with examples in Table 4.6. The RESTORE statement consists of the keyword RESTORE optionally followed by a label. If no label follows the keyword RESTORE, then the next READ statement accesses the first data item in the first DATA statement. If a label follows RESTORE, the next READ statement accesses the first data item in the DATA statement that immediately follows the specified label.

TABLE 4.6 - The RESTORE Statement	
General Form:	RESTORE label
	where **label** is blank, a label name, or a line number.
Purpose:	Allows the data in the program to be reread. If no label follows the keyword RESTORE then the next READ statement accesses the first data item in the first DATA statement.
	If a label follows RESTORE, the next READ statement accesses the first data item in the first DATA statement that immediately follows the specified label.
Examples:	RESTORE
	RESTORE record

The RESTORE statement causes the pointer to be moved backward or forward to a specified area in the data-sequence holding area. This is done so that the next READ statement executed will read the data from some other point in the sequence.

The RESTORE statement generally is used when it is necessary to perform several types of computations on the same data items. It can also be used to randomly access data located in DATA statements that have labels. The program in Figure 4.8 illustrates the use of the RESTORE statement.

FIGURE 4.8

An example of using the RESTORE statement.

```
 1   ' Use of the RESTORE Statement
 2   ' ****************************
 3   READ Item.1, Item.2, Item.3
 4   Sum = Item.1 + Item.2 + Item.3
 5   RESTORE   'Reset data pointer to first data item
 6   READ Item.4, Item.5, Item.6
 7   Product = Item.4, * Item.5 * Item.6
 8   PRINT Item.1, Item.2, Item.3, Sum
 9   PRINT Item.4, Item.5, Item.6, Product
10   ' ******* Data Follows *******
11   DATA 1, 3, 9

     [run]

     1              3              9              13
     1              3              9              27
```

When the first READ statement in line 3 is executed in the program in Figure 4.8, Item.1 is assigned the value of 1, Item.2 the value of 3, and Item.3 the value of 9 from the DATA statement in line 11. After a value for Sum is computed in line 4, the RESTORE statement in line 5 is executed. This resets the pointer to the beginning of the data-sequence holding area so that it points at the value of 1 again. When the second READ statement in line 6 is executed, the values of 1, 3, and 9 are reread and assigned to Item.4, Item.5, and Item.6.

4.4 THE PRINT STATEMENT

The PRINT **statement** is used to write information to the screen. It is commonly used to display the results from computations, to display headings and labeled information, and to plot points on a graph. In addition, the PRINT statement allows you to control the spacing and the format of the desired output.

The general form of the PRINT statement is given with examples in Table 4.7. The PRINT statement consists of the keyword, PRINT. It may also have an optional list of **print items** separated by mandatory commas or semicolons. The print items may be numeric or string constants, variables, expressions, or null items. In addition, the print items may include useful function references, such as the Integer and Square Root functions, INT and SQR.

TABLE 4.7 - The PRINT Statement	
General Form:	PRINT item pm item pm ... pm item
	where each **item** is a constant, variable, expression, function reference, or null, and each **pm** is a comma or semicolon.
Purpose:	Writes information to the screen.
Examples:	PRINT
	PRINT Emp.Name$
	PRINT Count; Discount, Employee$; Number
	PRINT Gender$; " "; Time; " "; Marital.Status$
	PRINT , , Height, Weight; Race$; Job(8);
	PRINT "X = "; X,"Y = "; Y
	PRINT "The answer is $"; H,
	PRINT TAB(10); (X + Y) / 4, INT(A)
	PRINT "The interest rate is"; Interest; "%"
	PRINT X; " "; 2 * X; " "; 3 * X; " "; 4 * X
Note:	Enter the question mark (?) and QBasic changes it to the keyword PRINT when the cursor is moved off the line. Enter one or more spaces between print items and QBasic inserts a semicolon between the print items when the cursor is moved off the line.

Print Zones and Print Positions

The most common use of the PRINT statement is to display values defined earlier in a program. Every sample program presented so far includes a PRINT statement. Listing items separated by commas within a PRINT statement

```
PRINT Product$, Original.Price, Rate, Discount, Sale.Price
```

causes the values of Product$, Original.Price, Rate, Discount, and Sale.Price to be displayed on a single line. QBasic displays the five values in print zones.

In the 80-column display, there are five print zones per line. Each **print zone** has 14 positions for a total of 70 positions per line. The **print positions** are numbered consecutively from the left, starting with position 1, as shown in Figure 4.9.

FIGURE 4.9

In the 80-column display mode, the print line is divided into five print zones.

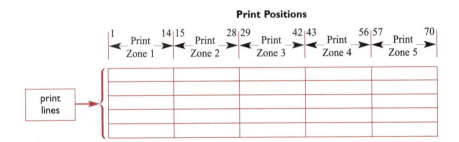

Representation of Numeric Output

Numeric constants, variables, expressions, and function references are evaluated to produce a string of characters consisting of a sign, the decimal representation of the number, and a trailing space. The sign is a leading space if the number is positive, or a leading minus sign if the number is negative.

Representation of String Output

String constants, string variables, string expressions, and string function references are displayed without any leading or trailing spaces. For example, when the following line

```
PRINT "Quick"; "BASIC"
```

is executed, the PC displays QuickBASIC in print positions 1 through 10. Unlike the way it treats numeric output, the PC does not insert a trailing space following the string constants in the output.

Use of the Comma Separator

Punctuation marks such as the comma and semicolon are placed between print items. As illustrated by lines 9 through 15 of Program 4.2 in Figure 4.10, the **comma separator** allows you to display values that are automatically positioned in tabular format. Each PRINT statement executed displays one line of information, unless one of the following conditions are true:

1. The number of print zones required by the PRINT statement exceeds five.
2. The PRINT statement ends with a comma or semicolon (see Program 4.2 in Figure 4.10, lines 9 and 10).

Two or more consecutive commas may be included in a PRINT statement (lines 14 and 15 in Figure 4.10) as a means of tabulating over print zones.

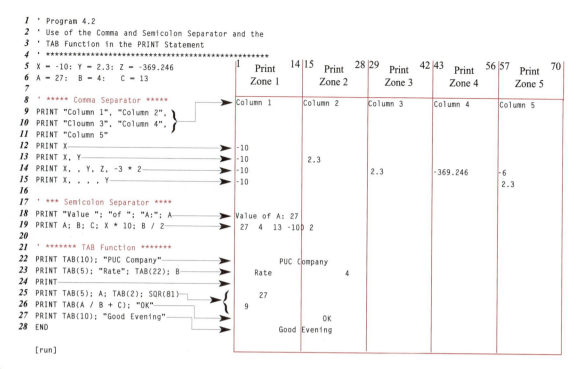

FIGURE 4.10

Program 4.1 effect of commas, semicolons, and the TAB function in PRINT statements with numeric and string expressions.

Use of the Semicolon Separator

While the comma separator allows you to tab to the next print zone, the **semicolon separator** does not. Instead, the semicolon in a PRINT statement causes the display of the value immediately to the right of the previous one. The semicolon allows you to display more than five items per line. Use of the semicolon separator is referred to as displaying values in a **packed** or **compressed format**.

Lines 18 and 19 in Figure 4.10 show the use of the semicolon separator. While each numeric value displayed is preceded by a leading sign and a trailing space, string values are displayed with no spaces separating them.

In line 19, all five print items are separated by the semicolon, and the values are all displayed within the first 18 print positions.

If a PRINT statement ends with a semicolon, the first item in the next PRINT statement displays on the same line in compressed form.

Creating Blank Lines

If a PRINT statement contains a null list, then a blank line results. For example,

```
PRINT
```

contains no print items and results in the display of a blank line. Line 24 in Figure 4.10 displays a blank line before the values displayed by line 25.

Use of the TAB Function

So far, PRINT statements have contained the comma and semicolon as separators among numeric and string expressions to display the values of these expressions in a readable format with correct spacing. Compact and exact spacing of output results also can be achieved by the use of the TAB and SPC functions.

The TAB **function** is used in the PRINT and LPRINT statements to specify the exact print positions for the various output results on a given line. The LPRINT statement is discussed in later paragraphs. Use of the TAB function

```
PRINT TAB(10); "PUC Company"
```

causes the string to be displayed beginning in exactly print position 10, as shown in line 22 in Figure 4.10 on the previous page.

The general form of the TAB function is

TAB(numeric expression);

where the numeric expression, the argument, may be a numeric constant, variable, expression, or function reference. The value of the argument determines the position on the line of the next character to be displayed. QBasic automatically appends a semicolon to the TAB function if you do not.

Line 25 in Figure 4.10 shows that backspacing is not permitted. If the argument is less than the current column position on the output device, then the PC positions the cursor or print head mechanism on the next line at a column position equal to the argument.

Study closely the remaining examples of the TAB function in lines 22 through 27 in Figure 4.10. Note that noninteger arguments are rounded. The following rules summarize the use of the TAB function:

TAB RULE 1	*The argument must be less than or equal to 32,767. An argument that is less than 1 is set equal to 1.*
TAB RULE 2	*A decimal argument is rounded to the nearest integer.*
TAB RULE 3	*Backspacing is not permitted with the TAB function. If the cursor or current print position is beyond the print position that equates to the argument, then the PC moves to the next line.*
TAB RULE 4	*If the argument is greater than the output width, then it is divided by the output width, and the remainder is used as the argument.*

Displaying Spaces — The SPC Function

The SPC **function** works in a fashion similar to the Spacebar on a keyboard. It may be used to insert spaces between print items. The general form of the SPC function is:

SPC(numeric expression)

Consider the following PRINT statement:

```
PRINT "Column 1"; SPC(3); "Column 2"; SPC(5); "Column 3"
```

The SPC(3) causes the insertion of three spaces between Column 1 and Column 2. The SPC(5) inserts five spaces between Column 2 and Column 3. The spaces inserted between results displayed often are called **filler**. The SPC function may be used any number of times in the same PRINT statement. However, it may be used only in PRINT or LPRINT statements.

Calculations within the PRINT Statement

QBasic permits calculations to be made within the PRINT statement. For instance, the sum, difference, product, quotient, modulo, and exponentiation of two numbers, such as 4 and 2, may be made in the conventional way by using LET statements or by using the PRINT statement, as in Program 4.3 presented in Figure 4.11.

FIGURE 4.11

Program 4.3, calculations within PRINT statements.

```
1    ' Program 4.3
2    ' Calculations within a PRINT Statement
3    ' ********************************************
4    PRINT 4 + 2; SPC(4); 4 - 2; SPC(4); 4 * 2; SPC(4); SQR(121)
5    PRINT 4 / 2; SPC(4); 4 \ 2; SPC(4); 4 MOD 2; SPC(4); 4 ^ 2
6    END

     [run]

     6       2       8       11
     2       2       0       16
```

Using the Immediate Window

As described in Chapter 2, QBasic has a narrow window at the bottom of the screen called the immediate window that permits your PC to act as a powerful desk calculator. To activate the immediate window, click anywhere in this window. Click the view window to activate the view window. To adjust the size of the immediate window, drag the line that separates the view window and the immediate window up or down.

Through the immediate window, statements such as the PRINT statement can be executed individually without being incorporated into a program. You merely enter the keyword PRINT followed by any numeric expression. As soon as you press the Enter key, the PC immediately computes and displays the value of the expression on the output screen.

The following example illustrates the computation of a complex expression in the immediate window:

```
PRINT (2 - 3 * 4 / 5) ^ 2 + 5 / (4 * 3 - 2 ^ 3)
 1.41
```

The value 1.41 displays on the output screen.

You can enter up to 10 lines in the immediate window, and each line may contain multiple statements separated by colons. Each line is executed independently of the others when you press the Enter key. You can move back and forth among the lines in the immediate window, executing them in any order.

Some programmers use the immediate window to test screen output before incorporating it into a large program. When the code is executing properly, it can be copied into the view window and made part of the current program.

You also can use the immediate window to **debug** the program in the view window. For example, if a program terminates unexpectedly, the PRINT statement can be used in the immediate window to display the values of variables used in the program in the view window. This use of the immediate window can be of great benefit in clearing up logical errors in a program. See Appendix C for a discussion of debugging a program that has errors.

The LPRINT Statement

While the PRINT statement displays results on the screen, the LPRINT **statement** prints the results on the printer. Everything that has been presented with respect to the PRINT statement in this chapter applies to the LPRINT statement as well. Obviously, to use this statement, you must have a printer attached to your PC and it must be in Ready mode.

4.5 THE PRINT USING STATEMENT FOR FORMATTED OUTPUT

The PRINT USING **statement** is far more useful than the PRINT statement in exactly controlling the format of a program's output. In Section 4.4, you were introduced to the comma, the semicolon, and the TAB and SPC functions for print-control purposes. For most applications, these print-control methods will suffice. However, when you are confronted with generating readable reports for nontechnical personnel, more control over the format of the output is essential. The PRINT USING statement gives you the desired capabilities to display information according to a predefined format instead of the free format provided by the PRINT statement.

Through the use of the PRINT USING statement, you can do the following:

1. Specify the exact image of a line of output.
2. Force decimal-point alignment when displaying numeric tables in columnar format.
3. Control the number of digits displayed for a numeric result.
4. Specify that commas be inserted into a number. (Starting from the units position of a number and progressing toward the left, digits are separated into groups of three by a comma.)
5. Specify that the sign status of the number be displayed along with the number (+ or blank if positive, – if negative).
6. Assign a fixed or floating dollar sign ($) to the number displayed.
7. Force a numeric result to be displayed in exponential form.
8. **Left-justify** or **right-justify** string values in a formatted field. (That is, align the leftmost or rightmost characters, respectively.)
9. Specify that only the first character of a string be displayed.
10. Round a value automatically to a specified number of decimal digits.

The general form of the PRINT USING statement is given with examples in Table 4.8.

TABLE 4.8 - The PRINT USING Statement

General Form:	PRINT USING string expression; list
	where **string expression** (sometimes called the descriptor field or format field) is either a string constant or a string variable; and
	list is a list of items to be displayed in the format specified by the descriptor field.
Purpose:	Provides for controlling the format of a program's output by specifying an image to which that output must conform.
Examples:	PRINT USING "The answer is #,###.##"; Cost
	PRINT USING "## divided by # is #.#"; Num; Den; Quot
	Format$ = "Total cost =======> $$,###.##-"
	PRINT USING Format$; Total
	Total.Line1$ = "**,###.##"
	PRINT USING Total.Line1$; Check;
	PRINT USING "\ \"; Cust.Name$
	PRINT USING "!. !. \ \"; First$; Middle$; Last$
	PRINT USING "Example _##"; Number
	PRINT USING "#.##^^^^"; Dis.1; Dis.2; Dis.3; Dis.4

Declaring the Format of the Output

To control the format of the displayed values, the PRINT USING statement is used in conjunction with a string expression that specifies the image to which the output must conform. The string expression is placed immediately after the words PRINT USING in the form of a string constant or string variable. If the format is described by a string variable, then the string variable must be assigned the format by a LET statement before the PRINT USING statement is executed in the program. Figure 4.12 illustrates the two methods for specifying the format for the PRINT USING statement.

FIGURE 4.12

The two methods for defining the format for a PRINT USING statement.

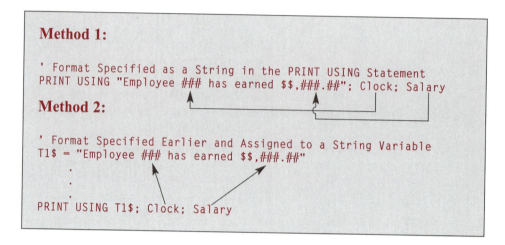

In Method 1 of Figure 4.12, the string following the keywords PRINT USING instructs the PC to display the values of Clock and Salary using the format found in that statement. In Method 2, the string constant has been replaced by the string variable T1$ that was assigned the desired format in the previous statement. If Clock is equal to 105 and Salary is equal to 4563.20, then the results displayed from the execution of either PRINT USING statement in Method 1 or Method 2 are as follows:

Format Symbols

Table 4.9 on the next page includes the format symbols available with QBasic. One or more consecutive format symbols appearing in a string expression is a **descriptor field**, or **format field**.

The Number Sign Symbol

The number sign (#) is the format symbol used to define a numeric descriptor field. Grouped number signs indicate exactly how many positions are desired in a numeric result during output. A number sign reserves space for a digit or sign. For example,

    # indicates one position in a numeric result
    ## indicates two positions in a numeric result
    #### indicates four positions in a numeric result
    ####.## indicates six positions, two of which are to the right of the decimal point

It is your responsibility to ensure that enough number signs are in the descriptor field to fit the output results in the prescribed format.

TABLE 4.9 - Format Symbols

SYMBOL	FUNCTION	EXAMPLES
#	Grouped number signs define a numeric descriptor field and cause the display of a numeric value in integer form.	# ### ####
.	The period is used for decimal-point placement. A decimal point in a numeric descriptor field causes the display of a numeric value in fixed point form.	###. ###.## .###
,	The comma is used for automatic comma placement. A comma in front of a decimal point in a numeric descriptor field causes the display of a numeric value with commas displayed to the left of the decimal point every three significant digits.	#,###,### ###,###.## #######,.##
^^^^	Four consecutive circumflexes to the right of a numeric descriptor field causes the display of a value in exponential notation (D or E format).	##^^^^ #,###^^^^ +##,###^^^^
+	A single plus sign to the left or right of a numeric descriptor field causes the display of a numeric value with a sign (plus or minus) immediately before or after the number.	+##,###.## ###+ #,###.##+
–	A single minus sign to the right of a numeric descriptor field causes the display of negative numbers with a trailing minus sign and positive numbers with a trailing space.	##.##– ###– ###,###.##–
$	A single leading dollar sign in a numeric descriptor field causes the display of a fixed dollar sign in that position, followed by a numeric value. (Note: The dollar sign may be substituted for any valid QBasic character listed in Table D.1 in Appendix D. Format symbols must be preceded by the underscore character.)	$### $##.## $#,###.##+
$$	Two leading dollar signs in a numeric descriptor field cause the display of a single dollar sign immediately to the left of the first significant digit of a numeric value.	$$##.## $$###.##– $$,###.##
**	Two leading asterisks in a numeric descriptor field cause the display of a numeric value with leading spaces, filled with asterisks, to the left of the numeric value.	**###.### **,###.## **.##
**$	Two leading asterisks followed by a single dollar sign in a numeric descriptor field combine the effects of the previous two symbols. These symbols (* * $) cause the display of a numeric value with leading spaces filled with asterisks, followed by a floating dollar sign immediately to the left of the numeric value.	**$######## **$#,###.##+
&	The ampersand causes the display of a complete string value left-justified.	&
!	The exclamation point causes the display of the first character of a string value.	!
_	The underscore causes the display of the next character in the descriptor field as if the character were a string constant. Any of the format symbols in this table can be displayed as a string constant.	_& _! _# #_# _$$##.##_#
\n spaces\	Two backslashes separated by n spaces cause the display of a string of characters left-justified and equal in length to 2 plus the number of spaces (n).	\\ \ \ \ \ \ \

Consider the example in Figure 4.13, where A = 10, B = –11, C = 12.75 and D = 4565.

FIGURE 4.13

Displaying numeric values through the use of the PRINT USING *statement. The character ḃ represents a blank character in the output results.*

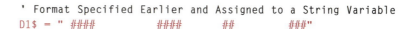
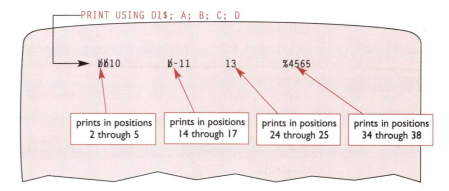

Table 4.10 summarizes the use of the number sign in various descriptor fields. The program in Figure 4.14 on page 117 gives examples of the use of the number sign.

DESCRIPTOR FIELD	DATA	OUTPUT	REMARKS
TABLE 4.10 – Use of the Number Sign (#) in a Descriptor Field			
####	10	ḃḃ10	Right-justify the digits in the field with leading
####	–11	ḃ-11	spaces. Note the floating minus sign.
##	12.75	13	The data is rounded to an integer, as only integers are specified by the descriptor field.
###	4565	%4565	Because the data is too large for the specified descriptor field, the value is displayed but is preceded by a percent sign (%) to indicate that an insufficient number of positions were reserved for this descriptor field.

If the string expression referenced in a PRINT USING statement contains fewer descriptor fields than print items in the list, QBasic reuses the string expression. For example, when the following line is entered in the immediate window

```
PRINT USING "##   "; -5; -7; -9
```

the PC displays

```
-5      -7      -9
```

If the string expression contains more descriptor fields than print items in the list, QBasic ignores the excess. For example,

```
PRINT USING "##        ##    ##    ##"; -5
```

results in -5 being displayed in print positions 1 and 2.

The Decimal Point (Period) Symbol

The period (.) in a numeric descriptor field places a decimal point in the output record at that character position in which it appears, and the format of the numeric result is aligned with the position of the decimal point. When number signs (#) precede the decimal point in a descriptor field, any leading zeros appearing in the data are replaced by spaces, except for a single leading zero immediately preceding the decimal point.

When number signs follow the decimal point, unused positions to the right of the decimal point are filled with trailing zeros. When the data contains more digits to the right of the decimal point than the descriptor field allows, the data is displayed rounded to the limits of the descriptor field.

Table 4.11 and the program in Figure 4.14 illustrate the use of the decimal point in various descriptor fields.

TABLE 4.11 - Use of the Decimal Point (.) in a Descriptor Field			
DESCRIPTOR FIELD	DATA	OUTPUT	REMARKS
####.##	217.5	ƀ217.50	Unspecified decimal fraction positions are
#####.##	-40	ƀƀ-40.00	filled with trailing zeros.
#####.##	23.458	ƀƀƀ23.46	Decimal fractional digits are rounded.
####.##	0.027	ƀƀƀ0.03	The last leading zero before the decimal point is not suppressed.

The Comma Symbol

A comma (,) to the left of the decimal point in a numeric descriptor field places a comma in front of every third digit to the left of the decimal point. A comma specifies a digit position within the descriptor field. If there are less than four significant digits to the left of the decimal point, the PC displays a space in place of the comma symbol. Table 4.12 and the program in Figure 4.14 illustrate the use of the comma in various descriptor fields.

If the descriptor field containing a comma has too few number signs, the comma is replaced by a digit.

TABLE 4.12 - Use of the Comma (,) in a Descriptor Field			
DESCRIPTOR FIELD	DATA	OUTPUT	REMARKS
#,###	4000	4,000	Comma displayed.
#,###,###	999999	ƀƀ999,999	Comma displayed.
#,###.##	−30.5	ƀƀ-30.50	Space displayed for comma when leading digits are blank.
########,.##	9876543.21#	9,876,543.21	Comma in front of a decimal point in descriptor field.

FIGURE 4.14

An example of using the number (#) sign, decimal point (.) and comma (,) format symbols.

```
1   ' Examples of the Use of the Number Sign
2   ' Decimal Point and Comma in a Descriptor Field
3   ' ********************************************
4   CLS  ' Clear Screen
5   DL1$ = "####   #,###   #,###.##   ########,.##"
6   READ Value, Constant#
7   PRINT USING DL1$; Value; Value; Value; Constant#
8   PRINT USING "####"; Value
9   PRINT USING "#,###"; Value
10  PRINT USING "#,###.##"; Value
11  ' ************** Data Follows ****************
12  DATA 1234.56, -1234567.87

    [run]

    1235    1,235    1,234.56     -1,234,567.87
    1235
    1,235
    1,234.56
```

The Plus and Minus Sign Symbols

A plus sign (+) as either the first or last character in a numeric descriptor field causes + to be displayed if the data item is positive, or – if the data item is negative. If the plus sign is the first character in the descriptor field, it is called a **floating sign**. If the plus sign is the last character in the descriptor field, it is called a **fixed sign**.

A minus sign (–) at the end of a numeric descriptor field, also called a fixed sign, causes negative numbers to be displayed with a trailing minus sign and positive numbers to be displayed with a trailing space.

Table 4.13 gives examples of the use of the plus and minus sign symbols in various numeric descriptor fields.

TABLE 4.13 – Use of the Plus (+) or Minus (–) Sign in a Descriptor Field			
DESCRIPTOR FIELD	**DATA**	**OUTPUT**	**REMARKS**
FIXED SIGNS			
###.##–	000.01	ᵇᵇ0.01ᵇ	The last leading zero before the decimal point is not suppressed.
###.##+	20.5	ᵇ20.50+	
###.##+	-8.236	ᵇᵇ8.24–	Automatic rounding when length of data exceeds descriptor-field specification.
###.##–	-456.0	456.00–	
FLOATING SIGNS			
+##.##	40.5	+40.50	
+##.##	7.07	ᵇ+7.07	
+###.##	-0.236	ᵇᵇ-0.24	
+##.##	-456.0	%-456.00	A percent sign (%) appears because the data is too large for the descriptor-field specification.

The Dollar Sign Symbol

A single dollar sign ($) appearing to the left of a numeric descriptor field causes a $ to be displayed in that position of the output record. A single dollar sign is called a **fixed dollar sign**.

Two leading dollar signs ($$) at the left of a numeric descriptor field causes a single dollar sign to float. The dollar sign will display to the left of the first significant digit. Two leading dollar signs appearing together are called a **floating dollar sign**. The leading dollar signs specify two positions in the numeric descriptor field. One position is filled by the dollar sign; the second sign reserves a digit position. Table 4.14 gives examples of the use of the dollar sign in various numeric descriptor fields.

TABLE 4.14 - Use of the Dollar Sign ($) in a Descriptor Field			
DESCRIPTOR FIELD	**DATA**	**OUTPUT**	**REMARKS**
FIXED DOLLAR SIGN			
$###.##	123.45	$123.45	
$###.##	98.76	$ƀ98.76	
$###.##−	40.613	$ƀ40.61ƀ	
$#,###.##−	−40.613	$ƀƀƀ40.61−	
$#,###.##+	40.613	$ƀƀƀ40.61+	
FLOATING DOLLAR SIGN			
$$###.##	1.23	ƀƀƀ$1.23	
$$,###.##	1234.68	$1,234.68	Second $ sign replaced by digit.
$$##.##−	−1.0	ƀƀ$1.00−	

The Asterisk Symbol

Two asterisks (* *) starting at the left side of a numeric descriptor field cause the value to be displayed in asterisk-filled format. The left side of the numeric field is filled with leading asterisks rather than leading spaces.

Leading asterisks often are used when monetary checks are being printed or when the result must be protected. Hence, leading asterisks are sometimes called **check protection asterisks**, and their use prevents someone from physically adding digits to the left side of a number. Table 4.15 gives examples of the use of the asterisk in various numeric descriptor fields.

TABLE 4.15 - Use of the Asterisk (*) in a Descriptor Field			
DESCRIPTOR FIELD	**DATA**	**OUTPUT**	**REMARKS**
**,###.##	10.15	****10.15	Asterisk displayed for comma when leading digits are zero.
**##−	−6.95	***7−	Data is rounded to an integer.
**###.##	4.58	****4.58	
**$#,###.##	50.258	*****$50.26	Dollar sign floats and leading zeros are displayed as asterisks.

Formatted Character String Output

Descriptor fields for string values are defined in terms of the ampersand (&), two backslashes (\\), the exclamation point (!), or the underscore (_), rather than the number sign (#). Table 4.9 on page 114 summarizes these four symbols with the other symbols already presented.

As a descriptor field, the ampersand represents a variable-length string field. The number of positions used to display the string is dependent on the internal size of the string. The ampersand indicates the beginning position in which the string is displayed and expansion is to the right in the line. Table 4.16 summarizes the use of the ampersand. The program in Figure 4.15 gives examples of the use of the ampersand. Note that the underscore (_) is used in line 10 to precede the exclamation point (!). This informs the PC that the exclamation point is a string constant to be displayed, not a descriptor field.

TABLE 4.16 - Use of the Ampersand (&) in a Descriptor Field			
DESCRIPTOR FIELD	DATA	OUTPUT	REMARKS
&	ABC	ABC	The character A is placed exactly in the line at the location specified by the ampersand. The B and C are placed in the next two positions of the line.
&	ABCDE	ABCDE	
&	A	A	

FIGURE 4.15

An example of using the ampersand (&) and underscore (_) format symbols.

```
 1    ' Use of the Ampersand and the
 2    ' Underscore as Descriptor Fields
 3    ' ******************************
 4    CLS  ' Clear Screen
 5    Short$ = "REM"
 6    Middle$ = "Remark"
 7    Long$ = "Remarkable"
 8    PRINT USING "The keyword &"; Short$
 9    PRINT USING "represents  &."; Middle$
10    PRINT USING "Isn't that  &_!"; Long$
11    PRINT USING "So &"; Short$;
12    PRINT USING "&"; "arkable"

[run]

The keyword REM
represents  Remark.
Isn't that  Remarkable!
So REMarkable
```

The exact number of positions to use for displaying a string value can be specified by using two backslashes separated by zero or more spaces. The number of positions in the descriptor field, including the two backslashes, indicate how many positions are to be used to display the string value. The string value is aligned in the descriptor field left-justified. If the internal value of the string contains fewer characters than the descriptor field, the string value is filled with spaces on the right in the print line. If the internal value of the string contains more characters than the descriptor field, the string value is truncated on the right. Table 4.17 on the next page summarizes the use of the backslash, and the program in Figure 4.16 gives examples of its use.

TABLE 4.17 - Use of the Backslash (\) in a Descriptor Field

DESCRIPTOR FIELD	NUMBER OF SPACES BETWEEN BACKSLASHES	DATA	OUTPUT	REMARKS
\ \	3	ABCDE	ABCDE	Size of descriptor field and string value are the same.
\ \	1	ABCDE	ABC	The last two characters are truncated.
\\	0	ABCDE	AB	The last three characters are truncated.
\ \	6	ABCDE	ABCDEℓℓℓ	Three spaces are appended to the right of the string value in the print line.

FIGURE 4.16

An example of using the backslash (\) format symbol.

```
 1   ' Use of Two Backslashes in a Descriptor Field
 2   ' *********************************************
 3   CLS  ' Clear Screen
 4   H1$ = "Name       Address     City-State   Zip Code"
 5   H2$ = "----       -------     ----------   --------"
 6   D1$ = "\        \ \       \ \          \ \          \"
 7   PRINT H1$
 8   PRINT H2$
 9   READ Cust.Name$, Cust.Street$, Cust.City$, Cust.Zip$
10   PRINT USING D1$, Cust.Name$; Cust.Street$; Cust.City$; Cust.Zip$
11   ' *************** Data Follows **************
12   DATA Jones J., 451 W 45th, "Hammond, IN", 46321-0452


[run]

Name       Address     City-State   Zip Code
----       -------     ----------   --------

Jones J.   451 W 45th Hammond, IN  46321-0452
```

Study closely the method used in lines 4 through 6 in the program in Figure 4.16 to align the fields. Collectively the three statements give you a good idea of what the output will eventually look like. This technique will be used throughout this book. Lines 7 and 8 print H1$ and H2$. These two variables are equal to the column headings as defined in lines 4 and 5. Line 10 displays the customer information using the format assigned to D1$ in line 6.

The exclamation point is used as a descriptor field to specify a one-position field in the print line. If the internal value of the string to be displayed is longer than one character, only the leftmost character is displayed. Table 4.18 summarizes the use of the exclamation point and the program in Figure 4.17 illustrates its use.

TABLE 4.18 - Use of the Exclamation Point (!) as a Descriptor Field

DESCRIPTOR FIELD	DATA	OUTPUT	REMARKS
!	JOE	J	First initial of name displayed.
!	XYZ	X	

```
1   ' Use of the Exclamation Point as a Descriptor Field
2   ' ****************************************************
3   CLS  ' Clear Screen
4   READ First.Name$, Middle.Name$, Last.Name$
5   PRINT USING "!. !. \        \"; First.Name$; Middle.Name$; Last.Name$
6   ' **************** Data Follows ******************
7   DATA George, Alfred, Smith

    [run]

    G. A. Smith
```

The LPRINT USING Statement

Like the LPRINT statement, the LPRINT USING **statement** prints the results on the printer. Everything that has been presented with respect to the PRINT USING statement also applies to the LPRINT USING statement. This statement gives you the capacity to print results directly on the printer according to a predefined format.

PROGRAMMING CASE STUDY 6 – Determining the Accounts Receivable Balance

This problem and its program solution incorporate much of the information discussed so far in this chapter, including the following useful techniques for formatting a report:

1. Align the detail lines with the column headings.
2. Force decimal-point alignment.
3. Control the number of digits displayed in a result.
4. Specify that commas and decimal points be displayed appropriately in numeric results.

Problem: Ron's Family Discount House would like its PC to generate a management report on the printer for the accounts receivable balance for a monthly billing period. The following formula is used to determine the balance:

End-of-Month Balance = Beginning of Month Balance – Payments + Purchases – Credits + Service Charge on Ending Unpaid Balance

The following formula is used to compute the Service Charge:

Service Charge = 19.5% Annually on the Unpaid Balance

or

= 0.01625 * (Beginning-of-Month Balance – Payments – Credits) per Month

Round the Service Charge to ensure consistency between the Beginning-of-Month Balance and End-of-Month Balance.

The input data for each customer includes customer number, beginning-of-month balance, payments, purchases, and credits. The following accounts receivable data is to be processed:

Customer Number	Beginning Balance	Payment	Purchases	Credit
14376172	$1,112.32	$35.00	$56.00	$ 0.00
16210987	30.00	30.00	15.00	0.00
18928384	125.50	25.00	0.00	12.50
19019293	120.00	12.00	12.00	23.00
19192929	10.00	7.00	2.50	1.50
EOF	0	0	0	0

The program should generate a report on the printer that includes report and column headings and a line of information for each customer. Each line is to include the five values read for each customer, the service charge, and the end-of-month balance as described on the **printer spacing chart** shown in Figure 4.18. Lines 1 through 4 of the printer spacing chart define the report and column headings. These are called **heading lines**. Line 6 defines the **detail line** that is displayed for each record processed: the row of Xs in line 6 describes an area for a string value, and the groups of 9s with commas and decimal points describe areas for numeric values. Finally, line 8 describes the end-of-job message. A line that includes summary information prior to an end-of-job message is called a **total line**. Total lines with summary information are presented in later chapters.

FIGURE 4.18

Output design for Programming Case Study 6.

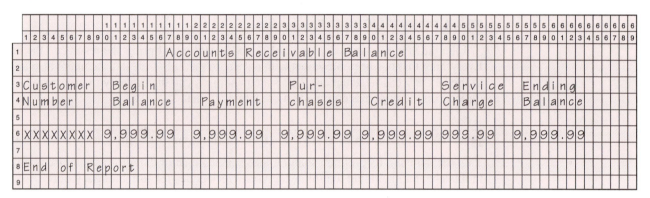

Following are a top-down chart (Figure 4.19), a list of the program tasks in outline form that correspond to the top-down chart, a program solution (Figure 4.20), and a discussion of the program solution.

FIGURE 4.19

A top-down chart for the solution to Programming Case Study 6.

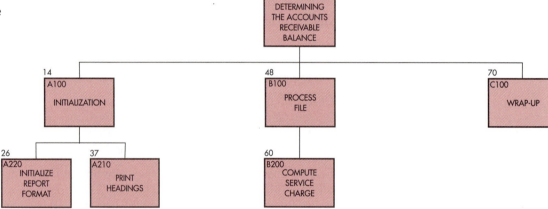

Program Tasks

The following program tasks correspond to the top-down chart in Figure 4.19:

1. A100.Initialization
   a. Clear the screen.
   b. Display a message on the screen that instructs the user to load paper into the printer and turn the printer on. After the printer is ready, accept the Enter key response via the INPUT statement to continue.
   c. Call A200.Initialize.Report.Format. In this subroutine, initialize the report format described on the printer spacing chart in Figure 4.18 to string variables. Use the string variables H1$, H2$, and H3$ for the heading lines, D1$ for the detail line, and T1$ for the total line.

    d. Call A210.Print.Headings. In this subroutine, use the `LPRINT` statement to print the heading lines H1$, H2$, and H3$.

2. B100.Process.File

    a. Read the first accounts receivable record; use the following variable names:

        Cus.No$ = Customer Number
        Beg.Bal   = Beginning Balance
        Pay   = Payments
        Pur   = Purchases
        Cr   = Credits

    b. Use a `DO WHILE` statement to establish a Do loop. The condition within the `DO WHILE` statement should allow the loop to be executed as long as Cus.No$ does not equal the sentinel value EOF (Cus.No$ < > "EOF").

      (1) Call B200.Compute.Service.Charge, which performs the following tasks:

        (a) Compute the unpaid balance from this formula:
            Unpaid.Bal = Beg.Bal – Pay – Cr

        (b) Compute the service charge from this formula:
            Serv.Chg = 0.01625 * Unpaid.Bal
            Round the service charge to the nearest cent using this formula:
            Serv.Chg = INT((Serv.Chg + 0.005) * 100) / 100

        (c) Compute the end-of-month balance from this formula:
            End.Bal = Unp.Bal + Pur + Serv.Chg

      (2) Use the `LPRINT USING` statement to print the seven values pertaining to the customer.

      (3) Read the next accounts receivable record.

3. C100.Wrap.Up – use the `LPRINT` statement to print T1$.

Program Solution

    Program 4.4 presented in Figure 4.20 lists the program solution for Programming Case Study 6. Figure 4.21 on the next page illustrates the report generated by the program.

FIGURE 4.20

Program 4.4, the solution to Programming Case Study 6.

```
 1   ' Program 4.4
 2   ' Determining the Accounts Receivable Balance
 3   ' *******************************************
 4   ' *               Main Program              *
 5   ' *******************************************
 6   GOSUB A100.Initialization
 7   GOSUB B100.Process.File
 8   GOSUB C100.Wrap.Up
 9   END
10
11   ' *******************************************
12   ' *               Initialization            *
13   ' *******************************************
14   A100.Initialization:
15      CLS ' Clear Screen
16      PRINT "Please make sure there is paper in the printer."
17      PRINT
18      INPUT "Press the Enter key when the printer is ready...", Control$
19      GOSUB A200.Initialize.Report.Format
20      GOSUB A210.Print.Headings
21   RETURN
22
```

(continued)

FIGURE 4.20
(continued)

string expressions
used in LPRINT and
LPRINT USING
statements

```
23    ' *********************************************
24    ' *          Initialize Report Format         *
25    ' *********************************************
26    A200.Initialize.Report.Format:
27       H1$ = "                Accounts Receivable Balance"
28       H2$ = "Customer  Begin                    Pur-          Service   Ending"
29       H3$ = "Number    Balance    Payment    chases   Credit   Charge    Balance"
30       D1$ = "\         \ #,###.##   #,###.##  #,###.## #,###.##   ###.## #,###.##"
31       T1$ = "End of Report"
32    RETURN
33
34    ' *********************************************
35    ' *               Print Headings              *
36    ' *********************************************
37    A210.Print.Headings:
38       LPRINT H1$
39       LPRINT
40       LPRINT H2$
41       LPRINT H3$
42       LPRINT
43    RETURN
44
45    ' *********************************************
46    ' *                Process File               *
47    ' *********************************************
48    B100.Process.File:
49       READ Cus.No$, Beg.Bal, Pay, Pur, Cr
50       DO WHILE Cus.No$ <> "EOF"
51          GOSUB B200.Compute.Service.Charge
52          LPRINT USING D1$; Cus.No$; Beg.Bal; Pay; Pur; Cr; Serv.Chg; End.Bal
53          READ Cus.No$, Beg.Bal, Pay, Pur, Cr
54       LOOP
55    RETURN
56
57    ' *********************************************
58    ' *            Compute Service Charge          *
59    ' *********************************************
60    B200.Compute.Service.Charge:
61       Unp.Bal = Beg.Bal - Pay - Cr
62       Serv.Chg = .01625 * Unp.Bal
63       Serv.Chg = INT((Serv.Chg + .005) * 100) / 100
64       End.Bal = Unp.Bal + Pur + Serv.Chg
65    RETURN
66
67    ' *********************************************
68    ' *                  Wrap-Up                   *
69    ' *********************************************
70    C100.Wrap.Up:
71       LPRINT
72       LPRINT T1$
73    RETURN
74
75    ' *************** Data Follows *************
76    DATA 14376172, 1112.32, 35,  56,    0
77    DATA 16210987,      30, 30,  15,    0
78    DATA 18928384,   125.5, 25,   0, 12.5
79    DATA 19019293,     120, 12,  12,   23
80    DATA 19192929,      10,  7, 2.5,  1.5
81    DATA EOF,            0,  0,   0,    0
82    ' ************* End of Program *************

      [run]
```

```
                          Accounts Receivable Balance

        Customer  Begin                     Pur-              Service  Ending
        Number    Balance     Payment     chases    Credit    Charge  Balance

        14376172 1,112.32       35.00      56.00      0.00     17.51 1,150.83
        16210987    30.00       30.00      15.00      0.00      0.00    15.00
        18928384   125.50       25.00       0.00     12.50      1.43    89.43
        19019293   120.00       12.00      12.00     23.00      1.38    98.38
        19192929    10.00        7.00       2.50      1.50      0.02     4.02

        End of Report
```

Discussion of the Program Solution

When Program 4.4 is executed, it transfers control to A100.Initialization, which begins by performing basic housekeeping tasks. The PC clears the screen and then displays the following messages to the user due to lines 16 through 18:

```
Please make sure there is paper in the printer.
Press the Enter key when the printer is ready...
```

Note that the INPUT statement temporarily halts the program until the user presses the Enter key in response to the message in the second line. After the user checks for paper in the printer and presses the Enter key, line 19 transfers control to A200.Initialize.Report.Format. Lines 27 through 31 assign the heading lines, detail line, and (total line described on the printer spacing chart in Figure 4.18 on page 122) to string variables.

Next, line 20 in A100.Initialization transfers control to A210.Print.Headings. The LPRINT statements (lines 38 through 42) print the report and column headings by referencing the string variables defined in A200.Initialize.Report.Format.

After A100.Initialization is complete, the GOSUB statement in line 7 invokes B100.Process.File. In line 49, the READ statement instructs the PC to read the first record found in line 76. Because the first record is not the end-of-file, the DO WHILE statement in line 50 passes control to line 51, and customer 14376172 is processed and printed.

After the second record is read in line 53, the LOOP statement in line 54 instructs the PC to loop back to line 50 to test for end-of-file. The second record is processed and printed before the PC reads the next record. This process continues until all of the accounts receivable records have been processed. When the trailer record is read, control returns to the Main Program, which then calls C100.Wrap.Up. After the message End of Report is printed, control returns to the Main Program which is terminated by the END statement in line 9.

The report (Figure 4.21) shows that through the use of the LPRINT USING statement in line 52, Program 4.4 prints all monetary values rounded to the nearest cent, with decimal points aligned and right-justified below the column headings. The customer number, which is defined to be a string variable, is displayed left-justified. The significance of taking the time to lay out the report on a printer spacing chart should be apparent in this Programming Case Study. After the printer spacing chart is complete, the format of the report can be copied directly into the program, as shown in lines 27 through 31 of Program 4.4. Note that in A200.Initialize.Report.Format the report format lines call for printing the first column of the report beginning in print position 1 — the position next to the left edge of the paper.

With the output techniques discussed so far in this chapter, you may now begin to dress up your output. Programmers often forget that most people using the results of computer-generated reports are unfamiliar with computers and are confused by poorly formatted output. You now have the capability in QBasic to produce high quality reports that are meaningful and easy to read.

4.6 THE LOCATE STATEMENT

The LOCATE **statement** may be used to position the cursor precisely at any position on the screen. It also may be used to turn the cursor on and off. Standard screens have 24 vertical lines (rows) and 80 horizontal print positions (columns). The LOCATE statement can position the cursor precisely on any one of the 1,920 positions on the screen.

The general form of the LOCATE statement is shown in Table 4.19. The values that follow the keyword LOCATE are called **parameters**.

TABLE 4.19 - The LOCATE Statement	
General Form:	LOCATE row, column, cursor
	where **row** represents the row and is a numeric expression between 1 and 24 for a standard screen;
	column represents the column and is a numeric expression between 1 and 80 in the 80-column display; and
	cursor is a numeric expression equivalent to 0 or 1. Zero makes the cursor invisible, and 1 makes the cursor visible.
Purpose:	To position the cursor precisely on the screen and to make the cursor visible or invisible.
Examples:	1. LOCATE 5, 10
	2. LOCATE 1, 1
	3. LOCATE 7
	4. LOCATE , 50
	5. LOCATE 4, 6, 0
	6. LOCATE , , 1

In Table 4.19, example 1 moves the cursor to column 10 on line 5. It makes no difference whether the cursor is above or below line 5 or to the right or left of column 10; when the statement is executed, the cursor is moved to line 5, column 10.

Example 2 moves the cursor to the **home position**: the leftmost column on line 1. Example 3 in Table 4.19 moves the cursor directly up or down to the same column on line 7. In example 4, the row is left blank and in this case, the PC moves the cursor to column 50 of the current line. When the row, column or cursor is left blank, the PC uses the current value.

Example 5 of Table 4.19 causes the PC to position the cursor in column 6 of line 4. Furthermore, the third parameter, zero, instructs the PC to make the cursor invisible. Example 6 makes the cursor visible at the current position.

The following revised version of Programming Case Study 4A presented in Chapter 3 illustrates the use of the PRINT USING and LOCATE statements. In addition, a new procedure for displaying messages on the screen is presented.

PROGRAMMING CASE STUDY 4B – Determining the Single Discount Rate with a Fixed Screen Format and End-of-File Test

Let's consider a refined program solution to Programming Case Study 4A, Determining the Single Discount Rate. Add the following to the original program specifications presented in Chapter 3 on page 63:

1. Redesign the output results to agree with the format shown on the **screen layout format** in Figure 4.22. A screen layout form is similar to a printer spacing chart in that it allows you to construct a skeleton of the output results for a screen, rather than the printer.
2. Format the single discount in percent form as shown in Figure 4.22.

3. Allow the user to decide whether he or she wishes to enter another series of discounts or terminate execution of the program (line 20, Figure 4.22).

Following are a top-down chart (Figure 4.23), a list of the additional program tasks, a program solution, and a discussion of the program solution.

FIGURE 4.22
Output for Programming Case Study 4B designed on a screen layout form.

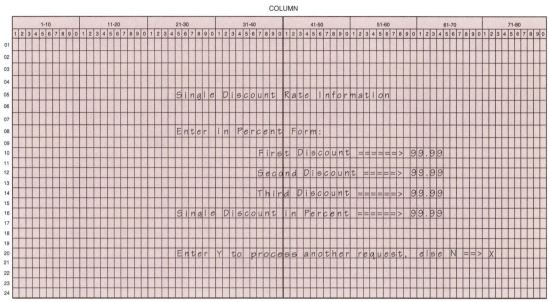

FIGURE 4.23
A top-down chart for Programming Case Study 4B.

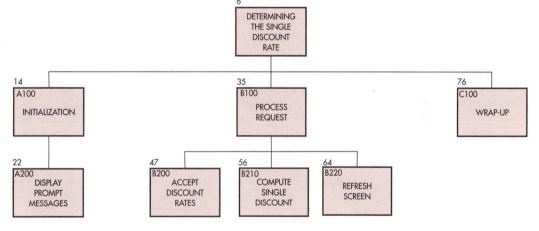

Additional Program Tasks

1. Use the LOCATE statement to position the cursor for each line displayed. Display all instructions and messages once in A100.Initialization. Leave the instructions and messages on the screen for the duration of the execution of the program. Use the LOCATE statement and the SPC function to blank out the results to the right of the instructions and messages before processing another series of discounts.
2. Use the PRINT USING statement to format the single discount.
3. Establish a Do loop within B100.Process.Request that executes the range of statements *before* testing for termination of the loop. That is, use a DO . . . LOOP UNTIL. (See Figure 4.5d on page 102.)

4. Use the condition, UCASE$(Control$) = "N", in the LOOP statement to determine whether to terminate the loop described in task 3. The UCASE$ function converts the value of Control$ to uppercase. (See Section 8.2 in Chapter 8 for more details on the UCASE$ function.) After displaying the single discount and before the LOOP statement, call upon a subroutine that uses the INPUT statement to accept a response from the user as to whether he or she wishes to determine another single discount. Assign the response to Control$ (Y to continue, N to terminate execution). Note that we are assuming the user will not enter any responses other than Y, y, N, or n. After accepting the response, clear the screen of the results from the previous inputs.

▌FIGURE 4.24

Program 4.5, the solution to Programming Case Study 4B.

```
 1   ' Program 4.5
 2   ' Determining the Single Discount Rate
 3   ' ************************************************
 4   ' *                 Main Program                *
 5   ' ************************************************
 6   GOSUB A100.Initialization
 7   GOSUB B100.Process.Request
 8   GOSUB C100.Wrap.Up
 9   END
10
11   ' ************************************************
12   ' *              Initialization                 *
13   ' ************************************************
14   A100.Initialization:
15      CLS  ' Clear Screen
16      GOSUB A200.Display.Prompt.Messages
17   RETURN
18
19   ' ************************************************
20   ' *            Display Prompt Messages          *
21   ' ************************************************
22   A200.Display.Prompt.Messages:
23      LOCATE 5, 25: PRINT "Single Discount Rate Information"
24      LOCATE 8, 25: PRINT "Enter in Percent Form:"
25      LOCATE 10, 37: PRINT "First Discount =====> "
26      LOCATE 12, 37: PRINT "Second Discount =====> "
27      LOCATE 14, 37: PRINT "Third Discount =====> "
28      LOCATE 16, 25: PRINT "Single Discount in Percent =====>"
29      LOCATE 20, 25: PRINT "Enter Y to process another request, else N ==>"
30   RETURN
31
32   ' ************************************************
33   ' *               Process Request               *
34   ' ************************************************
35   B100.Process.Request:
36      DO
37         GOSUB B200.Accept.Rates
38         GOSUB B210.Compute.Single.Discount
39         LOCATE 16, 59: PRINT USING " ##.##"; Rate
40         GOSUB B220.Refresh.Screen
41      LOOP UNTIL UCASE$(Control$) = "N"        ←  keeps user in
42   RETURN                                          loop until N or
43                                                   n is entered
44   ' ************************************************
45   ' *            Accept Discount Rates            *
46   ' ************************************************
47   B200.Accept.Rates:
48      LOCATE 10, 60: INPUT "", Rate1
49      LOCATE 12, 60: INPUT "", Rate2
50      LOCATE 14, 60: INPUT "", Rate3
51   RETURN
52
```

```
53   ' **********************************************
54   ' *            Compute Single Discount          *
55   ' **********************************************
56   B210.Compute.Single.Discount:
57      Rate = 1 - (1 - Rate1 / 100) * (1 - Rate2 / 100) * (1 - Rate3 / 100)
58      Rate = 100 * Rate
59   RETURN
60
61   ' **********************************************
62   ' *                Refresh Screen               *
63   ' **********************************************
64   B220.Refresh.Screen:
65      LOCATE 20, 72: INPUT "", Control$
66      LOCATE 10, 60: PRINT SPC(7);
67      LOCATE 12, 60: PRINT SPC(7);
68      LOCATE 14, 60: PRINT SPC(7);
69      LOCATE 16, 60: PRINT SPC(7);
70      LOCATE 20, 72: PRINT SPC(7);
71   RETURN
72
73   ' **********************************************
74   ' *                   Wrap-Up                    *
75   ' **********************************************
76   C100.Wrap.Up:
77      CLS   ' Clear Screen
78      LOCATE 12, 25: PRINT "End of Program - Have a Nice Day"
79   RETURN
80
81   '************* End of Program ****************
```

[run]

Discussion of the Program Solution

When Program 4.5 is executed, the GOSUB statement in line 6 transfers control to A100.Initialization, which has two subtasks: clear the screen, and display *all* of the messages specified on the screen layout form described in Figure 4.22 on page 127. Line 15 accomplishes the first subtask by clearing the screen; line 16 calls A200.Display.Prompt. Messages where lines 23 through 29 accomplish the second subtask. The display from these lines is shown in Figure 4.25.

FIGURE 4.25

The display from Program 4.5 due to the execution of lines 23 through 29.

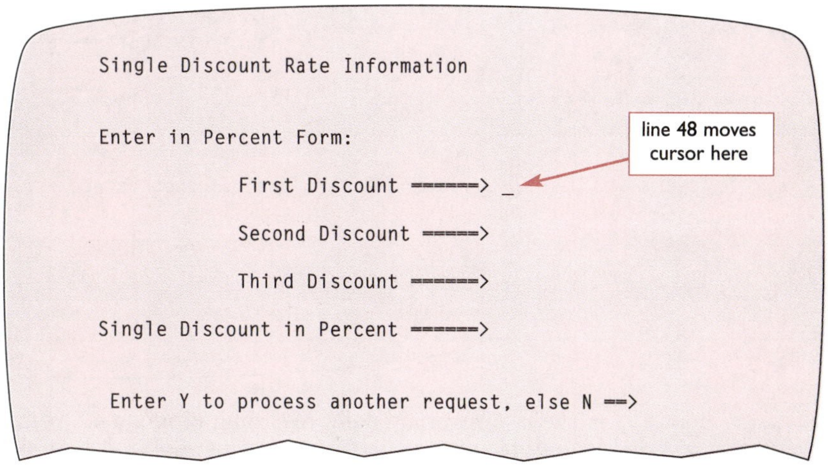

```
Single Discount Rate Information


Enter in Percent Form:                          line 48 moves
                                                cursor here
        First Discount ======>  _

        Second Discount =====>

        Third Discount ======>

Single Discount in Percent =====>


   Enter Y to process another request, else N ==>
```

Note that we did not place the first subtask of A100.Initialization, clear the screen, in a separate subroutine in Program 4.5. At coding time, potential subroutines that are only a few lines of code or that perform housekeeping tasks may be placed directly in the superior module. The decision as to whether a subtask should be a separate subroutine in a program becomes easier to make with experience.

After A100.Initialization displays the messages shown in Figure 4.25 on the previous page, control returns to line 7 in the Main Program. Line 7, in turn, transfers control to B100.Process.Request. The DO statement in line 36 does not include a condition, therefore, the range of statements (lines 37 through 40) is executed before testing for termination of the loop.

The first statement in the loop (line 37) transfers control to B200.Accept.Rates. In this lower-level subroutine, lines 48 through 50 employ the LOCATE and INPUT statements to accept the three discounts from the user. Recall that the LOCATE statement is capable of moving the cursor back to the end of the corresponding message that is already displayed on the screen. Each INPUT statement has the null string as the prompt message. The null string followed by a comma eliminates the question mark that displays when no prompt message is used.

After control passes back to line 38, Program 4.5 calls the next subroutine, B210.Compute.Single.Discount, which uses the three rates to compute the single rate. Next, the single rate is displayed (line 39). Line 40 then transfers control to B220.Refresh.Screen. The INPUT statement in line 65 of B220.Refresh.Screen causes the PC to halt execution until a response to continue is entered by the user. This gives the user time to read the results. When the user finishes reading the results, he or she enters a response.

If the user enters a Y or any other character other than N or n, as shown in Figure 4.26, then the PC will make another pass through the Do loop because of the condition in line 41. On the other hand, if the user enters N or n, control returns to the Main Program, and C100.Wrap.Up displays a message before the END statement in line 9 terminates execution of the program. Note in line 78 of C100.Wrap.Up, that a pleasant message to the user is displayed as part of the end-of-job routine.

FIGURE 4.26

Screen display from Program 4.5 when entering discounts of 40%, 20% and 10%.

```
Single Discount Rate Information


Enter in Percent Form:

          First Discount =======> 40

          Second Discount =====> 20

          Third Discount =======> 10

Single Discount in Percent ======> 56.80



Enter Y to process another request, else N ==> Y
```

The last important point regarding Program 4.5 concerns lines 66 through 70 in B220.Refresh.Screen. These lines are used to refresh the screen in preparation for the next set of data to be entered by the user. In each of these lines, the LOCATE statement is used to move the cursor to the exact position where previous data entered by the user is displayed on the screen. Following each LOCATE statement, the SPC function is used in a PRINT statement to blank out the previous data. SPC(7) blanks out seven positions to the right, beginning with the location of the cursor. If you plan to use this procedure to build screens, it is important to remember that the LOCATE statement does not clear the screen. Any old data will remain on the screen unless it is cleared. This is the purpose of B220.Refresh.Screen.

4.7 What You Should Know

1. A loop in a program instructs the PC to repeat a series of instructions.
2. A loop defined by the DO and LOOP statements is called a Do loop. The DO statement indicates the beginning of the loop and the LOOP statement the end of the loop. The condition can be placed in the DO or LOOP statements. (See Figure 4.5 on page 102 for examples of the different ways a Do loop can be constructed in QBasic.)
3. One execution of a loop is a pass.
4. A condition is a relationship that is either true or false. A condition is made up of two expressions separated by a relational operator. The six valid relational operators are: greater than (>); less than (<); equal to (=); greater than or equal to (>=); less than or equal to (<=); and not equal to (<>).
5. The DATA statement provides for the creation of a sequence of data items for use by the READ statement.
6. The DATA statement consists of the keyword DATA followed by a list of data items, which can be either numeric or string. If string data contains a leading or trailing blank or an embedded comma or colon, the data must be enclosed in quotation marks.
7. The DATA statement is a nonexecutable statement. The placement of DATA statements has no bearing on the execution of the program.
8. Data items from all DATA statements are collected and placed into one single data-sequence holding area. The order in which the data items appear among all DATA statements determines the order of the data items in the single data-sequence holding area.
9. The READ statement provides for the assignment of values to variables from a sequence of data items created from DATA statements.
10. The READ statement consists of the keyword READ followed by a list of variables separated by mandatory commas.
11. Every variable appearing in the program whose value is directly obtained by a READ statement must be listed in a READ statement before it is used in the program.
12. A program containing a READ statement also must have at least one DATA statement.
13. The RESTORE statement allows the data in a given program to be reread by READ statements as often as necessary.
14. The RESTORE statement consists of the keyword RESTORE followed by an optional label. If the label is not present, the pointer is restored to the first data item in the first DATA statement. If the label is present, then the pointer is set to the first data item in the DATA statement referenced by the specified label.
15. The PRINT statement consists of the keyword PRINT. It may also have an optional list of print items separated by mandatory commas or semicolons. The print items may be numeric or string constants, variables, expressions or null items. In addition, the print items may include useful functions such as INT or SQR.
16. The comma separator in a PRINT statement allows you to display output automatically positioned in a tabular format determined by five print zones in the 80-column display mode. Each print zone in the 80-column display mode has 14 positions.
17. If a PRINT statement contains no list of print items, then a blank line results.
18. The semicolon separator can be used to generate output in a compressed or packed format.
19. The TAB function is used in the PRINT statement to specify the exact print positions for the various output results on a given print line.
20. The SPC function is used to insert spaces (filler) between print items.
21. QBasic allows calculations to be made within the PRINT statement.

22. QBasic permits the PC to be used as a powerful desk calculator through the use of the immediate window. The immediate window also may be used to debug programs in the view window, as well as test lines of code before they are moved into the view window.

23. The PRINT USING statement is useful in controlling the output format.

24. One or more consecutive format symbols appearing in a string expression are a descriptor field, or field format.

25. Depending on the type of editing desired, numeric descriptor fields can include a number sign, decimal point, comma, dollar sign, plus or minus sign, asterisk, and four consecutive circumflexes. (See Table 4.9 on page 114.)

26. Descriptor fields for string values use the exclamation point, ampersand, underscore, and two backslashes separated by n spaces, which reserve n + 2 positions in the line, to display a string.

27. While the PRINT and PRINT USING statements display results on the screen, the LPRINT and LPRINT USING statements print the results on a printer.

28. The LOCATE statement is used to position the cursor on the screen. It also may be used to make the cursor visible or invisible.

4.8 Test Your QBasic Skills (Even-numbered answers are in Appendix E)

1. Study the valid programs listed below. Without using a computer, determine what is displayed if each is executed.

a.
```
' Exercise 4.1a
' MPG Comparisons
READ Car.Model$, Miles, Gallons
DO WHILE Car.Model$ <> "EOF"
    Mpg = Miles / Gallons
    PRINT "Car model ===> "; Car.Model$
    PRINT "Miles =======> "; Miles
    PRINT "Gallons =====> "; Gallons
    PRINT "Mpg =========> "; Mpg
    PRINT
    READ Car.Model$, Miles, Gallons
LOOP
PRINT "Job Finished"
' **** Data Follows ****
DATA A, 2604, 93
DATA B, 255,   8.5
DATA C, 2408, 68.8
DATA EOF,  0,  0
END
```

c.
```
' Exercise 4.1c
' Displaying Bye!
CLS    ' Clear Screen
Row = 12
Col = 23
Curs = 0
DO
    Col = Col + 4
    LOCATE Row, Col, Curs
    PRINT "Bye!"
    Row = Row + 1
LOOP UNTIL Row = 25
END
```

b.
```
' Exercise 4.1b
' ******** Main Module ********
GOSUB A100.Initialization
GOSUB B100.Process.File
GOSUB C100.Wrap.Up
END
' Data Follows
DATA 3, 8, 5, 9, 7, 11, 0, -2
'
' ****** Initialization *******
A100.Initialization
    CLS    ' Clear Screen
    A = 10
    B = 10
    Count = 10
RETURN
'
' ****** Process File *********
B100.Process.File
    READ X, Y
    DO WHILE Y >= 0
        A = A - X
        B = B - Y
        Count = Count + 2
        PRINT Count; A; B
        READ X, Y
    LOOP
RETURN
'
' ****** Wrap-Up **************
C100.Wrap.Up
    LOCATE 1, 14, 0
    PRINT USING "Count ====> ###"; Count
    LOCATE 3, 14, 1: PRINT "FINISHED"
RETURN
' ******* End of Program ******
```

```
d.  ' Exercise 4.1d
    READ X, Y
    DO WHILE X <> -1
       PRINT "Old value of X ="; X
       PRINT "Old value of Y ="; Y
       T = X
       X = Y
       Y = T
       PRINT "New value of X ="; X
       PRINT "New value of Y ="; Y
       PRINT
       READ X, Y
    LOOP
    PRINT "Job Finished"
    ' ***** Data Follows *****
    DATA 7, 11
    DATA 14, 18
    DATA -1, 0
    END
```

```
e.  ' Exercise 4.1e
    ' Nested Do Loops
    CLS     ' Clear Screen
    Row = 0
    DO
       Row = Row + 1
       Column = 0
       DO
          Column = Column + 1
          LOCATE Row, Column
          PRINT "*"
       LOOP UNTIL Column > 40
    LOOP UNTIL Row > 10
    END
```

2. Fix all the errors (syntax and logic) that you find in the following programs:

```
a.  ' Exercise 4.2a
    READ S, B,
    D = S - C
    TAB(3)
    LOKATE 26, 14, -1 : PRINT D
    END
    DATA 4, 6
```

```
b.  ' Exercise 4.2b
    DATA 1, 2, 5, 6, 8, 7, 1, 3, 2, 0
    READ X, Y, Z
    DO WHILE X > 0
       X1 = X * Y
       X1 = X1 * Z
       READ X, Y, Z
    LOOP WHILE X > 0
    PRINT X2
    END
```

3. Consider the following types of Do loops.

```
a. DO WHILE ... LOOP          b. DO UNTIL ... LOOP
c. DO ... LOOP WHILE          d. DO ... LOOP UNTIL
```

Answer the following questions for each type of Do loop:
(1) Is the test made before or after the range of statements is executed?
(2) What is the *minimum* number of times the range of statements is executed?
(3) Does the Do loop terminate when the condition is true or false?

4. Write a sequence of LOCATE and PRINT statements that will display the value of the variable A2 in column 7 of the second line and the value of B5 in column 45 of the fifth line.

5. Write a single PRINT statement to compute and display:
   a. square root of X   b. cubed root of X   c. fifth root of X

6. Write a PRINT USING statement that includes the string constant for the purpose of displaying the message The amount is followed by the value of the variable Amount. Include a numeric descriptor field with the following characteristics:
   a. Six digit positions, two to the right of the decimal point
   b. A floating dollar sign
   c. A sign status (+ or -) to the right of the number
   d. Two or more check protection asterisks

7. Determine whether the conditions below are true or false, given the following:
   Credit.Union = 30, Ins.Ded = 20, and Salary = 900.

```
a. Credit.Union >= 30              b. Salary / Ins.Ded > Credit.Union
c. Ins.Ded = Credit.Union - 5      d. Salary <> 800
e. 875 + Credit.Union <= Salary    f. Ins.Ded > 20
```

8. Write a sequence of statements that will clear the screen and display the value 8 in print position 8 of line 8.

9. Write `LOCATE` and `PRINT` statements that will cause the following to be displayed starting in column 12 of line 3: `Customer name =====>`

10. Indicate the location of the cursor immediately after the following two lines are executed:
```
LOCATE 6, 12, 1 : PRINT "QBasic"
LOCATE 14
```

11. Consider the valid programs listed below. Without using a computer, determine what displays if each is executed.
    a.
```
' Exercise 4.11a
CLS    'Clear Screen
PRINT "Net"; "      "; "Pay"
PRINT TAB(11); "Net Pay"
PRINT
PRINT "N"; SPC(3); "e"; SPC(3); "t"; SPC(3); "P";
PRINT SPC(3); "a"; SPC(3); "y"
END
```
    b.
```
' Exercise 4.11b
CLS    'Clear Screen
PRINT "Hours", "Gross", "FICA", "FIT"
PRINT "Hours"; "Gross"; "FICA"; "FIT"
PRINT : PRINT 10, 20, 30, 30 - 10
PRINT 10; 20; 30; 30 - 10
PRINT : PRINT TAB(10); "Hours"
PRINT "Hours"; TAB(40); "Gross"
END
```

12. What kind of graphic output displays from this program?
```
'Exercise 4.12
CLS 'Clear Screen
LOCATE 10, 38: PRINT "VVVVV"
LOCATE 11, 37: PRINT "X";  TAB(43); "X"
LOCATE 12, 36: PRINT "X";  TAB(39); "O"; TAB(41); "O"; TAB(44); "X"
LOCATE 13, 36: PRINT "X";  TAB(44); "X"
LOCATE 14, 36: PRINT "X";  TAB(40); "U"; TAB(44); "X"
LOCATE 15, 36: PRINT "X";  TAB(38); "("; TAB(42); ")"  TAB(44); "X"
LOCATE 16, 36: PRINT "X";  TAB(40); "-"; TAB(44); "X"
LOCATE 17, 37: PRINT "X";  TAB(43); "X"
LOCATE 18, 38: PRINT "XXXXX"
END
```

13. Write a program that will generate the following graphic output. Use the `LOCATE` statement to position the upper, left-most asterisk in column 33 of line 8.
```
************
Q B a s i c *
B L       N Q
a   E   R   B
s     A     a
i   E   R   s
c L       N i
* Q B a s i c
************
```

14. Write a `PRINT USING` statement that displays the value of Last.Name$ beginning in position 1 for each of the following:
    a. Only the first character of Last.Name$ is displayed.
    b. All of Last.Name$ is displayed.
    c. The first six characters of Last.Name$ are displayed.
    d. The first two characters of Last.Name$ are displayed.

15. Write a sequence of `LOCATE` and `PRINT` statements to display the following figure with the vertex at print position 20 on line 9. Clear the screen and make the cursor invisible before displaying the figure.

```
* * * * * * * * *
  *             *
    *         *
      *     *
        *
```

16. For each of the following descriptor fields and corresponding data, indicate what the PC displays. Use the letter b̸ to indicate the space character.

	Descriptor Field	Data	Result		Descriptor Field	Data	Result
a.	###	4.5		b.	#,###.##	24.7	
c.	$$,###.##-	-44.3		d.	$#,###.##-	213.45	
e.	**#,###.##	44.423		f.	#,###.#	4131.02	
g.	##.##-	1.532		h.	###.##	-246.4	
i.	##,###.####	24.3228		j.	##.##^^^^	433.43	
k.	!	WXYZ		l.	&	WXYZ	
m.	\ \(1 space)	WXYZ		n.	\ \(2 spaces)	WXYZ	

17. **PC Hands-On Exercise:** Load Program 4.1 (PRG4-1) from the Data Disk and do the following:
    a. Execute Program 4.1 and note the results displayed. Move the trailer record (line 64) to the top of the list of `DATA` statements (between lines 58 and 59). Execute the program and see what happens.
    b. Reload PRG4-1. Delete the trailer record; execute the program and see what happens. Note the importance of the trailer record. Do not save these program changes.

18. **PC Hands-On Exercise:** Load Program 4.1 (PRG4-1) from the Data Disk. Display and execute the program. Use the Search menu and replace all the `PRINT` statements with `LPRINT` statements. Turn on the printer and execute the program a second time.

19. **PC Hands-On Exercise:** Load Program 4.5 (PRG4-5) from the Data Disk. Display and execute the program. Enter the following sets of data:

    Set 1: 7%, 14%, 24%
    Set 2: 4%, 6%, 8%
    Set 3: 2.25%, 34.55%, 48.99%
    Set 4: 99.99%, 99.99%, 99.99%

    Step through the program and try to determine which statement the PC is attempting to execute when it suspends execution to accept the data.

4.9 QBasic Programming Problems

1. Determining the Price/Earnings (P/E) Ratio

Purpose: To become more familiar with the top-down approach, READ and DATA statements and Do loops.

Problem: Construct a top-down program to compute and display the P/E ratio for companies whose current stock prices and earnings per share are known. Process the companies listed in the table below until the Stock Name is equal to EOF.

The P/E ratio is a useful tool employed by stock market analysts in evaluating the investment potential of various companies. The P/E ratio is determined by dividing the price of a share of stock by the company's latest earnings per share.

(**Hint**: Use Program 4.1 as a guide to solving this problem.)

Input Data: Prepare and use the following sample data:

Stock Name	Price per Share	Latest Earnings
Microsoft	115	1.51
Compaq	27.25	.65
Novell	37.75	.55
IBM	118	4.22
Intel	85.75	2.08
EOF	0	0

Output Results: The output screen should appear as illustrated by Figure 4.27.

FIGURE 4.27
Output for Programming Problem 1.

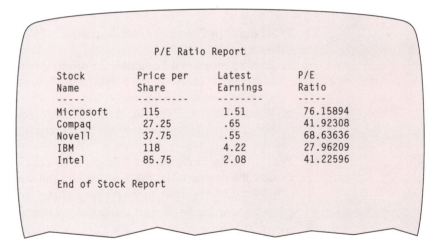

```
                        P/E Ratio Report

        Stock           Price per       Latest          P/E
        Name            Share           Earnings        Ratio
        -----           ---------       --------        -----

        Microsoft       115             1.51            76.15894
        Compaq          27.25           .65             41.92308
        Novell          37.75           .55             68.63636
        IBM             118             4.22            27.96209
        Intel           85.75           2.08            41.22596

        End of Stock Report
```

2. Inflation Gauge

Purpose: To become familiar with printing a report on the printer and the use of the DO WHILE, LOOP, READ, DATA, and PRINT USING statements.

Problem: Write a top-down program to read today's current price, the previous price, and the number of weeks between price quotes from DATA statements. Compute the sample annual inflation rate and the expected price of the item one year from today's current price. Use the following formulas:

Price Change = (Current Price – Previous Price) / Weeks * 52
Annual Inflation Rate = Price Change / Previous Price
Expected Price = Current Price + Annual Inflation Rate * Current Price

For each item processed, print the item, current price, computed inflation rate, and expected price in one year. For the current price and expected price in one year, use the descriptor field #,###.##. For the inflation rate, use the descriptor field ###.##.

(**Hint**: Use Program 4.4 as a guide to solving this problem.)

Input Data: Prepare and use the following sample data:

Item	Current Price	Previous Price	Number Weeks
1 doz. eggs	$0.98	$0.84	13
1 lb. butter	1.70	1.62	14
1 gal. milk	2.20	2.09	17
1 loaf bread	1.65	1.55	8

Output Results: The output screen should appear as illustrated by Figure 4.28

FIGURE 4.28

Output for Programming Problem 2.

```
                    Inflation Gauge Report

                    Current      Inflation      Price
          Item      Price        Rate in %      in 1 Yr.
          ----      -------      ---------      --------
          1 doz. eggs    0.98        66.67          1.63
          1 lb. butter   1.70        18.34          2.01
          1 gal. milk    2.20        16.10          2.55
          1 loaf bread   1.65        41.94          2.34

          End of Report
```

3. Determining the Point of Intersection

Purpose: To become familiar with Do loops, testing for end-of-file, and the READ and DATA statements.

Problem: Maximum profit or minimum cost often can be determined from equations based on known facts concerning a product. The point of intersection of the equations is significant. Write a top-down program to find the point of intersection for two first-degree equations in two variables (that is, two equations and two unknowns). The general form for the two equations is as follows:

$$a_1 x + b_1 y = c_1 \qquad a_2 x + b_2 y = c_2$$

The solutions are expressed as follows:

$$x = \frac{c_1 b_2 - c_2 b_1}{a_1 b_2 - a_2 b_1} \qquad y = \frac{c_2 a_1 - c_1 a_2}{a_1 b_2 - a_2 b_1}$$

The program should read the coefficients (a_1, b_1, c_1, a_2, b_2, and c_2, in this order) from a DATA statement; solve for x and y; display the values of a_1, b_1, and c_1 on one line, and a_2, b_2, c_2, x, and y on the next line. The program should loop back to read a set of data for the next system of equations.

Terminate the Do loop within the Process File module when a_1 is equal to –999. Make your program efficient by computing the denominator of x and y only once.

(**Hint**: Use Program 4.1 as a guide to solving this problem.)

Input Data: Prepare and use the following sample data:

	Equation 1 Coefficients			Equation 2 Coefficients		
System	a	b	c	a	b	c
1	3	2	8	2	1	1
2	1	−5	6	3	1	−8
3	0.4	−0.75	−6	0.4	0.125	0

Output Results: The output screen should appear as illustrated by Figure 4.29.

FIGURE 4.29
*Output for Programming
Problem 3.*

```
<------------Equations---------->     <---Intersection---->
Coeff A       Coeff B     Coeff C     X Value     Y Value
-------       -------     -------     -------     -------

3             2           8
2             1           1           -6          13


1             -5          6
3             1           -8          -2.125      -1.625


.4            -.75        -6
.4            .125        0           -2.142857   6.857143


End of Report
```

4. Determining the Eventual Cash Value of an Annuity

Purpose: To become familiar with the LOCATE statement, looping, the hierarchy of operations in a complex LET statement, and building a screen for data entry.

Problem: An annuity or installment plan is a series of payments made at equal intervals of time. Examples of annuities are pensions and premiums on life insurance. More often than not, the interest conversion period is unequal to the payment interval. The following formula determines the eventual cash value of an annuity of R dollars paid per year in P installments for N years, at an interest rate of J percent converted M times a year.

$$S = R \left[\frac{\left(1 + \frac{J}{M}\right)^{MN} - 1}{P\left[\left(1 + \frac{J}{M}\right)^{M/P} - 1\right]} \right]$$

where S = eventual cash value
R = payment per year
P = number of installments per year
N = duration of the annuity in years
J = nominal interest rate
M = conversions per year

Write a top-down program to determine the eventual cash value of an annuity rounded to the nearest dollar. After processing the first annuity, loop back to process the next annuity.

Prior to processing the first annuity, clear the screen and use the LOCATE statement to center the instructions and messages. Display the instruction and message portions only once. After the results for the first set of data are displayed, request that the user enter Y to process another set of data and N to terminate the program. If Y is entered, use the SPC function to clear the results, and then request the user to enter the next set of data.

(**Hint**: Use Program 4.5 as a guide to solving this problem.)

Input Data: Prepare and use the following sample data:

	Set 1	Data Set 2	Set 3
Description			
Payment per year	$3,000	$3,500	$4,500
Installments per year	12	12	12
Time in years	25	25	25
Interest rate in %	7.5	7	6.5
Conversions per year	2	4	12

Output Results: The results for Set 1 are shown below in Figure 4.30. Begin the screen title on line 5, column 25. After that, skip a line between each line displayed. Skip three lines prior to the last line. When the user requests that the program terminate, clear the screen and display an appropriate message. The eventual Cash value for Sets 2 and 3 are $234,764.00 and $280,814.00, respectively.

▌FIGURE 4.30
Output for Programming Problem 4, Set 1.

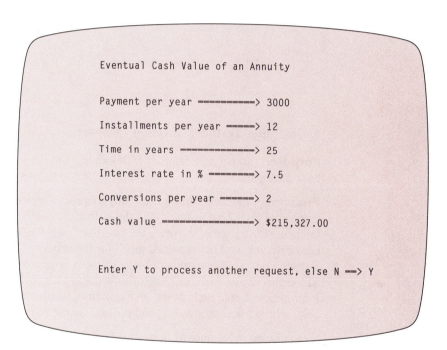

```
        Eventual Cash Value of an Annuity


        Payment per year ===========> 3000

        Installments per year ======> 12

        Time in years ==============> 25

        Interest rate in % ========> 7.5

        Conversions per year ======> 2

        Cash value ==============> $215,327.00



        Enter Y to process another request, else N ==> Y
```

5. Check Digit Calculation

Purpose: To become familiar with using the INT function to separate the digits in a number and to learn about elementary check digit calculations.

Problem: Companies that issue credit cards often use algorithms to create credit card numbers that people will have difficulty generating at random. One approach is to add the digits of a number and add 0 or 1 to make the sum of the digits even. For example, the number 45931 (that is, $4 + 5 + 9 + 3 + 1 = 22$ and is even) would be acceptable, but the number 37230 (that is, $3 + 7 + 2 + 3 + 0 = 15$ and is odd) would not. The last digit in the number, either a 1 or a 0, is called the **check digit**.

Write a top-down program that accepts a four-digit number, generates the check digit, and displays the original number, check digit number and five-digit credit card number.

(**Hint**: Use Program 4.1 as a guide to solving this problem. Use the INT function to determine the individual digits that make up the four-digit number and the check digit.)

Input Data: Prepare and use the following sample data in DATA statements:
2347, 4641, 4737, 2222, 9998

Output Results: The output screen should appear as illustrated by Figure 4.31.

FIGURE 4.31

Output for Programming Problem 5.

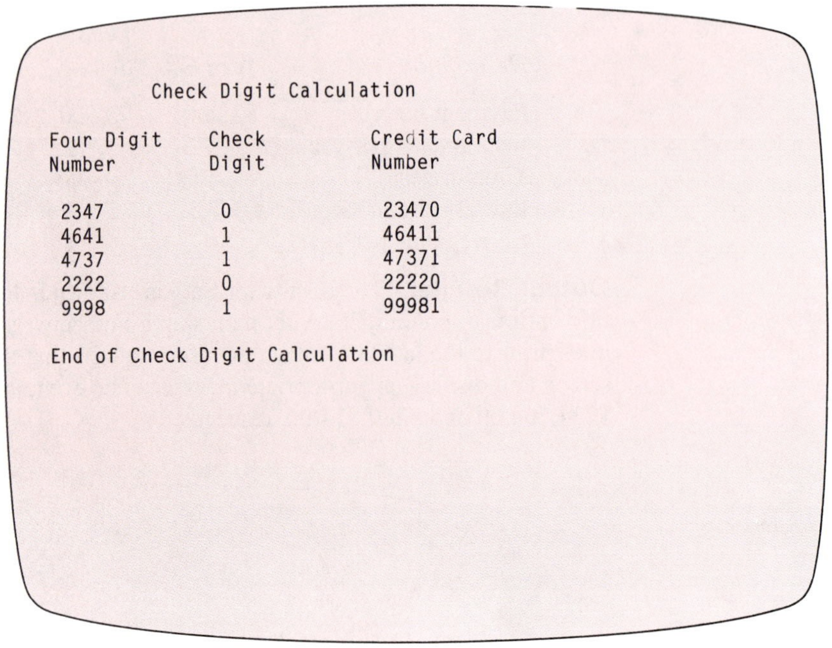

```
              Check Digit Calculation

   Four Digit    Check           Credit Card
   Number        Digit           Number

     2347          0               23470
     4641          1               46411
     4737          1               47371
     2222          0               22220
     9998          1               99981

   End of Check Digit Calculation
```

6. Computer Textbook Inventory Report

Purpose: To become familiar with looping and the use of the LPRINT USING, READ, and DATA statements.

Problem: Inventory control not only includes keeping track of the names of items, the number of each item in stock, and the individual cost of items, it also entails calculating the total cost of the items, the price the items will sell for, the total value of all the items within each category, and the expected profit for those items.

Using the sample input data below, write a program to generate a report on the printer. The report should include a line of information for each category of textbook. Each line of information should include the textbook title, number of textbooks on hand, unit cost, total cost, selling price, total value, and profit. Use the following formulas:

Total Cost = Number of Items on Hand * Unit Cost
Selling Price = 1 / (1 – Margin) * Unit Cost where Margin = 30%
Total Value = Selling Price * Number of Items on Hand
Profit = Total Value – Total Cost

(**Hint**: Use Program 4.4 as a guide to solving this problem.)

Input Data: Prepare and use the sample data that follows and add a trailer record using a sentinel value of your own choice.

Title	On Hand	Unit Cost
C Programming	180	19.25
Computer Concepts	567	32.25
Network Basics	98	23.00
Microsoft Office	34	13.25
QBasic	45	23.00
Visual JAVA	423	38.00
System Analysis	231	33.00

Output Results: The output report should appear as illustrated by Figure 4.32.

FIGURE 4.32
Printer output report for Programming Problem 6.

```
                    Computer Textbook Inventory

                    On   Unit    Total  Selling    Total
Title              Hand  Cost     Cost    Price     Value     Profit
-----              ----  ----    -----  -------    -----     ------
C Programming       180  19.25   3,465.00   27.50   4,950.00  1,485.00
Computer Concepts   567  32.25  18,285.75   46.07  26,122.50  7,836.75
Network Basics       98  23.00   2,254.00   32.86   3,220.00    966.00
Microsoft Windows    34  13.25     450.50   18.93     643.57    193.07
QBasic               45  23.00   1,035.00   32.86   1,478.57    443.57
Visual JAVA         423  38.00  16,074.00   54.29  22,962.86  6,888.86
Systems Analysis    231  33.00   7,623.00   47.14  10,890.00  3,267.00

End of Report
```

7. Payroll Problem IV: Biweekly Payroll Report

Purpose: To become familiar with looping and the use of the PRINT USING, READ, and DATA statements.

Problem: Modify Payroll Problem III (Programming Problem 6 in Chapter 3 on page 92) to generate a report that contains a line of information for each employee. Each line is to include employee number, gross pay, federal withholding tax, and net pay.

(**Hint**: Use Program 4.4 as a guide to solving this problem.)

Input Data: Use the sample data found in Payroll Problem III. Add a trailer record. Select your own sentinel value.

Output Results: The output screen should appear as illustrated by Figure 4.33.

FIGURE 4.33
Output for Programming Problem 7.

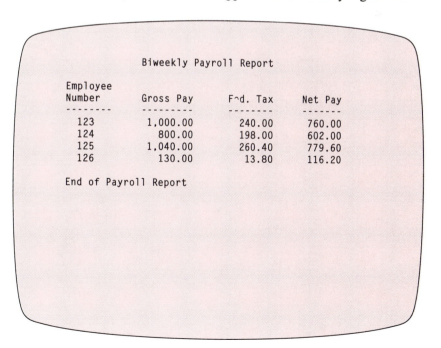

```
                  Biweekly Payroll Report

        Employee
        Number     Gross Pay     Fed. Tax    Net Pay
        --------   ---------     --------    -------
          123      1,000.00       240.00      760.00
          124        800.00       198.00      602.00
          125      1,040.00       260.40      779.60
          126        130.00        13.80      116.20

        End of Payroll Report
```

5

Structured Programming and Menu-Driven Programs

5.1 STRUCTURED PROGRAMMING

I t is appropriate at this time that we introduce you to some important concepts related to structured programming.

Structured programming is a methodology according to which all program logic can be constructed from a combination of the following three basic control structures:

1. **Sequence.** The most fundamental of the structures, it provides for two or more actions to be executed in the order in which they appear.
2. **If-Then-Else** or **Selection.** Provides a choice between two alternatives.
3. **Do-While** or **Repetition.** Provides for the repeated execution of a loop.

The following are two extensions to these control structures:

Do-Until. An extension of the Do-While structure.
Case. An extension of the If-Then-Else structure, in which the choice includes more than two alternatives.

So far in this book, the Sequence, Do-While, and Do-Until control structures have been used, although they have not been identified by their formal names.

The use of structured programming offers definite advantages. Computer professionals have found that when it is applied correctly in the construction of programs, structured programming confers the following benefits:

1. Programs are clearer and more readable.
2. Less time is spent debugging, testing, and modifying the program.
3. The programmer's productivity increases.
4. The quality, reliability, and efficiency of the program are improved.

Clearly, there are important payoffs in the use of structured programming.

Control Structures

In the previous chapter, the programs performed precisely the same computations for every set of data items that was processed. In some applications, it is not always desirable to process each set of data items in exactly the same way. For example, in a program that computes gross pay, some employees may be eligible for overtime, while others may not. Therefore, a decision must be made concerning which of two gross pay formulas to use.

The sequential flow of control within modules used in previous programs and shown in Figure 5.1 is not sufficient to solve problems that involve **decision making**. To develop an algorithm that requires deviation from sequential control, we need another control structure. This new structure, called If-Then-Else, is shown in Figure 5.2. It is also described in detail in Appendix A, Section A.3.

FIGURE 5.1

Sequence structure.

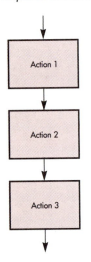

FIGURE 5.2

If-Then-Else structure.

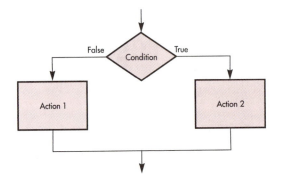

The flowchart representation of a decision is the diamond-shaped symbol. One flowline will always be shown entering the symbol, and two lines will always be shown leaving the symbol. A condition that must be either true or false is written within the decision symbol. Such a condition asks, for example, whether two variables are equal or whether an expression is within a certain range. If the condition is true, one path is taken; if not, the other path is taken. In Figure 5.2 we have adopted the convention of placing all the actions to the left of the diamond-shaped-symbol when the condition is false and all the actions to the right when the condition is true.

To instruct the PC to select actions on the basis of the values of variables, as illustrated in Figure 5.2, QBasic includes the IF statement. This chapter presents a number of examples to illustrate how IF statements are used to implement If-Then-Else structures.

The SELECT CASE statement may be used to implement an extension of the If-Then-Else structure, in which there are more than two alternatives. This extended version of the If-Then-Else structure is called the Case structure; it is illustrated in Figure 5.3 and described in Appendix A, Section A.3. As we shall see later in this chapter, the Case structure is commonly used to implement menu-driven programs. A **menu-driven program** is one in which a menu or series of menus is used to guide a user through a multifunction interactive program. The **menu** itself lists the functions that a program or a section of a program can perform.

FIGURE 5.3

Case structure.

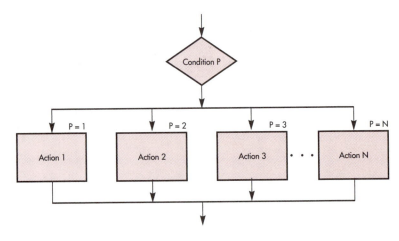

As we saw in Chapter 4, with looping it is necessary to include a decision to terminate the loop after a sufficient number of repetitions has occurred. Most computer professionals agree that the decision to terminate a loop should be located at the very top or very bottom of the loop. A loop that has the termination decision at the top is called a Do-While structure (Figure 5.4). We implement a Do-While structure in QBasic by using the DO WHILE and LOOP statements.

A loop that has the termination decision at the bottom is called a Do-Until structure (Figure 5.5). We implement a Do-Until structure by using the DO and LOOP UNTIL statements. (For additional information on the Do-While and Do-Until structures, see Figure 4.5 on page 102 and Section A.3 in Appendix A.)

FIGURE 5.4
Do-While structure.

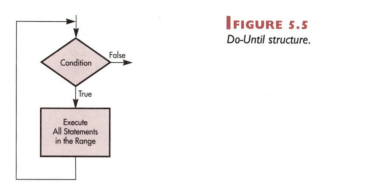

FIGURE 5.5
Do-Until structure.

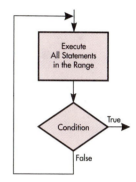

Combining Conditions

Logical operators, such as AND, OR, and NOT, may be used to combine conditions to reduce the number of statements required to implement certain If-Then-Else structures. In this chapter, we will discuss these three logical operators and three others — XOR, EQV, and IMP.

Logical operators are often used in the conditions of decision statements that verify that the data entered by the user is within a range that will generate valid results when the program is executed. This is called data validation.

Top-Down versus Structured

In Chapter 3, you studied concepts associated with the top-down, or modular, approach. In this chapter, you will study structured programming. Do not confuse structured programming with top-down programming; they are not the same. In designing a top-down solution, we use a top-down chart to determine *what must be done,* as described in Chapter 3. In designing a structured programming solution for a subtask, we use a program flowchart or some other logic tool to resolve the question of *how to implement* the subtask. Emphasis is placed on decision making and looping.

Upon successful completion of this chapter, you will be able to apply concepts related to structured programming and top-down programming. You will also be able to develop algorithms and write programs that include decisions, accumulators, logical operators, data-validation techniques, and menus.

5.2 THE IF STATEMENT

The IF statement is commonly regarded as one of the most powerful statements in QBasic. The function of this statement is to perform selection. In selection, the IF statement is used to let a program choose between two alternative paths, as illustrated in Figure 5.2. The general form of the IF statement is given in Table 5.1 on the next page.

TABLE 5.1 - The IF Statement

General Form: IF condition THEN clause ELSE clause

or

IF condition THEN
  clause
ELSE
  clause
END IF

where **condition** is a relation that is either true or false and **clause** is a statement or series of statements.

Purpose: If the condition is true, the PC executes the clause following the keyword THEN. If the condition is false and an ELSE clause is included, the PC executes the ELSE clause. After either clause is executed, control passes to the statement following the IF in the first form, known as a single-line IF statement, and to the statement following the corresponding END IF in the second form, known as a block IF statement.

Examples:

```
1. IF Age > 65 THEN PRINT Age ELSE Switch$ = "Y"
2. IF Tax >= 0 THEN
       Switch1$ = "Y"
       PRINT Gross.Pay
   ELSE
       Switch1$ = "N"
   END IF
3. IF Mar.Status$ = "M" THEN
       PRINT "Married"
   END IF
4. IF Gender.Code$ = "M" THEN
       IF Age >= 18 THEN
          PRINT "Male adult"
       ELSE
          PRINT "Male minor"
       END IF
   ELSE
       IF Age >= 18 THEN
          PRINT "Female adult"
       ELSE
          PRINT "Female minor"
       END IF
   END IF
```

Note: The IF statement may include the keyword ELSEIF to test for a series of different conditions. In situations where ELSEIF may be used, we will use SELECT CASE. (See Section 5.8 for a comparison between an IF statement using the keyword ELSEIF and the SELECT CASE statement.)

As indicated in Table 5.1, the IF statement is used to specify a decision. The condition appears between the keywords, IF and THEN. In determining whether the condition is true or false, the PC first determines the single value of each expression in the condition and then evaluates them both with respect to the relational operator. Table 4.3 on page 102 lists the relational operators used to indicate the type of comparison.

If the condition in an IF statement is true, the PC acts upon the THEN clause. If the condition is false, the PC acts upon the ELSE clause. In either case, after executing the statements making up the clause, control passes to the statement following the IF in the **single-line** IF statement, and to the statement following the corresponding END IF in the **block** IF statement. If no ELSE clause is present and the condition is false, then control passes immediately to the statement following the IF or corresponding END IF.

In Example 1 in Table 5.1, if Age is greater than 65, then the value of Age is displayed, and control passes to the statement following the IF statement. If Age is less than or equal to 65, Switch$ is assigned the value Y, and control passes to the statement following the IF statement. Note that the single-line IF statement does not include the END IF statement.

In Example 2 in Table 5.1, if Tax is greater than or equal to zero, the PC assigns Switch1$ the value Y and displays Gross.Pay. On the other hand, if Tax is less than zero, the PC assigns Switch1$ the value N. In either case, control passes to the statement following the corresponding END IF. Note that the block IF statement allows you to include as many statements as necessary in either clause.

In Example 3 in Table 5.1, if Mar. Status$ equals the value M, then the word Married displays, and control passes to the statement following the END IF. This IF statement does not include an ELSE clause. Hence, if the condition is false, control passes to the statement following the corresponding END IF without executing a clause.

Example 4 in Table 5.1 includes a nested IF statement. A **nested** IF statement is one in which a second IF statement is found within the THEN or ELSE clause. In Example 4, the nested IF statements cause the PC to print one of the four possible messages. The message displayed depends on the values of Gender.Code$ and Age. Note that each IF statement in Example 4 ends with a corresponding END IF statement.

Structured programming permits the nesting of the five control structures to any reasonable level. For example, you may nest an IF statement within a loop formed by a DO WHILE statement, and this may be nested within a loop formed by a DO UNTIL statement.

Comparing Numeric Expressions

If the condition in an IF statement includes two numeric expressions, the comparison is based on the algebraic values of the two expressions. That is, the PC evaluates not only the magnitude of each resultant expression, but also its sign. Examples 1 and 2 in Table 5.2 on the next page include conditions made up of numeric expressions.

Comparing String Expressions

If the condition in an IF statement includes two string expressions, the PC evaluates the two strings from left to right, one character at a time. As soon as one character in an expression is different from the corresponding character in the other expression, the comparison stops, and the PC decides which expression has a lower value, generally on the basis of numerical and alphabetical order. In other words, the PC evaluates two string expressions the same way you would. For example:

DOE is less than JOE   NO is not equal to No

JEFF is greater than JAFF YES is equal to YES

TAPE is greater than TAP

Two string expressions are considered equal if they are of the same length and contain an identical sequence of characters.

The PC determines which characters are *less than* other characters on the basis of the code that is used to store data in main memory. The code is called the **American Standard Code for Information Interchange (ASCII)**. A total of 256 different characters can be entered into main memory. The ASCII code and the collating sequence is shown in Appendix D, Table D.1. The **collating sequence** is the position of the character in relation to other characters. As Table D.1 shows, numbers are less than uppercase letters in value, which are in turn less than lowercase letters in value. The null character is considered to have the least value in the collating sequence. Examples 4 and 5 in Table 5.2 illustrate IF statements that include conditions made up of string expressions.

If you compare a numeric expression to a string expression in an IF statement, QBasic will display a dialog box with the diagnostic message Type mismatch when you attempt to execute the program.

		TABLE 5.2 - Examples of IF Statements	
EXAMPLE	**STATEMENT**	**VALUES OF VARIABLES**	**RESULT**
I	`IF Z = 0 THEN S = 4`	Z = 0	The variable S is assigned the value 4, and control passes to the line following the IF statement.

2	`IF X < Y THEN`
	`    PRINT A`
	`    Tax = Tax + 10`
	`ELSE`
	`    PRINT B`
	`    Tax = Tax + 5`
	`END IF`
		X = 7
		Y = 9
			The value of A is displayed; Tax is incremented by 10, and control passes to the line following the END IF.

3	`IF D <> A - B - 6 THEN`
	`    PRINT S`
	`END IF`
		D = 23
		A = 14
		B = −15
			Control passes to the line following the END IF.

4	`IF B$ > C$ + D$ THEN`
	`ELSE`
	`    PRINT Y`
	`END IF`
		B$ = "WINE"
		C$ = "WA"
		D$ = "TER"
			The THEN clause is null and control passes to the line following the END IF.

5	`IF A$ = "NO" THEN`
	`    PRINT A$`
	`END IF`
		A$ = "no"	Control passes to the line following the END IF. "NO" and "no" are not the same string.

Values of Conditions

Conditions are evaluated by the arithmetic-logic unit (ALU) in the PC. When the ALU evaluates a condition, it returns to the program -1 if the condition is true, or 0 if the condition is false. This is illustrated in the following program, which displays the values of the three conditions X < Y, X = Y, and X > Y. Prior to the PRINT statement, the program assigns X the value 10, and Y the value 20.

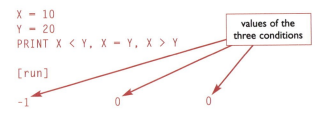

```
X = 10
Y = 20
PRINT X < Y, X = Y, X > Y

[run]

-1          0          0
```

values of the three conditions

Because X is less than Y, the first condition is equal to -1. The last two conditions are false; and therefore, zeros display.

Hence, each time an IF statement in a program executes, the ALU checks the condition. If the condition is true, the ALU returns -1 (true) to the program, and the PC executes the THEN clause. If the condition is false, the ALU returns 0 (false), and the PC executes the ELSE clause if it is present.

5.3 ACCUMULATORS

Most programs require **accumulators**, which are used to develop totals. Accumulators are numeric variables that are initialized to a predetermined value, such as zero, in the Initialization module, then incremented within the loop in the Process File module, and then manipulated or displayed in the Wrap-Up module. Although QBasic automatically initializes numeric variables to zero, good programming practice demands this be done prior to the loop in which they are incremented.

Two types of accumulators are counters and running totals. Both types are discussed in the sections that follow.

Counters

A **counter** is an accumulator that is used to count the number of times some action or event is performed. For example, appropriately placed within a loop, the statement

```
Emp.Count = Emp.Count + 1
```

causes the counter Emp.Count to increment by 1 each time a record is read. Associated with a counter is a statement placed in the Initialization module, which initializes the counter to some value. In most cases the counter is initialized to zero.

Running Totals

A **running total** is an accumulator that is used to sum the different values a variable is assigned during the execution of a program. For example, appropriately placed within a loop, the statement

```
Total.Gross = Total.Gross + Emp.Gross
```

causes Total.Gross to increase by the value of Emp.Gross. Total.Gross is called a running total. If a program is processing an employee file and the variable Emp.Gross is assigned the employee's gross pay each time a record is processed, then the variable Total.Gross represents the running total of the gross pay paid to all the employees in the file. As with a counter, a running total must be initialized to some predetermined value in the Initialization module. A running total normally is initialized to zero.

PROGRAMMING CASE STUDY 7A – Weekly Payroll and Summary Report

The following example incorporates both a counter and a running total, as well as some of the concepts discussed earlier in this chapter.

Problem: A payroll application requires that the employee number, the hours worked, the rate of pay, and the gross pay be printed for each of the following employees:

Employee Number	Hours Worked	Rate of Pay
124	40	$5.60
126	56	5.90
128	38	4.60
129	48.5	6.10

Also, the total gross pay, the total number of employees, and the average gross pay for this payroll are to be printed. The required report is described on the printer spacing chart shown in Figure 5.6 on the next page.

FIGURE 5.6

Output for Program 5.1, the solution to Programming Case Study 7A, designed on a printer spacing chart.

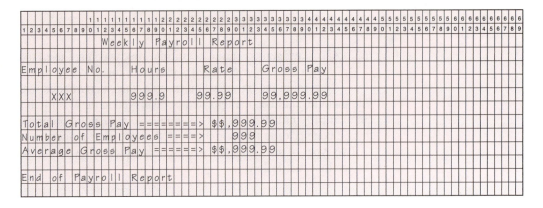

The gross pay is determined by multiplying the hours worked by the hourly rate of pay. Overtime, hours in excess of 40, is paid at 1.5 times the hourly rate.

Following are a top-down chart (Figure 5.7), two program flowcharts of subtasks (Figure 5.8), the program tasks in outline form, a program solution in Program 5.1, the program output results (Figure 5.10 on page 154), and a discussion of the program solution.

FIGURE 5.7

Top-down chart for the modules in Program 5.1.

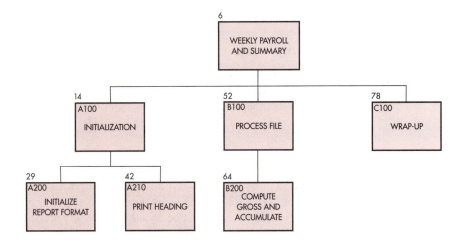

Program Tasks

The following program tasks correspond to the top-down chart in Figure 5.7.

1. A100.Initialization
   a. Initialize a counter (Emp.Count) and running total (Total.Gross) to zero. Use the counter to determine the total number of employees processed. Use the running total to determine the total gross pay.
   b. Clear the screen and display a message informing the user the report will print on the printer. After the user checks the printer, accept the Enter key response via the INPUT statement to continue.
   c. Initialize the report format — assign the heading lines, the detail line, and the total lines, described in Figure 5.6, to string variables.
   d. Print the report and column headings.

2. B100.Process.File
   a. Read an employee record. Use the following variable names for the employee record:

Emp.Number$:	employee number
Emp.Hours:	employee hours
Emp.Rate:	employee hourly rate

FIGURE 5.8

A flowchart for B100.Process.File and B200.Compute.Gross.And. Accumulate in Program 5.1.

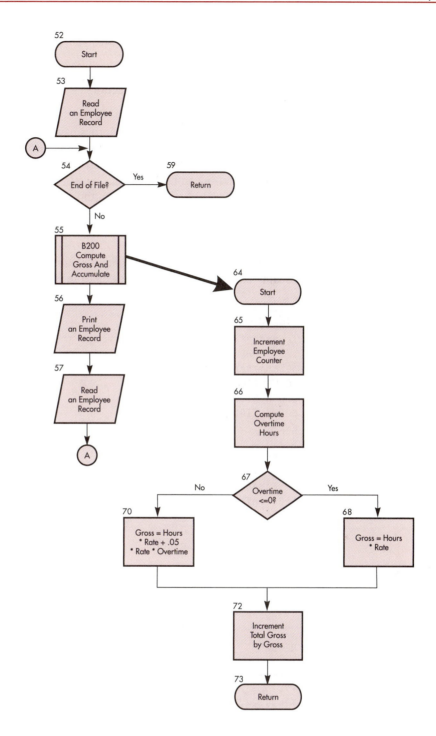

b. Use a `DO WHILE` statement to establish a loop for processing the employee records when Emp.Number$ does not equal the value EOF. If end-of-file, return control to the Main Program. If not end-of-file, do the following:

(1) Determine the gross pay and increment accumulators.

(a) Increment the counter Emp.Count by 1.

(b) Compute the employee overtime (Emp.Overtime).

(c) Determine the gross pay (Emp.Gross). If Emp.Overtime is less than or equal to zero, use this formula:

Emp.Gross = Emp.Hours * Emp.Rate

If Emp.Overtime is greater than zero, use this formula:

Emp.Gross = Emp.Hours * Emp.Rate + 0.5 * Emp.Rate * Emp.Overtime

(d) Increment the running total (Total.Gross) by the employee gross pay (Emp.Gross).
  (2) Print an employee record.
  (3) Read the next employee record.

3. C100.Wrap.Up

  a. Compute the average employee gross pay (Average.Gross).
  b. Print the values of the accumulators (Total.Gross and Emp.Count) and average employee gross pay (Average.Gross).
  c. Print an end-of-job message.
  d. Display an end-of-job message on the screen.

Program Solution

Program 5.1 in Figure 5.9 and the output results (Figure 5.10 on page 154) correspond to the preceding tasks and to the top-down chart in Figure 5.7.

FIGURE 5.9

Program 5.1, the solution to Programming Case Study 7A.

```
 1    ' Program 5.1
 2    ' Weekly Payroll and Summary Report
 3    ' **********************************************
 4    ' *                Main Program                *
 5    ' **********************************************
 6    GOSUB A100.Initialization
 7    GOSUB B100.Process.File
 8    GOSUB C100.Wrap.Up
 9    END
10
11    ' **********************************************
12    ' *             Initialization                 *
13    ' **********************************************
14    A100.Initialization:
15       Emp.Count = 0
16       Total.Gross = 0
17       CLS  ' Clear Screen
18       LOCATE 10, 20
19       PRINT "Please make sure there is paper in the printer."
20       LOCATE 12, 20
21       INPUT "Press Enter key when the printer is ready...", Control$
22       GOSUB A200.Initialize.Report.Format
23       GOSUB A210.Print.Headings
24    RETURN
25
26    ' **********************************************
27    ' *          Initialize Report Format          *
28    ' **********************************************
29    A200.Initialize.Report.Format:
30       H1$ = "           Weekly Payroll Report"
31       H2$ = "Employee No.   Hours      Rate      Gross Pay"
32       D1$ = "    \  \        ###.#     ##.##     ##,###.##"
33       T1$ = "Total Gross Pay ========> $$,###.##"
34       T2$ = "Number of Employees ====>    ###"
35       T3$ = "Average Gross Pay ======> $$,###.##"
36       T4$ = "End of Payroll Report"
37    RETURN
38
```

set accumulators to 0 in Initialization

```
39  ' *************************************************
40  ' *        Print Report and Column Headings       *
41  ' *************************************************
42  A210.Print.Headings:
43     LPRINT H1$
44     LPRINT
45     LPRINT H2$
46     LPRINT
47  RETURN
48
49  ' *************************************************
50  ' *                   Process File                *
51  ' *************************************************
52  B100.Process.File:
53     READ Emp.Number$, Emp.Hours, Emp.Rate
54     DO WHILE Emp.Number$ <> "EOF"
55        GOSUB B200.Compute.Gross.And.Accumulate
56        LPRINT USING D1$; Emp.Number$; Emp.Hours; Emp.Rate; Emp.Gross
57        READ Emp.Number$, Emp.Hours, Emp.Rate
58     LOOP
59  RETURN
60
61  ' *************************************************
62  ' *   Compute Gross Pay & Increment Accumulators   *
63  ' *************************************************
64  B200.Compute.Gross.And.Accumulate:
65     Emp.Count = Emp.Count + 1          ◀——— increment Emp.Count
66     Emp.Overtime = Emp.Hours - 40             by 1 each time a
67     IF Emp.Overtime <= 0 THEN                 record is processed
68        Emp.Gross = Emp.Hours * Emp.Rate
69     ELSE
70        Emp.Gross = Emp.Hours * Emp.Rate + .5 * Emp.Rate * Emp.Overtime
71     END IF
72     Total.Gross = Total.Gross + Emp.Gross  ◀——— increment
73  RETURN                                            Total.Gross by
74                                                    Emp.Gross
75  ' *************************************************
76  ' *                   Wrap-Up                      *
77  ' *************************************************
78  C100.Wrap.Up:
79     Average.Gross = Total.Gross / Emp.Count
80     LPRINT
81     LPRINT USING T1$; Total.Gross        ⎫
82     LPRINT USING T2$; Emp.Count          ⎬ ◀—— print accumulators
83     LPRINT USING T3$; Average.Gross      ⎭      before the program
84     LPRINT                                       terminates
85     LPRINT T4$
86     LOCATE 14, 20: PRINT "End of Job"
87  RETURN
88
89  ' *************** Data Follows ****************
90  DATA 124, 40,   5.60
91  DATA 126, 56,   5.90
92  DATA 128, 38,   4.60
93  DATA 129, 48.5, 6.10
94  DATA EOF,  0,   0    : ' This is the trailer record
95  ' ************** End of Program ****************

    [run]
```

FIGURE 5.10

The Weekly Payroll and Summary Report printed due to the execution of Program 5.1.

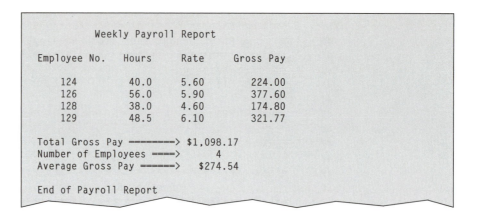

```
           Weekly Payroll Report

Employee No.    Hours    Rate    Gross Pay

    124         40.0     5.60      224.00
    126         56.0     5.90      377.60
    128         38.0     4.60      174.80
    129         48.5     6.10      321.77

Total Gross Pay ========> $1,098.17
Number of Employees =====>      4
Average Gross Pay =======>  $274.54

End of Payroll Report
```

Discussion of the Program Solution

The solution to the Weekly Payroll and Summary Report, as represented by Program 5.1, includes a few significant points that did not appear in previous programs. They are as follows:

1. The use of a counter (Emp.Count) and a running total (Total.Gross). Both are initialized to zero (lines 15 and 16) and are incremented each time an employee record is read. The counter is used to keep track of the total number of employees and is incremented in line 65. The running total is used to sum the gross pay and is incremented by the individual employee gross pay in line 72.
2. The A100.Initialization subroutine calls two subroutines. The first one, A200.Initialize.Report.Format (lines 29 through 37), assigns each output line, described on the printer spacing chart in Figure 5.6 on page 150, to a string variable. Later, these string variables are used in LPRINT and LPRINT USING statements to print the required output. The second subroutine (lines 42 through 47) prints the report and column headings according to the format established in the subroutine A200.Initialize.Report.Format.
3. A decision is made in line 67 to determine which one of the two formulas is to be used to compute the gross pay. If Emp.Overtime is less than or equal to zero, the PC uses the THEN clause. If Emp.Overtime is greater than zero, the PC uses the ELSE clause.
4. We are able to eliminate the recomputation of Emp.Overtime by calculating the overtime in line 66 and assigning it to the variable Emp.Overtime. Whenever a value is required several times in a program, it is better to compute it once and assign it to a variable, as in line 66, than to recompute it every time it is needed. (See Appendix C, Section C.3, Programming Tips 2 and 3.)
5. The C100.Wrap.Up subroutine (lines 78 to 87) involves calculating an average that is based on the total gross pay (Total.Gross) and the number of employees (Emp.Count) and printing these totals and the average.

Programming Styles

You should be aware that there are several ways to modularize and code Program 5.1. For example, some programmers prefer to place the single statement that reads a record (line 53 or line 57 in Program 5.1) and the statement that prints the detail line (line 56 in Program 5.1) in separate subroutines. We did not follow this programming style because it tends to increase the complexity of a program and creates confusion by containing too many unnecessary levels of subroutines.

We believe a program should be easy to read and understand while still maintaining its structure. We do not believe in using unnecessary subroutines merely for the sake of subroutine usage.

5.4 IMPLEMENTING THE DO-WHILE AND DO-UNTIL STRUCTURES

In designing and implementing a Do loop, think carefully about where to place the decision to terminate the loop. As mentioned earlier in Section 4.2 of Chapter 4, the decision to terminate should be at the very top or very bottom of the loop.

If, in the design of a solution, the logic requires that you test to terminate before making a pass on the loop (Do-While structure), then use the DO WHILE and LOOP statements to implement the loop. If, on the other hand, the design calls for a pass on the loop before testing for termination (Do-Until structure), use the DO and LOOP UNTIL statements. The partial flowcharts and programs in Figures 5.11 and 5.12 illustrate two different solutions to the same problem — summing the first 100 integers:

$$(1 + 2 + 3 + \ldots + 100)$$

In Figure 5.11, the DO WHILE and LOOP statements are used to implement the Do-While structure. In Figure 5.12, the DO and LOOP UNTIL statements are used to implement the Do-Until structure. Both programs generate identical results.

FIGURE 5.11

A Do-While control structure implemented using the DO WHILE *and* LOOP *statements.*

FIGURE 5.12

A Do-Until control structure implemented using the DO *and* LOOP UNTIL *statements.*

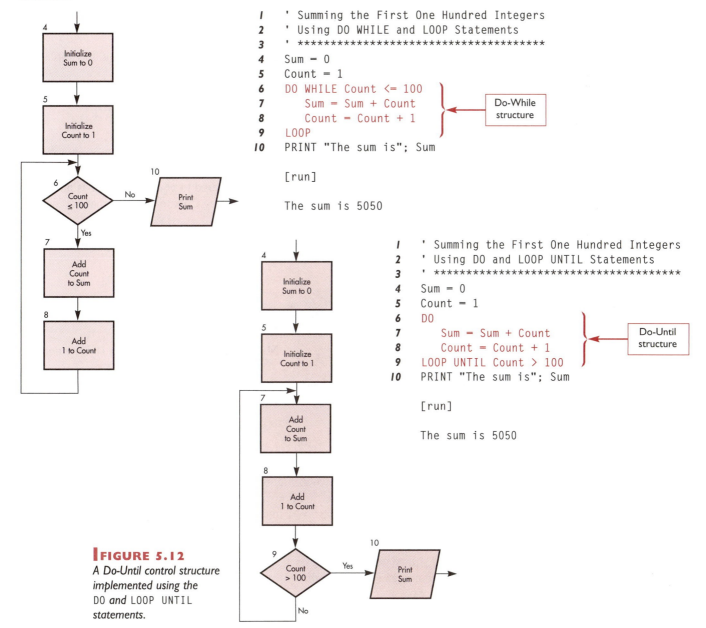

```
1   ' Summing the First One Hundred Integers
2   ' Using DO WHILE and LOOP Statements
3   ' ***************************************
4   Sum = 0
5   Count = 1
6   DO WHILE Count <= 100
7       Sum = Sum + Count
8       Count = Count + 1
9   LOOP
10  PRINT "The sum is"; Sum


[run]

The sum is 5050
```

Do-While structure

```
1   ' Summing the First One Hundred Integers
2   ' Using DO and LOOP UNTIL Statements
3   ' ***************************************
4   Sum = 0
5   Count = 1
6   DO
7       Sum = Sum + Count
8       Count = Count + 1
9   LOOP UNTIL Count > 100
10  PRINT "The sum is"; Sum


[run]

The sum is 5050
```

Do-Until structure

The WHILE and WEND Statements

QBasic also includes the WHILE and WEND statements for the purpose of implementing a Do-While loop in a program. This pair of statements works exactly the same as the DO WHILE and LOOP statements. The WHILE statement initiates a Do-While loop, and the WEND statement terminates it. Hence, in Figure 5.11 on the previous page, we can replace the DO WHILE statement in line 6 with the WHILE statement and the LOOP statement in line 9 with the WEND statement, and the program would function the same way as shown here:

```
6    WHILE Count <= 100
7       Sum = Sum + Count
8       Count = Count + 1
9    WEND
```

In this book we will use the DO WHILE and LOOP statements to implement the Do While structure. However, because of their popularity in earlier dialects of Microsoft BASIC, you should be aware that the WHILE and WEND statements exist.

5.5 IMPLEMENTING THE IF-THEN-ELSE STRUCTURE

This section describes the various forms of the If-Then-Else structure and the implementation of IF statements in QBasic.

Simple Forms of the If-Then-Else Structure

Consider the If-Then-Else structure in Figure 5.13 and the corresponding methods of implementing the logic in QBasic. Assume that Reg$ represents a person's voter registration status. If Reg$ is equal to the value Y, the person is registered to vote. If Reg$ does not equal Y, the person is not registered to vote. Reg.Cnt and Not.Reg.Cnt are counters that are incremented as specified in the flowchart.

FIGURE 5.13

Implementatin of the If-Then-Else structure with alternative processing for the true and false cases.

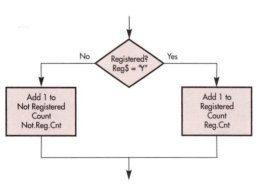

Method 1: Using a single IF statement.

```
IF Reg$ = "Y" THEN
   Reg.Cnt = Reg.Cnt + 1
ELSE
   Not.Reg.Cnt = Not.Reg.Cnt + 1
END IF
```

Method 2: Using two separate IF statements.

```
IF Reg$ = "Y" THEN
   Reg.Cnt = Reg.Cnt + 1
END IF
IF Reg$ <> "Y" THEN
   Not.Reg.Cnt = Not.Reg.Cnt + 1
END IF
```

In the first method of solution shown in Figure 5.13, an IF statement resolves the logic indicated in the partial flowchart. The first line compares Reg$ to the value Y. If Reg$ is equal to Y, then Reg.Cnt is incremented by 1 in the THEN clause. If Reg$ does not equal Y, Not.Reg.Cnt is incremented by 1 in the ELSE clause. Regardless of the counter incremented, control passes to the statement following the END IF.

Note that the first method could have been written as a single-line IF statement without the END IF. We recommend for readability purposes that you do not use the single-line IF statement.

In Method 2, Reg$ is compared to the value Y twice. In the first IF statement, the counter Reg.Cnt is incremented by 1 if Reg$ is equal to Y. In the second IF statement, the counter Not.Reg.Cnt is incremented by 1 if Reg$ does not equal Y.

Although both methods are valid and both satisfy the If-Then-Else structure, the first method is more efficient, as it involves fewer lines of code and less execution time. Therefore, the first method is recommended over the second.

As shown in Figures 5.14, 5.15, and 5.16, the If-Then-Else structure can take on a variety of appearances. In Figure 5.14, there is a task to perform only if the condition is true.

FIGURE 5.14

Implementation of an If-Then-Else structure with alternative processing for the true case.

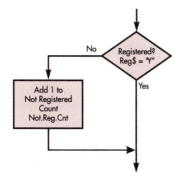

Method 1: Using an IF statement with no ELSE clause.

```
IF Reg$ = "Y" THEN
    Reg.Cnt = Reg.Cnt + 1
END IF
```

Method 2: Using an IF statement with a null ELSE clause.

```
IF Reg$ = "Y" THEN
    Reg.Cnt = Reg.Cnt + 1
ELSE
END IF
```

FIGURE 5.15

Implementation of an If-Then-Else structure with alternative processing for the false case.

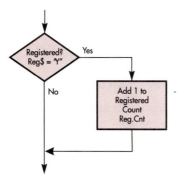

Method 1: Negating the condition in the decision symbol and using an IF statement.

```
IF Reg$ <> "Y" THEN
    Not.Reg.Cnt = Not.Reg.Cnt + 1
END IF
```

Method 2: Using an IF statement with a null THEN clause.

```
IF Reg$ = "Y" THEN
ELSE
    Not.Reg.Cnt = Not.Reg.Cnt + 1
END IF
IF Reg$ = "Y" THEN
    Reg.Cnt = Reg.Cnt + 1
    PRINT "Registered"
ELSE
    Not.Reg.Cnt = Not.Reg.Cnt + 1
    PRINT "Not Registered"
END IF
```

FIGURE 5.16

Implementation of an If-Then-Else structure with several statements for both the true and false cases.

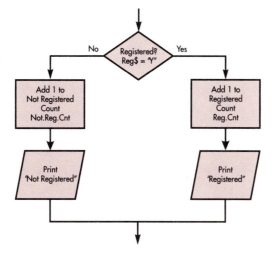

In Figure 5.14, the first method is preferred over the second, because it is more straightforward and involves fewer lines of code. Note that the second method involves a null ELSE clause.

The If-Then-Else structure in Figure 5.15 illustrates the incrementation of the counter Not.Reg.Cnt when the condition is false. In Method 1, the relation in the condition found in the partial flowchart has been negated. The condition Reg$ = "Y" has been modified to read Reg$ <> "Y" in the QBasic code. Negating the relation is usually preferred when additional tasks must be done as a result of the condition being false.

In Method 2, the relation is the same as in the decision symbol. When the condition `Reg$ = "Y"` is true, the null `THEN` clause simply passes control to the statement following the `END IF`. Either method is acceptable. Some programmers prefer always to include both a `THEN` and an `ELSE` clause, even when one of them is null. On the other hand, some prefer to negate the condition rather than include a null clause.

In Figure 5.16 on the previous page, each task in the If-Then-Else structure is made up of multiple statements. We have included in the figure a suggested method of implementation. If the condition `Reg$ = "Y"` is true, the two statements in the `THEN` clause are executed. If the condition is false, the two statements in the `ELSE` clause are executed.

Although there are alternative methods for implementing the If-Then-Else structure, the method presented is more straightforward and involves fewer lines of code.

Nested Forms of the If-Then-Else Structure

A nested If-Then-Else structure is one in which the action to be taken for the true or false case includes yet another If-Then-Else structure. The second If-Then-Else structure is considered to be nested, or layered, within the first.

Study the partial program that corresponds to the nested If-Then-Else structure in Figure 5.17. In the partial program in Figure 5.17, if the condition `Age >= 18` is true, control passes to the true task beginning with line 2. If the condition is false, the `ELSE` clause in line 9 is executed. If control does pass to line 2, then a second `IF` tests to determine if Reg$ equals the value Y. If the condition in line 2 is true, lines 3 and 4 are executed. If the condition is false, then the PC executes lines 6 and 7.

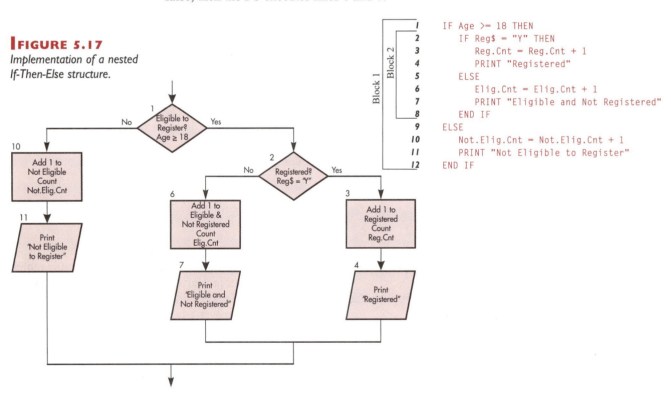

FIGURE 5.17

Implementation of a nested If-Then-Else structure.

QBasic requires that you end each block `IF` statement with an `END IF`. Hence, the `IF` in line 1 has a corresponding `END IF` in line 12, and the `IF` in line 2 has a corresponding `END IF` in line 8. This leads to the following rule.

IF RULE 1   *Each block `IF` statement must have a corresponding `END IF`.*

Note in Figure 5.17 that only one of the three alternative tasks is executed for each record processed. Regardless of the path taken, control eventually passes to the statement immediately following the last `END IF` in line 12.

If-Then-Else structures can be nested to any depth, but readability decreases as nesting increases. Consider the nested structure in Figure 5.18 and the corresponding implementation in QBasic. Figure 5.18 contains four nested If-Then-Else structures and six counters. The counters can be described in the following manner:

NE.Male:	totals the number of males not eligible to register
NE.Fem:	totals the number of females not eligible to register
NR.Male:	totals the number of males who are old enough to vote but have not registered
NR.Fem:	totals the number of females who are old enough to vote but have not registered
N.Vote:	the number of individuals who are eligible to vote but did not vote
Vote:	totals the number of individuals who voted

In the partial program in Figure 5.18, line 1 corresponds to the decision at the very top of the flowchart. Lines 2 through 14 handle the true case to the right in the flowchart. Lines 16 through 20 fulfill the false case to the left in the flowchart. Incorporating the logic and concepts found in Figure 5.18 into a complete program is left as an exercise for you at the end of this chapter. (See QBasic Programming Problem 3 at the end of this chapter.)

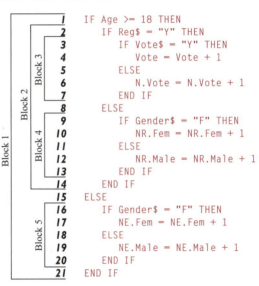

```
 1   IF Age >= 18 THEN
 2       IF Reg$ = "Y" THEN
 3           IF Vote$ = "Y" THEN
 4               Vote = Vote + 1
 5           ELSE
 6               N.Vote = N.Vote + 1
 7           END IF
 8       ELSE
 9           IF Gender$ = "F" THEN
10               NR.Fem = NR.Fem + 1
11           ELSE
12               NR.Male = NR.Male + 1
13           END IF
14       END IF
15   ELSE
16       IF Gender$ = "F" THEN
17           NE.Fem = NE.Fem + 1
18       ELSE
19           NE.Male = NE.Male + 1
20       END IF
21   END IF
```

FIGURE 5.18

Implementation of an If-Then-Else structure with several layers.

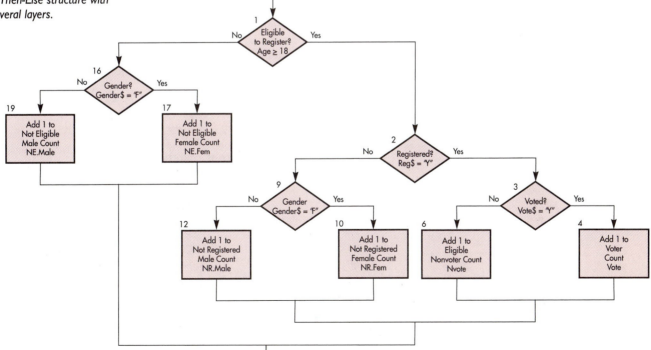

5.6 LOGICAL OPERATORS

In many instances, a decision to execute one alternative or another is based upon two or more conditions. In previous examples that involved two or more conditions, we tested each condition in a separate decision statement. In this section, we will discuss combining conditions within one decision statement by means of the logical operators AND, OR, XOR, EQV, and IMP. When two or more conditions are combined by these logical operators, the expression is called a **compound condition**. The logical operator NOT allows you to write a condition in which the truth value is **complemented**, or reversed.

The NOT Logical Operator

A condition made up of two expressions and a relational operator is sometimes called a **relational expression**. A relational expression that is preceded by the NOT **logical operator** forms a condition that is false when the relational expression is true. If the relational expression is false, then the condition is true. Consider the following IF statements:

Method 1: Using the NOT logical operator.

```
IF NOT A > B THEN
    READ A
END IF
```

Method 2: Using other relations to complement.

```
IF A <= B THEN
    READ A
END IF
```

Method 3: Using a null THEN.

```
IF A > B THEN
ELSE
    READ A
END IF
```

If A is greater than B, meaning the relational expression is true, then the condition NOT A > B is false. If A is less than or equal to B, meaning the relational expression is false, then the condition is true. All three methods are equivalent; however, Methods 1 and 2 are preferred.

Because the logical operator NOT can increase the complexity of the decision statement significantly, use it sparingly. As illustrated in Table 5.3, with QBasic you may write the complement, or reverse, of a condition by using other relations.

TABLE 5.3 - Use of Other Relations to Complement a Condition		
	COMPLEMENT OF CONDITION	
CONDITION	METHOD I	METHOD 2
A = B	A <> B	NOT A = B
A < B	A >= B	NOT A < B
A > B	A <= B	NOT A > B
A <= B	A > B	NOT A <= B
A >= B	A < B	NOT A >= B
A <> B	A = B	NOT A <> B

The following rule summarizes the use of the logical operator, NOT.

LOGICAL OPERATOR RULE 1   *The NOT logical operator requires that the relational expression be false for the condition to be true. If the relational expression is true, then the condition is false.*

The AND Logical Operator

The AND **logical operator** requires that both conditions be true for the compound condition to be true. Consider the following IF statements:

Method 1: Using the AND logical operator.

```
IF Gender$ = "M" AND Age > 20 THEN
    PRINT Emp.Name$
END IF
```

Method 2: Using nested IF statements.

```
IF Gender$ = "M" THEN
    IF Age > 20 THEN
        PRINT Emp.Name$
    END IF
END IF
```

If Gender$ is equal to the value M and Age is greater than 20, then Emp.Name$ is displayed before control passes to the line following the END IF. If either one of the conditions is false, then the compound condition is false, and control passes to the line following the END IF without Emp.Name$ being displayed. Although both methods are equivalent, Method 1 is more efficient, more compact, and more straightforward than Method 2.

Like a single condition, a compound condition can be only true or false. To determine the truth value of the compound condition, the PC must evaluate and assign a truth value to each individual condition. Then the truth value is determined for the compound condition.

For example, if Count equals 4 and Code$ equals "A", the PC evaluates the following compound condition in the manner shown:

```
IF Count = 3 AND Code$ = "A" THEN PRINT Emp.Soc.Sec
       1. false         2. true
              3. false
```

The PC first determines the truth value for each condition, then concludes that the compound condition is false because of the AND operator.

A compound condition can be made up of several conditions separated by AND operators. The flowchart in Figure 5.19 on the next page indicates that all three variables (T1, T2, and T3) must equal zero to increment Count by 1. The IF statement in Figure 5.19 illustrates the use of a compound condition to implement the logic. The AND operator requires that all three conditions be true for Count to be incremented by 1. If any one of the three conditions is false, control is transferred to the line following the END IF, and Count is not incremented by 1.

FIGURE 5.19
Use of two AND *operators.*

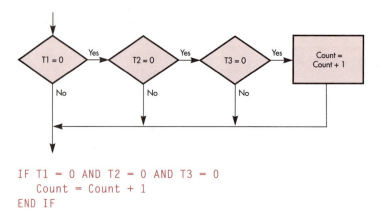

```
IF T1 = 0 AND T2 = 0 AND T3 = 0
    Count = Count + 1
END IF
```

The following rule summarizes the use of the logical operator AND.

LOGICAL OPERATOR RULE 2   *The* AND *logical operator requires that **all** conditions be true for the compound condition to be true.*

The OR Logical Operator

The OR **logical operator** requires only one of the two conditions be true for the compound condition to be true. If both conditions are true, the compound condition is also true. Likewise, if both conditions are false, the compound condition is false. The use of the OR operator is illustrated below:

Method 1: Using the OR logical operators.

```
IF Div = 0 OR Expo > 1E30 THEN
    PRINT "WARNING"
END IF
```

Method 2: Using two IF statements.

```
IF Div = 0 THEN
    PRINT "WARNING"
END IF
IF Expo > 1E30 THEN
    PRINT "WARNING"
END IF
```

In Method 1, if either Div equals 0 or Expo is greater than 1E30, the THEN clause is executed. If both conditions are true, the THEN clause is also executed. If both conditions are false, the THEN clause is bypassed and control passes to the line following the END IF.

Method 2 uses two IF statements to resolve the same problem. Both methods are basically equivalent. However, Method 1 is more straightforward than Method 2. Can you write a single nested IF statement without a logical operator that results in the same logic described in Methods 1 and 2?

FIGURE 5.20
Use of two OR *operators.*

Figure 5.20 illustrates a partial flowchart and the use of two OR operators to implement it.

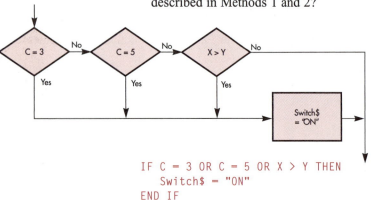

```
IF C = 3 OR C = 5 OR X > Y THEN
    Switch$ = "ON"
END IF
```

As with the AND logical operator, the truth values of the individual conditions in the IF statement in Figure 5.20 are first determined, and then the truth values for the conditions containing the OR logical operator are evaluated. For example, if C equals 4, X equals 4.9, and Y equals 4.8, the following condition is true:

```
IF   C = 3   OR   C = 5   OR   X > Y   THEN Switch$ = "ON"
     1. false      2. false      3. true
          4. false
                  5. true
```

In this IF statement, the PC first evaluates the individual conditions (steps 1, 2, and 3). The first and second conditions are false, and the third condition is true. Next, the PC evaluates the leftmost OR (step 4). Because the truth values of the first two conditions are false, the truth value of C = 3 OR C = 5 is also false.

Finally, the PC evaluates the truth value of the condition resulting from step 4 and the condition resulting from step 3 for the rightmost logical operator OR. Because the condition resulting from step 3 has a truth value of true, the entire condition is determined to be true.

The following rule summarizes the use of the logical operator OR.

LOGICAL OPERATOR RULE 3   *The OR logical operator requires **only one** of the conditions be true for the compound condition to be true. If both conditions are true, the compound condition is also true.*

The XOR, EQV, and IMP Logical Operators

Three logical operators rarely used are XOR (exclusive OR), EQV (equivalence), and IMP (implication).

The XOR **logical operator** requires one of the two conditions be true for the compound condition to be true. If both conditions are true, the compound condition is false. Likewise, if both conditions are false, the compound condition is also false. For example, if C = 3 and D = 4, then the following compound condition is false:

```
C = 3   XOR   D > 3
1. true        2. true
      3. false
```

The EQV **logical operator** requires both conditions be true or both conditions be false for the compound condition to be true. For example, if C = 4 and D = 3, then the following compound condition is true.

```
C = 3   EQV   D > 3
1. false       2. false
      3. true
```

The IMP **logical operator** requires that both conditions be true or both conditions be false, or the first condition be false and the second condition be true for the compound condition to be true. For example, if C = 4 and D = 5, then the following compound condition is true.

```
C = 3   IMP   D > 3
1. false       2. true
      3. true
```

Truth Tables

Truth tables for the six logical operators discussed in this section are summarized in Table 5.4. A summary of the order of precedence of all QBasic operators, including arithmetic, relational, and logical, can be found on page 5 of the Reference Card in the back of this book.

TABLE 5.4 - Truth Tables for Logical Operators where A and B Represent Conditions, T Represents True, and F Represents False

LOGICAL OPERATOR NOT

VALUE OF A	VALUE OF NOT A
T	F
F	T

LOGICAL OPERATOR XOR

VALUE OF A	VALUE OF B	VALUE OF A XOR B
T	T	F
T	F	T
F	T	T
F	F	F

LOGICAL OPERATOR AND

VALUE OF A	VALUE OF B	VALUE OF A AND B
T	T	T
T	F	F
F	T	F
F	F	F

LOGICAL OPERATOR EQV

VALUE OF A	VALUE OF B	VALUE OF A EQV B
T	T	T
T	F	F
F	T	F
F	F	T

LOGICAL OPERATOR OR

VALUE OF A	VALUE OF B	VALUE OF A OR B
T	T	T
T	F	T
F	T	T
F	F	F

LOGICAL OPERATOR IMP

VALUE OF A	VALUE OF B	VALUE OF A IMP B
T	T	T
T	F	F
F	T	T
F	F	T

Combining Logical Operators

Logical operators can be combined in a decision statement to form a compound condition. The formation of compound statements that involve more than one type of logical operator can create problems unless you fully understand the order in which the PC evaluates the entire condition. Consider the following decision statement:

```
IF X > Y OR T = D AND H < 3 OR NOT Y = R THEN
    Count = Count + 1
END IF
```

Does the PC evaluate operators from left to right or right to left or one type of operator before another?

The order of evaluation is a part of what is called the **rules of precedence**. Just as we have rules of precedence for arithmetic operations (Chapter 3), we also have rules of precedence for logical operators. (See page 5 of the Reference Card at the back of this book.)

PRECEDENCE RULE 3 *Reading from left to right, unless parentheses dictate otherwise, conditions containing arithmetic operators are evaluated first; then those containing relational operators; then those containing NOT operators; then those containing AND operators; then those containing OR or XOR operators; then those containing EQV operators, and finally those containing IMP operators.*

The compound condition in the previous IF statement is evaluated as follows. Assume that D = 3, H = 3, R = 2, T = 5, X = 3, and Y = 2:

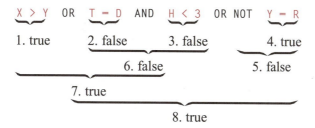

If you have trouble following the logic behind this evaluation, use this technique: Applying the rules of precedence, look, or scan, from *left to right* four different times. On the first scan, determine the truth value of each condition that contains a relational operator. On the second scan, moving from left to right again, evaluate all conditions that contain NOT operators. Y = R is true and NOT Y = R is false. On the third scan, moving again from left to right, evaluate all conditions that contain AND operators. T = D is false, as is H < 3; therefore, T = D and H < 3 is false. On the fourth scan, moving from left to right, evaluate all conditions that contain OR operators. The first OR yields a truth value of true. The second OR yields, for the entire condition, a final truth value of true.

The Effect of Parentheses in the Evaluation of Compound Conditions

Parentheses may be used to change the order of precedence. In QBasic, parentheses are normally used to avoid ambiguity and to group conditions with a desired logical operator. When there are parentheses in a compound condition, the PC evaluates that part of the compound condition within the parentheses first and then continues to evaluate the remaining compound condition according to the rules of precedence. For example, suppose variable C (below) has a value of 6, and D has a value of 3. Consider the following compound condition:

```
C = 7    AND   D < 4   OR   D <> 0
1. false       2. true       3. true
        4. false
                 5. true
```

Following the order of precedence for logical operators, the compound condition yields a truth value of true. If parentheses surround the latter two conditions in the compound condition, then the OR operator is evaluated before the AND condition, and the compound condition yields a truth value of false, as shown below.

```
C = 7   AND   (D < 4   OR   D <> 0)
4. false        1. true       2. true
                       3. true
        5. false
```

Parentheses may be used freely when the evaluation of a compound condition is in doubt. For example, if you wish to evaluate the compound condition

```
C > D AND S = 4 OR X < Y AND T = 5
```

you may incorporate it into a decision statement as it stands. You may also write it as

```
(C > D AND S = 4) OR (X < Y AND T = 5)
```

and feel more certain of the outcome of the decision statement.

5.7 DATA-VALIDATION TECHNIQUES

Up to this point, we have assumed the data used in the various programs is valid. However, a good program always checks the data to be sure it is accurate at initial input, especially when the INPUT statement is used. In information processing, Garbage In Garbage Out (GIGO, pronounced ge-go) is used to describe the generation of inaccurate information from the input of invalid data.

In this section, some definitions and techniques for testing data will be formalized so you will write programs that are characterized by Garbage Doesn't Get In (GDGI) rather than GIGO. **Data validation** is the process of ensuring that valid data is assigned to a program. The following four data-validation techniques are used:

1. The reasonableness check
2. The range check
3. The value or code check
4. The digit check

Before describing these data-validation techniques, we will examine the BEEP statement and its use in validation routines.

The BEEP Statement

When executed, the BEEP **statement** causes the PC's speaker to beep for a quarter of a second; several successive BEEP statements produce a constant beeping sound. For example, the following statement causes the PC to beep for one second.

```
BEEP : BEEP : BEEP : BEEP
```

The BEEP statement is often used in validation routines to alert the user that something is wrong. The general form of the BEEP statement is given in Table 5.5.

TABLE 5.5 - The BEEP Statement	
General Form:	BEEP
Purpose:	Causes the PC speaker to beep for a quarter of a second.
Examples:	BEEP
	BEEP : BEEP : BEEP : BEEP
Note:	The BEEP statement is represented by the ASCII decimal code of 7 as shown in Appendix D, Table D.1.

Additional examples of the BEEP statement are presented in the remainder of this section.

The Reasonableness Check

The **reasonableness check** ensures the legitimacy of data items that are entered from an external source, such as the keyboard. For example, a program may check a string variable to ensure a specific number of characters is assigned to it. Or a program may check a numeric variable representing a person's age to ensure that it is positive. If the data is not reasonable, the program can request the data be re-entered, or it can note the error in a report.

The following partial program requests that the user enter a five-character part number. If the string data item does not contain five characters, the user is requested to re-enter the part number.

```
1    INPUT "Five Character Part Number  =====> ", Part$
2    DO WHILE LEN(Part$) <> 5
3       BEEP : BEEP : BEEP : BEEP
4       PRINT "Part Number "; Part$; " in error, please re-enter"
5       INPUT "Five Character Part Number =====> ", Part$
6    LOOP

     [run]

     Five Character Part Number =====> 436A
     Part Number 436A in error, please re-enter
     Five Character Part Number =====> 436A2
```

invalid part number

Line 1 requests the user enter a part number. Line 2 uses the LEN function to test the length of the entry. If the length of Part$ is 5, control transfers to the line following the LOOP statement in line 6. If the length of Part$ is not 5, the PC enters the body of the Do-While loop. Within the loop, the speaker is beeped for one second; a diagnostic message is displayed, and the user is requested to re-enter the part number. The PC remains in the loop until a valid part number is entered or until the program is manually terminated.

If the LOCATE statement is used to specify exactly where the prompt message in the first INPUT statement is displayed on the screen, the following routine may be used in place of the previous one:

```
1    LOCATE 14, 10 : INPUT  "Five Character Part Number =====> ", Part$
2    DO WHILE LEN(Part$) <> 5
3       BEEP : BEEP : BEEP : BEEP
4       LOCATE 15, 10
5       PRINT "Part Number "; Part$; " in error, please re-enter"
6       LOCATE 14, 44 : PRINT SPC(10)
7       LOCATE 14, 44 : INPUT "", Part$
8       LOCATE 15, 10 : PRINT SPC(40)
9    LOOP
```

In this example, if an invalid entry is made, line 5 displays the diagnostic message, line 6 erases the previous user entry, and line 7 positions the cursor to the right of the prompt message displayed earlier by line 1. Following the next user entry, line 8 erases the diagnostic message displayed earlier by line 5.

The Range Check

The **range check** ensures data items entered from an external device fall within a range of valid values. A company may have a rule that all purchase order amounts must be less than $500.00. If so, then the program that processes the purchase order should verify that the amount is greater than zero and less than $500.00. This range check is shown in the partial program on the next page.

```
1   INPUT "Purchase Order Amount ($0.00 < Amount < $500.00) =====> ", Amt
2   DO WHILE Amt <= 0 OR Amt >= 500
3      BEEP : BEEP : BEEP : BEEP
4      PRINT "Amount"; Amt; "is in error, please re-enter"
5      INPUT "Purchase Order Amount ($0.00 < Amount < $500.00) =====> ", Amt
6   LOOP
```

out-of-range
purchase order
amount

```
[run]

Purchase Order Amount ($0.00 < Amount < $500.00) =====> 525.45
Amount 525.45 is in error, please re-enter
Purchase Order Amount ($0.00 < Amount < $500.00) =====> 425.45
```

The range check, defined by the condition in the DO WHILE statement in line 2, verifies that the value of the purchase order amount is positive and less than $500.00. If the purchase amount is within range, the Do-While loop is bypassed, and control transfers to the line following the LOOP statement in line 6. If the purchase amount is out of range, the PC enters the body of the loop. Line 3 beeps the speaker for one second. Line 4 displays a diagnostic message, and line 5 requests the user enter a valid amount. Note that the PC remains in the loop while invalid amounts are entered or until the program is manually terminated.

The Value or Code Check

The **value check** or **code check** ensures values or codes entered from an external source are valid. In a school registration system, for example, the value for class standing may be F for freshman, S for sophomore, J for junior, and G for senior, with all other entries considered invalid.

The following partial program requests that the user enter the class standing:

```
1   INPUT "Class Standing (F, S, J, OR G) =====> ", Class$
2   DO WHILE Class$ <> "F" AND Class$ <> "S" AND Class$ <> "J" AND Class$ <> "G"
3      BEEP : BEEP : BEEP : BEEP
4      PRINT "Class Standing "; Class$; " is invalid, please re-enter"
5      INPUT "Class Standing (F, S, J, OR G) =====> ", Class$
6   LOOP
```

```
[run]
```

invalid class-
standing code

```
Class Standing (F, S, J, OR G) =====> B
Class Standing B is invalid, please re-enter
Class Standing (F, S, J, OR G) =====> J
```

As illustrated in the compound condition in line 2, and because the values are seldom contiguous (meaning they seldom follow one another in the alphabet or, for that matter, in sequence), the logical operator AND and the relational operator <> are normally used to form the compound condition. If Class$ equals F, S, J, or G, control does not enter the Do-While loop; rather, it transfers to the line following the LOOP statement in line 6.

Any other value assigned to Class$ causes the PC to enter the Do-While loop. Line 3 beeps the speaker, line 4 displays the diagnostic message, and line 5 requests the user to enter a valid class standing.

The Digit Check

The **digit check** verifies the assignment of a special digit to a number. A company may use a procedure whereby all part numbers of items sold begin with the digit 2. The partial program below illustrates how the string function LEFT$ can be used to accept only part numbers that begin with a 2.

```
1   INPUT "Part Number =====> ", Part$
2   DO WHILE LEFT$(Part$, 1) <> "2"
3      BEEP : BEEP : BEEP : BEEP
4      PRINT "Part Number must begin with a 2, please re-enter"
5      INPUT "Part Number =====> ", Part$
6   LOOP
```

```
[run]
```

```
Part Number =====> 12389          invalid part
Part Number must begin with a 2, please re-enter    number
Part Number =====> 22389
```

In line 2, the expression LEFT$(Part$, 1) is equal to the first character of Part$. If the first character in Part$ is a 2, control bypasses the Do-While loop. If the first character is not a 2, control enters the Do-While loop. The PC beeps the speaker and displays a diagnostic message, and the user is requested to re-enter the part number.

5.8 THE SELECT CASE STATEMENT AND MENU-DRIVEN PROGRAMS

The SELECT CASE **statement** is used to implement the Case structure. The Case structure is an extension of the If-Then-Else structure. It is illustrated in Figure 5.21 on the next page and described in Appendix A, Section A.3.

Figure 5.21 shows two methods for implementing a Case structure, which determines a letter grade (Letter.Grade$) from a grade point average (GPA) using the following grading scale:

Grade Point Average	Letter Grade
GPA $\geq$ 90	A
80 $\leq$ GPA < 90	B
70 $\leq$ GPA < 80	C
60 $\leq$ GPA < 70	D
0 $\leq$ GPA < 60	F
GPA < 0	Error

In Method 1 of Figure 5.21, an IF statement with several ELSEIF clauses is used to implement the Case structure. Each ELSEIF is followed by a condition and a THEN clause. Only one of the THEN clauses or the ELSE clause, just before the END IF, is executed for each pass.

For example, if the variable GPA is equal to 74, then the condition in the second ELSEIF clause is true, and Letter.Grade$ is assigned the value C. After executing the THEN clause, the PC transfers control to the statement below the END IF. It does not test any of the conditions below the first condition that is true.

In Method 2 of Figure 5.21, the SELECT CASE statement is used to implement the grading scale. Notice how much easier it is to read through the SELECT CASE than the IF statement in Method 1. When the PC executes the SELECT CASE statement, it compares the variable GPA, which follows the keywords SELECT CASE to the expressions following the keyword CASE in each CASE clause. A CASE clause is also called a case. It begins the comparison with the first case and continues through the remaining ones until it finds a match. When a match is found, the range of statements immediately following the keyword CASE is executed. Following execution of the case, control transfers to the statement following the END SELECT. The PC does not search for additional matches in the remaining cases.

▌FIGURE 5.21
Implementation of a Case structure.

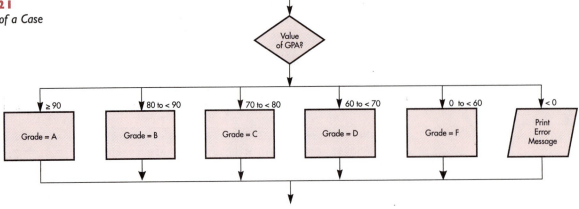

Method 1: Using an `IF` statement with an `ELSEIF` clause.

```
IF GPA >= 90 THEN
    Letter.Grade$ = "A"
ELSEIF GPA >= 80 THEN
    Letter.Grade$ = "B"
ELSEIF GPA >= 70 THEN
    Letter.Grade$ = "C"
ELSEIF GPA >= 60 THEN
    Letter.Grade$ = "D"
ELSEIF GPA >= 0 THEN
    Letter.Grade$ = "F"
ELSE
    PRINT "Negative grade average"
END IF
```

Method 2: Using a `SELECT CASE` statement.

```
SELECT CASE GPA
    CASE IS >= 90
        Letter.Grade$ = "A"
    CASE IS >= 80
        Letter.Grade$ = "B"
    CASE IS >= 70
        Letter.Grade$ = "C"
    CASE IS >= 60
        Letter.Grade$ = "D"
    CASE IS >= 0
        Letter.Grade$ = "F"
    CASE ELSE
        PRINT "Negative grade average"
END SELECT
```

For example, if GPA is equal to 89.6, then the PC finds a match in the second case. Therefore, it assigns Letter.Grade$ the value B and passes control to the statement following the `END SELECT`. If GPA equals a negative value, then no match is found, and the `PRINT` statement following the `CASE ELSE` is executed.

The general form of the `SELECT CASE` statement is given in Table 5.6.

TABLE 5.6 - The SELECT CASE Statement

General Form:
```
SELECT CASE testexpression
   CASE matchexpression
      [range of statements]
         .
         .
         .
   CASE ELSE
      [range of statements]
END SELECT
```
where **testexpression** is a string or numeric variable or expression that is matched with the matchexpression in the corresponding CASE clauses; and **matchexpression** is a numeric or string expression or a range of numeric or string expressions of the following form:
1. expression, expression, . . . , expression
2. expression TO expression
3. IS relational expression where relation is <, >, >=, <=, =, or <>.

Purpose: Causes execution of the range of statements that follow the CASE clause whose matchexpression matches the testexpression. If there is no match, then the range of statements in the CASE ELSE clause is executed. Following the execution of a range of statements, control passes to the statement following the END SELECT.

Examples: (Also see Table 5.7 for additional examples of the matchexpression in CASE clauses.)

```
1. SELECT CASE Age                     2. SELECT CASE Code$
      CASE IS  = 0                           CASE "A", "B", "D"
         CALL B200.Baby                         Interest = .015
      CASE IS  < 2                              Time = 24
         CALL B210.Toddler                   CASE "C", "G" TO "K"
      CASE IS  < 14                             Interest = .014
         CALL B220.Youngster                    Time = 36
      CASE IS  < 21                          CASE "L" TO "Z"
         CALL B230.Young.Adult                  Interest = .013
      CASE IS  >= 21                            Time = 48
         CALL B240.Adult                     CASE "E", "F"
      CASE ELSE                                 Interest = .012
         PRINT "INVALID AGE"                    Time = 60
   END SELECT                           END SELECT
```

Note: If the CASE ELSE clause is not included, as in Example 2, in a SELECT CASE statement, then it is the programmer's responsibility to ensure the testexpression falls within the range of one of the matchexpressions found in the accompanying CASE clauses, otherwise the diagnostic message CASE ELSE expected displays in a dialog box when a match is not found.

As indicated in Table 5.6, with the SELECT CASE you place the variable or expression you want to test after the keywords SELECT CASE. Next, you assign the group of values that make each alternative case true after the keyword CASE. Each case contains the range of statements to execute, and you may have as many cases as required. After the last case, end the SELECT CASE with an END SELECT.

Example 1 in Table 5.6 tests the variable Age against the matchexpressions, beginning with the first CASE clause and continuing downward until a match is found. If Age is equal to 0, then a match occurs on the first case and control transfers to the subroutine B200.Baby. The keyword IS is required when a relational operator, such as =, is used. When the RETURN statement in B200.Baby executes, control returns to the statement following the END SELECT. If Age is less than 2, control transfers to B210.Toddler. If Age is greater than or equal to 2, but less than 14, control transfers to the subroutine B220.Youngster. If Age is greater than or equal to 14, but less than 21, control transfers to the subroutine B230.Young.Adult. If Age is greater than or equal to 21, control transfers to the subroutine B240.Adult. If Age is less than 0, the CASE ELSE is executed, and the message INVALID AGE displays. Note that the CASE ELSE clause is the last one in the list of cases. The placement of the CASE ELSE clause can be stated as follows:

SELECT CASE RULE 1   *If a* CASE ELSE *clause is included, then it must be the last case.*

Note that in Example 1, if Age is equal to a value of 0, then all cases are true. However, only the range of statements that correspond to the first match is executed. This leads to the following rule:

SELECT CASE RULE 2   *Only the first matched case in a* SELECT CASE *is executed.*

In Example 2 of Table 5.6 on the previous page, the variable Code$ is matched against several different categories of letters. The first case is executed if Code$ is equal to the value A, B, or D. The commas in a list of expressions following the keyword CASE are mandatory. If Code$ is equal to the value C or the letters G through K, then the second case is executed. The keyword TO is required when specifying a range, such as "G" TO "K". If Code$ is equal to the values L through Z, the third case is executed. Finally, if Code$ is equal to the value E or F, then the last case is executed.

Note in this example that there is no CASE ELSE. The assumptions here are that Code$ contains no lowercase letters between A to Z; Code$ is validated prior to the execution of the SELECT CASE, and that Code$ is equal to an uppercase letter between A and Z. Hence, the CASE ELSE is not required. However, if you don't validate the expression, then always include a CASE ELSE. This leads to the following rule:

SELECT CASE RULE 3   *If there is no match and no* CASE ELSE, *then QBasic halts execution of the program and displays a diagnostic message in a dialog box.*

When specifying a range in a CASE clause, make sure the smaller value is listed first. For example, CASE 3 TO -1 is invalid. It should be stated as CASE -1 TO 3. The same applies to string values. Whereas, CASE "Greg" TO "Jeff" is valid, CASE "Jeff" TO "Greg" is not.

Valid Match Expressions

As indicated in Table 5.6, there are several ways to construct valid match expressions. Consider the match expressions in Table 5.7.

In Example 1 in Table 5.7, the match expression is a list made up of the letters F to H, the letter S, and the value of the variable Emp.Code$. In Example 2, the match expression includes Emp.Salary and the expression Max.Salary – 2000. As indicated earlier, if a relational operator is used, then the keyword IS is required. The second value in the list of Example 2 shows that expressions with arithmetic operators are allowed. The third example includes a list with the keywords IS and TO.

TABLE 5.7 - Valid Match Expressions	
EXAMPLE	**MATCH EXPRESSION**
1	CASE "F" TO "H", "S", Emp.Code$
2	CASE IS = Emp.Salary, IS = Max.Salary - 2000
3	CASE IS < 12, 20 TO 30, 48.6, IS > 100

It is easy to see why programmers use the SELECT CASE statement. A SELECT CASE statement is used when the design of a program includes a Case structure. Furthermore, nesting of Case structures is permitted as with the other structures. The following Programming Case Study illustrates a major use of the SELECT CASE statement — menu-driven programs.

PROGRAMMING CASE STUDY 8 – A Menu-Driven Program

It is common for programs to have multiple functions, or sets of logic. A menu, a list of the functions that a program can perform, often is used to guide a user through a multifunction program. Programs that display a menu of functions are menu-driven programs. Such a program displays a menu like the one illustrated on the screen layout form in Figure 5.22. The user can then choose the desired function from the list by entering a corresponding code. After the request is satisfied, the program again displays the menu. As illustrated in Figure 5.22, one of the codes (in this case 7) terminates execution of the program.

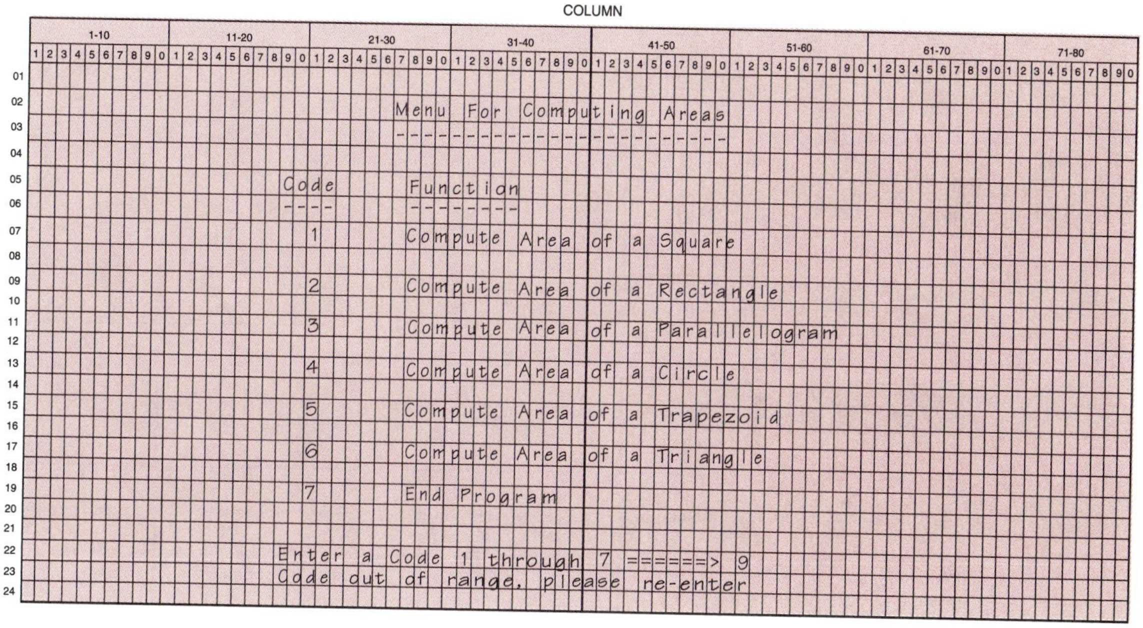

FIGURE 5.22

A menu of program functions designed on a screen layout form.

The following problem uses the menu illustrated in Figure 5.22.

Problem: A menu-driven program is to compute the area of a square, rectangle, parallelogram, circle, trapezoid, and triangle. The program should display the menu shown in Figure 5.22. After a code is entered, the program must do a range check to ensure that the code corresponds to one of the menu functions. After the selection of the proper function, the program should prompt the user for the necessary data, compute the area, and display it accordingly. The displayed results are to remain on the screen until the Enter key on the keyboard is pressed. After that, the program should display the menu again.

1. Area of a square: A = S * S where S is the length of a side of the square.
2. Area of a rectangle: A = L * W where L is the length and W is the width of the rectangle.
3. Area of a parallelogram: A = B * H where B is the length of the base and H is the height of the parallelogram.
4. Area of a circle: A = 3.141598 * R * R where R is the radius of the circle.
5. Area of a trapezoid: A = H * (B1 + B2) / 2 where H is the height, B1 is the length of the primary base, and B2 is the length of the secondary base of the trapezoid.
6. Area of a triangle: A = B * H / 2 where B is the base and H is the height of the triangle.

The Freeze Screen module at the fourth level of the top-down chart in Figure 5.23 has more than one superior subroutine. Recall from Chapter 3 that we identify lower level modules with more than one superior by darkening the upper right-hand corner of the process symbol. Furthermore, we assign a module with more than one superior the letter M for multiple superiors. The letter M is then followed by a level number that corresponds to its level in the top-down chart. At coding time, modules that begin with the letter M physically end up at the bottom of the list of subroutines.

FIGURE 5.23

A top-down chart for the solution to Programming Case Study 8.

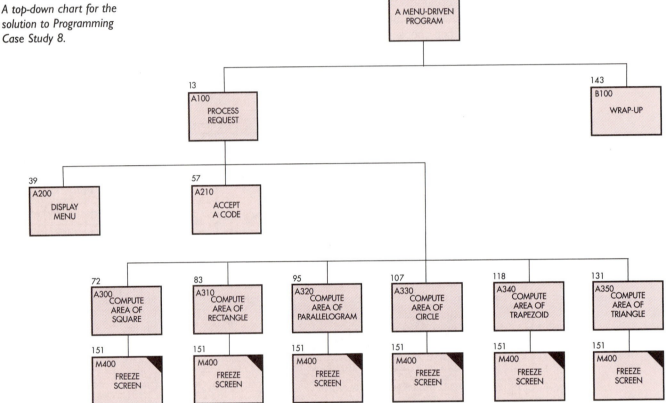

The general flowchart of the Process Request module in Figure 5.24 illustrates the six independent functions of the solution for Programming Case Study 8, Program 5.2. Each module reference includes its own input, processing, and output statements.

Program Tasks

The following program tasks correspond to the top-down chart in Figure 5.23:

1. A100.Process.Request
   a. Display the menu shown in Figure 5.22 using the LOCATE and PRINT statements.
   b. Accept a value for Code.
      (1) Request the user to enter a code. Assign the code to the integer variable Code%. (Make the variable an integer type to ensure that the code entered is an integer. If a decimal number is entered, the PC will only assign Code% the whole number portion of the number.)
      (2) Use a Do-While loop to validate the code. If the code is invalid, beep the speaker, display an appropriate diagnostic message, and again ask the user to select a function.

FIGURE 5.24

A flowchart for Process Request module of the solution to Programming Case Study 8, Program 5.2.

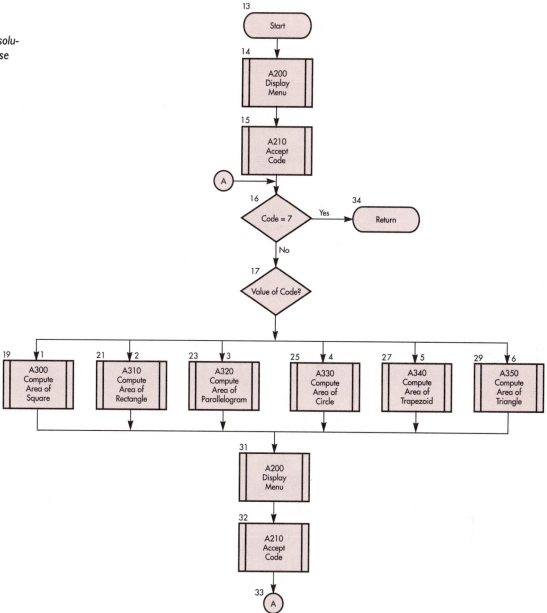

(3) When a valid code is entered, clear the screen, and return control to A100.Process.Request.

c. Establish a Do-While loop that executes while Code does not equal 7. Within the loop, use a SELECT CASE statement to transfer control to the subroutine that carries out the requested function. In this case, implement each of the 6 different area computations in separate subroutines. Within each subroutine do the following:

(1) Request the data using one or more INPUT statements.

(2) Compute the area. For efficiency, multiply by 0.5, rather than divide by 2, in the formulas that determine the areas of a trapezoid and triangle.

(3) Display the results.

(4) Prior to returning to A100.Process.Request, call a subroutine (M400.Freeze.Screen) to keep the information on the screen. Beep the speaker to alert the user to press the Enter key. Use the following prompt message to redisplay the menu:

```
Press Enter Key to Return to Menu ...
```

d. Display the menu as described earlier in 1a and accept a value for Code.

2. B100.Wrap.Up
    a. Clear the screen.
    b. Display a pleasant message prior to terminating the program.

Program Solution

Figure 5.25 presents Program 5.2, the solution to Programming Case Study 8, which corresponds to the preceding tasks and to the top-down chart illustrated in Figure 5.23.

FIGURE 5.25

Program 5.2, the solution to Programming Case Study 8.

```
 1  ' Program 5.2
 2  ' A Menu-Driven Program
 3  ' ****************************************************************
 4  ' *                        Main Program                        *
 5  ' ****************************************************************
 6  GOSUB A100.Process.Request
 7  GOSUB B100.Wrap.Up
 8  END
 9
10  ' ****************************************************************
11  ' *                     Process a Request                      *
12  ' ****************************************************************
13  A100.Process.Request:
14     GOSUB A200.Display.Menu
15     GOSUB A210.Accept.Code
16     DO WHILE Code% <> 7
17        SELECT CASE Code%
18           CASE 1
19              GOSUB A300.Area.Square
20           CASE 2
21              GOSUB A310.Area.Rectangle
22           CASE 3
23              GOSUB A320.Area.Parallelogram
24           CASE 4
25              GOSUB A330.Area.Circle
26           CASE 5
27              GOSUB A340.Area.Trapezoid
28           CASE 6
29              GOSUB A350.Area.Triangle
30        END SELECT
31        GOSUB A200.Display.Menu
32        GOSUB A210.Accept.Code
33     LOOP
34  RETURN
35
36  ' ****************************************************************
37  ' *                       Display Menu                         *
38  ' ****************************************************************
39  A200.Display.Menu:
40     CLS  ' Clear Screen
41     LOCATE 2, 27: PRINT "Menu For Computing Areas"
42     LOCATE 3, 27: PRINT "------------------------"
43     LOCATE 5, 19: PRINT "Code     Function"
44     LOCATE 6, 19: PRINT "----     --------"
45     LOCATE 7, 19: PRINT "  1      Compute Area of a Square"
46     LOCATE 9, 19: PRINT "  2      Compute Area of a Rectangle"
47     LOCATE 11, 19: PRINT "  3       Compute Area of a Parallelogram"
48     LOCATE 13, 19: PRINT "  4      Compute Area of a Circle"
49     LOCATE 15, 19: PRINT "  5      Compute Area of a Trapezoid"
50     LOCATE 17, 19: PRINT "  6      Compute Area of a Triangle"
51     LOCATE 19, 19: PRINT "  7      End Program"
52  RETURN
53
```

```
54   ' ***********************************************************
55   ' *                    Accept a Code                      *
56   ' ***********************************************************
57   A210.Accept.Code:
58      LOCATE 22, 19: INPUT "Enter a Code 1 through 7 ======> ", Code%
59      DO WHILE Code% < 1 OR Code% > 7
60         BEEP: BEEP: BEEP: BEEP
61         LOCATE 23, 19: PRINT "Code out of range, please reenter"
62         LOCATE 22, 52: PRINT SPC(10);
63         LOCATE 22, 52: INPUT "", Code%
64         LOCATE 23, 19: PRINT SPC(40);
65      LOOP
66      CLS
67   RETURN
68
69   ' ***********************************************************
70   ' *              Compute Area of a Square                 *
71   ' ***********************************************************
72   A300.Area.Square:
73      LOCATE 5, 24: PRINT "Compute Area of a Square"
74      LOCATE 8, 24: INPUT "Length of Side of Square ====> ", Side
75      Area = Side * Side
76      LOCATE 10, 24: PRINT "Area of Square ==============>"; Area; "Square Units"
77      GOSUB M400.Freeze.Screen
78   RETURN
79
80   ' ***********************************************************
81   ' *             Compute Area of a Rectangle               *
82   ' ***********************************************************
83   A310.Area.Rectangle:
84      LOCATE 5, 24: PRINT "Compute Area of a Rectangle"
85      LOCATE 8, 24: INPUT "Length of Rectangle =====> ", Length
86      LOCATE 10, 24: INPUT "Width of Rectangle ======> ", Wide
87      Area = Length * Wide
88      LOCATE 12, 24: PRINT "Area of Rectangle =======>"; Area; "Square Units"
89      GOSUB M400.Freeze.Screen
90   RETURN
91
92   ' ***********************************************************
93   ' *            Compute Area of a Parallelogram            *
94   ' ***********************************************************
95   A320.Area.Parallelogram:
96      LOCATE 5, 24: PRINT "Compute Area of Parallelogram"
97      LOCATE 8, 24: INPUT "Base of Parallelogram =====> ", Base1
98      LOCATE 10, 24: INPUT "Height of Parallelogram ===> ", Height
99      Area = Base1 * Height
100     LOCATE 12, 24: PRINT "Area of Parallelogram =====>"; Area; "Square Units"
101     GOSUB M400.Freeze.Screen
102  RETURN
103
104  ' ***********************************************************
105  ' *              Compute Area of a Circle                 *
106  ' ***********************************************************
107  A330.Area.Circle:
108     LOCATE 5, 24: PRINT "Compute Area of a Circle"
109     LOCATE 8, 24: INPUT "Radius of Circle =====> ", Radius
110     Area = 3.141598 * Radius * Radius
111     LOCATE 10, 24: PRINT "Area of Circle =======>"; Area; "Square Units"
112     GOSUB M400.Freeze.Screen
113  RETURN
114
```

(continued)

```
115  ' ************************************************************
116  ' *              Compute Area of a Trapezoid              *
117  ' ************************************************************
118  A340.Area.Trapezoid:
119     LOCATE 5, 24: PRINT "Compute Area of a Trapezoid"
120     LOCATE 8, 24: INPUT "Primary Base of Trapezoid =====> ", Base1
121     LOCATE 10, 24: INPUT "Secondary Base of Trapezoid ===> ", Base2
122     LOCATE 12, 24: INPUT "Height of Trapezoid ===========> ", Height
123     Area = Height * (Base1 + Base2) * .5
124     LOCATE 14, 24: PRINT "Area of Trapezoid ============>"; Area; "Square Units"
125     GOSUB M400.Freeze.Screen
126  RETURN
127
128  ' ************************************************************
129  ' *               Compute Area of a Triangle              *
130  ' ************************************************************
131  A350.Area.Triangle:
132     LOCATE 5, 24: PRINT "Compute Area of a Triangle"
133     LOCATE 8, 24: INPUT "Base of Triangle =====> ", Base1
134     LOCATE 10, 24: INPUT "Height of Triangle ===> ", Height
135     Area = Base1 * Height * .5
136     LOCATE 12, 24: PRINT "Area of Triangle =====>"; Area; "Square Units"
137     GOSUB M400.Freeze.Screen
138  RETURN
139
140  ' ************************************************************
141  ' *                        Wrap-Up                        *
142  ' ************************************************************
143  B100.Wrap.Up:
144     CLS
145     LOCATE 12, 24: PRINT "End of Program - Have a Nice Day!"
146  RETURN
147
148  ' ************************************************************
149  ' *                     Freeze Screen                     *
150  ' ************************************************************
151  M400.Freeze.Screen:
152     BEEP: BEEP: BEEP: BEEP
153     LOCATE 20, 24
154     INPUT "Press Enter Key to Return to Menu....", Control$
155  RETURN
156
157  ' ******************** End of Program ********************
```

[run]

When Program 5.2 is first executed, line 6 calls A100.Process.Request. In this subroutine, line 14 calls A200.Display.Menu, and line 15 calls A210.Accept.Code.

In A200.Display.Menu, line 40 clears the screen, and lines 41 through 51 display the menu illustrated in Figure 5.26. The last line of Figure 5.26 is displayed by line 58 in A210.Accept.Code. Assume code 3 is selected, as shown in the lower right corner of Figure 5.26.

When the Enter key is pressed, lines 59 through 65 validate the code. After a valid code is entered, line 66 again clears the screen before control is returned to the calling subroutine A100.Process.Request.

FIGURE 5.26

The menu displayed by A200.Display.Menu and A210.Accept.Code subroutines in Program 5.2.

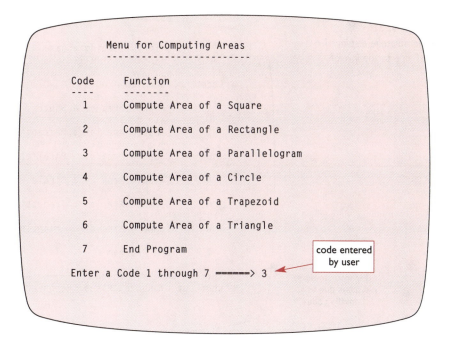

```
                    Menu for Computing Areas
                    -------------------------

        Code       Function
        ----       --------
          1        Compute Area of a Square

          2        Compute Area of a Rectangle

          3        Compute Area of a Parallelogram

          4        Compute Area of a Circle

          5        Compute Area of a Trapezoid

          6        Compute Area of a Triangle

          7        End Program

        Enter a Code 1 through 7 =======> 3
```

code entered by user

Because Code is not equal to 7, the DO WHILE statement in line 16 allows control to pass to the SELECT CASE statement in line 17. With Code equal to 3, control passes to A320.Area.Parallelogram (lines 95 through 102). Figure 5.27, for example, shows a base of 10 units and a height of 4 units to have been entered, which results in an area of 40 square units for the parallelogram. The subroutine (M400.Freeze.Screen) called by line 101 allows the user to view the results on the screen for as long as desired. Note that the speaker is beeped four times. Four beeps produces a constant beep that lasts for approximately one second. After the Enter key is pressed in response to line 154, the PC returns control to line 102, which then returns control to line 31. Line 31 redisplays the menu shown in Figure 5.26.

FIGURE 5.27

The display from the selection of code 3, Compute Area of a Parallelogram.

```
        Compute Area of a Parallelogram

        Base of Parallelogram =====> 10

        Height of Parallelogram ---> 4

        Area of Parallelogram =====> 40 Square Units

        Press Enter Key to Return to Menu ...
```

Figure 5.28 on the next page shows an out-of-range code which causes the PC to beep before displaying a diagnostic message. The beeping and display of the diagnostic message are due to lines 60 and 61. Line 62 is used to refresh that part of the screen where the incorrect code is displayed so that another code may be entered. After a valid code is entered in response to line 63, the screen is again cleared by line 66, and control returns to A100.Process.Request.

❙FIGURE 5.28

Diagnostic message displayed by line 61 due to the invalid code 9.

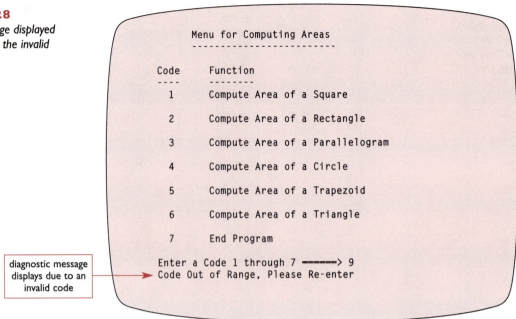

```
              Menu for Computing Areas
              --------------------------

      Code      Function
      ----      --------
        1       Compute Area of a Square

        2       Compute Area of a Rectangle

        3       Compute Area of a Parallelogram

        4       Compute Area of a Circle

        5       Compute Area of a Trapezoid

        6       Compute Area of a Triangle

        7       End Program

      Enter a Code 1 through 7 =======> 9
      Code Out of Range, Please Re-enter
```

diagnostic message
displays due to an
invalid code

If the user enters a code of 5 to compute the area of a trapezoid with a primary base of 18, secondary base of 9 and a height of 5, the display shown in Figure 5.29 occurs.

❙FIGURE 5.29

The display from the selection of code 5, Compute Area of a Trapezoid.

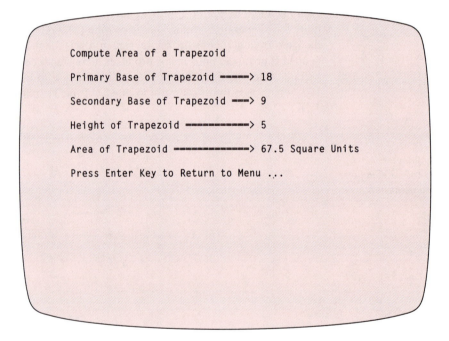

```
      Compute Area of a Trapezoid

      Primary Base of Trapezoid =======> 18

      Secondary Base of Trapezoid ====> 9

      Height of Trapezoid ============> 5

      Area of Trapezoid ==============> 67.5 Square Units

      Press Enter Key to Return to Menu ...
```

To terminate execution of Program 5.2, enter a code of 7. Line 7 in the Main Program calls B100.Wrap.Up, which displays an appropriate message before line 8 terminates execution of the program.

The preceding problem could have been solved by replacing the SELECT CASE statement with an IF statement containing ELSEIF clauses. Usually, however, when a series of three or more tests is to be performed in succession, the SELECT CASE statement is the better alternative for purposes of readability.

5.9 What You Should Know

1. Structured programming is a methodology according to which all program logic can be constructed from a combination of the following three basic control structures: Sequence, Selection (If-Then-Else or Case), and Repetition (Do-While or Do-Until).

2. The If-Then-Else structure is used in program design to specify a selection between two alternative paths.

3. The Case structure is an extension of the If-Then-Else structure, in which the choice includes more than two alternatives.

4. Most computer professionals agree the decision statement to terminate a loop should be located at the top or bottom of the loop.

5. A loop that has the termination decision statement at the top is called a Do-While structure. A loop that has the termination decision statement at the bottom is called a Do-Until structure.

6. Top-down programming and structured programming are not the same. Top-down programming describes a strategy for solving large, complex problems. To solve a problem top-down, you divide and conquer. Structured programming is used within modules to generate disciplined code. We improve the clarity and reduce the complexity by using only the five control structures — Sequence, If-Then-Else, Case, Do-While, and Do-Until.

7. The IF statement is used to implement the If-Then-Else structure.

8. The IF statement has two general forms — single line and block. A single-line IF statement must fit on one line and the END IF statement is not required. The block IF statement can include multiple lines in each clause and must end with an END IF statement.

9. In an IF statement, if the condition is true, the PC executes the THEN clause, and control passes to the statement following the corresponding END IF. If the condition is false, the PC executes the ELSE clause and control passes to the statement following the corresponding END IF. If the condition is false and no ELSE clause is included in the IF statement, then the PC passes control to the statement following the corresponding END IF.

10. If the condition in an IF statement contains two numeric expressions, then the comparison is based on the algebraic values of the two expressions.

11. If the condition in an IF statement contains two string expressions, the PC evaluates the two strings from left to right, one character at a time. As soon as one character in one expression is different from the corresponding character in the other expression, the PC decides which expression has a lower value.

12. QBasic uses the ASCII code. It is the collating sequence of the ASCII code that determines the position of a character in relation to other characters.

13. A null THEN or null ELSE clause in an IF statement is valid.

14. A counter is an accumulator used to count the number of times some action or event is performed.

15. A running total is an accumulator used to sum the different values a variable is assigned during the execution of a program.

16. All accumulators should be initialized to some value before they are used in a statement that tests the accumulator or adds to its value.

17. Depending on the problem to be solved, an If-Then-Else structure can have alternative processing for both the true case and the false case, alternative processing only for the true case, or alternative processing only for the false case.

18. Negating the relation in the condition of an If-Then-Else structure can sometimes simplify and clarify the IF statement.

19. A nested If-Then-Else structure is one in which the action to be taken for the true or false case includes yet another If-Then-Else structure.

20. In a nested block IF statement, each IF must have a corresponding END IF statement.

21. The truth value of the relational expression in a condition is complemented by the logical operator NOT.

22. The logical operator NOT requires the relational expression be false for the condition to be true. If the relational expression is true, then the condition is false.

23. When two or more conditions are combined by the logical operators AND, OR, XOR, EQV, or IMP, the expression is a compound condition.

24. The logical operator AND requires both conditions be true for the compound condition to be true.

25. The logical operator OR requires only one of the two conditions be true for the compound condition to be true. If both conditions are true, the compound condition is also true.

26. The XOR (exclusive OR) operator requires one of the two conditions be true for the compound condition to be true. If both are true, the condition is false.

27. The EQV (equivalence) operator requires both conditions be true or both conditions be false for the compound condition to be true.

28. The IMP (implication) operator requires both conditions be true or both conditions be false, or the first condition be false and the second true for the compound condition to be true.

29. Unless parentheses dictate otherwise, reading from left to right, conditions containing arithmetic operators are evaluated first, then those containing relational operators, then those containing NOT operators, then those containing AND operators, then those conditions containing OR and XOR operators, then those containing EQV operators, and finally those containing IMP operators.

30. The BEEP statement causes the PC's speaker to beep for one-fourth of one second.

31. Data validation is a technique used to ensure valid data is assigned to a program. Data can be validated, or checked, for reasonableness, range, value or code, and digit.

32. A reasonableness check is a technique used to ensure data items entered from an external device, such as the keyboard, are of reasonable and valid magnitudes.

33. A range check is a technique used to ensure data items entered from an external device fall within a range of valid values.

34. A value check or code check is a technique used to ensure values entered from an external source are valid.

35. A check digit is a technique used to verify the assignment of a special digit to a number. A check digit is an addition to a number that requires validation; this addition can be used to verify the rest of the digits.

36. Use the SELECT CASE statement to implement a case structure.

37. The SELECT CASE statement includes a test expression. When the test expression is evaluated, the PC attempts to match it to the match expressions in the corresponding CASE clauses. If a match is found, the range of statements for that CASE clause is executed. If a match is not found, the statements contained in the CASE ELSE are executed. Following the execution of one of the cases, control transfers to the statement following the corresponding END SELECT.

38. Match expressions can include a list of values separated by commas, a range of values using the keyword TO, or a relational operator preceded by the keyword IS and followed by a value.

39. A menu is a list of the functions that a program can perform. When a menu-driven program is first executed, it displays a menu of functions. Each time a requested function is satisfied, the program redisplays the menu.

5.10 Test Your QBasic Skills (Even-numbered answers are in Appendix E)

1. Consider the following valid programs. Without using a computer, determine what is displayed if each is executed.

a.
```
' Exercise 5.1a
' ****** Main Program *******
GOSUB A100.Initialization
GOSUB B100.Process.File
GOSUB C100.Wrap.Up
END


' ***** Initialization *****
A100.Initialization:
   Count1 = 0
   Count2 = 0
RETURN


' ****** Process File ******
B100.Process.File:
   READ Age, Weight
   DO WHILE Age >= 0
      Count1 = Count1 + 1
      IF Age >= 21 AND Weight >= 130 THEN
         Count2 = Count2 + 1
      END IF
      READ Age, Weight
   LOOP
RETURN


' ******** Wrap-Up *********
C100.Wrap.Up:
   PRINT "Number of People Evaluated:"; Count1
   PRINT "Number of Adults Weighing"
   PRINT "130 Pounds or more:"; Count2
RETURN


' **** Data Follows ****
DATA 10, 125, 24, 130, 21, 150, 30, 120
DATA 51, 225, 47, 175, 18, 130, -1, 0
' **** End of Program ******
```

b.
```
' Exercise 5.1b
A = 1  : PRINT A
DO WHILE A > 0
   IF A - 2 < 0 THEN
      A = 2
   ELSE
      GOSUB Sub1
   END IF
   PRINT A
LOOP
END

' *** Subroutine 1 ***
Sub1:
   IF A - 2 = 0 THEN
      A = 3
   ELSE
      GOSUB Sub2
   END IF
RETURN


' *** Subroutine 2 ***
Sub2:
   IF A - 4 < 0 THEN
      A = 4
   ELSE
      GOSUB Sub3
   END IF
RETURN


' *** Subroutine 3 ***
Sub3:
   IF A - 4 = 0 THEN
      A = 5
   ELSE
      A = 1
   END IF
RETURN
' ** End of Program **
```

c. Assume I is assigned the values 1, 4, 7, 2, 21, 20, –99.

```
' Exercise 5.1c
INPUT I
DO WHILE I <> -99
   SELECT CASE I
      CASE 1, 4, 7
         PRINT "Case 1"
      CASE IS < 8
         PRINT "Case 2"
      CASE 14 To 21
         PRINT "Case 3"
      CASE ELSE
         PRINT "Case 4"
   END SELECT
   INPUT I
LOOP
END
```

d.
```
' Exercise 5.1d
READ X, Y
DO WHILE X > 0
   IF X = Y AND Y >= 10 THEN
      PRINT "Both Conditions are True"
   END IF
   IF X = Y XOR Y >= 10 THEN
      PRINT "Only 1 of the 2 is True"
   END IF
   IF NOT X = Y AND NOT Y >= 10 THEN
      PRINT "Neither Condition is True"
   END IF
   READ X, Y
LOOP
PRINT "End of Job"
'********* Data Follows ********
DATA 3, 5, 8, 10, 15, 15, 4, 4, -1, 0
END
```

2. Write a QBasic statement that will initialize X to 0 and another that will initialize T to 10. Also, write additional QBasic statements that will consecutively increment these variables by the following:

   a. 1   b. 7   c. 2   d. double each value   e. minus 1

3. Given the following:
   Employee number E = 500
   Salary S = 700
   Job code J = 1
   Tax T = 60
   Insurance deduction I = 40

   Determine the truth value of the following compound conditions:

   a. E < 400 OR J = 1
   c. S - T = 640 AND J = 1
   e. NOT J < 0
   g. NOT (J = 1 OR T = 60)
   i. I <> 40 EQV S > 500
   k. S < 300 AND I < 50 OR J = 1
   m. NOT (NOT J = 1)

   b. S = 700 AND T = 500
   d. T + I = S - 500 OR J = 0
   f. NOT S > 500 AND NOT T > 80
   h. J = 1 XOR E >= 500
   j. S = 700 IMP T = 60
   l. S < 300 AND (I < 50 OR J = 1)

4. Determine the value of Q that will cause the condition in the IF statements below to be true:

   a. ```
      IF Q > 8 OR Q = 3 THEN
            Z = Z / 10
      END IF
      ```

   b. ```
      IF Q + 10 >= 7 AND NOT Q < 0 THEN
            PRINT "The answer is"; A
      END IF
      ```

   c. ```
      IF Q / 3 < 9 THEN
            Count = Count + 1
      END IF
      ```

   d. ```
      IF Q <> 3 XOR Q = 3 THEN
            Sum = Sum + Amt
      END IF
      ```

5. Write a series of statements to perform the logic indicated below:

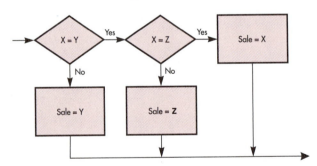

6. Construct partial programs for each of the structures found below:

   a.   b.

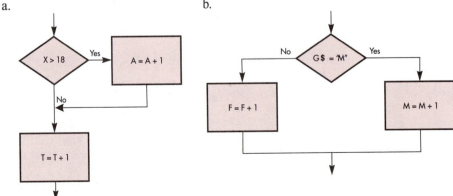

7. Construct partial programs for each of the logic structures found below:

a.

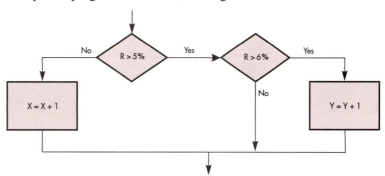

b.

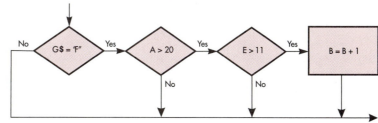

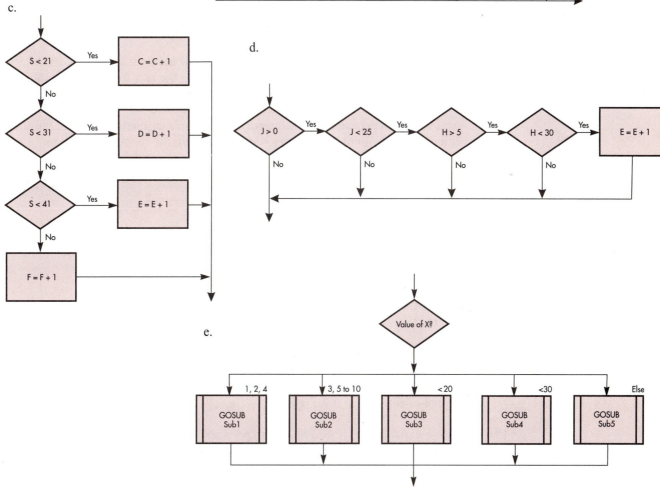

c.

d.

e.

8. Construct a partial flowchart for each of the following:

a. `NOT(S = Q) AND (X > 1 OR C < 3)`

b. `(K = 9 AND Q = 2) OR NOT Z = 3 OR T = 0`

9. Given the conditions, S = 0, Y = 4, B = 7, T = 8, and X = 3, determine the action taken for each of the following:

a. ```
IF S > 0 THEN
    GOSUB B200.Compute
END IF
```

b. ```
IF B = 4 OR T > 7 THEN
    IF X > 1 THEN
        GOSUB B200.Compute
    END IF
END IF
```

c. ```
IF X = 3 OR T > 2 THEN
    IF Y > 7 THEN
        GOSUB B200.Compute
    END IF
END IF
```

d. ```
IF X + 2 < 5 THEN
    IF B < Y + X THEN
        GOSUB B200.Compute
    END IF
END IF
```

e. ```
IF B <> 7 AND NOT(T = 6) THEN
    GOSUB B200.Compute
END IF
```

f. ```
IF T > X OR B <> S THEN
    GOSUB B200.Compute
END IF
```

10. Write a partial program for each of the following situations that requests the user to enter a value. After the value is entered, validate the value using a Do-While loop. If the value is invalid, display an appropriate diagnostic message and request the entry be re-entered.
    a. Request a percentage (Percent). If the percentage is negative or greater than 25, request the user to re-enter the value.
    b. Request a balance (Balance). Check if the balance is between $550.99 and $765.50 inclusive. If the balance is outside the range, request the user to re-enter the value.
    c. Request a customer code (Code$). Check to ensure that the code is an A, D, E, or F. If the code is invalid, request the user to re-enter the code.
    d. Request a customer number (Customer$) and check to ensure that the third left-most digit is a 4. If the third digit is not a 4, request the user to re-enter the number.

11. Assume P and Q are simple conditions. The following logical equivalences are known as DeMorgan's Laws:

    NOT (P OR Q) is equivalent to NOT P AND NOT Q
    NOT (P AND Q) is equivalent to NOT P OR NOT Q

    Use DeMorgan's Laws to write a logical equivalent for each of the following:

    a. NOT P OR NOT Q
    b. NOT((NOT P) OR Q)
    c. NOT (NOT P AND Q)
    d. NOT (NOT P AND NOT Q)

12. Write a program that determines the number of negative values (Negative), number of zero values (Zero) and number of positive values (Positive) in the following data set: 4, 2, 3, − 9, 0, 0, − 4, − 6, − 8, 3, 2, 0, 0, 8, − 3, 4. Use the sentinel value −999 to test for the end-of-file.

13. Given four variables, W, X, Y, and Z, with previously defined values, write an IF statement to increment the variable, Count, by 1 if all four variables have the exact value of 100.

14. The sequence of Fibonacci numbers begins with integers 1 and 1, and continues endlessly, with each number being the sum of the preceding two:

    1, 1, 2, 3, 5, 8, 13, 21, 34, ...

Construct a program to compute the first X integer numbers of the sequence where the value of X is entered in response to an INPUT statement. Accept only values for X that are greater than 3 and less than or equal to 190.

15. Given two positive-valued variables, A and B, write a sequence of statements to assign the variable with the larger value to Big and the variable with the smaller value to Small. If A and B are equal, assign either to Same.

16. The values of three variables, U, V, and W, are positive and not equal to each other. Using IF statements, determine which has the smallest value and assign this value to Little.

17. The symbol N! represents the product of the first N positive integers. Thus 5! = 5 * 4 * 3 * 2 * 1. This is called 5 factorial. The general equation is:
    N! = N * (N - 1) * (N - 2) * ... * 1
    When a result is defined in terms of itself, we call it a recursive definition.
    Construct a program that will accept from the keyboard a positive integer and compute its factorial. The recursive definition is as follows:
    If N = 1, then N! = 1, otherwise N! = N * (N - 1)!

18. Consider the following program:

```
' ******* Main Program *****
GOSUB A100.Initialization
GOSUB B100.Process.File
GOSUB C100.Wrap.Up
END
' ***** Initialization *****
A100.Initialization:
   Count = 0
   Sum = 0
RETURN
' ***** Process File ******
B100.Process.File:
   READ A, B, C
   DO WHILE A > 0
      IF A < B + 1 THEN
         Count = Count + 1
      ELSE
         IF A >= C + 2 THEN
            Sum = Sum + A
            Count = Count + 2
            PRINT Sum
         ELSE
            Count = Count +   2
         END IF
      END IF
      READ A, B, C
   LOOP
RETURN
' ***** Wrap-Up ******
C100.Wrap.Up:
   PRINT Count, Sum
   PRINT "End of Report"
RETURN
' ******* Data Follows **********
DATA 3, 5, 14, 9, 6, 5, 7, 2, 4
DATA 12, 8, 2, 11, 4, 1, -3, 0, 0
' ***** End of Program **********
```

a. Which variable is used to test for end-of-file?
b. What are the values of Count and Sum just before the LOOP statement is executed for the third time?

    c. How many lines are displayed by this program?
    d. What is the maximum value of Sum displayed?
    e. What is the maximum value of Count displayed?

19. The WEGOTU National Bank computes its monthly service charge on checking accounts by adding $0.60 to a value computed from the following:

    $0.14 per check for the first 10 checks
    $0.13 per check for the next 10 checks
    $0.12 per check for the next 10 checks
    $0.11 per check for all the rest of the checks

    Write a sequence of statements that includes a SELECT CASE statement and a PRINT statement to display the account number (Account), the number of checks cashed (Checks), and the computed monthly charge (Charge). The account number and the number of checks cashed are entered via INPUT statements prior to the execution of the SELECT CASE statement.

20. Write a partial program to set A = –1 if C and D are both zero, set A = –2 if neither C nor D is zero, and set A = –3 if either, but not both, C or D is zero.

21. In each of the following compound conditions, indicate the order of evaluation by the PC. (See the examples beginning on page 161. Beginning with 1, use numbers and truth values to show the order of evaluation.)
    a. S > 0 OR A > 0 OR T > 0
    b. S > 0 AND A > 0 AND NOT T > 0
    c. S > 0 IMP A > 0 EQV T > 0 AND P > 0
    d. NOT S > 0 AND T > 0 XOR P > 0

22. **PC Hands-On Exercise:** Load Program 5.1 (PRG5-1) from the Data Disk. Display the program and execute it. After the results are printed, modify the program by changing line 56 to a comment so that PRG5-1 prints only the summary totals.

    Reload PRG5-1. Modify it by changing lines 90 through 94 to comments. Execute the modified version of Program 5.1. Consider why it is important to have at least one line of data, excluding the trailer record, for this program.

23. **PC Hands-On Exercise:** Load Program 5.2 (PRG5-2) from the Data Disk. List the program, and then execute it. When requested, enter the following data:
    Data Set 1:   Code = 4, Radius = 6
    Data Set 2:   Code = 0 (a diagnostic message should display.)
    Data Set 3:   Code = 6, Base = 5, Height = 6
    Data Set 4:   Code = 7 (End program.)

5.11 QBasic Programming Problems

1. Employee Average Yearly Salary

Purpose: To illustrate the initialization and incrementing of a counter and a running total accumulator, looping, and testing for the last value in a set of data.

Problem: Construct a top-down program to read records, count records, accumulate salaries, and display a sequence of data consisting of employee numbers and salaries in a payroll file. After the sentinel value (EOF) is processed, display the total number of employees and the average yearly salary of all the employees processed.

(Hint: Use the top-down chart illustrated in Figure 5.7 on page 150 and Program 5.1 — PRG5-1 on the Data Disk — as a guide to solving this problem.)

Input Data: Prepare and use the following sample data in DATA statements:

Employee Number	Employee Salary
123	$16,000
148	18,126
184	14,800
196	17,400
201	18,950
EOF	0

Output Results: The output screen should appear as illustrated by Figure 5.30.

FIGURE 5.30

Output for Programming Problem 1.

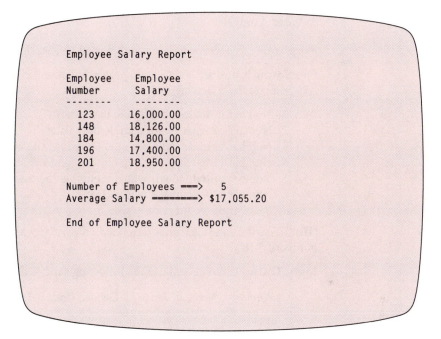

```
Employee Salary Report

Employee    Employee
Number      Salary
--------    --------
   123      16,000.00
   148      18,126.00
   184      14,800.00
   196      17,400.00
   201      18,950.00

Number of Employees ===>   5
Average Salary ========> $17,055.20

End of Employee Salary Report
```

2. Selecting the Best and Worst Salesperson

Purpose: To become familiar with decision-making logic, exchanging the values of string variables, and using the RESTORE statement.

Problem: Construct a top-down program that will determine and display the best and worst salesperson on the basis of total sales from a salesperson file.

(Hint: Use the top-down chart illustrated in Figure 5.7 and Program 5.1 — PRG5-1 on the Data Disk — as a guide to solving this problem.)

Input Data: Prepare and use the following sample data in DATA statements:

Salesperson Name	Total Sales
Franklin, Ed	$76,185
Smith, Susan	18,421
Stankie, Jim	75,856
Runaw, Jeff	32,146
Ray, Kathy	13,467
Doolittle, Frank	14,316
Zachery, Louis	48,615

Output Results: The output screen should appear as illustrated by Figure 5.31.

FIGURE 5.31
*Output for Programming
Problem 2.*

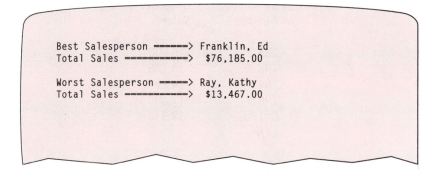

```
Best Salesperson =======> Franklin, Ed
Total Sales ============> $76,185.00

Worst Salesperson =====> Ray, Kathy
Total Sales ===========> $13,467.00
```

3. Voter Analysis

Purpose: To become familiar with nested If-Then-Else structures.

Problem: Construct a top-down program that will clear the screen, analyze a citizen file, and generate the following totals:

1. Number of males not eligible to register
2. Number of females not eligible to register
3. Number of males who are old enough to vote but have not registered
4. Number of females who are old enough to vote but have not registered
5. Number of individuals who are eligible to vote but did not vote
6. Number of individuals who did vote
7. Number of records processed

(**Hint:** Use the variable names described on page 159 and the If-Then-Else structure shown in Figure 5.18.)

Input Data: Prepare and use the following sample data in DATA statements:

Number	Age in Years	Gender Code	Registered	Voted
1812	23	M	Y	Y
1951	37	F	Y	Y
4516	15	F	N	N
1654	19	M	Y	N
2145	18	F	N	N
6233	21	F	Y	Y
9127	22	M	N	N
3215	26	F	Y	Y
2201	33	F	Y	N
7743	41	M	Y	Y
1121	51	F	Y	Y
1949	17	M	N	N

Output Results: The output screen should appear as illustrated by Figure 5.32.

4. Stockbroker's Commission

Purpose: To become familiar with the If-Then-Else structure and methods used to determine a stockbroker's commission.

Problem: Write a top-down program that will read a stock transaction and determine the stockbroker's commission. Each transaction includes the following data: the stock name, price per share, number of shares involved, and the stockbroker's name. The stockbroker's commission is computed in the following manner:

FIGURE 5.32
Output for Programming Problem 3.

```
Voter Analysis

Males Not Eligible to Register ==================> 1
Females Not Eligible to Register ================> 1

Males Old Enough to Vote but Not Registered ======> 1
Females Old Enough to Vote but Not Registered ====> 1

Individuals Eligible to Vote but Did Not Vote ===> 2
Individuals that Voted =========================> 6

Total Number of Records Processed ================> 12

End of Report
```

If the price per share P is less than or equal to $40.00, the commission rate is $0.17 per share; if P is greater than $40.00, the commission rate is $0.28 per share. If the number of shares sold is less than 125, the commission is 1.5 times the rate per share.

Each detail line of output to the printer is to include the stock transaction data set and the commission paid the stockbroker. Test the stock name for the EOF. Print the total commission earned.

(**Hint:** Use the top-down chart illustrated in Figure 5.7 on page 150 and Program 5.1 — PRG5-1 on the Data Disk — as a guide to solving this problem.)

Input Data: Prepare and use the following sample data in DATA statements:

Stock Name	Price per Share	Number of Shares	Stockbroker Name
Amoco	$56.25	250	Guinn, M.
PnWbrins	14.88	300	Myers, I.
EKodak	61.38	250	Banks, W.
Chrysler	44.25	150	Lucas, T.
McDnInvst	17.38	115	Lucas, B.
McDonalds	54.38	200	Dixon, D.

Output Results: The output report on the printer should appear as illustrated by Figure 5.33.

FIGURE 5.33
Printed output for Programming Problem 4.

```
               Stockbroker's Commission

Stock       Price       Number      Stockbroker
Name        per Share   of Shares   Name           Commission
-----       ---------   ---------   -----------    ----------
Amoco          56.25         250    Guinn, M.           70.00
PnWbrins       14.88         300    Myers, I.           51.00
EKodak         61.38         250    Banks, W.           70.00
Chrysler       44.25         150    Lucas, T.           42.00
McDnInvs       17.38         115    Lucas, B.           29.33
McDonalds      54.38         200    Dixon, D.           56.00

Total Commission Earned                              $318.33

End of Report
```

5. Aging Accounts

Purpose: To become familiar with data validation and with the concepts of aging accounts receivable using Julian Calendar dates (that is, using a number between 1 and 365 to signify a date).

Problem: Write a top-down program to compute the total amount due and percentage of the total amount of receivables that are as follows:

1. Less than 30 days past due (accounts due < 30 days)
2. Past due between 30 and 60 days (30 <= accounts due <= 60)
3. Past due more than 60 days (accounts due > 60)

Include in the output the number of accounts in each category. The first input value will be today's Julian date from the keyboard. Verify that the Julian date is a value between 1 and 365 inclusive. Assume no leap years. The account number, amount due, and the date due for each customer should be stored in one or more DATA statements.

(**Hint:** See Program 5.1 on page 152 or PRG5-1 on the Data Disk.)

Input Data: Prepare and use the following sample data. Assume today's Julian date is 225 (that is, the 225th day of the year).

Account Number	Amount Due	Date Due
1380	685.73	23
2456	1,231.10	166
3392	4,016.52	159
3867	7.25	192
5173	1,943.86	174
7549	81.90	148
9026	357.28	181

Output Results: The output screen should appear as illustrated by Figure 5.34.

|FIGURE 5.34
Output for Programming Problem 5.

```
Please Enter the Julian Date =====> 225


                    Aging Accounts for Day 225

Accounts            Number of       Total           Percent of
Past Due            Accounts        Amount Due      Total Amount
--------            ---------       ----------      ------------
Less Than 30 Days   0                    0.00              0.00
30 To 60 Days       4                3,539.49             42.52
Over 60 Days        3                4,784.15             57.48

Job Complete
```

6. Money Changer

Purpose: To illustrate the concepts of multiple loops and data validation.

Problem: Construct a top-down program that will make change from a one-dollar bill on a sale of less than or equal to one dollar. Have the program request the amount of the sale. If the sale amount is less than 1 cent or greater than 100 cents, display a diagnostic message and request that the amount of the sale be re-entered. The program is to display the number of half dollars, quarters, dimes, nickels, and pennies that are to be returned to the customer. Have the program return as many half dollars as possible, then as many quarters as possible, and so on. A sale amount of -99 indicates end-of-job.

Input Data: Enter the following sample data via INPUT statements:

$0.65, $0.11, $1.07, $0.10, $0.52, $1.50, $0.84, $0.32, $0.00, $0.63

Output Results: The output screen should appear as illustrated by Figure 5.35 for a sale amount of $0.65.

FIGURE 5.35

Output for a sale amount of $0.65 for Programming Problem 6.

```
Money Changer

Enter Amount of Sale as a Whole Number
Between 1 Cent and 100 Cents Inclusive ====> 65

Return to the Customer -   0 Half-Dollar(s)
                           1 Quarter(s)
                           1 Dime(s)
                           0 Nickel(s)
                           0 Pennies


Press Enter to Initiate a New Sale...
```

7. The Check Digit Problem

Purpose: To illustrate the concepts of generating check digits.

Problem: Construct a top-down program to create a check digit (sixth digit) for a part number and compare it to the existing check digit (sixth digit). The computation of the check digit involves multiplying every other digit of the first five existing digits by 2 and adding these digits and the remaining two digits of the part number together. The units digit of the result obtained is then subtracted from 10 to obtain the check digit.

To illustrate the process used, let us verify a part number by computing the check digit for the number 725465, where the last 5 is the current check digit. Using the first five digits, alternate digits, 7, 5, and 6, are first multiplied by 2:

$$7 \times 2 = 14$$
$$5 \times 2 = 10$$
$$6 \times 2 = 12$$

Then the remaining two digits (2 and 4) are included, and *all* the above digits are then added:

$$1 + 4 + 1 + 0 + 1 + 2 + 2 + 4 = 15$$

The 5 in 15 is then subtracted from 10 to give a check digit of 5, so the part number should be 725465. This confirms that the original part number was correct.

(**Hint:** The digits must be separated. You may separate digits through the use of the INT function. For example, the left-most digit [D1] can be determined from the following, where PART is the 6 digit value:

```
D1 = INT(PART / 100000)
```

and the second left-most digit [D2] is equal to:

```
D2 = INT((PART - D1 * 100000) / 10000)
```

Continue in this fashion, until the first five digits are extracted. A similar method is used to extract the digits from the partial products.)

Input Data: Using the following part numbers, check to see if the right-most digit is the correct check digit.

725465, 752465, 033332, 098792, 098798, 089798, 000000, 000001, 999999, 999995

Output Results: The output screen for 725465 should appear as illustrated by Figure 5.36.

FIGURE 5.36
Output for Programming Problem 7.

```
Validation of Check Digit

Enter Part Number ====> 725465

Part Number is Valid

To Continue Calidation, Enter Y, else N...N
```

8. A Menu-Driven Program with Multifunctions

Purpose: To become familiar with the SELECT CASE statement, a multifunction program, data validation, and the use of a menu.

Problem: Use top-down programming techniques to write a menu-driven program to compute the volume of a box, cylinder, cone, and sphere. The program should display the menu shown in Figure 5.37 under Output Results. After a code is entered, it must be validated.

After the selection of the proper function, the program should prompt the user for the necessary data, compute the volume, and display it accordingly. The displayed results are to remain on the screen until the Enter key on the keyboard is pressed. After that, the program should redisplay the menu.

Use the following formulas for the volumes:

1. Volume of a **box**: $V = L * W * H$ where L is the length, W is the width, and H is the height of the box.
2. Volume of a **cylinder**: $V = pi * R * R * H$, where pi equals 3.14159, R is the radius, and H is the height of the cylinder.
3. Volume of a **cone**: $V = (pi * R * R * H)/3$, where pi equals 3.14159, R is the radius of the base, and H is the height of the cone.
4. Volume of a **sphere**: $V = 4 * pi * R * R * R/3$, where pi equals 3.14159 and R is the radius of the sphere.

Input Data: Use the following sample data:

```
Code — 3, Radius = 7, Height = 9
Code — 4, Radius = 10
Code — 1, Length = 4.5, Width = 6.7, Height = 12
Code — 2, Radius = 8, Height = 15
Code — 7  (This code should return a diagnostic message.)
Code — 5  (End Program.)
```

Output Results: The output screen for the menu should appear as illustrated by Figure 5.37.

▌FIGURE 5.37
*Output menu for
Programming Problem 8.*

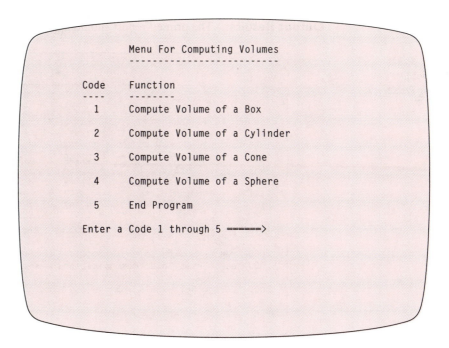

```
                    Menu For Computing Volumes
                    --------------------------

            Code     Function
            ----     --------
             1       Compute Volume of a Box

             2       Compute Volume of a Cylinder

             3       Compute Volume of a Cone

             4       Compute Volume of a Sphere

             5       End Program

          Enter a Code 1 through 5 ======>
```

9. Sales Forecasting

Purpose: To practice decision-making logic, exchanging values of string variables, and using the RESTORE statement.

Problem: Construct a top-down program to calculate and report to the printer forecasted sales for the years 2001, 2002, and 2003. The 2002 and 2003 forecast sales figures should be calculated only in cases where the 2000 sales are equal to or greater than 1500; otherwise, the 2002 and 2003 forecast sales figures should be zero. The information will be taken from a textbook data file, and the forecast sales figures will be calculated as follows:

2001 = 75% of 2000 sales
2002 = 50% of 2000 sales
2003 = 25% of 2000 sales

The program also should determine and report for 2000 the greatest number of units sold, the least number of units sold, and the average number of units sold, with the corresponding textbook titles.

Input Data: Prepare and use the following sample data in DATA statements:

Stock Number	Textbook Title	2000 Sales Figures
1057	Turbo C ++	11,229
4333	Algebra Starter	2,150
3982	Literature	1,650
7649	Windows 2000	11,149
2141	Communications	707
8156	Busy People	9,452

Output Results: The printed report should appear as illustrated by Figure 5.38.

FIGURE 5.38
Printed output for
Programming Problem 9.

```
                            Sales Forecasting Report

        Stock     Title of           2000      2001      2002      2003
        Number    Textbook           Sales     Sales     Sales     Sales
        ------    --------           -----     -----     -----     -----
        1057      Turbo C++          11,229    8,422     5,615     2,807
        4333      Algebra Starter     2,150    1,613     1,075       538
        3982      Literature I        1,650    1,238       825       413
        7649      Windows 2000       11,149    8,362     5,575     2,787
        2141      Communications        707      530         0         0
        8156      Busy People         9,452    7,089     4,726     2,363
                                     ------    ------    ------    ------
        Totals                       36,337    27,253    17,815     8,908

        2000 Greatest Units Sold: Turbo C++      ==>   11,229
        2000 Least Units Sold: Communications ======>     707

        2000 Average Units Sold ==>   6,056

        End of Sales Forecasting Report
```

10. Payroll Problem V — Biweekly Payroll Computations with Time and a Half for Overtime

Purpose: To become familiar with decision making and some payroll concepts.

Problem: Modify in a top-down fashion Payroll Problem IV on page 141 to include the following conditions:
1. Overtime (hours worked more than 80) is paid at 1.5 times the hourly rate.
2. Federal withholding tax is determined in the same manner as indicated in Payroll Problem III on page 92; however, assign a value of $0.00 if the gross pay less the product of the number of dependents and $40.46 is not positive.
3. After processing the employee records, display the total gross pay, federal withholding tax, and net pay.

(**Hint:** Use the top-down chart illustrated in Figure 5.7 on page 150 and Program 5.1 — PRG5-1 on the Data Disk — as a guide to solving this problem.)

Input Data: Use the sample data found in Payroll Problem III (Problem 6) in Chapter 3. Modify the DATA statement representing employee 126 so that the number of dependents equals 9.

Output Results: The output screen should appear as illustrated by Figure 5.39.

FIGURE 5.39
Output for Programming
Problem 10.

```
                          Biweekly Payroll Report

        Employee
        Number        Gross Pay        Fed. Tax      Net Pay
        --------      ---------        --------      -------
           123        1,000.00          238.96        761.04
           124          880.00          218.28        661.72
           125        1,040.00          259.88        780.12
           126          130.00            0.00        130.00

        Total Gross Pay ========>     3,050.00
        Total Withholding Tax ==>       717.12
        Total Net Pay ==========>     2,332.88

        End of Payroll Report
```

6

Sequential Files, Paging Reports, and Control-Break Processing

6.1 INTRODUCTION

In the first five chapters of this book, we stressed the importance of integrating data into the program. You learned that data may be entered into a program through the use of the LET statement, the INPUT statement, or the READ and DATA statements. This chapter presents a fourth method for entering data — the use of data files. With data files, the data is stored on auxiliary storage rather than in the program itself. This technique is used primarily for dealing with large amounts of data.

Processing large amounts of data often involves generating reports that are many pages in length. When the length of a report exceeds one page, the report and column headings, as well as a page number, should be printed at the top of each page. This chapter introduces you to writing programs that generate reports of more than one page or more than one screen.

The third topic presented in this chapter is control-break processing. A **control break** is a technique used to generate subtotals within a report. Most businesses are divided into units for the purpose of better management. To evaluate the performance of the units within each level, managerial reports are generated that show summaries, or minor totals for each sub-unit. This chapter illustrates programming techniques for generating these types of reports.

At the conclusion of this chapter, you should be able to design programs that write reports to auxiliary storage, build data files, process data files, and generate reports with paging and control breaks.

6.2 DATA FILES

In previous chapters, top-down program development was emphasized. Of equal concern are the organization and processing of data in the form of files. This is especially true in a business environment for the following three reasons:

1. Business applications, such as payroll, billing, order entry, and inventory, involve the processing of extensive amounts of data.
2. Data must be updated continually if management reports are to be useful.
3. The same data often is required for several applications such as payroll, personnel, pension plans, and insurance reporting.

Computer manufacturers have applied a great deal of effort in developing both hardware, such as auxiliary storage devices, and software, such as **file-handling statements**, to deal directly with the organization and processing of large amounts of data.

In programs in previous chapters, the LET statement, the INPUT statement, or the READ and DATA statements were used to enter data into the PC. A more efficient and convenient method of organizing data is to store it on an auxiliary storage device, such as a floppy disk or hard disk, and keep it separate from the programs that will process the data. Data stored in this fashion is a **file**, a group of related records. The number of records making up a file may range from just a few, to thousands or millions. Each record within the file contains related data items.

Figure 6.1 illustrates a partial list of data items that can be found within the records of a payroll file. Common data items occupy the same position in each record. This sequence within a record is important both for processing and updating a file.

FIGURE 6.1

A conceptual view of a file stored on a floppy disk, with each data item separated by a comma and each record separated by a carriage return character <cr>.

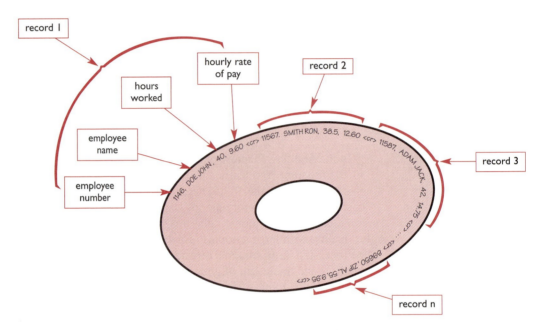

Creating a data file that is separate from the program yet accessible to it means the following:

1. Data can be used by different programs without having to be re-entered each time.
2. Records can be updated easily.
3. Many data files can be processed by a single program.
4. Programs can process a particular file for one run and another file for the next, provided the data items in the records of the files have some common organization.

QBasic includes a set of file-handling statements that allow a user to do the following:

1. Create data files.
2. Define the data files to be used by a program.
3. Open a file.
4. Read data from a file.
5. Write data to a file.
6. Test for the end-of-file.
7. Close a file.

File Organization

File organization is a method of arranging records on an auxiliary storage device. QBasic provides for two types of file organization — sequential and random.

A file organized sequentially is called a **sequential file** and is limited to sequential processing. This means the records can be processed only in the order in which they are placed in the file. Conceptually, a sequential file is identical to the use of DATA statements within a QBasic program. For example, the fourteenth record in a sequential file cannot be processed until after the previous thirteen records have been processed. Similarly, the fourteenth data item in a DATA statement of a QBasic program cannot be processed until the previous thirteen data items have been processed.

Sequential organization also can be used to write reports to auxiliary storage instead of to the screen or printer. After the report is in auxiliary storage, it can be displayed at any time and as often as needed. Writing reports to auxiliary storage is a common practice, especially with programs that generate multiple reports. In such programs, each report is written to a separate file.

The second type of file organization, random files, will be discussed in Chapter 9.

6.3 SEQUENTIAL FILE PROCESSING

This section presents the file-handling statements required to create and process sequential files. We also present sample programs to illustrate the following:

1. How reports can be written to auxiliary storage instead of to the screen or to the printer.
2. How to build sequential files that other programs can process.
3. How reports can be generated from data that is located in sequential files.

Later, in Chapter 9, we will show you how to update sequential files.

Opening Sequential Files

Before any file can be read from or written to, it must be opened by the OPEN statement. When executed, the OPEN **statement** carries out the following five basic functions:

1. Requests the PC to allocate a **buffer**. A buffer is a part of main memory through which data is passed between the program and auxiliary storage.
2. Identifies by name the file to be processed.
3. Indicates whether the file is to be read from or written to.
4. Assigns the file a filenumber.
5. Sets the *pointer* to the beginning of the file or to the end of the file.

The general form of the OPEN statement is shown in Table 6.1 on the next page. As described in Table 6.1, a sequential file may be opened for input, output, or append. Example 1 in Table 6.1 opens the file EMPLOYEE.DAT for input as filenumber 1. The file is located on the A drive. Because EMPLOYEE.DAT is opened for *input*, the program can only read records from it. An attempt to write a record to EMPLOYEE.DAT will result in the display of a dialog box with the following diagnostic message:

```
Bad file mode
```

If an attempt is made to open a nonexistent file for input, the following diagnostic message displays in a dialog box:

```
File not found
```

TABLE 6.1 - The OPEN Statement for Sequential Files

General Form: OPEN filespec FOR mode AS #filenumber

where **filespec** is the name of the file;

mode is one of the following:

APPEND specifies sequential output mode, where the pointer is positioned to the end of the file;

INPUT specifies sequential input mode, where the pointer is positioned at the beginning of the file,

OUTPUT specifies sequential output mode, where the pointer is positioned at the beginning of the file; and

filenumber is a numeric expression whose value is between 1 and 255. The filenumber is associated with the file (filespec) for as long as it is open. The filenumber is used by other file-handling statements to refer to the specific file.

Purpose: Allows a program to read records from or write records to a sequential data file.

Examples:
```
OPEN "A:EMPLOYEE.DAT" FOR INPUT AS #1
OPEN "payroll.lis" FOR OUPUT AS #2
OPEN "ACCOUNTS.DAT" FOR APPEND AS #3
OPEN Filename$ FOR INPUT AS #3
```

Note:
1. The OPEN statement also includes an ACCESS parameter for controlling access of files on a network. This parameter will not be used in this book.

2. QBasic provides for a second general form for the OPEN statement:
OPEN mode, #filenumber, filespec

This second general form is less contemporary than the general form specified at the top of this table, and therefore, will not be used in this book.

Example 2 in Table 6.1 opens PAYROLL.LIS on the default drive for output. Because PAYROLL.LIS is opened for *output*, the program can only write records to the sequential file. Opening a sequential file for output always creates a new file. If, for example, PAYROLL.LIS already exists, then it is deleted before it is opened. Because there are never any records in a newly opened output file, the data pointer is positioned at the beginning of the file.

In the third example in Table 6.1, the OPEN statement opens ACCOUNTS.DAT on the default drive for appending records to the end of the file. If ACCOUNTS.DAT exists, the data pointer is positioned after the last record. If ACCOUNTS.DAT does not exist, the PC creates it and positions the data pointer at the beginning of the file.

The **append mode** (APPEND) should be used in the OPEN statement whenever records are being added to a sequential file. For example, with an order-entry application, it may be desirable to maintain a weekly customer order file. Orders entered on a daily basis are appended to those which have been previously entered. At the end of the week, the customer order file will contain the orders for the week in the sequence entered.

The last example in Table 6.1 illustrates how the filespec may be defined in an OPEN statement as a string variable. This allows you to write an OPEN statement in a program without knowing the name of the sequential file. Of course, when the program is executed, the user must supply the filespec. This is usually done through the use of an INPUT statement. Consider the following partial program:

```
INPUT "Please enter filespec to process ====> ", Filename$
OPEN Filename$ FOR INPUT AS #3
```

The OPEN statement opens for input the file that corresponds to the string constant assigned to the string variable Filename$. Note that the user is responsible for the entire file specification — device name, folder or directory name, file name, and file extension. Through the use of the concatenation operator, which is discussed in Chapters 3 and 8, we can simplify the user entry as shown here:

```
INPUT "Name of the File to Process ====> ", Filename$
OPEN "A:" + Filename$ + ".DAT" FOR INPUT AS #3
```

In this case, the user enters only the file name. The concatenation operators in the OPEN statement append the device name to the front of the file name and the file extension to the end of the file name.

The filenumber in an OPEN statement must be an integer expression whose value is between 1 and 255.

The following rules summarize the use of the OPEN statement:

OPEN RULE 1	*A sequential file must be opened before it can be read from or written to.*
OPEN RULE 2	*A program can read only records from a sequential file that has been opened for input.*
OPEN RULE 3	*A sequential file must already exist if it is opened for input.*
OPEN RULE 4	*A program can write only records to a sequential file that has been opened for output or append.*
OPEN RULE 5	*A filenumber can be assigned to only one sequential file at a time.*

Closing Sequential Files

When a program is finished reading or writing to a file, it must close the file with the CLOSE statement. The CLOSE **statement** terminates the association between the file and the filenumber assigned in the OPEN statement and deallocates the part of main memory that is assigned to the buffer.

If a file is being written to, the CLOSE statement ensures that the last record is transferred from the buffer in main memory to auxiliary storage. The general form of the CLOSE statement is shown in Table 6.2 on the next page.

TABLE 6.2 - The CLOSE Statement	
General Form:	CLOSE or CLOSE #filenumber₁, ..., #filenumberₙ
Purpose:	Terminates the association between a filenumber and a file that was established in a previously executed OPEN statement. If the file is opened for output, the CLOSE statement ensures that the last record is transferred from main memory to auxiliary storage. If no filenumbers follow the keyword CLOSE, then all opened files are closed.
Examples:	CLOSE #1, #2, #3 CLOSE #1 CLOSE #2, #1 CLOSE

The CLOSE statement terminates access to a file. For example,

CLOSE #2, #3

causes the files assigned to filenumbers 2 and 3 to be closed. Any other files previously opened by the program remain open.

Following the close of a specified file, the filenumber may be assigned again to the same file or to a different file by an OPEN statement. Opening and closing a file more than once in a program is quite common. For example, many applications involve reading and processing the records in a sequential data file to compute an average. The file is then processed a second time to evaluate each record against the average. The term **rewind** is sometimes used to describe the technique of closing and then opening the file to begin processing again with the first record.

Note that when executed, the END statement closes all opened files before terminating execution of the program. It is good programming practice to close all opened files with the CLOSE statement, instead of relying on the execution of the END statement.

The following rule summarizes the CLOSE statement:

CLOSE RULE 1   *A file must be opened before it can be closed.*

Writing Reports to a Sequential File

The PRINT #n **and** PRINT #n, USING **statements** are used to write reports to sequential files. After it has been written to a file, the report can be displayed or printed as often as desired without the program being executed again. The general forms of the PRINT #n and PRINT #n, USING statements are shown in Tables 6.3 and 6.4, respectively.

TABLE 6.3 - The PRINT #n Statement	

General Form:	`PRINT #n, item pm item pm ... pm item`
	
	where **n** is a filenumber assigned to a file defined in an `OPEN` statement;
	   item is a constant, variable, expression, function reference, or null;
	   and
	   pm is a comma or semicolon.

Purpose:	Writes information to a sequential file in auxiliary storage.

Examples:	`PRINT #1,`
	`PRINT #2, Emp.Name$, Age, Weight`
	`PRINT #1, "Total Sales ======>"; Total`
	`PRINT #2, X + Y/4, C * B`
	`PRINT #3, Q1.Tax, Q2.Tax, Q3.Tax, Q4.Tax`
	`PRINT #2, Sum;`

Note:	Type the question mark (?), and QBasic changes it to the keyword `PRINT` when the cursor is moved off the line.

The `PRINT #n` and `PRINT #n, USING` statements work in exactly the same way as the `PRINT` and `PRINT USING` statements except that information is written to a sequential file on auxiliary storage rather than to the screen. For example, the statement

```
PRINT Record.Count, Total.Amount, Average
```

displays the values of Record.Count, Total.Amount, and Average on the screen in print zones 1, 2, and 3. Similarly, the statement

```
PRINT #1, Record.Count, Total.Amount, Average
```

creates and transmits a record image to the sequential file assigned to filenumber 1, with the values of Record.Count, Total.Amount, and Average beginning in zones 1, 2, and 3 of the record.

TABLE 6.4 - The PRINT #n, USING Statement	

General Form:	`PRINT #n, USING string expression; list`
	
	where **n** is a filenumber assigned to a file defined in an `OPEN` statement;
	   string expression (sometimes called the descriptor field, or format field)
	   is either a string constant or a string variable; and
	   list is a list of items to be displayed in the format specified by the format field.

Purpose:	Provides for controlling exactly the format of a program's output to a sequential file in auxiliary storage by specifying an image to which that output must conform.

Examples:	`PRINT #3, USING "The answer is #,###.##"; Cost`
	`PRINT #2, USING "## divided by # is #.#"; Num; Den; Quot`
	
	`T1$ = "Total cost =====> $$,###.##-"`
	`PRINT #7, USING T1$; Total`
	
	`D1$ = "**,###.##"`
	`PRINT #1, USING D1$; Check;`
	
	`PRINT #2, USING "\  \"; Cust.Name$`
	`PRINT #4, USING "Example _##"; NUMBER`
	`PRINT #9, USING "#.##^^^^"; Dis.1; Dis.2; Dis.3; Dis.4`

Note:	For more information on the descriptor field, see Table 4.9 on page 114.

PROGRAMMING CASE STUDY 7B – Writing the Weekly Payroll and Summary Report to Auxiliary Storage

In Chapter 5, the Weekly Payroll and Summary Report (Programming Case Study 7A) was introduced. In the solution (Program 5.1 in Figure 5.9 on page 152), the LPRINT and LPRINT USING statements printed the report. In the following modified solution, the report is written to a sequential file in auxiliary storage using the PRINT #n and PRINT #n, USING statements.

Program 6.1 is identical to Program 5.1, except for the inclusion of the following:

1. Line 20, which displays a message on the screen indicating that the report is being written to auxiliary storage
2. Line 21, which opens for output the sequential file REPORT.LIS on the A drive
3. Inclusion of filenumber 1 in each PRINT #n and PRINT #n, USING statement writing the report
4. Line 86, which closes REPORT.LIS
5. Lines 87 and 88, which display end-of-job information on the screen

Program Solution

Program 6.1, the solution to Programming Case Study 7B, is presented in Figure 6.2 and writes the weekly payroll and summary report to auxiliary storage.

FIGURE 6.2

Program 6.1, the solution to Programming Case Study 7B.

```
 1   ' Program 6.1
 2   ' Writing the Weekly Payroll and Summary Report
 3   ' to Auxiliary Storage
 4   ' Report File Name = REPORT.LIS
 5   ' *************************************************
 6   ' *                 Main Program                *
 7   ' *************************************************
 8   GOSUB A100.Initialization
 9   GOSUB B100.Process.File
10   GOSUB C100.Wrap.Up
11   END
12
13   ' *************************************************
14   ' *              Initialization                 *
15   ' *************************************************
16   A100.Initialization:
17      Emp.Count = 0
18      Total.Gross = 0
19      CLS  ' Clear Screen
20      LOCATE 10, 20: PRINT "Writing Payroll Report to Auxiliary Storage..."
21      OPEN "A:REPORT.LIS" FOR OUTPUT AS #1
22      GOSUB A200.Initialize.Report.Format
23      GOSUB A210.Print.Headings
24   RETURN
25
26   ' *************************************************
27   ' *          Initialize Report Format           *
28   ' *************************************************
29   A200.Initialize.Report.Format:
30      H1$ = "            Weekly Payroll Report"
31      H2$ = "Employee No.  Hours      Rate      Gross Pay"
32      D1$ = "   \  \       ###.#     ##.##    ##,###.##"
33      T1$ = "Total Gross Pay =======> $$,###.##"
34      T2$ = "Number of Employees ====>    ###"
35      T3$ = "Average Gross Pay ======> $$,###.##"
36      T4$ = "End of Payroll Report"
37   RETURN
38
```

```
39    ' ************************************************
40    ' *        Print Report and Column Headings        *
41    ' ************************************************
42    A210.Print.Headings:
43       PRINT #1, H1$
44       PRINT #1,
45       PRINT #1, H2$
46       PRINT #1,
47    RETURN
48
49    ' ************************************************
50    ' *                  Process File                  *
51    ' ************************************************
52    B100.Process.File:
53       READ Emp.Number$, Emp.Hours, Emp.Rate
54       DO WHILE Emp.Number$ <> "EOF"
55          GOSUB B200.Compute.Gross.And.Accumulate
56          PRINT #1, USING D1$; Emp.Number$; Emp.Hours; Emp.Rate; Emp.Gross
57          READ Emp.Number$, Emp.Hours, Emp.Rate
58       LOOP
59    RETURN
60
61    ' ************************************************
62    ' *  Compute Gross Pay & Increment Accumulators  *
63    ' ************************************************
64    B200.Compute.Gross.And.Accumulate:
65       Emp.Count = Emp.Count + 1
66       Emp.Overtime = Emp.Hours - 40
67       IF Emp.Overtime <= 0 THEN
68          Emp.Gross = Emp.Hours * Emp.Rate
69       ELSE
70          Emp.Gross = Emp.Hours * Emp.Rate + .5 * Emp.Rate * Emp.Overtime
71       END IF
72       Total.Gross = Total.Gross + Emp.Gross
73    RETURN
74
75    ' ************************************************
76    ' *                   Wrap-Up                      *
77    ' ************************************************
78    C100.Wrap.Up:
79       Average.Gross = Total.Gross / Emp.Count
80       PRINT #1,
81       PRINT #1, USING T1$; Total.Gross
82       PRINT #1, USING T2$; Emp.Count
83       PRINT #1, USING T3$; Average.Gross
84       PRINT #1,
85       PRINT #1, T4$
86       CLOSE #1
87       LOCATE 12, 20: PRINT "Report Stored Under File Name REPORT.LIS"
88       LOCATE 14, 20: PRINT "End of Job"
89    RETURN
90
91    ' *************** Data Follows ******************
92    DATA 124, 40,   5.60
93    DATA 126, 56,   5.90
94    DATA 128, 38,   4.60
95    DATA 129, 48.5, 6.10
96    DATA EOF, 0,   0   : ' This is the trailer record
97    ' *************** End of Program ****************
```

[run]

Discussion of the Program Solution

When Program 6.1 is executed, the information shown in Figure 6.3 displays on the screen to inform the user the report is being written to a sequential file in auxiliary storage under the name REPORT.LIS.

FIGURE 6.3

The display from the execution of Program 6.1.

```
Writing Payroll Report to Auxiliary Storage ...

Report Stored Under File Name REPORT.LIS

End of Job
```

The report written to auxiliary storage by Program 6.1 is illustrated in Figure 6.4. To view the report, use the Open command on the File menu to display REPORT.LIS in the view window, or quit QBasic and, if in Windows, use Notepad to view and print the file. If at the DOS prompt, use the TYPE or PRINT commands.

FIGURE 6.4

Results of Program 6.1 written to auxiliary storage under the file name REPORT.LIS.

```
                Weekly Payroll Report

    Employee No.      Hours      Rate      Gross Pay

        124           40.0       5.60        224.00
        126           56.0       5.90        377.60
        128           38.0       4.60        174.80
        129           48.5       6.10        321.77

    Total Gross Pay ========> $1,098.17
    Number of Employees =====>         4
    Average Gross Pay =======>    $274.54

    End of Payroll Report
```

FIGURE 6.5

Flowchart symbols for opening and closing files.

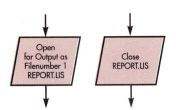

Flowchart of the OPEN and CLOSE Statements

The I/0 symbol is used to represent the OPEN and CLOSE statements. The flowchart symbol on the left in Figure 6.5 represents the OPEN statement in line 21 of Program 6.1, and the flowchart symbol on the right in Figure 6.5 represents the CLOSE statement in line 86 of Program 6.1.

Writing Data to a Sequential File

In Program 6.1, the PRINT #n and PRINT #n, USING statements were used to write a *report* to a sequential file on auxiliary storage. To write *data* to a sequential file, we use the WRITE #n statement. The WRITE #n **statement** writes data in a format required by the INPUT #n statement. The format requirement is similar to that of the READ and DATA statements —

all data items are separated by commas. The WRITE #n statement goes one step better by surrounding all string data items with quotation marks.

The following WRITE #n statement writes a record in the format required by the INPUT #n statement:

```
WRITE #1, Stock$, Location$, Desc$, Cost, Price, Quantity
```

This WRITE #n statement causes a comma to be placed between the data items in the record. Quotation marks are placed around the values of Stock$, Location$, and Desc$, and a carriage return character < cr > is appended to the last data item listed to form the record. For example, if Stock$ = C101, Location$ = 1, Desc$ = Roadhandler, Cost = 96.56, Price = 125.11, and Quantity = 25, then the previous WRITE #1, statement transmits the following record to the sequential file assigned to filenumber 1:

```
"C101","1","Roadhandler",96.56,125.11,25<cr>
```

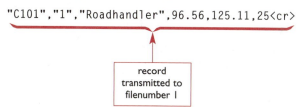

record transmitted to filenumber 1

Note that the string values are delimited with the quotation marks and that the usual leading and trailing spaces surrounding positive numbers are compressed out.

The general form of the WRITE #n statement is given in Table 6.5.

TABLE 6.5 - The WRITE #n Statement

General Form:	WRITE # n, list of variables
	where **n** is a filenumber assigned to a sequential file opened for output.
Purpose:	Writes data items separated by commas to a sequential file on auxiliary storage.
Examples:	WRITE #1, Cost, Margin, Price
	WRITE #2, Amount, Description$
	WRITE #3, Dependents, Tax,

PROGRAMMING CASE STUDY 9 – Creating a Sequential File

Problem: The PUC Company has requested that a sequential file (INVNTORY.DAT) be created from the inventory data that follows. The data must be written in a format that is consistent with the INPUT #n statement. Use a series of LOCATE and INPUT statements to display the screen shown in Figure 6.6.

FIGURE 6.6

The screen design for requesting user entry of inventory records for Programming Case Study 9.

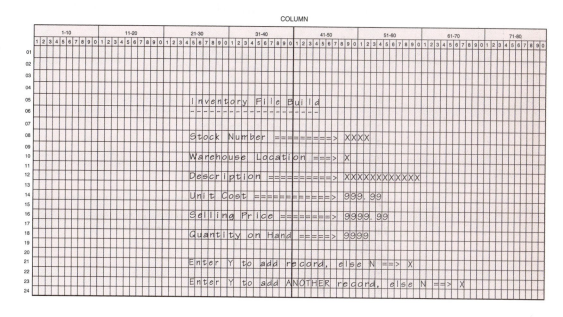

In the following inventory data, each line represents an inventory record:

Stock Number	Warehouse Location	Description	Unit Cost	Selling Price	Quantity on Hand
C101	1	Roadhandler	97.56	125.11	25
C204	3	Whitewalls	37.14	99.95	140
C502	2	Tripod	32.50	38.99	10
S209	1	Maxidrill	88.76	109.99	6
S416	2	Normalsaw	152.55	179.40	1
S812	2	Router	48.47	61.15	8
S942	4	Radialsaw	376.04	419.89	3
T615	4	Oxford-Style	26.43	31.50	28
T713	2	Moc-Boot	24.99	29.99	30
T814	2	Work-Boot	22.99	27.99	56

Following are a list of the program tasks in outline form, a program solution, and a discussion of the program solution.

Program Tasks

1. A100.Initialization
   a. Set Record.Count to zero.
   b. Open INVNTORY.DAT.

2. B100.Build.File — create a Do-Until loop that executes *until* the uppercase value of Control$ equals N.
   a. Call B200.Accept.Record.
   b. If the uppercase value of Add.Rec$ is equal to the value Y, then call the subroutine B210.Write.Record. In B210.Write.Record, do the following:
      (1) Write the record to INVNTORY.DAT.
      (2) Increment Record.Count by 1.

3. C100.Wrap.Up
   a. Close the file.
   b. Display the value of Record.Count and an end-of-job message.

Program Solution

Program 6.2, the solution to Programming Case Study 9, is presented in Figure 6.7.

FIGURE 6.7

Program 6.2, the solution to Programming Case Study 9.

```
 1   ' Program 6.2
 2   ' Creating a Sequential File
 3   ' Output File Name = INVNTORY.DAT
 4   ' ****************************************************************
 5   ' *                      Main Program                          *
 6   ' ****************************************************************
 7   GOSUB A100.Initialization
 8   GOSUB B100.Build.File
 9   GOSUB C100.Wrap.Up
10   END
11
12   ' ****************************************************************
13   ' *                      Initialization                        *
14   ' ****************************************************************
15   A100.Initialization:
16      Record.Count = 0
17      OPEN "A:INVNTORY.DAT" FOR OUTPUT AS #1
18   RETURN
19
```

```
20    ' *****************************************************************
21    ' *                       Build File                            *
22    ' *****************************************************************
23    B100.Build.File:
24       DO
25          GOSUB B200.Accept.Record
26          IF UCASE$(Add.Rec$) = "Y" THEN
27             GOSUB B210.Write.Record
28          END IF
29       LOOP UNTIL UCASE$(Control$) = "N"
30    RETURN
31
32    ' *****************************************************************
33    ' *                 Accept an Inventory Record                  *
34    ' *****************************************************************
35    B200.Accept.Record:
36       CLS  ' Clear Screen
37       LOCATE 5, 25: PRINT "Inventory File Build"
38       LOCATE 6, 25: PRINT "--------------------"
39       LOCATE 8, 25: INPUT "Stock Number =========> ", Stock$
40       LOCATE 10, 25: INPUT "Warehouse Location ===> ", Location$
41       LOCATE 12, 25: INPUT "Description ==========> ", Desc$
42       LOCATE 14, 25: INPUT "Unit Cost ============> ", Cost
43       LOCATE 16, 25: INPUT "Selling Price ========> ", Price
44       LOCATE 18, 25: INPUT "Quantity on Hand =====> ", Quantity
45       LOCATE 21, 25: INPUT "Enter Y to add record, else N ===> ", Add.Rec$
46       LOCATE 23, 25: INPUT "Enter Y to add ANOTHER record, else N ===> ", Control$
47    RETURN
48
49    ' *****************************************************************
50    ' *                 Write an Inventory Record                   *
51    ' *****************************************************************
52    B210.Write.Record:
53       WRITE #1, Stock$, Location$, Desc$, Cost, Price, Quantity
54       Record.Count = Record.Count + 1
55    RETURN
56
57    ' *****************************************************************
58    ' *                          Wrap-Up                            *
59    ' *****************************************************************
60    C100.Wrap.Up:
61       CLOSE #1
62       CLS  ' Clear Screen
63       LOCATE 10, 15: PRINT "Creation of Sequential File is Complete"
64       LOCATE 14, 15
65       PRINT "Total Number of Records in INVNTORY.DAT ===>"; Record.Count
66    RETURN
67
68    ' ********************** End of Program **********************

      [run]
```

Discussion of the Program Solution

When Program 6.2 is executed, line 17 opens INVNTORY.DAT for output as filenumber 1. In B100.Build.File, line 25 in the Do loop calls B200.Accept.Record. Figure 6.8 shows the display due to the execution of this subroutine for the first record entered by the user. Note the two messages at the bottom of the screen. The first message is generated by line 45 of the program and gives the user the opportunity to reject the data entered by assigning Add.Rec$ a value other than Y or y (see line 26). The second message is generated by line 46 and requests the user enter a Y to add another record to the inventory file.

FIGURE 6.8

The display after the first record is entered due to the execution of Program 6.2.

```
Inventory File Build
--------------------

Stock Number =========> C101

Warehouse Location ===> 1

Description ==========> Roadhandler

Unit Cost ============> 97.56

Selling Price ========> 125.11

Quantity on Hand =====> 25


Enter Y to add record, else N ===> Y

Enter Y to add ANOTHER record, else N ===> Y
```

Due to line 27 of the program, the inventory record is added by B210.Write.Record if the uppercase value of Add.Rec$ is equal to Y.

Line 29 controls the Do loop. If the uppercase value of Control$ equals N, then the Do loop terminates, and control returns to line 9 of the Main Program. If the uppercase value of Control$ is equal to any other value, then the Do loop continues.

In B210.Write.Record, line 53 includes the WRITE #n statement. This statement writes the record to the sequential file INVNTORY.DAT in a format consistent with that required by the INPUT #n statement documented in Table 6.6. Figure 6.9 shows the format of the data written to INVNTORY.DAT by Program 6.2.

FIGURE 6.9

A listing of INVNTORY.DAT created by Program 6.2.

```
"C101","1","Roadhandler",97.56,125.11,25
"C204","3","Whitewalls",37.14,99.95,140
"C502","2","Tripod",32.5,38.99,10
"S209","1","Maxidrill",88.76,109.99,6
"S416","2","Normalsaw",152.55,179.4,1
"S812","2","Router",48.47,61.15,8
"S942","4","Radialsaw",376.04,419.89,3
"T615","4","Oxford-Style",26.43,31.5,28
"T713","2","Moc-Boot",24.99,29.99,30
"T814","2","Work-Boot",22.99,27.99,56
```

In C100.Wrap.Up, line 61 closes INVNTORY.DAT. This ensures the last record entered by the user is moved from the buffer to the file in auxiliary storage. Figure 6.10 shows the display due to lines 63 through 65 of C100.Wrap.Up.

FIGURE 6.10

The display due to the execution of the Wrap-up module in Program 6.2.

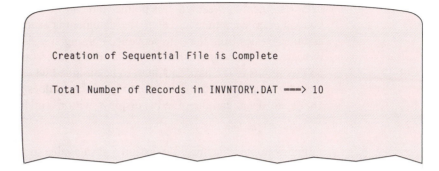

```
Creation of Sequential File is Complete


Total Number of Records in INVNTORY.DAT ===> 10
```

Data validation was purposely left out of this case study to present a clear-cut example of how to create a sequential file. In a production environment, reasonableness checks should always be considered for the stock number (Stock$), warehouse location (Location$), unit cost (Cost), selling price (Price), quantity on hand (Quantity), and user responses (Add.Rec$ and Control$). Data should always be validated before it is placed in a file as discussed in Chapter 5, Section 5.7.

The INPUT #n Statement

The INPUT #n **statement** is used to read data from a sequential file that has been created with the WRITE #n statement. The statement is the same as the READ statement, except that it reads data from a file instead of from DATA statements. The following partial program reads six data items from the sequential file INVNTORY.DAT.

```
OPEN "INVNTORY.DAT" FOR INPUT AS #1
    .
    .
    .
INPUT #1, Stock$, Location$, Desc$, Cost, Price, Quantity
```

For data to be read from a sequential file, the following must be true:

1. The file must already exist.
2. The file must be opened for input.
3. The data items in the file must be separated by a comma or by a carriage return character <cr>.

The general form of the INPUT #n statement is shown in Table 6.6.

TABLE 6.6 - The INPUT #n Statement	
General Form:	INPUT #n, list of variables
	where **n** is a filenumber assigned to an existing sequential file opened for input.
Purpose:	Reads data items from a sequential file on auxiliary storage and assigns them to variables.
Examples:	INPUT #1, Sum, Fix, Desc$, Price
	INPUT #3, Amount
	INPUT #2, Code$, Salary, Tax, Dependents

The INPUT #n statement causes the variables in its list to be assigned specific values, in order, from the data sequence found in the sequential file assigned to filenumber n. In order to visualize the relationship between the INPUT #n statement and the associated file, think of a **pointer** associated with the data items, as discussed in Chapter 4, page 104. When the OPEN statement is executed, this pointer indicates the first data item in the data-sequence holding area. Each time an INPUT #n statement is executed, the variables in the *list* are assigned values from the data-sequence holding area, beginning with the data item that is indicated by the pointer, and the pointer is advanced one value per variable. Hence, the pointer points to the next data item to be assigned when the INPUT #n statement is executed.

If the data type of the data item to be assigned does not agree with the variable in the INPUT #n statement, then the PC displays within a dialog box the diagnostic message

```
Type mismatch
```

For example, it is invalid to assign a string value to a numeric variable. In determining the actual value of a data item, the PC scans in the following manner:

1. For a numeric value: Leading spaces and carriage return characters < cr > are ignored. The first character that is not a space or a carriage return character is assumed to be the start of the numeric data item. A comma, carriage return, or space terminates the numeric value.
2. For a string value: Leading spaces and carriage return characters are ignored. The first character that is not a space or a carriage return character is assumed to be the start of the string data item. Spaces within a string are valid characters. If the first character is a quotation mark, the string data item will consist of all characters between the first quotation mark and the second. Also, if the first character is a quotation mark, the string cannot include a quotation mark. If the string is unquoted, the value terminates with a comma or a carriage return character.

The following rules summarize the material discussed in this section:

INPUT RULE 4   *Before the* INPUT #n *statement is executed, the filenumber n must be assigned to a sequential file that is opened for input.*

INPUT RULE 5   *Numeric variables in* INPUT #n *statements require numeric constants as data items, and string variables require quoted strings or unquoted strings as data.*

The EOF Function

When a sequential file that was opened for output is closed, the PC automatically adds an **end-of-file mark** after the last record written to the file. Later, when the same sequential file is opened for input, you can use the EOF(n) **function** to test for the end-of-file mark. The n indicates the filenumber assigned to the file in the OPEN statement.

If the EOF function senses the end-of-file mark, it returns a value of −1 (true). Otherwise, it returns a value of 0 (false). The EOF function can be used to control a Do loop. For example, consider the following partial program:

```
OPEN "INVNTORY.DAT" FOR INPUT AS #1
    .
    .
    .
DO WHILE NOT EOF(1)
    INPUT #1, Stock$, Location$, Desc$, Cost, Price, Quantity
    GOSUB B200.Compute.And.Accumulate
    GOSUB B210.Print.Record
LOOP
```

In the DO WHILE statement, the EOF(1) function is used to control the Do loop. Each time the DO WHILE statement is executed, the PC checks to see whether the data pointer is pointing to the end-of-file mark in INVNTORY.DAT.

When using the EOF function, it is important to organize your program so that the test for the end-of-file precedes the execution of the INPUT #n statement. Therefore, note in the preceeding partial program that only one INPUT #n statement is used, and that this statement is placed inside at the top of the Do loop. This is different from previous programs that used READ statements — one prior to the Do loop and one following the Do loop.

The logic exhibited by the Do loop also works when the file is empty (that is, when the file contains no records). If the INVNTORY.DAT file is empty, the OPEN statement in the preceeding partial program still opens the file for input. However, when the DO WHILE statement is executed, the EOF function immediately detects the end-of-file mark on the empty file, thereby causing the Do loop to pass control to the statement following the corresponding LOOP statement.

Two additional points must be considered regarding the EOF function:

1. It is invalid to precede the filenumber with a number sign (#). For example, the following is invalid:

```
WHILE NOT EOF(#1)    '   Invalid due to #
```

2. Filenumber n must be opened for input. It is invalid to test for the end-of-file mark on a file that is opened for output.

The following rule summarizes the placement of the EOF function in a program.

EOF FUNCTION RULE 1   *The* EOF *function should test for the end-of-file mark prior to the execution of an* INPUT *#n statement.*

(See Programs 6.3, 6.4, and 6.5 later in this chapter for examples on the use of the EOF function.)

6.4 PAGING A REPORT

Processing large amounts of data often results in generating reports that are many pages long or many screens long. In multiple-page reports, the report title, the column headings, and a page number should be printed at the top of every page or displayed at the top of every screen. This is called **paging** the report. Optionally, the current date and time may be printed or displayed on each page.

Additional programming logic is required for paging a report. For example, immediately after a detail or total line is printed, a **line counter** should be incremented to keep track of what line the printer is on. Prior to printing a detail or a series of total lines, an IF statement should be used to determine whether or not to start a new page. The condition in the IF statement compares the line counter to the maximum number of lines per page. The maximum number of lines per page can be assigned to a variable in the Initialization module.

The logic for single-spacing detail lines in a report follows:

1. If the line counter is greater than or equal to the maximum lines per page, call the Print Headings module.
2. Print the detail line.
3. Increment the line counter by 1. (Increment the line counter by 2 for double spacing and by 3 for triple-spacing.)

The logic for the Print Headings module follows:

1. Increment the page counter by 1.
2. Advance to new page (or clear the screen for a new page).
3. Print the report title, column headings, and page counter.
4. Set the line counter equal to the number of lines printed in this module plus 1.

When using the LPRINT statement, it is also important to be aware of some of the characteristics associated with most ink jet and laser printers attached to PCs.

1. A sheet of paper in a printer is normally 8.5 inches wide and 11 inches long.
2. Printers print six or eight lines per inch. The default value is six lines per inch.
3. In the Print Headings module, we instruct the printer to start a new page by printing a Form Feed character. The ASCII code for the **Form Feed character** is 12, as shown in Appendix D, Table D.1. There is no single key on the keyboard for this code; however, we can transmit the Form Feed character by using the CHR$ function. This function is discussed in detail in Chapter 8 on page 305. The following LPRINT statement starts a new page:

```
LPRINT CHR$(12);    ' Start a new page
```

The semicolon following the CHR$ function instructs the printer to stay on the current line rather than move down a line.

The following Programming Case Study requires data to be read and processed from the sequential file created by Program 6.2. The program solution illustrates printing a report on the printer, paging a report, and the use of the INPUT #n statement and the EOF function.

PROGRAMMING CASE STUDY 10 – Processing a Sequential Data File and Paging a Report

In this case study, we want to generate a report using the data in the sequential file INVNTORY.DAT. This file was created by Program 6.2, and its contents are shown in Figure 6.9 on page 210.

For each record in INVNTORY.DAT, the following items are to be printed on the printer by means of the LPRINT and LPRINT USING statements:

1. Stock number
2. Description
3. Unit cost
4. Selling price
5. Quantity on hand
6. Total item cost of a stock item (unit cost times quantity on hand)
7. Total selling price of a stock item (selling price times quantity on hand)

Print the total inventory cost and the total inventory selling price after all records have been processed.

Print the report title, column headings, and a page number at the top of each page. Print the inventory records on every other line; that is, double-space the report. Print a maximum of 20 lines per page. (We selected 20 lines per page to ensure a page break with the small data file used in this case study. Normally, the maximum lines per page for printed output is set at around 60.)

The printer-spacing chart in Figure 6.11 illustrates the design of the report to be printed.

Following are the program tasks in outline form, a program solution, and a discussion of the program solution.

Program Tasks

1. A100.Initialization
   a. Set Page.Count to zero.
   b. Set Max.Lines.Per.Page to 20.
   c. Set Grand.Tot.Cost and Grand.Tot.Price to zero.
   d. Display a message to load paper in the printer.
   e. Open INVNTORY.DAT.
   f. Call A200.Initialize.Report.Format.

```
                        Inventory Analysis                    Page:  99

                                                          Total
Stock              Unit  Selling  Quantity  Total         Selling
No.    Description Cost  Price    on Hand   Item Cost     Price
----   ----------- ----  -------  --------  -----------   --------
XXXX   XXXXXXXXXXX 999.99 9999.99   9999    99,999.99     99,999.99

Totals                                      999,999.99    999,999.99

Job Complete
```

FIGURE 6.11

The output for Programming Case Study 10 on a printer-spacing chart.

g. Call M300.Print.Headings. Because this subroutine is also called from any other subroutine that prints lines on the printer, assign a level number beginning with the letter M, which stands for multiple, followed by a number representing the lowest level at which it exists. Additionally, we place this subroutine below C100.Wrap.Up so it may be easily located. In M300.Print.Headings, do the following:
   (1) Increment Page.Count by 1.
   (2) If Page.Count is greater than 1, then start a new page.
   (3) Print the report title and Page.Count.
   (4) Print the column headings.
   (5) Set Line.Count to 7.

2. B100.Process.File — Establish a Do-While loop that executes while the EOF function does not detect the end-of-file mark in INVNTORY.DAT. In this loop do as follows:
   a. Read an inventory record.
   b. Call B200.Compute.And.Accumulate. In this subroutine, do the following:
      (1) Compute the total cost (Tot.Cost) and total price (Tot.Price).
      (2) Increment Grand.Tot.Cost and Grand.Tot.Price.
   c. Call B210.Print.Record. In this subroutine, do the following:
      (1) Compare Line.Count to Max.Lines.Per.Page + 1. If the condition is true, call M300.Print.Headings.
      (2) Print the inventory record.
      (3) Increment Line.Count by 2.

3. C100.Wrap.Up
   a. Close INVNTORY.DAT.
   b. Compare Line.Count to Max.Lines.Per.Page − 1. If the condition is true, then call M300.Print.Headings.
   c. Print Grand.Tot.Cost and Grand.Tot.Price.
   d. Print an end-of-job message to conclude the report.
   e. Display an end-of-job message on the screen.

Program Solution

Program 6.3, the solution to Programming Case Study 10, is illustrated in Figure 6.12 on the next page and corresponds to the requirements of the printer-spacing chart in Figure 6.11 and to the preceding program tasks.

▌FIGURE 6.12

Program 6.3, the solution to Programming Case Study 10.

```
 1  ' Program 6.3
 2  ' Processing a Sequential Data File
 3  ' Input File Name = INVNTORY.DAT
 4  ' ************************************************
 5  ' *                 Main Program                *
 6  ' ************************************************
 7  GOSUB A100.Initialization
 8  GOSUB B100.Process.File
 9  GOSUB C100.Wrap.Up
10  END
11
12  ' ************************************************
13  ' *                Initialization               *
14  ' ************************************************
15  A100.Initialization:
16     Page.Count = 0
17     Max.Lines.Per.Page = 20
18     Grand.Tot.Cost = 0
19     Grand.Tot.Price = 0
20     CLS   ' Clear Screen
21     LOCATE 10, 20
22     PRINT "Please make sure there is paper in the printer."
23     LOCATE 12, 20
24     INPUT "Press the Enter key when the printer is ready...", Control$
25     OPEN "A:INVNTORY.DAT" FOR INPUT AS #1
26     GOSUB A200.Initialize.Report.Format
27     GOSUB M300.Print.Headings
28  RETURN
29
30  ' ************************************************
31  ' *           Initialize Report Format          *
32  ' ************************************************
33  A200.Initialize.Report.Format:
34     H1$ = "                 Inventory Analysis          Page: ##"
35     H2$ = "                                                Total"
36     H3$ = "Stock                 Unit Selling Quantity Total       Selling"
37     H4$ = "No.   Description     Cost Price   on Hand  Item Cost   Price"
38     H5$ = "----- -------------   ---- ------- -------- ---------   -------"
39     D1$ = "\   \  \            \ ###.## ####.##    #### ##,###.## ##,###.##"
40     T1$ = "Totals                                  ###,###.## ###,###.##"
41     T2$ = "Job Complete"
42  RETURN
43
44  ' ************************************************
45  ' *                 Process File                *
46  ' ************************************************
47  B100.Process.File:
48     DO WHILE NOT EOF(1)
49        INPUT #1, Stock$, Location$, Desc$, Cost, Price, Quantity
50        GOSUB B200.Compute.And.Accumulate
51        GOSUB B210.Print.Record
52     LOOP
53  RETURN
54
```

```
55   ' **********************************************
56   ' *      Compute and Increment Accumulators     *
57   ' **********************************************
58   B200.Compute.And.Accumulate:
59      Tot.Cost = Cost * Quantity
60      Tot.Price = Price * Quantity
61      Grand.Tot.Cost = Grand.Tot.Cost + Tot.Cost
62      Grand.Tot.Price = Grand.Tot.Price + Tot.Price
63   RETURN
64
65   ' **********************************************
66   ' *            Print an Inventory Record        *
67   ' **********************************************
68   B210.Print.Record:
69      IF Line.Count >= Max.Lines.Per.Page + 1 THEN
70         GOSUB M300.Print.Headings
71      END IF
72      LPRINT USING D1$; Stock$; Desc$; Cost; Price; Quantity; Tot.Cost; Tot.Price
73      LPRINT
74      Line.Count = Line.Count + 2
75   RETURN
76
77   ' **********************************************
78   ' *                    Wrap-Up                  *
79   ' **********************************************
80   C100.Wrap.Up:
81      CLOSE #1
82      IF Line.Count >= Max.Lines.Per.Page - 1 THEN
83         GOSUB M300.Print.Headings
84      END IF
85      LPRINT
86      LPRINT USING T1$; Grand.Tot.Cost; Grand.Tot.Price
87      LPRINT
88      LPRINT T2$
89      LPRINT CHR$(12); ' Start a new page
90      LOCATE 14, 20: PRINT "Job Complete"
91   RETURN
92
93   ' **********************************************
94   ' *        Print Report and Column Headings     *
95   ' **********************************************
96   M300.Print.Headings:
97      Page.Count = Page.Count + 1
98      IF Page.Count > 1 THEN
99         LPRINT CHR$(12); ' Start a new page
100     END IF
101     LPRINT USING H1$; Page.Count
102     LPRINT
103     LPRINT H2$
104     LPRINT H3$
105     LPRINT H4$
106     LPRINT H5$
107     Line.Count = 7
108  RETURN
109
110  ' *************** End of Program ***************

     [run]
```

Discussion of the Program Solution

When Program 6.3 is executed, the report illustrated in Figure 6.13 is printed on the printer. The following points should be noted concerning the program solution represented by Program 6.3:

1. In line 16, Page.Count is initialized to zero; later, in line 97, it is incremented by 1 just prior to printing the report title. In line 17, Max.Lines.Per.Page is set equal to 20, the number of lines to be printed per page in this example.

2. In line 25, the OPEN statement opens INVNTORY.DAT for input as filenumber 1. The remaining file-handling statements, which are lines 49 and 81, reference INVNTORY.DAT by specifying the filenumber 1.

3. The Do-While loop, lines 48 through 52 in B100.Process.File, processes records while the EOF function does not detect the end-of-file mark.

4. The activity of printing an inventory record is in a separate subroutine (lines 68 through 75) because it involves several lines of code. This subroutine is called from line 51 in the Do-While loop. Study B210.Print.Record closely. Whenever a program pages a report, the line counter must be tested (line 69) before the detail line is printed. After printing the detail line and double-spacing, the line counter is incremented by 2 (line 74).

    Note that the line counter (Line.Count) is compared against a value that ensures that the required lines to be printed in the subroutine will fit on the page. The problem specifications indicated that only 20 physical lines were to be printed per page. Because Line.Count is initialized to 7 (line 107) and incremented by two each time a detail line is printed (line 74), Line.Count takes on the values 7, 9, 11, 13, 15, 17, 19, 21. When Line.Count is 19, there is enough room on the page to print another detail line. When Line.Count is 21, there is no more room on the page. Hence, in line 69 when Line.Count is greater than or equal to Max.Lines.Per.Page + 1, that is 21, we transfer control to M300.Print.Headings.

5. M300.Print.Headings is called from lines 27, 70, and 83. Top-down programming requires that a module called from two or more different places in a program be placed below the last called subroutine. Calls should always be made in a downward direction in the program. Additionally, because this module is called from several points in the program, its level number begins with M which stands for multiple, followed by a number denoting the lowest level at which the module exists.

    M300.Print.Headings, beginning at line 96, increments the page number (line 97), starts a new page if the first page has already been printed (line 99), prints the report and column headings (lines 101 through 106), and finally sets the line counter to 7 (line 107). Line.Count is set equal to the number of the next line to be printed.

6. Although the warehouse location is not manipulated or displayed by Program 6.3, it is necessary to include a variable (Location$) that represents the warehouse location in the list of the INPUT #n statement (line 49) because the data item is part of the record. You cannot be selective and input from a sequential data file only those data items which you plan to manipulate or display. All data items within the record must be assigned to variables in the INPUT #n statement, as shown in line 49.

Paging Output on the Screen

To display the output from Program 6.3 on the screen rather than sending it to the printer, requires very few changes. The following steps outline these changes:

1. Remove lines 21 through 24, 89, and 90.
2. Replace the LPRINT statement in line 99 with two statements; the following INPUT statement and a CLS statement:

```
INPUT "Press Enter to continue ", Control$
```

This INPUT statement holds the screen while you view the current page of output. When you press Enter, the screen will be cleared and ready for the next page of output.

FIGURE 6.13

The report generated by Program 6.3.

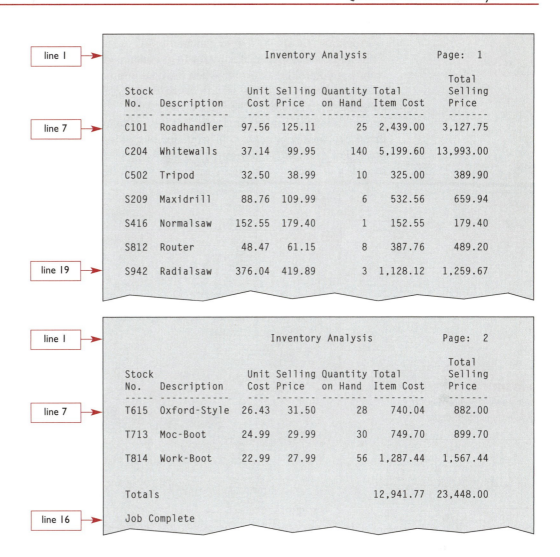

line 1

line 7

line 19

```
                        Inventory Analysis          Page:  1

                                                    Total
  Stock              Unit Selling Quantity Total    Selling
  No.   Description  Cost Price   on Hand  Item Cost Price
  ----- ------------ ---- ------- -------- --------- -------
  C101  Roadhandler  97.56 125.11      25  2,439.00  3,127.75

  C204  Whitewalls   37.14  99.95     140  5,199.60 13,993.00

  C502  Tripod       32.50  38.99      10    325.00    389.90

  S209  Maxidrill    88.76 109.99       6    532.56    659.94

  S416  Normalsaw   152.55 179.40       1    152.55    179.40

  S812  Router       48.47  61.15       8    387.76    489.20

  S942  Radialsaw   376.04 419.89       3  1,128.12  1,259.67
```

line 1

line 7

line 16

```
                        Inventory Analysis          Page:  2

                                                    Total
  Stock              Unit Selling Quantity Total    Selling
  No.   Description  Cost Price   on Hand  Item Cost Price
  ----- ------------ ---- ------- -------- --------- -------
  T615  Oxford-Style 26.43  31.50      28    740.04    882.00

  T713  Moc-Boot     24.99  29.99      30    749.70    899.70

  T814  Work-Boot    22.99  27.99      56  1,287.44  1,567.44

  Totals                                  12,941.77 23,448.00

  Job Complete
```

3. Replace all other LPRINT statements with PRINT statements

The QBasic output screen will display up to 24 lines of output. Thus, you must make certain that multiple-page reports that are displayed on the output screen contain no more than 24 lines per page. Because Program 6.3 used a maximum of 20 lines per page, no adjustments are needed to the value of Max.Lines.Per.Page. A modified version of Program 6.3 that displays the output report to the screen is located on your data disk under the name PRG6-3A.

6.5 CONTROL-BREAK PROCESSING

Most businesses are divided into smaller units for the purpose of better management. A retail company doing business on a national scale may have several levels of management with the levels headed by such people as a district manager, a store manager, and a department manager. To evaluate the performance of the units within each level, managerial reports are generated showing summaries, or minor totals, for each subunit. For example, a sales analysis report generated for the manager of a company often shows a summary sales total for each district within the company, as well as a grand sales total for the company.

Programs that are written to generate levels of subtotals use a technique involving control fields and control breaks. A **control field** contains data that is to be compared from record to record. A control break occurs when the data in the control field changes.

A control break may be used to display a summary line each time a selected data item, common to all records in the file, changes value. The variable assigned to the selected data item is called the **control variable**. For this technique to work successfully, it is essential that the records be processed in sequence, according to the data item that determines the break. For example, to generate the Sales Analysis Report shown in Figure 6.14, all the records that belong to District 1 must precede all the District 2 records.

FIGURE 6.14

Sales Analysis Report with a single-level control break.

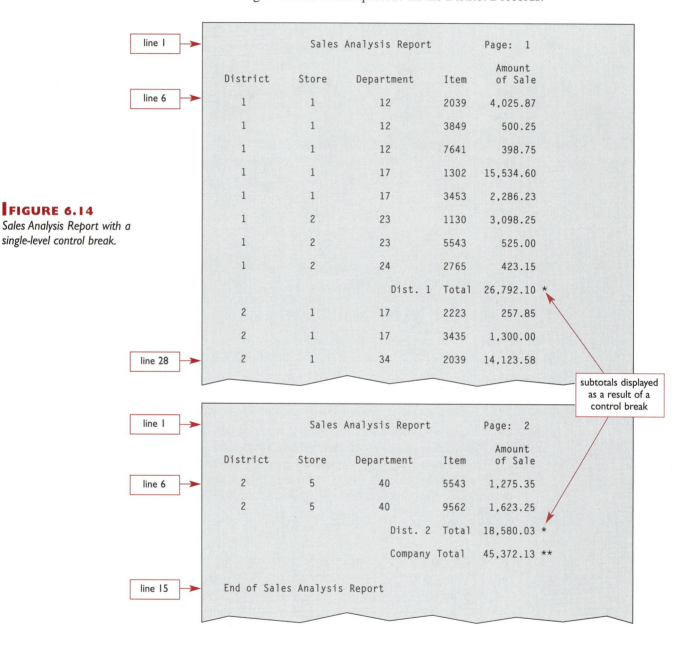

With the sales records in sequence, the program solution can check each sales record to see whether it is the first record of a new district. If the sales record represents an item from the *old* district (that is, if the current item and the previous one belong to the same district), then selected contents of that record are printed, and the PC adds the sales amount for that item to a district sales accumulator.

When a sales record that belongs to a *new* district is read, a control break occurs, and the current value of the district sales accumulator is printed. In addition, asterisks are often printed to the right of the totals to highlight a summary. One asterisk indicates the lowest level, two asterisks the next level, and so on. Before processing the sales record that caused the control break, the PC must add the district sales to the company sales total, which is displayed after all records in the file have been processed.

Furthermore, the control variable must be assigned the value of the next district number before the processing of the record is resumed. Finally, the variable that is used to sum the district sales must be reset to zero after each control break so that it can be used to sum the sales for the next district.

The following Programming Case Study pertains to generating the report found in Figure 6.14.

PROGRAMMING CASE STUDY 11A – Sales Analysis Report – Single-Level Control Break

Problem: The Sales Analysis department of the PUC Company has requested that a program be written to generate the Sales Analysis Report shown in Figure 6.14. Each record in the file includes a district, a store, a department, an item, and the sales amount, as shown in Figure 6.15(a).

The sales records are located in the data file SALES.DAT in ascending sequence by district, as illustrated in Figure 6.15(b). A data file like SALES.DAT may be created by a program that is similar to Program 6.2. Note that although the first four data items in each record of SALES.DAT are numeric, we have stored them as string values because we do not plan to do arithmetic using them.

FIGURE 6.15

(a) The sales data in ascending sequence by department within store within district.
(b) A listing of the sales data sorted in SALES.DAT.

District	Store	Dept.	Item	Amt. of Sale
1	1	12	2039	$ 4,025.87
1	1	12	3849	500.25
1	1	12	7641	398.78
1	1	17	1302	15,534.60
1	1	17	3453	2,286.23
1	2	23	1130	3,098.25
1	2	23	5543	525.00
1	2	24	2765	423.15
2	1	17	2223	257.85
2	1	17	3435	1,300.00
2	1	34	2039	14,123.58
2	5	40	5543	1,275.35
2	5	40	9562	1,623.25

(a)

```
"1","1","12","2039",4025.87
"1","1","12","3849",500.25
"1","1","12","7641",398.75
"1","1","17","1302",15534.6
"1","1","17","3453",2286.23
"1","2","23","1130",3098.25
"1","2","23","5543",525
"1","2","24","2765",423.15
"2","1","17","2223",257.85
"2","1","17","3435",1300
"2","1","34","2039",14123.58
"2","5","40","5543",1275.35
"2","5","40","9562",1623.25
```

(b)

The data items within each sales record are to be printed on the printer. Also to be printed are the sales total for each district before a new district is processed, and the final sales total for the company after all sales records have been processed. Print 30 lines to a page. At the top of each new page, print the report title, page number, and column headings as illustrated in Figure 6.14. Double-space the detail lines.

Figure 6.16 on the next page shows a top-down chart for the Sales Analysis report. Figure 6.17 on the next page shows a general flowchart of B100.Process.File. Following are a list of the program tasks in outline form, a program solution, and a discussion of the program solution.

FIGURE 6.16
A top-down chart for the Sales Analysis report program.

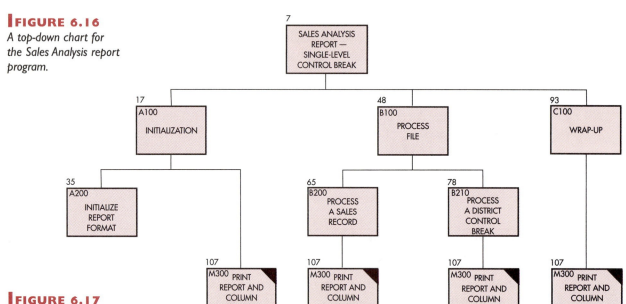

FIGURE 6.17
A general flowchart for the Sales Analysis report program.

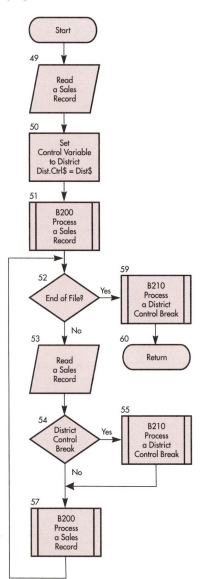

Program Tasks

The following program tasks correspond to the top-down chart in Figure 6.16, the flowchart in Fiugre 6.17 — and Program 6.4, the solution to Programming Case Study 11A:

1. A100. Initialization
   a. Set Page.Count to zero.
   b. Set Max.Lines.Per.Page to 30.
   c. Set Dist.Total and Cmpy.Total to zero.
   d. Clear the screen.
   e. Display a message instructing the user to make sure there is paper in the printer.
   f. Open SALES.DAT.
   g. Initialize report format and print the report headings.

2. B100.Process.File, if not end-of-file
   a. Read a sales record.
   b. Assign the value of Dist$ to Dist.Ctrl$.
   c. Call B200.Process.Record. Within this subroutine, do the following:
      (1) Increment Dist.Total by Amount.
      (2) If Line.Count is greater than or equal to Max.Lines.Per.Page, then print the report headings.
      (3) Print the detail line.
      (4) Increment Line.Count by 2 because the report is to be double-spaced.
   d. Establish a Do-While loop that executes while not end-of-file. Within this loop, do the following:
      (1) Read the next sales record.
      (2) Test for a control break (Dist$ <> Dist.Ctrl$). If a control break occurs, then call B210.District.Break. This subroutine must do the following:
         (a) Increment Cmpy.Total by Dist.Total.
         (b) If Line.Count is greater than or equal to Max.Lines.Per.Page, then print the report headings.

            (c) Print Dist.Total.

            (d) Set Dist.Ctrl$ equal to Dist$.

            (e) Reset Dist.Total to zero.

        (3) Call B200.Process.Record described in step 2c.

    e. Following the Do-While loop, process the last district.

3. C100.Wrap.Up

    a. Close SALES.DAT.

    b. If Line.Count is greater than or equal to Max.Lines.Per.Page − 2, then print the report headings.

    c. Print Cmpy.Total and an end-of-job message.

    d. Display an end-of-job message on the screen.

Program Solution

Program 6.4, the solution to Programming Case Study 11A, is presented in Figure 6.18.

▌FIGURE 6.18

Program 6.4, the solution to Programming Case Study 11A.

```
 1  ' Program 6.4
 2  ' Sales Analysis Report -- Single Level Control Break
 3  ' Input File Name = SALES.DAT
 4  ' *****************************************************
 5  ' *                    Main Program                  *
 6  ' *****************************************************
 7  GOSUB A100.Initialization
 8  IF NOT EOF(1) THEN
 9     GOSUB B100.Process.File
10  END IF
11  GOSUB C100.Wrap.Up
12  END
13
14  ' *****************************************************
15  ' *                  Initialization                  *
16  ' *****************************************************
17  A100.Initialization:
18     Page.Count = 0
19     Max.Lines.Per.Page = 30
20     Dist.Total = 0
21     Cmpy.Total = 0
22     CLS  ' Clear Screen
23     LOCATE 10, 20
24     PRINT "Please make sure there is paper in the printer."
25     LOCATE 12, 20
26     INPUT "Press the Enter key when the printer is ready...", Control$
27     OPEN "A:SALES.DAT" FOR INPUT AS #1
28     GOSUB A200.Initialize.Report.Format
29     GOSUB M300.Print.Headings
30  RETURN
31
32  ' *****************************************************
33  ' *             Initialize Report Format             *
34  ' *****************************************************
35  A200.Initialize.Report.Format:
36     H1$ = "                  Sales Analysis Report         Page: ##"
37     H2$ = "                                                Amount"
38     H3$ = "District     Store     Department     Item     Of Sale"
39     D1$ = "    \\           \\            \\          \ \    ##,###.##"
40     T1$ = "                                Dist. \\ Total ###,###.## *"
41     T2$ = "                                Company Total ####,###.## _**"
42     T3$ = "End of Sales Analysis Report"
43  RETURN
44
```

(continued)

```
45   ' **************************************************
46   ' *                   Process File                      *
47   ' **************************************************
48   B100.Process.File:
49      INPUT #1, Dist$, Store$, Dept$, Item$, Amount          initialize control
50      Dist.Ctrl$ = Dist$  ◄─────────────────────────              variable
51      GOSUB B200.Process.Record     ' Process first record
52      DO WHILE NOT EOF(1)
53         INPUT #1, Dist$, Store$, Dept$, Item$, Amount       test for
54         IF Dist$ <> Dist.Ctrl$ THEN  ◄──────────────    control break
55            GOSUB B210.District.Break   ' Process a District Control Break
56         END IF
57         GOSUB B200.Process.Record
58      LOOP
59      GOSUB B210.District.Break
60   RETURN
61
62   ' **************************************************
63   ' *              Process a Sales Record                 *
64   ' **************************************************
65   B200.Process.Record:
66      Dist.Total = Dist.Total + Amount
67      IF Line.Count >= Max.Lines.Per.Page THEN
68         GOSUB M300.Print.Headings
69      END IF
70      LPRINT USING D1$; Dist$; Store$; Dept$; Item$; Amount
71      LPRINT
72      Line.Count = Line.Count + 2
73   RETURN
74
75   ' **************************************************
76   ' *            Process a District Control Break         *
77   ' **************************************************
78   B210.District.Break:
79      Cmpy.Total = Cmpy.Total + Dist.Total
80      IF Line.Count >= Max.Lines.Per.Page THEN
81         GOSUB M300.Print.Headings
82      END IF                                            print district
83      LPRINT USING T1$; Dist.Ctrl$; Dist.Total  ◄──────     total
84      LPRINT
85      Line.Count = Line.Count + 2
86      Dist.Ctrl$ = Dist$
87      Dist.Total = 0
88   RETURN
89
90   ' **************************************************
91   ' *                   Wrap-Up                           *
92   ' **************************************************
93   C100.Wrap.Up:
94      CLOSE #1
95      IF Line.Count >= Max.Lines.Per.Page - 2 THEN
96         GOSUB M300.Print.Headings
97      END IF
98      LPRINT USING T2$; Cmpy.Total
99      LPRINT : LPRINT : LPRINT T3$
100     LPRINT CHR$(12);        ' Form feed last page
101     LOCATE 14, 20: PRINT "Job Complete"
102  RETURN
103
```

```
104   ' *************************************************
105   ' *          Print Report and Column Headings      *
106   ' *************************************************
107   M300.Print.Headings:
108      Page.Count = Page.Count + 1
109      IF Page.Count > 1 THEN
110         LPRINT CHR$(12); ' Start a new page
111      END IF
112      LPRINT USING H1$; Page.Count
113      LPRINT
114      LPRINT H2$
115      LPRINT H3$
116      LPRINT
117      Line.Count = 6
118   RETURN
119
120   ' *************** End of Program ******************

      [run]
```

Discussion of the Solution

When Program 6.4 is executed, the PC prints the report shown in Figure 6.14 on page 220. Note these important points regarding the control-break processing in Program 6.4.

1. In A100.Initialization, lines 20 and 21 initialize the district and the company accumulators.
2. In the Main Program, B100.Process.File is called by line 9 only if SALES.DAT is not empty. The IF statement is required in line 8 because the first statement in B100.Process.File (line 49) is the INPUT #n statement.
3. In B100.Process.File, line 49 reads the first sales record and line 50 sets the control variable (Dist.Ctrl$) equal to the first district (Dist$). Line 51 causes the first sales record to be processed.

   The DO WHILE statement in line 52 tests to determine whether there are any records left in SALES.DAT. Within the Do-While loop, line 53 reads the next sales record. Line 54 compares the district of the most recently read sales record to the control variable. If they are different, a control break has occurred and B210.District.Break is called. Whether or not a control break occurs, line 57 processes the sales record last read by line 53.

   Following the processing of a record line 58 returns control to the DO WHILE statement in line 52. When the end-of-file mark finally is detected, the DO WHILE statement transfers control to line 59 and the totals for the last district in the file are processed.
4. In B210.District.Break, the four requirements for processing a control break are fulfilled in the following way:
   a. Line 79 increments the company sales accumulator (Cmpy.Total) by the district sales accumulator (Dist.Total).
   b. Line 80 tests for a page break. Lines 83 through 85 print the value of the district sales accumulator and increment Line.Count. Note that line 83 uses the control variable (Dist.Ctrl$) rather than the variable Dist$ to print the district number. Can you explain why we do not print Dist$?
   c. Line 86 assigns the control variable (Dist.Ctrl$) the value of the new district.
   d. Line 87 sets the district sales accumulator (Dist.Total) to zero in preparation for processing the next district.
5. In C100.Wrap.Up, the company sales total (Cmpy.Total) is printed.

PROGRAMMING CASE STUDY 11B – Sales Analysis Report – Two Levels of Control Breaks

Four classifications of control breaks include: minor, intermediate, major, and multiple. A report may include one break (minor), as was the case in the previous example; two breaks (intermediate); three breaks (major); or multiple (more than three breaks).

The next program solution illustrates the generation of a sales analysis report that is the same as the one shown in Figure 6.14 on page 220, except that it includes two levels of control breaks. Each control break causes a number of summaries to be printed, depending on the level of the break. A store change (minor) causes one summary to be printed. A district change (major) causes both the last store total and the district total to be printed. When the end-of-file mark is sensed, all summaries that relate to the last store and district are printed, along with the grand total sales for the company.

The logic employed in a program involving multilevel control breaks is similar to that shown in Program 6.4. It makes little difference whether there are two, three, or more levels to consider. The program need only include additional decision statements and accumulators for each control-break summary. The comparison should be structured so that the major level is considered first, then the intermediate levels, and so forth down to the minor level.

Finally, it is important that the sales records be in ascending sequence by store within district. That is, within each district, the stores must be in ascending sequence. Study carefully the sequence of the sales records in SALES.DAT shown in Figure 6.15(a) on page 221.

A list of the additional program tasks required to modify Program 6.4 so that it will generate the new report are listed below. The program solution, the Sales Analysis Report, and a discussion of the program solution follow.

Program Tasks in Addition to Those Listed for Programming Case Study 11A

1. A100.Initialization

    a. Set Max.Lines.Per.Page to 36 rather than 30.
    b. Set Store.Total to zero.
    c. In A200.Initialize.Report.Format, add an extra total line to print the value of Store.Total when a minor control break occurs.

2. B100.Process.File

    a. Set Store.Ctrl$ equal to Store$ after the first record is read.
    b. Within the Do-While loop, add a test for a minor control break (Store$ <> Store.Ctrl$) nested immediately after the test for the major control break (Dist$ <> Dist.Ctrl$).
    c. As the first statement in the control-break test in B100.Process.File, add a call to B220.Store.Break. (Whenever there is a district control break, there must be a store control break.)
    d. Add the subroutine B220.Store.Break. This subroutine is nearly identical to B210.District.Break; the only difference is that the reference to all variables is at the store level rather than at the district level.

Program Solution

Program 6.5, the soluton to Programming Case Study 11B, is presented in Figure 6.19 and contains the modifications to Program 6.4 described by the preceding additional tasks.

FIGURE 6.19

Program 6.5, the solution to Programming Case Study 11B.

```
 1  ' Program 6.5
 2  ' Sales Analysis Report -- Two Levels of Control Breaks
 3  ' Input File Name = SALES.DAT
 4  ' ****************************************************
 5  ' *                  Main Program                  *
 6  ' ****************************************************
 7  GOSUB A100.Initialization
 8  IF NOT EOF(1) THEN
 9     GOSUB B100.Process.File
10  END IF
11  GOSUB C100.Wrap.Up
12  END
13
14  ' ****************************************************
15  ' *                 Initialization                 *
16  ' ****************************************************
17  A100.Initialization:
18     Page.Count = 0
19     Max.Lines.Per.Page = 36
20     Store.Total = 0
21     Dist.Total = 0
22     Cmpy.Total = 0
23     CLS  ' Clear Screen
24     LOCATE 10, 20
25     PRINT "Please make sure there is paper in the printer."
26     LOCATE 12, 20
27     INPUT "Press the Enter key when the printer is ready...", Control$
28     OPEN "A:SALES.DAT" FOR INPUT AS #1
29     GOSUB A200.Initialize.Report.Format
30     GOSUB M300.Print.Headings
31  RETURN
32
33  ' ****************************************************
34  ' *            Initialize Report Format            *
35  ' ****************************************************
36  A200.Initialize.Report.Format:
37     H1$ = "               Sales Analysis Report        Page: ##"
38     H2$ = "                                              Amount"
39     H3$ = "District      Store       Department    Item    Of Sale"
40     D1$ = "   \\           \\            \\          \ \   ##,###.##"
41     T1$ = "                            Store \\ Total ###,###.## *"
42     T2$ = "                            Dist. \\ Total ###,###.## *_*"
43     T3$ = "                            Company Total ####,###.## *_**"
44     T4$ = "End of Sales Analysis Report"
45  RETURN
46
47  ' ****************************************************
48  ' *                  Process File                  *
49  ' ****************************************************
50  B100.Process.File:
51     INPUT #1, Dist$, Store$, Dept$, Item$, Amount
52     Dist.Ctrl$ = Dist$
53     Store.Ctrl$ = Store$
54     GOSUB B200.Process.Record     ' Process first record
55     DO WHILE NOT EOF(1)
56        INPUT #1, Dist$, Store$, Dept$, Item$, Amount
57        IF Dist$ <> Dist.Ctrl$ THEN          test for major
                                                control break first
58           GOSUB B220.Store.Break         ' Process a Store Control Break
59           GOSUB B210.District.Break      ' Process a District Control Break
60        ELSE
```

(continued)

```
61              IF Store$ <> Store.Ctrl$ THEN
62                  GOSUB B220.Store.Break        ' Process a Store Control Break
63              END IF
64          END IF
65          GOSUB B200.Process.Record
66      LOOP
67      GOSUB B220.Store.Break          ' Process last Store Control Break
68      GOSUB B210.District.Break       ' Process last District Control Break
69  RETURN
70
71  ' *****************************************************
72  ' *              Process a Sales Record               *
73  ' *****************************************************
74  B200.Process.Record:
75      Store.Total = Store.Total + Amount
76      IF Line.Count >= Max.Lines.Per.Page THEN
77          GOSUB M300.Print.Headings
78      END IF
79      LPRINT USING D1$; Dist$; Store$; Dept$; Item$; Amount
80      LPRINT
81      Line.Count = Line.Count + 2
82  RETURN
83
84  ' *****************************************************
85  ' *          Process a District Control Break         *
86  ' *****************************************************
87  B210.District.Break:
88      Cmpy.Total = Cmpy.Total + Dist.Total
89      IF Line.Count >= Max.Lines.Per.Page THEN
90          GOSUB M300.Print.Headings
91      END IF
92      LPRINT USING T2$; Dist.Ctrl$; Dist.Total
93      LPRINT
94      Line.Count = Line.Count + 2
95      Dist.Ctrl$ = Dist$
96      Dist.Total = 0
97  RETURN
98
99  ' *****************************************************
100 ' *            Process a Store Control Break          *
101 ' *****************************************************
102 B220.Store.Break:
103     Dist.Total = Dist.Total + Store.Total
104     IF Line.Count >= Max.Lines.Per.Page THEN
105         GOSUB M300.Print.Headings
106     END IF
107     LPRINT USING T1$; Store.Ctrl$; Store.Total
108     LPRINT
109     Line.Count = Line.Count + 2
110     Store.Ctrl$ = Store$
111     Store.Total = 0
112 RETURN
113
114 ' *****************************************************
115 ' *                    Wrap-Up                        *
116 ' *****************************************************
117 C100.Wrap.Up:
118     CLOSE #1
119     IF Line.Count >= Max.Lines.Per.Page - 2 THEN
120         GOSUB M300.Print.Headings
```

```
121     END IF
122     LPRINT USING T3$; Cmpy.Total
123     LPRINT : LPRINT : LPRINT T4$
124     LPRINT CHR$(12);      ' Form feed last page
125     LOCATE 14, 20: PRINT "Job Complete"
126 RETURN
127
128 ' ****************************************************
129 ' *          Print Report and Column Headings        *
130 ' ****************************************************
131 M300.Print.Headings:
132     Page.Count = Page.Count + 1
133     IF Page.Count > 1 THEN
134         LPRINT CHR$(12); ' Start a new page
135     END IF
136     LPRINT USING H1$; Page.Count
137     LPRINT
138     LPRINT H2$
139     LPRINT H3$
140     LPRINT
141     Line.Count = 6
142 RETURN
143
144 ' **************** End of Program ******************

    [run]
```

Discussion of the Program Solution

When Program 6.5 is executed, the report shown in Figure 6.20 on the next page is generated. The main difference between the report in Figure 6.20 and the one in Figure 6.14 on page 220 is that in Figure 6.20 there are two levels of control breaks. Following the processing of all Store 1, District 1 records, a total for Store 1 prints. Following a district control break, both the totals for the store and district print. Printing the store and district totals each time they change continues until the entire file has been processed.

The following specific points should be noted concerning Program 6.5:

1. In B100.Process.File, line 57 tests for a district control break. If a district control break occurs, control transfers to B220.Store.Break (line 58). After the store control break has been processed, control returns to B100.Process.File. The subroutine B210.District.Break is then called (line 59), and the district control break is processed. Line 58 ensures that a store control break is processed whenever a district control break occurs.
2. If the condition testing for a district control break in line 57 is false, line 61 tests to determine whether there is a store control break. If there is a minor control break, control transfers to B220.Store.Break.

When a sales record causes a district control break, the condition in line 61 that tests for a store control break will not be tested and need not be tested because Store.Ctrl$ is equal to Store$, owing to the major control break.

As an addition to this program solution, in QBasic Programming Problem 6 on page 237 you are asked to generate a triple-control-break report with the same file (SALES.DAT) that was used in Programming Case Studies 11A and 11B. The report requires three control breaks that include department, within store, within district. A close look at SALES.DAT in Figure 6.15(b) on page 221 reveals that the file is in ascending sequence by department, within store, within district.

FIGURE 6.20

Sales Analysis Report with two levels of control breaks.

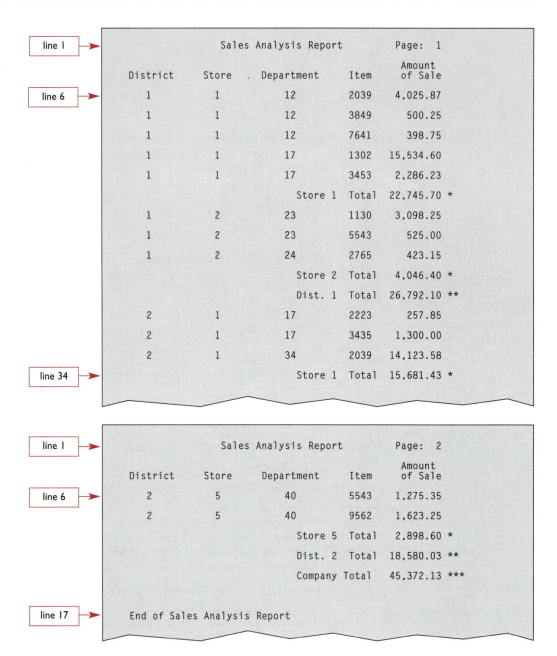

```
line 1  →                      Sales Analysis Report              Page:  1

                                                            Amount
            District     Store   . Department     Item      of Sale
line 6  →      1           1          12          2039      4,025.87
               1           1          12          3849        500.25
               1           1          12          7641        398.75
               1           1          17          1302     15,534.60
               1           1          17          3453      2,286.23
                                         Store 1   Total   22,745.70 *
               1           2          23          1130      3,098.25
               1           2          23          5543        525.00
               1           2          24          2765        423.15
                                         Store 2   Total    4,046.40 *
                                         Dist. 1   Total   26,792.10 **
               2           1          17          2223        257.85
               2           1          17          3435      1,300.00
               2           1          34          2039     14,123.58
line 34 →                                Store 1   Total   15,681.43 *
```

```
line 1  →                      Sales Analysis Report              Page:  2

                                                            Amount
            District     Store     Department     Item      of Sale
line 6  →      2           5          40          5543      1,275.35
               2           5          40          9562      1,623.25
                                         Store 5   Total    2,898.60 *
                                         Dist. 2   Total   18,580.03 **
                                         Company Total      45,372.13 ***

line 17 →   End of Sales Analysis Report
```

6.6 What You Should Know

1. In QBasic, the four following techniques can be used to integrate data into a program:
   a. The INPUT statement and keyboard or any other external input device
   b. The READ and DATA statements
   c. The INPUT #n statement and data files
   d. The LET statement
2. A file is a group of related records. Each record within a file contains related data items.
3. QBasic provides for two types of file organization — sequential and random. A file that is organized sequentially is limited to sequential processing. Random files will be discussed in Chapter 9.
4. A filespec identifies a file in auxiliary storage.
5. Before a file can be read from or written to, it must be opened by the OPEN statement.
6. When a program is finished reading from or writing to a file, it must close the file with the CLOSE statement.

7. A sequential file can be opened for input, output, or append. If a file is opened for input, the pointer is placed at the beginning of the file, and the program can only read records from it. If a file is opened for output, the pointer is placed at the beginning of the file, and the program can only write records to the file. If a file is opened for append, the pointer is placed after the last record in the file and the program can only write records to the file.

8. If a file is opened for input, the file must already exist. If a file is opened for output and it already exists, the PC deletes the file before it opens it. The file may or may not exist prior to the execution of the OPEN statement for appending records. If the file exists, the pointer is placed after the last record in the file. If the file does not exist, then APPEND is the same as OUTPUT.

9. The PRINT #n and PRINT #n, USING statements are used to write information to a sequential file in the form of a report.

10. The WRITE #n statement is used to write data to a file in the format required by the INPUT #n statement. The format requirement is similar to that of the READ and DATA statements: all data items must be separated by commas.

11. The INPUT #n statement reads data from a sequential file.

12. When a file opened for output is closed by the CLOSE or END statement, an end-of-file mark is added after the last record. Later, when a program reads records from the file, the EOF(n) function may be used to test for the end-of-file mark on the file that is associated with filenumber n. It is important that the test be made prior to the attempt to read a record.

13. Paging a report involves printing the report and column headings along with a page number at the top of the first page, or screen, and then each time after a predetermined number of lines has been printed.

14. Paging a report requires two accumulators: a line counter and a page counter.

15. Programs that are written to generate levels of subtotals use control fields and control breaks. A control field contains data that is to be compared from record to record. A control break occurs when the data in the same control field changes.

16. To display subtotals when control breaks occur, the records within a file must be in sorted sequence, ascending or descending, according to the control field.

17. There are four classifications of control breaks: one break (minor); two breaks (intermediate); three breaks (major); and multiple breaks (more than three).

6.7 Test Your QBasic Skills (Even-numbered answers are in Appendix E)

1. Consider the valid program below, then explain its function. Assume that the values in the table below are entered in response to the INPUT statements in the program.

Stock Item	Selling Price	Discount Code
138	$ 78.56	2
421	123.58	3
617	475.65	2
812	23.58	1
917	754.56	4

```
' Exercise 6.1
OPEN 'EX61.DAT" FOR OUTPUT AS #1
DO
    CLS      'Clear Screen
    INPUT "Stock Item =====> ", Item$
    INPUT "Selling Price ===> ", Price
    INPUT "Discount Code ===> ", Code$
    WRITE #1, Item$, Price, Code$
    INPUT "Add ANOTHER record? (Y or N)", Control$
LOOP UNTIL UCASE(Control$) = "N"
CLOSE #1
PRINT : PRINT "Job Complete"
END
```

2. Fill in the blanks in the following sentences:
   a. The _____ statement with a mode of _____ or _____ must be executed before a PRINT #n, PRINT #n, USING, or WRITE #n statement is executed.
   b. The _____ statement with a mode of _____ must be executed before an INPUT #n statement is executed.
   c. A file can be opened as often as required, provided it is _____ before each subsequent open.
   d. The function _____ is used to test for the end-of-file mark with a sequential file.
   e. When records are to be added to the end of a sequential file, the _____ mode is used in the OPEN statement.

3. Explain the purpose of the EOF function. Also indicate where it should be located in a program in relation to the INPUT #n statement.

4. A program is to read records from one of three sequential data files: SALES1.DAT, SALES2.DAT, and SALES3.DAT. The three files are stored on the floppy disk in the A drive. Write three OPEN statements that would allow the program to read records from any of the three sequential files.

5. Construct a WRITE #n statement that would write the values of A, B, X$, and D to a sequential file in the format required by the INPUT #n statement.

6. Which of the following are invalid file-handling statements? Why?
   a. OPEN FOR OUTPUT "A:SAL.DAT" AS #1
   b. OPEN File$ FOR APPEND AS #3
   c. PRINT #1,
   d. PRINT #1, A,
   e. PRINT #1 USING "####.##"; Cost
   f. CLOSE
   g. DO WHILE NOT EOF(#2)
   h. INPUT #2, Amount,

7. Assume that the following line is located in the Print a Detail Line module and prints the detail line for a report:

   LPRINT Emp.Number$, Emp.Name$, Emp.Soc.Sec$, Emp.Salary

   Write the line that would immediately follow it if:

   a. Double-spacing where required.
   b. Triple-spacing where required.

8. Write a statement that would properly increment the line counter (Line.Count) for each of the requirements below. This statement would follow the LPRINT statement in Exercise 7 in the Print a Detail Line module.

   a. Single-space the detail line.
   b. Double-space the detail line.
   c. Triple-space the detail line.

9. Write the IF statement that would test to determine whether the report title and column headings should be printed for each of the requirements below. This IF statement would precede the LPRINT statement in Exercise 7 in the Print a Detail Line module. Assume Line.Count was initialized to 2 in the Print Headings module.

   a. Max.Lines.Per.Page = 10 and triple-spacing
   b. Max.Lines.Per.Page = 45 and double-spacing
   c. Max.Lines.Per.Page = 54 and single-spacing

10. **PC Hands-On Exercise:** Do the following:
    a. Load Program PRG6-3A from the Data Disk and execute the program. Notice the paging that occurs on the screen. Delete the statement, Line.Count = Line.Count + 2, in B210.Print.Record and execute the program again. Do you understand why it is important to increment the line counter? Exit the program without saving it.

b. Load Program PRG6-3A again. In A100.Initialization, change the statement Page.Count = 0 to Page.Count = 99. Execute the program and examine the page numbers on the report. How would you adjust the definition of H1$ to ensure that page numbers up to 999 will print correctly?

c. Load Program PRG6-3A again. In A100.Initialization, set Max.Lines.Per.Page to 10. Execute the program. Do you agree that by modifying the value of this variable you can change the number of lines printed or displayed per page?

11. **PC Hands-On Exercise**: Load Program 6.4 (PRG6-4) from the Data Disk. Display and execute Program 6.4. Delete line 50 illustrated in Figure 6.18 (pages 223-229) and execute the program a second time. Study the output results and explain the important function of line 50.

12. **PC Hands-On Exercise**: Load Program 6.5 (PRG6-5) from the Data Disk. Display and execute Program 6.5. Delete line 58 illustrated in Figure 6.19 (pages 227-229)and execute the program a second time. Study the output results. Do you understand that when there is a major control break, all lower-level control breaks must also be processed?

6.8 QBasic Programming Problems

1. Creating a Master File

Purpose: To become familiar with creating a sequential file that is consistent with the format required by the INPUT statement. Use of the OPEN, CLOSE, and WRITE # statements is required.

Problem: Construct a top-down program to create a sequential file named EX61PAY.DAT that represents the payroll master file for the PUC Company. A **master file** is one that is, for the most part, permanent or includes data that is required each time an application such as payroll is processed. Each record in the file describes an employee, including the year-to-date (YTD) payroll information, as shown under the Input Data.

Write the data to the file in the format required by the INPUT #n statement. Have the user enter Y (or y) to add the record entered and displayed on the screen before writing it to the file. After completing each record entry, have the user enter Y (or y) to add another record, else N (or n). As part of the end-of-job routine, display a message indicating that the file was created, as well as the total number of records written to the file.

(**Hint:** Use Program 6.2 — PRG6-2 on the Data Disk — as a guide to solving this problem.)

Input Data: Prepare and use the following sample data.

| Employee | | Depend- | Marital | Rate | Year-to-Date | | |
No.	Name	ents	Status	of Pay	Gross Pay	Federal With. Tax	Social Security
123	Col Joan	2	M	12.50	25,345.23	10,256.45	1,938.91
124	Fiel Don	1	S	18.00	50,725.00	15,546.45	3,880.46
125	Dim Lisa	1	S	13.00	52,115.23	14,035.78	3,924.45
126	Snow Joe	9	M	5.50	11,510.05	854.34	880.52
134	Hi Frank	0	M	8.75	9,298.65	2,678.25	711.35
167	Bri Edie	3	S	10.40	8,190.45	2,017.50	626.57
210	Liss Ted	6	M	8.80	7,098.04	2,120.55	543.00
234	Son Fred	2	M	6.75	1,350.00	405.00	100.00
244	John Tom	3	M	8.75	0.00	0.00	0.00

Output Results: The sequential file EX61PAY.DAT is created on auxiliary storage on the default drive. The results are shown in Figure 6.21 for the first payroll record and for the termination of the program.

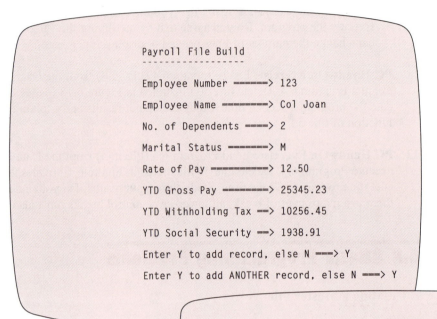

```
Payroll File Build
------------------

Employee Number ======> 123

Employee Name =========> Col Joan

No. of Dependents =====> 2

Marital Status ========> M

Rate of Pay ==========> 12.50

YTD Gross Pay ========> 25345.23

YTD Withholding Tax ==> 10256.45

YTD Social Security ==> 1938.91

Enter Y to add record, else N ===> Y

Enter Y to add ANOTHER record, else N ===> Y
```

```
Creation of Sequential Data File is Complete

Total Number of Records in EX61PAY.DAT ===> 9

Job Complete
```

FIGURE 6.21
The output results for the first record and for termination of the program for Programming Problem 1.

2. Master File List

Purpose: To become familiar with reading records in a sequential file, printing the records on the printer, and paging a report. Use of the OPEN, CLOSE, INPUT #n, PRINT, and PRINT USING statements and the EOF function is required.

Problem: Write a top-down program that prints the data items found in each employee record of the sequential file EX61PAY.DAT created in QBasic Programming Problem 1. Page the report. Print a maximum of 18 lines to a page. Double-space the detail lines and single-space the total lines. As part of the end-of-job routine, display the following totals: employee record count, YTD gross pay, YTD federal withholding tax, and YTD social security tax.

(**Hint:** Use PRG6-3A on the Data Disk as a guide in solving this problem.)

Input Data: Use the sequential file EX61PAY.DAT created in Problem 1. (If you did not complete QBasic Programming Problem 1, then use EX61PAY.DAT found on the Data Disk.)

Output Results: The output screens should appear as illustrated by Figure 6.22.

FIGURE 6.22
Output for Programming Problem 2.

```
                         Payroll File List          Page:  1

      Employee         Marital Rate of <-------Year-to-Date-------->
      No. Name    Dep. Status Pay     Gross Pay With. Tax Soc. Sec.
      ---  -------- ----  -------  -------   ---------  ---------  ---------
      123 Col Joan   2     M      12.50  25,345.23 10,256.45  1,938.91

      124 Fiel Don   1     S      18.00  50,725.00 15,546.45  3,880.46

      125 Dim Lisa   1     S      13.00  52,115.23 14,035.78  3,924.45

      126 Snow Joe   9     M       5.50  11,510.05    854.34    880.52

      134 Hi Frank   0     M       8.75   9,298.65  2,678.25    711.35

      167 Bri Edie   3     S      10.40   8,190.45  2,017.50    626.57

      210 Liss Ted   6     M       8.80   7,098.04  2,120.55    543.00
```

```
                         Payroll File List          Page:  2

      Employee         Marital Rate of <-------Year-to-Date-------->
      No. Name    Dep. Status Pay     Gross Pay With. Tax Soc. Sec.
      ---  -------- ----  -------  -------   ---------  ---------  ---------
      234 Son Fred   2     M       6.75   1,350.00    405.00    100.00

      244 John Tom   3     M       8.75       0.00      0.00      0.00

      Total Number of Records ========>          9
      Total YTD Gross Pay =============> 165,632.65
      Total YTD Withholding Tax =======>  47,914.32
      Total YTD Social Security =======>  12,605.26

      Job Complete
```

3. Writing a Report to Auxiliary Storage

Purpose: To become familiar with writing a report to a sequential file. Use of the OPEN, CLOSE, INPUT #n, PRINT #n, and PRINT #n, USING statements and the EOF function is required.

Problem: Same as QBasic Programming Problem 2, except write the report to the sequential file EX63RPT.LIS. Later, display the report on the screen and print the report on the printer.

Input Data: Use the sequential file EX61PAY.DAT that was created in QBasic Programming Problem 1. (If you did not complete QBasic Programming Problem 1, then use EX61PAY.DAT found on the Data Disk.)

Output Results: The sequential file EX63RPT.LIS is created in auxiliary storage. Figure 6.23 on the next page illustrates the termination message that should display at end-of-job time.

▌FIGURE 6.23
Output termination message for Programming Problem 3.

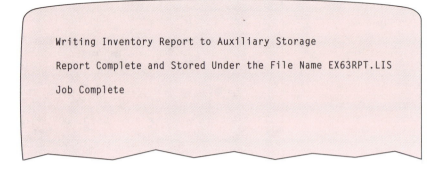

```
Writing Inventory Report to Auxiliary Storage

Report Complete and Stored Under the File Name EX63RPT.LIS

Job Complete
```

4. Appending Records to the End of a File

Purpose: To become familiar with appending records to the end of a sequential file. Use of the OPEN, CLOSE, and WRITE #n statements is required.

Problem: The sequential file EX64PAY.DAT found on the Data Disk is a duplicate of EX61PAY.DAT, created by QBasic Programming Problem 1. Append to EX64PAY.DAT the new employee records described under Input Data.

Input Data: Prepare and use the following sample data:

Employee Number	Employee Name	Dependents	Marital Status	Rate of pay
345	Lie Jeff	2	M	6.60
612	Abe Mike	1	S	8.75

Because these are new employees, assign all year-to-date items a value of zero.

Output Results: The screen display should be the same as shown in the Output Results for QBasic Programming Problem 1. Figure 6.24 illustrates what is displayed at end-of-job.

▌FIGURE 6.24
End of job message for Programming Problem 4.

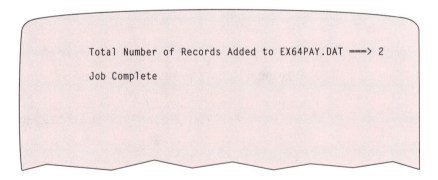

```
Total Number of Records Added to EX64PAY.DAT ===> 2

Job Complete
```

5. Computing the Average Age of Employees with a Minor Control Break

Purpose: To become familiar with a method of testing for a control break in a file. Use of the OPEN, CLOSE, and INPUT #n statements and the EOF function is required.

Problem: Construct a top-down program that will find the average age of those employees less than 40 years old and the average age of those greater than or equal to 40 years old. The program should do the following:

1. Read a department number and a person's age from the sequential data file EX65EMP.DAT found on the Data Disk. The employee records found in EX65EMP.DAT are shown under Input Data.
2. Test to see whether the department number is the same as the previous one.

3. If the department number is the same, determine whether the age is greater than or equal to 40, or less than 40. Use an IF statement to transfer control so that the age is added to an appropriate total, and a variable representing a counter has its value incremented by 1.

4. If the department number changes (control break occurs), transfer control to determine the average ages of those employees below 40, and of those 40 and above; display a summary line; reset counters and the control variable; and then continue processing the next department.

(**Hint:** Use the top-down chart illustrated in Figure 6.16 on page 222 and Program 6.4 — PRG6-4 on the Data Disk — as a guide to solving this problem.)

Input Data: The sequential data file EX65EMP.DAT is stored on the Data Disk. The file contains the following 20 sample data items:

Dept. No.	Age	Dept. No.	Age	Dept. No.	Age	Dept. No.	Age
A	22	A	61	B	63	B	29
A	33	A	24	B	28	C	32
A	27	A	35	B	30	C	28
A	44	B	44	B	42	C	31
A	52	B	47	B	45	C	56

Output Results: Figure 6.25 illustrates the output results for Programming Problem 5.

FIGURE 6.25
Output results for Programming Problem 5.

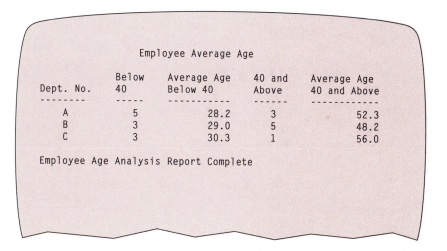

```
                    Employee Average Age

                Below    Average Age    40 and    Average Age
    Dept. No.    40       Below 40      Above     40 and Above
    ---------   -----    -----------    ------    ------------
        A         5          28.2         3           52.3
        B         3          29.0         5           48.2
        C         3          30.3         1           56.0

    Employee Age Analysis Report Complete
```

6. Sales Analysis Report with Three Levels of Control Breaks

Purpose: To become familiar with paging a report, the LPRINT and LPRINT USING statements, and the concepts of multilevel control breaks and sequential file processing.

Problem: Write a top-down program that prints a report with three levels of control breaks. The program is to process the sequential data file SALES.DAT used earlier in the chapter by Program 6.5 and stored on the Data Disk. Print totals for department, store, district, and company. A listing of SALES.DAT is shown in Figure 6.15 on page 221. Note that the records are in sequence by department, within store, within district. The report should be similar to the one shown in Figure 6.20 on page 230. Page the report. Print a maximum of 36 lines per page.

(**Hint:** See Program 6.5 or PRG6-5 on the Data Disk.)

Input Data: Use the sequential data file SALES.DAT that is located on the Data Disk.

Output Results: The output results should be similar to the report shown in Figure 6.20 on page 230 with the inclusion of a department control break.

7. Checking the Sequence of Customer Numbers

Purpose: To devise an efficient method of checking the sequence in ascending order of records in a sequential data file.

Problem: A sequential data file EX67CUS.DAT on the Data Disk contains customer records. Each record contains a customer number and the balance due. The records must be checked to ensure that all are in ascending sequence on the basis of the customer number. The program must not compare the first customer number against the customer number of 0 or 1, or any predetermined fixed number. Beginning with the second record, each customer number should be compared to the previous customer number in sequence.

If a customer record is out of order, the following is to be displayed:

```
Out of Order =====> XXXXX
```

where the Xs represent the customer number of the record that is out of order. If a duplicate customer number is detected, the following is to be displayed:

```
Duplicate ========> XXXXX
```

If the customer record is in ascending order, processing continues. Duplicate customer numbers are not out of order. When the last customer number is processed, display the total customer records that have been sequence-checked in ascending order.

Input Data: Use the sequential data file EX67CUS.DAT on the Data Disk. Listed below are the first five records. You can use the Open command on the File menu to display the entire file.

Customer Number	Balance Due
03000	$ 43.25
03012	132.00
03013	5.65
03015	354.98
03014	99.80

Output Results: Figure 6.26 illustrates output results for Programming Problem 7.

FIGURE 6.26

Output results for Programming Problem 7.

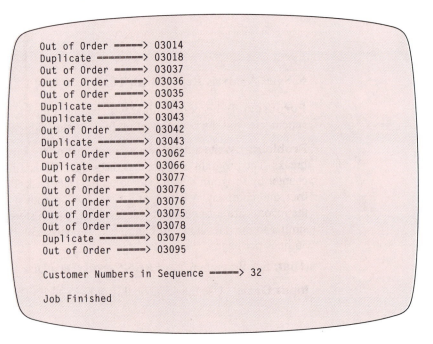

```
Out of Order =====> 03014
Duplicate ========> 03018
Out of Order =====> 03037
Out of Order =====> 03036
Out of Order =====> 03035
Duplicate ========> 03043
Duplicate ========> 03043
Out of Order =====> 03042
Duplicate ========> 03043
Out of Order =====> 03062
Duplicate ========> 03066
Out of Order =====> 03077
Out of Order =====> 03076
Out of Order =====> 03076
Out of Order =====> 03075
Out of Order =====> 03078
Duplicate ========> 03079
Out of Order =====> 03095

Customer Numbers in Sequence =====> 32

Job Finished
```

8. Payroll Problem VI: Social Security Computations and Multiple-File Processing

Purpose: To become familiar with multiple-file processing and paging a report.

Problem: Modify Payroll Problem V (Problem 10) in Chapter 5 to determine the Social Security deduction. The Social Security deduction is equal to 7.65% of the gross pay, to a maximum of $5,377.95 (7.65% of $70,300) for the year. Modify the solution to Payroll Problem V by adding this additional computation as a subroutine. Include the following:

1. Use the master payroll file EX61PAY.DAT created in QBasic Programming Problem 1 of this chapter to obtain year-to-date information and the rate of pay for each employee. (If you did not complete QBasic Programming Problem 1, then use EX61PAY.DAT found on the Data Disk.)
2. Use the transaction file EX68TRA.DAT on the Data Disk. A **transaction file** is one that contains temporary data. In this case, the temporary data is the employee number and hours worked for the pay period, as shown under Input Data.
3. Write a new master file EX68PAY.DAT that includes the updated year-to-date values for each employee.
4. Page the report. Print a maximum of 18 lines to a page.
5. Round the Social Security tax and withholding tax to the nearest cent.

You may assume that the records in EX61PAY.DAT and EX68TRA.DAT are in ascending sequence and that there is exactly one record in each file per employee. That is, each record in EX61PAY.DAT has a match in EX68TRA.DAT.

Input Data: Use the sequential data files described below. Both files are stored on the Data Disk.

1. EX61PAY.DAT as the master payroll file (see the Input Data for QBasic Programming Problem 1).
2. EX68TRA.DAT as the transaction file. EX68TRA.DAT contains the following data:

Employee Number	Hours Worked
123	88
124	96
125	72
126	80
134	80
167	70.5
210	80
234	32
244	40

Output Results: A new master payroll file is created as EX68PAY.DAT. Figure 6.27 on the next page illustrates the report that is printed on the printer.

FIGURE 6.27
*Output results for
Programming Problem 8.*

```
                        Biweekly Payroll Report            Page:  1

        Employee
        Number      Gross Pay      Fed. Tax     Soc. Sec.    Net Pay
        --------    ---------      --------     ---------    -------
          123       1,150.00        277.96         87.97      784.07

          124       1,872.00        476.20        143.21    1,252.59

          125         936.00        232.84         71.60      631.56

          126         440.00         19.72         33.66      386.62

          134         700.00        182.00         53.55      464.45

          167         733.20        159.07         56.09      518.04

          210         704.00        119.92         53.86      530.22
```

```
                        Biweekly Payroll Report            Page:  2

        Employee
        Number      Gross Pay      Fed. Tax     Soc. Sec.    Net Pay
        --------    ---------      --------     ---------    -------
          234         216.00         35.12         16.52      164.36

          244         350.00         59.44         26.77      263.79


        Total Gross Pay ========>   7,101.20
        Total Withholding Tax ==>   1,562.27
        Total Social Security ==>     543.23
        Total Net Pay ==========>   4,995.70

        End of Payroll Report
```

7

FOR Loops, Arrays,
Sorting, and Table Processing

7.1 INTRODUCTION

In earlier chapters, loops were implemented (coded) with the DO and LOOP statements. This chapter presents a second method for implementing certain types of loops using the FOR and NEXT statements.

Also in previous chapters, the programs used simple variables such as Amount, Price, and Code$ to store and access data. Each variable was assigned a single value in an INPUT, LET, or READ statement. Another technique that can make a program shorter, easier to code, and more general is the use of arrays. In this chapter, we will discuss the advantages gained by grouping similar data into an array. In QBasic, an **array** is a string or numeric variable that is allocated a specified number of storage locations, each of which can be assigned a unique value. In other words, an array allows a programmer to store more than one value under the same variable name. Arrays are used commonly in programming for sorting and table processing.

A report usually is easier to work with and more meaningful if the information is generated in some sequence, such as first to last, largest to smallest, or oldest to newest. Arranging data according to order or sequence is called **sorting**.

In information processing terminology, a **table** is a collection of data in which each item is uniquely identified by a label, by its position relative to other items, or by some other means. Income tax tables, insurance tables, airline schedules, and telephone directories are examples of tables that present data that is concise, yet easy to read and understand. Storing table elements in arrays allows a programmer to organize the entries and to write efficient code for retrieving each individual element.

Upon successful completion of this chapter, you will be able to code certain types of loops more efficiently. You also will be able to develop programs that demand that large amounts of data, stored in an orderly fashion, be available to the PC during the entire execution of the program.

7.2 THE FOR AND NEXT STATEMENTS

The FOR and NEXT statements make it possible to loop through a range of statements with automatic changes in the value of a variable during each pass through the loop. In Chapters 4, 5, and 6, the DO and LOOP statements were used to implement a loop structure that repeatedly executed a section of a program. Whenever you develop a **counter-controlled loop**, a loop that executes based on the value of a counter, the coding requires statements for initializing, incrementing, and testing for a counter. Any counter-controlled loop may be written with the FOR and NEXT statements. When these two statements are used to establish a loop, it is called a **For loop**.

The Do-While Loop versus the For Loop

The two partial programs in Figure 7.1 illustrate the similarity between the use of the DO WHILE and LOOP statements and the FOR and NEXT statements. Both partial programs compute the sum of the integers from 1 to 100.

▌FIGURE 7.1

Comparing the use of the (a) Do-While and (b) For loop.

(a) Using a Do-While loop

```
 1    ' Looping Using DO WHILE
 2    ' and LOOP Statements
 3    ' **********************
 4    CLS  ' Clear Screen
 5    Sum = 0
 6    Count = 1
 7    DO WHILE Count <= 100
 8        Sum = Sum + Count
 9        Count = Count + 1
10    LOOP
11    PRINT "The sum is"; Sum

      [run]

      The sum is 5050
```

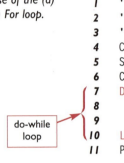

(b) Using a For loop

```
 1    ' Looping Using FOR
 2    ' and NEXT Statements
 3    ' *******************
 4    CLS  ' Clear Screen
 5    Sum = 0
 6    FOR Count = 1 TO 100 STEP 1
 7        Sum = Sum + Count
 8    NEXT Count
 9    PRINT "The sum is"; Sum

      [run]

      The sum is 5050
```

for loop

do-while loop

The partial program in Figure 7.1(a) uses the DO WHILE and LOOP statements. Lines 5 and 6 initialize the running total (Sum) to 0 and the counter (Count) to 1. Line 7 tests to determine whether the value of Count is less than or equal to 100. If the condition is true, Sum is incremented by the value of Count, and Count is incremented by 1 before control transfers back to line 7. When the condition in the DO WHILE statement is false, the PC terminates the loop, and line 11 displays the value of Sum.

The partial program in Figure 7.1(b) incorporates the FOR and NEXT statements to define the For loop (lines 6 through 8). Read through this partial program carefully and note how compact it is and how superior it is to the partial program in Figure 7.1(a). Using a single FOR statement, as in line 6 of Figure 7.1(b), we can consolidate the functions of lines 6, 7, and 9 of the partial program in Figure 7.1(a).

As well as using less main memory and being easier to read than the one in Figure 7.1(a), the For loop is also more efficient; it executes faster than the Do-While loop. In Chapter 8, we will illustrate performance differences among various versions of a For loop.

The Execution of a For Loop

The execution of the For loop in Figure 7.1(b) involves the following:

1. When the FOR statement is executed for the first time, the For loop becomes active, and Count is set equal to 1.

2. Count is compared to 100. Because it is less than or equal to 100, the statements in the For loop, in this case line 7, are executed.
3. Control returns to the FOR statement, where the value of Count is incremented by 1, the value that follows the keyword STEP.
4. If the value of Count is less than or equal to 100, execution of the For loop continues.
5. When the value of Count is greater than 100, control transfers to the statement (line 9) following the corresponding NEXT statement.

The general forms of the FOR and NEXT statements are given in Tables 7.1 and 7.2.

TABLE 7.1 - The FOR Statement	
General Form:	FOR k = initial value TO limit value STEP increment value
	or
	FOR k = initial value TO limit value
	where **k** is a simple numeric variable called the **loop variable**, and the **initial value**, **limit value**, and **increment value** are numeric expressions.
Purpose:	Causes the statements between the FOR and NEXT statements to be executed repeatedly in a loop until the value of k exceeds the limit value. When k exceeds the limit value, control transfers to the line immediately following the corresponding NEXT statement.
	If the increment value is negative, the test is reversed. The value of k is decremented each time through the loop, and the loop is executed until k is less than the limit value.
Examples:	FOR Item = 1 TO 20
	FOR Amount = -5 TO 15 STEP 2
	FOR Count = 10 TO -5 STEP -3
	FOR Tax = 0 TO 10 STEP 0.1
	FOR Total = Start TO Finish STEP Increment
	FOR S = A + 5 TO C / D STEP F * B
	FOR I = 20 TO 20
	FOR J = 20 TO 1 STEP -1
Note:	If the keyword STEP is not used, then the increment value defaults to 1.

TABLE 7.2 - The NEXT Statement	
General Form:	NEXT k
	where **k** is the same variable as the loop variable in the corresponding FOR statement.
Purpose:	Identifies the end of a For loop.
Examples:	NEXT Item
	NEXT Amount

The terminology used to describe the FOR statement is shown in Figure 7.2.

FIGURE 7.2

The terminology used to describe the FOR *and* NEXT *statements.*

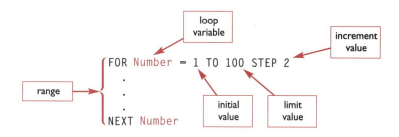

As shown in Figure 7.2 on the previous page, the **range** of a For loop is the set of statements beginning with the FOR statement and continuing up to and including the NEXT statement that has the same loop variable.

Flowchart Representation of a For Loop

The flowchart representation of a For loop is the Do-While structure (Figure 7.3). In the first process symbol, the loop variable is assigned the initial value. Next a test is made. If the condition is true, the loop is terminated and control transfers to the statement that follows the NEXT statement.

If the condition is false, control passes into the body of the For loop. After the statements in the For loop are executed, the loop variable is incremented by the increment value, and control transfers back up to the decision symbol again to test whether the loop variable exceeds the limit value.

If the increment value is negative, the test is reversed. The value of the loop variable is decremented each time through the loop, and the loop is executed while the loop variable is equal to or greater than the limit value. Figure 7.4 illustrates the flowchart that corresponds to the program in Figure 7.1(b) on page 242.

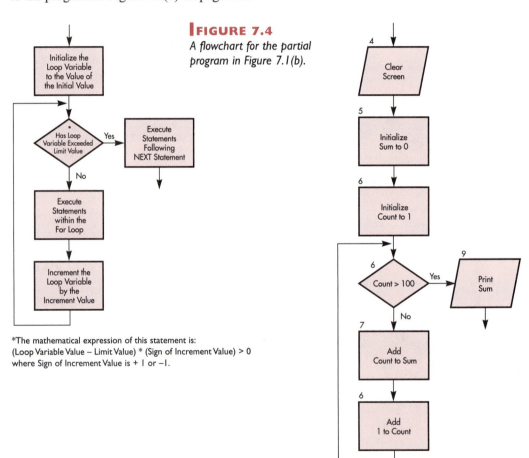

FIGURE 7.3

General flowchart representation of a For loop.

FIGURE 7.4

A flowchart for the partial program in Figure 7.1(b).

*The mathematical expression of this statement is:
(Loop Variable Value − Limit Value) * (Sign of Increment Value) > 0
where Sign of Increment Value is + 1 or −1.

Valid Values in the FOR Statement

The examples presented in Table 7.1 on the previous page indicate that the initial, limit, and increment values of a FOR statement can take on a variety of representations. This section is divided into subsections that illustrate these representations.

Stepping by 1

Many applications call for incrementing, or **stepping**, the loop variable by 1 each time the For loop is executed. You may write such a FOR statement as follows:

```
FOR Rate = 1 TO 12 STEP 1
```

or

```
FOR Rate = 1 TO 12
```

Subroutine B300.Determine.Amount (line 3) illustrated in Figure 7.5 includes a FOR statement (line 8) without the STEP parameter. The subroutine uses the value of the variable Principal to compute the amount of an investment (Amount), compounded annually, for whole number interest rates (Rate) between 1% and 12%, inclusive. Assume that the value 500 is assigned to Principal in Figure 7.5 prior to the execution of the subroutine.

FIGURE 7.5

Using a For loop to determine various amounts.

```
 1    ' Stepping by 1 in a FOR Statement
 2    ' *******************************
 3    B300.Determine.Amount:
 4       PRINT USING "Principal: #,###,##"; Principal
 5       PRINT
 6       PRINT "Rate        Amount"
 7       D1$ = "##.#      ##,###.##"
 8       FOR Rate = 1 TO 12
 9          Amount = Principal * (1 + Rate / 100)
10          PRINT USING D1$; Rate, Amount
11       NEXT Rate
12       PRINT "Job Complete"
13    RETURN

[run]

Principal:  500.00

Rate          Amount
  1.0         505.00
  2.0         510.00
  3.0         515.00
  4.0         520.00
  5.0         525.00
  6.0         530.00
  7.0         535.00
  8.0         540.00
  9.0         545.00
 10.0         550.00
 11.0         555.00
 12.0         560.00
Job Complete
```

Line 4 in the subroutine in Figure 7.5 displays the value of Principal, which is assigned before the subroutine is called. Line 8 activates the For loop and assigns Rate a value of 1 (that is, 1%). Line 9 computes the amount of the investment, and line 10 displays the interest rate and amount. The loop variable Rate is incremented by 1, and the loop is executed repeatedly until Rate exceeds 12. When this occurs, control transfers to line 12.

As with Do-While loops, the statements between FOR and NEXT should be indented by three spaces for the purpose of readability, as illustrated by lines 9 and 10 in Figure 7.5. This style allows you to scan a For loop quickly and simplifies the debugging effort.

Stepping by a Value Other than 1

Some applications call for the loop variable to be incremented by a value other than 1. If line 8 of Figure 7.5 on the previous page is modified to

```
FOR Rate = 1 TO 12 STEP 3
```

the program computes the amount of an investment, compounded annually, for interest rates of 1%, 4%, 7%, and 10%. The loop terminates when the loop variable Rate becomes 13 because this is greater than the value of the limit, which is 12.

Initializing the Loop Variable to a Value Other than 1

It is not necessary to initialize the loop variable to 1. If line 8 in Figure 7.5 is modified to

```
FOR Rate = 8 TO 16 STEP 2
```

the program generates a report that shows the even-valued interest rates between 8% and 16%, inclusive.

Some applications call for initializing the loop variable to zero or some negative value. For example, the statements

```
FOR Temp = 0 TO 10
```

or

```
FOR Temp = -6 TO 12
```

are both valid. The first example causes the For loop to execute 11 times. The second example causes the For loop to execute 19 times.

Decimal Fraction Values in a FOR Statement

The values in a FOR statement can be decimal fraction numbers. If line 8 in Figure 7.5 is modified to

```
FOR Rate = 11.5 TO 12.5 STEP .1
```

the program computes the amount of an investment compounded annually for interest rates between 11.5% and 12.5%, inclusive, in increments of one-tenth of one percent.

Be careful with decimal fraction parameters because the PC cannot always store the exact binary representation of a decimal number. Stepping by a decimal fraction can, in some instances, result in one less or one more time through the For loop than you expect.

Negative Values in a FOR Statement

The values in a FOR statement can be negative. If line 8 in Figure 7.5 is modified to

```
FOR Rate = 8 TO 0 STEP -1
```

the program generates a report in which the interest rates are decremented from 8% to 0%. The negative step value in the FOR statement causes the test to be reversed, and the loop variable is decremented until it is less than the limit value.

Variables in a FOR Statement

The subroutine in Figure 7.6 shows that the values in a FOR statement can be variables as well as numeric constants. Lines 4 through 6 display the initial, terminal, and increment values (Rate1, Rate2, and Increment) that are assigned prior to the subroutine being called. Also, a value of 3000 is assigned to Prinicpal prior to calling the subroutine.

FIGURE 7.6

Variable values for a FOR statement.

```
 1    ' Variable Values in a FOR Statement
 2    ' ***********************************
 3    B340.Determine.Amount:
 4       PRINT USING "Initial Rate:    ###.##%"; Rate1
 5       PRINT USING "Limit Rate:      ###.##%"; Rate2
 6       PRINT USING "Increment Rate: ###.##%"; Increment
 7       PRINT USING "Principal:    #,###.##"; Principal
 8       PRINT
 9       PRINT "Rate         Amount"
10       D1$ = "##.#     ##,###.##"
11       FOR Rate = Rate1 TO Rate2 STEP Increment
12          Amount = Principal * (1 + Rate / 100)
13          PRINT USING D1$; Rate, Amount
14       NEXT Rate
15       PRINT "Job Complete"
16    RETURN

      [run]

      Initial Rate:    10.00%
      Limit Rate:      12.50%
      Increment Rate:   0.50%
      Principal:    3,000.00

      Rate         Amount
      10.0      3,300.00
      10.5      3,315.00
      11.0      3,330.00
      11.5      3,345.00
      12.0      3,360.00
      12.5      3,375.00
      Job Complete
```

Be sure that the increment value is assigned a value other than zero. An increment value of zero creates an infinite loop or endless loop and forces you to press the Ctrl+Break keys to terminate further processing of the program on the PC.

Expressions as Values in a FOR Statement

The values in a FOR statement may be complex numeric expressions. For example, the following FOR statements are valid:

```
FOR X = A * B TO S / T STEP C * 2
FOR Y = (A + B) ^ C TO P * (F - G) * C STEP 5 * V
```

If C is zero, what do you think happens in the two FOR statements above?

Initial Entry into a For Loop

Control must not transfer into the range of a For loop from any statement outside its range. For example, you cannot use a GOSUB statement to transfer into the middle of a For loop without executing the FOR statement itself.

Redefining For Loop Values

After the FOR statement is executed, the initial, limit, and increment values are set and cannot be altered while the For loop is active. QBasic simply disregards any attempt to redefine them. The For loop illustrated in Figure 7.7 on the next page executes ten times, even though the variables in the FOR statement are changed by lines 6 through 8.

```
1   Initial = 1
2   Limit = 10
3   Increment = 1
4   FOR Loop.Variable = Initial to Limit STEP Increment
5       PRINT Loop.Variable, Initial, Limit, Increment
6       Initial = 5
7       Limit = 1
8       Increment = 4
9   NEXT Loop.Variable
```

do not change
the values in the
FOR statement

On the second pass, the values displayed for Initial, Limit, and Increment by line 5 are 5, 1, and 4. However, the actual values of Initial, Limit, and Increment in the FOR statement are assigned 1, 10, and 1, by lines 1 to 3, respectively.

Exiting a For Loop Prematurely — the EXIT Statement

Certain looping situations require a premature exit from the For loop. QBasic includes the EXIT **statement** for terminating a For loop early. Consider the program in Figure 7.8, which requests the user to enter five values for Amount, one each time through the For loop. If the user enters a value that is less than or equal to zero, the For loop terminates prematurely due to the EXIT FOR statement in line 8.

```
1    ' Premature Exit from a For Loop
2    ' *****************************
3    Total.Amount = 0
4    FOR Loop.Variable = 1 TO 5
5       INPUT "Amount value"; Amount
6       IF Amount <= 0 THEN
7           PRINT "Amount <= 0 ... Program terminating"
8           EXIT FOR
9       END IF
10      Total.Amount = Total.Amount + Amount
11   NEXT Loop.Variable
12   PRINT : PRINT "Value of Loop.Variable is"; Loop.Variable
13   END

[run]

Amount value? 23
Amount value? 12
Amount value? -6
Amount <= 0 ... Program terminating

Value of Loop.Variable is 3
```

When the program in Figure 7.8 executes, the condition in the IF statement in line 6 is false for the first two Amount values, 23 and 12. When the user enters the third value (–6), the condition in line 6 is true, and the diagnostic message displays due to line 7. Next, line 8 causes the PC to exit the For loop and continue execution with the PRINT statement in line 12. This is called a **premature exit** from the For loop. Note that when the PC exits the For loop, the value of the loop variable is available for further processing, as shown by the last output line displayed due to line 12.

The general form of the EXIT statement is given in Table 7.3.

TABLE 7.3 - The EXIT Statement	
General Form:	EXIT statement
	where statement is FOR, DO, DEF, FUNCTION, SUB.
Purpose:	Exit a For or Do loop, function, or subroutine prematurely.
Examples:	EXIT FOR
	EXIT DO

Rules that summarize the FOR statement are listed below.

FOR RULE 1

If the increment value following the keyword STEP is positive, or if the keyword STEP is not used, then the PC executes the For loop while the loop variable is less than or equal to the limit value. If the increment value is negative, the test is reversed. The value of the loop variable is decremented each time through the loop, and the loop is executed until the loop variable is less than the limit value.

FOR RULE 2

The value of the increment value must not be zero.

FOR RULE 3

A valid initial entry into a For loop can be accomplished only by transferring control to the FOR statement.

FOR RULE 4

A normal exit from a For loop leaves the current value of the loop variable equal to its value the last time the NEXT statement was executed plus the increment value.

FOR RULE 5

A premature exit from a For loop leaves the current value of the loop variable equal to its value the last time the NEXT statement was executed.

FOR RULE 6

Statements located in the range of a For loop cannot change the initial, limit, and increment values.

Iterations in a For Loop

The number of **iterations**, or repetitions, specified by a FOR statement may be computed with the following formula:

$$\text{Number of Iterations} = \frac{\text{Limit value} - \text{Initial value}}{\text{Increment value}} + 1$$

where the ratio is performed in integer arithmetic so that the quotient is truncated to the next lowest integer.

How many iterations are performed by a For loop with the following FOR statement?

```
FOR TEMP = -2 TO 30 STEP 2
```

Using the formula, the number of iterations is

$$\frac{30 - (-2)}{2} + 1 = 16 + 1 = 17$$

Another Look at the For Loop

The For loop in QBasic corresponds to a Do-While structure. (See Figure 7.3 on page 244.) The test for whether the value of the loop variable exceeds the limit value is carried out at the beginning of the loop. This means that the body of the For loop will not be executed if the initial value is greater than the limit value.

For example, in the partial program presented in Figure 7.9, when the FOR statement is encountered, control immediately transfers to the line below the NEXT statement. The For loop is executed zero times, and the loop variable is equal to the initial value.

FIGURE 7.9

Initial value greater than the limit value in a For loop.

10 is greater than the limit, 1

```
Count = 0
FOR I = 10 TO 1 STEP 2
    Count = Count + 1
NEXT I
PRINT "The loop variable is equal to"; I
PRINT "The For loop is executed"; Count; "times"

[run]

The loop variable is equal to 10
The For loop is executed 0 times
```

On the other hand, if the increment value is –2 in the FOR statement, the loop variable is equal to 0 when the For loop is deactivated, and the For loop is executed five times.

Re-examine Figure 7.3 and note that the mathematical expression used to terminate the looping in a For loop is

(Loop Variable Value – Limit Value) * (Sign of Increment Value) > 0

where the sign of the increment value is either +1 or –1.

Nested For Loops

Just as there are nested expressions and nested subroutines in QBasic, there are nested For loops. When the statements of one For loop lie within the range of another For loop, the loops are said to be **nested**, or **embedded**. Furthermore, the outer For loop may be nested in the range of still another For loop, and so on.

The program in Figure 7.10 utilizes two For loops. The inner For loop, formed by lines 5 through 7, is written so that all the statements in its range also lie within the range of the outer For loop, lines 3 through 9.

When line 3 is executed in the partial program in Figure 7.10, the outer For loop becomes active. The loop variable X is set to 1, and line 4 displays that value. When line 5 is executed, the inner For loop becomes active. The loop variable Y is set to 1, and line 6 displays the values of both X and Y. With X equal to 1, control remains within the inner loop, which is executed three times, until Y exceeds 3. At this point, the inner loop is satisfied, and control passes to the outer For loop, which executes line 8.

Control then passes back to line 3, where the loop variable X is incremented by 1 to become 2. After line 4 displays the new value of X, line 5 is executed, and the inner For loop becomes active again. The loop variable Y is initialized to 1, and the process repeats itself.

FIGURE 7.10

A nested For loop.

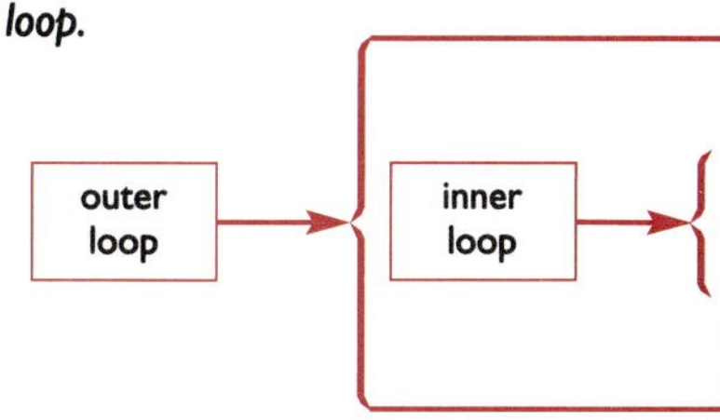

```
 1    ' Nested For loops
 2    ' ****************
 3    FOR X = 1 TO 4
 4       PRINT "OUTER LOOP ---- X ="; X
 5       FOR Y = 1 TO 3
 6          PRINT "   INNER LOOP - X = "; X; "AND Y ="; Y
 7       NEXT Y
 8       PRINT
 9    NEXT X
10    END

[run]

OUTER LOOP ---- X = 1
   INNER LOOP - X = 1 AND Y = 1
   INNER LOOP - X = 1 AND Y = 2
   INNER LOOP - X = 1 AND Y = 3

OUTER LOOP ---- X = 2
   INNER LOOP - X = 2 AND Y = 1
   INNER LOOP - X = 2 AND Y = 2
   INNER LOOP - X = 2 AND Y = 3

OUTER LOOP ---- X = 3
   INNER LOOP - X = 3 AND Y = 1
   INNER LOOP - X = 3 AND Y = 2
   INNER LOOP - X = 3 AND Y = 3

OUTER LOOP ---- X = 4
   INNER LOOP - X = 4 AND Y = 1
   INNER LOOP - X = 4 AND Y = 2
   INNER LOOP - X = 4 AND Y = 3
```

When the outer loop is satisfied, control passes to line 10. In Figure 7.10, the outer For loop executes a total of four times, and the inner For loop executes a total of 3 times 4 or 12.

As another example of a program with nested For loops, consider the program in Figure 7.11 on the next page, which generates the multiplication table. Each time the loop variable in the outer For loop (lines 6 through 12) is assigned a new value, the inner For loop (lines 8 through 10) computes and displays one row of the table. The two loop variables, Row and Column, are multiplied together in line 9 to form the various products in the multiplication table.

The PRINT statements in lines 7 and 9 end with the semicolon separator. Recall from Chapter 3 that when a PRINT statement ends with a semicolon, the cursor remains on the same line. Each time the inner loop is satisfied, the null PRINT statement in line 11 moves the cursor to the beginning of the next line.

▌FIGURE 7.11

Generating the multiplication table using a nested For loop.

```
1    ' Generating the Multiplication Table
2    ' ********************************
3    CLS  ' Clear Screen
4    PRINT "  x !  0   1   2   3   4   5   6   7   8   9  10  11  12"
5    PRINT "-----+------------------------------------------------"
6    FOR ROW = 0 TO 12
7       PRINT USING "###  _!"; Row;
8       FOR Column = 0 TO 12
9          PRINT USING "####"; Row * Column;
10      NEXT Column
11      PRINT
12   NEXT Row
13   PRINT
14   PRINT "End of Multiplication Table"
15   END
```

[run]

x !	0	1	2	3	4	5	6	7	8	9	10	11	12
0 !	0	0	0	0	0	0	0	0	0	0	0	0	0
1 !	0	1	2	3	4	5	6	7	8	9	10	11	12
2 !	0	2	4	6	8	10	12	14	16	18	20	22	24
3 !	0	3	6	9	12	15	18	21	24	27	30	33	36
4 !	0	4	8	12	16	20	24	28	32	36	40	44	48
5 !	0	5	10	15	20	25	30	35	40	45	50	55	60
6 !	0	6	12	18	24	30	36	42	48	54	60	66	72
7 !	0	7	14	21	28	35	42	49	56	63	70	77	84
8 !	0	8	16	24	32	40	48	56	64	72	80	88	96
9 !	0	9	18	27	36	45	54	63	72	81	90	99	108
10 !	0	10	20	30	40	50	60	70	80	90	100	110	120
11 !	0	11	22	33	44	55	66	77	88	99	110	121	132
12 !	0	12	24	36	48	60	72	84	96	108	120	132	144

End of Multiplication Table

Valid Nesting of For Loops

When nesting occurs, all statements in the range of the inner For loop also must be in the range of the outer For loop. QBasic does not allow the range of an inner For loop to extend past the end of the range of an outer For loop. If this type of error occurs, QBasic displays a dialog box with the diagnostic message

```
NEXT without FOR
```

When one For loop is nested within another, the name of the loop variable for each For loop must be different. Figure 7.12 illustrates valid and invalid nesting of For loops.

▌FIGURE 7.12

Valid and invalid nesting of For loops.

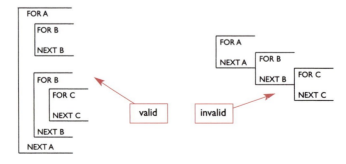

The usefulness of the FOR and NEXT statements for looping purposes should be apparent from the examples and illustrations presented so far. However, you will see an even greater use for them in applications involving the manipulation of arrays, which are discussed in the following sections of this chapter. The material in this section can be summarized in the following rules:

FOR RULE 7 — *If the range of a For loop includes another For loop, all statements in the range of the inner For loop also must be within the range of the outer For loop.*

FOR RULE 8 — *When one For loop is within another, the name of the loop variable for each For loop must be different.*

7.3 ARRAYS VERSUS SIMPLE VARIABLES

Arrays permit a programmer to represent many values with one variable name. The variable name assigned to represent an array is called the **array name**. The elements in the array are distinguished from one another by subscripts. In QBasic, the subscript is written inside a set of parentheses and is placed immediately to the right of the array name. Recall from Chapter 3, page 60, that QBasic allows two different types of variables: simple and subscripted. While simple variables are used to store and reference values that are independent of one another, **subscripted variables** are used to store and reference values that have been grouped into an array.

Consider the problem of writing a program that is to manipulate the monthly sales for a company and generate a year-end report. Figure 7.13 illustrates the difference between using an array to store the monthly sales and using simple variables.

FIGURE 7.13

Utilizing an array (a) versus simple variables (b).

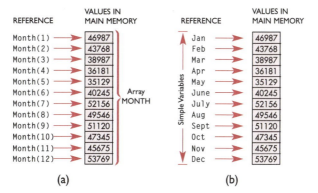

The monthly sales stored in an array require the same storage allocation as the sales represented as independent variables. The difference lies in the programming techniques that can access the different values. For example, the programmer may assign the values of simple variables in a READ statement in this manner:

```
READ Jan, Feb, Mar, Apr, May, June, July, Aug, Sept, Oct, Nov, Dec
```

Each simple variable must explicitly appear in a LET or PRINT statement if the monthly sales are to be summed or displayed. Not only will the programming consume time, but also the variables *must* be placed properly in the program.

The same function can be accomplished by entering all 12 values into the array Month:

```
FOR Number = 1 TO 12
   READ Month(Number)
NEXT Number
```

In the FOR statement, Number is initialized to 1. The READ statement assigns the first value in the data holding area to Month(1) and is read as *Month sub 1*. Then Number is incremented to 2, and the next value is assigned to Month(2). This continues until Month(12) is assigned to the twelveth value in the data holding area.

Month2 and Month(2) are different from each other. Month2 is a simple variable, no different from Sale, Increment, Digit, or Cost. Whereas, Month(2) is the second element in the array Month, and the manner in which it is called upon in a program differs from the fashion in which a simple variable is called.

7.4 DECLARING ARRAYS

Before arrays can be used, the amount of main memory to be reserved must be declared in the program. This is the purpose of the DIM **statement**. The keyword DIM is an abbreviation of **dimension**. The DIM statement also declares the **lower-bound value** and **upper-bound value** of the subscript. The upper- and lower-bound values define the **range** of permissible values to which a subscript may be assigned.

The DIM Statement

The main function of the DIM statement is to declare to the PC the necessary information about the allocation of storage locations in memory for arrays used in a program. Good programming practice dictates that every program that utilizes array elements should have a DIM statement that properly defines the arrays.

The general forms of the DIM statement are given in Table 7.4. In Table 7.4, Example 1 reserves storage for a one-dimensional numeric array, Balance, which consists of five elements, or storage locations. A one dimensional array requires only one subscript per element. These elements — Balance(0), Balance(1), Balance(2), Balance(3), and Balance(4) — can be used in a program in much the same way as a simple variable can be used. For this DIM statement, elements Balance(5), Balance(6), and Balance(-4) are not valid.

Example 2 in Table 7.4 establishes a one-dimensional string array named Code$. Code$ has eight elements — Code$(1), Code$(2), Code$(3), Code$(4), Code$(5), Code$(6), Code$(7), and Code$(8). In this DIM statement, both the lower-bound value (1) and the upper-bound value (8) are specified using the keyword TO.

Example 3 declares two one-dimensional arrays, Pick and Job$, and one two-dimensional array, Time. A two-dimensional array requires two subscripts per element. The DIM statement reserves storage locations for 10 elements for the array Pick, which has negative lower and upper bounds; 201 elements for the array Job$; and 400 elements for the array Time.

The fourth example in Table 7.4 declares three arrays. The first array, Cost, is a one-dimensional array consisting of a negative lower bound and 51 elements. The last two, K$ and Amount, are three-dimensional arrays. Multidimensional arrays, such as K$ and Amount, are discussed in Section 7.6.

TABLE 7.4 - The DIM Statement	

General Form: DIM array name(size),..., array name(size)

or

DIM array name(lb$_1$ TO ub$_1$),..., array name(lb$_1$ TO ub$_1$,..., lb$_n$ TO ub$_n$)

where **array name** represents a numeric or string variable name,

     size in the first general form defines the upper-bound value of each subscript of the array. Size may be a positive integer or numeric variable for one-dimensional arrays. Size may be a series of positive integers or a series of numeric variables separated by commas for multidimensional arrays.

In the second general form, **lb$_n$** may be a positive or negative integer or numeric variable that serves as the lower-bound value of the array, and **ub$_n$** may be a positive or negative integer or numeric variable that serves as the upper-bound value.

Purpose: To reserve storage locations for arrays.

Examples:
1. DIM Balance(4)
2. DIM Code$(1 TO 8)
3. DIM Pick(-10 TO -1), Job$(200), Time(1 TO 20, 1 TO 20)
4. DIM Cost(-5 TO 45), K$(X TO 50, Y, Z),
   Amount(2, 1 TO 75, 7)

Notes:
1. In the first general form, the lower bound of each dimension is 0, unless you include an OPTION BASE statement.
2. In QBasic, the maximum number of dimensions is 60.
3. The DIM statement can declare the type of array (that is, integer, single precision, etc.). For additional information, load QBasic, click Help, select the hyperlink Index, and select the keyword DIM.

To ensure the proper placement of DIM statements, it is customary to put them at the beginning of the program.

DIM RULE 1   *The DIM statement can be located anywhere before the first use of an array element in a program.*

A single DIM statement will be sufficient for most programs in this chapter. If four different arrays are to be declared, all four arrays can be listed in the same DIM statement as follows:

```
DIM X(1 TO 20), Code(15 TO 28), Temp(Row, Column, Plane), Desc$(25)
```

Four separate DIM statements also can be used in the program to declare the arrays individually:

```
DIM X(1 TO 20)
DIM Code(15 TO 28)
DIM Temp(Row, Column, Plane)
DIM Desc$(25)
```

The OPTION BASE Statement

When only the upper bound is specified, QBasic automatically allocates the zero element for each dimension of the array. Thus,

```
DIM Month(12), Time(20, 20)
```

actually reserves 13 elements for the array Month and 21 elements for each dimension of the array Time, or 441 elements. The extra array element is Month(0) for the array Month. For Time, the extra elements are Time(0, n) and Time(n, 0), where n is a value from 0 to 20. Although additional elements will not present a problem to your program, the OPTION BASE **statement** allows you to control the lower bound of arrays that are declared when you specify only the upper-bound value in a DIM statement.

An alternative to using the OPTION BASE statement is to use the TO option in the DIM statement and specify both the upper- and lower-bound values for each array.

The general form of the OPTION BASE statement is found in Table 7.5.

TABLE 7.5 - The OPTION BASE Statement	
General Form:	OPTION BASE n
	where **n** is either 0 or 1.
Purpose:	To assign a lower bound of 0 or 1 to all arrays in a program.
Examples:	OPTION BASE 0
	OPTION BASE 1
Note:	If the OPTION BASE statement is not used, the lower-bound value is set to zero for all arrays declared with only an upper-bound value.

When considering the placement of an OPTION BASE statement in a program, the following rules can be stated:

OPTION BASE RULE 1

The OPTION BASE statement can be used only once in a program and it must precede any DIM statement in a program.

OPTION BASE RULE 2

The OPTION BASE statement affects only dimensions within arrays that are declared without a lower-bound value.

Dynamic Allocation of Arrays

Some applications call for dynamically-dimensioned arrays. A **dynamically-dimensioned array** is one that has a variable or expression, rather than a constant, as the lower bound or upper bound. For example, a program may manipulate 60 elements of a one-dimensional array during one run, 100 elements the next time, and so on. Rather than modify the value of the size of a DIM statement each time the number of elements changes, QBasic permits the size of an array in a DIM statement to be written as a simple variable, as in

```
DIM Code(Size)
```

This DIM statement reserves a variable number of elements for the one-dimensional array Code. Usually an INPUT or READ statement is used before the DIM statement to assign a value to the variable used to determine the size of the array. After Size is assigned a value, the DIM statement allocates the actual number of elements to the array Code. Any FOR statements involved in the manipulation of the array must contain as their limit value the same simple variable, Size.

Variables also may be used as the lower- and upper-bound values for an array dimensioned using the keyword TO. For example, the following DIM statement is valid:

```
DIM Code(Lower TO Upper)
```

Here again, the variables Lower and Upper must be assigned values prior to the execution of the DIM statement.

7.5 MANIPULATING ARRAYS

In this section, several sample programs that manipulate the elements of arrays will be discussed. Before the programs are presented, however, it is important that you understand the syntax and limitations of subscripts.

Subscripts

As indicated in Section 7.3, the elements of an array are referenced by assigning a subscript to the array name. The subscript is written within parentheses and is placed immediately to the right of the array name. The subscript may be any valid number, variable, or numeric expression within the range of the array. This leads to the following rule:

DIM RULE 2   *Subscripts must be within the lower and upper bounds of an array.*

If an array Tax is declared as

```
DIM Tax(1 TO 50)
```

it is invalid to reference Tax(-3), Tax(51), or other elements that are outside the lower and upper bounds of the array.

Noninteger subscripts are rounded to the nearest integer to determine the element to be manipulated. Table 7.6 illustrates some additional examples of subscripts.

TABLE 7.6 - Examples of Subscripts	
ARRAY REFERENCE	**COMMENT**
Tax(1)	Valid, provided 1 is within the range of the array.
Tax(-3)	Valid, provided –3 is within the range of the array.
Tax(X + Y)	Valid, provided X + Y is within the range of the array.
Tax(-X)	Valid, provided –X is within the range of the array.
Tax(12.7)	Valid, provided the array has been declared with an upper bound of at least 13.
Tax(0)	Valid, provided the zero element exists.
Tax(Cost(2))	Valid, provided Cost(2) is within the range of the array. Subscripted subscripts are allowed to any valid dimension level in QBasic.
Tax(X(2,3), Y(1,3))	Valid, provided X(2, 3) and Y(1, 3) are within the range of the array.
Tax(X + Y/3 + 5^X)	Valid, provided $X + Y / 3 + 5 \wedge X$ is within the range of the array.

You must decide which variables will be subscripted in any program and then use them consistently throughout the program. For example, if the array element is Month(Number), the variable name Month cannot be used by itself without a subscript, nor could it be used with two subscripts. On the PC, either of these actions would cause the program to halt and display a dialog box with a diagnostic message indicating the type of error.

The program in Figure 7.14 reads data into an array and then displays the value of each element in the array.

FIGURE 7.14

Declaring, loading, and printing the elements of an array.

```
 1   ' Monthly Sales Analysis I
 2   ' ************************
 3   DIM Month(1 TO 12)
 4   CLS  ' Clear Screen
 5   ' ****** Read Monthly Sales into Month ******
 6   FOR Number = 1 TO 12
 7      READ Month(Number)
 8   NEXT Number
 9   ' ********** Display Monthly Sales **********
10   FOR Number = 1 TO 12
11      PRINT Month(Number),
12   NEXT Number
13   ' ************** Data Follows **************
14   DATA 46987, 43768, 38987, 36181, 35129, 40245
15   DATA 52156, 49546, 51120, 47345, 45675, 53769
16   END

     [run]

     46987        43768        38987        36181        35129
     40245        52156        49546        51120        47345
     45675        53769
```

In Figure 7.14, line 3 reserves 12 elements or storage locations for the array Month. Valid subscripts for Month range from 1 to 12. Line 6 activates the first For loop and assigns Number a value of 1. Line 7 reads the first data item, 46987, from the data holding area and assigns it to Month(1). Number is incremented to 2, and line 8 returns control to the FOR statement in line 6. The READ statement in line 7 then assigns the second data item to Month(2). This loop continues until Month(12) is assigned the twelfth data item, 53769.

Line 10 activates the second For loop and resets Number to 1. This For loop then proceeds to display the values assigned to the array Month, as shown.

Summing the Elements of an Array

Many applications call for summing the elements of an array. In the program in Figure 7.15, the monthly sales are summed; an average is computed; and the sales are displayed four to a line.

FIGURE 7.15

Summing the elements of an array.

```
 1   ' Monthly Sales Analysis II
 2   ' *************************
 3   DIM Month(1 TO 12)
 4   CLS  ' Clear Screen
 5   Total.Sales = 0
 6   ' ******* Read Monthly Sales into Month and Sum Monthly Sales *******
 7   FOR Number = 1 TO 12
 8      READ Month(Number)
 9      Total.Sales = Total.Sales + Month(Number)
10   NEXT Number
11   ' *********** Compute and Display Average Monthly Sales ***********
12   Avg.Sales = Total.Sales / 12
13   PRINT USING "The average of the monthly sales is $$##,###.##"; Avg.Sales
14   PRINT
15   ' ******************** Display Monthly Sales **********
```

```
16   FOR Number = 1 TO 12 STEP 4
17      PRINT Month(Number), Month(Number + 1), Month(Number + 2), Month(Number + 3)
18   NEXT Number
19   PRINT
20   PRINT "Job Complete"
21   ' ************************ Data Follows *************************
22   DATA 46987, 43768, 38987, 36181, 35129, 40245
23   DATA 52156, 49546, 51120, 47345, 45675, 53769
24   END
```

[run]

The average of the monthly sales is $45,075.67

```
    46987         43768         38987         36181
    35129         40245         52156         49546
    51120         47345         45675         53769
```

Job Complete

In Figure 7.15, line 9 is used to sum the values of the array elements. For example, when line 7 activates the For loop, Number is assigned the value of 1. Line 8 reads the first data item, 46987, and assigns it to Month(1). Line 9 increments Total.Sales by Month(1). Number is incremented to 2, and line 10 returns control to the FOR statement in line 7.

After the READ statement, Total.Sales is assigned the sum of Total.Sales and Month(2). This process continues until the twelfth element is added to the sum of the first 11 elements of the array Month. Line 12 computes the average, and line 13 displays it.

The For loop found in lines 16 through 18 displays the monthly sales, four to a line. The first time through the loop, Number is equal to 1; and Month(1), Month(2), Month(3), and Month(4) display on one line. The next time through the loop, Number is equal to 5; and Month(5), Month(6), Month(7), and Month(8) display on the next line. Finally, Number is set equal to 9; and Month(9), Month(10), Month(11), and Month(12) display on the third line. The subscripts in line 17 are in the form of numeric expressions.

PROGRAMMING CASE STUDY 12 – Analysis of Monthly Sales

The following programming case study illustrates the use of parallel arrays and the selection of elements that meet a certain criterion. **Parallel arrays** are two or more arrays that have corresponding elements, that is, elements that are related in some manner. This case study also shows how arrays may be used to store data that is used many times during the execution of a program.

Problem: Ray's Roofing Company has stored the past year's monthly sales on a floppy disk in a sequential file called MONTHSAL.DAT. The file is made up of 12 records as shown below:

"January", 46987	"May", 35129	"September", 51120
"February", 43768	"June", 40245	"October", 47345
"March", 38987	"July", 52156	"November", 45675
"April", 36181	"August", 49546	"December", 53769

The company would like to have a program that displays annual sales information. The following is to be included in the report:

1. The average monthly sales for the past year
2. A list of the months in which the sales exceeded the average monthly sales. (Include the sales figures for these months and their deviation from the average sales.)
3. The month name with the most sales and the month name with the fewest sales. (No two months have equal monthly sales.)

A top-down chart and a flowchart for each subtask are illustrated in Figures 7.16 and 7.17. The program tasks that correspond to the top-down chart, a program solution, and a discussion of the program solution follow.

FIGURE 7.16

Top-down chart for Program 7.1, the solution to Programming Case Study 12.

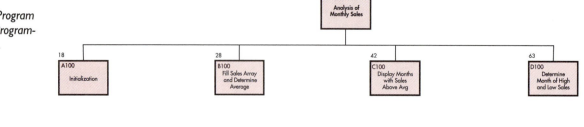

FIGURE 7.17

Flowcharts for the modules in Program 7.1, the solution to Programming Case Study 12.

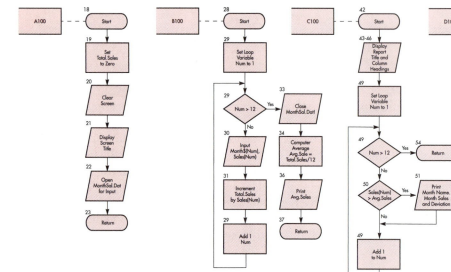

Program Tasks

The following program tasks correspond to the top-down chart in Figure 7.16.

1. Main Program
    a. Dimension two parallel arrays, Month$ and Sales, to 12 elements (1 to 12). Use the array Month$ to store the 12 month names and the array Sales to store the 12 monthly sales.
    b. Call subordinate subroutines.

2. A100.Initialization
    a. Initialize a running total (Total.Sales) to zero. Use Total.Sales to sum the 12 monthly sales.
    b. Clear the screen and display a screen title.
    c. Open the sequential data file MONTHSAL.DAT for input as filenumber 1.

3. B100.Fill.Sales.Array.and.Determine.Avg

   a. Use a For loop with an initial value of 1 and a limit value of 12 to read the 12 month names and corresponding sales into the parallel arrays Month$ and Sales. Within the loop, increment Total.Sales by each monthly sales.

   b. Close the MONTHSAL.DAT file.

   c. Determine the average monthly sales (Avg.Sales) by dividing Total.Sales by 12.

   d. Display the average monthly sales.

4. C100.Display.Months.With.Sales.Above.Avg

   a. Display report title and column headings.

   b. With an initial value of 1 and limit value of 12, use a For loop to test each month's sales against the average monthly sales. If the month's sales are greater than the average monthly sales, display the month name, the month's sales, and deviation of the month's sales from the average monthly sales.

5. D100.Determine.High.and.Low.Sales

   a. Assume that the first month has the highest and lowest sales.

     (1) Set the variable High to the first month's sales. Initialize the variable Subh to the value 1. Subh is used later as a subscript to access the month name with the most sales.

     (2) Set the variable Low to the first month's sales. Initialize the variable Subl to the value 1. Subl is used later as a subscript to access the month name with the lowest sales.

   b. Use a For loop with an initial value 2 and limit value 12 to test the sales of the second through twelfth months against the value of the variable High. If a month's sales are greater than the value of High, assign the month's sales to High and the value of the loop variable (Num) to Subh. Also include within the For loop a test in which the month's sales are compared against the value of Low. If the month's sales are less than the value of Low, assign the month's sales to Low and the value of the loop variable (Num) to Subl.

   c. Display the month with the most sales – Month$(Subh).

   d. Display the month with the fewest sales – Month$(Subl).

Program Solution

    The solution to Programming Case Study 12, Program 7.1, is illustrated in Figure 7.18 and corresponds to the previously defined tasks and to the top-down chart in Figure 7.16. The output from Program 7.1 is illustrated in Figure 7.19.

FIGURE 7.18

Program 7.1, the solution to Programming Case Study 12.

```
1    ' Program 7.1
2    ' Programming Case Study 12
3    ' Analysis of Monthly Sales
4    ' Input File Name = MONTHSAL.DAT
5    ' *************************************************************
6    ' *                     Main Program                       *
7    ' *************************************************************
8    DIM Month$(1 TO 12), Sales(1 TO 12)
9    GOSUB A100.Initialization
10   GOSUB B100.Fill.Sales.Array.and.Determine.Avg
11   GOSUB C100.Display.Months.With.Sales.Above.Avg
12   GOSUB D100.Determine.High.and.Low.Sales
13   END
14
15   ' *************************************************************
16   ' *                     Initialization                     *
17   ' *************************************************************
18   A100.Initialization:
19      Total.Sales = 0
20      CLS   ' Clear Screen
```

(continued)

```
21       LOCATE 1, 8: PRINT "Analysis of Monthly Sales"
22       OPEN "A:MONTHSAL.DAT" FOR INPUT AS #1
23    RETURN
24
25    ' ************************************************************
26    ' *           Fill Sales Array and Determine Average        *
27    ' ************************************************************
28    B100.Fill.Sales.Array.and.Determine.Avg:
29       FOR Num = 1 TO 12
30          INPUT #1, Month$(Num), Sales(Num)
31          Total.Sales = Total.Sales + Sales(Num)
32       NEXT Num
33       CLOSE #1
34       Avg.Sales = Total.Sales / 12
35       LOCATE 3, 1
36       PRINT USING "The average monthly sales is $$##,###.##"; Avg.Sales
37    RETURN
38
39    ' ************************************************************
40    ' *           Display Months with Sales Above Average       *
41    ' ************************************************************
42    C100.Display.Months.With.Sales.Above.Avg:
43       LOCATE 6, 1
44       PRINT "Months in which Sales are Above Average"
45       PRINT
46       PRINT "Month              Sales          Deviation"
47       PRINT
48       D1$ = "\          \     ##,###.##           ##,###.##"
49       FOR Num = 1 TO 12
50          IF Sales(Num) > Avg.Sales THEN
51             PRINT USING D1$; Month$(Num); Sales(Num); Sales(Num) - Avg.Sales
52          END IF
53       NEXT Num
54    RETURN
55
56    ' ************************************************************
57    ' *        Determine Month of Highest and Lowest Sales      *
58    ' *                                                         *
59    ' * Assume First Month has the Highest and Lowest Sales     *
60    ' * Subh = Subscript of Highest Sales, High = Highest Sales *
61    ' * Subl = Subscript of Lowest Sales,  Low  = Lowest Sales  *
62    ' ************************************************************
63    D100.Determine.High.and.Low.Sales:
64       High = Sales(1)
65       Subh = 1
66       Low = Sales(1)
67       Subl = 1
68       FOR Num = 2 TO 12
69          IF Sales(Num) > High THEN
70             High = Sales(Num): Subh = Num
71          END IF
72          IF Sales(Num) < Low THEN
73             Low = Sales(Num): Subl = Num
74          END IF
75       NEXT Num
76       PRINT
77       PRINT "Month of Highest Sales - "; Month$(Subh)
78       PRINT "Month of Lowest Sales  - "; Month$(Subl)
79       PRINT : PRINT "Job Complete"
80    RETURN
81
82    ' *************** End of Program ****************
```

[run]

FIGURE 7.19

The display due to the execution of Program 7.1.

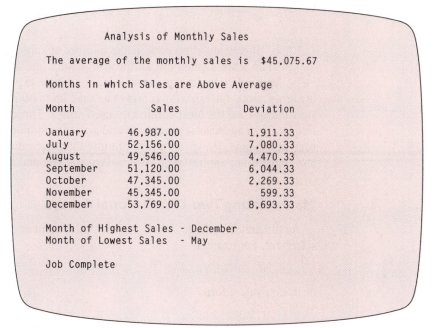

```
                    Analysis of Monthly Sales

        The average of the monthly sales is  $45,075.67

        Months in which Sales are Above Average

        Month              Sales            Deviation

        January          46,987.00          1,911.33
        July             52,156.00          7,080.33
        August           49,546.00          4,470.33
        September         51,120.00          6,044.33
        October          47,345.00          2,269.33
        November         45,345.00            599.33
        December         53,769.00          8,693.33

        Month of Highest Sales - December
        Month of Lowest Sales  - May

        Job Complete
```

Discussion of the Program Solution

In Program 7.1 presented in Figure 7.18, the arrays Month$ and Sales are declared in the Main Program by the DIM statement in line 8. The B100.Fill.Sales.Array.and.Determine.Avg subroutine is similar to the program in Figure 7.15 on page 258. The For loop (lines 29 through 32) loads the two arrays with values and sums the monthly sales. Line 33 closes MONTHSAL.DAT. At this point, the entire file is loaded into the parallel arrays Month$ and Sales. Line 34 computes the average; line 36 displays the average monthly sales.

The For loop in lines 49 through 53 tests each of the monthly sales found in the array Sales against the average monthly sales, Avg.Sales. If the value of an element in the array is greater than the average, then the PC is instructed to display the corresponding month name, the monthly sales, and the monthly sales deviation from the average:

Sales(Num) - Avg.Sales.

In the last subroutine of Program 7.1, lines 64 through 78 illustrate a technique that determines and displays the month in which the sales are the highest and the month in which the sales are the lowest. In lines 64 through 67, the first month's sales are assumed to be the highest as well as the lowest. The For loop, lines 68 through 75, tests the remaining months against the highest sales (line 69) and the lowest sales (line 72).

If a month's sales — Sales(Num) — are greater than the current highest sales (High), the month's sales are assigned as the current highest sales, and the variable Subh is assigned the value of the subscript Num. When the For loop is satisfied, Subh is the subscript that represents the element in the array Sales that has the highest sales. Subl is the subscript that represents the element in the array Sales that has the lowest sales. Because Month$ and Sales are parallel arrays, the corresponding month with the highest and lowest sales can be obtained by referencing Month$(Subh) and Month$(Subl).

7.6 MULTIDIMENSIONAL ARRAYS

The dimension of an array is the number of subscripts required to reference an element in an array. Up to now, all the arrays were one-dimensional, and an element was referenced by an integer, a variable, or a single expression in the parentheses following the array name. QBasic allows arrays to have up to 60 dimensions. One- and two-dimensional arrays are the most commonly used arrays. Three-dimensional arrays are used less frequently in business applications, and arrays with more than three dimensions are rarely used in business. However, arrays of more than three dimensions are used often in scientific and engineering applications, such as heat transfer and fluid dynamics.

Manipulating Two-Dimensional Arrays

As illustrated in Table 7.4 on page 255, the number of dimensions is declared in the `DIM` statement. For example,

```
DIM Cost(1 TO 2, 1 TO 5)
```

or its equivalent form

```
OPTION BASE 1
DIM Cost(2, 5)
```

declares an array to be two dimensional. A two-dimensional array usually is illustrated in the form of a table. The first subscript tells how many rows there are, and the second subscript tells how many columns. Figure 7.20 shows a 2 x 5 array (read *2 by 5 array*). Cost(1, 1) is read as *Cost sub one one* and references the element found in the first row and first column.

FIGURE 7.20
Conceptual view of the storage locations reserved for a 2 x 5 two-dimensional array called Cost, with the name of each element specified.

ROWS \ COLUMNS	1	2	3	4	5
1	COST(1, 1)	COST(1, 2)	COST(1, 3)	COST(1, 4)	COST(1, 5)
2	COST(2, 1)	COST(2, 2)	COST(2, 3)	COST(2, 4)	COST(2, 5)

Cost(2, 3) is read as *Cost sub two three* and references the element found in the second row and third column.

FIGURE 7.21
A 2 x 5 array with each element assigned a value.

ROWS \ COLUMNS	1	2	3	4	5
1	6	12	-52	3.14	0.56
2	8	2	5	6	2

Assuming that the elements of the array Cost are assigned the values shown in Figure 7.21, the following statements are true:

Cost(1, 2) is equal to 12.
Cost(2, 4) is equal to 6.
Cost(2, 2) is equal to 2.
Cost(1, 1) is equal to Cost(2, 4).
Cost(3, 5) is outside the range of the array; it does not exist.
Cost(2, 6) is outside the range of the array; it does not exist.
Cost(–2, –5) is outside the range of the array; it does not exist.

Initializing Arrays

You may write the code below to initialize to 0, row by row, all the elements in a 4 x 3 array called Area.

```
DIM Area(1 TO 4, 1 TO 3)
FOR Row = 1 TO 4
   FOR Column = 1 TO 3
      Area(Row, Column) = 0
   NEXT Column
NEXT Row
```

To initialize to 1 all elements on the main diagonal of a 5 x 5 array called Table, you may write the following:

```
DIM Table(1 TO 5, 1 TO 5)
FOR Row = 1 TO 5
   Table(Row, Row) = 1
NEXT Row
```

As a result, elements Table(1, 1), Table(2, 2), Table(3, 3), Table(4, 4), and Table(5, 5) are assigned the value of 1.

Two-dimensional arrays often are used to classify data. For example, if a company makes five models of a particular product and the production of each model involves a certain amount of processing time on six different machines, the processing time can be summarized in a table of five rows and six columns, as illustrated in Figure 7.22.

The following statement reserves storage in memory for a two-dimensional array that will accommodate the data in the table shown in Figure 7.22.

```
DIM Time(1 TO 5, 1 TO 6)
```

FIGURE 7.22

A table showing the processing time each model spends on a machine.

PRODUCT PROCESSING MINUTES		Machine					
		1	2	3	4	5	6
	1	13	30	5	17	12	45
	2	23	12	13	16	0	20
Model	3	45	12	28	16	10	13
	4	21	16	15	22	19	26
	5	23	50	17	43	15	18

If Model represents the model number (row of the table) and Machine represents the machine (column of the table), then the subscripted variable Time(Model, Machine) gives the time it takes for a model to be processed on a particular machine. The value of Model can range from 1 to 5, and the value of Machine can range from 1 to 6. If Model is equal to 4 and Machine is equal to 5, the table tells us the product processing time is 19 minutes. That is, model number 4 involves 19 minutes of processing on machine 5.

To sum all the elements in column 2 of the table in Figure 7.22 into a running total Sum2 and to sum all the elements in row 4 into a running total Sum4, you can write the following:

```
DIM Time(1 TO 5, 1 TO 6)
Sum2 = 0
Sum4 = 0
FOR Model = 1 TO 5
   Sum2 = Sum2 + Time(Model, 2)
NEXT Model
FOR Machine = 1 TO 6
   Sum4 = Sum4 + Time(4, Machine)
NEXT Machine
```

These last three partial programs should give you an idea of how you can handle elements that appear in various rows and columns of two-dimensional arrays.

Arrays with More than Two Dimensions

The table in Figure 7.22 is for one product with five different models. Now suppose we want to consider comparable tables for two different products, each of which has five different model numbers and all of which utilize the six machines. To construct such a table, we can modify the array Time so it is a three-dimensional array.

```
DIM Time(1 TO 5, 1 TO 6, 1 TO 2)
```

Now the subscripted variable Time(Model, Machine, Product) refers to the time it takes for a given model number (Model) on a particular machine (Machine) for a specific product (Product). Figure 7.23 represents a conceptual view of some of the storage locations for a 5 x 6 x 2 array called Time. This three-dimensional array contains five rows, six columns, and two planes, for a total of 60 elements.

FIGURE 7.23

Conceptual view of some of the storage locations reserved for a 5 x 6 x 2 three-dimensional array called Time.

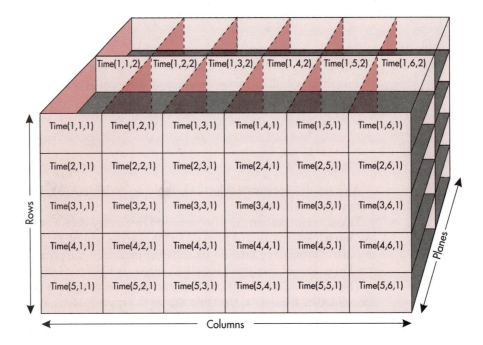

If we want to take into account the production differences at three different sites, we can make Time a four-dimensional array:

```
DIM Time(1 TO 5, 1 TO 6, 1 TO 2, 1 TO 3)
```

Now the subscripted variable Time(Model, Machine, Product, Site) refers to the processing time it takes for a given model number, on a particular machine, for a specific product, at a given site. If factors other than site, product, model, and machine are required, we can add even more dimensions.

Determining the Lower- and Upper-Bound Subscript Values of an Array

QBasic includes two functions that allow you to determine during the execution of a program the lower- and upper-bound subscript values of an array. LBOUND**(array name, N)** returns the lower-bound subscript value, and UBOUND**(array name, N)** returns the upper-bound subscript value. N specifies the Nth dimension. If N is omitted, QBasic uses 1. As an example of these two functions, consider the partial program in Figure 7.24, which is self-explanatory.

```
 I    ' Displaying the Lower- and Upper-bound
 2    ' Subscript Values of Arrays
 3    ' ************************************
 4    OPTION BASE 1
 5    DIM S(-5 TO 4), T(5 TO 10, 8), A(7, 3, 4 TO 7)
 6    PRINT "Array S:"
 7    PRINT TAB(3); "Upper-bound value ===>", UBOUND(S, 1)
 8    PRINT TAB(3); "Lower-bound value ===>", LBOUND(S, 1)
 9    PRINT
10    PRINT "Array T:"
11    PRINT TAB(3); "Upper-bound values ===>", UBOUND(T, 1), UBOUND(T,2)
12    PRINT TAB(3); "Lower-bound values ===>", LBOUND(T, 1), UBOUND(T,2)
13    PRINT
14    PRINT "Array A:"
15    PRINT TAB(3); "Upper-bound values ==>", UBOUND(A, 1), UBOUND(A,2), UBOUND(A, 3)
16    PRINT TAB(3); "Lower-bound values ==>", LBOUND(A, 1), LBOUND(A,2), LBOUND(A, 3)

      [run]

      Array S:
         Upper-bound value ===>       4
         Lower-bound value ===>      -5

      Array T:
         Upper-bound values ==>      10          8
         Lower-bound values ==>       5          1

      Array A:
         Upper-bound values ==>       7          3          7
         Lower-bound values ==>       1          1          4
```

FIGURE 7.24
Using the UBOUND and LBOUND functions.

7.7 SORTING

Sorting data into alphabetical or numerical order is one of the more frequently executed operations in a business information processing environment. It is a time-consuming operation, especially when large amounts of data are involved. Although most computer operating systems supply you with a sort program today, this has not always been the case. Computer professionals have spent a great deal of time developing algorithms to speed up the sorting process. Usually, the faster the process, the more complex the algorithm. In this section, we will discuss two of the more common sort algorithms: the **bubble sort** and the **Shell sort**, named after its author, Donald Shell. These algorithms will assist you in better understanding arrays and the manipulation of data.

Figure 7.25 illustrates the difference between unsorted data and the same data in ascending and descending sequence. Data in sequence from lowest to highest in value is in **ascending sequence**. Data in sequence from highest to lowest in value is in **descending sequence**.

FIGURE 7.25
Data in various sequences.

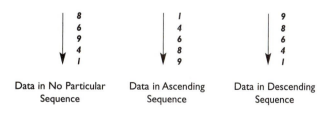

Data in No Particular Sequence   Data in Ascending Sequence   Data in Descending Sequence

The Bubble Sort

The bubble sort is a straightforward method of sorting data items that have been placed in an array. To illustrate the logic of a bubble sort, we will sort the data found in Figure 7.25 on the previous page into ascending sequence. Assume that the data has been assigned to the array B, as illustrated in Figure 7.26.

The bubble sort involves comparing adjacent elements and **swapping** (that is, interchanging) the values of those elements when they are out of order. For example, B(1) is compared to B(2). If B(1) is less than or equal to B(2), no swap occurs. If B(1) is greater than B(2), the values of the two elements are swapped. B(2) is then compared to B(3), and so on, until B(4) is compared to B(5). One complete time through the array is called a **pass**. At the end of the first pass, the largest value is in the last element of the array B, as illustrated in Figure 7.27. Its box has been shaded to show that it is in its final position and will not move again.

FIGURE 7.26

Original order of unsorted data in array B.

B(1)	8
B(2)	6
B(3)	9
B(4)	4
B(5)	1

FIGURE 7.27

First pass through array B.

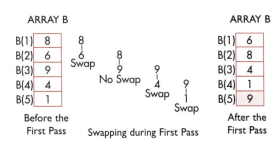

FIGURE 7.28

Second pass through array B.

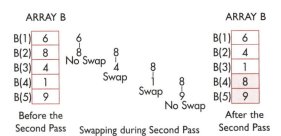

The maximum number of passes necessary to sort the elements in an array is equal to the number of elements in the array less 1. Because array B has 5 elements, four passes at most are made on the array. Keep in mind that the minimum number of passes to sort the elements in an array may be one. This occurs when the array elements initially are stored in sorted sequence.

Figures 7.28, 7.29, and 7.30 illustrate the second, third, and fourth passes made on the array B. The swapping pushes the larger values down in the illustrations, and as a side effect, the smaller numbers *bubble* up to the top of the array.

FIGURE 7.29

Third pass through array B.

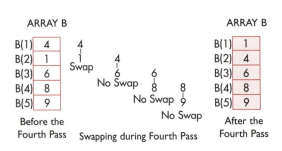

FIGURE 7.30

Fourth pass through array B, which is now in ascending sequence.

The SWAP Statement

To exchange the values of two storage locations in a program, we can use the SWAP **statement**. The general form of the SWAP statement is shown in Table 7.7.

TABLE 7.7 - The SWAP Statement	
General Form:	SWAP variable1, variable2
	where **variable**1 and **variable**2 are of the same type.
Purpose:	Exchanges the values of two variables or two elements of an array.
Examples:	1. SWAP Old.Balance, New.Balance
	2. SWAP Array(Size), Array(Size + 1)
	3. SWAP Code1$(Row, Col), Code2$(Row, Col)

In Table 7.7, example 1 exchanges the values of the two simple variables, Old.Balance and New.Balance. Prior to the execution of the SWAP statement, if Old.Balance is equal to 500 and New.Balance is equal to 600, then after its execution, Old.Balance is equal to 600 and New.Balance is equal to 500.

In example 2 of Table 7.7, the values of the two subscripted variables, Array(Size) and Array(Size + 1), are exchanged. Exchanging the values of two adjacent elements of an array is a common practice with sort algorithms.

Finally, in example 3 of Table 7.7, the SWAP statement exchanges the values of the two corresponding string elements of tables, Code1$ and Code2$.

Implementing the Bubble Sort

The statement that compares two adjacent elements in an array and exchanges them when necessary is

```
IF B(I) > B(I + 1) THEN
   SWAP B(I), B(I + 1)
END IF
```

One pass on the array, which compares all adjacent elements, can be implemented by using the following For loop:

```
FOR I = 1 TO 4
   IF B(I) > B(I + 1) THEN
      SWAP B(I), B(I + 1)
   END IF
NEXT I
```

Finally, as illustrated in Figures 7.27 through 7.30, the elements of the array are sorted by completing four passes on the array. This can be accomplished with a pair of nested For loops. To make the routine more general, we have also included an expression for the limit parameters in each For loop as follows:

```
Limit = 5
FOR J = 1 TO (Limit - 1)
   FOR I = 1 TO (Limit - 1)
      IF B(I) > B(I + 1) THEN
         SWAP B(I), B(I + 1)           inefficient
      END IF                           algorithm
   NEXT I
NEXT J
```

Although the nested For loops sort the values of the elements in array B, the algorithm is highly inefficient for the two following reasons. First, the values of the elements in the array may already be in ascending sequence before the sort routine is initiated. This inefficient technique would still make four passes on the sorted array.

Second, during a pass, all the values of the elements in the array beyond the last interchange may be in sequence. For example, assume 100 numbers are being sorted, and on the first pass the *last interchange* is made between the 59th and 60th elements in the list. On the next pass, elements beyond the 58th and 59th need not be compared because they will be in the proper sequence.

To minimize the number of passes it takes to sort an array, a variable called a switch is required. The switch is used to halt the sort routine when the array is sorted. The **switch** is a simple string variable that takes on two values during the duration of the loop. If Switch$ is the variable that represents the switch, then when the switch is on, meaning Switch$ equals the value ON, another pass is required. When the switch is off, meaning Switch$ equals the value OFF, the array is sorted and the loop is terminated. The switch is turned on whenever two adjacent elements are exchanged, and this means that another pass is required. If a pass is made, meaning all adjacent elements are compared, and the switch remains off, then the array is sorted.

In the previous algorithm, the outer For loop controlled the number of passes. If a switch is used to control the number of passes, then the For loop should be replaced by a Do-While loop. To sort on the next pass only to the point where the last interchange occurred, a variable called Last is required. Last is assigned the current value of the loop variable I whenever an interchange is made. When the For loop is satisfied, the value of Last is assigned to the Limit value of the For loop.

The partial program code presented in Figure 7.31 will *efficiently* sort the elements of array B into ascending sequence.

FIGURE 7.31
Efficient bubble sort logic.

```
27   ' ******************************
28   ' *        Bubble Sort        *
29   ' ******************************
30   B100.Bubble.Sort:
31     Limit = Number
32     Switch$ = "ON"
33     DO WHILE Switch$ = "ON"
34       Switch$ = "OFF"
35       FOR I = 1 TO (Limit - 1)
36         IF B(I) > B(I + 1) THEN
37           SWAP B(I), B(I + 1)
38           Switch$ = "ON"
39           Last = I
40         END IF
41       NEXT I
42       Limit = Last
43     LOOP
44   RETURN
```

These two statements substantially improve the efficiency of the sort, especially when some of the data is already in order.

The variable Switch$ controls whether another pass will be done on the array. Line 32 assigns Switch$ a value of ON. Because Switch$ equals ON, line 33 passes control into the body of the Do-While loop. Line 34 assigns Switch$ a value of OFF just before the For loop makes a pass on the loop. If Switch$ is not modified later in the loop (line 38), the values in the array are in sequence, and the next time that line 33 is executed control transfers to line 44.

The FOR statement in line 35 initializes I to 1. The first element B(1) is then compared to B(2). If B(1) is greater than B(2), the THEN clause swaps the values of the two elements and assigns Switch$ a value of ON. Next, B(2) is compared to B(3) and so on.

The number of comparisons per pass is equal to the number of elements to compare minus 1. Because the number of data items to sort is five, the limit parameter in the FOR statement is set to 4.

Program 7.2 illustrated in Figure 7.32 incorporates the logic found in this partial program to sort the values 8, 6, 9, 4, and 1. To make the sort algorithm more general, a variable can be used for the size of the array. Line 17 dynamically allocates storage for array B. Because array B is dynamically allocated on the basis of Number, we placed the DIM statement in A100.Initialization instead of in the Main Program.

The For loop, made up of lines 20 through 23, loads and displays the unsorted elements of the array. The B100.Bubble.Sort subroutine (lines 30 through 44) sorts the numeric array. The C100.Display.Sorted.Array subroutine (lines 49 through 54) displays the elements after the array has been sorted.

FIGURE 7.32

Program 7.2, sorting numeric data using the bubble sort technique.

```
1    ' Program 7.2
2    ' Sorting Numeric Data Using the
3    ' Bubble Sort Technique
4    ' ****************************
5    ' *         Main Program         *
6    ' ****************************
7    GOSUB A100.Initialization
8    GOSUB B100.Bubble.Sort
9    GOSUB C100.Display.Sorted.Array
10   END
11
12   ' ****************************
13   ' *         Initialization         *
14   ' ****************************
15   A100.Initialization:
16      READ Number
17      DIM B(1 TO Number)
18      CLS   ' Clear Screen
19      PRINT "Unsorted -";
20      FOR I = 1 TO Number
21         READ B(I)
22         PRINT B(I);
23      NEXT I
24      PRINT : PRINT
25   RETURN
26
27   ' ****************************
28   ' *         Bubble Sort         *
29   ' ****************************
30   B100.Bubble.Sort:
31      Limit = Number
32      Switch$ = "ON"
33      DO WHILE Switch$ = "ON"
34         Switch$ = "OFF"
35         FOR I = 1 TO (Limit - 1)
36            IF B(I) > B(I + 1) THEN
37               SWAP B(I), B(I + 1)
38               Switch$ = "ON"
39               Last = I
40            END IF
41         NEXT I
42         Limit = Last
43      LOOP
44   RETURN
45
46   ' ****************************
47   ' *    Display Sorted Array    *
48   ' ****************************
```

bubble sort code presented in Figure 7.31

(continued)

```
49    C100.Display.Sorted.Array:
50      PRINT "Sorted   -";
51      FOR I = 1 TO Number
52        PRINT B(I);
53      NEXT I
54    RETURN
55
56    ' ******** Data Follows ********
57    DATA 5 : ' Number of values to sort
58    DATA 8, 6, 9, 4, 1
59    ' ****** End of Program ********

      [run]

      Unsorted - 8  6  9  4  1

      Sorted   - 1  4  6  8  9
```

The advantage to studying sort algorithms is that they raise the question of algorithm efficiency. In the next section, we will discuss the Shell sort, which offers a vast improvement over the bubble sort algorithm.

The Shell Sort

The bubble sort algorithm works well for a small number of data items, but it can take too much processing time for a large number of data items. The problem with this algorithm is that the smaller data items move only one position at a time because only adjacent elements are compared. The Shell sort provides a faster means of sorting a large number of data items. The longer the list to be sorted, the greater the advantage of the Shell sort over the bubble sort.

The Shell sort is similar to the bubble sort, but instead of comparing and swapping adjacent elements B(I) and B(I + 1), it compares and swaps nonadjacent elements B(I) and B(I + Gap), where Gap starts out considerably greater than 1.

Prior to the loop that swaps the elements, Gap is set to one-half the length of the array. When a swap is made, a big improvement takes place. When no swap is made on a pass, the Gap is halved again for the next pass. Finally, the Gap becomes 1, as in the bubble sort, and adjacent elements are compared and swapped.

The Shell sort is used in Program 7.3 illustrated in Figure 7.33 to sort a list of fifteen data items. In the B100.Shell.Sort subroutine, line 31 begins by assigning the Gap to one-half the size of the list. Line 32 initiates a loop that has as its body the bubble sort with some minor modifications. Within the For loop (lines 37 through 45), the integer I in the bubble sort algorithm is replaced by the variable Gap.

FIGURE 7.33

Program 7.3, sorting numeric data using the Shell sort technique.

```
1    ' Program 7.3
2    ' Sorting Numeric Data Using the
3    ' Shell Sort Technique
4    ' *****************************
5    ' *        Main Program        *
6    ' *****************************
7    GOSUB A100.Initialization
8    GOSUB B100.Shell.Sort
9    GOSUB C100.Display.Sorted.Array
10   END
11
12   ' *****************************
13   ' *       Initialization       *
14   ' *****************************
```

```
15   A100.Initialization:
16      READ Number
17      DIM B(1 TO Number)           ◄─── array B
                                          declared
18      CLS  ' Clear Screen
19      PRINT "Unsorted -";
20      FOR I = 1 TO Number
21         READ B(I)
22         PRINT B(I);
23      NEXT I
24      PRINT : PRINT
25   RETURN
26
27   ' *****************************
28   ' *         Shell Sort        *
29   ' *****************************
30   B100.Shell.Sort:
31      Gap = Number \ 2       'Integer Division   ◄─── Gap is
                                                        initialized
32      DO WHILE Gap > 0
33         Limit = Number
34         Switch$ = "ON"
35         DO WHILE Switch$ = "ON"
36            Switch$ = "OFF"
37            FOR I = 1 TO Limit - Gap
38               IF B(I) > B(I + Gap) THEN
39                  SWAP B(I), B(I + Gap)
40                  Switch$ = "ON"
41                  Last = I
42               END IF
43            NEXT I
44            Limit = Last
45         LOOP
46         Gap = Gap \ 2       ◄─── Gap is
                                     recalculated
47      LOOP
48   RETURN
49
50   ' *****************************
51   ' *    Display Sorted Array    *
52   ' *****************************
53   C100.Display.Sorted.Array:
54      PRINT "Sorted   -";
55      FOR I = 1 TO Number
56         PRINT B(I);
57      NEXT I
58   RETURN
59
60   ' ******** Data Follows ********
61   DATA 15 : ' Number of Values to Sort
62   DATA 18, 13, 6, 4, 19, 12, 67, 1
63   DATA 11, 13, 27, 32, 2, 17, 55
64   ' ******* End of Program *******

     [run]

     Unsorted - 18  13  6  4  19  12  67  1  11  13  27  32  2  17  55

     Sorted   - 1  2  4  6  11  12  13  13  17  18  19  27  32  55  67
```

To make the Shell sort even faster, all the numeric variables could have been declared as integer data type for the limited data that required sorting.

7.8 TABLE PROCESSING

Many applications call for the use of data that is arranged in tabular form. Rates of pay, tax brackets, part costs, and insurance rates are examples of tables that contain systematically arranged data. Arrays make it easier to write programs for applications involving tables.

Table Organization

Tables are organized on the basis of how the data items, also called **table functions**, are to be referenced. In **positionally-organized tables**, table functions can be accessed by their position in the table. In **argument-organized tables**, table functions are accessed by the value that corresponds to the desired table function.

Positionally-Organized Tables

To illustrate a positionally-organized table, a program can be written that displays the name of the month in response to a month number, 1 through 12. Figure 7.34 shows the basic concept behind accessing a table function in a positionally organized table.

FIGURE 7.34

Accessing a table function in a positionally organized table.

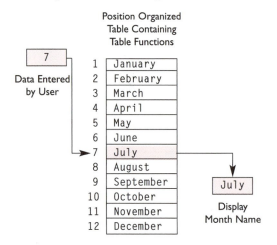

In Figure 7.34, the month name is selected from the table on the basis of its location. A value of 1, entered by the user, equates to January, 2 to February, and so on. To write a program that uses table processing techniques, you must do the following:

1. Define the table by declaring an array.
2. Load the table functions into the array.
3. Write statements to access the table entries.

Program 7.4, presented in Figure 7.35, illustrates how to declare, load, and access the table of month names described in Figure 7.34. Line 6 defines the table by declaring the one-dimensional string array Month$ to 12. Lines 16 through 18 load the table functions — in this case, the month names — into the array. Line 52 in the B210.Access.Table.Function subroutine accesses the desired table function.

FIGURE 7.35

Program 7.4, accessing functions in a positionally organized table.

```
 1   ' Program 7.4
 2   ' Accessing Functions in a Positionally Organized Table
 3   ' ******************************************************
 4   ' *                    Main Program                    *
 5   ' ******************************************************
 6   DIM Month$(1 TO 12)            ' Declare the Table
 7   GOSUB A100.Initialization
 8   GOSUB B100.Process.Request
 9   GOSUB C100.Wrap.Up
10   END
11
12   ' ******************************************************
13   ' *                  Initialization                    *
14   ' ******************************************************
```

```
15   A100.Initialization:
16      FOR Number = 1 TO 12
17         READ Month$(Number)     ' Load the Table
18      NEXT Number
19   RETURN
20
21   ' ********************************************************
22   ' *                 Process a Request                  *
23   ' ********************************************************
24   B100.Process.Request:
25      DO
26         GOSUB B200.Accept.Operator.Input
27         GOSUB B210.Access.Table.Function
28      LOOP UNTIL UCASE$(Control$) = "N"
29   RETURN
30
31   ' ********************************************************
32   ' *                 Accept Operator Input              *
33   ' ********************************************************
34   B200.Accept.Operator.Input:
35      CLS  ' Clear Screen
36      LOCATE 3, 15
37      INPUT "Month Number (Enter 1 through 12) =====> ", Num
38      DO WHILE Num < 1 OR Num > 12
39         LOCATE 5, 15: PRINT "Month Number Invalid, Please Reenter"
40         BEEP: BEEP: BEEP: BEEP
41         LOCATE 3, 56: PRINT SPC(15);
42         LOCATE 3, 56: INPUT "", Num
43         LOCATE 5, 15: PRINT SPC(40);
44      LOOP
45   RETURN
46
47   ' ********************************************************
48   ' *                 Access the Table Function          *
49   ' ********************************************************
50   B210.Access.Table.Function:
51      LOCATE 5, 15
52      PRINT "Month Name ============================> "; Month$(Num)
53      LOCATE 7, 15
54      INPUT "Enter Y to process another month number, else N... ", Control$
55   RETURN
56
57   ' ********************************************************
58   ' *                     Wrap-Up                        *
59   ' ********************************************************
60   C100.Wrap.Up:
61      CLS  ' Clear Screen
62      PRINT : PRINT "Job Complete"
63   RETURN
64
65   ' ************** Table Entries Follow *****************
66   DATA January, February, March, April, May, June, July
67   DATA August, September, October, November, December
68   ' *************** End of Program ********************

     [run]
```

The routine to access the table function in Program 7.4 is straightforward. The user enters a value for Num. A range check (lines 38 through 44) ensures the value is between 1 and 12. After a valid value is entered, line 52 references the corresponding element of the array that contains the table functions. Figures 7.36 and 7.37 show the results displayed as a result of entering the month numbers 7 and 12 in response to a request by Program 7.4.

FIGURE 7.36

The display by Program 7.4 due to entering the month number 7.

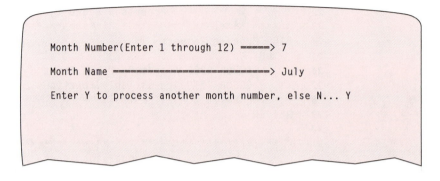

```
Month Number(Enter 1 through 12) ======> 7

Month Name ================================> July

Enter Y to process another month number, else N... Y
```

FIGURE 7.37

The display by Program 7.4 due to entering the month number 12.

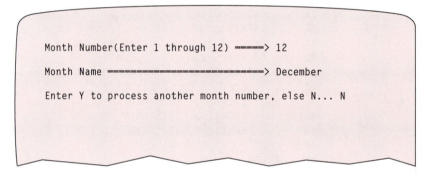

```
Month Number(Enter 1 through 12) ======> 12

Month Name ===============================> December

Enter Y to process another month number, else N... N
```

Positionally-organized tables, such as Month$ in Program 7.4, are not difficult to understand. Unfortunately, few tables can be constructed on the basis of the relative position of the table functions. Months, days of the week, and job classes are examples of systematic data that can be organized into positional tables.

Argument-Organized Tables

In most applications, tables are characterized by entries made up of multiple functions. Multiple-function entries are accessed by means of a **search argument**. The search argument is entered by the user much as the month number was in Program 7.4. The search argument is compared to the **table argument**, a table entry, to retrieve the corresponding table function. Figure 7.38 illustrates the composition of a table that is organized by arguments.

The table argument is assigned to a one-dimensional array. Functions are assigned to parallel arrays. Unlike a positionally-organized table, in which the value entered is used to obtain the table function, an argument-organized table must be searched until the search argument agrees with one of the table arguments. This search is a **table search**, or a **table lookup**.

FIGURE 7.38

Conceptual view of an argument organized table.

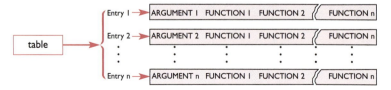

Two methods for searching a table are: the serial search and the binary search. A **serial search** begins by comparing the search argument to the first table argument. If the two agree, the search is over. If they do not agree, then the search argument is compared to the second table argument, and so on, until the table argument either is found or not found. In the serial search, the table arguments may be either in sorted or unsorted order, or arranged in a predetermined order based on frequency of use.

In general, a **binary search** begins the search in the middle of the table and determines whether the table argument that agrees with the search argument is in the upper half or the lower half of the table. The half that contains this table argument is then halved again. This process continues until there is nothing left to divide in half. At that point, the binary search is complete. The table argument either has been found or not found. The binary search, which requires that the table arguments be in sorted order, that is in ascending or descending sequence, will be discussed in greater detail later.

Serial Search

A serial search, sometimes called a **linear search** or **sequential search**, is a procedure that all of us use in everyday life. Suppose, for example, that you have a parts list that contains the part numbers and corresponding part descriptions and part costs. If you have a part number, one method for finding the part description and cost is to read through the part number list until you find the part number for which you are searching. You can then read off the description and cost that correspond to the part number. Figure 7.39 illustrates the basic concept of a serial search.

FIGURE 7.39

Conceptual view of a serial search.

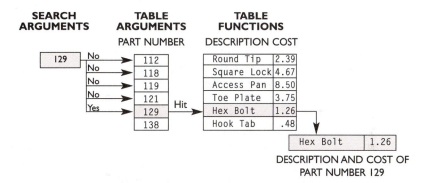

The search argument is tested against each of the table arguments, beginning with the first, until a *hit* (that is, a match) is made. At that point, the corresponding part description and part cost are selected from the table.

A program that completes the serial search illustrated in Figure 7.39 first needs to have the table defined. Because each entry is made up of a table argument and two functions, we declare three parallel arrays — Part, Desc$, and Cost, as shown in line 16 of the partial program below. The variable Entries is assigned the number of parts in the parts list by line 15.

```
15    READ Entries
16    DIM Part(1 TO Entries), Desc$(1 TO Entries), Cost(1 TO Entries)
```

The array Part is assigned the part numbers, the array Desc$ the part descriptions, and the array Cost the part costs. A For loop is used to load the table, as follows:

```
17    FOR Number = 1 TO Entries
18        READ Part(Number), Desc$(Number), Cost(Number)
19    NEXT Number
```

Each time the READ statement is executed, one entry is loaded into the parallel arrays. Each entry in the table consists of an argument and two functions. The partial program presented in Figure 7.40 on the next page searches the argument table and causes either the part description and part cost or a diagnostic message to be displayed. Assume that the user has assigned the part number that is to be looked up to the variable Search.Argument.

FIGURE 7.40

Access table functions in a serial search.

```
41   ' *********************************************************
42   ' *            Access the Table Function              *
43   ' *********************************************************
44   B210.Access.Table.Function:
45      FOR Number = 1 TO Entries
46         IF Search.Argument = Part(Number) THEN
47            EXIT FOR                  ' Process a Table Hit
48         END IF
49      NEXT Number
50      IF Number <= Entries THEN
51         GOSUB B300.Display.Table.Function
52      ELSE
53         LOCATE 7, 15
54         PRINT "Part Number"; Search.Argument; "NOT FOUND"
55      END IF
56      LOCATE 11, 15
57      INPUT "Enter Y to look up another part number, else N... ", Control$
58   RETURN
59
60   ' *********************************************************
61   ' *              Display Table Function               *
62   ' *********************************************************
63   B300.Display.Table.Function:
64      LOCATE 7, 15
65      PRINT "Description =====> "; Desc$(Number)
66      LOCATE 9, 15
67      PRINT USING "Cost ============> $$#.##"; Cost(Number)
68   RETURN
```

serial search

A For loop (lines 45 through 49) is used to implement the serial search algorithm. The IF statement in line 46 compares Search.Argument against the part numbers in the table Part(Number). When a hit, or match, occurs, the EXIT FOR statement in line 47 causes a premature exit from the For loop. In this case, Number is equal to the desired subscript. If no hit occurs, then the For loop runs its normal course, and Number is greater than the limit value Entries.

The IF statement following the For loop in line 50 compares Number to Entries. If Number is less than or equal to Entries, then the search was successful and control transfers to the B300.Display.Table.Function subroutine. Number is used in lines 65 and 67 to display the corresponding part description and part cost found in the parallel arrays. If Number is greater than Entries in line 50, then the search was unsuccessful, and the diagnostic message in line 54 displays.

The complete program, Program 7.5, is illustrated in Figure 7.41.

FIGURE 7.41

Program 7.5, Serial Search of an Argument organized table.

```
1    ' Program 7.5
2    ' Serial Search of an Argument Organized Table
3    ' *********************************************************
4    ' *                  Main Program                     *
5    ' *********************************************************
6    GOSUB A100.Initialization
7    GOSUB B100.Process.Request
8    GOSUB C100.Wrap.Up
9    END
10
11   ' *********************************************************
12   ' *                 Initialization                    *
13   ' *********************************************************
14   A100.Initialization:
15      READ Entries
16      DIM Part(1 TO Entries), Desc$(1 TO Entries), Cost(1 TO Entries)
```

```
17      FOR Number = 1 TO Entries
18        READ Part(Number), Desc$(Number), Cost(Number)
19      NEXT Number
20   RETURN
21
22   ' **********************************************************
23   ' *                 Process a Request                      *
24   ' **********************************************************
25   B100.Process.Request:
26      DO
27         GOSUB B200.Accept.Operator.Input
28         GOSUB B210.Access.Table.Function
29      LOOP UNTIL UCASE$(Control$) = "N"
30   RETURN
31
32   ' **********************************************************
33   ' *                Accept Operator Input                   *
34   ' **********************************************************
35   B200.Accept.Operator.Input:
36      CLS  ' Clear Screen
37      LOCATE 5, 15
38      INPUT "Part Number =====> ", Search.Argument
39   RETURN
40
41   ' **********************************************************
42   ' *                Access the Table Function               *
43   ' **********************************************************
44   B210.Access.Table.Function:
45      FOR Number = 1 TO Entries
46         IF Search.Argument = Part(Number) THEN
47            EXIT FOR                   ' Process a Table Hit
48         END IF
49      NEXT Number
50      IF Number <= Entries THEN
51         GOSUB B300.Display.Table.Function
52      ELSE
53         LOCATE 7, 15
54         PRINT "Part Number"; Search.Argument; "NOT FOUND"
55      END IF
56      LOCATE 11, 15
57      INPUT "Enter Y to look up another part number, else N... ", Control$
58   RETURN
59
60   ' **********************************************************
61   ' *                Display Table Function                  *
62   ' **********************************************************
63   B300.Display.Table.Function:
64      LOCATE 7, 15
65      PRINT "Description =====> "; Desc$(Number)
66      LOCATE 9, 15
67      PRINT USING "Cost ============> $$#.##"; Cost(Number)
68   RETURN
69
70   ' **********************************************************
71   ' *                     Wrap-Up                            *
72   ' **********************************************************
73   C100.Wrap.Up:
74      CLS  ' Clear Screen
75      PRINT : PRINT "Job Complete"
76   RETURN
77
```

load parallel arrays

serial search

(continued)

```
78  ' ****************** Table Entries ******************
79  DATA 6 : ' Number of Table Entries
80  DATA 112, Round Tip,   2.39
81  DATA 118, Square Lock, 4.67
82  DATA 119, Access Pan,  8.5
83  DATA 121, Toe Plate,   3.75
84  DATA 129, Hex Bolt,    1.26
85  DATA 138, Hook Tab,     .48
86  ' ***************** End of Program ******************

[run]
```

Figure 7.42 illustrates the display that is due to a part number of 129, and Figure 7.43 illustrates the display that is due to the invalid part number 122.

▌FIGURE 7.42

The display from Program 7.5 due to valid part number 129.

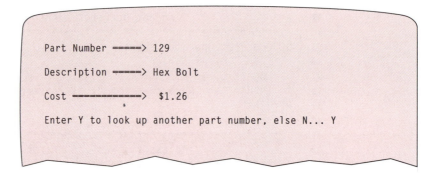

```
Part Number =====> 129

Description =====> Hex Bolt

Cost ============> $1.26

Enter Y to look up another part number, else N... Y
```

▌FIGURE 7.43

The display from Program 7.5 due to invalid part number 122.

```
Part Number =====> 122

Part Number 122 NOT FOUND

Enter Y to look up another part number, else N... N
```

Ordering the Table Arguments for a Serial Search

For a serial search, it is not always necessary that the table arguments be in sequence. If it is known that some table entries are requested more often than others, then the table entries requested most often should be placed at the beginning of the table. For example, assume that a frequency analysis uncovered the following pattern of requests regarding the part-number table entries illustrated in Figure 7.39 on page 277.

Part Number	% Requested
112	10
118	4
119	15
121	40
129	25
138	6

According to the frequency analysis, the description and cost for part number 121 are requested 40% of the time, and the description and cost for part number 118 are requested only 4% of the time.

If we load the table according to the frequency analysis, then the table entry for part number 121 is at the beginning of the table, and the table entry for part number 118 is at the end of the table. This is shown in Figure 7.44. In contrast to the search done earlier in Figure 7.39, the same search takes three fewer comparisons in Figure 7.44. If we load the table according to the frequency analysis, 65% of the requests will require, at most, two comparisons.

FIGURE 7.44
A serial search of a table loaded according to a frequency analysis.

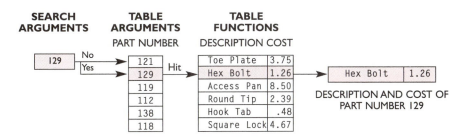

Binary Search

A serial search is useful for short tables, but not for long ones. For example, suppose the names in a telephone book were not listed alphabetically. If there were 15,000 names, it would take an average of 7,500 comparisons to find a specific telephone number. Some numbers might require only a few comparisons to find, while others might require nearly 15,000 comparisons.

Because telephone books are arranged alphabetically, any name listed therein can be located quickly and easily. When the arguments in a table are in alphabetical or numerical order, an efficient algorithm, known as the binary search, can be used. A binary search begins the search in the middle of the table. If the search argument is less than the middle table argument, the search continues by halving the lower valued half of the table. If the search argument is greater than the middle table argument, the search continues by halving the higher valued half of the table. If the search argument is equal to the middle table argument, the search is over. The binary search algorithm continues to narrow the table until it either finds a match or determines there is no match.

Figure 7.45 illustrates how the binary search algorithm works with a table of part numbers and corresponding part costs. Follow carefully the arrows numbered 1 to 4. Part number

FIGURE 7.45
A conceptual view of a binary search.

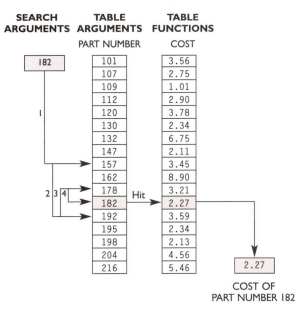

COST OF
PART NUMBER 182

182 is first compared against the ninth element of the 17-element array. Because 182 is greater than 157, the match is located in the higher valued half of the table. Part number 182 is next compared to the 13th element, halfway between 10 and 17. The part number is less than 192, and the confined area between 10 and 13 is halved again. On the next comparison, 182 is greater than 178, and the area is reduced by half. On the fourth comparison, a match is found. A serial search for part number 182 would have taken 12 comparisons before a match had been found. The difference in the number of comparisons between the two algorithms becomes even greater as the size of the table increases.

Program 7.6 illustrated in Figure 7.46 employs the binary search algorithm to search the table described in Figure 7.45 on the previous page. In the B210.Access.Table.Function subroutine (lines 44 through 65), the variables Low and High are initialized to the beginning and end of that section of the array Part to which the search is confined. Line 45 initializes Low to 1. Line 46 initializes High to Entries, which is equal to the number of entries in the table. Line 47 initializes Middle to 1 to ensure that Part(Middle) in line 48 is within the range of the array.

FIGURE 7.46

Program 7.6, a binary search of an argument-organized table.

```
 1    ' Program 7.6
 2    ' Binary Search of an Argument-Organized Table
 3    ' **********************************************************
 4    ' *                    Main Program                       *
 5    ' **********************************************************
 6    GOSUB A100.Initialization
 7    GOSUB B100.Process.Request
 8    GOSUB C100.Wrap.Up
 9    END
10
11    ' **********************************************************
12    ' *                   Initialization                      *
13    ' **********************************************************
14    A100.Initialization:
15       READ Entries
16       DIM Part(1 TO Entries), Cost(1 TO Entries)   ' Declare the table
17       FOR Number = 1 TO Entries
18          READ Part(Number), Cost(Number)           ' Load the Table
19       NEXT Number
20    RETURN
21
22    ' **********************************************************
23    ' *                  Process a Request                    *
24    ' **********************************************************
25    B100.Process.Request:
26       DO
27          GOSUB B200.Accept.Operator.Input
28          GOSUB B210.Access.Table.Function
29       LOOP UNTIL UCASE$(Control$) = "N"
30    RETURN
31
32    ' **********************************************************
33    ' *                 Accept Operator Input                 *
34    ' **********************************************************
35    B200.Accept.Operator.Input:
36       CLS  ' Clear Screen
37       LOCATE 5, 15
38       INPUT "Part Number =====> ", Search.Argument
39    RETURN
40
41    ' **********************************************************
42    ' *               Access the Table Function               *
43    ' **********************************************************
44    B210.Access.Table.Function:
45       Low = 1
46       High = Entries
47       Middle = 1
48       DO WHILE Search.Argument <> Part(Middle) AND Low <= High
49          Middle = (Low + High) \ 2
50          IF Search.Argument < Part(Middle) THEN
51             High = Middle - 1
52          END IF
```

```
53          IF Search.Argument > Part(Middle) THEN
54              Low = Middle + 1
55          END IF
56      LOOP
57      LOCATE 7, 15
58      IF Search.Argument = Part(Middle) THEN
59          PRINT USING "Cost ==============> $$#.##"; Cost(Middle)
60      ELSE
61          PRINT "Part Number"; Search.Argument; "NOT FOUND"
62      END IF
63      LOCATE 9, 15
64      INPUT "Enter Y to look up another part number, else N... ", Control$
65   RETURN
66
67   ' ******************************************************
68   ' *                      Wrap-Up                       *
69   ' ******************************************************
70   C100.Wrap.Up:
71      CLS   ' Clear Screen
72      PRINT : PRINT "Job Complete"
73   RETURN
74
75   ' ************* Table Entries Follow ******************
76   DATA 17 : ' Number of Table Entries
77   DATA 101, 3.56, 107, 2.75, 109, 1.01, 112, 2.9,  120, 3.78
78   DATA 130, 2.34, 132, 6.75, 147, 2.11, 157, 3.45, 162, 8.9
79   DATA 178, 3.21, 182, 2.27, 192, 3.59, 195, 2.34, 198, 2.13
80   DATA 204, 4.56, 216, 5.46
81   ' *************** End of Program *********************
```

[run]

The Do-While loop (lines 48 through 56) carries out the search. The compound condition in line 48 terminates the Do-While loop when Search.Argument is equal to Part(Middle) or when Low exceeds High. Immediately following the Do-While loop, line 58 tests to determine which of the two conditions caused the Do-While loop to terminate. If the search ends because Search.Argument is equal to Part(Middle), the search is successful. If the search ends because Low exceeds High, the search is unsuccessful.

Figure 7.47 shows the results that display when a part number of 182 is entered by the user. This corresponds to the example illustrated earlier in Figure 7.45. Figure 7.48 shows the results that display when an invalid part number is entered.

FIGURE 7.47
The display from Program 7.6 due to entering part number 182.

```
Part Number ------> 182

Cost --------------> $2.27

Enter Y to look up another part number, else N... Y
```

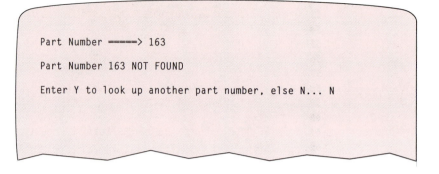

```
Part Number =====> 163

Part Number 163 NOT FOUND

Enter Y to look up another part number, else N... N
```

Combining Table-Access Methods

By itself, a binary search is not always the best method for searching large tables. This is especially true if the most sought after entries can be isolated. For example, the following frequency analysis of a part-number table with 650 table entries suggests that the table be divided into two tables — one small table in which the six most requested entries are ordered by request, and one large table containing 644 entries, in which the arguments are in ascending sequence.

Part Number	% Requested
112	8
118	4
119	10
121	40
129	25
138	6
Remaining 644 Part Numbers	7

A serial search is first used with the smaller table. If this search is unsuccessful, then a binary search is used on the larger table. This concept can be expanded further to include several tables and an algorithm that searches one table — a directory table — to determine the table that contains the entry and is to be searched next.

Some Formulae for Searching

When a serial search is used, the average number of searches may be found from the following formula:

$$s = n / 2$$

where n = total number of elements

    s = average number of searches

The table on the right illustrates the effects of this formula.

Total number of elements	Average number of searches
2	1
4	2
8	4
16	8
32	16
64	32
128	64
.	.
.	.
.	.

The word *binary* is given to the binary search algorithm because this algorithm keeps splitting into two sorted lists of elements until either a match has been found or not found, as illustrated earlier in the telephone book analogy. The following table illustrates the effects of the binary search algorithm:

Total number of elements	Average number of searches
2	1
4	2
8	3
16	4
32	5
64	6
128	7
.	.
.	.
.	.

The formula for determining the average number of searches when a binary search is used can be derived as follows:

$$n = 2^s$$
$$\log_2 n = s$$

or

$$s = \log_2 n$$

where n = total number of elements

s = average number of searches

Hence, on the average, a binary search is faster than a serial search when the size of the total number of elements increases.

7.9 What You Should Know

1. The FOR and NEXT statements are used to set up counter-controlled loops.
2. If the increment value following the keyword STEP is positive or the keyword STEP is not used, then the PC executes the For loop until the loop variable exceeds the limit value. If the increment value is negative, the test is reversed. The value of the loop variable is decremented each time through the loop, and the loop is executed until the loop variable is less than the limit value.
3. The FOR statement may be located anywhere before the corresponding NEXT statement.
4. A valid initial entry into a For loop can be accomplished only by transferring control to the FOR statement.
5. If the range of a For loop includes another For loop, all the statements that are in the range of the inner For loop must also be within the range of the outer For loop.
6. When one For loop is within another, the name of the control variable for each For loop must be different.
7. The EXIT statement may be used to prematurely exit a For loop.
8. An array is a variable that allocates a specified number of storage locations in memory, each of which can be assigned a unique value.
9. The elements in the array are distinguished from one another by subscripts. The subscript, written in parentheses, can be a numeric constant, a numeric variable, or a numeric expression.

10. The dimension of an array is the number of subscripts required to reference an element in an array.
11. Before an array can be used in a program, the DIM statement should be used to declare the number of storage locations in main memory that must be reserved for the array.
12. The DIM statement may be located anywhere before the first occurrence of a subscripted variable in a program.
13. Several arrays may be dimensioned in the same DIM statement.
14. The programmer has the choice in a DIM statement of specifying only the upper bound of an array or both the lower and upper bounds. If only the upper bound is specified, then the lower bound is zero, unless the OPTION BASE statement is used. To specify both bounds, use the keyword TO.
15. The OPTION BASE statement is used to assign a lower bound of 0 or 1 to all arrays dimensioned with only an upper bound. If the OPTION BASE statement is not used, the lower bound for all arrays is set to zero.
16. The subscript that references an array element must be within the range of the array. The range is the number of elements in the array.
17. Noninteger subscripts are rounded to the nearest integer.
18. An array is usually loaded with data using a READ or INPUT statement inside a For loop.
19. Parallel arrays are two or more arrays that have related corresponding elements.
20. QBasic permits arrays to be allocated dynamically. In the DIM statement, a variable is placed within the parentheses to indicate the size of the array. Before the DIM statement, the variable is assigned a value to which the array is dimensioned.
21. A two-dimensional array is one that requires two subscripts to reference any element. The first subscript designates the row of that element, and the second subscript designates the column of that element.
22. QBasic allows up to 60 dimensions. One- and two-dimensional arrays are the most commonly used arrays in business applications.
23. Sorting is the arranging of data in accordance with some certain order or sequence. Data in sequence from lowest to highest is in ascending sequence; data in sequence from highest to lowest is in descending sequence.
24. The LBOUND and UBOUND functions may be used to determine the lower- and upper-bound subscript values of an array.
25. The SWAP statement is used to interchange the values of two variables or elements of an array.
26. Both the bubble sort and Shell sort algorithms work on arrays that contain numeric or string data.
27. Regardless of the sort algorithm used, three steps are required in a program to sort data: dimension the array, load the array with data, and apply an algorithm to manipulate the elements in the array.
28. Tables are organized on the basis of how the data is to be referenced. In positionally-organized tables, table functions can be accessed by their position in the table. In argument-organized tables, table functions are accessed by looking up a desired value that corresponds to them. To retrieve these corresponding table functions, a search argument is compared against the table argument. When the search argument matches the table argument, the corresponding table functions are selected and used.
29. To utilize table-processing techniques in a program, you must (1) declare the table by dimensioning arrays for the table entries, (2) use a READ or an INPUT statement inside a For loop to load the table entries, and (3) code appropriate statements to access the table entries.
30. Serial and binary search methods are normally used to access data stored in tables.
31. A serial search, which normally begins at the top of the table, does not require the data to be in any sequence.
32. A binary search, which begins in the middle of the table, requires the data to be in ascending or descending sequence.

7.10 Test Your QBasic Skills (Even-numbered answers are in Appendix E)

1. Consider the four valid programs listed below. What is displayed if each program is executed?

a.
```
' Exercise 7.1a
Between0.50 = 0
Between50.100 = 0
Greater100 = 0
READ Num
FOR I = 1 TO Num
   READ Score
   IF Score >= 0 AND Score < 50 THEN
      Between0.50 = Between0.50 + 1
   END IF
   IF Score >= 50 AND Score <= 100 THEN
      Between50.100 = Between50.100 + 1
   END IF
   IF Score > 100 THEN
      Greater100 = Greater100 + 1
   END IF
NEXT I
PRINT Between0.50, Between50.100, Greater100
' ********** Data Follows **********
DATA 11
DATA 150, 99, 100, 50, 0, 25, 88, 40
DATA 42, 101, 10
END
```

b.
```
' Exercise 7.1b
F = 0
FOR I = 1 TO 4
   G = 0
   F = F + 1
   FOR J = 1 TO 3
      G = G + F
      PRINT F, G
   NEXT J
NEXT I
END
```

c.
```
' Exercise 7.1c
CLS ' Clear Screen
DIM A(1 TO 5), B(1 TO 5), C(1 TO 5)
FOR I = 1 TO 5
   READ A(I), B(I)
NEXT I
FOR I = 1 TO 5
   C(I) = A(I) * B(I)
   PRINT C(I);
NEXT I
' ******** Data Follows ********
DATA 1, 4, 2, 3, 4, 4, 2, 3, 3, 5
END
```

d.
```
' Exercise 7.1d
CLS ' Clear Screen
OPTION BASE 1
READ X, Y
DIM A(X, Y)
FOR I = 1 TO X
   FOR J = 1 TO Y
      READ A(I, J)
      PRINT A(I, J);
   NEXT J
   PRINT
NEXT I
' **** Data Follows ****
DATA 4, 3
DATA 2, 1, 6, 9, 5
DATA 6, 2, 1, 6, 8, 4, 2
END
```

2. Assume that array L is dimensioned in a program by the statement DIM L(1 TO 5, 1 TO 5). Also assume the elements of the array L are assigned the following values: Write the subscripted variable name that references the following values found in the array L:

a. 12   b. 70   c. 15   d. 45
e. 60   f. 7   g. 14   h. 22

ARRAY L

2	5	14	30	50
7	12	21	70	10
5	15	70	60	0
19	20	30	10	20
22	45	20	40	50

3. Identify the syntax and logic error(s), if any, in each of the following FOR statements:

   a. FOR Amount = -1 TO 10 STEP -1
   b. FOR Var = 1 TO -6
   c. FOR Vector = 1 TO SQR(25)
   d. FOR Pint$ = 0 TO 7
   e. FOR Value = 10 TO 1
   f. FOR Quad = A TO B STEP -B

4. Explain what the following partial program does:

```
' Exercise 7.4
OPTION BASE 1
DIM A(3, 4), B(3, 4)
      .
      .
      .
FOR I = 1 TO 3
   FOR J = 1 TO 4
      B(I, J) = A(I, J)
   NEXT J
NEXT I
PRINT LBOUND(A, 1), UBOUND(A, 1), LBOUND(B, 2), UBOUND(B, 2)
```

5. Assume that array A has 4 rows and 4 columns and that the elements of array A are assigned the following values:

   ARRAY A

1	2	3	4
5	6	7	8
9	10	11	12
13	14	15	16

   Note: A(1, 1) = 1 and A(3, 2) = 10.

   What will be the final arrangement of array A after the following program is executed? Select your answer from the choices below:

```
' Exercise 7.5
FOR I = 1 TO 4
   FOR J = 1 TO 4
      A(I, J) = A(J, I)
   NEXT J
NEXT I
```

   a.

1	2	3	4
5	6	7	8
9	10	11	12
13	14	15	16

   b.

16	15	14	13
12	11	10	9
8	7	6	5
4	3	2	1

   c.

1	2	2	4
5	6	6	8
9	10	10	12
13	14	14	16

   d.

1	5	9	13
5	6	10	14
9	10	11	15
13	14	15	16

   e. None of these

6. Refer to the initial array A given in Exercise 5. What will be the final arrangement of array A after each of the following patial programs is executed? Select your answer from the choices given in Exercise 5.

a.
```
' Exercise 7.6a
FOR I = 1 TO 4
    A(I, 3) = A(I, 2)
NEXT I
```

b.
```
' Exercise 7.6b
J = 2
FOR I = 1 TO 4
    A(I, J + 1) = A(I, J)
NEXT I
```

c.
```
' Exercise 7.6c
FOR I = 1 TO 4
    A(I, I) = A(I - 2, I + 2)
NEXT I
```

d.
```
' Exercise 7.6d
FOR I = 1 TO 4
    FOR J = 1 TO 4
        A(I, J) = A(I, J)
    NEXT J
NEXT I
```

7. Refer to the initial array A given in Exercise 5. What will be the final arrangement of array A after the following program is executed? Select your answer from the choices given in Exercise 5. Assume that array B has been declared the same as array A.

```
' Exercise 7.7
FOR I = 1 TO 4
    FOR J = 1 TO 4
        B(I, J) = A(I, J)
    NEXT J
NEXT I
X = 0
FOR I = 4 TO 1 STEP -1
    Y = 0
    X = X + 1
    FOR J = 4 TO 1 STEP -1
        Y = Y + 1
        A(X, Y) = B(I, J)
    NEXT J
NEXT I
```

8. Given the one-dimensional array Number, consisting of 50 elements, write a partial program that will count the number of elements in array Number that have a value between 0 and 18, inclusive, between 26 and 29, inclusive, and between 42 and 47, inclusive. Use the following counters:

Low: count of elements with a value between 0 and 18, inclusive
Mid: count of elements with a value between 26 and 29, inclusive
High: count of elements with a value between 42 and 47, inclusive

Use the subscript I to help reference the elements.

9. Given an array F that has been declared to have 10 elements, assume that each element of array F has been assigned a value. Write a partial program to shift all the values up one location. That is, assign the value of F(1) to F(2), F(2) to F(3), and F(10) to F(1). Do not use any array other than array F. Be sure not to destroy a value before it is shifted.

10. Given the three arrays A, B, and C, each declared to have 100 elements, assume that the elements of arrays A and B have been assigned values. Write a partial program that compares each element of array A to its corresponding element in array B. Assign 1, 0, or –1 to the corresponding element in the array C, as follows:

1 if A is greater than B
0 if A is equal to B
-1 if A is less than B

11. Identify the error(s), if any, in each of the following partial programs:

    a.
    ```
    ' Exercise 7.11a
    DIM X(50 TO 500)
    FOR I = 1 TO 500
        READ X(I)
    NEXT I
    ```

    b.
    ```
    ' Exercise 7.11b
    DIM X(1 TO 700)
    FOR K = 700 TO 1 STEP -1
        READ X(K)
    NEXT K
    ```

12. Given the two two-dimensional arrays R and S, each of which have 20 rows and 20 columns, write a partial program to compute the sum (Sum) of the elements of the two arrays that have equal subscript values. That is, find the following:

    $$Sum = R(1,1) + R(2,2) + \dots + R(20,20) + S(1,1) + S(2,2) + \dots S(20,20)$$

13. A program utilizes four arrays B(I), K(J), L(Q), and M(Q, J). The maximum values for I, J, and Q are 15, 36, and 29. The minimum values for I, J, and Q are –10, 5, and 3. Write a correct DIM statement.

14. How many lines will be displayed by the following program?
    ```
    ' Exercise 7.14
    FOR C = 1 TO 20
        FOR A = 1 TO 10
            FOR Q = 1 TO 7
                PRINT C, A, Q
            NEXT Q
        NEXT A
    NEXT C
    END
    ```

15. Write a partial program for each of the following expressions and display the result:
    a. $1 + 1/2 + 1/4 + 1/8 + \dots + 1/2^{10}$ b. $11 + 22 + 33 + 44 + 55 + 66$

16. Given the one-dimensional array A, consisting of 50 elements, write the DIM statement and the For loop to count the number of elements with negative, positive, and zero values in the array.

17. Write a partial program to find the salesperson who has the least total sales for a given period. Assume that the total sales are in the array Sales, that the corresponding salespersons' names are in the array Person$, and that each array has been dimensioned to a lower bound of 1 and an upper bound of 30.

18. Write a partial program to find the salesperson who has the greatest total sales for a given period. Use the same arrays as in exercise 17.

19. Write a partial program to generate the first six rows of **Pascal's triangle**. Each entry in a given row of the triangle is generated by adding the two adjacent entries in the immediately preceding row. For example, the third entry in row 4 is the sum of the second and third entries in row 3. The first six rows of Pascal's triangle follow. To eliminate the complexity of spacing, display each row starting in column 1.

```
            1
         1     1
      1     2     1
   1     3     3     1
1     4     6     4     1
1   5   10      10    5     1
```

20. Write a program to display the item number and gross sales for all items that have gross sales greater than $3,000. Assume that the item number is stored in the array Item$ and that the corresponding gross sales are stored in the array Sales. Declare a lower bound of 1 and an upper bound of 100 for the arrays. Do not write the code to load the arrays.

21. Consider the valid program below. What displays when the program is executed?

```
' Exercise 7.21
DIM Fib(1 TO 10)
PRINT "N", "NTH FIBONACCI NO."
Fib(1) = 1
Fib(2) = 1
PRINT 1, Fib(1)
PRINT 2, Fib(2)
FOR Num = 3 TO 10
   Fib(Num) = Fib(Num - 2) + Fib(Num - 1)
   PRINT Num, Fib(Num)
NEXT Num
END
```

22. **PC Hands-On Exercise:** Enter the program in Figure 7.1(b) on page 242. Modify the initial, limit, and increment values in the FOR statement according to the sets listed below. Execute the program for each set. If the PC goes into an endless loop, press the Ctrl + Break keys to terminate processing.

Set	Initial	Limit	Increment	Set	Initial	Limit	Increment
1	1	1,000	2	6	1	10	0.1
2	25	75	5	7	1	- 10	-1
3	5	5	1	8	1	10	0
4	5	1	1	9	-5	- 20	remove the
5	5	1	-1				keyword STEP

23. **PC Hands-On Exercise:** Enter the program in Figure 7.11 on page 252. Display and execute the program. Change the limit value to 16 in the FOR statements in lines 6 and 8. Execute the program and see what happens.

24. **PC Hands-On Exercise:** Enter the program in Figure 7.14 on page 258. Delete line 3. Execute the program and see what happens. Re-enter line 3 and replace line 10 with the following statement:

```
For Number = 12 TO 1 STEP -1
```

Execute the program. Compare the sequence of the monthly sales to the original results displayed in Figure 7.14.

25. **PC Hands-On Exercise:** Load Program 7.2 (PRG7-2) from the Data Disk. Change the relation in line 36 from *greater than* to *less than*. Execute the program. Compare the sequence of the sorted numbers to that originally displayed by Program 7.2 on page 272. Now do you understand the difference between ascending sequence and descending sequence?

26. **PC Hands-On Exercise:** Load Program 7.6 (PRG7-6) from the Data Disk. Turn on the trace feature in the Debug menu. Execute the program and enter the same part numbers shown in Figures 7.47 and 7.48 on pages 283 and 284. See if you can follow the sequence of statements executed in Program 7.6 from the displayed results. (See Appendix C for a discussion of tracing and other debugging features of QBasic.)

7.11 QBasic Programming Problems

1. Sum of a Series of Numbers

Purpose: To become familiar with the implementation of counter-controlled loops by means of the FOR and NEXT statements.

Problem: Write five different programs (like the one in Figure 7.1(b) on page 242) as described below.

PART A: Construct a program to compute and display the sum of the following series: $1 + 2 + 3 + \ldots + 150$. Use a For loop to create these integers, and sum them.
PART B: Same as Part A, except sum all the even numbers from 2 to 150, inclusive.
PART C: Same as Part A, except input the lower and upper limits.
PART D: Same as Part C, except include a variable step.
PART E: Same as Part A, except construct a one-statement QBasic program in the immediate window to compute directly, instead of iteratively, the sum of the numbers from 1 to 100.

Input Data: For Parts A, B, and E, there is no input. For C, input a lower limit of 15 and an upper limit of 40. For Part D, input a lower limit of 20, an upper limit of 80, and a step of 5.

Output Results: Display the result of each program in sentence form. For Parts A and E, the sum is 11,325; for Part B, the sum is 5,700; for Part C, the sum is 715; for Part D, the sum is 650.

2. Credit Card Verification

Purpose: To become familiar with declaring, loading, and serially searching a table.

Problem: Write a top-down program that will accept a six-digit credit card number and verify this number is in a table. If the credit card number is in the table, display a message indicating that the credit card number is valid. If the credit card number is not in the table, display a message indicating that the credit card is invalid, alert the manager, and beep the speaker several times. Declare the credit card number table to Number elements. Use the following 15 credit card numbers.

131416	238967	384512	583214	172319
345610	410001	672354	194567	351098
518912	691265	210201	372198	562982

The number of credit cards (15) and the credit card numbers are stored in a data file under the name EX72CARD.TBL on the Data Disk.

Input Data: Use the following sample data for testing:

372198	518912	102002	672354	210200	000000	999999

Output Results: Output results are shown in Figure 7.49 for credit card numbers 372198 and 210200.

FIGURE 7.49
*Output results for
Programming Problem 2.*

```
Credit Card Verification

Credit Card Number =====> 372198

Credit Card Number is Valid

Enter Y to verify another Credit Card Number, else N... Y
```

```
Credit Card Verification

Credit Card Number =====> 210200

**Error** Credit Card Number is Invalid - Alert Your Manager

Enter Y to verify another Credit Card Number, else N... Y
```

3. Wind Chill Table Lookup

Purpose: To become familiar with accessing data from a positionally-organized table.

Problem: As every resident of cold weather climates knows, the real enemy in terms of the weather is not the near-zero temperatures, but the wind chill factor. Meteorologists give both the temperature and the wind chill factor. So important is the wind chill factor that calm air at -40° Fahrenheit is less likely to cause frostbite than air just below freezing that is blowing at gale force. Basically, two factors determine the wind chill factor: the velocity of wind and the temperature.

Write a top-down program that accepts from the user a temperature between -20° F and 15° F and a wind velocity between 5 mph and 30 mph, both in multiples of five. The program should look up the wind chill factor in a positionally-organized table and display it. Use the following table of wind chill factors:

Table of Wind Chill Factors

Temperature in Fahrenheit	Wind Velocity in Miles per Hour					
	5	10	15	20	25	30
-20	-26	-46	-58	-67	-74	-79
-15	-21	-40	-51	-60	-66	-71
-10	-15	-34	-45	-53	-59	-64
-5	-10	-27	-38	-46	-51	-56
0	-5	-22	-31	-39	-44	-49
5	0	-15	-25	-31	-36	-41
10	7	-9	-18	-24	-29	-33
15	12	-3	-11	-17	-22	-25

In your program, use the INPUT #n statement and the data file EX73TABL.TBL on the Data Disk to fill the table. Use the DIM statement in the Main Program to declare the two-dimensional array.

Input Data: Use the following sample data:

Temperature (°F)	Wind Velocity (mph)
-15	10
0	30
-5	40
-40	25
5	10

Output Results: Output results are shown in Figure 7.50 for the first set of data items.

▌FIGURE 7.50

Output results for Programming Problem 3.

```
Wind Chill Table Lookup

Temperature (Between -20 and 15) =====> -15

Velocity (Between 5 and 30) ===========> 10

Wind chill Factor ====================> -40

Enter Y to determine another wind chill factor, else N... Y
```

4. Week-Ending Department and Store Receipts

Purpose: To become familiar with the use of arrays for determining totals.

Problem: Businesses usually are subdivided into smaller units for the purpose of better organization. The Tri-Quality retail store is subdivided into four departments. Each department submits its receipts at the end of the day to the store manager. Using an array consisting of five rows and six columns, write a top-down program that is assigned the daily sales. Use the fifth row and sixth column to accumulate the totals. After accumulating the totals, display the entire array.

Input Data: Use the following sample data:

Dept.	Monday	Tuesday	Wednesday	Thursday	Friday
1	$2,146	$6,848	$8,132	$8,912	$5,165
2	8,123	9,125	6,159	5,618	9,176
3	4,156	5,612	4,128	4,812	3,685
4	1,288	1,492	1,926	1,225	2,015

In your program, use the INPUT #n statement and the data file EX74SAL.DAT to fill the array. EX74SAL.DAT is stored on the Data Disk. Use the DIM statement in the Main Program to declare the arrays.

Output Results: Output results are shown in Figure 7.51.

FIGURE 7.51
Output results for Programming Problem 4.

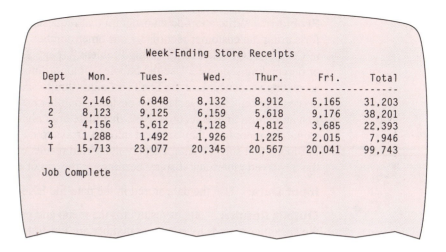

```
                    Week-Ending Store Receipts

       Dept    Mon.     Tues.     Wed.     Thur.     Fri.     Total
      --------------------------------------------------------------
        1      2,146    6,848    8,132    8,912    5,165    31,203
        2      8,123    9,125    6,159    5,618    9,176    38,201
        3      4,156    5,612    4,128    4,812    3,685    22,393
        4      1,288    1,492    1,926    1,225    2,015     7,946
        T     15,713   23,077   20,345   20,567   20,041    99,743

      Job Complete
```

5. Merging Lists

Purpose: To become familiar with the operation of merging.

Problem: Merging is the process of combining two sorted lists into a single sorted list. Obviously, one list can be appended to the other, and the new list can then be sorted. This process, however, is not always the most efficient. Write a top-down program that merges two arrays, X and Y, into array Z. Assume that arrays X and Y have been presorted and are in ascending sequence. Declare array X to have N elements, array Y to have M elements, and array Z to have N + M elements. Display the contents of array Z as part of the end-of-job routine.

(**Hint:** Be sure to take into consideration that the two arrays are not the same size. That is, when the shorter of the two arrays has been processed, assign the remaining elements of the longer array to array Z.)

Input Data: Use the following sample data.

Array X: 15 elements — 4, 9, 12, 15, 22, 33, 44, 66, 72, 84, 87, 92, 96, 98, 99
Array Y: 12 elements — 6, 8, 12, 16, 24, 31, 68, 71, 73, 74, 81, 93

Output Results: Output results are shown in Figure 7.52. Note that the format of your results may vary slightly.

FIGURE 7.52
Output results for Programming Problem 5.

```
      The merged array, Z, has 27 elements.  Their values are:
       4   6   8   9  12  12  15  16  22  24  31  33  44  66  68  71  72
      73  74  81  84  87  92  93  96  98  99

      Job Complete
```

6. Sorting Customer Numbers

Purpose: To become familiar with sorting data into ascending or descending sequence and to gain a better understanding of the bubble and Shell sort algorithms.

Problem: Write a top-down program that requests the selection from a menu of functions for sorting the customer records by customer number. Use the file EX67CUS.DAT described in Chapter 6, QBasic Programming Problem 7 (page 238), and sort it into either ascending or descending sequence. Use the bubble sort algorithm to sort the customer numbers into ascending sequence. Use the Shell sort algorithm to sort the customer numbers into descending sequence. Declare the customer number array so that the program can sort up to a maximum of 100 records. Note that there are only 43 records in the customer file. Count the records as they are read into the arrays to determine the limit parameter for the For loops that sort the data. Display the sorted results on the screen. Number the pages in the displayed report and display headings at the top of each page as illustrated below.

Input Data: Use the data stored in the data file EX67CUS.DAT on the Data Disk.

Output Results: Output results for the menu and patial results for the ascending sort of the customer records by customer number are illustrated in Figure 7.53.

FIGURE 7.53

Output menu and partial results for the ascending sort for Programming Problem 6.

```
              Menu for Sorting Customer Numbers
              ------------------------------------

              Code              Function
              ----              --------
               1                Ascending Sequence
               2                Descending Sequence
               3                End Program

              Enter a Code 1 through 3 =====> 1
```

```
      Sorted Customer List          Page 1
      --------------------

      Customer      Balance
      --------      -------
       03000         43.25
       03012        132.00
       03013          5.65
       03014         99.80
       03015        354.98
       03016        123.56
       03017          0.00
       03018         87.05
       03018          7.93
       03019        145.00
       03020         50.00
       03034          2.25
       03035         12.30
       03036          0.67
       03037          9.99

      Press Enter to Continue
```

7. Determining the Mean, the Variance, and the Standard Deviation

Purpose: To apply the concepts of array elements to a statistical problem.

Problem: Construct a top-down program to find the mean (M), the variance (V), and the standard deviation (SD) of a variable number of student grades (G1, G2, G3, . . . , Gn). Use the following three formulas:

$$M = (G1 + G2 + G3 + \ldots + Gn) / n$$

$$V = [(G1 - M)^2 + (G2 - M)^2 + \ldots + (Gn - M)^2] \; / (n - 1)$$

$$SD = \text{Square Root of V}$$

where n is the total number of grades.

Input Data: Use READ and DATA statements for the student grades to fill an array that contains 12 elements.

Student grades: 94, 92, 87, 93, 96, 88, 78, 95, 96, 87, 84, 86

Output Results: Output results are shown in Figure 7.54.

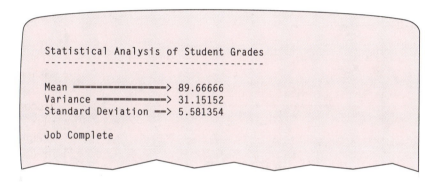

```
Statistical Analysis of Student Grades
----------------------------------------

Mean =================> 89.66666
Variance =============> 31.15152
Standard Deviation --> 5.581354

Job Complete
```

8. Payroll Problem VII: Bonus Table Lookup Computations

Purpose: To become familiar with table utilization and program modification.

Problem: Modify Payroll Problem VI (Programming Problem 8 on page 239) in Chapter 6 to compute a bonus for each employee. Add the bonus to the gross pay defined in Payroll Problem VI. Adjust the report to include the bonus. Also, print the total bonus paid to all employees.

The bonus is computed by multiplying a factor times the original gross pay. The factor is based on a job class that is found in each employee payroll transaction record. After computing the gross pay for an employee, use the job class to search the bonus table for the bonus factor to multiply times the gross pay to determine the bonus. If the job class is not in the table, assign the employee a bonus of $25.00. The bonus table follows:

Job Class	Bonus Factor
01	.025
03	.0315
06	.04
07	.045
09	.05
10	.0525
12	.055

The data that makes up the bonus table is stored under the name EX78RATE.TBL on the Data Disk. The very first data item in EX78RATE.TBL is 7, the number of table entries. Use this value to dimension the parallel arrays used to store the table.

Each record in the transaction file contains an employee number, the number of hours worked, and a job class. The transaction file contains the following nine records:

Employee Number	Hours Worked	Job Class
123	88	06
124	96	03
125	72	07
126	80	07
134	80	12
167	70.5	02
210	80	03
234	32	09
244	40	03

FIGURE 7.55
Output results for
Programming Problem 8.

```
                  Biweekly Payroll Report           Page:  1

Employee
Number    Bonus   Gross Pay    Fed. Tax  Soc. Sec.   Net Pay
--------  -----   ---------    --------  ---------   -------
  123     46.00   1,196.00      289.92      91.49    814.59

  124     58.97   1,930.97      491.53     147.72  1,291.72

  125     42.12     978.12      243.79      74.83    659.50

  126     19.80     459.80       24.87      35.17    399.76

  134     38.50     738.50      192.01      56.50    489.99

  167     25.00     758.20      165.57      58.00    534.63

  210     22.18     726.18      125.69      55.55    544.94
```

```
                  Biweekly Payroll Report           Page:  2

Employee
Number    Bonus   Gross Pay    Fed. Tax  Soc. Sec.   Net Pay
--------  -----   ---------    --------  ---------   -------
  234     10.80     226.80       37.93      17.35    171.52

  244     11.03     361.02       62.31      27.62    271.10


Total Bonus ==============>      274.39
Total Gross Pay ===========>   7,375.59
Total Withholding Tax ==>      1,633.62
Total Social Security ==>        564.23
Total Net Pay =============>   5,177.73

End of Payroll Report
```

The transaction file is stored with the name EX78TRA.DAT on the Data Disk. The employee master file EX61PAY.DAT is the same as for Payroll Problem VI in Chapter 6. You may assume that the records in EX61PAY.DAT and EX78TRA.DAT are in ascending sequence and that there is exactly one record in each file per employee. (That is, each record in EX61PAY.DAT has a match in EX78TRA.DAT.)

Input Data: Use the following three sequential data files, described under Problem and stored on the Data Disk:

File Name	Description
EX78RATE.TBL	Bonus Table Entries
EX61PAY.DAT	Employee Payroll Master File
EX78TRA.DAT	Employee Payroll Transaction File

Output Results: A master employee payroll file, as described in Payroll Problem VI in Chapter 6, is created as EX78PAY.DAT. Figure 7.55 illustrates the report that is printed on the printer.

CHAPTER 8

More on Strings and Functions

8.1 INTRODUCTION

Computers were originally built to perform mathematical calculations. They are still used for that purpose; however, today computer applications process string data as well. Sections 3.5 and 4.6 briefly introduced five string functions — LEFT$, MID$, RIGHT$, LEN, and UCASE$ — giving some indication of the capability of QBasic to manipulate string data. As you shall see in this chapter, QBasic includes several additional string functions, string statements, and special variables for manipulating letters, numbers, words, and phrases.

QBasic also includes numeric functions to handle common mathematical calculations. Section 3.5 introduced you to two numeric functions — INT and SQR. In this chapter, we discuss additional frequently used numeric functions.

A second type of function discussed in Chapter 8 is the user-defined function. With a function that is defined by the user, numeric or string functions can be created to perform a task needed often by the programmer. User-defined functions can be defined and called in the same program or defined as a distinct unit of code in the same fashion as a subprograms (introduced in Chapter 11) and called by any program.

Finally, this chapter introduces you to **system event trapping**. This activity requires the PC to check for the occurrence of an event — for example, the user pressing one of the function keys — as it executes a program. When the event occurs, the PC immediately transfers control to an event-assigned subroutine. After the subroutine has been completed, the PC continues execution of the program where it left off when the event occurred.

8.2 STRING FUNCTIONS AND STATEMENTS

A list of the frequently used QBasic string functions, along with their areas of use, are shown in Table 8.1 on the next page. To be used, these functions need only be referred to by name in a LET, PRINT, or IF statement. For a complete listing of the string functions and statements, see the Reference Card at the back of this book.

TABLE 8.1 - Frequently Used QBasic String Functions

FUNCTION	FUNCTION VALUE
ASC(X$)	Returns a two-digit numeric value equivalent in ASCII code to the first character of the string argument X$.
CHR$(N)	Returns a single string character equivalent in ASCII code to the numeric argument N.
DATE$	Returns the system date as a string in the form mm-dd-yyyy.
INKEY$	Accepts a single character from the keyboard without suspending execution of the program or waiting for the Enter key to be pressed.
INPUT$(N)	Suspends execution of the program until N number of characters from the keyboard are entered.
INSTR(P, X$, S$)	Returns the beginning position of the substring S$ in string X$. P indicates the position the search begins in X$ and may be omitted from the argument list. If the search for S$ in X$ is unsuccessful, INSTR returns a value of zero.
LCASE$(X$)	Returns X$ in lowercase.
LEFT$(X$, N)	Extracts the leftmost N characters of the string argument X$.
LEN(X$)	Returns the length of the string argument X$.
LTRIM$(X$)	Returns X$ with leading blanks trimmed away.
MID$(X$, P, N)	Extracts N characters of the string argument X$ beginning at position P.
RIGHT$(X$, N)	Extracts the rightmost N characters of the string argument X$.
RTRIM$(X$)	Returns X$ with trailing blanks trimmed away.
SPACE$(N)	Returns N number of spaces.
SPC(N)	Displays N spaces. May be used only in a PRINT or LPRINT statement.
STR$(N)	Returns the string equivalent of the numeric argument N.
STRING$(N, X$)	Returns N times the first character of X$.
TIME$	Returns the time of day in 24-hour notation as a string in the form hh:mm:ss.
UCASE$(X$)	Returns X$ in uppercase.
VAL(X$)	Returns the numeric equivalent of the string argument X$.

Concatenation, Substrings, and Character Counting Revisited — +, LEN, LEFT$, RIGHT$, and MID$ Functions

The extraction of substrings from a large string and the combining of two or more strings are important in manipulating nonnumeric data. In Section 3.5 on page 72, the concatenation operation (+) and the LEN, LEFT$, RIGHT$, and MID$ functions were briefly introduced. Recall that concatenation (+) is the only string operation allowed in QBasic. It *joins* two strings to form a new string. It does *not* add two strings. For example,

```
Join$ = "ABC" + "DEF"
```

assigns Join$ the value ABCDEF. The second string is joined to the right end of the first string to form the result, which is then assigned to Join$. More than one concatenation operator may appear in a single assignment statement.

For example, if Phrase1$ = "Resist " and Phrase2$ = "the urge " and Phrase3$ = "to code.", then

```
Phrase$ = Phrase1$ + Phrase2$ + Phrase3$
```

assigns Phrase$ the string,
```
Resist the urge to code.
```
The LEN function returns the length of the argument. The argument may be a string constant, a string variable, or a string expression. Table 8.2 and the partial program in Figure 8.1 illustrate the use of the LEN function.

TABLE 8.2 - Examples of the LEN Function

VALUE OF VARIABLE	STATEMENT	RESULTS
Comp1$ = "Dell"	Len1 = LEN(Comp1$)	Len1 = 4
Comp2$ = "Compaq"	Len2 = LEN(Comp2$)	Len2 = 6
	Len3 = LEN("Clone")	Len3 = 5
	Len4 = LEN(" ")	Len4 = 1
Noth$ = "" (null)	Len5 = LEN(Noth$)	Len5 = 0

FIGURE 8.1

Examples of the use of the LEN function.

```
 1  ' Examples of the Use of the LEN function
 2  ' ***************************************
 3  CLS  ' Clear Screen
 4  Word1$ = "Structured"
 5  Word2$ = "Programming"
 6  Length = LEN(Word1$)
 7  PRINT Word1$; " has"; Length; "characters."
 8  PRINT Word2$; " has"; LEN(Word2$); "characters."
 9  PRINT Word1$ + " " + Word2$; " has";
10  PRINT LEN(Word1$ + " " + Word2$); "characters."

[run]

Structured has 10 characters.
Programming has 11 characters.
Structured Programming has 22 characters.
```

In Figure 8.1, LEN(Word1$) in line 6 assigns the variable Length a value of 10. In line 8, LEN(Word2$) is displayed as 11. In line 10, the LEN function returns the length of the string expression WORD1$ + " " + WORD2$ as 22.

The LEFT$, MID$, and RIGHT$ string functions may be used to extract substrings from a string constant, a string variable, or a string expression. A **substring** is a part of a string. For example, some substrings of Galaxie Quest are Galaxie, Quest, ala, Qu, and est. All three functions reference substrings on the basis of the position of characters within the string argument, where the leftmost character of the string argument is position 1; the next is position 2, and so on. For example, in the string Galaxie Quest, the substring Galaxie begins in position 1, and the substring Quest begins in position 9.

LEFT$(X$, N) extracts a substring starting with the leftmost character (position 1) of the string X$. The length of the substring is determined by the integer value of the length argument N. For example, the following statement assigns a value of Galaxie to Sub1$:

```
Sub1$ = LEFT$("Galaxie Quest", 7)
```

Galaxie begins in position 1 and has a length of 7. The quotation marks are not part of the string.

RIGHT$(X$, N) extracts a substring starting with the rightmost character of the string argument X$. The length of the substring is determined by the value of the length argument N. For example, if Movie$ is equal to the string Stuart Little, then the following statement assigns Sub2$ the substring Little:

```
Sub2$ = RIGHT$(Movie$, 6)
```

MID$(X$, P, N) extracts a substring beginning with the character in position P of X$. The length of the substring is determined by the value of the length argument N. For example, if Phrase$ is equal to the string, Every dog must have his day, then the following statement assigns Sub3$ the substring, dog must have:

```
Sub3$ = MID$(Phrase$, 7, 13)
```

If the length argument is not included in the list for the MID$ function, then the PC returns a substring that begins with the position argument and ends with the last character in the string argument. For example, if Phrase$ is equal to the string

```
Today is the tomorrow I worried about yesterday
```

then the following statement assigns Sub4$ the substring I worried about yesterday:

```
Sub4$ = MID$(Phrase$, 23)
```

Table 8.3 on the next page illustrates the use of the LEFT$, RIGHT$, and MID$ functions.

TABLE 8.3 - Examples of the LEFT$, RIGHT$, and MID$ Functions

Assume S$ is equal to: `If something can go wrong, it will`

EXAMPLE	STATEMENT	RESULTS
1	C$ = LEFT$(S$, 12)	C$ = If something
2	F$ = LEFT$(S$, 1.7)	F$ = If
3	H$ = LEFT$(S$, 0)	H$ = null
4	J$ = RIGHT$(S$, 7)	J$ = it will
5	P$ = RIGHT$(S$, -1)	Illegal function call
6.	R$ = RIGHT$(S$, 50)	R$ = S$
7	T$ = MID$(S$, -1, 6)	Illegal function call
8	U$ = MID$(LEFT$(S$, 4), 2, 1)	U$ = f
9	V$ = MID$(S$, 75, 4)	V$ = null
10	X$ = MID$(S$, 18)	X$ = go wrong, it will
11	Y$ = MID$(S$, 32768)	Illegal function call

In Example 2 in Table 8.3, the argument 1.7 is rounded to 2. In Example 3, the numeric argument 0 causes the PC to assign H$ the null string. In Example 5, the negative argument (–1) causes the PC to display a dialog box with a diagnostic message. Example 6 shows that if the length argument is greater than the length of the string argument, the function returns a substring that begins at the specified position and includes the remaining portion of the string.

In Example 7, the position argument, –1, is invalid. Example 8 shows that you may include a string function as the string argument. Example 9 illustrates that a null string is returned when the specified beginning position in the MID$ function is greater than the length of the argument string. Example 10 shows that when the length argument is not included in the MID$ function, the PC returns a substring beginning with the specified position and ending with the last character of the string argument. Finally, Example 11 causes a dialog box to display with a diagnostic message because the position argument is greater than 32,767. The position argument must be in the range 1 to 32,767.

QBasic interprets the position argument P and the length argument N of the LEFT$, MID$, and RIGHT$ functions according to the following rules:

STRING FUNCTION RULE 1   *If the position argument P or the length argument N is a decimal fraction, the value of N or P is rounded to an integer.*

STRING FUNCTION RULE 2   *If the length argument N is less than 0 or greater than 32,767, then the function call is illegal. If N is equal to zero, the function returns a null string.*

STRING FUNCTION RULE 3   *If the length argument N is greater than the remaining length of the string argument, the function returns a substring that begins at the specified position and includes the remaining portion of the string.*

STRING FUNCTION RULE 4   *If the position argument P is greater than the length of the string argument, the function returns a null string. If the position argument P is less than 1 or greater than 32,767, then the function call is illegal.*

The partial program in Figure 8.2 makes use of the LEN and MID$ functions. The basic purpose of the program is to search for words in a sentence. Each time a word is found, the program displays it on a separate line. The program assumes that each word, except for the last, is followed by a space.

FIGURE 8.2

Using the LEN *and* MID$
functions.

```
 I   ' Displaying Each Word in a Sentence
 2   ' ********************************
 3   CLS  ' Clear Screen
 4   PRINT "Enter the sentence without punctuation:"
 5   PRINT : INPUT "", Sentence$
 6   Begin = 1
 7   PRINT : PRINT "Words in the sentence:"
 8   FOR Character = 1 TO LEN(Sentence$)
 9      IF MID$(Sentence$, Character, 1) = " " THEN
10         PRINT TAB(23); MID$(Sentence$, Begin, Character - Begin)
11         Begin = Character + 1
12      END IF
13   NEXT Character
14   ' ****** Display the Last Word ******
15   PRINT TAB(23); MID$(Sentence$, Begin)
16   PRINT "Job Complete"
```

```
[run]

Enter the sentence without punctuation:

If an experiment works something has gone wrong

Words in the sentence:
                        If
                        an
                        experiment
                        works
                        something
                        has
                        gone
                        wrong
Job Complete
```

When the partial program in Figure 8.2 is executed, line 4 displays a prompt message. Line 5 accepts the sentence and assigns it to the variable Sentence$. In line 6, the variable Begin is assigned a value of 1. This variable is used later in line 10 to indicate the beginning position of each word and in line 15 to display the last word in the sentence.

Line 9 in the For loop tests each character in the sentence to determine whether it is a space. If a character is a space, then the word beginning at position Begin with length of Character - Begin is displayed, and Begin is set equal to a value that is equivalent to the beginning position of the next word. Because the last word in the sentence does not end with a space, line 15, instead of line 10, is used to display the last word.

Substring Searching and Replacement — INSTR Function and MID$ Statement

QBasic includes the INSTR **function** to search a string argument for a particular substring. INSTR(P, X$, S$) returns the beginning position of the substring S$ in X$. The search begins at position P of X$. For example, the following partial program causes the variable Count1 to be assigned the value 4:

```
Phrase$ = "To be or not to be"
Count1 = INSTR(1, Phrase$, "be")
```

The second line in the partial program assigns Count1 the position of the first character of the substring be in the string Phrase$. If there are no occurrences of the substring, INSTR returns the value zero.

The INSTR function always returns the leftmost position of the first occurrence of the substring. If the following statement is added to the previous partial program,

```
Count2 = INSTR(5, Phrase$, "be")
```

then Count2 is assigned a value of 17. The first occurrence of be is bypassed because the search begins at position 5, rather than position 1.

The position argument P may be omitted. For example, the statement Count1 = INSTR(Phrase$, "be") is identical to Count1 = INSTR(1, Phrase$, "be"). That is, the search begins at position 1, by default, and assigns Count1 a value of 4. Table 8.4 illustrates some additional examples of the INSTR function.

TABLE 8.4 - Examples of the INSTR Function	
Assume that S$ is equal to: It is better to be right than to be popular	
STATEMENT	RESULTS
Pos1 = INSTR(1, S$, "than")	Pos1 = 26
Pos2 = INSTR(Start, S$, "be")	Pos2 = 34 (assume Start = 22)
Pos3 = INSTR(S$, "is")	Pos3 = 4

The MID$ **statement** is used for substring replacement. Do not confuse the MID$ statement with the MID$ function. The MID$ function returns a substring, but the MID$ statement replaces a series of characters within a string with a designated substring. The general form of the MID$ statement is given in Table 8.5.

TABLE 8.5 - The MID$ Statement	
General Form:	MID$(X$, P, N) = S$
	where **X$** is the string in which the replacement takes place; **P** is the position at which the replacement begins; **N** is the number of characters to replace; and **S$** is the replacement substring.
Purpose:	To replace a substring within a string.
Examples:	1. MID$(Phrase$, 3, 4) = Substr$
	2. MID$(Word1$, 1, 5) = "Y" (1 character replaced)
	3. MID$(Wd1$, 30, 2) = "abcde" (2 characters replaced)
	4. MID$(E$, 4, 5) = A$ + B$

As illustrated by the general form in Table 8.5, a substring of X$, specified by the beginning position P and the length N, is replaced by the substring S$. In example 1, if Phrase$ is equal to inprocment and Substr$ is equal to vest, then the following statement

```
MID$(Phrase$, 3, 4) = Substr$
```

assigns Phrase$ the value investment. The substring vest replaces the substring proc.

Example 2 in Table 8.5 shows that if the replacement substring is shorter than the substring designated by the length argument in the MID$ statement, then only those characters that are designated by the replacement substring are actually replaced. For example, if Word1$ is equal to Beast, then the statement

```
MID$(Word1$, 1, 5) = "Y"
```

assigns Word1$ the value Yeast.

If the replacement substring has a length greater than that specified by N in the MID$ statement, then the PC replaces only N characters. The rightmost excess characters in the replacement substring are not used.

The partial program in Figure 8.3 modifies a line of text through the use of the INSTR function and the MID$ statement. The program searches for all occurrences of the substring ne. Each time the substring is found, it is replaced with the substring in.

FIGURE 8.3

Use of the INSTR *function and* MID$ *statement.*

```
 I    ' Searching and Replacing Strings
 2    ' ******************************
 3    Phrase$ = "The rane in Spane stays manely in the plane"
 4    PRINT "Old text ===> "; Phrase$
 5    Position = INSTR(Phrase$, "ne")
 6    DO WHILE Position <> 0
 7       MID$(Phrase$, Position, 2) = "in"
 8       Position = INSTR(Position + 2, Phrase$, "ne")
 9    LOOP
10    PRINT
11    PRINT "New text ===> "; Phrase$


      [run]

      Old text ===> The rane in Spane stays manely in the plane

      New text ===> The rain in Spain stays mainly in the plain
```

Line 5 in Figure 8.3 assigns the variable Position the value 7, which is the beginning position of the first occurrence of the substring ne. Line 7 replaces the substring ne that begins in position 7 with the substring in. Line 8 searches for the next occurrence of the substring ne. The search begins one position to the right of the previous occurrence.

The next occurrence of the substring ne begins at position 16. Therefore, the INSTR function assigns Position a value of 16. The loop continues, with line 7 making the next replacement.

This process continues until all the occurrences of ne have been changed to in. At this point, line 8 assigns Position a value of zero, and the loop terminates. The modified value of Phrase$ is then displayed by line 11.

If Phrase$ is assigned a value without the substring ne, the Do-While loop (lines 6 through 9) will not execute. The INSTR function in line 5 returns a value of zero when the substring is not found. With Position equal to zero, the DO WHILE statement in line 6 causes execution to continue at line 10. In this case, the new text and old text are identical.

Converting Character Codes — ASC and CHR$ Functions

The ASC and CHR$ **functions** facilitate the manipulation of individual characters. The ASC(X$) function returns a two-digit numeric value that corresponds to the ASCII code for the first character of the string argument X$. As explained in Chapter 5 on page 147, each character in QBasic has a corresponding ASCII numeric code the PC uses for storing the character in main memory or auxiliary storage. For example, the character A has an ASCII code of 65, the character B has an ASCII code of 66, and so on. The following statement displays the result 67:

```
PRINT ASC("C")
67
```

CHR$(N) can be described as the reverse of the ASC function. It returns a single string character equivalent in ASCII code to the numeric argument N. For example, the following statement displays the character B:

```
PRINT CHR$(66)
B
```

A total of 256 different characters are represented by the ASCII code. (See Appendix D, Table D.1.) The CHR$ function allows you to enter any of the 256 characters by using the corresponding ASCII code as the argument.

For example, the following partial program

```
FOR I = 1 TO 10
    PRINT CHR$(7);
NEXT I
PRINT CHR$(12)
```

causes the PC to beep 10 times and clear the first 24 lines of the screen because the ASCII code 7 corresponds to the bell character (beep), and the ASCII code 12 corresponds to the character for a form feed.

Table 8.6 illustrates several examples of the ASC and CHR$ functions. Below, Programming Case Study 13 makes use of both functions to decipher a coded message.

TABLE 8.6 - Examples of the ASC and CHR$ Functions		
VALUE	STATEMENT	RESULTS
	Code1= ASC("5")	Code1 = 53
C$ = "" (null)	D1 = ASC(C$)	Illegal function call
D$ = "ABC"	E = ASC(D$)	E = 65
	Kay$ = CHR$(75)	Kay$ = K
D = -3	Y$ = CHR$(D)	Illegal function call

Changing Case — LCASE$ and UCASE$ Functions

The LCASE$ and UCASE$ **functions** are used to convert alphabetic characters in a string expression to uppercase or lowercase. For example, if Phrase$ is equal to 1580 FOULIS Court, then LCASE$(Phrase$) is equal to 1580 foulis court. Note that the digits 1580, the spaces after 1580 and FOULIS, and the lowercase characters ourt are not affected by the LCASE$ function.

The UCASE$ function is the opposite of the LCASE$ function. UCASE$(Phrase$) returns the string 1580 FOULIS COURT. Here again, the digits, spaces, and uppercase characters in Phrase$ are not affected by the UCASE$ function. Only the lowercase characters ourt are changed to uppercase.

Table 8.7 shows additional examples of the LCASE$ and UCASE$ functions.

Programming Case Study 4B on page 126 introduced the UCASE$ function. The user is asked to enter Y or N to control a looping process. For example,

```
LOOP UNTIL UCASE$(Control$) = "N"
```

determines if a Do-Until loop should continue.

TABLE 8.7 - Examples of the LCASES$ and UCASE$ Functions		
VALUE	STATEMENT	RESULTS
L$ = "QBasic"	U$ = UCASE$(L$)	U$ = QBASIC
	L$ = LCASE$("12A4B&3")	L$ = 12a4b&3
L$ = "msO1Cr?"	U$ = UCASE$(L$)	U$ = MSO1CR?

PROGRAMMING CASE STUDY 13 – Deciphering a Coded Message

Messages often are coded by having one letter represent another. The coded message is called a **cryptogram**, and an algorithm is used to decipher the message into readable form.

The objective here is to take a coded message and have the PC display the corresponding deciphered message in lowercase. The algorithm calls for subtracting 3 from the numeric code that represents each character in the coded message. After each character in the message is deciphered, it is to be displayed in lowercase. Obviously, the algorithm can be, and usually is, more complex. The coded message is WKH#IRUFH#EH#ZLWK#XV.

Following are an analysis of the problem, a program solution, and a discussion of the program solution.

Program Tasks

1. A100.Initialization
   a. Clear the screen.
   b. Accept the coded message.

2. B100.Process.Code — Change and display the coded message. Use a For loop that includes the following:
   a. A limit parameter of LEN(Code$).
   b. The MID$ function to extract each character.
   c. The ASC function to determine the numeric value equivalent to the ASCII code of the extracted character.
   d. Subtraction of 3 from the numeric value determined in 2c.
   e. The CHR$ function to change the numeric value in 2d to a character.
   f. Displaying the character in lowercase using the LCASE$ function.

3. C100.Wrap.Up — Print End of Job message.

Program Solution

Program 8.1, the solution to Programming Case Study 13, is illustrated in Figure 8.4 and corresponds to the preceding tasks.

FIGURE 8.4

Program 8.1, the solution to Programming Case Study 13.

```
1   ' Program 8.1
2   ' Deciphering a Coded Message
3   ' ******************************************
4   ' *              Main Program              *
5   ' ******************************************
6   GOSUB A100.Initialization
7   GOSUB B100.Process.Code
8   GOSUB C100.Wrap.Up
9   END
10
11  ' ******************************************
12  ' *              Initialization            *
13  ' ******************************************
14  A100.Initialization:
15    CLS   ' Clear Screen
16    PRINT : INPUT "Coded message =======> ", Code$
17    PRINT : PRINT "The message is =======> ";
18  RETURN
19
20  ' ******************************************
21  ' *              Process Code              *
22  ' ******************************************
23  B100.Process.Code:
24    FOR Char = 1 TO LEN(Code$)
25       Number = ASC(MID$(Code$, Char, 1))
26       Number = Number - 3
27       Letter$ = CHR$(Number)
28       PRINT LCASE$(Letter$);
29    NEXT Char
30  RETURN
31
```

(continued)

FIGURE 8.4
(continued)

```
32  ' *****************************************
33  ' *                 Wrap-Up                *
34  ' *****************************************
35  C100.Wrap.Up:
36     PRINT : PRINT
37     PRINT "End of Job"
38  RETURN

    [run]

    Coded message ========> WKH#IRUFH#EH#ZLWK#XV

    The message is =======> the force be with us

    End of Job
```

Discussion of the Program Solution

Program 8.1 accepts a coded message, deciphers it one character at a time, and displays the corresponding message one character at a time in lowercase.

In line 24, LEN(Code$) is the limit value for the For loop. Line 25 determines the numeric value that corresponds to the ASCII code for the character selected by the MID$ function. It is valid for a string function to be part of the argument for another string function. Line 26 subtracts 3 from the value of Number, and in line 27 the CHR$ function returns the corresponding character. Finally, the LCASE$ function is used in the PRINT statement in line 28 to display the deciphered character in lowercase before the next character in the message is processed.

Modifying Data Types — STR$ and VAL Functions

The PC cannot add a string value to a numeric value. The STR$ and VAL **functions** allow this restriction to be circumvented. The STR$(N) function returns the string equivalent of the numeric value N. VAL(X$) returns the numeric equivalent of the string X$. Thus, STR$(52.3) returns the string "52.3", and VAL("310.23") returns the numeric value 310.23. If the argument for the STR$ function is negative, the function returns a leading negative sign. If the argument for the VAL function does not represent a number, the function returns a value of 0. For example, the value displayed by the following statement is zero:

```
PRINT VAL("HTML")
0
```

Table 8.8 gives examples of both the STR$ and VAL functions. These two functions are used primarily in instances where a substring of numeric digits within an identification number — such as a credit card number or an invoice number — needs to be extracted for computational purposes, and the result has to be transformed back as a string value.

TABLE 8.8 - Examples of the STR$ and VAL Functions		
VALUE	**STATEMENT**	**RESULTS**
	A$ = STR$(34)	A$ = 34
B = 64.543	S$ = STR$(B)	S$ = 64.543
C = -3.21	Z$ = STR$(C)	Z$ = -3.21
	F = VAL("766.321")	F = 766.321
K$ = "12E-3"	Q = VAL(K$)	Q = 12E-3
P$ = "ABC"	W = VAL(P$)	W = 0

Note: Any numeric value assigned to a string variable is actually a string, not a number.

Duplicating Strings — SPACE$ and STRING$ Functions

The SPACE$ and STRING$ **functions** are used to duplicate string data. The SPACE$(N) function returns N spaces or blank characters. It is similar to the SPC function discussed in Chapter 3. For example, the two statements

```
PRINT "STAR"; SPC(4); "TREK"
```

and

```
PRINT "STAR"; SPACE$(4); "TREK"
```

display identical results. The advantage of the SPACE$ function over the SPC function is that SPACE$ may be used in statements other than the PRINT or LPRINT statements. For example, the following statement

```
Sp$ = SPACE$(25)
```

assigns Sp$ a string value of 25 spaces. If the argument is equal to or less than zero, the function returns the null string.

The STRING$(N, X$) function returns N times the first character of the string X$. The STRING$ function may be used to duplicate any character. For example, the following statement

```
PRINT STRING$(72, "*")
```

displays a line of 72 asterisks. The second argument may also be represented in ASCII code. That is, the statement

```
PRINT STRING$(72, 42)
```

is identical to the previous PRINT statement because 42 is the ASCII code representation for the asterisk character.

Table 8.9 gives examples of both the SPACE$ and STRING$ functions.

VALUE	STATEMENT	COMMENT
TABLE 8.9 - Examples of the SPACE$ and STRING$ Functions		
N = 50	PRINT SPACE$(N); "A"	Displays 50 spaces, followed by the character A in position 51.
	Sp$ = SPACE$(12)	Assigns 12 spaces to Sp$.
	Null$ = SPACE$(0)	Assigns Null$ the null string.
C = 45	PRINT STRING$(C, "-")	Displays 45 minus signs.
	A$ = STRING$(5,65)	Assigns A$ the string value AAAAA.

Trimming Blank Characters — LTRIM$ and RTRIM$ Functions

The LTRIM$ and RTRIM$ **functions** remove leading or trailing blank characters from a string expression. LTRIM$(X$) returns X$ with leading (left) blank characters removed. RTRIM$(X$) returns X$ with trailing (right) blank characters removed. For example, in the following partial program,

```
1   Phrase1$ = "   Leading Blanks"
2   Phrase2$ = "Trailing Blanks   "
3   Phrase.LTrim$ = LTRIM$(Phrase1$)
4   Phrase.RTrim$ = RTRIM$(Phrase2$)
```

line 3 assigns Phrase.LTrim$ the value Leading Blanks without the leading blank characters that were part of the string value in line 1. Line 4 assigns Phrase.RTrim$ the value Trailing Blanks without the trailing blank characters that were part of the string value in line 2.

Accessing the System Time and Date — DATE$ and TIME$ Functions

The DATE$ and TIME$ **functions** return the system date and system time, respectively. DATE$ is equal to the current system date as a string value in the form mm-dd-yyyy. The first two characters, mm, represent the month. The fourth and fifth characters, dd, represent the day. The last four characters, yyyy, represent the year. For example, if the date is December 25, 2002, then the statement

```
Todays.Date$ = DATE$
```

assigns Todays.Date$ the string 12-25-2002.

TIME$ is equal to the time of day, in twenty-four hour notation, as a string value in the form hh:mm:ss. The first two characters, hh, represent the hours (range 00-23). The fourth and fifth characters, mm, represent the minutes (range 00-59). The last two characters, ss, represent the seconds (range 00-59). If the time is 11:35:42 *at the instant* the statement

```
PRINT "The time is "; TIME$
```

executes, then the following displays:

```
The time is 11:35:42
```

The key phrase in the last sentence is *at the instant*, because one second later the time will be different.

Table 8.10 gives examples of both the DATE$ and TIME$ functions.

TABLE 8.10 - Examples of the DATE$ and TIME$ Functions	
Assume DATE$ = 09-15-2002 **and** TIME$ = 15:26:32	
STATEMENT	**RESULTS**
Td$ = DATE$	Td$ = 09-15-2002
Tt$ = TIME$	Tt$ = 15:26:32
Month$ = MID$(DATE$, 1, 2)	Month$ = 09
Day$ = MID$(DATE$, 4, 2)	Day$ = 15
Year$ = MID$(DATE$, 9, 2)	Year$ = 02
Hour$ = MID$(TIME$, 1, 2)	Hour$ = 15
Minute$ = MID$(TIME$, 4, 2)	Minute$ = 26
Second$ = MID$(TIME$, 7, 2)	Second$ = 32

Note: Any numeric value assigned to a string variable is actually a string, not a number.

The DATE$ and TIME$ functions are used frequently to display the date and time as part of report headings. The DATE$ function also may be used in business-related applications to verify that a payment date, birth date, or hire date is valid.

PROGRAMMING CASE STUDY 14 – Validating Payment Dates

The following program solution illustrates how to verify that a payment date is the present date or an earlier date, not a future date.

Problem: The following customer payment records are stored in the sequential file ACCREC.DAT on the Data Disk. The payment dates are of the form mmddyyyy.

Customer Number	Customer Payment	Payment Date
31245381	$101.55	09152003
46371230	95.25	06122002
71209824	25.00	06242002
96012567	38.00	05302002

The accounts receivable department has requested a program to verify the payment date for each record in ACCREC.DAT is not a date in the future. The program should verify each payment date against today's date. If today's date is greater than or equal to the payment date, then the payment date is valid. If today's date is less than the payment date, then the payment date is invalid. For each record, display the customer number, the payment, the payment date, and a message indicating whether the payment date is valid or invalid. The results are to be in report form with one line displayed for each record read. Assume that today's date is June 22, 2002. (You may change your system date to this date or use the DATE$ statement, which is discussed in the next section.) To compare the two dates, the most significant part of the date (years) must be at the far left, followed by the next most significant part (months), followed by the least significant part (days). That is, the program must rearrange the two dates before it can compare them, as follows:

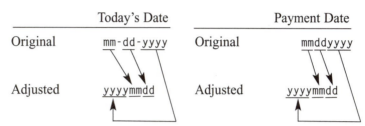

To rearrange the substrings within each date, the MID$ function and the concatenation operator may be used. After the two fields have been adjusted, today's date can be compared against the customer payment date.

Following are a list of the program tasks, a program solution, and a discussion of the program solution.

Program Tasks

1. A100.Initialization
   a. Set To.Date$ to DATE$.
   b. Use this expression to rearrange today's date:

```
Today$ = MID$(To.Date$, 7, 4) + MID$(To.Date$, 1, 2) + MID$(To.Date$, 4, 2)
```

   c. Call A200.Initialize.Report.Format.
   d. Call A210.Print.Headings.
   e. Open ACCREC.DAT.

2. B100.Process.File — Establish a Do-While loop to do the following:
   a. Read a payment record.
   b. Call B200.Validate.Payment.Date:
      (1) Adjust the customer payment date (C.Date$). Use the following statement:

```
Adj.Date$ = MID$(C.Date$, 5, 4) + MID$(C.Date$, 1 , 2) + MID$(C.Date$, 3, 2)
```

      (2) If Today$ >= Adj.Date$, then Message$ equals Date OK. Otherwise, Message$ equals Date NOT OK.
   c. Display the customer number, the payment, the payment date, and the message. Format the payment date in the form mm-dd-yyyy.

3. C100.Wrap.Up
   a. Close ACCREC.DAT.
   b. Display an end-of-job message.

Program Solution

Program 8.2, the solution to Programming Case Study 14, is illustrated in Figure 8.5 on the next page and corresponds to the preceding tasks.

FIGURE 8.5

Program 8.2, the solution to Programming Case Study 14.

```
1    ' Program 8.2
2    ' Validating Payment Dates
3    ' Input File Name = ACCREC.DAT
4    ' *********************************************************
5    ' *                        Main Program                  *
6    ' *********************************************************
7    GOSUB A100.Initialization
8    GOSUB B100.Process.File
9    GOSUB C100.Wrap.Up
10   END
11
12   ' *********************************************************
13   ' *                      Initialization                  *
14   ' *********************************************************
15   A100.Initialization:
16      To.Date$ = DATE$
17      Today$ = MID$(To.Date$, 7, 4) + MID$(To.Date$, 1, 2)
18      Today$ = Today$ + MID$(To.Date$, 4, 2)
19      CLS  ' Clear Screen
20      GOSUB A200.Initialize.Report.Format
21      GOSUB A210.Print.Headings
22      OPEN "A:ACCREC.DAT" FOR INPUT AS #1
23   RETURN
24
25   ' *********************************************************
26   ' *                Initialize Report Format              *
27   ' *********************************************************
28   A200.Initialize.Report.Format:
29      H1$ = "   Validating Payment Dates For "
30      H2$ = "Customer                   Payment"
31      H3$ = "Number      Payment       Date            Comment"
32      H4$ = "--------    -------      -------        -------"
33      D1$ = "\        \  #,###.##    \\-\\-\ \     \              \"
34      T1$ = "End of Report"
35   RETURN
36
37   ' *********************************************************
38   ' *                Initialize Report Format              *
39   ' *********************************************************
40   A210.Print.Headings:
41      PRINT H1$; DATE$
42      PRINT SPC(3); STRING$(39, "-")
43      PRINT
44      PRINT H2$
45      PRINT H3$
46      PRINT H4$
46   RETURN
48
49   ' *********************************************************
50   ' *                      Process File                    *
51   ' *********************************************************
52   B100.Process.File:
53      DO WHILE NOT EOF(1)
54         INPUT #1, C.Num$, C.Pay, C.Date$
55         GOSUB B200.Validate.Payment.Date
56         Month$ = LEFT$(C.Date$, 2)
57         Day$ = MID$(C.Date$, 3, 2)
58         Year$ = RIGHT$(C.Date$, 4)
59         PRINT USING D1$; C.Num$; C.Pay; Month$; Day$; Year$; Message$
60      LOOP
61   RETURN
62
```

```
63    ' ********************************************************
64    ' *                 Validate Payment Date                *
65    ' ********************************************************
66    B200.Validate.Payment.Date:
67       Adj.Date$ = MID$(C.Date$, 5, 4) + MID$(C.Date$, 1, 2)
68       Adj.Date$ = Adj.Date$ + MID$(C.Date$, 3, 2)
69       IF Today$ >= Adj.Date$ THEN
70          Message$ = "Date OK"
71       ELSE
72          Message$ = "Date NOT OK"
73       END IF
74    RETURN
75
76    ' ********************************************************
77    ' *                       Wrap-Up                        *
78    ' ********************************************************
79    C100.Wrap.Up:
80       CLOSE #1
81       PRINT : PRINT T1$
82    RETURN
83
84    ' ****************** End of Program ******************
```

```
[run]
```

Discussion of the Program Solution

In Program 8.2, line 16 assigns To.Date$ today's date. Lines 17 and 18 rearrange the substrings of To.Date$ in the format yyyymmdd and assigns the result to Today$. Lines 67 and 68 rearrange the substrings of the customer payment date into the same format. Line 69 compares today's date to the customer payment date. If Today$ is greater than or equal to Adj.Date$, then Message$ is set equal to Date OK. If Today$ is less than Adj.Date$, then the payment date is a future date and Message$ is set equal to Date NOT OK. Pay particular attention to lines 17 and 18, and 67 and 68. Rearranging substrings is a common characteristic of programs that validate dates.

The report generated by Program 8.2 is shown in Figure 8.6. Note that the payment dates are formatted on the basis of the descriptor field in line 33 and the use of the string functions in lines 56 through 58.

FIGURE 8.6
The report generated by Program 8.2.

```
Validating Payment Dates For 06-22-2002
-------------------------------------------

Customer              Payment
Number     Payment    Date          Comment
--------   -------    -------       -------
31245381   101.55     09-15-2003    Date NOT OK
46371230    95.25     06-12-2002    Date OK
71209824    25.00     06-24-2002    Date NOT OK
96012567    38.00     05-30-2002    Date OK

End of Report
```

Setting the Time and Date — DATE$ and TIME$ Statements

While the DATE$ and TIME$ functions are equal to the system's current date and time, the DATE$ and TIME$ **statements** allow you to set the PC's date and time. These two statements override the system date and time. The general forms for the DATE$ and TIME$ statements are given in Tables 8.11 and 8.12.

TABLE 8.11 - The DATE$ Statement	
General Form:	DATE$ = string expression
	where **string expression** is one of the following forms:
	mm-dd-yy
	mm-dd-yyyy
	mm/dd/yy
	mm/dd/yyyy
Purpose:	To set the system date.
Examples:	DATE$ = "07-06-99"
	DATE$ = "7/6/2002"
	DATE$ = "06-22-2008"
	DATE$ = "1/25/99"
	DATE$ = Cur.Date$
Note:	The year must be in the range 1980 to 2099. If you enter a two-digit year, then the PC assumes 19yy. You may enter one digit for the month or day. If only one digit is entered, then the PC assumes a leading zero.

TABLE 8.12 - The TIME$ Statement		
General Form:	TIME$ = string expression	
	where **string expression** is one of the following forms:	
	hh	Set the hour (range 0 to 23).
	hh:mm	Set the hour and minute (minute range 0 to 59).
	hh:mm:ss	Set the hour, minute, and second (second range 0 to 59).
Purpose:	To set the system time.	
Examples:	TIME$ = "10"	
	TIME$ = "1:23"	
	TIME$ = "20:00:23"	
	TIME$ = "0:25"	
	TIME$ = Cur.Time$	
Note:	You may enter one digit for the hour, minute, or second. If one digit is entered, then the system assumes a leading zero.	

If you assign values that are out of the designated ranges described in Tables 8.11 and 8.12, the PC will display a dialog box with the following diagnostic message:

```
Illegal function call
```

If the expression assigned to the DATE$ or TIME$ statements is not a valid string, the PC displays a dialog box with the following diagnostic message:

```
Type mismatch
```

Accepting String Data — LINE INPUT Statement, INKEY$ and INPUT$ Functions

The LINE INPUT **statement** accepts a line entered from the keyboard as a string value and assigns it to a specified string variable. The LINE INPUT statement ignores the usual delimiters, namely the quotation mark and the comma. That is, if the string value

```
She said, "Terminate the program!"
```

is entered in response to the statement

```
LINE INPUT "What did she say? "; Statement$
```

then Statement$ is assigned the entire string of characters

```
She said, "Terminate the program!"
```

including the comma and the quotation marks.

The general form of the LINE INPUT statement is shown in Table 8.13.

TABLE 8.13 - The LINE INPUT Statement

General Form:	LINE INPUT string variable or LINE INPUT "input prompt message"; string variable or LINE INPUT #n, string variable
Purpose:	Provides for the assignment to a single string variable of an entire line (up to 255 characters), including commas and quotation marks, entered from an external source such as the keyboard or auxiliary storage.
Examples:	

LINE INPUT Statement	Data from an External Source
LINE INPUT Cus.Rec$	"123","Adams Joe",44,0520
LINE INPUT "What? "; Stat$	"Don't do it", Amanda Said
LINE INPUT "Weight ===> "; Wgt$	126.5 lbs.
LINE INPUT #2, Complete.Line$	"John Smith", 46, "3", 12

Note:	A question mark is not displayed as part of the prompt unless it is included in the input prompt message.

The major differences between the LINE INPUT statement and the INPUT statement are:

1. The LINE INPUT statement does not automatically prompt the user with the question mark and trailing space, as the INPUT statement does.
2. The LINE INPUT statement can accept data for only one string variable. The INPUT statement can have more than one variable in the list, and the variables may be either numeric or string or both.

When executed, an INPUT or LINE INPUT statement instructs the PC to suspend execution of the program until the Enter key is pressed. That is, with each of these two statements, the PC must always be signaled by pressing the Enter key when you have finished entering the requested data. The INKEY$ and the INPUT$ functions do not require pressing the Enter key for the program to accept input.

The INKEY$ **function** *does not* suspend execution of the program; instead, it checks the keyboard to determine whether a character is pending — that is, whether a key was pressed since the last time it executed an expression with INKEY$ or since the beginning of the program if it is the first INKEY$ encountered. The following statement

```
Pending$ = INKEY$
```

assigns Pending$ the character that corresponds to the last key pressed. If no character is pending, then INKEY$ assigns the null string to Pending$.

Consider the following example, in which the INKEY$ function is used to control a looping process. The values of Number and Number MOD 7 are displayed until the user presses a key or until an overflow condition occurs.

```
Number = 1
DO WHILE INKEY$ = ""
    PRINT Number, Number MOD 7
    Number = Number + 1
LOOP
```

In this partial program, the INKEY$ function is used in the DO WHILE statement to control the loop. As long as no character is pending from the keyboard, the PC continues to execute the loop.

The INKEY$ function is useful for applications requiring a program not to be interrupted and yet accept responses from the keyboard. This method of processing is essential for video game programs. In games, objects on the monitor are in constant motion, and at the same time, the games must check for user input such as the firing of a phaser or torpedo. Later in this chapter, we will study additional statements that can be used to trap similar events.

The INPUT$(N) **function** is even more sophisticated than the INKEY$ function because it accepts N characters from the keyboard. However, unlike INKEY$, INPUT$(N) suspends execution of the program until the user has pressed N number of keys. For example, the statement

```
Char$ = INPUT$(1)
```

causes the PC to suspend execution of the program and wait until a key is pressed.

The characters entered in response to the INPUT$ function are *not* displayed on the screen. To display the response, the statement that contains the function should be followed with a PRINT statement. For example,

```
CHAR$ = INPUT$(5)
PRINT CHAR$
```

displays the five characters entered by the user.

Table 8.14 illustrates examples of the INKEY$ and the INPUT$ functions.

TABLE 8.14 - Examples of the INKEY$ and the INPUT$ Functions		
STATEMENT	KEYBOARD RESPONSE	RESULTS
Pending$ = INKEY$	J	Pending$ = J
Keyboard$ = INKEY$	No Response	Keyboard$ = null
Char$ = INPUT$(4)	A1B2	Char$ = A1B2
One.Char$ = INPUT$(1)	3	One.Char$ = 3

A common use of the INPUT$ function is to suspend the execution of a program at the conclusion of a task so the information on the screen may be read before it disappears. For example, if a program displays a long list of items, you may want to suspend execution of the program after every 20 or so lines display. The message

```
Press any key to continue...
```

often is used in this context. The INPUT$ simplifies the entry by not requiring the Enter key to be pressed. The following partial program shows how to incorporate this technique into a QBasic program:

```
PRINT "Press any key to continue..."
Char$ = INPUT$(1)
```

The first line displays the message, and the second line suspends execution of the program. Execution continues when the user presses any key on the keyboard except Ctrl+Break, Num Lock, Shift, Alt, and other passive keys.

8.3 NUMERIC FUNCTIONS

The most frequently used QBasic numeric functions are listed in Table 8.15. (For a complete listing of the numeric functions, see the Reference Card at the back of this book.)

TABLE 8.15 - Some QBasic Numeric Functions	
FUNCTION	**FUNCTION VALUE**
ABS(N)	Returns the absolute value of the argument N.
ATN(N)	Returns the angle in radians whose tangent is the value of the argument N.
CINT(N)	Returns the value of N rounded to an integer.
COS(N)	Returns the cosine of the argument N where N is in radians.
CSRLIN	Returns the current cursor row position.
EXP(N)	Returns e (2.718281...) raised to the argument N.
FIX(N)	Returns the value of N truncated to an integer.
INT(N)	Returns the largest integer that is less than or equal to the argument N.
LOG(N)	Returns the natural log of the argument N where N is greater than 0.
POS(N)	Returns the current cursor column position.
RND	Returns a random number between 0 (inclusive) and 1 (exclusive).
SCREEN(R, C)	Returns the ASCII code for the character at the specified row (R) and column (C) on the screen.
SGN(N)	Returns the sign of the argument N: −1 if the argument N is less than 0; 0 if the argument N is equal to 0; or + 1 if the argument N is greater than 0.
SIN(N)	Returns the sine of the argument N where N is in radians.
SQR(N)	Returns the positive square root of the argument N.
TAN(N)	Returns the tangent of the argument N where N is in radians.
TIMER	Returns a value equal to the number of seconds elapsed since midnight.

In the discussion that follows, several examples of each numeric function are presented.

Arithmetic Functions — ABS, FIX, INT, CINT, and SGN

The functions classified as **arithmetic** include ABS (absolute value), FIX (fixed integer), INT (integer), CINT (rounded integer), and SGN (sign).

The ABS **function** takes any numeric expression and returns its positive value. For example, if N is equal to -4, then ABS(N) is equal to 4. Additional examples of the ABS function are shown in Table 8.16.

The FIX(N) **function** returns the truncated integer portion of the argument N. When the argument is positive, the FIX function is identical to the INT **function**. For example, if N is equal to 13.45, then FIX(N) returns 13. However, when the argument is negative, the two functions return a different result. For example, if N is equal to-4.45, then FIX(N) returns -4, and INT(N) returns -5. The INT function returns an integer less than or equal to the argument.

Like the FIX(N) and INT(N) functions, the CINT(N) **function** returns an integer. However, the CINT function returns the rounded integer portion of the argument. Additional examples of the FIX, INT, and CINT functions are shown in Table 8.16.

The SGN(N) **function** returns a value of + 1 if the argument N is positive, 0 if the argument is 0, and -1 if the argument N is negative. Table 8.16 shows examples of the SGN function.

TABLE 8.16 - Examples of the ABS, FIX, INT, CINT, and SGN Functions		
VALUE OF VARIABLE	**STATEMENT**	**RESULTS**
N = -3	P = ABS(N)	P = 3
C = 4.5	M = ABS(C)	M = 4.5
C = 4, D = -6	A = C + ABS(D)	A = 10
G = 25.567	B = CINT(G)	B = 26
G = -25.567	C = CINT(G)	C = -26
G = 25.567	F = FIX(G)	F = 25
G = -25.567	X = FIX(G)	X = -25
G = -25.567	I = INT(G)	I = -26
G = -25.567	K = INT(ABS(G))	K = 25
D = 4	E = SGN(D)	E = 1
P = -5	F = 5 + SGN(P)	F = 4

Generalized Procedures for Rounding and Truncation

As you recall, some fundamentals of rounding and truncation were discussed in Section 3.5 on page 70. Although QBasic allows for automatic rounding through the use of the PRINT USING statement, it is sometimes more convenient for the programmer to control the process of rounding and truncation. The CINT and FIX functions may be used to write generalized expressions for rounding or truncating a number to any decimal place. The generalized expression for rounding numbers is

```
CINT(N * 10 ^ E) / 10 ^ E
```

The generalized expression for truncating numbers is

```
FIX(N * 10 ^ E) / 10 ^ E
```

where **N** is the value to be rounded or truncated, and **E** is the number of decimal places desired.

To determine what value should be assigned to E, begin counting from the decimal point as illustrated below.

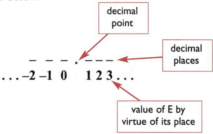

For example, if you want to round a result N to the nearest hundredths place, you assign E a value of 2. The generalized expression for rounding to the nearest hundredths place becomes the following:

```
CINT(N * 10 ^ 2) / 10 ^ 2
```

or

```
CINT(N * 100) / 100
```

For truncating a result N to the nearest hundredths place, the generalized expression becomes the following:

```
FIX(N * 10 ^ 2) / 10 ^ 2
```

or

```
FIX(N * 100) / 100
```

See QBasic Programming Problem 3 at the end of this chapter for an example of the use of these generalized expressions for rounding and truncating values.

Exponential Functions — SQR, EXP, and LOG

The functions classified as **exponential** include the SQR (square root), EXP (exponential), and LOG (logarithmic).

The SQR(N) **function** computes the square root of the argument N. Table 8.17 shows several examples of computing the square root of a number.

TABLE 8.17 - Examples of the SQR Function		
VALUE OF VARIABLE	**STATEMENT**	**RESULTS**
	Root = SQR(9)	Root = 3
Value = 0	R1 = SQR(Value)	R1 = 0
Cube = 625	R2 = SQR(SQR(Cube))	R2 = 5
Bus(1) = 1.15129	R3 = SQR(Bus(1))	R3 = 1.072982
X = 3, Y = 4	Hyp = SQR(X ^ 2 + Y ^ 2)	Hyp = 5
Neg = -49	Posi = SQR(ABS(Neg))	Posi = 7
N = -25	Root = SQR(N)	Illegal Function Call

The symbol **e** in mathematics represents the **Napierian base** (2.718281...), where the three dots show the fractional part of the constant is not a repeating sequence of digits. In QBasic, the keyword EXP is used to represent this constant, which is raised to the power given as the argument in parentheses following the function name. The EXP **function** can be used, for example, to determine the value of $e^{1.14473}$. The following statement,

```
Pi = EXP(1.14473)
```

results in the variable Pi being assigned a value of 3.141593, which is a close approximation of π. If the value of the argument for the EXP function exceeds 88.72283, then an overflow condition occurs.

The natural log ($\log_e$ or ln) of a number can be determined by using the LOG **function**. For example, the value of X in the equation

$$e^x = 3.141593$$

can be determined by using the following statement:

```
X = LOG(3.141593)
```

The resulting value of X is 1.14473 and therefore,

$$e^{1.14473} = 3.141593$$

This function also can be used to determine the logarithm to the base 10 by multiplying the LOG function by 0.434295. For example, in the statement

```
Log10 = 0.434295 * LOG(3)
```

Log10 is assigned the value 0.4771218, the base 10 logarithm of 3.

Of the three exponential functions, programmers use the square root function more than the exponential or logarithmic. However, the latter two functions are essential in some advanced applications. The following programming case study is an example of the use of the LOG function.

PROGRAMMING CASE STUDY 15 - Determining the Time to Double an Investment

The formula for computing the amount of an investment compounded annually for a given number of years is $A = P(1 + J)^N$ where A is the total amount, P is the initial investment, J is the annual rate of interest, and N is the number of years.

This formula can be rewritten to solve for the number of years N:

$$N = \frac{\log\left(\dfrac{A}{P}\right)}{\log(1 + J)}$$

If the number of years it takes to double an investment is to be determined, then the amount A is equal to twice the investment P, or A = 2P. The formula for determining the number of years to double an investment can further be simplified to the following:

$$N = \frac{\log 2}{\log(1 + J)}$$

The ensuing problem uses the LOG function to compute the number of years it takes to double an investment.

Problem: The WESAVU National Bank requests that a program be written to display a table of annual interest rates and the corresponding years it will take to double an investment compounded annually for integer interests rates from 4% through 14%, inclusive. Display the number of years to the nearest tenths place.

Program Solution

The solution to Programming Case Study 15, Program 8.3, is presented in Figure 8.7 and generates the specified report.

FIGURE 8.7

Program 8.3, the solution to Programming Case Study 15.

```
 1   ' Program 8.3
 2   ' Determining the Time to Double an Investment
 3   ' *********************************************
 4   ' *               Main Program                *
 5   ' *********************************************
 6   GOSUB A100.Initialization
 7   GOSUB B100.Generate.Table
 8   GOSUB C100.Wrap.Up
 9   END
10
11   ' *********************************************
12   ' *               Initialization              *
13   ' *********************************************
14   A100.Initialization:
15      CLS   ' Clear Screen
16      GOSUB A200.Initialize.Report.Format
17      GOSUB A210.Display.Headings
18   RETURN
19
20   ' *********************************************
21   ' *          Initialize Report Format         *
22   ' *********************************************
23   A200.Initialize.Report.Format:
24      H1$ = "Doubling an Investment"
25      H2$ = "----------------------"
26      H3$ = "Interest    Number"
27      H4$ = "Rate in %   of Years"
28      H5$ = "---------   --------"
29      D1$ = "   ##          ##.#"
30      T1$ = "End of Report"
31   RETURN
32
33   ' *********************************************
34   ' *     Display Report and Column Headings     *
35   ' *********************************************
36   A210.Display.Headings:
37      PRINT H1$
38      PRINT H2$
39      PRINT
40      PRINT H3$
```

```
41        PRINT H4$
42        PRINT H5$
43    RETURN
44
45    ' **********************************************
46    ' *                 Generate Table             *
47    ' **********************************************
48    B100.Generate.Table:
49        Numerator = LOG(2)
50        FOR Interest = 4 TO 14
51            Time = Numerator / LOG(1 + Interest / 100)
52            PRINT USING D1$; Interest; Time
53        NEXT Interest
54    RETURN
55
56    ' **********************************************
57    ' *                    Wrap-Up                 *
58    ' **********************************************
59    C100.Wrap.Up:
60        PRINT : PRINT T1$
61    RETURN
62
63    ' ****************** End of Program ******************

      [run]
```

Discussion of the Program Solution

The results displayed by Program 8.3 are shown in Figure 8.8. With slight modifications to the values in the FOR statement (line 50) in Program 8.3, the number of years it takes to double an investment compounded annually can be determined for a variety of interest rates. The argument for the LOG function in line 49 may be changed to other numbers, such as 3 or 4, to determine how long it takes to triple or quadruple an investment compounded annually. See QBasic Programming Problem 3 at the end of this chapter to determine the number of years it takes to double an investment compounded quarterly.

FIGURE 8.8
The display due to the execution of Program 8.3.

```
          Doubling an Investment
          ----------------------

          Interest    Number
          Rate in %   of Years
          ---------   --------
              4        17.7
              5        14.2
              6        11.9
              7        10.2
              8         9.0
              9         8.0
             10         7.3
             11         6.6
             12         6.1
             13         5.7
             14         5.3

          End of Report
```

Trigonometric Functions — SIN, COS, TAN, and ATN

In QBasic the SIN, COS, and TAN **functions** can be used to determine the sine, cosine, and tangent of the angle X expressed in **radians**. For these functions to work correctly, the angle X *must* be expressed in radians. Because angles usually are expressed in degrees, the following statements relating angles and radians should prove helpful:

1 radian = 180 / π degrees = 180 / 3.141593 degrees
1 degree = π / 180 radians = 3.141593 / 180 radians

When using these three functions, remember that if the argument is in units of degrees, it must first be multiplied by 3.141593 / 180 to convert it into units of radians before the function can evaluate it. In mathematics, if the equation X = sin 30° is evaluated, then X = 0.5. Evaluating the same equation in QBasic requires the following:

```
Rads = 30 * 3.141593 / 180
X = SIN(Rads)
```

or

```
X = SIN(30 * 3.141593 / 180)
```

TABLE 8.18 - Determining the Cosecant, Secant, and Cotangent	
TO FIND THE	**USE**
Cosecant	1 / SIN(X)
Secant	1 / COS(X)
Cotangent	1 / TAN(X)

QBasic does not have corresponding functions for the cosecant, the secant, and the cotangent. These three trigonometric functions must be evaluated by combinations of the SIN, COS, and TAN functions. Table 8.18 illustrates the combinations.

The fourth trigonometric function available in QBasic is the arctangent. The ATN **function** returns a value that is the angle, in units of radians, that corresponds to the argument in the function. For example,

```
Angle = ATN(1)
```

results in Angle being assigned the value of 0.7853982 radians. Multiplying this number by 180/3.141593 yields an angle of 45°.

Utility Functions — POS, CSRLIN, and SCREEN

The POS **function** returns the current column position of the cursor relative to the left edge of the display screen. The value returned is an integer in the range 1 to 40, or 1 to 80, depending on the current screen width setting. For example,

```
PRINT TAB(15);
PRINT POS(0)
```

causes the PC to display the value 15. The value of the argument plays no role in the value returned by the POS function.

The CSRLIN **function** is equal to the current row (line) the cursor is on relative to the top of the display screen. The value of CSRLIN varies in the range 1 to 25. For example, the following statement entered in the immediate mode

```
LOCATE 5, 6 : PRINT CSRLIN
5
```

displays the current line position.

The CSRLIN and POS functions are used in applications where a value must be displayed at a position on the screen other than the current one, followed by the return of the cursor to the former position. Consider the following partial program:

```
Row = CSRLIN
Col = POS(0)
LOCATE 1, 20 : PRINT "Aim the arrow carefully"
LOCATE Row, Col
```

The first line assigns Row the line the cursor is on. The second line assigns Col the column the cursor is in. The LOCATE statement in the third line moves the cursor to column 20 of line 1 and displays the message. The last line returns the cursor to its former position on the screen.

The SCREEN **function** allows you to determine which character currently is displayed at the intersection of a row and a column on the screen. The function returns the ASCII code for the character found at the specified location. For example, the following partial program assigns Char the value 66, because that is the ASCII code for the character B:

```
LOCATE 15, 16 : PRINT "B"
Char = SCREEN(15, 16)
```

This function also may be used to return the color attribute at the intersection of the specified row and column. For additional information on the SCREEN statement, load QBasic, click Help, click Index, and then select the keyword SCREEN.

Performance Testing — TIMER Function

The TIMER **function** returns a single-precision numeric value representing the number of seconds that have elapsed since midnight. The following For loop illustrates values returned by the TIMER function:

```
TIME$ = "12:00:00"
FOR I = 1 TO 10
    PRINT "Time = "; TIME$, "Timer ="; TIMER
NEXT I

[run]

Time = 12:00:00      Timer = 43200.21
Time = 12:00:00      Timer = 43200.32
Time = 12:00:00      Timer = 43200.43
Time = 12:00:00      Timer = 43200.54
Time = 12:00:01      Timer = 43200.6
Time = 12:00:01      Timer = 43200.71
Time = 12:00:01      Timer = 43200.82
Time = 12:00:01      Timer = 43200.93
Time = 12:00:01      Timer = 43201.04
```

The first statement resets the system time to 12:00 noon (43,200 seconds past midnight). In the For loop, the PRINT statement displays both the system time and the number of seconds elapsed since midnight. A close look at the results shows that, on the average, it takes 0.11 seconds to make a pass on the For loop in this partial program.

The time it takes to make a pass on a given loop will vary slightly between runs and will depend greatly on the type of PC used. For this reason, when benchmarking an algorithm, you should take the average duration of time it takes to accomplish the same task over many runs of the program under the same conditions. **Benchmarking** is the activity of comparing the performance of algorithms or applications that are running under similar conditions on one or more computer systems.

The following two partial programs make use of the TIMER function to determine the difference between using a single-precision variable and an integer variable as the loop variable in a For loop. Both the partial programs in Figures 8.9 and 8.10 on the next page execute empty For loops 32,766 times. The results of these two programs will vary greatly depending upon the speed of the computer system used.

FIGURE 8.9
Timing for a Loop in single precision.

```
 I   ' Timing a For Loop
 2   ' in Single Precision
 3   ' *******************
 4   CLS  ' Clear Screen
 5   '
 6   Start = TIMER
 7   FOR Count = 1 TO 32766
 8   NEXT Count
 9   Finish = TIMER
10   '
11   Duration = Finish - Start
12   PRINT "For loop time ==>";
13   PRINT USING "##.##"; Duration;
14   PRINT " seconds"

     [run]

     For loop time ==> 1.78 seconds
```

FIGURE 8.10
Timing for a Loop in integer precision.

```
 I   ' Timing a For Loop
 2   ' in Integer Precision
 3   ' *******************
 4   CLS  ' Clear Screen
 5   '
 6   Start = TIMER
 7   FOR Count% = 1 TO 32766
 8   NEXT Count%
 9   Finish = TIMER
10   '
11   Duration = Finish - Start
12   PRINT "For loop time ==>";
13   PRINT USING "##.##"; Duration;
14   PRINT " seconds"

     [run]

     For loop time ==>  .09 seconds
```

The duration of time it takes for the processor to execute the For loop in the partial program in Figure 8.9 is 1.78 seconds. With the For loop in the partial program in Figure 8.10, the duration of time is 0.09 seconds. In other words, the For loop that uses an integer variable for the loop variable (Figure 8.10) executes 20 times faster than the same For loop that uses a single-precision variable for the loop variable (Figure 8.9). Hence, if you desire to speed up the execution of For loops in your program, you should declare the loop variable as type integer. From now on, we will declare all our loop variables to be type integer unless decimal fraction values are used.

In the partial programs in Figures 8.9 and 8.10, line 6 sets the variable Start to the value returned by the TIMER function. At the conclusion of each loop, the variable Finish is set equal to TIMER. In both programs, line 11 assigns Duration the time required to execute the particular loop.

Random Number Function and the RANDOMIZE Statement

The RND **function** is important to the programmer involved in the development of programs that simulate situations described by a random process. The owners of a shopping mall, for example, may want a program written to simulate the number of cars that would enter their parking lots during a particular period of the day. Or, perhaps the manager of a grocery store wants a program to model unpredictable values that represent people standing in line waiting to check out. The unpredictable values could be supplied by the RND function. Actually, the random numbers generated by the PC are provided by a repeatable process, and for this reason they often are called **pseudo-random numbers**.

The RND **function** returns an unpredictable decimal fraction number between 0 (inclusive) and 1 (exclusive). Each time the function is referenced, any number between 0 and less than 1 has an equal probability of being returned by the function. For example, the statement

```
Random = RND
```

assigns Random a random number. The partial program in Figure 8.11 illustrates the generation of five random numbers.

FIGURE 8.11

Generating random numbers.

```
1    ' Generating Random Numbers
2    ' *************************
3    CLS   ' Clear Screen
4    FOR I% = 1 TO 5
5       PRINT RND,
6    NEXT I%

     [run]

      .7151002    .683111    .4821425    .9992938    .6465093
```

Each time the RND function is referenced in line 5, a random number between 0 and < 1 is displayed.

The INT and RND functions can be combined to create random digits over a specified range. The following expression allows for the generation of random digits over the range C < n < D:

```
INT((D - C + 1) * RND + C)
```

For example, to generate random digits over the range 1 to 10, inclusive, change line 5 in Figure 8.11 to

```
PRINT INT((10 - 1 + 1) * RND + 1)
```

or

```
PRINT INT(10 * RND + 1)
```

The partial program in Figure 8.12 simulates tossing a coin 20 times. The expression INT (2 * RND) returns a zero (heads) or a one (tails). The expression in line 7 returned 12 zeros (heads) and 8 ones (tails).

FIGURE 8.12

Using the RND function to simulate coin tosses.

```
1    ' Simulation of Coin Tossing
2    ' 0 is a Head and 1 is a Tail
3    ' The Coin is Tossed 20 Times
4    ' **************************
5    CLS   ' Clear Screen
6    FOR I% = 1 TO 20
7       PRINT INT(2 * RND);
8    NEXT I%

     [run]

      1 0 1 0 0 0 1 1 0 1 0 0 0 0 1 0 0 1 1 0
```

The partial program in Figure 8.12 can be enhanced to allow a user to enter the number of simulated coin tosses desired and to display the total number of heads and tails. This is illustrated in the partial program in Figure 8.13 on the next page.

FIGURE 8.13

Enhanced program using the RND function to simulate coin tosses.

```
1    ' Simulation of Coin Tossing
2    ' 0 is a Head and 1 is a Tail
3    ' User Enters Number of Times Coin is Tossed
4    ' ********************************************
5    CLS  ' Clear Screen
6    Head = 0
7    Tail = 0
8    INPUT "How many tosses ===> ", Tosses
9    FOR Number% = 1 TO Tosses
10       Rand.No = INT(2 * RND)
11       IF Rand.No = 0 THEN
12          Head = Head + 1
13       ELSE
14          Tail = Tail + 1
15       END IF
16   NEXT Number%
17   PRINT "Number of Heads ===>"; Head
18   PRINT "Number of Tails ===>"; Tail


[run]


How many tosses ===> 500
Number of Heads ===> 259
Number of Tails ===> 241
```

When executed, the partial program in Figure 8.13 requests the user to enter the number of coin tosses to be simulated. Depending on the value assigned to Rand.No, line 11 determines whether to increment Head (head counter) or Tail (tail counter) by 1. At the conclusion of the For loop, lines 17 and 18 display the total number of heads and total number of tails. As illustrated by the results of the partial program in Figure 8.13, out of 500 simulated coin tosses, 259 are heads and 241 are tails.

Every time this partial program is executed, it will display the same results because the PC generates random numbers from a starting value called the **seed**. Unless the seed is changed, the PC continues to generate the same set of random numbers in the same sequence each time the same program is executed. When a program containing the RND function is ready for production, the RANDOMIZE **statement** can be used to instruct the PC to generate random numbers from a different seed each time the program is executed. The general form of the RANDOMIZE statement is shown in Table 8.19.

TABLE 8.19 - The RANDOMIZE Statement	
General Form:	RANDOMIZE or RANDOMIZE Numeric expression
Purpose:	To supply a new seed for the generation of random numbers by the RND function.
Examples:	RANDOMIZE RANDOMIZE TIMER RANDOMIZE 396.5 RANDOMIZE VAL(RIGHT$(TIME$,2))
Note:	If you do not include a parameter following the keyword RANDOMIZE, then the PC suspends execution of the program and requests a value between –32768 and 32767.

The rule for the execution of the RANDOMIZE statement in a program follows:

RANDOMIZE RULE 1	*The* RANDOMIZE *statement must be executed prior to any reference to the* RND *function.*

PROGRAMMING CASE STUDY 16 – Guess a Number between 1 and 100

The RND function can be used in a program to instruct the PC to simulate a popular guessing game in which the player attempts to guess a number between 1 and 100. Incorporating the RANDOMIZE statement ensures that the RND function will return a new set of random numbers each time the program is executed.

Figure 8.14 presents the solution to Programming Case Study 16, Program 8.4. A discussion of the program solution follows the figure.

FIGURE 8.14

Program 8.4, the solution to Programming Case Study 16.

```
1    ' Program 8.4
2    ' Guess a Number Between 1 and 100
3    ' ***********************************************
4    ' *                Main Program                 *
5    ' ***********************************************
6    GOSUB A100.Initialization:
7    GOSUB B100.Guess.Number:
8    GOSUB C100.Wrap.Up:
9    END
10
11   ' ***********************************************
12   ' *               Initialization                *
13   ' ***********************************************
14   A100.Initialization:
15      CLS  ' Clear Screen
16      RANDOMIZE TIMER
17      Random.Number = INT(100 * RND + 1)
18      PRINT "***********************************"
19      PRINT "*                                 *"
20      PRINT "* Guess a number between 1 and 100. *"
21      PRINT "* I will tell you if your guess is  *"
22      PRINT "* too high or too low.              *"
23      PRINT "*                                 *"
24      PRINT "***********************************"
25      PRINT
26   RETURN
27
28   ' ***********************************************
29   ' *               Guess a Number                *
30   ' ***********************************************
31   B100.Guess.Number:
32      INPUT "Guess a number ====> ", Guess
33      Guess.Count = 1
34      DO WHILE Guess <> Random.Number
35         IF Guess > Random.Number THEN
36            PRINT "Too High"
37         ELSE
38            PRINT "Too Low"
39         END IF
40         INPUT "Guess a number ====> ", Guess
41         Guess.Count = Guess.Count + 1
42      LOOP
43   RETURN
44
```

(continued)

FIGURE 8.14
(continued)

```
45   ' ***********************************************
46   ' *                   Wrap-Up                   *
47   ' ***********************************************
48   C100.Wrap.Up:
49      PRINT : PRINT "Your guess is correct."
50      PRINT "It took you"; Guess.Count; "guesses."
51   RETURN
52   ' ************* End of Program *****************
```

[run]

Discussion of the Program Solution

When Program 8.4 is executed, line 16 in A100.Initialization ensures that the program does not generate the same set of random numbers it generated the last time the program was executed. The seed is based on the value returned by the TIMER function. The chances of generating the same set of random numbers from one run of Program 8.4 to the next are very small.

Line 17 assigns Random.Number the number to be guessed (94 in this case). Lines 18 through 24 display the instructions for the game as shown at the top of the screen in Figure 8.15. Line 32 in B100.Guess.Number accepts a value for Guess from the user. Line 33 sets the guess counter (Guess.Count) to 1. If Guess is equal to Random.Number in line 34, the program terminates after one guess. If Guess does not equal Random.Number, the PC executes the Do-While loop and displays an appropriate message before requesting the next guess and incrementing Guess.Count. When the user finally guesses the number, control passes to C100.Wrap.Up, and a message and the value of Guess.Count display.

FIGURE 8.15

The display due to the execution of Program 8.4.

```
*************************************
* Guess a number between 1 and 100. *
* I will tell you if your guess is  *
* too high or too low.              *
*                                   *
*************************************

Guess a number ====> 50
Too Low
Guess a number ====> 75
Too Low
Guess a number ====> 87
Too Low
Guess a number ====> 95
Too High
Guess a number ====> 93
Too Low
Guess a number ====> 94

Your guess is correct.
It took you 6 guesses.
```

8.4 USER-DEFINED FUNCTIONS

In addition to numeric and string functions, QBasic allows you to define new string or numeric functions that relate to a particular application. This type of function, known as a **user-defined function**, is written directly into the program. The user-defined function may be written as a one-line statement or as a series of statements. One way QBasic recognizes a user-defined function is by the keywords DEF FN, for *define function,* which initiate the function in the program. For example, the DEF FN statement

```
DEF FNY(X) = X * (X + 1) / 2
```

defines a one-line, user-defined function, x(x + 1) / 2, whose name is FNY. The parentheses following the name of the function surround a simple variable known as a **function parameter**. The expression to the right of the equal sign indicates which operations are to be performed with the value of X when the function is referenced in such statements as LET, PRINT, LPRINT, CASE SELECT, and IF. For example, either

```
Result = FNY(Value) + 5
```

or

```
PRINT FNY(Part / 3)
```

found in the same program with the user-defined function FNY described earlier will reference the FNY function.

Multiple-line, user-defined functions allow the user to define more complex algorithms. When more than one line is required, the user-defined function ends with the END DEF statement. The following user-defined function includes an IF statement that returns the value ON or OFF, depending on the value of Amount:

```
DEF FNSWITCH$(Amount)
    IF Amount > 500 THEN
        FNSWITCH$ = "ON"
    ELSE
        FNSWITCH$ = "OFF"
    END IF
END DEF
```

The following statement uses the FNSWITCH$ function to assign Flag$ the value ON or OFF, depending on the value of the variable Cost:

```
Flag$ = FNSWITCH$(Cost)
```

Defining your own function reduces programming effort and makes your program compact and efficient. Instead of writing a common formula or algorithm over and over again, you simply define it once as a function, give it a name, and then reference it by that name whenever you need it.

The DEF FN Statement

Table 8.20 on the next page shows that the DEF FN **statement** permits the creation of user-defined functions. The name of the function follows DEF, and it must begin with the two letters FN, followed by a variable name that is consistent with the rules used for naming variables. When subprograms are used, the DEF FN must be placed in the Main Program; that is, you cannot define a function in a subprogram. Subprograms are discussed in Chapter 11.

TABLE 8.20 - The DEF Statement

General Form:

```
DEF FNx(p₁ , ..., pₙ) = expression
```

or

```
DEF FNx(p₁ , ..., pₙ)
    [range of statements]
END DEF
```

where **x** is a simple variable that must agree in type with the expression, and **p₁ through pₙ** are simple variables called function parameters.

Purpose:

To define a function that is relevant to a particular application that can be referenced as frequently as needed in the program in which it is defined. In the second general form, the function FNx must be assigned a value by one of the statements within the multiple-line function.

Examples:

```
1.  DEF FNCUBE(Y, Z) = Y ^ 3 + Z ^ 3
2.  DEF FNPI = 3.141593
3.  DEF FNSUB$(Stng$, P, H) = MID$(Stng$, P, N)
4.  DEF FNFUTUREVALUE(P, I, C, N)
      I = R / C
      M = C * N
      FNFUTUREVALUE = P * (1 + I) ^ M
    END DEF
```

Notes:

1. To be consistent with the QBasic functions, capitalizing all letters in the name of the function is recommended.

2. A user-defined numeric function is declared integer, long integer, single precision, or double precision on the basis of the following:

Special Character Appended to Name	Type
Percent Sign (%)	Integer
Ampersand (&)	Long Integer
Exclamation Point (!) or no special character	Single precision
Number Sign (#)	Double precision

The parameters in a user-defined function are called **dummy variables** because they are assigned the values of the corresponding arguments when reference is made to the function. For example, the following partial program contains two user-defined functions. The first one rounds the value assigned to Number to the nearest cent. The second one truncates the value assigned to Number to the nearest cent.

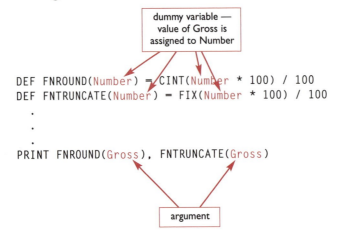

```
                 dummy variable —
                 value of Gross is
                 assigned to Number

DEF FNROUND(Number) = CINT(Number * 100) / 100
DEF FNTRUNCATE(Number) = FIX(Number * 100) / 100
    .
    .
    .
PRINT FNROUND(Gross), FNTRUNCATE(Gross)

                      argument
```

The value of the variable Gross in the PRINT statement is used in place of the variable Number when the first user-defined function FNROUND is called. The same applies when the user-defined function FNTRUNCATE is called by the second item in the PRINT statement.

It is possible to define functions through the use of variables other than the parameters because variables used within the body of a DEF FN statement are global to the program. **Global** means that a variable name in both the user-defined function and in the calling program or subroutine references the same storage location. For example, in the following partial program

```
DEF FNC(A) = A * B * C
    .
    .
    .
READ A, B, C
```

the variables A, B, and C in the DEF FN are the same as the variables A, B, and C in the READ statement. That is, when the READ statement is executed, the variables A, B, and C in the DEF FN statement are assigned values.

A function with no parameters may be defined. Such functions may be used to define constants or expressions that do not require a variable, as shown below:

```
DEF FNPI#    = 3.14159265
DEF FNCENTI  = 2.54
DEF FNRANDOM = INT(10 * RND + 1)
```

The first user-defined function defines FNPI# equal to pi (π) in double precision. FNCENTI is defined to be equal to the number of centimeters in an inch. FNRANDOM returns a random number between 1 and 10.

The rules regarding DEF FN statements in a program follow.

DEF FN RULE 1 — *A user-defined function must be located in the Main Program in such a way that it is evaluated by the PC before it is called.*

DEF FN RULE 2 — *The same user-defined function may be defined as often as required. The last definition executed is used.*

DEF FN RULE 3 — *A user-defined function definition cannot reference itself.*

DEF FN RULE 4 — *A multiple-line, user-defined function must include a statement that assigns the function name a value.*

QBasic also allows the user to define functions using the FUNCTION statement. (For a comparison between the DEF FN and FUNCTION statements, see Section 11.4 in Chapter 11.)

Referencing User-Defined Functions

User-defined functions are referenced in the same way as numeric functions. The following program determines the effective rates of interest for the nominal rates 5.5%, 6.5%, 7.5%, 8.5%, and 9.5%, using the following formula:

$$R = \left(1 + \frac{J}{C}\right)^c - 1$$

where R is the effective rate;
C is the number of conversions per year; and
J is the nominal rate.

The partial program in Figure 8.16 calculates and displays the effective rates to two decimal places for nominal rates converted semiannually, quarterly, monthly, and daily. (Assume 365 days per year.)

FIGURE 8.16

Referencing a user-defined function.

```
 1   ' Determining the Effective Rate of Interest
 2   ' Using a User-Defined Function
 3   ' **********************************************
 4   DEF FNRATE(Comp) = 100 * ((1 + Rate / (Comp * 100)) ^ Comp - 1)
 5   CLS  ' Clear Screen
 6   PRINT "                    Effective Rates Compounded"
 7   PRINT "             ----------------------------------------"
 8   PRINT "Nominal Rate   Semiannually  Quarterly  Monthly  Daily"
 9   PRINT "------------   ------------  ---------  -------  -----"
10   D1$ = "   ##.##         ##.#        ##.##     ##.##    ##.##"
11   FOR Rate = 5.5 TO 9.5
12      PRINT USING D1$; Rate; FNRATE(2), FNRATE(4), FNRATE(12), FNRATE(365)
13   NEXT Rate
14   PRINT : PRINT "End of Report"

     [run]
```

function definition

function references

When the partial program in Figure 8.16 is executed, the display shown in Figure 8.17 is generated. The usefulness of the DEF FN statement is apparent in this program. Instead of having to code the formula four times to determine the corresponding effective rates for a nominal rate, the DEF FN statement allows you to code the formula once (line 4) and then reference it four times (line 12). The constant used as the argument in each function reference in line 12 is assigned to Comp in the DEF FN statement in line 4.

FIGURE 8.17

The display due to the execution of the partial program in Figure 8.16.

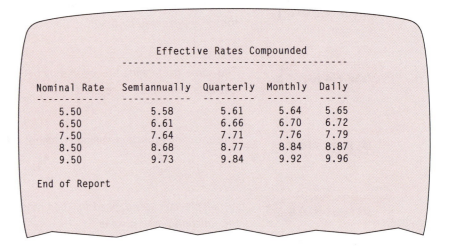

```
                    Effective Rates Compounded
             ----------------------------------------

Nominal Rate   Semiannually  Quarterly  Monthly  Daily
------------   ------------  ---------  -------  -----
    5.50           5.58         5.61      5.64    5.65
    6.50           6.61         6.66      6.70    6.72
    7.50           7.64         7.71      7.76    7.79
    8.50           8.68         8.77      8.84    8.87
    9.50           9.73         9.84      9.92    9.96

End of Report
```

PROGRAMMING CASE STUDY 17 – Computer Simulation – Beat the House Roller

The following programming case study incorporates the use of both the RND function and a user-defined function.

Problem: Beat the House Roller is a simple but popular dice game in which the house roller throws a pair of dice. The customer then throws the dice, trying to roll a higher score. If the customer rolls a lower score or the same score as the house roller, the house wins. The imaginary bet is $5.00 for each game.

An accumulator is included to keep track of the customer's winnings. Also, the customer's winnings are displayed at the end of each roll. A means of temporarily stopping the game is included so that the customer can decide if he or she desires to continue playing. On the following pages are an analysis of the problem, a program solution, and a discussion of the program solution.

Program Tasks

1. Main Module
   a. Call appropriate subroutines.

2. A100.Initialization
   a. Reseed the random number generator.
   b. Use the following user-defined function to generate random numbers between 1 and 6 to represent the sides of a die:
      ```
      DEF FNRANDOM = INT(6 * RND + 1)
      ```
   c. Set Winnings to zero.

3. B100.Roll.Dice — Establish a Do-Until loop to do the following:
   a. Reference the user-defined function FNRANDOM twice in succession for the house roller. Determine the customer's score in the same manner. Display both scores.
   b. Determine the winner, and increment or decrement Winnings by $5.00.
   c. Display Winnings.

4. C100.Wrap.Up — Display a message on the basis of the customer's winnings. If the customer owes money, display the message, Better luck next time! If the customer does not owe any money, display the message, You are pretty lucky!

Program Solution

The solution to Programming Case Study 17, Program 8.5, is presented in Figure 8.18 and corresponds to the preceding tasks.

FIGURE 8.18

The solution to Programming Case Study 17, Program 8.5.

```
 1   ' Program 8.5
 2   ' Computer-Simulated Dice Game
 3   ' ****************************************
 4   ' *              Main Program            *
 5   ' ****************************************
 6   GOSUB A100.Initialization
 7   GOSUB B100.Roll.Dice
 8   GOSUB C100.Wrap.Up
 9   END
10
11   ' ****************************************
12   ' *              Initialization          *
13   ' ****************************************
14   A100.Initialization:
15      CLS   ' Clear Screen
16      RANDOMIZE TIMER
17      DEF FNRANDOM = INT(6 * RND + 1)
18      Winnings = 0
19   RETURN
20
```

(continued)

FIGURE 8.18
(continued)

```
21    ' *******************************
22    ' *          Roll The Dice            *
23    ' *******************************
24    B100.Roll.Dice:
25       DO
26          ' **** Determine House Roller Score ****
27          House = FNRANDOM + FNRANDOM
28          PRINT : PRINT "The house rolls =======>"; House
29          ' **** Determine the Customer's Score ****
30          Customer = FNRANDOM + FNRANDOM
31          PRINT "Your score ==============>"; Customer
32          ' **** Determine the Winner ****
33          IF Customer > House THEN
34             Winnings = Winnings + 5
35          ELSE
36             Winnings = Winnings - 5
37          END IF
38          PRINT USING "Your winnings ===========>$$##.##"; Winnings
39          INPUT "Enter Y to roll the dice again, else N... ", Control$
40       LOOP UNTIL UCASE$(Control$) = "N"
41    RETURN
42
43    ' *****************************************
44    ' *                Wrap-Up                  *
45    ' *****************************************
46    C100.Wrap.Up:
47       PRINT : PRINT
48       IF Winnings > 0 THEN
49          PRINT "You are pretty lucky!"
50       ELSE
51          PRINT "Better luck next time!"
52       END IF
53    RETURN
54    ' ************ End of Program *************
```

```
[run]

The house rolls =======> 6
Your score ==============> 9
Your winnings ===========> $5.00
Enter Y to roll the dice again, else N... Y

The house rolls =======> 7
Your score ==============> 11
Your winnings ===========> $10.00
Enter Y to roll the dice again, else N... Y

The house rolls =======> 7
Your score ==============> 4
Your winnings ===========> $5.00
Enter Y to roll the dice again, else N... Y

The house rolls =======> 9
Your score ==============> 11
Your winnings ===========> $10.00
Enter Y to roll the dice again, else N... N

You are pretty lucky!
```

Discussion of the Program Solution

The solution to the Computer-Simulated Dice Game is represented by Program 8.5, which includes the following significant points:

1. Line 17 of A100.Initialization defines a function that is referenced four times (lines 27 and 30 of B100.Roll.Dice) for each pass through the loop.
2. Line 33 of B100.Roll.Dice tests to determine whether the running total, Winnings, should be incremented or decremented by $5.00.
3. Lines 48 through 52 of C100.Wrap.Up display an end-of-game message. The message displayed depends on the value of Winnings.

8.5 TRAPPING EVENTS

Some applications require the PC to halt execution of a subroutine and execute a subroutine when a specific event has occurred. The RETURN statement in the subroutine transfers control back to the line label the PC was about to execute when control was transferred to the subroutine. Table 8.21 summarizes specific **event-trapping statements** that are available in QBasic.

TABLE 8.21 - A Summary of Event-Trapping Statements*	
STATEMENT	**PURPOSE**
ON COM(n) GOSUB label	Transfers control to label when data fills the communications buffer (n).
ON KEY(n) GOSUB label	Transfers control to label when the function key or cursor control key (n) is pressed.
ON PEN GOSUB label	Transfers control to label when the light pen is activated.
ON PLAY(n) GOSUB label	Transfers control to label when a note (n) is sensed. Plays continuous background music.
ON STRIG(n) GOSUB label	Transfers control to label when one of the joystick buttons (n) is pressed.
ON TIMER(n) GOSUB label	Transfers control to label when the specified period of time (n) in seconds has passed.

* Label can be a line label or line number.

Execute event-trapping statements prior to the first possible occurrence of the event, and place the statement at the beginning of A100.Initialization.

All the statements in Table 8.21 require the execution of a second statement to activate the trap. The corresponding statement that activates the trap for the ON KEY(n) GOSUB statement is KEY ON(n). Consider the following:

```
ON KEY(3) GOSUB Function.Key.F3
KEY(3) ON
```

The first line informs the PC of the subroutine to branch to when the F3 key is pressed. The second line instructs the PC to begin checking for the event that is specified in the first line.

When the F3 key is pressed following the execution of the two lines, the PC saves the location of the line it was about to execute. It then executes the subroutine Function.Key.F3. The RETURN statement transfers control to the location of the line saved by the PC when the event was encountered.

As another example, consider the use of the ON TIMER(n) GOSUB statement. In some menu-driven applications, it is useful to display an accurate system time on the screen. The partial program in Figure 8.19 on the next page illustrates how you can instruct the PC to refresh the time displayed on the screen every five seconds without interfering with the interaction between the user and the program.

FIGURE 8.19

An example of refreshing the time displayed on the screen every five seconds.

```
 1    ' ************************************************
 2    ' *                 Main Program                *
 3    ' ************************************************
 4    GOSUB A100.Initialization
         .
         .
         .
 5    END
 6
 7    ' ************************************************
 8    '                Initialization
 9    ' ************************************************
10    A100.Initialization:
11       CLS  ' Clear Screen
12       LOCATE 1, 70: PRINT TIME$
13       ON TIMER(5) GOSUB M200.Refresh.Time
14       TIMER ON
15    RETURN
         .
         .
         .
16    ' ************************************************
17    '             Refresh Time Subroutine           *
18    ' ************************************************
19    M200.Refresh.Time:
20       Row = CSRLIN
21       Col = POS(0)
22       LOCATE 1, 70: PRINT TIME$
23       LOCATE Row, Col
24    RETURN

    [run]
```

Line 11 clears the screen, and line 12 displays the system time in the format hh:mm:ss. Line 13 establishes the subroutine to branch to every five seconds. Note that n, the time interval, is specified in seconds. The value n may range between 1 and 86,400. The upper limit of n is equal to the number of seconds in 24 hours.

Line 14 activates the interval timer trap. Thereafter, as long as the program is executing, the PC branches to the subroutine M200.Refresh.Time every five seconds and refreshes the time displayed on the screen.

If you desire, you may decrease the value of n, the time interval, to three seconds or something smaller to display the time more frequently and more accurately. However, be aware that if the value of n is too small, the performance of your program may degrade because the PC is being used to frequently update the time on the screen.

Note how the CSRLIN and POS functions are used in lines 20 and 21 to determine the current position of the cursor. Then in line 23, the cursor is moved back to the position it had before control passed to the subroutine.

You may also instruct the PC to turn off an event or to continue keeping track of the event but bypass trapping it. For example,

    TIMER OFF

causes the PC to stop tracking TIMER activity, and no trapping takes place. The following statement

    TIMER STOP

also instructs the PC to disregard trapping the interval timer. However, with the latter statement, TIMER activity is still tracked, so an immediate trap occurs when TIMER ON is later executed.

8.6 What You Should Know

1. QBasic includes several string functions and string statements that place it among the better programming languages for manipulating letters, numbers, words, and phrases. (See Table 8.1 on page 300 for a list of the string functions.)
2. The MID$ statement replaces a substring within a string.
3. The DATE$ and TIME$ statements may be used to set the system date and time.
4. The LINE INPUT statement accepts an entire line from the keyboard as a string value and assigns it to a specified string variable name.
5. QBasic includes numeric functions to handle common mathematical calculations. (See Table 8.15 on page 317 for a list of the most frequently used numeric functions.)
6. The RANDOMIZE statement supplies a new seed for the generation of random numbers by the RND function.
7. In addition to the built-in functions, QBasic allows you to define other numeric and string functions that relate to a particular application. This second type of function, known as a user-defined function, is written directly into the program.
8. User-defined functions begin with the keyword DEF FN. If the function is more than one line long, then the definition ends with an END DEF statement.
9. All user-defined function names begin with the two letters FN, followed by a variable name that is consistent with the rules used for naming numeric variables.
10. User-defined functions must be defined in the same program in which they are called. Furthermore, when the program is executed, user-defined functions must be evaluated before they are called.
11. User-defined functions are called upon in a LET, PRINT, LPRINT, CASE SELECT, or IF statement in the same way that numeric and string functions are called upon.
12. QBasic includes several event-trapping statements that instruct the PC to interrupt its normal execution of a program and execute a subroutine when a certain event has occurred.

8.7 Test Your QBasic Skills (Even-numbered answers are in Appendix E)

1. Consider the valid programs below. What is displayed if each program is executed?

    a.
    ```
    ' Exercise 8.1a
    CLS ' Clear Screen
    State$ = "Michigan"
    FOR I% = 1 TO LEN(State$)
       LOCATE I%, I%: PRINT LEFT$(State$, I%)
    NEXT I%
    END
    ```

    b. Assume that the system time is exactly 11:45:03.

    ```
    ' Exercise 8.1b
    Clock = VAL(LEFT$(TIME$, 2))
    IF Clock < 12 THEN
       Id$ = "am"
       IF Clock = 0 THEN
          Clock = 12
       END IF
    ELSE
       Id$ = "pm"
       IF Clock <> 12 THEN
          Clock = Clock - 12
       END IF
    END IF
    Tim$ = STR$(Clock) + MID$(TIME$, 3, 6) + SPACE$(1) + Id$
    PRINT "The time is "; Tim$
    END
    ```

c.
```
' Exercise 8.1c
Code$ = "08<NC74NOAA>FN20A45D;;H"
CLS    'Clear screen
PRINT "Coded message =====>"; Code$
PRINT : PRINT "The message is ====> ";
FOR I% = 1 to LEN(Code$)
    Mesg = ASC(MID$(Code$, I%, 1))
    Mesg = Mesg + 17
    Char$ = CHR$(Mesg)
    PRINT LCASE$(Char$);
NEXT I%
END
```

d.
```
' Exercise 8.1d
CLS ' Clear Screen
Phrase1$ = "TODAY IS THE TOMORROW YOU "
Phrase2$ = "WORRIED ABOUT YESTERDAY"
Phrase3$ = Phrase1$ + Phrase2$
LOCATE 12, 15: PRINT LEFT$(Phrase3$, 1);
FOR I% = 2 TO LEN(Phrase3$)
    Upper = ASC(MID$(Phrase3$, I%, 1))
    IF Upper <> 32 THEN
        Upper = Upper + 32
    END IF
    Lower$ = CHR$(Upper)
    PRINT Lower$;
NEXT I%
PRINT "."
END
```

2. Evaluate each of the following. Assume that Phr$ is equal to the following string:

```
If I have ran further it is because I have been carried in the arms of giants
```

a. LEN(Phr$)

b. RIGHT$(Phr$, 100)

c. LEFT$(Phr$, 5)

d. MID$(Phr$, 11, 3)

e. VAL("36.8")

f. ASC(MID$(Phr$, 4, 1))

g. CHR$(71)

h. STRING$(14, "A")

i. STR$(-13.691)

j. INSTR(10, Phr$, "u")

k. MID$(Phr$, 72, 7) = "friends"

l. SPACE$(4)

3. Evaluate each of the following. Assume that Num is equal to 2 and that Phr$ is equal to the following string:

```
Programming is a lot of fun
```

a. LEN(Phr$)

b. RIGHT$(Phr$, 3)

c. RIGHT$(Phr$, 30)

d. LEFT$(Phr$, 50)

e. LEFT$(Phr$, 1.5)

f. LEFT$(Phr$, Num)

g. MID$(Phr$, Num, 3)

h. MID$(Phr$, Num^3, 2)

i. MID$(Phr$, 1, 5 * Num)

j. INSTR(Phr$, "is")

k. INSTR(Num, Phr$, "t")

l. INSTR(2 * Num, Phr$, "r")

4. Evaluate each of the following:

a. VAL("99")

b. ASC("+")

c. CHR$(63)

d. STR$(44.5)

e. CLS : PRINT CSRLIN

f. PRINT UCASE$("xyz")

g. CHR$(37)

h. ASC(":")

i. PRINT TAB(15); POS(0)

j. LOCATE 23, 41: PRINT POS(0) + CSRLIN

5. What does the following program display when executed? What value must be assigned to Control$ to terminate the program?

```
' Exercise 8.5
Char$ = "r"
Control$ = ""
DO WHILE Control$ <> "&"
   FOR I% = 1 To 80
      PRINT Char$;
   NEXT I%
   Control$ = INKEY$
   IF Control$ <> "" THEN
      Char$ = Control$
   END IF
LOOP
END
```

6. Using the concepts in this chapter, write a series of statements that will display the sum of the digits in the customer number Num$. Assume that Num$ is equal to the string value 2587.

7. Assuming that the system time is exactly 11:59:59 p.m. and that the system date is December 1, 2002, evaluate each of the following:

   a. Clock$ = TIME$ b. Day$ = DATE$ c. Sec = TIMER

8. What does the following program display when executed? Explain the algorithm that is used in this program.

```
' Exercise 8.8
CLS ' Clear Screen
PRINT "Prime numbers between 1 and 100 -";
PRINT 2;
FOR I% = 3 TO 100
   FOR K% = 2 TO INT(SQR(I%))
      IF I% MOD K% = 0 THEN
         K% = 12
      END IF
   NEXT K%
   IF K% < 12 THEN
      PRINT I%;
   END IF
NEXT I%
END
```

9. What does the following program display when executed?

```
' Exercise 8.9
CLS ' Clear Screen
FOR K% = 1 TO 24
   FOR J% = 1 TO 10
      LOCATE 12, 36: PRINT "Wake Up ";
      FOR I% = 1 TO 5
         PRINT CHR$(7);
      NEXT I%
   NEXT J%
   PRINT
NEXT K%
END
```

10. Write a single QBasic statement for each of the following. Use numeric functions wherever possible. Assume that the value of X is a real number.

    a. $p = \sqrt{a^2 + b^2}$

    b. $b = \sqrt{|\tan X - 0.51|}$

    c. $q = 8 \cos^2 X + 4 \sin X$

    d. $y = e^X + \log_e (1 + X)$

11. What is the numeric value of each of the following?

    a. `INT(-18.5)`

    b. `ABS(-3)`

    c. `INT(16.9)`

    d. `ABS(6.7)`

    e. `EXP(1)`

    f. `LOG(0)`

12. Write separate QBasic statements for each of the following:

    a. Determine the sign of $2X^3 + 3X + 5$.

    b. Determine the integer part of $4X + 5$.

    c. Round X to two decimal places, then to one decimal place.

13. Write a program that displays the values for X and `SIN X` where X varies between 0° and 180°. Increment X in steps of 5.

14. Explain the purpose of the `POS`, `CSRLIN`, and `SCREEN` functions.

15. Characterize the four methods of accepting input through the keyboard — `INPUT`, `LINE INPUT`, `INKEY$`, and `INPUT$(N)` — in terms of suspension of program execution, type and length of data that may be assigned, and whether the Enter key must be pressed.

16. Write a program that will generate and display 100 random numbers between 1 and 75, inclusive.

17. Explain the purpose of the `RANDOMIZE` statement. Why is the `TIMER` function a good choice for determining the seed?

18. Write a user-defined function that will determine a 10% discount on the amount of purchase (Purchase) in excess of $200.00. The discount applies to the excess, not the entire purchase.

19. Explain the function of the following partial program:

```
ON KEY(5) GOSUB M200.Function.Key.F5
KEY(5) ON
```

20. Is the following program valid or invalid? If it is valid, indicate the output. If it is invalid, indicate why.

```
' Exercise 8.20
DEF FNW(B) = B * 6
DEF FNA(B) = FNW(B) - 2
DEF FNX(B) = FNA(B) * 2
PRINT FNX(4)
END
```

21. Given the following program:

```
' Exercise 8.21
FOR I% = 1 TO 5
    READ X
    PRINT TAB(5); X, (complete this portion)
NEXT I%
DATA 1.1, 10000.5, 100.3, 1000.4, 10.2
END
```

Complete the PRINT statement so that the results displayed in the second column are right justified, as shown below:

```
1.1                    1.1
10000.5             10000.5
100.3                100.3
1000.4              1000.4
10.2                  10.2
```

Do not use the PRINT USING statement.

(**Hint:** Use the LOG function.)

22. **PC Hands-On Exercise:** Enter the partial program in Figure 8.3 on page 305. In line 8, change the string ne to en. Execute the program and compare the results to those displayed in Figure 8.3.

23. **PC Hands-On Exercise:** Load Program 8.1 (PRG8-1) from the Data Disk. Delete lines 25 through 27 and insert the following statement in place of line 28:

```
PRINT LCASE$(CHR$(ASC(MID$(CODE$, CHAR, 1)) - 3));
```

Execute the program and enter the following coded message:

ZKR#LV#WKH#VKDGRZB

Do you agree that it is valid to have functions as the arguments of other functions?

24. **PC Hands-On Exercise:** Load Program 8.3 (PRG8-3) from the Data Disk. Change the argument of the LOG function in line 49 to 10 so that the PC determines the number of years it takes to increase an investment tenfold at the given interest rates. Execute the program.

25. **PC Hands-On Exercise:** Load Program 8.4 (PRG8-4) from the Data Disk and try your luck at guessing a number between 1 and 100. If you get bored with the game, modify PRG8-4, lines 17 and 20, to guess a number between 1 and 1,000.

26. **PC Hands-On Exercise:** Load Program 8.5 (PRG8-5) from the Data Disk. Execute the program and try your luck at Beat the House Roller.

8.8 QBasic Programming Problems

1. Palindromes

Purpose: To become familiar with the manipulation of strings through the use of the LEN and MID$ functions.

Problem: A palindrome is a word or phrase that is the same when read either backward or forward. For example, NOON is a palindrome, but MOON is not. Write a top-down program that requests the user to enter a string of uppercase characters and then determines whether the string is a palindrome or not.

Input Data: Use the following sample data:

9876556789
ABLE WAS I ERE I SAW ELBA
I
BOB DAD BOB
WOW LIL DAD POP
WORDS ARE BACKWARDS AND FORWARDS
PROFESSOR OTTO ROSSEFORP
RADAR
!@#$$@#!
()
A PROGRAM IS A MIRROR IMAGE OF THE MIND

Output Results: Figure 8.20 illustrates partial output results.

FIGURE 8.20

Partial output results for Programming Problem 1.

```
String? 9876556789
9876556789 is a palindrome.

Enter Y to continue, else N... Y


    .
    .
    .


String? A PROGRAM IS A MIRROR IMAGE OF THE MIND
A PROGRAM IS A MIRROR IMAGE OF THE MIND is not a palindrome.

Enter Y to continue, else N... N
```

2. English to Pig-Latin Conversion

Purpose: To become familiar with string manipulation.

Problem: In pig Latin, a word such as computer is converted to omputercay. For this problem, the translation from English to pig Latin calls for taking the first consonant of the word and moving it to the end of the word, followed by an appended "ay." If a word begins with a vowel, then the vowel remains in its beginning position, and the string "way" is appended to the end of the word. For example, apple becomes appleway.

Write a top-down program that displays the pig Latin translation for a string of English words (uppercase). Also display the number of words that begin with a vowel, the total number of words in the string, and the percentage of words that begin with a vowel. Do not include punctuation.

Input Data: Use the following sample data. Do not press the Enter key until you have entered the entire phrase.

LIKE A RIVER A PERSON WHO TAKES THE COURSE OF LEAST RESISTANCE WILL END UP CROOKED

Output Results: Figure 8.21 illustrates the output for Programming Problem 2.

```
Enter the English Sentence without Punctuation
-------------------------------------------------
LIKE A RIVER A PERSON WHO TAKES THE COURSE OF LEAST RESISTANCE
WILL END UP CROOKED

The Sentence in Pig Latin is:
-----------------------------
IKELAY AWAY IVERRAY AWAY ERSONPAY HOWAY AKESTAY HETAY OURSECAY
OFWAY EASTLAY ESISTANCERAY ILLWAY ENDWAY UPWAY ROOKEDCAY

Words beginning with a vowel ========>     5
Total number of words ===============>    16
Percentage beginning with a vowel ===>    31.25000

Job Complete
```

3. Time to Double an Investment Compounded Quarterly

Purpose: To become familiar with the use of numeric functions and user-defined functions, and the concepts of rounding and truncation.

Problem: Write a top-down program that will determine the time it takes to double an investment compounded quarterly for the following annual interest rates: 4%, 5%, 6%, and 7%. The formula for computing the time is as follows:

$$N = \frac{\log 2}{M(\log(1 + J/M))}$$

where N = time in years
J = annual interest rate
M = number of conversion periods

After the time has been determined for a given interest rate, use the generalized expressions for rounding and truncation given on page 318 in Section 8.3 to round and truncate the answer to two decimal places. Define both expressions as user-defined functions in your program.

Input Data: None.

Output Results: Figure 8.22 illustrates the output for Programming Problem 3.

```
                 Time to Double an Investment
                     Compounded Quarterly
                 ----------------------------

                       Years            Years
        Annual        to Double        to Double
        Interest      (Rounded)        (Truncated)
        --------      ---------        -----------
           4%           17.42             17.41
           5%           13.95             13.94
           6%           11.64             11.63
           7%            9.99              9.98

        Job Complete
```

4. Order Entry Simulation

Purpose: To become familiar with the use of the random number function RND, the RANDOMIZE statement, the TIMER function, the INPUT$ function, and computer simulation.

Problem: Order entry is the process of receiving customer orders and producing shipping orders. The Ainsworth Company has three clerks in its Order Entry Department. On the average, the three clerks can process 207 customer orders a day. Management has requested the Information Systems Department to simulate the activities of the Order Entry Department over a four-week period (20 working days). The following statistics were compiled over the same four-week period during the previous year:

Customer Orders Received	Frequency in Days	Relative Frequency	Cumulative Frequency
195	1	0.05	0.05
200	5	0.25	0.30
205	6	0.30	0.60
210	4	0.20	0.80
215	3	0.15	0.95
220	1	0.05	1.00

Assuming that the four-week period (day 1 through day 20) begins with no backlog orders, write a top-down program that will print on the printer the simulation of the following:

1. Number of orders received each day
2. Number of orders processed (the day's order plus backlog orders)
3. Orders not processed
4. Number of days in which orders go unprocessed

The orders received are to be simulated by employing the RND function. When the program is working properly, add the statement, RANDOMIZE TIMER, so a new seed will be used to generate the random numbers each time the program is executed.

The random number returned by the RND function should be passed through a SELECT CASE statement to determine whether it is less than or equal to the cumulative frequencies for orders compiled from the previous year. The logic for these tests is shown in Figure 8.23.

FIGURE 8.23
The logic for the Order Entry Simulation.

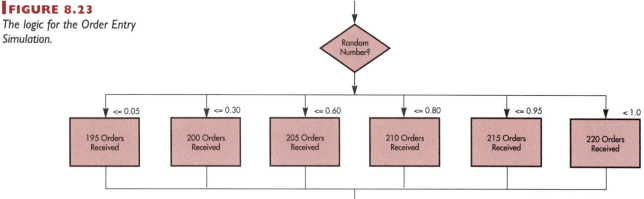

Input Data: None.

Output Results: Display the following message on the screen to the user:

```
Press any key when the printer is ready ...
```

Figure 8.24 illustrates the partial printed output of a sample run. Note that your answers will vary, depending on the random numbers generated on the basis of the value of TIMER.

```
                    Order Entry Simulation
              Maximum Orders Processed Per Day 207

                 Orders        Orders       Orders Not
        Day      Received      Processed    Processed
        ---      --------      ---------    ----------
         1         200           200            0
         2         200           200            0
         3         210           207            3
         4         200           203            0
         .          .             .             .
         .          .             .             .
         .          .             .             .
        18         210           207            7
        19         200           207            0
        20         205           205            0

      Number of days orders went unprocessed =======> 15
      End of Report
```

5. Cryptograms

Purpose: To become familiar with concatenation, table searching, and string manipulation of cryptograms.

Problem: In Section 8.2, you were introduced to a method of substituting characters in a coded message and determining the contents of the message. The direct substitution method, based on a table of substitutes, may also be used with cryptograms. Write a top-down program that uses the following table of substitutes to decode a given message:

Coded Characters: 9 G Q 6 V L P N W X A 8 T # H Z J M (U 3) R I S B F K D
Regular Characters: A B C D E F G H I J K L M N O P Q R S T U V W X Y Z - ∅ .

The coded characters and their corresponding regular characters are stored in EX85CODE.TBL on the Data Disk. View the file EX85CODE.TBL to determine the order in which the data is stored. Assume that all coded messages are in uppercase. The letter K represents the blank character.

Input Data: Use the following sample coded messages.

```
Message 1:   G9(WQKW(KV9(S
Message 2:   LW#6W#PKUNVK6VVZK(WTZ8WQWUWV(KW#K9K
             QHTZ8WQ9UV6KQH88VQUWH#KHLKUNW#P(K
             UHKGVK6H#(VKW(KUNVKQMV9UW)WUSKW#K
             ZMHPM9TTW#(PKFKND6DTW88(
```

Output Results: Figure 8.25 on the next page presents the output results for Message 1 in Programming Problem 5.

FIGURE 8.25
*Output for Message 1 in
Programming Problem 5.*

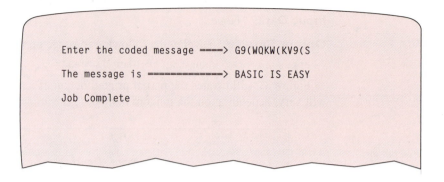

```
Enter the coded message ====> G9(WQKW(KV9(S

The message is ============> BASIC IS EASY

Job Complete
```

6. Soundex Code

Purpose: To become familiar with character transformation, Soundex, and the use of the LINE INPUT statement.

Problem: Companies that allow their customers to telephone or write for information regarding their account status frequently have only the customer's name to aid them in locating a record in the account file. Sometimes the name itself is not clear because of illegible handwriting or poor voice communications in a telephone conversation. Also, when customers call to request information about their accounts, some companies like to ask as few questions as possible to give callers the impression that they are special customers.

Soundex is the name of a method for transforming the sound of a name into a successful and efficient search for a customer record. Developed by M. Odell and R. Russell, the method involves assigning a code, called the **Soundex code**, to a surname when a record is first added to a file, and placing this code in the record for access purposes. The Soundex code for a name is determined from the following rules:

1. Retain the first letter and drop all occurrences of a, e, h, i, o, u, w, and y in other positions of the name.
2. Assign the following digits to the remaining letters:

Digits	Letters
1	b, f, p, v
2	c, g, j, k, q, s, x, z
3	d, t
4	l
5	m, n
6	r

3. If two or more letters with the same code are adjacent in the original name, drop all but the first letter.
4. Convert the name to the form, *letter, digit, digit, digit,* by adding trailing zeros if there are less than three digits, or by dropping rightmost digits if there are more than three digits. The following examples of names have these corresponding Soundex codes:

Last Name	Code	Last Name	Code
Case	C200	Knuth	K530
Cash	C200	Smith	S530
Caise	C200	Smyth	S530
Gauss	G200	Smythe	S530

This system will work for most names and will reduce the time it takes to search a file with many records.

Write a top-down program that builds an account file in which each record contains the customer number, customer name, Soundex code, and balance due. The program should request from the user the customer number, name, and balance due. From the last name, the program should determine the Soundex code and display it. Then the program should write the record to a sequential file EX86DATA.DAT.

Input Data: Use the following sample data. Be sure to include the comma (,) as part of the customer name.

Customer Number	Customer Name	Balance Due	Customer Number	Customer Name	Balance Due
1783	Allen, John	$55.00	3401	Smith, Amanda	45.00
1934	Smit, Joan	0.00	3607	Cass, Lou	0.00
2109	Conn, Jim	5.00	4560	Smythe, Alice	4.00
2134	Allen, Bill	35.00	5590	Ellen, Boyd	7.80
2367	Allan, Fred	65.00	6498	Case, Nikole	5.30
2568	Canne, Edie	87.00	7591	Kane, Judy	0.00

Output Results: The records above are written to the sequential file EX86DATA.DAT. Figure 8.26 illustrates partial results for Programming Problem 6.

FIGURE 8.26
Partial results for Programming Problem 6.

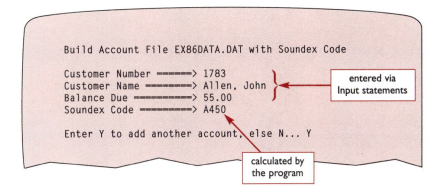

```
Build Account File EX86DATA.DAT with Soundex Code

Customer Number ======> 1783
Customer Name ========> Allen, John          entered via
Balance Due ==========> 55.00                Input statements
Soundex Code =========> A450

Enter Y to add another account, else N... Y
```

calculated by the program

7. Payroll Problem VIII: Spelling Out the Net Pay

Purpose: To become familiar with table utilization, use of the zero element of an array, the INT and STR$ functions, and spelling out numbers.

Problem: Construct a top-down program that spells out the net pay for check-writing purposes. For example, the net pay $5,078.45 is written out on a check as follows:

Five Thousand Seventy-Eight Dollars and 45 Cents

Assume that the net pay does not exceed $9,999.99.

Hint: Use the INT function to separate the integer portion of the net pay into single digits. Use the single digits to access the words from one of two positionally organized tables. If the digit represents the thousands, hundreds, or units position, then access the word from the following table:

Digit	Word	Digit	Word
0	Null	10	Ten
1	One	11	Eleven
2	Two	12	Twelve
3	Three	13	Thirteen
4	Four	14	Fourteen
5	Five	15	Fifteen
6	Six	16	Sixteen
7	Seven	17	Seventeen
8	Eight	18	Eighteen
9	Nine	19	Nineteen

If the digit represents the tens position, then access the word from the following table:

Digit	Word	Digit	Word
0	Null	5	Fifty
1	Ten	6	Sixty
2	Twenty	7	Seventy
3	Thirty	8	Eighty
4	Forty	9	Ninety

The word entries for both tables are found in the sequential file EX87TAB.TBL on the Data Disk. The entries for the thousands, hundreds, and units table are first in the sequential file, followed immediately by the entries for the tens table.

Use the INT and STR$ functions to determine the fraction portion of the net pay. Use the concatenation operator to string the words together. If there are no dollars or cents, display the word, No, accordingly.

Input Data: Use the sequential file EX87DATA.DAT on the Data Disk. The data file includes the following sample data:

Employee Number	Net Pay
123	$8,462.34
124	987.23
125	78.99
126	6,000.23
127	1,003.00
128	4,037.00
129	4.67
130	0.02

Output Results: Figure 8.27 illustrates the output for Programming Problem 7.

FIGURE 8.27

Output for Programming Problem 7.

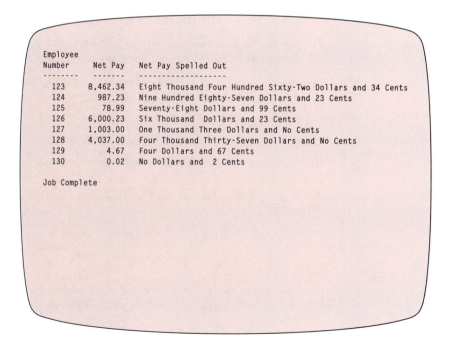

```
Employee
Number    Net Pay    Net Pay Spelled Out
--------  -------    -------------------
   123    8,462.34   Eight Thousand Four Hundred Sixty-Two Dollars and 34 Cents
   124      987.23   Nine Hundred Eighty-Seven Dollars and 23 Cents
   125       78.99   Seventy-Eight Dollars and 99 Cents
   126    6,000.23   Six Thousand  Dollars and 23 Cents
   127    1,003.00   One Thousand Three Dollars and No Cents
   128    4,037.00   Four Thousand Thirty-Seven Dollars and No Cents
   129        4.67   Four Dollars and 67 Cents
   130        0.02   No Dollars and  2 Cents

Job Complete
```

CHAPTER 9

File Maintenance, Random File Processing, and Simulated-Indexed Files

9.1 INTRODUCTION

In Chapter 6, you were introduced to sequential file processing. Topics included writing reports to auxiliary storage and building and processing sequential data files. In this chapter, we discuss file maintenance. **File maintenance** means updating files in one or more of the following ways:

1. *Adding* new records
2. *Deleting* unwanted records
3. *Changing* or updating data within records

This chapter also concentrates on two additional methods of file organization — random and simulated-indexed files.

Random Files

A file that is organized randomly is called a **random file** or a **relative file**. The sequence of processing a random file has no relationship to the sequence in which the records are stored. If the tenth record in a file is required by a program, the record can be accessed directly without processing the preceeding nine records. However, the program must indicate to the PC the location of the record relative to the beginning of the file. For example, to access the tenth record instead of the third or fourth record, the program must explicitly indicate to the PC that the tenth record is requested for processing.

Indexed Files

A third type of file organization, known as **indexed,** also is widely used in data processing. A file organized by an index is an **indexed file**. An indexed file is organized around a specified data item called the **key**, which is common to each record. In an airline reservation file, the key may be the flight number. In an inventory file, the key may be the part number or a part description.

Indexed files have one advantage over random files: the program need supply only the key of the record to be accessed instead of the record's relative location. Although indexed files are not available with QBasic, this method of organization may be simulated by using both a sequential file and a random file, as illustrated in Programming Case Study 22 later in this chapter.

Indexed files and random files are used primarily for on-line activities where the applications call for random processing of the data. In airline reservation systems, inventory systems, management information systems, and customer credit checks, indexed or random organization of a file has important advantages over sequential organization.

9.2 FILE MAINTENANCE

File maintenance is one of the most important activities in data processing. The programming techniques that are used to update a file usually are based on the type of file organization under which the file was created. To update sequential files, the record additions, deletions, and changes normally are entered into another data file called a **transaction file**. A transaction file, therefore, contains data of a temporary, or transient nature. After the updates have been completed, the transaction file can be archived and deleted.

The file that is updated is called the **master file**. A master file contains data that usually is permanent. **Current master file** refers to the master file before updating, and **new master file** refers to the updated version of the current master file. A file maintenance program that updates a sequential file must deal with at least three files, as illustrated in the system flowchart in Figure 9.1.

FIGURE 9.1

A system flowchart representing file maintenance of a sequential file.

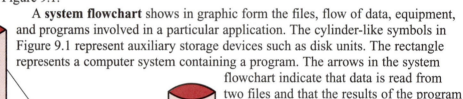

A **system flowchart** shows in graphic form the files, flow of data, equipment, and programs involved in a particular application. The cylinder-like symbols in Figure 9.1 represent auxiliary storage devices such as disk units. The rectangle represents a computer system containing a program. The arrows in the system flowchart indicate that data is read from two files and that the results of the program are written to another file.

To use the file maintenance technique described in Figure 9.1 for a sequential file, both the master and transaction files must be in the same sequence, based on one of the data items common to both files. For example, an inventory master file and a corresponding inventory transaction file may be in sorted ascending sequence by stock number.

For the sake of simplicity, the presentation of file maintenance has been divided into two problems and two corresponding program solutions. In the first set, Programming Case Study 18, a method of adding records to the current master file to form a new master file is illustrated. In Programming Case Study 19 later in the chapter, record deletion and update are illustrated. QBasic Programming Problem 1 at the end of this chapter requires the completion of all the file maintenance activities in one program.

PROGRAMMING CASE STUDY 18 – File Maintenance I – Adding Records by Merging Files

Problem: Programming Case Study 9, on page 207 in Chapter 6, created a sequential data file called INVNTORY.DAT from the inventory data in Table 9.1.

TABLE 9.1 - Inventory Data Used to Create the Master File INVNTORY.DAT					
STOCK NUMBER	WAREHOUSE LOCATION	DESCRIPTION	UNIT COST	SELLING PRICE	QUANTITY ON HAND
C101	1	Roadhandler	97.56	125.11	25
C204	3	Whitewalls	37.14	99.95	140
C502	2	Tripod	32.50	38.99	10
S209	1	Maxidrill	88.76	109.99	6
S416	2	Normalsaw	152.55	179.40	1
S812	2	Router	48.47	61.15	8
S942	4	Radialsaw	376.04	419.89	3
T615	4	Oxford-Style	26.43	31.50	28
T713	2	Moc-Boot	24.99	29.99	30
T814	2	Work-Boot	22.99	27.99	56

New stock items are to be added to the inventory master file INVNTORY.DAT created in Programming Case Study 9. The new stock items are shown in Table 9.2 and are in the file TRAINV.DAT. The program should merge the records of the two files to create the new inventory master file. **Merging** is the process of combining two or more files that are *in the same sequence* into a single file that maintains that same sequence for a given data item found in each record. The two files are each in ascending sequence according to the stock number.

TABLE 9.2 - Inventory Data in the Transaction File TRAINV.DAT					
STOCK NUMBER	WAREHOUSE LOCATION	DESCRIPTION	UNIT COST	SELLING PRICE	QUANTITY ON HAND
C103	2	Saw-Blades	5.06	6.04	15
C206	1	Square	4.56	5.42	34
S210	3	Microscope	31.50	41.99	8
S941	2	Hip-Boot	26.95	32.50	12
T615	4	Oxford-Style	26.43	31.50	28
T731	1	Sandals	6.75	9.45	52

The transaction file can be created by modifying line 17 in Program 6.2 on page 208 as follows:

```
OPEN "A:TRAINV.DAT" FOR OUTPUT AS #1
```

and entering the records in Table 9.2 in response to the modified Program 6.2.

Also assume that the name of the current master file INVNTORY.DAT has been changed to CURINV.DAT, using Explorer in Windows, the MS-DOS command RENAME, or the QBasic NAME statement. For example, use the MS-DOS command

```
RENAME A:INVNTORY.DAT A:CURINV.DAT
```

or the QBasic statement

```
NAME "A:INVNTORY.DAT" AS "A:CURINV.DAT"
```

The NAME statement may be entered in the immediate window or placed in A100.Initialization.

By changing the name of the current master file, its former name INVNTORY.DAT then can be assigned to a new master file.

For adding records to a current master file, it is an error for a record in the transaction file to have the same stock number as a record in the current master file. If this happens, an appropriate diagnostic message, including the stock number and description, should display. Also, a count of the number of records in the new master file should display before the program is terminated.

A top-down chart showing the organization of the program used to solve the problem is illustrated in Figure 9.2. Recall that recurring subtasks are identified by darkening the upper right-hand corner of the process symbol. At implementation time, recurring subtasks are coded once and called upon as often as needed. Following are the program tasks that specify how to solve the problem on the basis of the top-down chart, a program solution, and a discussion of the program solution.

FIGURE 9.2

Top-down chart for the solution to Programming Case Study 18.

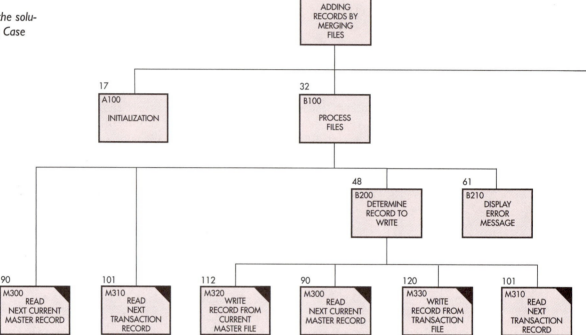

Program Tasks

1. A100.Initialization
    a. Set Record.Count to zero.
    b. Set two end-of-file switches, Master.Eof$ for the current master file and Transaction.Eof$ for the transaction file, to the value OFF. Set either switch to the value ON when the end-of-file mark is sensed in the corresponding file.
    c. Open CURINV.DAT, TRAINV.DAT, and INVNTORY.DAT.
    d. Display an appropriate screen title.

2. B100.Process.Files
    a. Read the first record in the current master file and the first record in the transaction file. Use the following variable names:

Current Master File		Transaction File	
M.Stock$	= stock number	T.Stock$	= stock number
M.Location$	= location	T.Location$	= location
M.Desc$	= description	T.Desc$	= description
M.Cost	= cost	T.Cost	= cost
M.Price	= price	T.Price	= price
M.Quantity	= quantity	T.Quantity	= quantity

b. Establish a Do-While loop that executes while both Master.Eof$ and Transaction.Eof$ are equal to the value OFF. Within the loop, compare M.Stock$ to T.Stock$ and do the following:

(1) If the stock number M.Stock$ is equal to the stock number T.Stock$, then display a diagnostic message and read the next transaction record.

(2) If the stock number M.Stock$ is less than the stock number T.Stock$, then write the current master record to the new master file, increment counter Record.Count by 1, and read the next current master record.

(3) If the stock number M.Stock$ is greater than the stock number T.Stock$, then write the transaction record to the new master file, increment counter Record.Count by 1, and read the next transaction record.

3. C100.Wrap.Up

a. One of the two input files may still contain records that need to be written to the new master file. This procedure is often referred to as **flushing the files**.

b. Close all files.

c. Display the value of Record.Count as well as an end-of-job message.

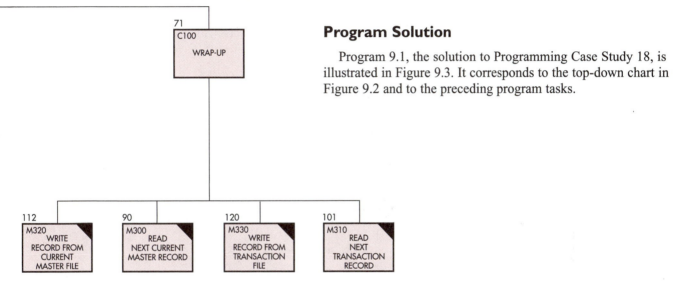

Program Solution

Program 9.1, the solution to Programming Case Study 18, is illustrated in Figure 9.3. It corresponds to the top-down chart in Figure 9.2 and to the preceding program tasks.

FIGURE 9.3

Program 9.1, the solution to Programming Case Study 18.

```
 1   ' Program 9.1
 2   ' File Maintenance I  - Adding Records by Merging Files
 3   ' Current Master File = CURINV.DAT
 4   ' Transaction File     = TRAINV.DAT
 5   ' New Master File      = INVNTORY.DAT
 6   ' ************************************************************
 7   ' *                       Main Program                     *
 8   ' ************************************************************
 9   GOSUB A100.Initialization
10   GOSUB B100.Process.Files
11   GOSUB C100.Wrap.Up
12   END
13
```

(continued)

FIGURE 9.3

(continued)

```
14  ' ****************************************************************
15  ' *                       Initialization                       *
16  ' ****************************************************************
17  A100.Initialization:
18     Record.Count = 0
19     Master.Eof$ = "OFF"
20     Transaction.Eof$ = "OFF"
21     OPEN "A:CURINV.DAT" FOR INPUT AS #1
22     OPEN "A:TRAINV.DAT" FOR INPUT AS #2
23     OPEN "A:INVNTORY.DAT" FOR OUTPUT AS #3
24     CLS  ' Clear Screen
25     LOCATE 5, 15: PRINT "Adding Records to Inventory File"
26     LOCATE 6, 15: PRINT "-------------------------------"
27  RETURN
28
29  ' ****************************************************************
30  ' *                       Process Files                        *
31  ' ****************************************************************
32  B100.Process.Files:
33     GOSUB M300.Read.Master.Record
34     GOSUB M310.Read.Transaction.Record
35     DO WHILE Master.Eof$ = "OFF" AND Transaction.Eof$ = "OFF"
36        IF M.Stock$ <> T.Stock$ THEN
37           GOSUB B200.Determine.Record.To.Write
38        ELSE
39           GOSUB B210.Display.Error.Message
40           GOSUB M310.Read.Transaction.Record
41        END IF
42     LOOP
43  RETURN
44
45  ' ****************************************************************
46  ' *           Determine Record to Write to Master File         *
47  ' ****************************************************************
48  B200.Determine.Record.To.Write:
49     IF M.Stock$ < T.Stock$ THEN
50        GOSUB M320.Write.Master.Record
51        GOSUB M300.Read.Master.Record
52     ELSE
53        GOSUB M330.Write.Transaction.Record
54        GOSUB M310.Read.Transaction.Record
55     END IF
56  RETURN
57
58  ' ****************************************************************
59  ' *                    Display Error Message                    *
60  ' ****************************************************************
61  B210.Display.Error.Message:
62     PRINT
63     PRINT "********** Transaction Record Already in Current Master File"
64     PRINT "*   ERROR  * Stock Number = "; T.Stock$
65     PRINT "********** Description  = "; T.Desc$
66  RETURN
67
68  ' ****************************************************************
69  ' *                         Wrap-Up                            *
70  ' ****************************************************************
```

```
71  C100.Wrap.Up:
72     DO WHILE Master.Eof$ = "OFF"
73        GOSUB M320.Write.Master.Record
74        GOSUB M300.Read.Master.Record
75     LOOP
76     DO WHILE Transaction.Eof$ = "OFF"
77        GOSUB M330.Write.Transaction.Record
78        GOSUB M310.Read.Transaction.Record
79     LOOP
80     CLOSE
81     PRINT
82     PRINT "The number of records in the new master file is"; Record.Count
83     PRINT
84     PRINT "INVNTORY.DAT Update Complete"
85  RETURN
86
87  ' ******************************************************************
88  ' *              Read Next Current Master Record                 *
89  ' ******************************************************************
90  M300.Read.Master.Record:
91     IF EOF(1) THEN
92        Master.Eof$ = "ON"
93     ELSE
94        INPUT #1, M.Stock$, M.Location$, M.Desc$, M.Cost, M.Price, M.Quantity
95     END IF
96  RETURN
97
98  ' ******************************************************************
99  ' *               Read Next Transaction Record                   *
100 ' ******************************************************************
101 M310.Read.Transaction.Record:
102    IF EOF(2) THEN
103       Transaction.Eof$ = "ON"
104    ELSE
105       INPUT #2, T.Stock$, T.Location$, T.Desc$, T.Cost, T.Price, T.Quantity
106    END IF
107 RETURN
108
109 ' ******************************************************************
110 ' *           Write Record from Current Master File              *
111 ' ******************************************************************
112 M320.Write.Master.Record:
113    WRITE #3, M.Stock$, M.Location$, M.Desc$, M.Cost, M.Price, M.Quantity
114    Record.Count = Record.Count + 1
115 RETURN
116
117 ' ******************************************************************
118 ' *            Write Record from Transaction File                *
119 ' ******************************************************************
120 M330.Write.Transaction.Record:
121    WRITE #3, T.Stock$, T.Location$, T.Desc$, T.Cost, T.Price, T.Quantity
122    Record.Count = Record.Count + 1
123 RETURN
124
125 ' ******************** End of Program ************************
```

[run]

Discussion of the Program Solution

Because merging two files into one is a complex process, we recommend that you pay particular attention to the top-down chart in Figure 9.2 on page 352. Stepping through both the program tasks and the top-down chart will give you a better understanding of the algorithm used to merge the two files.

Figures 9.4 and 9.5 show the contents of the current master file CURINV.DAT and the transaction file TRAINV.DAT.

FIGURE 9.4

A list of the records in the current master file, CURINV.DAT.

```
"C101","1","Roadhandler",97.56,125.11,25
"C204","3","Whitewalls",37.14,99.95,140
"C502","2","Tripod",32.5,38.99,10
"S209","1","Maxidrill",88.76,109.99,6
"S416","2","Normalsaw",152.55,179.4,1
"S812","2","Router",48.47,61,15,8
"S942","4","Radialsaw",376.04,419.89,3
"T615","4","Oxford-Style",26.43,31.5,28
"T713","2","Moc-Boot",24.99,29.99,30
"T814","2","Work-Boot",22.99,27.99,56
```

FIGURE 9.5

A list of the records in the transaction file, TRAINV.DAT.

```
"C103","2","Saw-Blades",5.06,6.04,15
"C206","1","Square",4.56,5.42,34
"S210","3","Microscope",31.50,41.99,8
"S941","2","Hip-Boot",26.95,32.50,12
"T615","4","Oxford-Style",26.43,31.50,28
"T731","1","Sandals",6.75,9.45,52
```

When Program 9.1 is executed, line 9 in the Main Program calls the subroutine A100.Initialization. Line 18 initializes the counter Record.Count to zero. Record.Count is equal to the number of records written to the new master file INVNTORY.DAT. Lines 19 and 20 assign the end-of-file switches Master.Eof$ and Transaction.Eof$ the value of OFF. These two switches are used to control the Do-While loops in the program.

Lines 21 and 22 open for input the two files CURINV.DAT and TRAINV.DAT. Line 23 opens for output the new master file INVNTORY.DAT. Line 24 clears the screen, and lines 25 and 26 display a screen title.

Following the return of control to the Main Program, line 10 calls the subroutine B100.Process.Files. Lines 33 and 34 cause the PC to read the first record in each file. Within the Do-While loop, line 36 compares the stock number (M.Stock$) in the record read from the master file to the stock number (T.Stock$) in the record read from the transaction file. The comparison determines which record will be written to the new master file INVNTORY.DAT. The logic proceeds as follows:

1. If M.Stock$ is equal to T.Stock$, then control transfers to the subroutine B210.Display.Error.Message (lines 61 through 66), and a diagnostic message displays indicating that the record from TRAINV.DAT already exists in the data file CURINV.DAT. In line 40, the next record in TRAINV.DAT is read before control passes back to the top of the Do-While loop.

2. If M.Stock$ does not equal T.Stock$, then control passes to the subroutine B200.Determine.Record.To.Write beginning at line 48, and another comparison is made between the two variables to determine which record should be written to the new master file. The following procedure is used:
   a. If M.Stock$ is less than T.Stock$, then control transfers to the subroutine M320.Write.Master.Record (lines 112 through 115), which writes the record from CURINV.DAT. The counter Record.Count is incremented by 1 before control returns to line 51, and the next record in CURINV.DAT is read. Control then returns to B100.Process.Files.

b. If M.Stock$ is greater than T.Stock$, then control transfers to the subroutine M330.Write.Transaction.Record (lines 120 through 123), which writes the record from TRAINV.DAT. The counter Record.Count is incremented by 1 before control returns to line 54, and the next record in TRAINV.DAT is read. Control then returns to B100.Process.Files.

When the PC senses the end-of-file mark on either file, the end-of-file switch representing the exhausted file is assigned a value of ON, and control returns to the Main Program. Line 11 in the Main Program transfers control to C100.Wrap.Up.

If the end-of-file is sensed on TRAINV.DAT, then lines 72 through 75 flush any records remaining in CURINV.DAT. If the end-of-file is sensed on CURINV.DAT, then the Do-While loop (lines 76 through 79) flushes any records that remain in TRAINV.DAT.

It is important to note that the main Do-While loop in B100.Process.Files and both Do-While loops that flush the files in C100.Wrap.Up are controlled by switches and not by the EOF function. If you use the EOF function instead of the two switches to directly control the loops, the last record in each file may not be written to the new master file.

A close look at Figures 9.4 and 9.5 reveals that the fifth record in TRAINV.DAT has the same stock number as the eighth record in CURINV.DAT. This causes the display of a diagnostic message as shown in Figure 9.6.

FIGURE 9.6

The results displayed due to the execution of Program 9.1.

```
               Adding Records to Inventory Files
               --------------------------------


*********** Transaction Record Already in Current Master File
*   ERROR  * Stock Number = T615
*********** Description  = Oxford-Style

The number of records in the new master file is 15

INVNTORY.DAT Update Complete
```

Figure 9.7 shows the contents of the new master file INVNTORY.DAT created by Program 9.1.

FIGURE 9.7

A list of the records in the merged, new master file INVNTORY.DAT.

```
"C101","1","Roadhandler",97.56,125.11,25
"C103","2","Saw-Blades",5.06,6.04,15
"C204","3","Whitewalls",37.14,99.95,140
"C206","1","Square",4.56,5.42,34
"C502","2","Tripod",32.5,38.99,10
"S209","1","Maxidrill",88.76,109.99,6
"S210","3","Microscope",31.5,41.99,8
"S416","2","Normalsaw",152.55,179.4,1
"S812","2","Router",48.47,61.15,8
"S941","2","Hip-Boot",26.95,32.5,12
"S942","4","Radialsaw",376.04,419.89,3
"T615","4","Oxford-Style",26.43,31.5,28
"T713","2","Moc-Boot",24.99,29.99,30
"T731","1","Sandals",6.75,9.45,52
"T814","2","Work-Boot",22.99,27.99,56
```

PROGRAMMING CASE STUDY 19 – File Maintenance II – Deleting and Changing Records by Matching Records

In Programming Case Study 18, you were introduced to one category of file maintenance — adding new records to the master file. In the following programming case study, you are introduced to the two remaining categories of file maintenance — deletion of unwanted records and changing data within records in the master file. Here again, records will be read from two files, and a new master file will be created. A process known as **matching records** will be used. Matching records involves processing two or more related files that are in the same sequence according to a common data item.

As records are read from the two related files, the PC acts upon them in the following manner:

1. If the stock numbers in both records are equal, then the action indicated on the transaction record is carried out. Either the current master record is deleted by not writing it to the new master file, or the data is changed in the current master record, as indicated on the transaction record, and the modified current master record is written to the new master file.
2. If the stock number in the current master record is less than the stock number in the transaction record; that is, if the transaction file contains no modifications to the current master record, then the current master record is written to the new master file.
3. If the stock number in the current master file is greater than the stock number in the transaction record; that is, if the transaction record has no match, then the transaction record is in error and a diagnostic message is displayed.

This process of matching records is illustrated in the following problem.

Problem: Given the current master file shown in Figure 9.7 on the previous page and the transaction file shown in Table 9.3, a program that updates the current master file and creates a new master file will be illustrated. Both the current master file and the transaction file are in ascending sequence by stock number.

TABLE 9.3 - Inventory Data in the Transaction File TRAINV-2.DAT						
STOCK NUMBER	TRANSACTION CODE	WAREHOUSE LOCATION	DESCRIPTION	UNIT COST	SELLING PRICE	QUANTITY ON HAND
C204	D	Null Char.	Null Char.	-1	-1	-1
C402	C	3	Null Char.	33.50	40.50	-1
S812	C	Null Char.	ROUTER-II	-1	-1	12
T615	D	Null Char.	Null Char.	-1	-1	-1
T731	C	Null Char.	Null Char.	6.50	-1	-1

Change the name of the current master file in Figure 9.7 to CURINV-2.DAT. Use the name TRAINV-2.DAT to identify the transaction file. Call the new master file INV-2.DAT.

With respect to the contents of the transaction file TRAINV-2.DAT, remember the following:

1. The transaction code D indicates that the corresponding record in the current master file is to be deleted, and the code C indicates changes. (Assume C and D are the only two transaction codes.)
2. Data items that are *not* to be changed in the current master file are designated in the transaction file with a value of –1 if the item is numeric, and by a null character if the item is a string.
3. In order for the INPUT statement to read the transaction file properly, all data items are assigned a value, including those within records representing a delete.
4. With minor modifications, Program 6.2 on page 208, can be used to build the transaction file.

If a record in the transaction file has no matching record in the current master file, then the diagnostic message

```
** ERROR ** Transaction record with stock number xxxx has no match.
```

is displayed. As part of the end-of-job routine, the total number of records deleted and the number of records changed are displayed.

Because the algorithm for matching records is similar to the algorithm for merging files that was presented in Programming Case Study 18 (page 350) a top-down chart and a list of the program tasks are not included in Programming Case Study 19. The program solution follows.

Program Solution

Program 9.2, the solution to Programming Case Study 19, is illustrated in Figure 9.8. It matches records between the current master file CURINV-2.DAT and the transaction file TRAINV-2.DAT, and builds the new master file INV-2.DAT.

FIGURE 9.8

Program 9.2, the solution to Programming Case Study 19.

```
1   ' Program 9.2
2   ' File Maintenance II -- Deleting Records and Changing Fields
3   ' Current Master File =  CURINV-2.DAT
4   ' Transaction File    =  TRAINV-2.DAT
5   ' New Master File      =  INV-2.DAT
6   ' ******************************************************************
7   ' *                       Main Program                          *
8   ' ******************************************************************
9   GOSUB A100.Initialization
10  GOSUB B100.Process.Files
11  GOSUB C100.Wrap.Up
12  END
13
14  ' ******************************************************************
15  ' *                       Initialization                        *
16  ' ******************************************************************
17  A100.Initialization:
18     Delete.Count = 0
19     Change.Count = 0
20     Record.Count = 0
21     Master.Eof$ = "OFF"
22     Transaction.Eof$ = "OFF"
23     OPEN "A:CURINV-2.DAT" FOR INPUT AS #1
24     OPEN "A:TRAINV-2.DAT" FOR INPUT AS #2
25     OPEN "A:INV-2.DAT" FOR OUTPUT AS #3
26     CLS  ' Clear Screen
27     PRINT "Deleting Records and Changing Fields in Inventory File"
28     PRINT "---------------------------------------------------------"
29  RETURN
30
31  ' ******************************************************************
32  ' *                       Process Files                         *
33  ' ******************************************************************
34  B100.Process.Files:
35     GOSUB M400.Read.Master.Record
36     GOSUB M410.Read.Transaction.Record
37     DO WHILE Master.Eof$ = "OFF" AND Transaction.Eof$ = "OFF"
38        IF M.Stock$ = T.Stock$ THEN
39           GOSUB B200.Determine.Maintenance.Type
40        ELSE
41           GOSUB B210.Write.Cur.Master.Or.Error.Message
42        END IF
43     LOOP
44  RETURN
45
```

(continued)

FIGURE 9.8
(continued)

```
46   ' ****************************************************************
47   ' *                 Determine Maintenance Type                 *
48   ' ****************************************************************
49   B200.Determine.Maintenance.Type:
50     IF T.Type$ = "D" THEN
51        GOSUB B300.Delete.Record
52     ELSE
53        GOSUB B310.Change.Record
54     END IF
55   RETURN
56
57   ' ****************************************************************
58   ' *          Write Current Master or Error Message             *
59   ' ****************************************************************
60   B210.Write.Cur.Master.Or.Error.Message:
61     IF M.Stock$ < T.Stock$ THEN
62        GOSUB M420.Write.New.Master.Record
63        GOSUB M400.Read.Master.Record
64     ELSE
65        GOSUB M430.Display.Error.Message
66        GOSUB M410.Read.Transaction.Record
67     END IF
68   RETURN
69
70   ' ****************************************************************
71   ' *                      Delete Record                         *
72   ' ****************************************************************
73   B300.Delete.Record:
74     Delete.Count = Delete.Count + 1
75     GOSUB M400.Read.Master.Record
76     GOSUB M410.Read.Transaction.Record
77   RETURN
78
79   ' ****************************************************************
80   ' *                      Change Record                         *
81   ' ****************************************************************
82   B310.Change.Record:
83     IF T.Location$ <> "" THEN
84        M.Location$ = T.Location$
85     END IF
86     IF T.Desc$ <> "" THEN
87        M.Desc$ = T.Desc$
88     END IF
89     IF T.Cost <> -1 THEN
90        M.Cost = T.Cost
91     END IF
92     IF T.Price <> -1 THEN
93        M.Price = T.Price
94     END IF
95     IF T.Quantity <> -1 THEN
96        M.Quantity = T.Quantity
97     END IF
98     Change.Count = Change.Count + 1
99     GOSUB M420.Write.New.Master.Record
100    GOSUB M400.Read.Master.Record
101    GOSUB M410.Read.Transaction.Record
102  RETURN
103
```

```
104   ' ****************************************************************
105   ' *                        Wrap-Up                             *
106   ' ****************************************************************
107   C100.Wrap.Up:
108      DO WHILE Master.Eof$ = "OFF"
109         GOSUB M420.Write.New.Master.Record
110         GOSUB M400.Read.Master.Record
111      LOOP
112      DO WHILE Transaction.Eof$ = "OFF"
113         GOSUB M430.Display.Error.Message
114         GOSUB M410.Read.Transaction.Record
115      LOOP
116      CLOSE
117      PRINT
118      PRINT "Total Number of Records Deleted ==========>"; Delete.Count
119      PRINT "Total Number of Records Changed ==========>"; Change.Count
120      PRINT "Total Number of Records in New Master ====>"; Record.Count
121      PRINT
122      PRINT "INV-2.DAT Update Complete"
123   RETURN
124
125   ' ****************************************************************
126   ' *              Read Next Current Master Record               *
127   ' ****************************************************************
128   M400.Read.Master.Record:
129      IF EOF(1) THEN
130         Master.Eof$ = "ON"
131      ELSE
132         INPUT #1, M.Stock$, M.Location$, M.Desc$, M.Cost, M.Price, M.Quantity
133      END IF
134   RETURN
135
136   ' ****************************************************************
137   ' *               Read Next Transaction Record                 *
138   ' ****************************************************************
139   M410.Read.Transaction.Record:
140      IF EOF(2) THEN
141         Transaction.Eof$ = "ON"
142      ELSE
143         INPUT #2, T.Stock$, T.Type$, T.Location$, T.Desc$, T.Cost, T.Price, T.Quantity
144      END IF
145   RETURN
146
147   ' ****************************************************************
148   ' *              Write Record to New Master File               *
149   ' ****************************************************************
150   M420.Write.New.Master.Record:
151      WRITE #3, M.Stock$, M.Location$, M.Desc$, M.Cost, M.Price, M.Quantity
152      Record.Count = Record.Count + 1
153   RETURN
154
155   ' ****************************************************************
156   ' *                   Display Error Message                    *
157   ' ****************************************************************
158   M430.Display.Error.Message:
159      PRINT
160      PRINT "** ERROR ** Transaction Record with stock number ";
161      PRINT T.Stock$; " has no match."
162   RETURN
163
164   ' ****************** End of Program ************************
      [run]
```

Discussion of the Program Solution

When Program 9.2 is executed, line 9 in the Main Program transfers control to A100.Initialization. Lines 18 through 22 initialize counters to zero and end-of-file switches to OFF. Line 23 opens for input the current master file CURINV-2.DAT shown in Figure 9.7 on page 357. Line 24 opens for input the transaction file TRAINV-2.DAT. The file TRAINV-2.DAT contains the records shown in Figure 9.9. Line 25 opens the new master file INV-2.DAT. After the screen clears and the title displays, control returns to the Main Program.

FIGURE 9.9

A list of records in the sequential file TRAINV-2.DAT.

```
"C204","D","","",-1,-1,-1
"C402","C", 3,"",33.50,40.50,-1
"S812","C","","ROUTER-II",-1,-1,12
"T615","D","","",-1,-1,-1
"T731","C","","",6.50,-1,-1
```

Next, line 10 in the Main Program transfers control to B100.Process.Files. Lines 35 and 36 call upon the subroutines to read the first current master record and the first transaction record. Within the Do-While loop, line 38 compares the two stock numbers M.Stock$ and T.Stock$. If M.Stock$ is equal to T.Stock$, then the transaction represents a change or delete, and control passes to B200.Determine.Maintenance.Type (lines 49 through 55). In line 50, the transaction type is compared to the value D. If the record represents a delete, then control transfers to B300.Delete.Record (lines 73 through 77). Otherwise, the record represents a change, and control transfers to B310.Change.Record (lines 82 through 102).

If in line 38 M.Stock$ does not equal T.Stock$, then control passes to line 60 B210.Write.Cur.Master.Or.Error.Message. In this subroutine, the PC determines whether the current master record should be written to the new master or whether the transaction record is in error.

In B310.Change.Record lines 83 through 97 test each value assigned to the variables that correspond to the transaction record. If any of the numeric variables T.Cost, T.Price, or T.Quantity equal -1, then the corresponding variables in the current master file are *not* changed. If they equal any other value, the IF statements result in the assignment of new values to the variables making up the current master record. Line 83 compares T.Location$ to the null character. The null character signifies that the description field in the current master record is not to be changed. If T.Location$ does not equal a null character, then T.Location$ is assigned to M.Location$.

After each variable is tested, except for the stock number which cannot be changed, line 98 increments the change field counter (Change.Count) by 1, and line 99 causes the PC to write the modified current master record to the new master file. In M420.Write.New.Master.Record, line 152 increments the new master file record count (Record.Count) by 1. Finally, lines 100 and 101 read the next current master record and the next transaction record. Control then returns to B100.Process.Files.

Now let us go back to line 38 and discuss what happens if the current master record and transaction record do not match. If M.Stock$ does not equal T.Stock$, then control transfers to B210.Write.Curr.Master.Or.Error.Message (lines 60 through 68). Line 61 determines whether the stock number in the current master record M.Stock$ is less than the stock number T.Stock in the transaction record. If M.Stock$ is less than T.Stock$, then control transfers to M420.Write.New.Master.Record defined by lines 150 through 153, and the current master record is written to the new master file before Record.Count is incremented by 1. When control returns to the calling subroutine, line 63 reads the next record in the current master file.

In line 61, if M.Stock$ is not less than T.Stock$, then it is greater than T.Stock$. In this case, control transfers to M430.Display.Error.Message (lines 158 through 162), which displays an appropriate diagnostic message. The diagnostic message states that the transaction record has no corresponding match in the current master file. Following a return from M430.Display.Error.Message, the PC reads the next transaction record.

B100.Process.Files maintains control of the PC until end-of-file is sensed on either the current master file or the transaction file. Here again, the switches Master.Eof$ and Transaction.Eof$, not the EOF function, are used to control the Do-While loops. If the EOF function is used to control the looping, it is possible that the last record in either input file will not be processed.

After the end-of-file mark is sensed on either input file, the appropriate end-of-file switch is set equal to the value ON and control passes back to the Main Program. C100.Wrap.Up then flushes either file that may have records remaining. If records remain in the current master file, then they are written to the new master file. If records remain in the transaction file, then they have no match and are considered to be in error.

Figure 9.10 shows the display due to the execution of Program 9.2.

FIGURE 9.10

The display due to the execution of Program 9.2.

```
Deleting Records and Changing Fields in Inventory File
--------------------------------------------------------

** ERROR ** Transaction Record with stock number C402 has no match.

Total Number of Records Deleted ============> 2
Total Number of Records Changed ============> 2
Total Number of Records in New Master =====> 13

INV-2.DAT Update Complete
```

In the results displayed by Program 9.2, one of the five records in the transaction file, stock number C402, does not have a corresponding match in the current master file. Of the other four transaction records, two call for deleting records, and two for modifying the current master records. The new master file INV-2.DAT contains 13 records as shown in Figure 9.11.

FIGURE 9.11

A list of the records in the sequential file INV-2.DAT following the execution of Program 9.2.

```
"C101","1","Roadhandler",97.56,125.11,25
"C103","2","Saw-Blades",5.06,6.04,15
"C206","1","Square",4.56,5.42,34
"C502","2","Tripod",32.5,38.99,10
"S209","1","Maxidrill",88.76,109.99,6
"S210","3","Microscope",31.5,41.99,8
"S416","2","Normalsaw",152.55,179.4,1
"S812","2","ROUTER-II",48.47,61.15,12
"S941","2","Hip-Boot",26.95,32.5,12
"S942","4","Radialsaw",376.04,419.89,3
"T713","2","Moc-Boot",24.99,29.99,30
"T731","1","Sandals",6.5,9.45,52
"T814","2","Work-Boot",22.99,27.99,56
```

9.3 RANDOM FILE PROCESSING

Recall from Section 9.1 that the sequence of processing a randomly organized file has no relationship to the sequence in which the records are stored in the file. Random files have several advantages over sequential files, even though fewer program steps are required to create and access records within sequential files than for the same procedure within random files. For example, random files require less space in auxiliary storage because numbers are stored in a compressed format and no commas are required between data items.

The main advantage of random files over sequential files is that their records may be processed randomly. In other words, processing a record in the middle of the file does not require all the records prior to that one to be read. This is true because each record within a random file has a key associated with it. The key indicates the position of the record from the beginning of the random file.

This section presents the file handling statements, functions, and programming techniques necessary to create and process files that can be accessed randomly.

Opening and Closing Random Files

As with sequential files, random files must be opened before they are read from or written to. When a program is finished with a random file, it must close the file. The general form of the OPEN statement for random files is shown in Table 9.4. The general form of the CLOSE statement is the same as for sequential files and is shown in Table 6.2 on page 202.

TABLE 9.4 - The OPEN Statement for Random Files	
General Form:	OPEN filespec FOR RANDOM AS #filenumber LEN = recl
	where **filespec** is the name of the random file;
	filenumber is a numeric expression whose value is between 1 and 255; and
	recl is a value equal to the length of the record.
Purpose:	Allows a program to read from or write records to a random file.
Examples:	1. OPEN "ACCOUNT.DAT" FOR RANDOM AS #2 LEN = 59
	2. OPEN "WHSEDATA.DAT" FOR RANDOM AS #1 LEN = LEN(Warehouse)
	3. OPEN "EX101PAY.DAT" FOR RANDOM AS #1
	4. OPEN Filename AS #1
Note:	QBasic provides a second general form for the OPEN statement:
	OPEN "R", #filenumber, filespec, recl
	This second general form is less contemporary than the general form specified at the top of this table, and therefore is not used in this book.

In Example 1 of Table 9.4, ACCOUNT.DAT is opened as a random file. Filenumber 2 is assigned to ACCOUNT.DAT. Recall from Chapter 6 that the filenumber is used in file handling statements to reference the associated file. The length parameter LEN specifies that each record in ACCOUNT.DAT is exactly 59 bytes. If ACCOUNT.DAT does not exist in auxiliary storage, then it is created. If ACCOUNT.DAT already exists as a random file, records may be added, read, and rewritten.

In Example 2 of Table 9.4, the LEN function is used to assign the random file WHSEDATA.DAT a **record length** equal to the length of the variable Warehouse. As shown in the next section, this technique for specifying the record length is commonly used.

Example 3 does not include a record length. In this case, QBasic assigns a default length of 128 bytes. Finally, Example 4 shows that the keywords FOR RANDOM are optional. That is, if a mode is not specified in an OPEN statement, then QBasic opens the file as a random file.

Creating the Record Structure for a Random File — The TYPE Statement

Fields, or data items, that make up the record to be read from or written to a random file must be defined with a TYPE statement. Each field is assigned a **field name** using the same rules as for variable names, except that the period (.) and trailing special characters (%, &, !, #, and $) are not allowed. Collectively, the fields are called the **record layout** or **record structure**, or **structure**. These field names then are used to access the data in the record. The TYPE statement is used to assign collectively the fields to a **label name** and to identify the fields with respect to their name, size, type, and location within the record. The label name follows the same rules as for field names.

Let us assume that the random file WHSEDATA.DAT contains a record for each warehouse that our company owns. Each record includes four fields:

Field	Type	Number of Characters
Warehouse Name	String	18
Street Address	String	17
City, State, Zip Code	String	20
Total Square Feet	Numeric	4

The following TYPE statement may be used to describe each field within the record:

```
TYPE WarehouseStructure
   Title AS STRING * 18
   Address1 AS STRING * 17
   Address2 AS STRING * 20
   Area AS SINGLE
END TYPE
```

The TYPE statement allocates the first 18 bytes (positions) in the record to the field Title (warehouse name); the next 17 bytes to Address1 (street address); the next 20 bytes to Address2 (city, state, zip code); and the last 4 bytes to Area (total square feet). A field name assigned a type SINGLE is allocated 4 bytes for a numeric value (as a single precision number).

To use the field names in WarehouseStructure, the DIM statement must be used to declare a **record variable** as the same type as WarehouseStructure. The following statement

```
DIM Warehouse AS WarehouseStructure
```

declares the record variable Warehouse as the same type as WarehouseStructure. The TYPE statement allows you to identify fields with respect to their name, size, and location within the record, but it is the DIM statement that actually reserves main memory for the record to move through on its way to and from auxiliary storage. The rules regarding the creation of record variable names is the same as for field and label names.

After data is read into the record variable Warehouse, the data items may be referenced by the names Warehouse.Title, Warehouse.Address1, Warehouse.Address2, and Warehouse.Area. Note that the record variable name in the DIM statement is *joined* to the field names in the TYPE statement by a period (.) to form the variable name. Also, these same variable names may be used to assign data items to the record before writing it to auxiliary storage.

The general form of the TYPE statement is shown in Table 9.5 on the next page. Valid field types in a TYPE statement include INTEGER (short integer, 2 byte length); LONG (long integer, 4 byte length); SINGLE (single precision, 4 byte length); DOUBLE (double precision, 8 byte length); STRING (character); or another user-defined data type. Table 3.4 on page 58 lists the range and precision characteristics of these field types.

The field type STRING defines the field name as string. You must follow the keyword STRING by an asterisk and a factor equal to the number of bytes you want to allocate. For example, Title AS STRING * 18 allocates 18 bytes to the field name Title.

	TABLE 9.5 - The TYPE Statement

General Form:	TYPE label name
	    field name₁ AS as field type
	       .
	       .
	       .
	    field nameₙ AS as field type
	END TYPE
	
	where **label name** is the name of the user-defined data type that identifies the group of field names;
	    field nameₙ names each field; and
	    field type is the field name's type: INTEGER, LONG, SINGLE, DOUBLE, STRING, or another user-defined data type.

Purpose:	To create user-defined data types. The TYPE statement is often used for identifying the group of fields in a record layout (structure) for a random file.

Example:	TYPE TownshipStructure
	    Number AS INTEGER
	    Title AS STRING * 20
	    Size AS SINGLE
	    Value AS DOUBLE
	END TYPE

Note:	Use the DIM statement to declare a record variable as the same type as the label name. For example, DIM Township AS TownshipStructure allocates storage for the record variable Township and assigns it the user-defined data type TownshipStructure. To access the field names in the structure, use the variable name *record variable.field name*.

The following rules summarize the use and proper placement of the TYPE statement in a program:

TYPE RULE 1	*Label names and field names in a TYPE statement follow the same rules as for variable names, except they may not include a period (.) or trailing special characters (%, &, !, #, and $).*
TYPE RULE 2	*Following the TYPE statement, the label name that identifies the structure must be assigned to a record variable name through the use of the DIM statement. Record variable names must abide by the same rules as field and label names.*
TYPE RULE 3	*To reference the field names in a TYPE statement, use the record variable name followed by a period (.) and the field name — record variable.field name.*
TYPE RULE 4	*The TYPE and DIM statements that define and declare the structure must precede the OPEN statement for the random file.*

The GET and PUT Statements

The GET **statement** reads and transfers a record from a random file. The PUT **statement** writes a record to a random file.

The general forms of the GET and PUT statements are shown in Tables 9.6 and 9.7 (on the next page).

TABLE 9.6 - The GET Statement	
General Form:	GET #filenumber, record number, record variable
	where **filenumber** is the number assigned to the random file in the OPEN statement; **record number** is the number of the record to read from the random file; and **record variable** is the variable assigned the user-defined structure.
Purpose:	To read a record from the random file assigned to filenumber and assign it to record variable.
Examples:	GET #1, Record.Number, Warehouse GET #2, , Department GET #FILE, Rec, Account GET #3, 15, Part
Note:	If the record number is not included in the GET statement as in Example 2, then the next record in the random file is read into the record variable.

The partial program in Figure 9.12 illustrates the steps involved in accessing a random file and the relationships between the TYPE, DIM, OPEN, and GET statements.

|FIGURE 9.12

The steps in accessing a random file and the relationships between the TYPE, DIM, OPEN, and GET statements.

Step 1: Use a TYPE statement to define the structure.

```
TYPE WarehouseStructure
    Title AS STRING * 18
    Address1 AS STRING * 17
    Address2 AS STRING * 20
    Area AS SINGLE
END TYPE
```

Step 2: Use a DIM statement to declare *Warehouse* as having the same data type as *WarehouseStructure*.

```
DIM Warehouse AS WarehouseStructure
```

Step 3: Use an OPEN statement to open the random file WHSEDATA.DAT as filenumber 1 with a length of *Warehouse*.

```
OPEN "A:WHSEDATA.DAT" FOR RANDOM AS #1 LEN = LEN(Warehouse)
```

reference to record variable Warehouse

Step 4: Use a GET statement to read a record from filenumber 1 (record 34 in this example into *Warehouse*).

```
GET #1, 34, Warehouse
```

Step 5: To display the field names defined in the TYPE statement, use the prefix of the record variable *Warehouse*, separated by a period.

```
PRINT Warehouse.Title, Warehouse.Address1
PRINT Warehouse.Address2, Warehouse.Area
```

If Record.Number has a value of 29 when the statement

```
GET #1, Record.Number, Warehouse
```

is executed, then the twenty-ninth record in the random file assigned to filenumber 1 is read into the record variable Warehouse.

Records from a random file may be read sequentially, beginning at any record in the file. For example, if in the following partial program

```
Record.Number = 26
GET #2, Record.Number, Warehouse
   .
   .
   .
GET #2, , Warehouse
   .
   .
   .
GET #2, , Warehouse
```

then the first GET reads the twenty-sixth record, the next GET reads the twenty-seventh record, and the third one, the twenty-eighth record. If the first GET following an OPEN statement has no record number, then the first record in the random file is read and assigned to the record variable.

As indicated in Table 9.7, the PUT statement writes the value of record variable to a random file. Thus, the statement

```
PUT #2, 62, Hospital
```

writes the value of Hospital to filenumber 2 as record 62.

TABLE 9.7 - The PUT Statement	
General Form:	PUT #filenumber, record number, record variable
Purpose:	To write the value of record variable to the random file assigned to filenumber.
Examples:	PUT #1, Record.Number, Warehouse PUT #2, 567, Order PUT #Filenum, , Count

The LOC and LOF Functions

The LOC(n) **function** returns the record number of the last record read or written to the random file assigned to filenumber n. For example, in the following partial program

```
GET #3, Record.Number, Model
Last.Record = LOC(3)
```

the variable Last.Record is assigned the value of Record.Number because Record.Number is the record number of the last record read from the random file assigned to filenumber 3.

The LOF(n) **function** returns information regarding the character size of the random file assigned to filenumber n. This value then may be used to determine the number of records in a random file by dividing the record variable length into whatever the LOF function returns.

For example, assume you want to append records to an existing random file, but you do not know the last record number; the following partial program will accomplish the task:

```
Record.Number = LOF(2) \ LEN(Warehouse)
   .
   .
   .
PUT #2, Record.Number + 1, Warehouse
```

The first statement assigns Record.Number the number of records in the random file assigned to filenumber 2. The `PUT` statement then writes the next record to the random file after the last record, thereby not destroying any records in the random file.

PROGRAMMING CASE STUDY 20 – Creating a Random File

In earlier programming case studies, each record in INVNTORY.DAT included a number to indicate the warehouse in which the stock item was located. The warehouse numbers (location) varied between 1 and 4. The following problem creates a random file in which each record includes a warehouse name, an address, and a total number of square feet for warehouses 1, 2, 3, and 4.

Problem: The PUC Company requests a program that creates a random file in which each record represents one of its warehouses. Each record includes the following data items.

Field	Type	Number of Characters
Warehouse Name	String	18
Street Address	String	17
City, State, Zip Code	String	20
Total Square Feet	Numeric, single precision	4

The actual data for each record is shown below:

Warehouse Location	Warehouse Name	Street Address	City, State, Zip Code	Total Square Feet
1	PUC Gyte Whse	1498 Baring Ave.	Whitley, IN 46325	80,000
2	PUC Anderson Whse	612 45th St.	Calcity, IL 60618	220,000
3	PUC Potter Whse	1329 Olcot St.	Pointe, IN 46367	85,900
4	PUC Porter Whse	15 E 63rd St.	Polk, IN 45323	92,500

The user enters the warehouse number (location) to indicate the record that is to be created. The warehouse number is not to be part of the record.

Following are the program tasks in outline form, a program solution, and a discussion of the program solution.

Program Tasks

1. Main Program — Call the subroutines A100.Initialization, B100.Create.Random.File, and C100.Wrap.Up.

2. A100.Initialization

   a. Use the `TYPE` statement to define the record structure.

   b. Use the `DIM` statement to to assign a record variable (Warehouse) the same data type as the label name in the `TYPE` statement.

   c. Open the file WHSEDATA.DAT for random access as filenumber 1 with a record length of Warehouse.

3. B100.Create.Random.File — Establish a Do-Until loop that executes until Control$ equals an N or n. Within the loop, do the following:

   a. Call B200.Accept.Warehouse.Record. In this subroutine, use `INPUT` statements to accept the warehouse number (Record.Number); warehouse name (Warehouse.Title); warehouse street address (Warehouse.Address1); warehouse city, state, zip code (Warehouse.Address2); and warehouse square feet (Warehouse.Area).

   b. Call B210.Write.Warehouse.Record. In this subroutine, use the `PUT` statement with the key Record.Number to write the record variable Warehouse to WHSEDATA.DAT.

c. Use an INPUT statement to assign Control$ the value Y or y if the user wants to enter another record.

4. C100.Wrap.Up

a. Close the random file WHSEDATA.DAT.
b. Display an end-of-job message.

Program Solution

Figure 9.13 presents Program 9.3, the solution to Programming Case Study 20. The program corresponds to the preceding tasks.

FIGURE 9.13

Program 9.3, the solution to Programming Case Study 20.

```
 1   ' Program 9.3
 2   ' Creating a Random File
 3   ' Random File Created = WHSEDATA.DAT
 4   ' ********************************
 5   ' *          Main Program          *
 6   ' ********************************
 7   GOSUB A100.Initialization
 8   GOSUB B100.Create.Random.File
 9   GOSUB C100.Wrap.Up
10   END
11
12   ' ********************************
13   ' *          Initialization          *
14   ' ********************************
15   A100.Initialization:
16      ' ***** Define Record Structure *****
17      TYPE WarehouseStructure
18         Title AS STRING * 18
19         Address1 AS STRING * 17
20         Address2 AS STRING * 20
21         Area AS SINGLE
22      END TYPE
23
24      ' ***** Declare Record Variable *****
25      DIM Warehouse AS WarehouseStructure
26
27      ' ****** Open Warehouse File *****
28      OPEN "A:WHSEDATA.DAT" FOR RANDOM AS #1 LEN = LEN(Warehouse)
29   RETURN
30
31   ' ********************************
32   ' *          Create Random File          *
33   ' ********************************
34   B100.Create.Random.File:
35      DO
36         GOSUB B200.Accept.Warehouse.Record
37         GOSUB B210.Write.Warehouse.Record
38         LOCATE 14, 10
39         INPUT "Enter Y to add another record, else N... ", Control$
40      LOOP UNTIL UCASE$(Control$) = "N"
41   RETURN
42
43   ' ********************************
44   ' *     Accept a Warehouse Record     *
45   ' ********************************
46   B200.Accept.Warehouse.Record:
47      CLS     ' Clear Screen
48      LOCATE 2, 10
```

```
49       PRINT "Warehouse Location Random File Create"
50       LOCATE 4, 10
51       INPUT "Warehouse Number ==============> ", Record.Number
52       LOCATE 6, 10
53       INPUT "Warehouse Name ================> ", Warehouse.Title
54       LOCATE 8, 10
55       INPUT "Warehouse Street ==============> ", Warehouse.Address1
56       LOCATE 10, 10
57       INPUT "Warehouse City, State, Zip ===> ", Warehouse.Address2
58       LOCATE 12, 10
59       INPUT "Warehouse Total Square Feet ==> ", Warehouse.Area
60    RETURN
61
62    ' *********************************
63    ' *     Write a Warehouse Record     *
64    ' *********************************
65    B210.Write.Warehouse.Record:
66       PUT #1, Record.Number, Warehouse
67    RETURN
68
69    ' *********************************
70    ' *               Wrap-Up                 *
71    ' *********************************
72    C100.Wrap.Up:
73       CLOSE #1
74       LOCATE 16, 10: PRINT "Random file WHSEDATA.DAT created"
75       LOCATE 18, 10: PRINT "Job Complete"
76    RETURN
77
78    ' *********** End of Program *******

      [run]
```

Discussion of the Program Solution

When Program 9.3 is executed, lines 17 through 22 define the record structure, line 25 declares the record variable Warehouse to be the same data type as WarehouseStructure, and line 28 opens the random file WHSEDATA.DAT as filenumber 1. As shown in Figure 9.14, B200.Accept.Warehouse.Record (lines 46 through 60) accepts the user's responses. The PUT statement in line 66 writes the record that corresponds to the warehouse number (Record.Number). Finally, line 39 in B100.Create.Random.File accepts a user response that determines whether the program should continue.

FIGURE 9.14

Display from the execution of Program 9.3 for warehouse location 2.

```
Warehouse Location Random File Create

Warehouse Number ==============> 2

Warehouse Name ================> PUC Anderson Whse

Warehouse Street ==============> 612 45th St.

Warehouse City, State, Zip ===> "Calcity, IL 60618"

Warehouse Total Square Feet ==> 220000

Enter Y to add another record, else N... Y
```

Program 9.3 can be written without the user being required to enter the warehouse number (Record.Number). In such a version, line 66 is modified to

```
PUT #1, , Warehouse
```

A PUT statement without a record number writes the record as the next record. However, the user would then be required to enter the records in sequence. As it now stands, Program 9.3 will properly create the random file regardless of the order in which the records are entered. For example, warehouse location number 4 can be entered before warehouse number 1.

Because it requests a warehouse number, Program 9.3 can be used later to add new warehouse records or to modify existing warehouse records. For example, if a fifth warehouse is added by the PUC Company, Program 9.3 can be used to add this new record. Unlike sequential files, whose original contents are automatically deleted when opened for output, random files exist until they are physically deleted by a system command.

In the creation of random files, it is not necessary for a record to be entered for every record number. It is valid to number warehouses 1, 3, 6, and 10. When a random file like that is created without contiguous record numbers, the PC reserves areas for records 2, 4, 5, 7, 8, and 9. These areas are called **empty cells**.

PROGRAMMING CASE STUDY 21 – Accessing Records in a Random File

The following problem includes a program that accesses records in the random file WHSEDATA.DAT created in Programming Case Study 20 (page 369).

Problem: The PUC Company has requested a program to be written to access and display records from the random file WHSEDATA.DAT. Following are the program tasks in outline form, a program solution, and a discussion of the program solution.

Program Tasks

1. Main Program — Call A100.Initialization, B100.Process.Request, and C100.Wrap.Up.
2. A100.Initialization
   a. Use the TYPE statement to define the record structure.
   b. Use the DIM statement to assign a record variable (Warehouse) the same data type as the label name in the TYPE statement.
   c. Open the file WHSEDATA.DAT for random access as filenumber 1 with a record length of Warehouse.
3. B100.Process.Request — Establish a Do-Until loop that executes until Control$ equals the value N or n. Within the loop, do the following:
   a. Call B200.Accept.Request. Within the subroutine, display a program title, and use the INPUT statement to accept the warehouse number (Record.Number).
   b. Call B210.Get.And.Display.Record. Within this subroutine, use the GET statement to access the requested record (Record.Number). Next, display the variables listed in the record structure.
   c. Use an INPUT statement to assign Control$ the value Y or y if the user wants to display another record.
4. C100.Wrap.Up
   a. Close the random file WHSEDATA.DAT.
   b. Display an end-of-job message.

Program Solution

Figure 9.15 presents the solution to Programming Case Study 21, Program 9.4. The program corresponds to the preceding tasks.

FIGURE 9.15

Program 9.4, the solution to Programming Case Study 21.

```
1    ' Program 9.4
2    ' Accessing Records in a Random File
3    ' Random File = WHSEDATA.DAT
4    ' **********************************
5    ' *            Main Program         *
6    ' **********************************
7    GOSUB A100.Initialization
8    GOSUB B100.Process.Request
9    GOSUB C100.Wrap.Up
10   END
11
12   ' **********************************
13   ' *          Initialization         *
14   ' **********************************
15   A100.Initialization:
16      ' ***** Define Record Structure *****
17      TYPE WarehouseStructure
18         Title AS STRING * 18
19         Address1 AS STRING * 17
20         Address2 AS STRING * 20
21         Area AS SINGLE
22      END TYPE
23
24      ' ***** Declare Record Variable *****
25      DIM Warehouse AS WarehouseStructure
26
27      ' ***** Open Warehouse File *****
28      OPEN "A:WHSEDATA.DAT" FOR RANDOM AS #1 LEN = LEN(Warehouse)
29   RETURN
30
31   ' **********************************
32   ' *          Process a Request      *
33   ' **********************************
34   B100.Process.Request:
35      DO
36         GOSUB B200.Accept.Request
37         GOSUB B210.Get.And.Display.Record
38         LOCATE 14, 10
39         INPUT "Enter Y to access another record, else N... ", Control$
40      LOOP UNTIL UCASE$(Control$) = "N"
41   RETURN
42
43   ' **********************************
44   ' *          Accept a Request       *
45   ' **********************************
46   B200.Accept.Request:
47      CLS  ' Clear Screen
48      LOCATE 2, 10
49      PRINT "Warehouse Location Random File Access"
50      LOCATE 4, 10
51      INPUT "Warehouse Number =============> ", Record.Number
52   RETURN
53
```

(continued)

FIGURE 9.15

(continued)

```
54   ' ***********************************
55   ' *        Get and Display Record      *
56   ' ***********************************
57   B210.Get.And.Display.Record:
58     GET #1, Record.Number, Warehouse
59     LOCATE 6, 10
60     PRINT "Warehouse Name ===============> "; Warehouse.Title
61     LOCATE 8, 10
62     PRINT "Warehouse Street =============> "; Warehouse.Address1
63     LOCATE 10, 10
64     PRINT "Warehouse City, State, Zip ===> "; Warehouse.Address2
65     LOCATE 12, 10
66     PRINT USING "Warehouse Total Square Feet ==> ###,###"; Warehouse.Area
67   RETURN
68
69   ' ***********************************
70   ' *             Wrap-Up              *
71   ' ***********************************
72   C100.Wrap.Up:
73     CLOSE #1
74     LOCATE 16, 10: PRINT "Job Complete"
75   RETURN
76
77   ' ********* End of Program **********

     [run]
```

Discussion of the Program Solution

Figure 9.16 shows the results displayed when warehouse number 2 is entered for Program 9.4. Line 58 in B210.Get.And.Display.Record reads the record that corresponds to the number entered by the user and assigned to Record.Number in line 51. Lines 60 through 66 show that the values found in a record can be displayed by using the field names preceded by the record variable name and a period.

It is important to note that records in WHSEDATA.DAT may be accessed in any desired order. After displaying warehouse location number 2, you may request 1, 3, 4, or 2 again, and the PC can respond immediately without rewinding the file or reading records between the previously accessed record and the next record.

FIGURE 9.16

Results displayed due to entering warehouse location number 2 for Program 9.4.

```
Warehouse Location Random File Access

Warehouse Number ==============> 2

Warehouse Name ===============> PUC Anderson Whse

Warehouse Street =============> 612 45th St.

Warehouse City, State, Zip ===> "Calcity, IL 60618"

Warehouse Total Square Feet ==> 220,000

Enter Y to access another record, else N... Y
```

9.4 SIMULATED-INDEXED FILES

Provided the record number is known, any record can be accessed in a random file. Unfortunately, few applications use integers, such as 1, 2, and 3, to represent the employee numbers, customer numbers, or stock numbers that commonly identify the record to be accessed in a file. More often, these keys are made up of several digits and letters that have no relationship to the location of the record in a random file. However, many applications require random access on the basis of these types of keys.

In many programming languages, such as COBOL and RPG, indexed files — a third type of file organization — allow a relationship between a key and the record location to automatically be established. With QBasic, indexed files are not available, and therefore, the relationship between the key and the record location must be handled by the programmer.

PROGRAMMING CASE STUDY 22 – Using a Simulated-Indexed File for Inventory Retrieval and Update

Problem: The Stores department of the PUC Company has requested computerized access to inventory records by stock number. Their request involves two separate parts. In the first part a program must be designed and coded to create a simulated-indexed file. In the second part another program must be created to update and maintain the file. Parts 1 and 2 and their associated programs, Program 9.5 and Program 9.6, are illustrated by the system flowchart in Figure 9.17.

FIGURE 9.17
A system flowchart representing the Programs 9.5 and 9.6, the solutuions to Part 1 and Part 2 of Progamming Case Study 22.

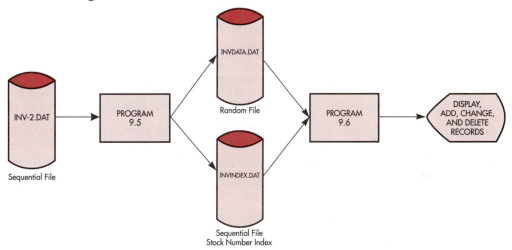

The program for Part 1 should create an index for up to 100 keys and a corresponding random file from the sequential file INV-2.DAT created earlier by Program 9.2 (presented in Figure 9.8 on pages 359-361 and containing the data shown in Figure 9.11 on page 363). Each record of INV-2.DAT contains the following fields:

Field	Type	Field Size
Stock Number	String	4
Warehouse Location	String	1
Description	String	15
Unit Cost	Single	4
Selling Price	Single	4
Quantity on Hand	Single	4

The program for the second part should permit the user to display, add, change, and delete records in the file, provided the stock number is known.

Following are the program tasks for Part 1 of the problem, the solution to Part 1, and a discussion of the solution.

Part 1 Tasks: Build Index File

1. Main Program

   a. Call the subroutines A100.Initialization, B100.Build.Data.Portion.Of.Index.File, and C100.Wrap.Up.

2. A100.Initialization

   a. Use the following TYPE statement to define the record structure:

   ```
   TYPE InventoryStructure
       Stock AS STRING * 4
       Location AS STRING * 1
       Desc AS STRING * 15
       Cost AS SINGLE
       Price AS SINGLE
       Quantity AS SINGLE
   END TYPE
   ```

   b. Use the following DIM statement to declare the record variable:

   ```
   DIM Inventory As InventoryStructure
   ```

   c. Declare the array Index$ to 100 elements.

   d. Use a For loop to set each element in the array Index$ equal to the string value Empty.

   e. Set Record.number% to zero.

   f. Open INV-2.DAT and INVDATA.DAT. Records will be read from the sequential file INV-2.DAT and written to the random file INVDATA.DAT.

3. B100.Build.Data.Portion.Of.Index.File — Establish a Do-While loop that executes until end-of-file on INV-2.DAT. Within the loop, do the following:

   a. Read a record from INV-2.DAT.

   b. Call B200.Assign.Stock.Number.To.Index. In this subroutine, increment Record.number% by 1 and set Index$(Record.number%) equal to the stock number (M.Stock$).

   c. Call B210.Write.Record.To.Random.File. In this subroutine, do the following:

   (1) Set the field names in the record variable equal to the corresponding values from the record read from INV-2.DAT.

   (2) Use the PUT statement to write the record to the random file INVDATA.DAT with the value of Record.number%.

4. C100.Wrap.Up

   a. Close the random file INVDATA.DAT.

   b. Display the number of records (Record.number%) written to INVDATA.DAT.

   c. Call C200.Create.File.Of.Keys. In this subroutine, open the sequential file INVINDEX.DAT. Use a For loop to write the elements of the array Index$ to INVINDEX.DAT.

   d. Close INVINDEX.DAT and display the message Job Complete.

FIGURE 9.18

Program 9.5, Create initial sequential index file and random file.

```
 1   ' Program 9.5
 2   ' Create Initial Sequential Index File and Random File
 3   '
 4   ' This program reads the sequential file INV-2.DAT and creates
 5   ' the random file INVDATA.DAT.  The stock number (Stock$) is
 6   ' assigned to the element in array Index$ that corresponds to
 7   ' the record number.  As part of the end-of-file routine, array
 8   ' Index$ is written to the sequential file INVINDEX.DAT.  The
 9   ' maximum no. of records that INVINDEX.DAT can contain is 100.
10   '
11   ' ********************************************************************
12   ' *                        Main Program                           *
13   ' ********************************************************************
14   GOSUB A100.Initialization
15   GOSUB B100.Build.Data.Portion.Of.Index.File
16   GOSUB C100.Wrap.Up
17   END
18
19   ' ********************************************************************
20   ' *                        Initialization                         *
21   ' ********************************************************************
22   A100.Initialization:
23      CLS  ' Clear Screen
24
25      ' ***** Define Record Structure *****
26      TYPE InventoryStructure
27         Stock AS STRING * 4
28         Location AS STRING * 1
29         Desc AS STRING * 15
30         Cost AS SINGLE
31         Price AS SINGLE
32         Quantity AS SINGLE
33      END TYPE
34      DIM Inventory AS InventoryStructure '  Declare Record Variable
35      DIM Index$(1 TO 100)
36      FOR Record.number% = 1 TO 100
37         Index$(Record.number%) = "Empty"
38      NEXT Record.number%
39      Record.number% = 0
40
41      ' ********** Open Files **********
42      OPEN "A:INV-2.DAT" FOR INPUT AS #1
43      OPEN "A:INVDATA.DAT" FOR RANDOM AS #2 LEN = LEN(Inventory)
44   RETURN
45
46   ' ********************************************************************
47   ' *              Build Data Portion of Index File                 *
48   ' ********************************************************************
49   B100.Build.Data.Portion.Of.Index.File:
50      DO WHILE NOT EOF(1)
51         INPUT #1, M.Stock$, M.Location$, M.Desc$, M.Cost, M.Price, M.Quantity
52         GOSUB B200.Assign.Stock.Number.To.Index
53         GOSUB B210.Write.Record.To.Random.File
54      LOOP
55   RETURN
56
```

(continued)

▌FIGURE 9.18
(continued)

```
57    ' ****************************************************************
58    ' *              Assign Key to Index$(Record.Number%)           *
59    ' ****************************************************************
60    B200.Assign.Stock.Number.To.Index:
61       Record.number% = Record.number% + 1
62       Index$(Record.number%) = M.Stock$
63    RETURN
64
65    ' ****************************************************************
66    ' *                Write Record to INVINDEX.DAT                 *
67    ' ****************************************************************
68    B210.Write.Record.To.Random.File:
69       Inventory.Stock = M.Stock$
70       Inventory.Location = M.Location$
71       Inventory.Desc = M.Desc$
72       Inventory.Cost = M.Cost
73       Inventory.Price = M.Price
74       Inventory.Quantity = M.Quantity
75       PUT #2, Record.number%, Inventory
76    RETURN
77
78    ' ****************************************************************
79    ' *                          Wrap-Up                           *
80    ' ****************************************************************
81    C100.Wrap.Up:
82       CLOSE
83       PRINT "The number of records in the file is"; Record.number%
84       GOSUB C200.Create.File.Of.Keys
85       PRINT : PRINT "Job Complete"
86    RETURN
87
88    ' ****************************************************************
89    ' *                     Create File of Keys                    *
90    ' ****************************************************************
91    C200.Create.File.Of.Keys:
92       OPEN "A:INVINDEX.DAT" FOR OUTPUT AS #1
93       FOR Record.number% = 1 TO 100
94          WRITE #1, Index$(Record.number%)
95       NEXT Record.number%
96       CLOSE
97    RETURN
98
99    ' ******************** End of Program ************************

      [run]

      The number of records in the file is 13

      Job Complete
```

Discussion of the Solution to Part 1

When Program 9.5 is executed, line 14 calls A100.Initialization. After the screen is cleared, the TYPE statement (lines 26 through 33) defines the record structure InventoryStructure, and the DIM statement (line 34) declares the record variable Inventory as the same type as InventoryStructure. Next the array Index$ is declared and lines 36 through 38 initialize all elements of the array Index$ to the string value Empty. Following the For loop, the record counter (Record.number%) is set equal to zero. Finally, the two files are opened in lines 42 and 43.

B100.Build.Data.Portion.Of.Index.File maintains control of the program until the end-of-file mark is sensed on the master file INV-2.DAT. Within the loop, a record from INV-2.DAT is read, the stock number (M.Stock$) is assigned to the next element in Index$, and the data portion of the master record is written to INVDATA.DAT. Note the relationship established between the Record.number% element of the array Index$ and the Record.number% record in the random file INVDATA.DAT.

As part of C100.Wrap.Up, the array Index$ is written to the sequential file INVINDEX.DAT. This file contains 100 data items, some of which are equal to stock numbers and others of which are equal to the string value Empty. In part 2 of this programming case study, the array Index$ is used to determine the locations of records with corresponding stock numbers. The fact that unused elements of the array Index$ are equal to the string value Empty will be helpful both for adding and for deleting records.

Part 2: Displaying and Updating Records in the Simulated-Indexed File

This second program displays and updates records in the simulated-indexed file created by Program 9.5 (page 377). A top-down chart (Figure 9.19), a list of the corresponding Part 2 tasks, the Part 2 solution (Program 9.6 on page 381), and a discussion of the solution follow.

After reading this section, you are encouraged to load Program 9.6 (PRG9-6) from the Data Disk and execute it.

FIGURE 9.19

A top-down chart for Program 9.6.

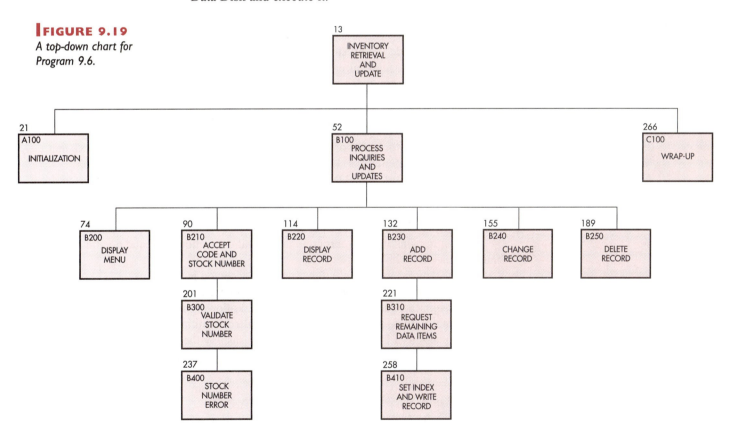

Part 2: Tasks

The following tasks correspond to the top-down chart in Figure 9.19.

1. Main Program

   a. Call the subroutines A100.Initialization, B100.Process.Inquiries.And.Updates, and C100.Wrap.Up.

2. A100.Initialization
   a. Use the same TYPE statement and DIM statement that were used in Program 9.5 to define the record structure and declare the record variable.
   b. Open the sequential file INVINDEX.DAT and random file INVDATA.DAT. INVINDEX.DAT contains the stock numbers; INVDATA.DAT contains the data that corresponds to the stock numbers.
   c. Use a DIM statement to declare the array Index$ to 100 elements.
   d. Use a For loop to read the 100 stock numbers in INVINDEX.DAT into the array Index$.
   e. Close INVINDEX.DAT.

3. B100.Process.Inquiries.And.Updates
   a. Call B200.Display.Menu. In this subroutine, display a menu with the following valid codes:

Code	Function
1	Display Record
2	Add Record
3	Change Record
4	Delete Record
5	End Program

   b. Call B210.Accept.Code.And.Stock.Number. In this subroutine, accept a function code (Code%) and stock number (Stock.Number$). Both Code% and Stock.Number$ must be validated. Code% must equal one of the valid function codes displayed by the menu.

   The stock number Stock.Number$ is validated by comparing it to the elements of the array Index$. If the function code Code% equals 1, 3, or 4, then Stock.Number$ must equal the value of one of the elements of Index$. Assign Record.Number% the value of the subscript of the element of the array Index$ that is equal to the stock number. Use Record.Number% in B220.Display.Record, B240.Change.Record, and B250.Delete.Record to access the corresponding record in the random file INVDATA.DAT.

   If the function code equals 2 (add record), then the stock number must not equal the value of an element in the array Index$.

   Control remains in this subroutine until a valid function code and a valid stock number are entered by the user.

   c. On the basis of the value of the function code accepted in B210, use a SELECT CASE statement to call the subroutines B220.Display.Record, B230.Add.Record, B240.Change.Record, or B250.Delete.Record. Following return of control from one of these subroutines, B200.Display.Menu is called to initiate the next user request.
   (1) The function of B220.Display.Record is to display the record that corresponds to the stock number entered by the user in B200.Display.Menu. In this subroutine, do the following:
       (a) Read the Record.Number% record in the random file INVDATA.DAT.
       (b) Display the record read from INVDATA.DAT.
       (c) Use the INPUT$ function to suspend execution so the user may view the record before the menu is displayed again.
   (2) The function of B230.Add.Record is to add a record to INVDATA.DAT and a corresponding stock number to the array Index$. In this subroutine, do the following:
       (a) Redisplay the stock number entered by the user.
       (b) Determine the first element of Index$ that is equal to the string value Empty.
       (c) If no element of Index$ is equal to the string value Empty, then the array is full, an appropriate diagnostic message is displayed, and control is returned to the menu.

(d) If an element of Index$ equals the value `Empty`, then assign the stock number (Stock.Number$) to the Record.Number% element of Index$ and request the remaining items that belong to this new record.

(e) Use the `PUT` statement to write the record to INVDATA.DAT that corresponds to Record.Number%. The record is written to INVDATA.DAT only after the user is given the opportunity to terminate the addition.

(3) The function of B240.Change.Record is to allow the user to change any item in the record except the stock number. In this subroutine, do the following:

(a) Use the `GET` statement to read the record in the random file INVDATA.DAT which corresponds to Record.Number%.

(b) Request the user to enter changes. If an item is to remain the same in the record, then the user responds by entering a –1 for the item in question.

(c) Check each response. If a response is not equal to –1, assign the response to the corresponding field name.

(d) Write the modified record to INVDATA.DAT only after the user has been given the opportunity to terminate the record change.

(4) The function of B250.Delete.Record is to delete an unwanted record. To delete a record, assign Index$(Record.Number%) the string value `Empty` only after giving the user the opportunity to terminate the record deletion. Note that nothing is done to the corresponding record in INVDATA.DAT. However, because Index$(Record.Number%) is assigned the string value `Empty`, this element may be used for a record addition at a later date; at this time, the record in the random file is changed.

4. C100.Wrap.Up

a. Close the random file INVDATA.DAT.

b. Open the sequential file INVINDEX.DAT for output.

c. Use a For loop to write the 100 elements of the array Index$ to INVINDEX.DAT.

d. Close the sequential file INVINDEX.DAT.

e. Display an end-of-job message.

FIGURE 9.20

Program 9.6, Inventory Record Display, Add, Update, and Deletion.

```
1   ' Program 9.6
2   ' Inventory Record Retrieval and Update
3   '
4   ' This program displays or updates records in a simulated-indexed file.
5   ' The data for the simulated-indexed file is located in the random file
6   ' INVDATA.DAT.  The records in the random file are accessed by a key
7   ' (stock number) that is entered by the user.  Records may be displayed,
8   ' added to the file, deleted from the file, or changed.
9   '
10  ' *******************************************************************
11  ' *                         Main Program                          *
12  ' *******************************************************************
13  GOSUB A100.Initialization
14  GOSUB B100.Process.Inquiries.And.Updates
15  GOSUB C100.Wrap.Up
16  END
17
18  ' *******************************************************************
19  ' *                        Initialization                         *
20  ' *******************************************************************
21  A100.Initialization:
22     CLS  ' Clear Screen
23
24     ' ******** Define Record Structure ********
25     TYPE InventoryStructure
26        Stock AS STRING * 4
27        Location AS STRING * 1
```

(continued)

▮FIGURE 9.20
(continued)

```
28          Desc AS STRING * 15
29          Cost AS SINGLE
30          Price AS SINGLE
31          Quantity AS SINGLE
32       END TYPE
33
34       ' ******** Declare Record Variable ********
35       DIM Inventory AS InventoryStructure
36
37       ' ************* Open Files ***************
38       OPEN "A:INVINDEX.DAT" FOR INPUT AS #1
39       OPEN "A:INVDATA.DAT" FOR RANDOM AS #2 LEN = LEN(Inventory)
40
41       ' ***** Declare and Load Array Index$ *****
42       DIM Index$(1 TO 100)
43       FOR Record.Number% = 1 TO 100
44          INPUT #1, Index$(Record.Number%)  ' Read Stock Numbers into Array
45       NEXT Record.Number%
46       CLOSE #1
47    RETURN
48
49    ' ********************************************************************
50    ' *                  Process Inquiries and Updates                 *
51    ' ********************************************************************
52    B100.Process.Inquiries.And.Updates:
53       GOSUB B200.Display.Menu
54       GOSUB B210.Accept.Code.And.Stock.Number
55       DO WHILE Code% <> 5
56          SELECT CASE Code%
57             CASE 1
58                GOSUB B220.Display.Record
59             CASE 2
60                GOSUB B230.Add.Record
61             CASE 3
62                GOSUB B240.Change.Record
63             CASE 4
64                GOSUB B250.Delete.Record
65          END SELECT
66          GOSUB B200.Display.Menu
67          GOSUB B210.Accept.Code.And.Stock.Number
68       LOOP
69    RETURN
70
71    ' ********************************************************************
72    ' *                         Display Menu                           *
73    ' ********************************************************************
74    B200.Display.Menu:
75       CLS
76       LOCATE 2, 19: PRINT "Menu for Inventory Retrieval And Update"
77       LOCATE 3, 19: PRINT "-------------------------------------"
78       LOCATE 5, 19: PRINT "   Code          Function"
79       LOCATE 6, 19: PRINT "   ----          --------"
80       LOCATE 7, 19: PRINT "    1            Display Record"
81       LOCATE 9, 19: PRINT "    2            Add Record"
82       LOCATE 11, 19: PRINT "    3            Change Record"
83       LOCATE 13, 19: PRINT "    4            Delete Record"
84       LOCATE 15, 19: PRINT "    5            End Program"
85    RETURN
86
```

```
87    ' *******************************************************************
88    ' *                  Accept Code and Stock Number                   *
89    ' *******************************************************************
90    B210.Accept.Code.And.Stock.Number:
91       DO
92          Switch$ = "ON"
93          LOCATE 17, 52: PRINT SPC(10);
94          LOCATE 17, 19: INPUT "Enter a Code 1 through 5 ======> ", Code%
95          DO WHILE Code% < 1 OR Code% > 5
96             BEEP: BEEP: BEEP: BEEP
97             LOCATE 18, 19: PRINT "Code out of range, please re-enter"
98             LOCATE 17, 52: PRINT SPC(10);
99             LOCATE 17, 52: INPUT "", Code%
100            LOCATE 18, 19: PRINT SPC(40);
101         LOOP
102         IF Code% <> 5 THEN
103            LOCATE 19, 19
104            INPUT "Stock Number =================> ", Stock.Number$
105            GOSUB B300.Validate.Stock.Number
106         END IF
107      LOOP UNTIL Switch$ = "ON"
108      CLS
109   RETURN
110
111   ' *******************************************************************
112   ' *                       Display Record                            *
113   ' *******************************************************************
114   B220.Display.Record:
115      GET #2, Record.Number%, Inventory
116      PRINT : PRINT "Stock Number =============> "; Stock.Number$
117      PRINT : PRINT "Warehouse Location =======> "; Inventory.Location
118      PRINT : PRINT "Description ==============> "; Inventory.Desc
119      PRINT
120      PRINT USING "Unit Cost ===============>#,###.##"; Inventory.Cost
121      PRINT
122      PRINT USING "Selling Price ===========>#,###.##"; Inventory.Price
123      PRINT
124      PRINT USING "Quantity on Hand ========>#,###"; Inventory.Quantity
125      PRINT : PRINT "Press any key to continue..."
126      A$ = INPUT$(1)
127   RETURN
128
129   ' *******************************************************************
130   ' *                         Add Record                              *
131   ' *******************************************************************
132   B230.Add.Record:
133      PRINT : PRINT "Stock Number =============> "; Stock.Number$
134      Record.Number% = 0
135      FOR I% = 1 TO 100   ' Search for "Empty" element in array Index$
136         IF Index$(I%) = "Empty" THEN
137            Record.Number% = I%
138            EXIT FOR
139         END IF
140      NEXT I%
141      IF Record.Number% <> 0 THEN
142         Inventory.Stock = Stock.Number$
143         RETURN B310.Request.Remaining.Data.Items
144      ELSE
145         PRINT
146         PRINT "** ERROR ** Index is full"
147         PRINT : PRINT "Press any key to continue..."
```

(continued)

|FIGURE 9.20
(continued)

```
148          A$ = INPUT$(1)
149       END IF
150    RETURN
151
152    ' *****************************************************************
153    ' *                        Change Record                        *
154    ' *****************************************************************
155    B240.Change.Record:
156       GET #2, Record.Number%, Inventory
157       PRINT : PRINT "Stock Number ============> "; Stock.Number$
158       PRINT
159       PRINT "**** Enter a -1 if you do not want to change a data item ****"
160       PRINT : INPUT "Warehouse Location =======> ", T.Location$
161       IF T.Location$ <> "-1" THEN
162          Inventory.Location = T.Location$
163       END IF
164       PRINT : INPUT "Description =============> ", T.Desc$
165       IF T.Desc$ <> "-1" THEN
166          Inventory.Desc = T.Desc$
167       END IF
168       PRINT : INPUT "Unit Cost ==============> ", T.Cost
169       IF T.Cost <> -1 THEN
170          Inventory.Cost = T.Cost
171       END IF
172       PRINT : INPUT "Selling Price ===========> ", T.Price
173       IF T.Price <> -1 THEN
174          Inventory.Price = T.Price
175       END IF
176       PRINT : INPUT "Quantity on Hand =========> ", T.Quantity
177       IF T.Quantity <> -1 THEN
178          Inventory.Quantity = T.Quantity
179       END IF
180       PRINT : INPUT "Enter Y to update record, else N... ", Control$
181       IF UCASE$(Control$) = "Y" THEN
182          PUT #2, Record.Number%, Inventory
183       END IF
184    RETURN
185
186    ' *****************************************************************
187    ' *                        Delete Record                        *
188    ' *****************************************************************
189    B250.Delete.Record:
190       PRINT
191       PRINT "Are you sure you want to delete stock number "; Stock.Number$
192       PRINT : INPUT "Enter Y to delete record, else N... ", Control$
193       IF UCASE$(Control$) = "Y" THEN
194          Index$(Record.Number%) = "Empty"
195       END IF
196    RETURN
197
198    ' *****************************************************************
199    ' *            Determine if Stock Number Is Valid               *
200    ' *****************************************************************
201    B300.Validate.Stock.Number:
202       Record.Number% = 0
203       FOR I% = 1 TO 100
204          IF Stock.Number$ = Index$(I%) THEN
205             IF Code% = 2 THEN
206                GOSUB B400.Stock.Number.Error.Routine
207             ELSE
208                Record.Number% = I%
```

```
209             EXIT FOR
210           END IF
211         END IF
212     NEXT I%
213     IF Record.Number% = 0 AND Code% <> 2 THEN
214         GOSUB B400.Stock.Number.Error.Routine
215     END IF
216   RETURN
217
218   ' *********************************************************************
219   ' *                  Request Remaining Data Items                    *
220   ' *********************************************************************
221   B310.Request.Remaining.Data.Items:
222     PRINT : INPUT "Warehouse Location =======> ", Inventory.Location
223     PRINT : INPUT "Description ============> ", Inventory.Desc
224     PRINT : INPUT "Unit Cost ============> ", Inventory.Cost
225     PRINT : INPUT "Selling Price ==========> ", Inventory.Price
226     PRINT : INPUT "Quantity on Hand =======> ", Inventory.Quantity
227     PRINT : INPUT "Enter Y to add record, else N... ", Control$
228     Inventory.Stock = Stock.Number$
229     IF UCASE$(Control$) = "Y" THEN
230         GOSUB B410.Set.Index.And.Write.Record
231     END IF
232   RETURN
233
234   ' *********************************************************************
235   ' *                  Stock Number Error Routine                      *
236   ' *********************************************************************
237   B400.Stock.Number.Error.Routine:
238     BEEP: BEEP: BEEP: BEEP
239     IF Code% = 2 THEN
240         LOCATE 20, 19
241         PRINT "Stock Number Already Exists"
242     ELSE
243         LOCATE 20, 19: PRINT "Stock Number Is Invalid"
244     END IF
245     LOCATE 22, 19
246     PRINT "Press any key to re-enter Code and Stock Number..."
247     A$ = INPUT$(1)
248     LOCATE 17, 52: PRINT SPC(10);
249     LOCATE 19, 52: PRINT SPC(10);
250     LOCATE 20, 19: PRINT SPC(50);
251     LOCATE 22, 19: PRINT SPC(50);
252     Switch$ = "OFF"
253   RETURN
254
255   ' *********************************************************************
256   ' *                  Set Index Array and Write Record                *
257   ' *********************************************************************
258   B410.Set.Index.And.Write.Record:
259     Index$(Record.Number%) = Stock.Number$
260     PUT #2, Record.Number%, Inventory
261   RETURN
262
263   ' *********************************************************************
264   ' *                            Wrap-Up                               *
265   ' *********************************************************************
266   C100.Wrap.Up:
267     CLOSE
```

(continued)

FIGURE 9.20
(continued)

```
268    OPEN "A:INVINDEX.DAT" FOR OUTPUT AS #1
269    FOR Record.Number% = 1 TO 100  ' Write New Index to INVINDEX.DAT
270       WRITE #1, Index$(Record.Number%)
271    NEXT Record.Number%
272    CLOSE
273    PRINT "Inventory Retrieval and Update Program Terminated"
274    PRINT : PRINT "Job Complete"
275 RETURN
276
277 ' ************************* End of Program *************************
```

```
[run]
```

Discussion of the Part 2 Solution

When Program 9.6 is executed, the menu shown in Figure 9.21 displays.

FIGURE 9.21
Menu displayed by Program 9.6.

```
        Menu For Inventory Retrieval and Update
        ----------------------------------------

             Code            Function
             ----            --------
              1            Display Record

              2            Add Record

              3            Change Record

              4            Delete Record

              5            End Program

        Enter a Code 1 through 5 =====>
```

If a function code of 1 through 4 is entered, then line 104 requests the user to enter a stock number by displaying the following message:

```
Stock Number ================>
```

B300.Validate.Stock.Number (lines 201 through 216) verifies the stock number. If a function code of 2 is entered, then Stock.Number$ must not equal the value of any of the elements of the array Index$. If a function code of 1, 3, or 4 is entered, then Stock.Number$ must be equal to one of the elements of the array Index$. An additional function of this validation process, when the function code is 1, 3, or 4, is to establish the record number (Record.Number%) of the corresponding record to be displayed, changed, or deleted.

If a function code of 1 and the stock number S941 are entered by the user, then B220.Display.Record (lines 114 through 127) displays the information shown in Figure 9.22.

FIGURE 9.22

The display from entering a function code of 1 (Display Record) and the stock number S941.

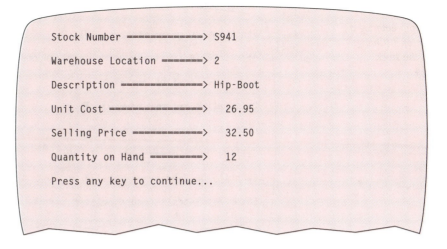

```
Stock Number ===============> S941

Warehouse Location =========> 2

Description ================> Hip-Boot

Unit Cost =================>    26.95

Selling Price =============>    32.50

Quantity on Hand =========>     12

Press any key to continue...
```

If a function code of 2 and the stock number S429 are entered by the user, then B230.Add.Record (lines 132 through 150) requests the remaining items that make up this new record. This is shown in Figure 9.23.

FIGURE 9.23

The display from entering a function code of 2 (Add Record) and the data items for stock number S429.

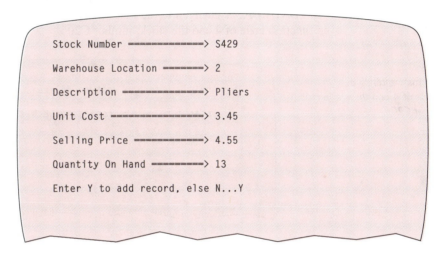

```
Stock Number ===============> S429

Warehouse Location =========> 2

Description ================> Pliers

Unit Cost =================> 3.45

Selling Price =============> 4.55

Quantity On Hand =========> 13

Enter Y to add record, else N...Y
```

Lines 135 through 140 determine the first element of Index$ that is equal to the string `Empty`. The subscript of this element is then used to indicate the record number in the PUT statement in line 260. Just before line 260, line 259 assigns the stock number Stock.Number$ to Index$(Record.Number%).

If a function code of 3 and the stock number T814 are entered, then B240.Change.Record (lines 155 through 184) reads the record that corresponds to Record.Number%, requests changes, and rewrites the record. Figure 9.24 shows the display for changing the selling price to 29.95 and the quantity on hand to 32 for record T814.

```
Stock Number ==============> T814

**** Enter a -1 if you do not want to change a data item ****

Warehouse Location ========> -1

Description ===============> -1

Unit Cost ================> -1

Selling Price ============> 29.95

Quantity On Hand =========> 32

Enter Y to update record, else N...Y
```

If a function code of 4 and the stock number of C206 are entered, then the subroutine B250.Delete.Record (lines 189 through 196) assigns the string `Empty` to the element of Index$ that corresponds to Record.Number%. Note that the data record in INVDATA.DAT is not changed in any way. Later, when a new record is added, the record deleted in INVDATA.DAT is changed to the new record. Figure 9.25 shows the display due to entering a function code of 4 and the stock number C206.

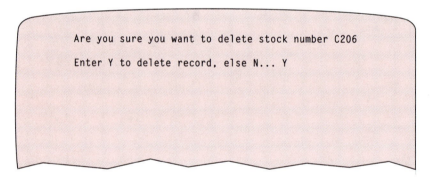

```
Are you sure you want to delete stock number C206

Enter Y to delete record, else N... Y
```

If a function code of 5 is entered in response to B200.Display.Menu, then the subroutine C100.Wrap.Up writes the array Index$ to the sequential file INVINDEX.DAT, closes the files, and displays the messages shown in Figure 9.26.

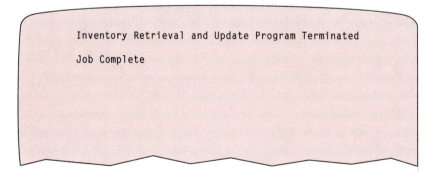

```
Inventory Retrieval and Update Program Terminated

Job Complete
```

9.5 What You Should Know

1. QBasic allows for two types of file organization — sequential and random. A file that is organized sequentially is limited to sequential processing. A file that is organized randomly can be processed either sequentially or in a random fashion. The sequence in which a random file is processed bears no relationship to the sequence in which the records are stored in it.

2. Indexed file organization is widely used in data processing. Although it is not directly available in QBasic, indexed files may be simulated by using both a sequential file and a random file.

3. File maintenance is the process of updating files, by one or more of the following ways:
   a. Adding new records
   b. Deleting unwanted records
   c. Changing data within records

4. A transaction file contains data of a temporary nature.

5. A master file contains data that is, for the most part, permanent.

6. A file maintenance program that updates a sequential file must deal with at least three files: a transaction file, the current master file, and a new master file.

7. A system flowchart shows in graphic form the files, the flow of data, the equipment, and the programs involved in a particular application.

8. Merging is the process of combining two or more files that are in the same sequence into a single file that maintains that same sequence for a given data item in each record.

9. Matching records involves two or more related files that are in the same sequence according to a common data item. If a record in the transaction file matches a record in the current master file, then the current master record may be updated. If there is no match, appropriate action must be taken, depending on the application.

10. Like sequential files, random files must be opened before they are read from or written to. When a program finishes with a random file, it must close the file. The OPEN statement for a random file must include a record length. Never write a record that is longer than the assigned record length. You can, however, write records that are shorter than the length that is specified in the OPEN statement.

11. The TYPE statement is used to define fields with respect to their name, size, type, and location within the record. Collectively, the field names are assigned to a label name and are called the record layout, record structure, or structure. The label name is also referred to as a user-defined data type.

12. Following the TYPE statement, the label name that identifies the structure must be assigned to a record variable name through the use of the DIM statement.

13. Follow the same rules for label names, field names, and record variables that you follow for variable names, except that the period (.) and trailing special characters (%, &, !, #, and $) are not allowed.

14. To reference the field names in a TYPE statement, use the record variable name followed by a period (.) and the field name — record variable.field name.

15. The TYPE and DIM statements that define and declare the structure must precede the OPEN statement for the random file.

16. In the OPEN statement for the random file, use the LEN function to assign the length of record variable to the LEN parameter.

17. The GET #n, r, v statement reads the rth record from the random file assigned to filenumber n into record variable v.

18. The PUT #n, r, v statement writes the rth record to the random file assigned to filenumber n from record variable v.

19. If the second parameter in a GET or PUT statement is not included, then the PC reads or writes the next record in sequence in the random file.

20. The LOC(n) function returns the record number of the last record read or written to the random file assigned to filenumber n.

21. The LOF(n) function returns information regarding the character size of the random file assigned to filenumber n.

9.6 Test Your QBasic Skills (Even-numbered answers are in Appendix E)

1. If the last record accessed in a program was record 10 of a random file assigned previously to filenumber 1, which record is accessed next by the following GET statements? (Assume that each GET statement is affected by the previous one.)

   a. `GET #1, ,RecVar`   b. `GET #1, 20, RecVar`   c. `GET #1, , RecVar`
   d. `GET #1, 86, Recvar`   e. `GET #1 , , RecVar`

2. Fill in the following:

   a. The GET statement reads a record into the _____ defined by the _____ statement.
   b. The _____ statement is used to define the field names for the record structure for a random file, and the _____ statement is used to declare the record variable.
   c. Assign the length of the corresponding _____ to the length parameter in the OPEN statement for a random file.
   d. The _____ function returns the record number of the last record read or written to the random file assigned as the argument.

3. Use a TYPE statement to construct a structure using the following field names and corresponding types and sizes. Call the structure Person.

Variable	Type	Size
Soc	String	9
Code	String	1
Value1	Numeric	Double Precision
Value2	Numeric	Single Precision
Value3	Numeric	Integer

4. Explain the difference between the label name in a TYPE statement and the record variable in the corresponding DIM statement.

5. The number of active records in the random file TABLE.DAT varies between 0 and 100 each day. Active records begin with 1 and continue by 1 until the last active record is reached. The number of the last active record in TABLE.DAT is always located in the first field of record 101. The active records each contain three data items defined in the TYPE statement by the names Fld1, Fld2, and Fld3 and assigned the type SINGLE. Use the label name DailyStructure and the variable name Daily.

   Write a partial program that first reads record 101 in TABLE.DAT, then dynamically dimensions the parallel arrays Item1, Item2, and Item3 to the number of active records. Finally, read the active records in TABLE.DAT and assign the three values in each record to the elements of arrays Item1, Item2, and Item3 in the order in which the values are located in the record. Use filenumber 1.

6. Which of the following are invalid file handling statements? Why?

   a. `OPEN "SALES.DAT" FOR RANDOM AS #1 LEN = Sales`
   b. `GET #2, , Inventory`
   c. `GET #1, Recno`
   d. `GET #2, Recno$, Sales`
   e. `PUT #3, ,Inventory`
   f. `DIM Inventory AS Inventory.Structure`
   g. `GET #1, LOC(1)`
   h. `GET FileNo, RecNo, RecVar`

7. Write a statement that assigns the random file EXPENSE.DAT to filenumber 2. The record variable name is ExRec.

8. Describe how a sequential data file, a random data file, and an array are used to simulate an indexed file.

9. **PC Hands-On Exercise:** Load Program 9.1 (PRG9-1) from the Data Disk. Use the NAME statement in the immediate window to rename CURINV.DAT as CURINVSA.DAT and INVNTORY.DAT as CURINV.DAT. Execute the program and note the diagnostic messages. Do not forget to rename the files with their original names when you are finished.

10. **PC Hands-On Exercise:** Load Program 9.2 (PRG9-2) from the Data Disk. In line 21, assign the variable Master.Eof$ the value ON. Execute the program and see what happens. Do you understand the importance of the switches defined in lines 21 and 22?

11. **PC Hands-On Exercise:** Load Program 9.3 (PRG9-3) from the Data Disk. Execute the program and add warehouse number (record number) 6. Use your first name as the name of the warehouse, your address, and a square-foot area of 100,000.

12. **PC Hands-On Exercise:** Load Program 9.4 (PRG9-4) from the Data Disk. Execute the program and request record number 6 — the one you added in question 11. After record number 6 displays, request record number 5 and see what happens. Can you explain the display?

9.7 QBasic Programming Problems

1. Adding, Changing, and Deleting Records in the Master File

Purpose: To become familiar with the maintenance of a sequential file.

Problem: Write a top-down program to match and merge the current payroll master file EX61PAY.DAT built in QBasic Programming Problem 1 on page 233 in Chapter 6 with the transaction file EX91TRA.DAT described below under Input Data. Call the new master file EX91PAY.DAT. Include the following diagnostic messages:

```
**ERROR** Addition Invalid - Employee XXX already in master file.
**ERROR** Transaction Invalid - Employee XXX not in master file.
```

Display as part of the end-of-job routine the total number of additions, changes, deletions, errors, and transactions and the number of records in the new master file.

Input Data: The master file EX61PAY.DAT and the transaction file EX91TRA.DAT are on the Data Disk. The contents of the transaction file EX91TRA.DAT are shown in Figure 9.27. The transaction code A represents an addition, C a record change, and D a record delete. *Null* represents the null character.

│FIGURE 9.27

Contents of the transaction file EX91TRA.DAT.

Tran. Code	Employee No.	Employee Name	Dependents	Marital Status	Rate of Pay	Gross Pay	Year-to-Date Federal With. Tax	Year-to-Date Social Security Tax
C	124	Null	4	Null	-1	$6,345.20	-1	-1
A	126	Fish, Joe	1	M	$6.00	0	0	0
D	134	Null	-1	Null	-1	-1	-1	-1
A	143	Byrd, Ed	3	S	9.00	0	0	0
C	168	Null	0	Null	-1	-1	-1	-1
C	225	Null	-1	S	-1	-1	-1	-1
D	250	Null	-1	Null	-1	-1	-1	-1

Output Results: The new master file EX91PAY.DAT is created. Figure 9.28 illustrates the output results from Programming Problem 1.

```
Payroll File Maintenance
------------------------

**ERROR** Addition Invalid - Employee 126 already in master file.

**ERROR** Transaction Invalid - Employee 168 not in master file.

**ERROR** Transaction Invalid - Employee 225 not in master file.

**ERROR** Transaction Invalid - Employee 250 not in master file.

Total Number of Records Added ==============> 1
Total Number of Records Changed ============> 1
Total Number of Records Deleted ============> 1
Total Number of Transaction Errors =======> 4
Total Number of Transactions ==============> 7
Total Number of Records in New Master ====> 9

New master file EX91PAY.DAT build complete
```

2. Creating a Random File for Quarterly Payroll Totals

Purpose: To become familiar with creating a random file.

Problem: Write a top-down program that creates a random file with four records. Each record contains payroll information with respect to the following time periods:

Record Number	Time Period	
1	January	— March
2	April	— June
3	July	— September
4	October	— December

Each record is made up of the following quarterly employee totals: gross pay, withholding tax, and Social Security tax. To ensure accuracy, use double-precision variables. Define the field names in the TYPE statement. Use the label name QuarterlyStructure and the record variable Quarterly. Call the random file EX92DAT.DAT.

Give the user the opportunity to cancel the record addition after the data is entered and displayed on the screen.

Input Data: Use the following sample data:

Quarter	Gross Pay	Withholding Tax	Social Security
1	$11,231.12	$3,998.34	$1,121.45
2	8,345.23	2,456.23	913.75
3	13,891.75	2,554.64	1,585.11
4	0.00	0.00	0.00

Output Results: The random file EX92DAT.DAT is created in auxiliary storage. Figure 9.29 illustrates partial results for the first record entered.

FIGURE 9.29
Patial display for Programming Problem 2.

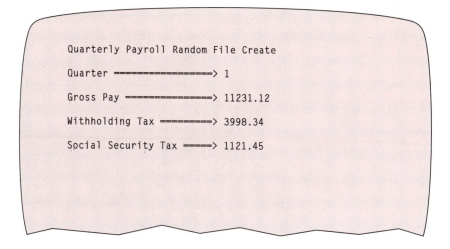

```
Quarterly Payroll Random File Create

Quarter ================> 1

Gross Pay ===============> 11231.12

Withholding Tax =========> 3998.34

Social Security Tax =====> 1121.45
```

3. Random Access of Quarterly Payroll Totals

Purpose: To become familiar with accessing records in a random file.

Problem: Write a program that will randomly access any record in the random file EX92DAT.DAT created in the previous exercise. If the user enters 2, then the program should display the payroll totals for the second quarter. If the user enters 1, then the program should display the payroll totals for the first quarter.

Input Data: Use the random file EX92DAT.DAT created in Programming Problem 2.

Output Results: Figure 9.30 presents the results displayed for quarter 2.

FIGURE 9.30
Quarter 2 display for Programming Problem 3.

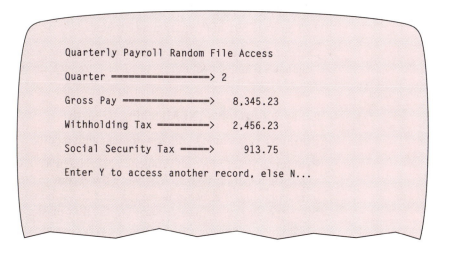

```
Quarterly Payroll Random File Access

Quarter ==================> 2

Gross Pay ===============>   8,345.23

Withholding Tax =========>   2,456.23

Social Security Tax =====>     913.75

Enter Y to access another record, else N...
```

4. Employee Record Retrieval and Update — A Simulated-Indexed File

Purpose: To become familiar with the use of indexed files.

Problem: Create two programs. The first program is to take the file EX61PAY.DAT created in QBasic Programming Problem 1 of Chapter 6 (page 233) and build an index in a sequential file made up of the employee numbers. The program should also build a corresponding random file made up of the data in EX61PAY.DAT. Declare 200 elements for the array written to the sequential file.

(**Hint:** See Program 9.5 on pages 377-378.)

(continued)

Call the sequential file EX94IND.DAT and the random file EX94DAT.DAT. Use the following TYPE statement and corresponding DIM statement for the random file:

```
TYPE EmployeeStructure
   Number AS STRING * 3
   FullName AS STRING * 20
   Dep As INTEGER
   Status AS STRING * 1
   Rate AS SINGLE
   YTDGross AS DOUBLE
   YTDFedTax AS DOUBLE
   YTDSocSec AS DOUBLE
END TYPE
DIM Employee AS EmployeeStructure
```

Ask your instructor whether the first program is required. Copies of EX94IND.DAT and EX94DAT.DAT are on the Data Disk.

The second program is to be a menu-driven program that allows the user to display, add, change, and delete records on a random basis. The user informs the PC of the record to access by entering the employee number. (See Program 9.6 on pages 381-386.)

The menu-driven program should accept the following function codes:

Code	Function	Code	Function
1	Display record	4	Delete record
2	Add record	5	End program
3	Change record		

Input Data: For program 1, use the file EX61PAY.DAT as input to create the index and the random files. For program 2, update the payroll file with the sample data given in Figure 9.27 on page 391 in Programming Problem 1.

Output Results: The program should generate results similar to those generated by Program 9.6 and shown in Figures 9.21 through 9.26 (pages 386-388).

5. Payroll Problem IX: Matching Records

Purpose: To become familiar with matching records.

Problem: Modify Payroll Problem VI (Problem 8) in Chapter 6 to display diagnostic messages when there is no match between the record in the master file and the record in the transaction file. If a record in the master file has no corresponding match in the transaction file, write the current master record to the new master file and display the message

```
** NOTE ** Employee XXX has no time card
```

If a record in the transaction file has no corresponding match in the master file, display the message

```
** ERROR ** Employee XXX has no master record
```

(**Hint:** The logic regarding matching records is similar to the logic in Program 9.2 on pages 359-361.)

Page the report and print 21 lines per page.

Input Data: Use EX61PAY.DAT as the current master file. This is the same file that was used in Payroll Problem VI. The transaction file EX95TR.DAT is on the Data Disk. The transaction file contains the following records:

Employee Number	Hours Worked
123	88
125	74
126	80
134	80
167	70.5
168	68
210	80
234	34

Output Results: A new master payroll file is created as EX95PAY.DAT. Figure 9.31 illustrates the results that are printed on the printer.

FIGURE 9.31

Printed report for Programming Problem 5.

```
                              Preliminary
                      Biweekly Payroll Report          Page:  1

        Employee
        Number       Gross Pay       Fed. Tax      Soc. Sec.     Net Pay
        --------     ---------       --------      ---------     -------
          123        1,150.00         277.96          87.97      784.07

        ** NOTE ** Employee 124 has no time card

          125          962.00         239.60          73.59      648.81

          126          440.00          19.72          33.66      386.62

          134          700.00         182.00          53.55      464.45

          167          733.20         159.07          56.09      518.04

        ** ERROR ** Employee 168 has no master record
```

```
                              Preliminary
                      Biweekly Payroll Report          Page:  2

        Employee
        Number       Gross Pay       Fed. Tax      Soc. Sec.     Net Pay
        --------     ---------       --------      ---------     -------
          210          704.00         119.92          53.86      530.22

          234          229.50          38.63          17.56      173.31

        ** NOTE ** Employee 244 has no time card


        Total Gross Pay ========>    4,918.70
        Total Withholding Tax ==>    1,036.90
        Total Social Security ==>      376.28
        Total Net Pay ==========>    3,505.52

        End of Payroll Report
```

C H A P T E R 10

Computer Graphics and Sound

10.1 INTRODUCTION

The value of the computer for displaying information in the form of charts, figures, and graphs as opposed to printed characters, has long been recognized. For many years, however, the cost of equipment kept most users from incorporating computer graphics into their programs. With the advent of the PC and advances in software, this has all changed.

As you will see in this chapter, QBasic has statements with considerable graphics capabilities. Figures 10.1 through 10.4 show a variety of different business-type charts, figures, and graphs that can be displayed on your PC. Business-type graphics are used commonly to summarize data. They are an effective way to show amounts or trends. Figure 10.5 on page 399 shows nonbusiness-type graphics that also may be displayed on your PC. Although no attempt is made here to present sophisticated graphics, at the conclusion of this chapter you will have enough knowledge of the graphics features of QBasic to start using them in the programs you write.

This chapter also explores the QBasic statements that allow you to play music and create sound and animation effects.

FIGURE 10.1
Line graph (used to show business trends).

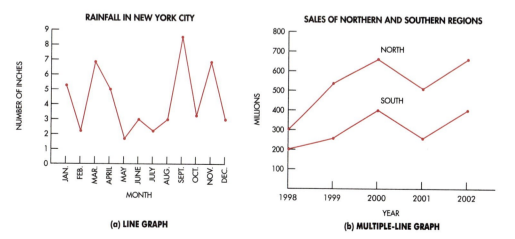

(a) LINE GRAPH

(b) MULTIPLE-LINE GRAPH

FIGURE 10.2

Bar graphs (compare two or more amounts).

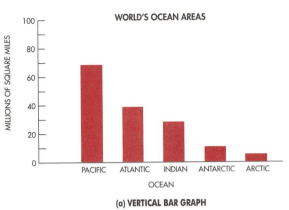

(a) VERTICAL BAR GRAPH

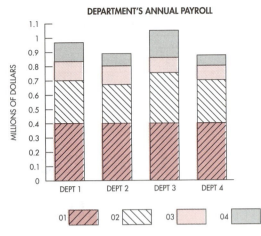

(b) STACKED-BAR GRAPH

FIGURE 10.3

Pie charts (show how 100% is divided).

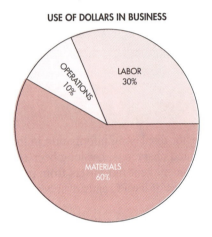

(a) PIE CHART

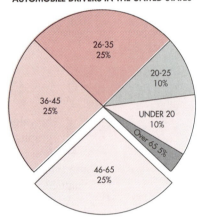

(b) EXPLODED PIE CHART

FIGURE 10.4

Plotting an equation (shows relationship between two variables).

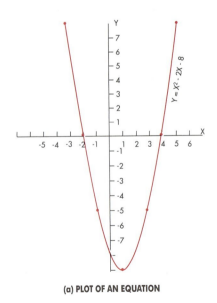

(a) PLOT OF AN EQUATION

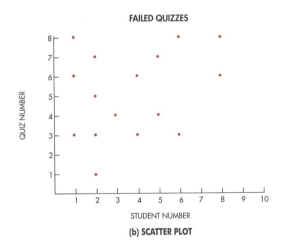

(b) SCATTER PLOT

FIGURE 10.5

Logo and animation.

(a) LOGO

(b) ANIMATION

PC Graphics Modes

Depending on the display device (monitor) and display adapter (graphics board), the PC can provide up to five different graphics modes: **text**, **medium resolution**, **high resolution**, **enhanced resolution**, and **very-high resolution**. As described in Table 10.1, text mode is available on all PCs. Medium-resolution and high-resolution graphics are available on all the configurations except the first one in Table 10.1.

TABLE 10.1 - Graphics Capabilities with Different Hardware Configurations			
DISPLAY DEVICE	**DISPLAY ADAPTOR**	**GRAPHICS CAPABILITIES**	**SCREEN MODE**
1. IBM Compatible Monochrome (black and white) Display	IBM Compatible Monochrome Display Adaptor (MDA)	Only text mode with a width of 40 or 80 characters. Black and white character graphics.	0
2. IBM Compatible Monochrome (black and white) Display	Color/Graphics Adaptor (CGA)	Shades of black and white in text, medium resolution, and high resolution.	0,1,2
3. Standard Color Monitor	Color/Graphics Adaptor (CGA)	Color graphics in text and medium resolution. Black and white graphics in high resolution.	0,1,2
4. Monochrome (black and white) Display	Enhanced Color Adaptor (EGA)	Shades of black and white in text, medium and high resolution.	0,10
5. Standard Color Monitor	Enhanced Color Adaptor (EGA)	Color graphics in text; medium, high, and enhanced resolution.	0,1,2 7,8
6. Enhanced Color Monitor	Enhanced Color Adaptor (EGA)	Color graphics in text; medium, high, and enhanced resolution.	0,1,2 7,8,9
7. Video Graphics Array (VGA and SVGA) Monitor	Video Graphics Array Adaptor (VGA and SVGA)	Color graphics in text; medium, high, enhanced, and very-high resolution.	0,1,2 7,8,9 10,11 12,13
8. Multicolor Graphics Array (MCGA) Monitor	Multicolor Graphics Array Adaptor (MCGA)	Color graphics in text; medium, high, and very-high resolution.	0,1,2 11,13

Enhanced resolution and very-high resolution are available with the more expensive graphics hardware (EGA, VGA, Super VGA, MCGA, and XGA). Many PCs sold today have at least a Color/Graphics Adaptor (CGA). Because the more advanced graphics hardware also can operate in CGA mode, this chapter concentrates on CGA hardware graphics capabilities — text graphics, medium-resolution graphics, and high-resolution graphics.

The last column in Table 10.1 on the previous page indicates the **screen mode** associated with each graphics mode. As shown later in this chapter, you tell QBasic which graphics mode to work in by the screen mode you specify in the SCREEN statement.

Text mode is the one used in earlier chapters. In this mode, the screen is divided into either 25 rows and 80 columns, or 25 rows and 40 columns, as illustrated in Figures 10.6(a) and 10.6(b). At the intersection of each row and column, the PC can display any one of the 256 characters shown in Table D.1 in Appendix D. Each intersection of a row and column is called a **character position**. In this mode, the PRINT statement and the ASCII character set are used to display figures and graphs, as well as nongraphical information such as words and sentences. If you have the proper hardware, you also can display the characters in 16 different colors. You often use text mode to create logos and simple animated designs.

▌FIGURE 10.6

Layout of the screen and color availability for the text mode, medium-resolution graphics mode, and high-resolution graphics mode.

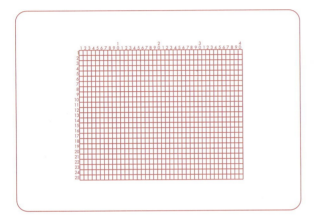

(a) SCREEN 0 : WIDTH 40
```
     Mode:      Text
     Rows:      25
     Columns:   40
     Colors:    16 Foreground
                 8 Background
                16 Border
```

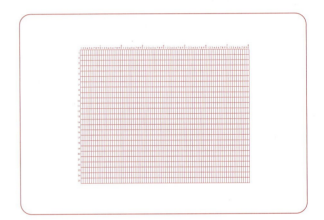

(b) SCREEN 0 : WIDTH 80
```
     Mode:      Text
     Rows:      25
     Columns:   80
     Colors:    16 Foreground
                 8 Background
                16 Border
```

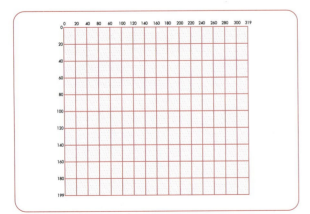

(c) SCREEN 1
```
     Mode:               Medium Resolution
     Rows:               200
     Columns:            320
     Characters per line: 40
     Colors:              8 Foreground
                         16 Background
```

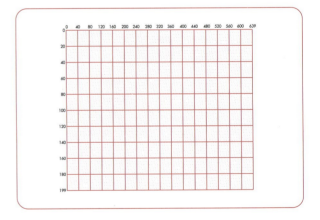

(d) SCREEN 2
```
     Mode:               High Resolution
     Rows:               200
     Columns:            640
     Characters per line: 80
     Colors:             Black and White
```

With medium-resolution graphics, the screen is divided into 200 rows and 320 columns as shown in Figure 10.6(c). Each intersection of a row and column represents a small dot which can be turned on or off by QBasic statements. The dots on the screen are called **pixels** (picture elements). The total number of pixels is 64,000 (200 × 320). Forty characters per line are displayed in this mode. If you have a color monitor, each pixel can be assigned any one of 16 colors (256 colors if you have VGA and MCGA hardware). In this mode you can plot points, draw figures, and create high-quality animated designs.

High-resolution graphics mode divides the screen into 200 rows and 640 columns, as shown in Figure 10.6(d). The total number of pixels is 128,000 (200 × 640). Eighty characters per line are displayed in this mode. With CGA hardware, only monochrome colors are available in this mode — black and white, or amber, or green. EGA hardware allows for 16 colors. With VGA or MCGA hardware, 256 colors are available.

If your PC allows for enhanced-resolution graphics and you select this mode, then the screen is divided into 350 rows and 640 columns, for a total of 320,000 pixels. This very high-resolution graphics mode divides the screen into 480 rows and 640 columns, for a total of 639,480 pixels. The greater number of pixels across the screen allows you to draw figures that require finer detail than is available with other graphics modes.

The SCREEN and WIDTH Statements

When QBasic is started, the PC is in text mode. The SCREEN **statement** then may be used to select between modes as described in Table 10.2. If you select a mode that is not available on your PC (Table 10.1 on page 399), then a dialog box with the diagnostic message Illegal function call displays when the SCREEN statement executes.

TABLE 10.2 - SCREEN Value Descriptions*			
STATEMENT	**COLUMNS**	**ROWS**	**CHARACTERS PER LINE**
SCREEN 0	40	25	40
	or		
	80	25	80
SCREEN 1	320	200	80
SCREEN 2	640	200	40
SCREEN 7	320	200	40
SCREEN 8	640	200	80
SCREEN 9	640	350	80
SCREEN 10	640	350	80
SCREEN 11	640	480	80
SCREEN 12	640	480	80
SCREEN 13	320	200	40

*With SCREEN 0, use the WIDTH statement to set the characters per line to 40 or 80. SCREEN statements that result in the same number of columns, rows, and characters per line have different color capabilities.

The SCREEN statement may be entered in immediate mode or as part of a program. Each time the SCREEN statement is executed, the screen is erased and the color is set to white on black. However, nothing is changed on the screen if the mode in the SCREEN statement is the same as the current one. If there is a QBasic program in main memory, it is not erased when you switch from one mode to another.

The general form of the SCREEN statement is shown in Table 10.3 on the next page.

TABLE 10. 3 - The SCREEN Statement	
General Form:	SCREEN mode, color switch, active page, visual page
	where **mode** is one of the following: 0, 1, 2, 7, 8, 9, 10, 11, 12, 13;
	color switch is 0 (disables color) or any other number (enables color) in text mode. With medium resolution, 0 enables color, and any other number disables color;
	active page is an integer expression (in the range 0 to 7 for width 40 characters, and 0 to 3 for width 80) which specifies the page to be written to by output statements; and
	visual page is an integer expression in the same range as active page that selects the page to be displayed.
Purpose:	Selects the screen attributes to be used by subsequent output statements.
Examples:	1. SCREEN 1
	2. SCREEN ,,2, 3
	3. SCREEN 0, 1, 1, 0
	4. SCREEN 0,, 0, 1
	5. SCREEN 1, 1
	6. SCREEN 2
Note:	The parameters active page and visual page are valid only in text mode, that is, mode = 0.

Example 1 in Table 10.3 clears the screen and switches to the medium-resolution mode. If any parameter is omitted in the SCREEN statement, the PC maintains the current status for each parameter.

In Example 2, the mode remains the same and all future output statements are directed to page 2. Page 3 is displayed immediately. Here, the term *page* refers to a 2K (width = 40) or 4K (width = 80) byte area of the 16K display buffer. Note that in this example we are preparing to have the PC build one page (page 2) while displaying another (page 3). This form of flip-flopping the screens may be used in text mode to create animations.

In Example 3 of Table 10.3, the mode is switched to text, color is enabled, all future output statements are directed to page 1, and page 0 is displayed. In Example 4, the mode is switched to text, color maintains its status, future output statements are directed to page 0, and page 1 is displayed. Example 5 switches the PC to medium resolution, and the color is disabled. Finally, line 6 switches the PC to high resolution.

Figure 10.6 on page 400 illustrates how the screen is subdivided for modes 0, 1, 2.

The WIDTH Statement

The PC automatically sets the maximum characters per line to 40 or 80, depending on the selected screen mode. (See Table 10.2 on the previous page.) It also sets the maximum number of lines on the screen to 25. You can change the maximum characters per line to 40 or 80 through the use of the WIDTH statement. In the 40-column display mode, the characters are displayed in a larger form and, therefore, are easier to read. However, the PC can display only half as many characters.

Depending on your display adaptor and selected screen mode, you can use the WIDTH statement to change the maximum number of lines to 25, 30, 43, 50, or 60.

The WIDTH statement also can be used to change the maximum number of columns on the printer. The general form of the WIDTH statement is given in Table 10.4.

TABLE 10.4 - The WIDTH Statement	
General Form:	WIDTH columns, lines or WIDTH LPRINT columns
Purpose:	The first general form clears the screen and sets the maximum number of columns (40 or 80) and the number of lines (25, 30, 43, 50, or 60). The second general form sets the number of columns for the printer.
Examples:	WIDTH 40 WIDTH 80 WIDTH 40, 50 WIDTH LPRINT 132
Notes:	1. When the statement WIDTH 40 is executed in high resolution, the PC switches to medium resolution. When the statement WIDTH 80 is executed in medium resolution, the PC switches to high resolution. 2. The WIDTH statement also may be used to set the maximum number of columns in a file. This form of the statement will not be used in this book.

10.2 TEXT-MODE GRAPHICS

You can produce interesting and useful graphics on any PC with the PRINT and PRINT USING statements, the CHR$ function, and the ASCII character set. Some elementary text mode graphics using the typewriter keys (letters, numbers, and punctuation marks) were presented in Chapter 4, Exercises 12 and 13, on page 134.

The program in Figure 10.7 shows how you can access additional graphics characters (ASCII codes 128 through 255, also called the **USA character set** or **extended ASCII character set**) through the use of the CHR$ function. Recall from Chapter 8 that the CHR$ function returns a character that is equivalent in ASCII code to the numeric argument.

FIGURE 10.7

Displaying the last half of the ASCII characters set.

```
1    ' Displaying the Last Half of the ASCII Character Set
2    ' *****************************************************
3    CLS  ' Clear Screen
4    FOR CODE% = 128 TO 255
5       PRINT USING "### !"; CODE%, CHR$(CODE%)
6    NEXT CODE%
7    END

     [run]
```

When the program in Figure 10.7 is executed, the For loop (lines 4 through 6) causes the PC to display the last half of the ASCII character set, as shown in Table D.1 in Appendix D. Through the use of the CHR$ function, these characters may be used in text mode to draw various figures. In addition to characters made up of curved lines, you can choose characters that range from a solid dark color (codes 219 through 223) to a lighter shade (codes 176, 177 and 178) for drawing bar graphs.

Another way to print the extended ASCII characters is to create them as characters in a PRINT statement by holding down the Alt key and entering the decimal value of the desired character via the numeric keypad. For example, to create the character ■ , enter the following:

```
PRINT "(hold down Alt and enter 219)"
```

The above statement will appear on the screen as follows:

```
PRINT " ■ "
```

Do not forget the quotation marks in the PRINT statement.

The cursor control keys also have ASCII values. You can use the INKEY$ function to return the proper ASCII value of the cursor control keys. For example, if a user presses one of the cursor control keys, the INKEY$ function returns a character string of length two. The first character is set to zero, and the second character is set to the ASCII value as follows:

Cursor Control Key	ASCII Value of Second Character
Up Arrow ↑	72
Down Arrow ↓	80
Left Arrow ←	75
Right Arrow →	77
Page Up	73
Page Down	81
Home	71
End	79

If a key corresponding to a standard ASCII character is pressed, then the INKEY$ function returns a character string of length one with the proper ASCII value.

PROGRAMMING CASE STUDY 23 – Logo for the Bow-Wow Dog Food Company

The following case study pertains to the display of a logo that uses some of the graphics characters that make up the last half of the ASCII character set.

Problem: On a recent tour through the main office, Mr. Bowser, president of the Bow-Wow Dog Food Company, noticed the large number of PCs in use. To brighten the office area, he has requested the Computer Information Systems Department to display the company logo, shown in Figure 10.8, on all idle PCs.

The program that displays the logo must chain to (call) a menu-driven program called MAINMENU when the user presses any key. (For a discussion of how a program chains to another program, see Section 11.5 on page 477.)

Following are a top-down chart (Figure 10.9), a list of the program tasks in outline form, a program solution, and a discussion of the program solution.

FIGURE 10.8

The Bow-Wow Dog Food Company logo designed on a screen layout form with a width of 40 characters.

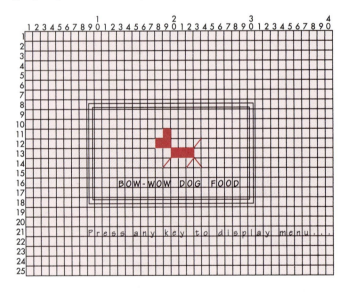

FIGURE 10.9

A top-down chart for the solution to Programming Case Study 23.

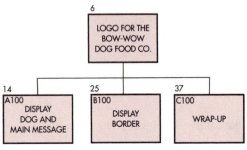

Program Tasks

The following program tasks correspond to the top-down chart in Figure 10.9:

1. A100.Display.Dog.And.Main.Message

    a. Use the WIDTH statement to set the display mode of the screen to 40 characters per line.

    b. Use the LOCATE and PRINT statements to position the dog and main message on the screen. Use the CHR$ function and the following ASCII character codes for the dog's body parts:

Body Part	ASCII Code	Character
Nose	220	▪
Head	219	▪
Body	219 (three)	▪▪▪
Tail	47	/
Legs pointing left	47 (two)	/
Leg pointing right	92	\

2. B100.Display.Border

Use the LOCATE and PRINT statements to display the border surrounding the dog and the main message. Use the CHR$ function and the following ASCII character codes for the border:

Border Part	ASCII Code	Character
Upper left corner	201	╔
Lower left corner	200	╚
Upper right corner	187	╗
Lower right corner	188	╝
Vertical border	186	║
Horizontal border	205	=

3. C100.Wrap.Up

    a. Display the message "Press any key to display menu..."

    b. Use the INPUT$ function to suspend execution until the user presses a key.

    c. Set the display mode of the screen to 80 characters per line.

4. Use the following statement in place of the END statement in the Main Program to chain to MAINMENU (see Section 11.5 on page 477).

```
CHAIN "A:MAINMENU"
```

Program Solution

Program 10.1, the solution to Programming Case Study 23, is presented in Figure 10.10. It corresponds to the top-down chart in Figure 10.9 and to the preceding program tasks.

▌FIGURE 10.10

Program 10.1, the solution to Programming Case Study 23.

```
 1   ' Program 10.1
 2   ' Logo for Bow-Wow Dog Food Company
 3   ' ********************************
 4   ' *          Main Program        *
 5   ' ********************************
 6   GOSUB A100.Display.Dog.And.Main.Message
 7   GOSUB B100.Display.Border
 8   GOSUB C100.Wrap.Up
 9   CHAIN "A:MAINMENU"      ' Call Program Mainmenu
10
```

(continued)

FIGURE 10.10
(continued)

```
11   ' ********************************
12   ' *  Display Dog and Main Message  *
13   ' ********************************
14   A100.Display.Dog.And.Main.Message:
15      WIDTH 40        ' Switch to 40-Column Display
16      LOCATE 12, 17: PRINT CHR$(220); CHR$(219); SPC(3); CHR$(47)
17      LOCATE 13, 19: PRINT STRING$(3, 219)
18      LOCATE 14, 18: PRINT CHR$(47); SPC(2); CHR$(47); CHR$(92)
19      LOCATE 16, 12: PRINT "BOW-WOW DOG FOOD"
20   RETURN
21
22   ' ********************************
23   ' *            Display Border           *
24   ' ********************************
25   B100.Display.Border:
26      LOCATE 8, 9: PRINT CHR$(201); STRING$(20, 205); CHR$(187)
27      FOR I% = 9 TO 17
28         LOCATE I%, 9: PRINT CHR$(186)
29         LOCATE I%, 30: PRINT CHR$(186)
30      NEXT I%
31      LOCATE 18, 9: PRINT CHR$(200); STRING$(20, 205); CHR$(188)
32   RETURN
33
34   ' ********************************
35   ' *              Wrap-Up              *
36   ' ********************************
37   C100.Wrap.Up:
38      LOCATE 21, 9: PRINT "Press any key to display menu...";
39      Halt$ = INPUT$(1)
40      WIDTH 80   ' Switch to 80-Column Display
41   RETURN
42
43   ' ********* End of Program *******

     [run]
```

Discussion of the Program Solution

When Program 10.1 is executed, line 15 clears the screen and switches the screen to the 40-column display mode. Lines 16 and 18 use the CHR$ function to display the various graphics characters. Note that in line 17 the STRING$ function causes three solid dark characters to display.

FIGURE 10.11

The logo displayed through the execution of Program 10.1.

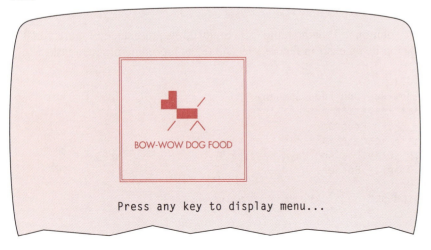

Lines 25 through 32 in B100.Display.Border use a For loop to display the vertical lines. In C100.Wrap.Up, the INPUT$ function is used to suspend execution until the user wants to display the main menu. Line 9 of the Main Program chains to MAINMENU before Program 10.1 terminates execution.

The logo displayed by Program 10.1 is shown in Figure 10.11.

PROGRAMMING CASE STUDY 24 – Horizontal Bar Graph of Monthly Sales

The program solution to the following problem illustrates the capability of QBasic to display information in the form of a horizontal bar graph (Figure 10.12).

Problem: The Sales Analysis Department of the ISCP Company wants to display a horizontal bar graph to illustrate the monthly sales trends of the previous year. Each month name and its sales are stored in the sequential data file MONSALES.DAT. The contents of MONSALES.DAT are as follows:

Month	Sales	Month	Sales
January	$41,000	July	$30,000
February	33,000	August	25,000
March	21,000	September	33,000
April	11,000	October	38,000
May	17,000	November	46,000
June	23,000	December	53,000

FIGURE 10.12

Output for the solution to Progamming Case Study 24.

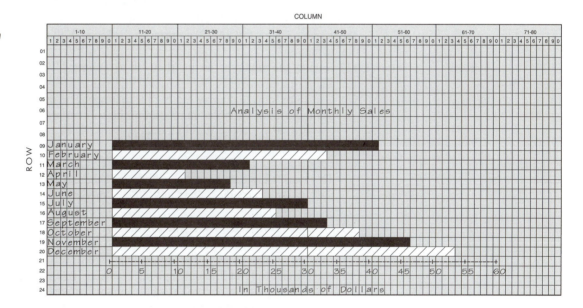

Following are a top-down chart, a list of the program tasks in outline form, a program solution, and a discussion of the program solution.

FIGURE 10.13

A top-down chart for the solution to Programming Case Study 24.

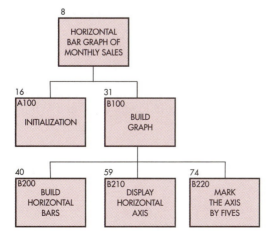

Program Tasks

The following program tasks correspond to the top-down chart in Figure 10.13 on the previous page:

1. Main Program

   a. Dimension the parallel arrays Month$ and Sales to 12.
   b. Call A100.Initialization and B100.Build.Graph.

2. A100.Initialization

   a. Open MONSALES.DAT for input.
   b. Use a For loop to read the month names and corresponding sales into the parallel arrays Month$ and Sales.
   c. Close MONSALES.DAT.
   d. Clear the screen and display the bar graph title.

3. B100.Build.Graph

   a. Call B200.Build.Horizontal.Bars. Within this subroutine, use a For loop with a loop variable of Mon% to display the 12 monthly names and corresponding bars. Use alternate shadings for each bar. Use the ASCII code 219 (■) to shade the first bar (January). Use the ASCII code 177 (▨) to shade the next bar (February). Set the variable Char$ to CHR$(219) prior to the loop. Within the For loop, do the following:

      (1) Display the month name and then tab to column 11. Hold the cursor at column 11.
      (2) Use a For loop to display the bar for the month being processed. In the For loop, use the control variable Num%, an initial value of 1, and a limit value of Sales(Mon%) / 1000. Within the loop, print Char$ and keep the cursor on the same line.
      (3) Following the inner For loop, use an IF statement to switch the value of Char$. This causes the next bar to be a different shade. If Char$ is equal to CHR$(219), then assign Char$ the value CHR$(177); otherwise, assign Char$ the value CHR$(219).

   b. B210.Display.Horizontal.Axis. Tab to column 10. Use a For loop with a control variable of Ticks%, an initial value of 0, and a limit value of 60. Within the For loop, use an IF statement to display a minus sign if Ticks% is not a multiple of 5. If Ticks% is a multiple of 5, then display a plus sign. In either case, the PRINT statement should end with a semicolon so the cursor remains on the same line. The plus sign marks off the horizontal line in multiples of 5. These marks are called **ticks**.

   c. Call B220.Mark.Axis.By.Fives. Use a For loop with a loop variable of Mark%, an initial value of 0, a limit value of 60, and a step of 5. Within the loop, use a PRINT statement and TAB function to display multiples of 5, beginning with 0. At the conclusion of the For loop, label the horizontal axis as illustrated in Figure 10.12 on the previous page.

Program Solution

Program 10.2, the solution to Programming Case Study 24, is presented in Figure 10.14. It corresponds to the top-down chart in Figure 10.13 and to the preceding program tasks.

FIGURE 10.14

Program 10.2, the solution to Programming Case Study 24.

```
1    ' Program 10.2
2    ' Horizontal Bar Graph of Monthly Sales
3    ' Input File Name = MONSALES.DAT
4    ' ****************************************************
5    ' *                   Main Program                 *
6    ' ****************************************************
7    ' **** Declare month names and month sales arrays ****
8    DIM Month$(1 TO 12), Sales(1 TO 12)
9    GOSUB A100.Initialization
10   GOSUB B100.Build.Graph
11   END
12
13   ' ****************************************************
14   ' *                  Initialization                *
15   ' ****************************************************
16   A100.Initialization:
17      OPEN "A:MONSALES.DAT" FOR INPUT AS #1
18      ' ********* Read Names and Sales into Arrays *********
19      FOR Mon% = 1 TO 12
20         INPUT #1, Month$(Mon%), Sales(Mon%)
21      NEXT Mon%
22      CLOSE #1
23      CLS  ' Clear Screen
24      LOCATE 6, 29: PRINT "Analysis of Monthly Sales"
25      LOCATE 9
26   RETURN
27
28   ' ****************************************************
29   ' *                  Build Graph                   *
30   ' ****************************************************
31   B100.Build.Graph:
32      GOSUB B200.Build.Horizontal.Bars
33      GOSUB B210.Display.Horizontal.Axis
34      GOSUB B220.Mark.Axis.By.Fives
35   RETURN
36
37   ' ****************************************************
38   ' *              Build Horizontal Bars             *
39   ' ****************************************************
40   B200.Build.Horizontal.Bars:
41      Char$ = CHR$(219)
42      FOR Mon% = 1 TO 12
43         PRINT Month$(Mon%); TAB(11);
44         FOR Num% = 1 TO Sales(Mon%) / 1000
45            PRINT Char$;
46         NEXT Num%
47         PRINT
48         IF Char$ = CHR$(219) THEN
49            Char$ = CHR$(177)          ' Light Shaded Character
50         ELSE
51            Char$ = CHR$(219)          ' Dark Shaded Character
52         END IF
53      NEXT Mon%
54   RETURN
55
56   ' ****************************************************
57   ' *              Display Horizontal Axis           *
58   ' ****************************************************
59   B210.Display.Horizontal.Axis:
60      PRINT TAB(10);
61      FOR Ticks% = 0 TO 60
62         IF Ticks% / 5 = Ticks% \ 5 THEN
```

(continued)

FIGURE 10.14
(continued)

```
63              PRINT "+";
64          ELSE
65              PRINT "-";
66          END IF
67      NEXT Ticks%
68      PRINT
69  RETURN
70
71  ' ********************************************************
72  ' *                Mark the Axis by Fives                *
73  ' ********************************************************
74  B220.Mark.Axis.By.Fives:
75      FOR Mark% = 0 TO 60 STEP 5
76          PRINT TAB(Mark% + 9); Mark%;
77      NEXT Mark%
78      PRINT
79      PRINT : PRINT TAB(30); "In Thousands of Dollars"
80  RETURN
81
82  ' *************** End of Program ********************
```

    [run]

Discussion of the Program Solution

When Program 10.2 is executed, A100.Initialization fills the parallel arrays Month$ and Sales with the 12 month names and corresponding monthly sales.

In B200.Build.Horizontal.Bars, line 41 assigns Char$ the dark-shaded graphics character with an ASCII code 219. The outer For loop (lines 42 through 53) builds a bar on each pass. The inner For loop (lines 44 through 46) builds each individual bar. After each bar displays, lines 48 through 52 switch the shade of the character assigned to Char$. The new shade is used to build the next bar.

B210.Display.Horizontal.Axis (lines 59 through 69) displays the horizontal axis. Finally, B220.Mark.Axis.By.Fives (lines 74 through 80) assigns a multiple of 5, beginning with 0, to each tick.

The horizontal bar graph displayed by Program 10.2 is shown in Figure 10.15.

FIGURE 10.15

The horizontal bar graph displayed due to the execution of Program 10.2.

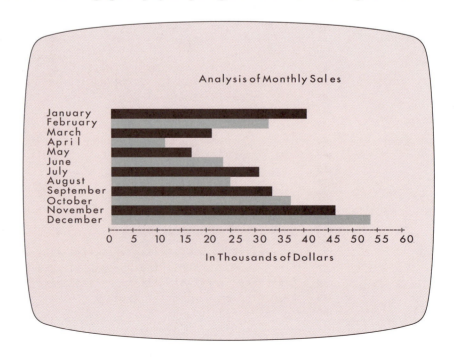

The COLOR Statement for Text Mode

The four general forms for the COLOR statements are: one for text mode (SCREEN 0); one for medium-resolution graphics mode (SCREEN 1); one for screen modes 7 through 10; and one for screen modes 12 and 13. In this section, we discuss the COLOR statement for text mode. In the next section, we cover color in the medium-resolution graphics mode.

The COLOR **statement** allows you to select colors for the foreground, background, and border of the screen. As illustrated in Figure 10.16, the **background** is that part of the screen against which the characters are displayed. Displayed characters are the **foreground**. The **border** is the edge of the screen. EGA, VGA, and MCGA do not support a border color.

❚FIGURE 10.16
The background, foreground, and border of the screen.

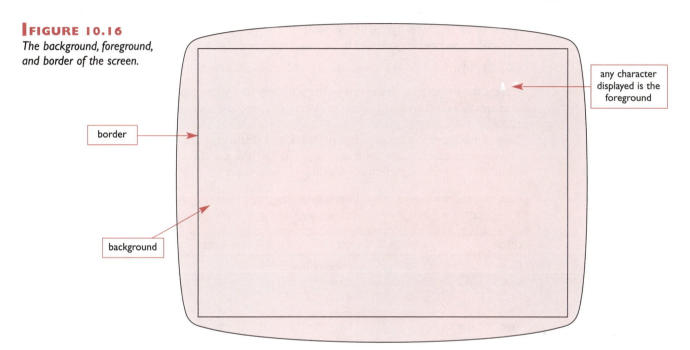

border

background

any character displayed is the foreground

When you first enter QBasic, the color of the output screen is set to white on black; that is, the foreground is set to white, and the background and border are set to black. The COLOR statement may then be used in the immediate mode or as a statement in a program to change the colors of the output screen as often as desired. The general form of the COLOR statement for text mode is shown in Table 10.5.

TABLE 10.5 - The COLOR Statement for Text Mode	
General Form:	COLOR foreground, background, border
	where **foreground** is a numeric expression in the range 0 to 31;
	background is a numeric expression in the range 0 to 7; and
	border is a numeric expression in the range 0 to 15.
Purpose:	Sets the color for the foreground, background, and border of the screen. The foreground and border may be set equal to any of the 16 colors described in Table 10.6. Adding the number 16 to the foreground value causes the characters to blink in that color. Only the colors with numbers 0 through 7 may be selected for the background.
Examples:	1. COLOR 14, 2, 6 ' Yellow on Green with a Brown Border
	2. COLOR 12 ' Light Red Foreground
	3. COLOR ,, 14 ' Yellow Border
	4. COLOR 7, 0, 0 ' White on Black
	5. COLOR 0, 7 ' Black on White
	6. COLOR 0, 0, 0 ' Black on Black
Note:	EGA, VGA, Super VGA, MCGA, and XGA do not support a border color.

Example 1 in Table 10.5 on the previous page sets a yellow foreground, a green background, and a brown border screen. Example 2 changes the foreground to light red; the background and border colors remain as they were. Example 3 changes only the border color to yellow. Example 4 resets the colors to the normal white on black. In this case, the background and border are the same. Example 5 reverses the colors; that is, it changes them to black on white. With Example 6, the foreground, background, and border are the same color; therefore, character images sent to the screen will not display. This method may be used to prevent the display of sensitive and confidential information, such as passwords, as they are entered via the keyboard.

When the COLOR statement is executed, all previously displayed characters remain in the original color. The new colors are used for future displays. For this reason, the COLOR statement is often followed by the CLS statement. The CLS statement causes the entire background and border to immediately display in the newly assigned colors. For example,

```
COLOR 14, 7, 2 : CLS 'Yellow on White with Green Border
```

instructs the PC to change the screen immediately to a white background and green border. All characters displayed as a result of listing or executing a program will display in the color yellow.

If you have a monochrome display (black and white or green or amber color) and a color/graphics adaptor, the color settings in Table 10.6 are still useful, but different colors will display in various patterns of shading on your screen.

TABLE 10.6 – The 16 Colors Available with a Color Monitor and Color/Graphics Adaptor					
COLOR	NUMBER	COLOR	NUMBER	COLOR	NUMBER
Black	0	Magenta (purplish)	5	Light Cyan	11
Blue	1	Brown	6	Light Red	12
Green	2	White	7	Light Magenta	13
Cyan	3	Grey	8	Yellow	14
(greenish blue)		Light Blue	9	Bright White	15
Red	4	Light Green	10		

The COLOR statement substantially improves the quality of the results displayed by a program. For example, if the following statement

```
COLOR 15, 1, 4 ' Bright White on Blue with Red Border
```

is added before the CLS statement in A100.Initialization of any of the previous menu driven programs in this book, then the main menu displays in bright white on a blue background with a red border. Other color combinations can be considered for submenus and the results displayed by a program.

Color monitors, sometimes called RGB **monitors**, create colors. The colors are determined by three independent bits representing the additive primary colors of red, green, and blue (hence, the term RGB), and a fourth bit representing the intensity (I). Collectively, these bits are called the **IRGB** color bits, and the color composition is referred to as the IRGB color. These bits form the 16 colors (2^4) in Table 10.6 by being on (1) or off (0) as shown in Table 10.7.

TABLE 10.7 - IRGB Colors

NUMBER	I	R	G	B	COLOR	COMPOSITION
0	0	0	0	0	Black	
1	0	0	0	1	Blue	Blue
2	0	0	1	0	Green	Green
3	0	0	1	1	Cyan	Green + Blue
4	0	1	0	0	Red	Red
5	0	1	0	1	Magenta	Red + Blue
6	0	1	1	0	Brown	Red + Green
7	0	1	1	1	White	Red + Green + Blue
8	1	0	0	0	Grey	Intensity
9	1	0	0	1	Light Blue	Intensity + Blue
10	1	0	1	0	Light Green	Intensity + Green
11	1	0	1	1	Light Cyan	Intensity + Green + Blue
12	1	1	0	0	Light Red	Intensity + Red
13	1	1	0	1	Light Magenta	Intensity + Red + Blue
14	1	1	1	0	Yellow	Intensity + Red + Green
15	1	1	1	1	Bright White	Intensity + Red + Green + Blue

TABLE 10.8 - QBasic Color Codes in Text Mode

NUMBER	COLOR FOREGROUND	COLOR BACKGROUND	COLOR BORDER
0	Black	Black	Black
1	Blue	Blue	Blue
2	Green	Green	Green
3	Cyan (greenish blue)	Cyan	Cyan
4	Red	Red	Red
5	Magenta (purplish)	Magenta	Magenta
6	Brown	Brown	Brown
7	White	White	White
8	Grey		Grey
9	Light Blue		Light Blue
10	Light Green		Light Green
11	Light Cyan		Light Cyan
12	Light Red		Light Red
13	Light Magenta		Light Magenta
14	Yellow		Yellow
15	Bright White		Bright White
16	Blinking Black		
17	Blinking Blue		
18	Blinking Green		
19	Blinking Cyan		
20	Blinking Red		
21	Blinking Magenta		
22	Blinking Brown		
23	Blinking White		
24	Blinking Grey		
25	Blinking Light Blue		
26	Blinking Light Green		
27	Blinking Light Cyan		
28	Blinking Light Red		
29	Blinking Light Magenta		
30	Blinking Yellow		
31	Blinking Bright White		

The three additive primary colors can be mixed or added in various combinations to form the first eight colors in Table 10.7. The intensity control yields an additional eight colors, each a brighter version of its non-intensified counterpart.

You may instruct the PC to blink characters by adding the number 16 to the foreground color: For example,

```
COLOR 31, 4 : CLS 'Blinking Bright
White on Red
```

causes the PC to blink bright white characters on a red background. All of these colors are summarized in Table 10.8 for the foreground, background, and border.

The partial program presented in Figure 10.17 displays the 32 foreground colors shown in Table 10.8 through the use of the COLOR statement.

FIGURE 10.17

Displaying the 32 foreground colors.

```
1    ' Displaying the 32 Foreground Colors
2    ' **********************************
3    SCREEN 0
4    WIDTH 40
5    FOR Fg = 0 TO 31
6       COLOR Fg, 0          ' Set Foreground Color
7       PRINT CHR$(219);     ' Print a Colored Block
8    NEXT Fg
```

```
[run]
```

When the partial progam in Figure 10.17 is executed, the FOR loop (lines 5 through 8) cause the PC to display horizontally, in the foreground a total of 32 colored blocks, represented by the ASCII decimal code of 219.

Suspending Execution of a Program

Some programs concerned with animation require the execution of a program to be suspended for a short time. This duration may range from a fraction of a second to several seconds. Sometimes the execution of a program is suspended until a key on the keyboard is pressed.

The temporary suspension of a program's execution is sometimes required to *slow down* the visual output from a program or to create an illusion in conjunction with the animation appearing on the screen.

In QBasic there are several ways to suspend temporarily the execution of a graphics program or *slow down* the program and, therefore, delaying the display of visual output. One way is to construct a time delay For loop as follows:

```
FOR Time.Delay% = 1 TO 500
NEXT Time.Delay%
```

This For loop has no statements between the FOR and NEXT statements. The main purpose of this For loop is to delay the display of visual output for a short duration.

Depending on the speed (MHz) of the CPU (see page 7), this delay may be a fraction of a second or longer. The problem with using a time-delayed For loop is that the limit value (500 in the example) must be adjusted as the speed of the CPU increases for the various models of the IBM PC and compatibles.

Another way to suspend temporarily the execution of a program is through the use of the SLEEP **statement** as shown in Table 10.9. The execution of the SLEEP statement is independent of the speed of the CPU.

TABLE 10.9 - The SLEEP Statement	
General Form:	SLEEP
	or
	SLEEP seconds
	where **seconds** indicates the length of time in seconds.
Purpose:	Suspends the execution of the program for an indicated period of time. If seconds is 0 or is omitted, the program is suspended until a key is pressed.
Examples:	1. SLEEP 5
	2. SLEEP 1
	3. SLEEP 0
	4. SLEEP

Example 1 in Table 10.9 instructs the PC to suspend the execution of the program for five seconds. It doesn't matter if the program is being executed on a 300 MHz, 500 MHz, or 700 MHz PC, the program is suspended for five seconds.

In Example 2, the execution of the program is suspended for one second. In both Examples 3 and 4, the execution of the program is suspended until a key is pressed.

The SLEEP statement will be used in this chapter to suspend temporarily the execution of a program and delay the appearance of visual output.

PROGRAMMING CASE STUDY 25 – Animating an Inchworm Creeping across the Screen

We can use the SCREEN statement in text mode to build different pages and display them one after another. As illustrated in the following case study, this page switching allows us to instruct the PC to animate objects formed with characters.

▌FIGURE 10.18

All five positions of the creeping inchworm.

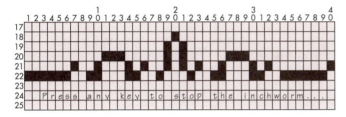

Problem: Use the SCREEN statement to animate an inchworm creeping across the screen in a left-to-right direction. The five positions of the inchworm are shown by the filled-in squares in Figure 10.18.

Use the 40-column display and build each position of the inchworm on a different page. After all the pages have been built, display the pages in sequence until the user intervenes.

Following are a top-down chart, a list of the program tasks in outline form, a program solution, and a discussion of the program solution.

Program Tasks

The following program tasks correspond to the top-down chart in Figure 10.19.

1. A100.Initialization
   a. Use the SCREEN statement to select text mode.
   b. Set the width of a line to 40 characters.

2. B100.Build.Inchworm — Build each position of the inchworm on a separate page. Note the similarity of positions 1 and 5 and positions 2 and 4 of the inchworm in Figure 10.18. By adjusting the columns and the page number, the same code may be used to build the identical positions of the inchworm.

▌FIGURE 10.19

Top-down chart for the solution to Programming Case Study 25.

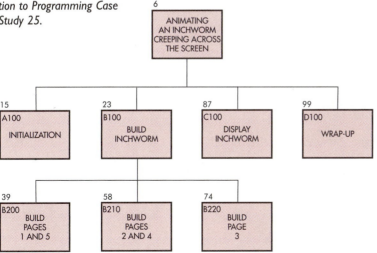

a. Call B200.Build.Pages.1.5 — Use the SCREEN statement to write to page 1 or 5 while displaying page 0. (Page 0 is blank.) For page 1, set the column to 1. For page 5, set the column to 34. Use the LOCATE and PRINT statements and the shaded rectangle (ASCII code = 219) to build the inchworm. Color the body green (COLOR 2) and the head red (COLOR 4). The message that is located on line 24 of Figure 10.18 is then written to page 5.

b. Call B210.Build.Pages.2.4 — Use the SCREEN statement to write to pages 2 and 4 while displaying page 0. For page 2, set the column to 9. For page 4, set the column to 25. Use the same statements and color described in 2a to build the inchworm.

c. Call B220.Build.Page.3 — Use the SCREEN statement to write to page 3 while displaying page 0. Use the statements and color in 2a to build the inchworm.

3. C100.Display.Inchworm — Establish a Do-While loop that executes until the user presses a key. Use the statement DO WHILE INKEY$ = "" to control the loop. Within the loop, use a For loop like the one below to display pages 1 through 5:

```
FOR Page% = 1 TO 5
   SCREEN , , , Page%
   SLEEP 1
NEXT Page%
```

The SCREEN statement displays pages 1 through 5. The SLEEP statement delays the display of the next page for one second. The display of the pages in sequence at a set time interval animates the inchworm creeping across the screen from left-to-right.

4. D100.Wrap.Up

    a. Use the SCREEN statement to write to page 0 and display page 0.

    b. Set the width of a line to 80 characters.

    c. Set the color to white on black.

    d. Clear the screen.

Program Solution

Program 10.3, the solution to Programming Case Study 25, is presented in Figure 10.20. It corresponds to the top-down chart in Figure 10.19 and to the preceding tasks.

FIGURE 10.20

Program 10.3, the solution to Programming Case Study 25.

```
 1   ' Program 10.3
 2   ' Animating an Inchworm Creeping across the Screen
 3   ' **********************************************
 4   ' *               Main Program               *
 5   ' **********************************************
 6   GOSUB A100.Initialization
 7   GOSUB B100.Build.Inchworm
 8   GOSUB C100.Display.Inchworm
 9   GOSUB D100.Wrap.Up
10   END
11
12   ' **********************************************
13   ' *               Initialization             *
14   ' **********************************************
15   A100.Initialization:
16      SCREEN 0
17      WIDTH 40
18   RETURN
19
20   ' **********************************************
21   ' *               Build Inchworm             *
22   ' **********************************************
23   B100.Build.Inchworm:
24      Page% = 1
25      GOSUB B200.Build.Pages.1.5
26      Page% = 2
27      GOSUB B210.Build.Pages.2.4
28      Page% = 3
29      GOSUB B220.Build.Page.3
30      Page% = 4
31      GOSUB B210.Build.Pages.2.4
32      Page% = 5
33      GOSUB B200.Build.Pages.1.5
34   RETURN
35
```

```
36  ' ************************************************
37  ' *                Build Pages 1 and 5              *
38  ' ************************************************
39  B200.Build.Pages.1.5:
40     SCREEN , , Page%, 0
41     IF Page% = 1 THEN
42        Col = 1
43     ELSE
44        Col = 34
45     END IF
46     LOCATE 22, Col: COLOR 2: PRINT STRING$(6, 219);
47     LOCATE 21, Col + 6: COLOR 4: PRINT CHR$(219)
48     IF Page% = 5 THEN
49        LOCATE 24, 3
50        COLOR 15
51        PRINT "Press any key to stop the inchworm..."
52     END IF
53  RETURN
54
55  ' ************************************************
56  ' *                Build Pages 2 and 4              *
57  ' ************************************************
58  B210.Build.Pages.2.4:
59     SCREEN , , Page%, 0
60     IF Page% = 2 THEN
61        Col = 9
62     ELSE
63        Col = 25
64     END IF
65     LOCATE 22, Col: COLOR 2: PRINT STRING$(2, 219); SPC(3); STRING$(2, 219)
66     LOCATE 21, Col + 1: PRINT CHR$(219); SPC(3); CHR$(219)
67     LOCATE 20, Col + 2: PRINT STRING$(3, 219)
68     LOCATE 21, Col + 7: COLOR 4: PRINT CHR$(219)
69  RETURN
70
71  ' ************************************************
72  ' *                  Build Page 3                   *
73  ' ************************************************
74  B220.Build.Page.3:
75     SCREEN , , Page%, 0
76     LOCATE 22, 18: COLOR 2: PRINT CHR$(219); SPC(3); CHR$(219)
77     LOCATE 21, 19: PRINT CHR$(219); SPC(1); CHR$(219)
78     LOCATE 20, 19: PRINT CHR$(219); SPC(1); CHR$(219)
79     LOCATE 19, 19: PRINT CHR$(219); SPC(1); CHR$(219)
80     LOCATE 18, 20: PRINT CHR$(219)
81     LOCATE 21, 23: COLOR 4: PRINT CHR$(219)
82  RETURN
83
84  ' ************************************************
85  ' *                Display Inchworm                 *
86  ' ************************************************
87  C100.Display.Inchworm:
88     DO WHILE INKEY$ = ""
89        FOR Page% = 1 TO 5
90           SCREEN , , , Page%
91           SLEEP 1
92        NEXT Page%
93     LOOP
94  RETURN
95
```

(continued)

FIGURE 10.20
(continued)

```
96  ' ************************************************
97  ' *                    Wrap-Up                  *
98  ' ************************************************
99  D100.Wrap.Up:
100    SCREEN , , 0, 0: WIDTH 80: COLOR 7  ' Reset Screen
101    CLS  ' Clear Screen
102  RETURN
103
104  ' ************** End of Program ****************
```

[run]

FIGURE 10.21

The five positions of the inchworm creeping across the screen, superimposed on one screen.

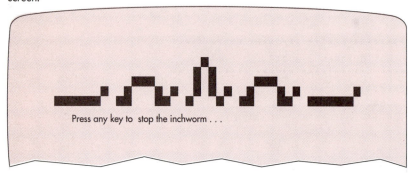

Press any key to stop the inchworm . . .

When Program 10.3 is executed, the five positions of the inchworm shown in Figure 10.21 are displayed from left to right, one after the other.

Discussion of the Program Solution

The five positions of the inchworm are each built on separate pages because of the calls made in the subroutine B100.Build.Inchworm. Each subroutine called from B100.Build.Inchworm begins with a SCREEN statement that establishes the page to write to and the page to display. It is important to include the parameter 0 for the visual page because the visual page defaults to the active page if no value is specified.

In C100.Display.Inchworm, the Do-While loop causes the inchworm to creep across the screen from left to right, over and over again, until the user presses a key on the keyboard. Within the loop, the five pages are displayed one after the other. The SLEEP statement in line 91 delays the display of the next page for one second.

In the solution to Programming Case Study 25, we were able to build all the required positions on separate pages before displaying the animation. This is not always possible because most animations require more pages than are available (eight pages for 40-column display and four pages for 80-column display). When the number of required positions exceeds the number of available pages, the program must build one page while displaying another page.

10.3 MEDIUM-RESOLUTION AND HIGH-RESOLUTION GRAPHICS

To change to medium-resolution graphics mode, enter the statement SCREEN 1. In this mode, the screen is divided into 200 rows and 320 columns (see Figure 10.6(c) on page 400). To change to high-resolution graphics mode, enter the statement SCREEN 2. In the high-resolution graphics mode, the screen is divided into 200 rows and 640 columns (see Figure 10.6(d) on page 400).

Consider these important points regarding medium-resolution and high-resolution graphics modes:

1. These two graphics modes are available only if your PC has a Color/Graphics Adaptor.
2. To send graphical designs to the printer, you must have one that emulates the IBM graphics printer. Also, you must enter the MS-DOS command GRAPHICS before you start QBasic.

3. With a color monitor, medium-resolution graphics allow you to color objects on the screen. High-resolution graphics allow displays in only black and white, but with much greater detail.

4. In either of the two graphics modes, the intersection of a row and column is a point, or pixel. You plot points and draw lines and curves by instructing the PC to turn on selected pixels.

5. The PC is given information about the points, lines, and curves to draw in the form of coordinates, such as (x, y), where x is the column (horizontal axis) and y is the row (vertical axis).

6. Coordinates are specified with the column first, then the row. This is different from the LOCATE statement in text mode, which requires the row first, then the column.

7. Rows and columns are numbered beginning with 0, rather than 1.

8. There are two ways to indicate the coordinates of a point on the screen: absolute form and relative form. Coordinates of the form (x, y) are absolute in relation to the origin (0, 0). Coordinates of the form STEP(x, y) are relative to the last point referenced by the last graphics statement executed.

9. If you enter WIDTH 80 in medium-resolution graphics mode, the PC will switch to high-resolution graphics mode. If you enter WIDTH 40 in high-resolution graphics mode, the PC will switch to medium-resolution graphics mode.

In the sections that follow, several graphics statements and examples are presented.

The COLOR Statement for Medium-Resolution Graphics Mode

The general form of the COLOR statement for medium-resolution graphics mode is given in Table 10.10.

In Table 10.10, Example 1 sets the background color to light blue and selects palette 1 for the foreground. Graphics statements that follow the COLOR statement in Example 1 may select cyan (color number 1 in Table 10.10), magenta (2), white (3), or the background color (0) for the foreground. Selecting the background color turns off the referenced pixel(s).

Example 2 leaves the background color the same, and palette 0 is selected for the foreground. Graphics statements that follow this COLOR statement may select the foreground color from green (1), red (2), brown (3), or the background color (0). Finally, Example 3 in Table 10.10 selects the background color on the basis of the value of Back and a palette on the basis of whether Pal is odd (palette 1) or even (palette 0).

TABLE 10.10 - The COLOR Statement for the Medium-Resolution Graphics Mode		
General Form:	COLOR background, palette	
	where **background** is a numeric expression in the range 0 to 15, and **palette** is a numeric expression. If the expression is an even number, then palette 0 is selected for the foreground; otherwise, palette 1 is selected.	
Purpose:	Sets the background color of the screen and selects one of two palettes of color for the foreground. The background may be set equal to any of the 16 colors described in Table 10.6 on page 412. The choice of palettes for the foreground is as follows:	
	Palette 0	**Palette 1**	**Number**
	Background Color	Background Color	0
	Green	Cyan	1
	Red	Magenta	2
	Brown	White	3
Examples:	1. COLOR 9, 1 2. COLOR , 0 3. COLOR Back, Pal	
Note:	The COLOR statement selects the palette (0 or 1) for the foreground. Graphics statements that follow the COLOR statement select the color number from the palette. If no color number is selected, then the default color number 3 is used for medium resolution, and the color number 1 is used for high resolution. In medium resolution the border is always the same color as the background.	

The PSET and PRESET Statements

The PSET (point set) and PRESET (point reset) **statements** can be used to set a point on the screen to one of the four colors in the active palette. The general forms of the PSET and PRESET statements are given in Table 10.11.

TABLE 10.11 - The PSET and PRESET Statements	
General Form:	PSET (x, y), color and PRESET (x, y), color where **(x, y)** are the coordinates of the point to be plotted (turned on), and **color** is an integer expression in the range 0 to 3. The color number selects the color from the active palette. (See Table 10.10 on the previous page.)
Purpose:	To plot a point on the screen.
Examples:	1. PSET (34, 72), 2 2. PSET (Col, Row) 3. PSET STEP (X, 5), 0 4. PRESET STEP (40, 90), Kolor 5. PRESET (34, 72)
Notes:	1. The coordinates (x, y) may be absolute, without STEP and from the origin, or relative, with STEP and from the current coordinates. 2. The PC ignores points referenced outside the range of the screen. 3. PSET and PRESET are identical statements except for the default color number when the color parameter is not included. With the PSET statement, the color number defaults to 3. With the PRESET statement, the color number defaults to 0, the background color. Thus, PSET (X, Y), 0 is identical to PRESET (X, Y).

Example 1 in Table 10.11 plots the point at the intersection of column 34 and row 72. Depending on which palette is active, the point is colored red or magenta. Example 2 plots the point (Col, Row) using the default color number 3 of the active palette. Examples 3 and 5 in Table 10.11 erase the point defined by the specified coordinates. Recall that a color number of 0 or a lack of the color parameter in the PRESET statement instructs the PC to use the background color. (That is, the pixel is turned off.) Example 4 plots the point that is 40 columns and 90 rows from the last point referenced. The color of the point is based upon the value of Kolor and the active palette.

FIGURE 10.22

Plotting a line and points.

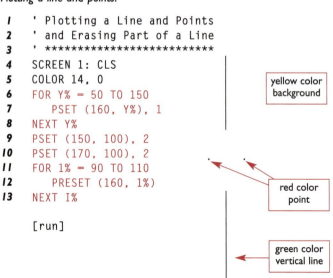

```
1   ' Plotting a Line and Points
2   ' and Erasing Part of a Line
3   ' *************************
4   SCREEN 1: CLS
5   COLOR 14, 0
6   FOR Y% = 50 TO 150
7       PSET (160, Y%), 1
8   NEXT Y%
9   PSET (150, 100), 2
10  PSET (170, 100), 2
11  FOR I% = 90 TO 110
12      PRESET (160, I%)
13  NEXT I%

[run]
```

yellow color background

red color point

green color vertical line

Consider the partial program and the results due to its execution in Figure 10.22. Line 4 switches the PC to medium-resolution graphics mode and clears the screen. Line 5 sets the background color to yellow and selects palette 0. The For loop (lines 6 through 8) draws a green vertical line. The color number in line 7 selects the color green from palette 0. Lines 9 and 10 plot two points using the color red on the left and right sides of the green, vertical line. Finally, the second For loop (lines 11 through 13) erases part of the line drawn by the first For loop.

As we see in the next section, QBasic has a LINE statement that simplifies drawing lines such as the one drawn by the partial program in Figure 10.22.

The LINE Statement

The LINE **statement** can be used to draw a line or a box on the screen. The general form of the LINE statement is given in Table 10.12.

In Table 10.12, Example 1 draws a line from the point defined by the intersection of column 50 and row 70 to the point defined by the intersection of column 90 and row 100. The color of the line is either red (palette 0) or magenta (palette 1). Example 2 draws a line from the last point referenced to the point (65, 90) in the default color on the active palette.

Example 3 in Table 10.12 draws a diagonal line from the upper left-hand corner to the lower right-hand corner of the screen. If palette 0 is active, the color of the line is brown. Example 4 draws a box around the outer edge of the screen. If palette 0 is active, the lines making up the box are colored green. Otherwise, the lines of the box are colored cyan. Example 5 also draws a box. The location of the box on the screen is dependent on the values assigned to Col1, Row1, Col2, and Row2. The parameter BF instructs the PC to fill the box with the default color for the active palette. Example 6 draws a dotted box. If palette 0 is active, the dots forming the box are colored green; otherwise, the dots are colored cyan.

TABLE 10.12 - The LINE Statement	
General Form:	LINE (x_1, y_1) - (x_2, y_2), color, box, style
	where (x_1, y_1) is the starting point;
	(x_2, y_2) is the ending point;
	color selects the color for the line from the active palette;
	box is B or BF,
	where **B** instructs the PC to draw a box, rather than a line with (x_1, y_1) and (x_2, y_2) as opposite coordinates; and
	BF is similar to B, except that the box is filled with color; and
	style is a 16-bit integer used to determine the type of line — dotted, dashed, or solid — to be drawn.
Purpose:	Connects two points with a line or draws a box, filled or unfilled, on the screen.
Examples:	1. LINE (50, 70)-(90, 100), 2
	2. LINE -(65, 90)
	3. LINE (0, 0)-(319, 199), 3
	4. LINE (0, 199)-(319, 0), 1, B
	5. LINE (Col1, Row1)-(Col2, Row2),, BF
	6. LINE (10, 10)-(50, 50), 1, B, &H1111
Notes:	1. Lines that extend beyond the range of the screen are **clipped**; that is, the PC determines the intersection of the line with the edge of the screen and draws the line up to the edge.
	2. The style parameter cannot be used with filled boxes (BF).

Consider the partial program in Figure 10.23 on the next page and the right triangle displayed as a result of its execution. In the partial program, line 3 switches the PC to medium resolution graphics mode and clears the screen. Line 4 changes the background of the screen to blue and selects palette 1. Line 5 draws the base of the triangle. Line 6 draws the altitude, and line 7 draws the hypotenuse. Because none of the LINE statements include a color number, the default color number 3 (white for palette 1) is used. Note also that lines 6 and 7 both draw lines from the last point referenced.

FIGURE 10.23

Drawing a right triangle.

```
1    ' Drawing a Right Triangle
2    ' ***********************
3    SCREEN 1: CLS
4    COLOR 1, 1
5    LINE (20, 75) - (100, 75)
6    LINE -(100, 25)
7    LINE -(20, 75)

     [run]
```

blue color background

white color line

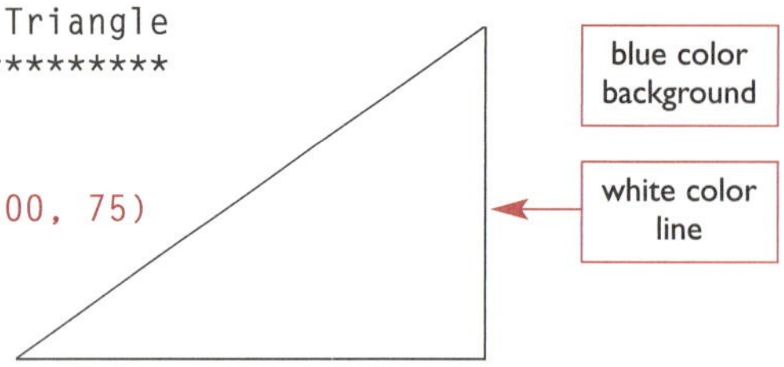

As two more examples of the use of the LINE statement, consider the partial programs in Figure 10.24. Partial program (a) instructs the PC to draw five boxes, one of which is inside another. Line 3 switches the PC to medium-resolution graphics mode and clears the screen. Line 4 selects a black background and palette 0.

FIGURE 10.24

Drawing boxes.

(a)

```
1    ' Drawing Boxes
2    ' *************
3    SCREEN 1: CLS
4    COLOR 0, 0
5    LINE (20, 10)-(40, 30), 1, B
6    LINE (20, 40)-(60, 80), 2, BF
7    LINE (30, 50)-(50, 70), 0, BF
8    LINE (70, 0)-(90, 80), 1, BF
9    LINE (110, 20)-(170, 40), , BF

     [run]
```

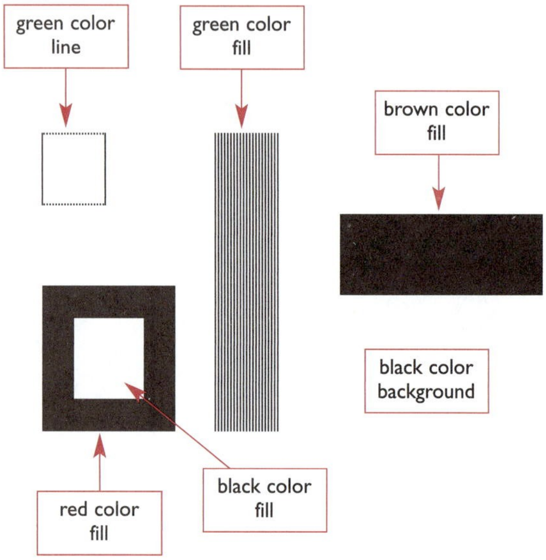

green color line

green color fill

brown color fill

red color fill

black color fill

black color background

(b)

```
1    ' Drawing Boxes with Dashed Lines
2    ' ******************************
3    SCREEN 1: CLS
4    LINE (5, 5)-(285, 185), , B, &HE724 ' Outermost box
5    LINE (25, 25)-(265, 165), , B, &H1111
6    LINE (45, 45)-(245, 145), , B, &HF0F0
7    LINE (65, 65)-(22S, 125), , B, &HFFCC ' Innermost box

     [run]
```

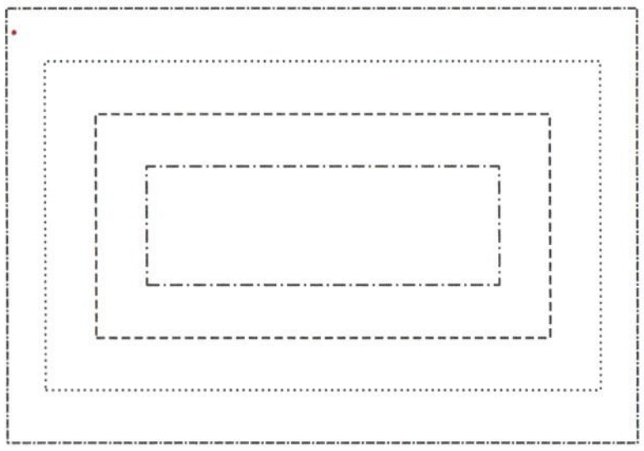

The first LINE statement in Figure 10.24(a) draws the small, unfilled square box with opposite coordinates of (20, 10) and (40, 30) using the color green. Line 6 draws the large filled square box, using the color red. Next, line 7 draws a filled square within the square drawn by line 6. Because the background color is used in line 7, the red pixels are turned off to leave an unfilled Square within the large red square.

Line 8 in Figure 10.24(a) draws the filled vertical box, using the color green. Finally, line 9 draws the filled horizontal box using the default color brown on palette 0. The style of a line consists of a series of pixels that are on (1) or off (0). In the LINE statement, the style consists of a 16-bit integer mask representing 16 consecutive pixels, and this pattern is used to construct the style of the line, which can be a dotted or dashed line or a box.

The 16-bit pattern repeats as necessary for the entire length of the line or the entire perimeter of a box. The style is specified by a 4-digit hexadecimal number that represents the desired pattern. The four steps involved in representing a pattern are as follows:

1. Create the 16-bit pattern on paper. Assume that the following dashed-line pattern is desired:

● ● ● ● ○ ○ ○ ○ ● ● ● ● ○ ○ ○ ○

where the solid dot represents an on-pixel and the open dot represents an off-pixel.

2. Substitute a zero for each open dot and a one for each solid dot:

1111000011110000

3. Divide the 16-bit pattern into four sets of 4-bit patterns where each of the four bits becomes a hexadecimal digit according to the conversion:

4-Bit Pattern	ASCII Value of Hexadecimal Digit	4-Bit Pattern	ASCII Value of Hexadecimal Digit
0000	0	1000	8
0001	1	1001	9
0010	2	1010	A
0011	3	1011	B
0100	4	1100	C
0101	5	1101	D
0110	6	1110	E
0111	7	1111	F

Hence, the 4-bit patterns become:

1111   0000   1111   0000
F   0   F   0

4. Type &H in front of the first hexadecimal number as shown:

&HF0F0

This now becomes a valid style for a LINE statement such as line 6 in Figure 10.24(b).

The partial program in Figure 10.24(b) instructs the PC to draw four dotted or dashed-line boxes, each inside of one another. Line 3 switches the PC to medium resolution graphics mode and clears the screen. Lines 4 through 7 draw the boxes with dotted or dashed lines by adding a style to the LINE statement.

The CIRCLE Statement

The CIRCLE **statement** draws circles, ellipses, arcs, and wedges. The general form of the CIRCLE statement is given in Table 10.13 on the next page.

TABLE 10.13 - The CIRCLE Statement

General Form:	CIRCLE (x, y), radius, color, start, end, shape
	where **(x, y)** is the center of the curved figure;
	radius is the distance from the center to the outer edge of the curved figure, as measured in points (pixels);
	color selects the color for the curved figure from the active palette;
	start and **end** are the two ends of the arc to be drawn (The measures are angles in radians and can range between -2 * 3.141593 and 2 * 3.141593. Negative values [-0 is not allowed] cause a wedge or pie slice to be drawn. If these two parameters are omitted, the PC draws the entire curved figure.); and
	shape is the ratio of the radius in the y direction to the radius in the x direction (height/width). This parameter is used to draw ellipses. If this parameter is omitted, the PC draws a partial or complete circle, depending on the start and end parameters.
Purpose:	To draw circles, ellipses, arcs, and wedges.
Examples:	1. CIRCLE (160, 100) , 20
	2. CIRCLE (60, 40), 30, 1
	3. CIRCLE (20, 20), 50
	4. CIRCLE (Col, Row), Red, Kolor
	5. CIRCLE (120, 120), 35,, 0, 1.5708
	6. CIRCLE (160, 100), 50, 1, -3.141593, -4.7124
	7. CIRCLE (100, 100), 40,,,, 5/18
Notes:	1. The last point referenced after the CIRCLE statement is executed is the center point (x, y).
	2. If you want to draw a radius to angle 0 (a horizontal line), then use a small nonzero value, such as -0.0001, rather than -0 or -2 * 3.141593.

In Table 10.13, Example 1 instructs the PC to draw a circle with a center at column 160 and row 100 and with a radius of 20 points. The default color number 3 on the active palette is used to draw the circle. In Example 2, a circle with a center at (60, 40) with a radius of 30 points is drawn in green or cyan.

Example 3 in Table 10.13 draws a circle that is clipped because part of the circle goes beyond the screen. Example 4 causes a circle to be drawn, using the color number Kolor, with center at (Col, Row) and radius of Red points.

Example 5 draws an arc from 0° to 90° with a center at (120, 120) and a radius of 35 points. The default color on the active palette is used to color the curved figure. Example 6 draws a wedge. The negative start and end parameters instruct the PC to connect the center to the ends of the arc to form a wedge. The wedge extends from 180° to 270°. Figure 10.25 shows the relationship between radians and slices of a circle.

FIGURE 10.25

A circle is composed of 2π or 6.28 radians, or 360°. (Note that the decimal fraction values are rounded to the nearest hundredths place.)

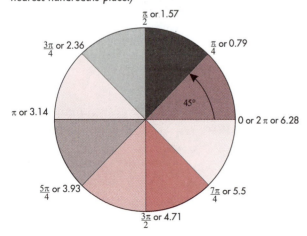

Example 7 in Table 10.13 draws a horizontal, flatter ellipse. The center of the ellipse is at (100, 100). Because the shape is less than 1, the radius parameter is the x radius. The product of the shape (5/18) and the radius parameter is the y radius.

In mathematics, when the shape is equal to 1, a circle is defined. A shape that is less than 1 causes the ellipse to be horizontal (flatter). A shape greater than 1 causes the ellipse to be vertical (taller).

Because the pixel length for the PC screen is not the same in both the x and y direction (320 × 200 for medium resolution), the default value of the shape that draws a circle is 5/6 (5 rows for every 6 columns) in medium resolution and 5/12 (5 rows for every 12 columns) in high resolution. With this in mind, you must adjust slightly the mathematical definition of the term *shape*.

For example, the following statement

```
CIRCLE (160, 100), 50,,,, 1
```

does not result in a circle even though the shape is 1. The CIRCLE statement draws an ellipse that is slightly taller than it is wide. The following statement draws a circle because the PC uses a default value of 5/6 for the shape:

```
CIRCLE (160, 100), 50
```

See the partial program in Figure 10.26 on the next page for additional examples of CIRCLE statements that draw ellipses.

The PAINT Statement

Another color statement available with QBasic is the PAINT statement. The **PAINT statement** paints (fills) an area on the screen with the selected color. The general form of the PAINT statement is given in Table 10.14.

TABLE 10.14 - The PAINT Statement	
General Form:	PAINT (x, y), paint, boundary
	where **(x, y)** are the coordinates of a point within the area to be filled with color; **paint** is a numeric expression or a string expression (If paint is a numeric expression, then it must be within the range 0 to 3 for medium resolution and 0 or 1 for high resolution. The numeric expression determines the color the PC uses to paint the area on the screen. The default for medium resolution is 3 and for high resolution 1. If paint is a string expression, then it describes a tiling pattern for the area.); and **boundary** is a numeric expression that defines the color of the edges of the area to be filled.
Purpose:	Paints an area defined by the boundary color on the screen with the selected color.
Examples:	1. PAINT (50, 25), 2, 1 2. PAINT (Col, Row), Kolor, Edge 3. PAINT (200, 100) 4. PAINT (100, 150), Tile$
Notes:	1. The area defined by the boundary color must be completely enclosed, or the entire screen is painted. 2. In high resolution, the paint parameter should not be different from the boundary parameter.

Assuming that in medium resolution palette 0 is active, Example 1 in Table 10.14 paints the area with the color red that is bounded by the color green in which the point with coordinates (50, 25) is located. If there is no green boundary surrounding (50, 25), the entire screen is painted red. Example 1 is invalid in high resolution because the paint parameter is not 0 or 1.

In either medium resolution or high resolution, Example 2 paints the area encompassing the point with coordinates (Col, Row) and bounded by the color number Edge with the color associated with Kolor. Example 3 colors the area that includes the point with coordinates (200, 100) with the default color (3 in medium resolution and 1 in high resolution). If the edge of the area is not equal to the default color, the entire screen is painted.

Consider the partial program and the results due to its execution in Figure 10.26. In the partial program in Figure 10.26, line 5 switches the PC to medium solution graphics mode. The COLOR statement in line 6 selects a blue background and activates palette 0. Line 8 draws the circle in the upper left corner of the output results. Line 9 paints the circle brown. Note that the boundary parameter in line 9 is equal to the color number used to draw the circle in line 8.

```
 1    ' Drawing Circles, Arcs,
 2    ' Wedges, and Ellipses
 3    ' *********************
 4    Pi = 3.141593
 5    SCREEN 1: CLS
 6    COLOR 1, 0
 7    ' **** Draw Circle ****
 8    CIRCLE (40, 40), 20, 1
 9    PAINT (40, 40), 3, 1
10    ' ****** Draw Arc *****
11    CIRCLE (80, 40), 20, 1, 0, Pi / 2
12    ' **** Draw Wedge *****
13    CIRCLE (120, 40), 20, 3, -.0001, -Pi / 2
14    PAINT (125, 35), 1, 3
15    ' ** Draw Horizontal Ellipse **
16    CIRCLE (40, 100), 30, 3, , , 7 / 18
17    PAINT (40, 100), 2, 3
18    ' ** Draw Vertical Ellipse **
19    CIRCLE (90, 100), 30, 3, , , 18 / 7
20    PAINT (95, 95), 1, 3
21    ' ** Draw Circle within Box **
22    LINE (120, 70) - (180, 130), 3, B
23    CIRCLE (150, 100), 20, 3
24    PAINT (125, 75), 2, 3

      [run]
```

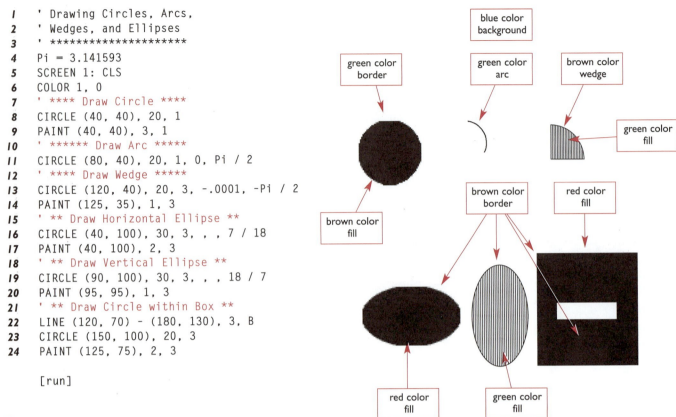

FIGURE 10.26

Examples of the COLOR and PAINT statements.

Line 11 in the partial program draws an arc from 0° to 90° with a center at (80, 40). Line 13 draws the wedge illustrated in Figure 10.26. Line 14 paints the wedge green. Rather than using –2 * Pi as the value for the start parameter in line 13, –0.0001 is used. Recall from Table 10.13 that the negative start and end parameters instruct the PC to draw lines from the center point to the end points of the arc to form a wedge. A start parameter of –2 * Pi, which is the same as 0°, is represented in line 13 by the decimal fraction value -0.0001. Assigning the start parameter of –2 * Pi, or –0, causes a dialog box to display with the diagnostic message Illegal function call. Here a value (–0.0001) was selected that is very close to –2 * Pi, or –0.

Line 16 draws a horizontal ellipse. Line 19 draws a vertical ellipse. Both ellipses are shown in the output results in Figure 10.26. Each of the two CIRCLE statements is followed by a PAINT statement that paints the ellipses. Line 17 paints the horizontal ellipse the color red, and line 20 paints the vertical ellipse the color green.

The lower right figure in Figure 10.26 displays because of lines 22 through 24. Line 22 draws the box. Line 23 draws the circle within the box. Both figures are drawn using the color brown (palette 0, color 3). Line 24 uses the color red to paint the area within the box and outside the circle. Painting continues in all directions until the brown border is reached.

Tiling

Example 4 in Table 10.14 on the previous page causes the area to be tiled instead of painted. **Tiling** involves covering a specified area on the screen with a pattern. The pattern is uniformly repeated over the entire area.

The pattern of the tile is based on a series of binary digits assigned to the paint parameter in the form of a string expression. The string expression may contain from 1 to 64 bytes. Each byte, called a **tile mask**, contains 8 binary digits. A single tile mask is formed in a QBasic program by means of the CHR$ function as follows:

```
CHR$(Decimal Number Representing the Tile Mask)
```

A series of tile masks is assigned to a string variable used as the paint parameter. An example of a tile pattern is shown in Figure 10.27. Each tile represents a single row of pixels.

FIGURE 10.27

An example of a tile pattern and the corresponding string expression assigned to the paint parameter Tile$.

	Bit Pattern	
	7 6 5 4 3 2 1 0	**CHR$ Argument**
Tile 0	*1 0 1 0 1 0 1 0*	*170*
Tile 1	*1 1 1 1 1 1 1 1*	*255*
Tile 3	*0 1 0 0 0 1 0 0*	*68*

```
Tile$ = CHR$(170) + CHR$(255) + CHR$(68)
```

With high resolution, every bit represents a pixel. If the bit is on (1), then the corresponding pixel is turned on; otherwise, the bit is assigned the background color (turned off). By scanning the bit pattern in Figure 10.27, you can get a feel for what each row in the pattern looks like in high resolution.

With medium resolution, every 2 bits represent a pixel, for a total of 4 pixels across per tile byte. Table 10.15 on the next page shows the binary color numbers for the foreground colors found on the two palettes and the equivalent CHR$ decimal representation for drawing solid lines. A solid line is defined as a single row of pixels.

Consider the partial programs (a) and (b) and their corresponding output results in Figure 10.28.

FIGURE 10.28

Partial programs (a) and (b) and their corresponding output results.

(a)

```
1   ' Tiling a Box in Medium Resolution
2   ' *******************************
3   Tile$ = CHR$(170) + CHR$(255) + CHR$(68)
4   SCREEN 1: CLS
5   COLOR 1, 1
6   LINE (40, 70)-(120, 120), 3, B
7   PAINT (117, 80), Tile$, 3

    [run]
```

(b)

```
1   ' Tiling a Wedge in High Resolution
2   ' *******************************
3   Pi = 3.141593
4   Tile$ = CHR$(170) + CHR$(170) + CHR$(255) + CHR$(68) + CHR$(68)
5   SCREEN 2: CLS
6   CIRCLE (320, 100), 150, , -3 * Pi / 4, -Pi
7   PAINT (300, 95), Tile$

    [run]
```

In Figure 10.28(a), line 7 tiles the box defined by line 6. The pattern of the tile is assigned to the string variable Tile$ in line 3 and corresponds to the one described earlier in Figure 10.27. Tile$ describes a pattern of three lines. The first two are solid lines, and the third is of alternating colors. The first line is in the color magenta. The second line is in the color white. The third line is alternating between cyan and the background color blue.

In Figure 10.28(b), line 4 defines the pattern of the tile. Line 5 switches the PC to high resolution. Line 6 instructs the PC to draw a wedge. Finally, line 7 tiles the wedge by turning on the pixels described by the series of binary digits described in line 4.

Developing reasonable patterns for either graphics mode becomes easier with practice. Enter the partial programs in Figure 10.28 into your PC and experiment with changing the patterns in the two partial programs.

		BINARY COLOR NUMBER	SOLID LINE PATTERN	CHR$ DECIMAL REPRESENTATION FOR SOLID LINE
PALETTE 0	**PALETTE I**			
Background	Background	00	00000000	0
Green	Cyan	01	01010101	85
Red	Magenta	10	10101010	170
Brown	White	11	11111111	255

TABLE 10.15 - The Binary Color Numbers for Tiling and Equivalent CHR$ Decimal Values for Solid Lines

The DRAW Statement

The DRAW **statement** instructs the PC to draw an object defined by a string expression. The string expression is made up of a series of easy-to-code commands (Table 10.17). You can use the commands to draw lines, plot points, set colors, and perform other special operations — all within one statement. For example, DRAW "L75 U100" draws a horizontal line 75 columns (pixels) long in a left direction of the last point referenced. It then draws a line 100 points long upward toward the top of the screen, beginning at the leftmost point of the first line. The last point referenced is based on the most recently executed graphics statement, or it is at the center of the screen following the execution of the program or a CLS statement. Recall that the center of the screen is at (160, 100) for medium resolution and (320, 100) for high resolution.

The general form for the DRAW statement is shown in Table 10.16. The list of DRAW commands that can be assigned to the string expression in the DRAW statement is given in Table 10.17.

TABLE 10.16 - The DRAW Statement

General Form: DRAW string expression

where **string expression** is a command or series of commands as described in Table 10.17.

Purpose: To draw an object as specified in the string expression.

Examples:
1. DRAW "BM75,120 M200,50 M100,150 M75,120"
2. DRAW "U100 R100 D100 L100"
3. DRAW "E=" + VARPTR$(S1) + "U25"
4. DRAW DESIGN$

Note: A DRAW command such as U or R may be followed by a constant or variable. If a variable is used, then surround the command (and equal sign, if required) with quotation marks and join to the command the function VARPTR$ with the variable as the argument. (See the first command in Example 3.)

TABLE 10.17 - DRAW Commands

COMMAND	FUNCTION	EXAMPLES
Mx,y	Moves and draws to (x,y).	M20,50
M ± x, ± y	Moves and draws to (X + x, Y + y), where (X,Y) is the last referenced point.	M+30,+50
Un	Moves and draws up n rows.	U70
Dn	Moves and draws down n rows.	D35
Rn	Moves and draws right n columns.	R45
Ln	Moves and draws left n columns.	L27
En	Moves and draws diagonally up and right, where n = diagonal distance.	E40
Fn	Moves and draws diagonally down and right, where n = diagonal distance.	F90
Gn	Moves and draws diagonally down and left, where n = diagonal distance.	G10
Hn	Moves and draws diagonally up and left, where n = diagonal distance.	H36
B	Causes the next move command to move without drawing.	BM20,50
N	Instructs the PC to return to the current point after the next move command.	NR75
An	Sets angle n, where n ranges from 0 to 3. 0 = 0 degrees, 1 = 90 degrees, 2 = 180 degrees, and 3 = 270 degrees. Rotates next object drawn through the specified angle.	A2
Tn	Turns angle n for subsequent drawings, where n is in the range -360 to 360; n > 0 turns angle counterclockwise, n < 0 turns angle clockwise.	T30
Sn	Scales subsequent drawings, where n varies between 1 and 255. (All line lengths are multiplied by n/4.)	S24
Cn	Selects color from active palette.	C2
Pp,b	Fills area using color number p to boundary b.	P1,2
"X" + v	Executes a subcommand, where v is equal to the VARPTR$ function with a string variable containing additional commands as the argument. *	"X" + VARPTR$ (Design2$)

* A command may be followed by a constant or variable. If a variable is used, then surround the command (and equal sign, if required) with quotation marks and join to the command the function VARPTR$ with the variable as the argument.

Partial programs (a), (b), and (c) in Figure 10.29 on the next page illustrate the use of the DRAW statement to instruct the PC to draw three simple figures — a bicycle wheel, a sailboat, and a flower.

Partial program (a) in Figure 10.29 uses the DRAW statement in high-resolution graphics mode to draw the bicycle wheel shown to the right of the program. Line 4 draws the rim with a center at (320, 100) and a radius of 60 points. The For loop (lines 5 through 7) draws the spokes. The loop variable Angle% starts at 0 and steps by 10 until it reaches 360. Each time through the loop, the TA command in line 6 causes the PC to rotate counterclockwise the direction of the next line drawn. Because we want to use the variable Angle%, rather than a constant, with the TA command, it is required that we use the VARPTR$ function. Note that the ratio of the length of a spoke to the radius of the circle is equal to 5/12. This ratio is required because the screen does not have the same number of rows (200) as columns (640).

FIGURE 10.29

Examples of the DRAW statement.

(a)

black color background

white color spokes

```
1    ' Draw a Bicycle Wheel
2    ' *********************
3    SCREEN 2: CLS
4    CIRCLE (320, 100), 60
5    FOR Angle% = 0 TO 360 STEP 10
6        DRAW "TA=" + VARPTR$(Angle%) + "NU25"
7    NEXT Angle%

     [run]
```

(b)

light blue color background

white color sail

center of screen

magenta color boat

```
1    ' Draw a Sailboat
2    ' ***************
3    SCREEN 1: CLS
4    COLOR 9, 1
5    DRAW "C2 L10 F10 R20 E10 L30 BU1 C3 U40 F30 L30"
6    PAINT (160, 105), 2, 2
7    PAINT (165, 85), 3, 3

     [run]
```

(c)

```
1    ' Draw a Flower
2    ' *************
3    SCREEN 1: CLS
4    COLOR 1, 1
5    BOX$ = "U50 R38 D50 L38"
6    FOR I = 1 TO 360 STEP 20
7        DRAW "TA=" + VARPTR$(I) + "X" + VARPTR$(BOX$)
8    NEXT I

     [run]
```

Partial program (b) in Figure 10.29 uses the DRAW statement in medium resolution to draw a sailboat on a light blue background. The boat is drawn first, then the sail. The color of the boat is magenta and the sail is white. The 11 commands in the string expression of the DRAW statement in line 5 do this: (1) C2 — select the color magenta for the boat; (2) L10 — move and draw to the left 10; (3) F10 — move and draw down and to the right 10; (4) R20 — move and draw right 20; (5) E10 — move and draw up and to the right 10; (6) L30 — move and draw left 30; (7) BU1 — move up one row; (8) C3 — select the color white for the sail; (9) U40 — draw and move up 40; (10) F30 — draw and move down and to the right 30; (11) L30 — move and draw to the left 30.

Two important points to remember about partial program (b): First, prior to the DRAW statement, the last point referenced is the center of the screen. Hence, the second command moves and draws a line 10 columns to the left of the center. Second, command 7 (BU1) is required so the sail does not intersect the boat. If the sail intersects the boat, the color magenta used in line 7 to paint the boat would leak out and would cover the entire screen except for the sail.

Partial program (c) in Figure 10.29 uses the DRAW statement in medium resolution to draw the flower shown to the right of the program. This program rotates a box about a central point, thereby producing the flower.

The WINDOW Statement

The WINDOW **statement** redefines the coordinates of the screen. In both medium resolution and high resolution, the physical coordinates are such that the upper left corner is the origin (0, 0) and the coordinate system extends down and to the right. This is called the **physical coordinate system**.

The WINDOW statement allows you to draw graphs and other objects in a different coordinate space called the **world coordinate system**. After the WINDOW statement modifies the coordinate system, subsequent figures are scaled to the new system. QBasic automatically converts the world coordinates into the normal physical coordinates so the figure can be displayed on the screen.

The general form of the WINDOW statement is given in Table 10.18.

TABLE 10.18 - The WINDOW Statement

General Form:	WINDOW (x_1, y_1) - (x_2, y_2) or WINDOW SCREEN (x_1, y_1) - (x_2, y_2) where (x_1, y_1) are the upper left coordinates and (x_2, y_2) are the lower right coordinates of the screen, as described below. 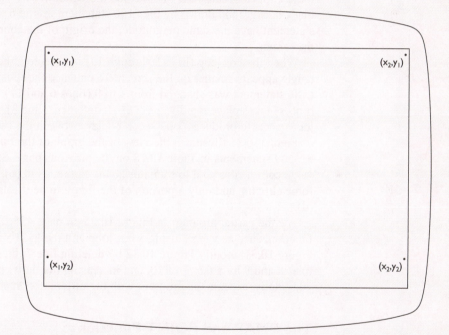 Active window coordinates are mapped onto any viewpoints subsequently opened by the VIEW statement. If the SCREEN parameter is not included in the WINDOW statement, then the screen is the normal Cartesian coordinate system, with x increasing to the right and y increasing upward. Furthermore, if the x and y values have the same magnitude, then the origin (0, 0) of the newly defined coordinate system is at the center of the screen. If the SCREEN parameter is included, then the coordinates are not inverted, and y values increase downward from the origin.
Purpose:	Redefines the coordinates of the viewpoint. Allows one to *zoom* and *pan* a figure. Subsequent PSET, PRESET, LINE, and CIRCLE statements reference the new coordinate system.
Examples:	WINDOW (-1, 1)-(1, -1) WINDOW (-4, 4)-(4, -4) WINDOW (0, 9)-(10, 0) WINDOW SCREEN (0, 0)-(10, 9)
Notes:	1. All possible pairs of x and y are valid. The only restriction is that x_1 cannot equal x_2 and y_1 cannot equal y_2. The SCREEN or WINDOW statements, with no parameters, return the screen to its normal physical coordinates with the origin (0, 0) at the upper left corner. 2. The DRAW statement always references the physical coordinates of the screen.

The partial program in Figue 10.30 shows how changing the window size changes the size of a figure drawn on the screen. The effect is one of *zooming* in and out.

FIGURE 10.30

A program for zooming in and out.

```
 1   ' Zooming In And Out
 2   ' ******************
 3   SCREEN 2
 4   FOR X = 50000 TO 100 STEP -50
 5      WINDOW (-X, X) - (X, -X)
 6      LINE (100, 100) - (120, 120), 1, BF
 7   NEXT X
 8   SLEEP 1
 9   FOR X = 100 TO 50000 STEP 50
10      WINDOW (-X, X) - (X, -X)
11      LINE (100, 100) - (120, 120), 0, BF
12   NEXT X

     [run]
```

When the partial program in Figure 10.30 is executed, the For loop (lines 4 through 7) causes the window to get smaller and the figure to become larger on the screen until parts of it are clipped because they lie outside the window. The figure is a filled white rectangle on a black background drawn by the LINE statement in line 6. Because the values of the WINDOW statement have the same magnitude, the origin of the coordinate system is at the center of the screen.

When the For loop (lines 9 through 12) is executed, the window gets larger and the rectangle appears smaller on the screen. To enhance the illusion, the color parameter in the LINE statement was changed from 1 to 0 (lines 6 and 11). Because the zooming in and out process takes place rapidly, a SLEEP 1 statement (line 8) was included between the two For loops so as to produce a one-second delay between the two processes.

Figure 10.31 illustrates the view of the graph of the function $y = x^2$ through the various WINDOW statements in Table 10.18 on the previous page. Study Figure 10.31 closely. Larger value coordinates tend to miniaturize the figure, as in (b), while smaller value coordinates force clipping and only a portion of the figure to be displayed and magnified as in (c) and (d).

See the partial program in Figure 10.32 on page 435 for an example of how to graph a function, such as $y = x^2$, using a For loop and the PSET statement. To display the screens in Figure 10.31, modify Figure 10.32 by deleting line 7, increasing the non-zero coordinates in lines 8 and 9 by a factor of 10, and increasing the limit parameter in line 10 by a factor of 10. Finally, execute the program with the different WINDOW statements shown in Figure 10.31.

The PMAP and POINT Functions

The PMAP and POINT functions are useful for determining screen characteristics when the WINDOW statement is used to change the coordinate system of the screen.

The PMAP **function** maps the specified physical coordinate to a world coordinate, or a specified world coordinate to a physical coordinate. That is, you can determine the physical coordinate that corresponds to a world coordinate, and vice versa.

The general form of the PMAP function is

```
numeric variable = PMAP(c, n)
```

where c is the x or y coordinate of the point that is to be mapped from one coordinate system to the other, and n is in the range 0 to 3. The descriptions of the permissible values of n are given in Table 10.19.

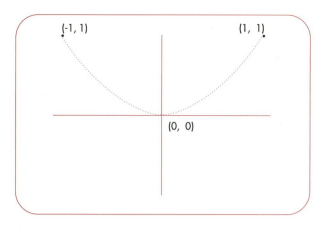

(a) WINDOW (-1, 1)-(1, -1)

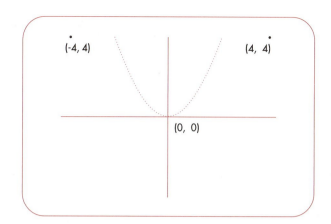

(b) WINDOW (-4, 4)-(4, -4)

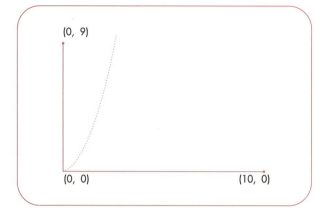

(c) WINDOW (0, 9)-(10, 0)

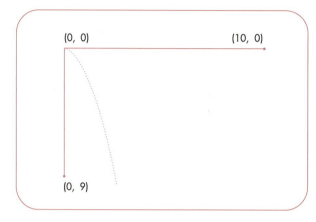

(d) WINDOW SCREEN (0, 0)-(10, 9)

FIGURE 10.31
Viewing the graph of the funciton $y = x^2$ through different window coordinates.

TABLE 10.19 – Descriptions of the Permissible Values for n for the PMAP Function	
VALUE OF n	**DESCRIPTION**
0	Returns the physical coordinate that corresponds to the world coordinate x.
1	Returns the physical coordinate that corresponds to the world coordinate y.
2	Returns the world coordinate that corresponds to the physical coordinate x.
3	Returns the world coordinate that corresponds to the physical coordinate y.

The POINT **function** has two general forms, as follows:

numeric variable = POINT(x, y)

or

numeric variable = POINT(n)

For the first general form, the PC returns the foreground color attribute of the point (x, y). If a WINDOW statement is active, then the point refers to the world coordinates.

The second general form returns the x or y coordinate of the last point referenced. The descriptions of the permissible values of n are given in Table 10.20 on the next page.

TABLE 10.20 - Descriptions of the Permissible Values for n for the POINT Function	
VALUE OF n	**DESCRIPTION**
0	Returns the physical x coordinate of the last point referenced.
1	Returns the physical y coordinate of the last point referenced.
2	Returns the world x coordinate that corresponds to the last point referenced (physical x coordinate if no WINDOW statement is active).
3	Returns the world y coordinate that corresponds to the last point referenced (physical y coordinate if no WINDOW statement is active).

The VIEW Statement

The VIEW **statement** defines a viewport, or rectangular subset of the screen, onto which figures can be displayed. The active window coordinates are mapped onto the viewport. Subsequent figures drawn in the viewport are scaled to the window coordinates. The general form of the VIEW statement is given in Table 10.21.

TABLE 10.21 - The VIEW Statement	
General Form:	VIEW (x_1, y_1) - (x_2, y_2), color, boundary or VIEW SCREEN (x_1, y_1) - (x_2, y_2), color, boundary where **(x_1, y_1)** are the upper left and **(x_2, y_2)** are the lower right coordinates of the viewport; (the coordinates must be defined in terms of the actual physical coordinates of the screen); **color** is a number (0 to 3 for medium resolution and 0 or 1 for high resolution) that corresponds to a color used to paint the viewport; and **boundary** is a number (0 to 3 for medium resolution and 0 or 1 for high resolution) that corresponds to a color used to draw a boundary around the viewport. If the SCREEN parameter is omitted, all points are relative to the viewport; otherwise, they are absolute.
Purpose:	Defines a viewport, or rectangular subset of the screen, onto which figures can be displayed. The VIEW statement causes subsequent figures to be scaled to fit the viewport.
Examples:	VIEW (75, 75) - (200, 100), 2, 3 VIEW (100, 100) - (150, 150) VIEW SCREEN (25, 50) - (100, 150)
Notes:	1. Only one viewport is active at a time. The CLS statement only clears the active viewport. Initial execution or the execution of a SCREEN statement disables the viewports. VIEW with no parameters defines the entire screen as the viewport. 2. A viewport is scaled according to the most recently executed WINDOW statement.

Consider the partial program in Figure 10.32 and the results displayed from its execution. Line 4 selects medium-resolution graphics mode and clears the output screen. Line 5 colors the screen background light blue and selects palette 0.

The WINDOW statement in line 6 redefines the coordinates of the screen. The new coordinate system has its origin (0, 0) exactly in the middle of the screen, with both the x-axis and y-axis extending from –1 to 1. The screen represents the Cartesian coordinate system magnified near the origin.

Line 7 of the partial program in Figure 10.32 defines and activates a second viewport with upper left coordinates of (100, 50) and lower right coordinates of (250, 150). These coordinates are not based on the coordinate system established by the WINDOW statement in line 6.

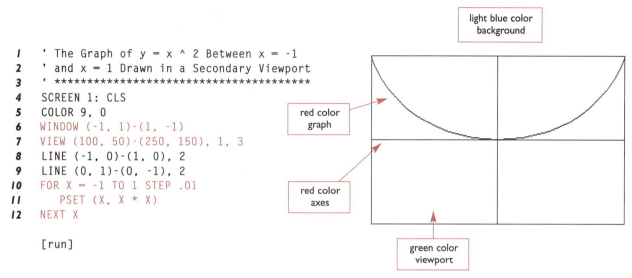

```
 1    ' The Graph of y = x ^ 2 Between x = -1
 2    ' and x = 1 Drawn in a Secondary Viewport
 3    ' ****************************************
 4    SCREEN 1: CLS
 5    COLOR 9, 0
 6    WINDOW (-1, 1)-(1, -1)
 7    VIEW (100, 50)-(250, 150), 1, 3
 8    LINE (-1, 0)-(1, 0), 2
 9    LINE (0, 1)-(0, -1), 2
10    FOR X = -1 TO 1 STEP .01
11       PSET (X, X * X)
12    NEXT X

      [run]
```

FIGURE 10.32

Multiple viewports.

Instead they relate to the original coordinate system, where the origin is at the upper left corner. However, except for its being scaled down, the coordinate system in the viewport is identical to the one defined by the WINDOW statement in line 6. The viewport has a green color.

Because only one viewport is active at a time, lines 8 and 9 draw red lines representing the x and y axes within the second viewport defined by line 7. The For loop (lines 10 through 12) graphs the equation $y = x^2$ between x = –1 and x = 1, with a point plotted every one-hundredth of one unit. The points making up the graph are colored red.

The GET and PUT Statements for Graphics

The GET and PUT statements are used for high-speed object motion. With these two statements, you can save and recall the contents of any rectangle on the screen. The activity of saving and recalling images in medium or high resolution can be very useful for producing high-quality computer animation.

The GET **statement** reads the colors of the points in the specified area of the screen into an array. The PUT **statement** writes the colors of the points in the array onto an area of the screen. The idea behind these two statements is that you can instruct the PC to draw a figure on the screen, use the GET statement to store the figure in a numeric array, then move the figure from one location to another with the PUT statement. The general forms of the GET and PUT statements are given in Table 10.22 and Table 10.23 on the next page.

TABLE 10.22 - The GET Statement for Graphics	
General Form:	GET (x_1, y_1) - (x_2, y_2), array name where (x_1, y_1) and (x_2, y_2) are the opposite coordinates of a rectangle on the screen (the coordinates may be absolute or relative;) and **array name** is the name of a numeric array into which the GET statement reads the information about the points in the specified area.
Purpose:	Reads the colors of the points in the specified area on the screen into an array.
Examples:	GET (250, 50) - (300, 100), Animation1 GET (0, 0) - (319, 199), Screen1% GET (0, 100) - (160, 199), Animation2
Note:	The required size of the array in bytes is as follows: 4 + H * INT((W * bits + 7) / 8) where **H** is the height (number of rows) of the rectangle; **W** is the width (number of columns) of the rectangle; and **bits** is 2 in medium resolution and 1 in high resolution. Recall that there are 2 bytes per element in an integer array; 4 bytes per element in a single-precision array; and 8 bytes per element in a double-precision array.

TABLE 10.23 - The PUT Statement for Graphics

General Form: PUT (x, y), array name, action

where **(x, y)** are the coordinates of the top left corner of the rectangular area on the screen, where the pixel pattern in **array name** is displayed; and **action** specifies the manner in which the pixel pattern is displayed on the existing screen background. The action parameter may be one of the following:

PSET   - Puts the pixel pattern on the screen exactly as defined in array name.
PRESET - Puts the inverse pixel pattern in array name (negative image) on the screen.
AND   - Turns *on* those pixels that are both *on* in array name and *on* on the screen.
OR   - Superimposes the pixel pattern in array name onto the existing pattern on the screen.
XOR   - Turns *on* those pixels that are *on* in array name and *off* on the screen or *off* in array name and *on* on the screen. (If the action parameter is not used, then XOR is the default value.)

Purpose: Writes the colors of the points in the array onto an area of the screen.

Example:
```
PUT (25, 50) - (75, 100), Animation1
PUT (0, 0) - (220, 99), Screen1%, XOR
PUT (0, 50) - (60, 199), Animation2, OR
PUT (160, 100) - (319, 199), Array1, PSET
```

With the PUT statement, the action parameter XOR is the most interesting because if you use it twice in succession, the original scene within the specified area will reappear. This is critical to computer animation when you are required to move an object across the screen. Before you can move an image to a new location on the screen, you must return the current location to its old scene. Two successive PUT statements with the XOR action parameter and a slight time delay in between gives us the desired action.

Here is a step-by-step algorithm for moving an object across the screen:

1. Draw the desired image on the screen.
2. Use the GET statement to store the image into an array.
3. Clear the screen.
4. Draw background figures that will remain constant during the animation.
5. Establish a For loop that determines the coordinates at which the image is to appear. Within the loop, do the following:
   a. Use the PUT statement with the action parameter XOR to put the image at the desired location.
   b. Use a SLEEP statement or a For loop to delay execution of the next statement so that the figure may be seen.
   c. Use the PUT statement with the action parameter XOR to erase the image at the current location.

Consider the animation of a bus traveling on a highway, right to left, produced in medium-resolution graphics mode by the partial program in Figure 10.33. Lines 7 through 13 plot the bus in the upper left corner of the screen. Line 15 stores the points within the rectangle defined by the coordinates (26, 40) and (71, 53) into the integer array Bus%.

The formula given in Table 10.22 is used to determine the size of Bus%. For example, from lines 7 through 11 it can be determined that the minimum size rectangle that includes the bus (plus the wheels) is 71 - 26 + 1 = 46 points wide and 53 - 40 + 1 = 14 points high. Furthermore, we are working in medium resolution, which requires 2 bits per point. Hence, the formula after substitution looks like this:

```
4 + 14 * INT((46 * 2 + 7) / 8) = 172
```

With an integer array, divide the byte requirement by 2. The result is that 86 elements are required in Bus%.

Lines 17 through 23 of the partial program in Figure 10.33 clear the screen, display a message, and then draw the highway and telephone poles. Finally, lines 25 through 31 animate the bus driving on the highway over and over again until the user presses any key on the keyboard.

The first PUT statement (line 27) in the For loop plots the bus to the far right and just above the highway. Line 28 delays the next PUT statement (line 29) for one second. This second PUT statement erases the bus plotted by line 27. The next time line 27 is executed, it plots the bus 50 points to the left. This plotting and erasing continues until the bus is near the left side of the screen. At this point, the Do-While loop starts the bus back at the right side of the screen. This animation continues until the user intervenes.

▌FIGURE 10.33

Computer animation in medium-resolution graphics mode of a bus traveling down a highway, right to left.

```
1    ' Animating a Moving Bus
2    ' *********************
3    DIM Bus%(1 TO 86)
4    CLS : SCREEN 1
5    COLOR 0, 0
6    ' ******* Draw Bus Body ********
7    LINE (31, 40)-(71, 50), 2, BF
8    LINE (26, 45)-(31, 50), 2, BF
9    ' ****** Draw Bus Wheels *******
10   CIRCLE (29, 50), 3, 3
11   CIRCLE (66, 50), 3, 3
12   PAINT (29, 50), 3, 3
13   PAINT (66, 50), 3, 3
14   ' ****** Store Bus Image *******
15   GET (26, 40)-(71, 53), Bus%
16   ' ** Draw Highway with Telephone Poles ***
17   CLS
18   LOCATE 15, 7: PRINT "Press any key to stop bus..."
19   LINE (0, 100)-(319, 100), 2
20   FOR Col% = 5 TO 319 STEP 40
21      LINE (Col%, 100)-(Col%, 85)
22      LINE (Col% - 3, 88)-(Col% + 2, 88)
23   NEXT Col%
24   ' ******** Animate Bus *********
25   DO WHILE INKEY$ = ""
26      FOR Animation% = 250 TO 0 STEP -50
27         PUT (Animation%, 87), Bus%, XOR
28         SLEEP 1
29         PUT (Animation%, 87), Bus%, XOR
30      NEXT Animation%
31   LOOP

[run]
```

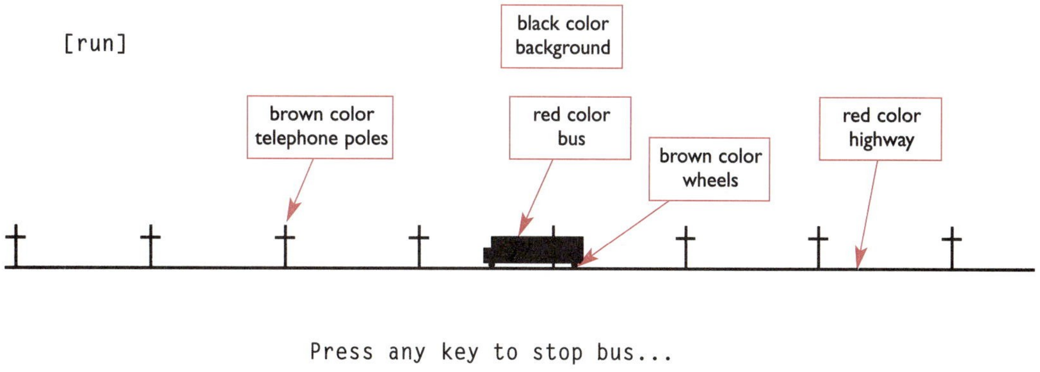

Press any key to stop bus...

10.4 SOUND AND MUSIC

A speaker is located toward the front of the system unit of the PC. Though this speaker is smaller than the stereo speakers that you may have attached to your PC, it is capable of producing a variety of sounds. For example, in Chapter 5 we used the BEEP statement to produce a high-pitched sound and draw the user's attention to data-entry errors. In this section, we explore two additional statements that can activate the speaker under program control. They are the SOUND and PLAY statements. Stereo speakers for your PC (Figure 1.2 on page 2) are available to create enhanced sounds and stereo-quality music.

The SOUND Statement

The SOUND **statement** is used to create a sound of variable frequency and duration. The general form of the SOUND statement is given in Table 10.24.

TABLE 10.24 - The SOUND Statement	
General Form:	SOUND frequency, duration where **frequency** is a numeric expression between 37 and 32767 specifying the pitch of the sound in hertz (cycles per second); and **duration** is a numeric expression in the range 0 to 65535 specifying the length of time in clock ticks to play the tone. There are 18.2 clock ticks per second. A duration of zero turns off the current sound.
Purpose:	To generate sound through the speaker.
Examples:	1. SOUND 1000, 91 2. SOUND 32767, 0 3. SOUND Freq%, Dur%

Example 1 in Table 10.24 plays a tone of 1,000 hertz for five seconds (91 clock ticks/18.2 clock ticks per second = 5 seconds). Example 2 turns off the current sound because the duration is zero. Example 3 causes the generation of a sound at a frequency of Freq% cycles per second for a duration of Dur% clock ticks.

The partial program in Figure 10.34 illustrates the use of the SOUND statement to generate a siren sound. Line 3 changes the width to 40 characters and clears the output screen. Line 4 selects a blinking, red foreground on a black background. Lines 5 and 6 display messages. The Do-While loop (lines 7 through 11) executes until the user presses a key on the keyboard.

The For loop (lines 8 through 10) in the partial program in Figure 10.34 generates a siren-like sound, using the PC's speaker(s). Each time through the For loop, the frequency increases until it reaches 1,100 hertz (cycles per second).

FIGURE 10.34
Generating a siren sound.

```
 1    Using the Speaker as a Siren
 2  ' **************************
 3    WIDTH 40
 4    COLOR 20, 0
 5    LOCATE 13, 8: PRINT "EMERGENCY!! EMERGENCY!!"
 6    LOCATE 24, 4: PRINT "Press any key to stop the siren...";
 7    DO WHILE INKEY$ = ""
 8       FOR Freq% = 500 TO 1100 STEP 20
 9          SOUND Freq%, .05
10       NEXT Freq%
11    LOOP
12    WIDTH 80: COLOR 7, 0

    [run]
```

The partial program in Figure 10.35 produces 25 random sounds whose frequency ranges from 37 to 6,000 hertz and whose duration ranges from one clock tick to one second.

FIGURE 10.35
Generating 25 random sounds.

```
 1  ' Using the Speaker for 25 Random Sounds
 2  ' **************************************
 3  FOR Cycle% = 1 TO 25
 4     Freq% = INT(5964 * RND) + 37
 5     Dur% = INT(173 * RND) / 10 + 1
 6     SOUND Freq%, Dur%
 7  NEXT Cycle

    [run]
```

The PLAY Statement

The PLAY **statement** converts your PC into a piano. Like the DRAW statement, the PLAY statement instructs the PC to play music that is defined by a string expression. The string is made up of a series of easy-to-code commands (Table 10.26 on the next page.) The music you compose may be as simple as a single note or as complex as the counterpoint in Bach or a symphony by Beethoven. The general form of the PLAY statement is shown in Table 10.25.

Example 1 in Table 10.25 plays the C scale. The greater than sign (>) causes the PC to climb to the next octave. The less than sign (<) has the opposite effect. Example 2 plays the song "Stepping Up Stepping Down." The L command establishes the length of all subsequent notes played. The command E2 changes the length only for that note.

TABLE 10.25 - The PLAY Statement	
General Form:	PLAY string expression where **string expression** is a command or series of commands, as described in Table 10.26.
Purpose:	Plays music as specified in the string expression.

Examples:	1. PLAY "C D E F G A B >C C <B A G F E D C"
	2. PLAY "L4 C D E2 L4 E D L2 C D E C"
	3. PLAY Music$
	4. Mary$ = "E D C D"
	   PLAY "O3 T90 L8 X" + VARPTR$(Mary$) + "E E E P8"
	5. PLAY "L =" + VARPTR$(Length) + "X" + VARPTR$(Chorus$)
	   PLAY "X" + VARPTR$(Bridge$) + "X" + VARPTR$(Chorus$)

Note:	A PLAY command such as L or E may be followed by a constant or variable. If a variable is used, then surround the command (and equal sign, if required) with quotation marks and join to the command the function VARPTR$ with the variable as the argument (see Examples 4 & 5).

Example 3 in Table 10.25 plays the tune definition assigned to Music$. Example 4 plays the first measure of "Mary Had a Little Lamb." Example 5 illustrates how you can instruct the PC to execute a series of subcommands. This can be useful when you want to play a chorus after each bridge as shown in Figure 10.36.

As a sample program that uses the PLAY statement, consider the partial program in Figure 10.36. This program plays the tune "Twinkle Twinkle Little Star" over and over again until the user presses a key on the keyboard. Both the chorus and the bridge are defined prior to the PLAY statement in lines 6 and 8. In lines 11 through 13, the PLAY statement uses the X command to reference the subcommands assigned to Chorus$ and Bridge$.

FIGURE 10.36
Playing a tune with the PC.

```
1   ' Twinkle Twinkle Little Star
2   ' ***************************
3   CLS
4   LOCATE 13, 25: PRINT "Press any key to stop the song..."
5   ' ****** Define Chorus ******
6   Chorus$ = "L4 C C G G A A L2 G L4 F F E E D D L2 C"
7   ' ****** Define Bridge ******
8   Bridge$ = "L4 G G F F E E L2 D L4 G G F F E E L2 D"
9   ' ******** Play Song ********
10  DO WHILE INKEY$ = ""
11     PLAY "X" + VARPTR$(Chorus$)
12     PLAY "X" + VARPTR$(Bridge$)
13     PLAY "X" + VARPTR$(Chorus$)
14  LOOP

    [run]
```

	TABLE 10.26 - PLAY Commands	
COMMAND	**FUNCTION**	**EXAMPLES**
A to G with optional #, +, or –	Plays the specified note in the current octave. A number sign (#) or plus sign (+) appended to the letter indicates a sharp; a minus sign (–) indicates a flat.	C A+ D-
On	Sets the octave for the notes that follow. There are 7 octaves, numbered 0 to 6. Octave 4 is the default. Each octave goes from C to B, and octave 3 starts with middle C.	O2
>n or <n	The greater than sign (>) instructs the PC to climb to the next octave and play note n. The less than sign (<) lowers the octave by 1. Either sign affects all notes that follow.	>C <D-
Nn	Plays note n, where n ranges from 0 to 84. This serves as an alternative to using the O command followed by the note name. N0 is a *rest*.	N27 N0
Ln	Sets the length of the notes that follow. The parameter n can range from 1 to 64. The PC interprets n as 1/n. The length of a note may also follow the note. For example, C4 is the same as L4C.	L4 L=S;
Pn	Pause. The parameter n can range from 1 to 64. As with the L command, the PC interprets n as 1/n.	P16 P=R;
.	Dot. Placed after a note, the dot causes the note to be played as a dotted note. Multiple dots are valid.	A. C+..
Tn	Tempo. Defines the number of quarter notes per minute. The parameter n can range from 32 to 255. The default is 120.	T110 T=NU;
MF	Music foreground. The music created by the SOUND or PLAY statement runs in the foreground. The program is put into a wait state until the music statement is finished. A note does not start until the previous note is finished. MF is the default.	MF
MB	Music background. The music created by the SOUND or PLAY statement runs in the background. That is, the QBasic program continues to execute while the music plays in the background.	MB
ML	Music legato. Each note that follows plays the full period set by L.	ML
MN	Music normal. Each note that follows plays 7/8 of the time specified by L. Default between MN, ML, and MS.	MN
MS	Music staccato. Each note that follows plays 3/4 of the time specified by L.	MS
"X" + v	Executes a subcommand, where v is equal to the VARPTR$ function with a string variable that contains additional commands as the argument.	"X" + VARPTR$ (Music$)

10.5 What You Should Know

1. The PC provides five graphics modes — text, medium resolution, high resolution, enhanced resolution, and very-high resolution.

2. When you enter QBasic, the PC is in text mode. In this mode, the output screen has 25 lines (rows) of 80 columns each. You can switch to the 40-column display by using the WIDTH statement.

3. The SCREEN statement can be used to switch among the different graphics modes. The SCREEN statement also can be used in text mode to do simple animation through the use of the active and visual pages.

4. In medium-resolution graphics mode, the screen is divided into 200 rows and 320 columns. In high-resolution graphics mode, the screen is divided into 200 rows and 640 columns. Each intersection of a column and row defines a point (pixel), which can be turned on or off.

5. Text mode often is used to create logos and simple animations. Medium-resolution graphics mode is used to plot points, draw figures, and create sophisticated animated designs. High-resolution graphics mode allows you to draw very detailed designs.

6. In text mode, you can produce interesting and useful graphics with the PRINT and PRINT USING statements, the CHR$ function, and the ASCII character set.

7. If you have a color monitor and a color/graphics adaptor, you can enhance your displays in the text and medium-resolution graphics modes with a variety of colors. With high resolution, figures can be displayed only in black and white or green or amber.

8. In text mode, the COLOR statement sets the color for the foreground, background, and border. The foreground and border can be set to 16 different colors and the background to eight colors. By adding the number 16 to the foreground color number, all displayed characters will blink.

9. In text mode, a CLS statement should follow the COLOR statement to ensure the color takes effect immediately over the entire screen.

10. To send graphics designs to the printer, you must have one that emulates the IBM graphics printer. You also must enter the system command GRAPHICS before you start QBasic.

11. In both medium and high resolutions, you plot points and draw lines by instructing the PC to turn on pixels. Lines and curves are defined in the form of coordinates, such as (x, y), where x is the column and y is the row. Each pixel has a unique set of coordinates.

12. Two ways to indicate the coordinates of a point are: absolute form and relative form.

13. The COLOR statement for medium resolution allows you to select from 16 different background colors and 1 of 2 palettes of colors for the foreground. Each palette carries four colors, numbered 0 through 3.

14. The PSET and PRESET statements are used to turn individual points (pixels) on or off. The PC turns off a point by assigning it the background color.

15. The LINE statement is used to draw lines and boxes in a color selected off the active palette. When the LINE statement is used to draw a box, you can instruct the PC to fill the box with the color selected off the active palette. In high resolution, the active palette has no meaning.

16. The CIRCLE statement is used to draw circles, ellipses, arcs, and wedges.

17. The PAINT statement can be used to paint an enclosed area. In medium resolution, the colors on the active palette are available. In high resolution, only black and white are available.

18. The PAINT statement also can be used to tile an enclosed area on the screen. The tile pattern is based on the binary value of the tile mask. The CHR$ function is used to establish the tile mask in a program.

19. The DRAW statement is used to draw complicated objects on the basis of commands assigned to a string expression.

20. The normal coordinates of the screen are called physical coordinates. The WINDOW statement can be used to redefine the coordinates into what are called world coordinates. Any viewpoint subsequently opened by the VIEW statement is defined in terms of the world coordinates.

21. Depending on the argument, the PMAP and PAINT functions return either physical or world coordinates.

22. The GET and PUT statements are used for high-speed object motion. These statements can be very useful in producing high-quality computer animation.

23. The SOUND statement generates sound through the speaker.
24. The PLAY statement converts your PC into a piano. The music you compose in the form of a string expression may be as simple as a single note or as complex as the counterpoint in Bach or a symphony by Beethoven.

10.6 Test Your QBasic Skills (Even-numbered answers are in Appendix E)

1. Consider the following six valid programs. What is displayed or produced if each is executed?

a.
```
' Exercise 10.1a
SCREEN 2: CLS
WINDOW (-100, 100) - (100, -100)
LINE (-100, 0) - (100, 0)
LINE (0, 100) - (0, -100)
FOR X% = -50 TO 50 STEP 1
   Y% = X% + 8
   PSET (X%, Y%)
NEXT X%
END
```

b.
```
' Exercise 10.1b
SCREEN 1: CLS
COLOR 1,0
WINDOW (-10, 10) - (100, -10)
LINE (-10, 0) - (10, 0)
LINE (0, 10) - (0, -10)
FOR X% = 1 TO 7
   CIRCLE (0, 0), X%, 2
NEXT X%
END
```

c.
```
' Exercise 10.1c
CLS
WIDTH 40
COL = 2
FOR COUNT = 1 TO 21 STEP 2
   PRINT TAB(COL);
   FOR STARS = 1 TO COUNT
      PRINT "*";
   NEXT STARS
   PRINT
   COL = COL + 1
NEXT COUNT
END
```

d.
```
' Exercise 10.1d
CLS
WIDTH 80
INPUT "ENTER THE ROW & COLUMN FOR UPPER LEFT CORNER "; ROW, COL
INPUT "ENTER THE WIDTH AND HEIGHT OF THE BOX "; BWIDTH, HEIGHT
CLS
LOCATE ROW, COL
PRINT "/";
FOR COUNT = 1 TO (BWIDTH - 2)
   PRINT "*";
NEXT COUNT
PRINT "\"
FOR COUNT = 1 TO HEIGHT
   PRINT TAB(COL); "¦"; TAB(COL + BWIDTH - 1); "¦"
NEXT COUNT
PRINT TAB(COL); "\";
FOR COUNT = 1 TO (BWIDTH - 2)
   PRINT "*";
NEXT COUNT
PRINT "/"
END
```

```
e. ' Exercise 10.1e
   CLS
   FOR K% = 500 TO 1200 STEP 5
      SOUND K%, K% / 1000
   NEXT K%
   SLEEP 1
   END
```

```
f. ' Exercise 10.1f
   SCREEN 1: CLS
   DRAW "S12"
   DRAW "TA -30"
   DRAW "U40 R30 D40 L30"
   END
```

2. Use PSET, LINE, and CIRCLE statements to draw the following figures. Assume that the PC is in the medium-resolution graphics mode.

a.

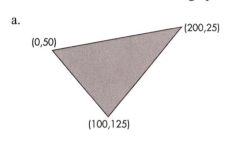

b.

c.

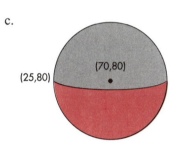

d.

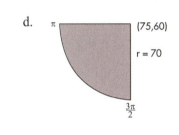

3. Use the DRAW statement to draw the figures in 2(a) and 2(b). Use the scale factor to double the size of each figure.

4. Describe the appearance of the screen after each of the following is executed:
   a. SCREEN 0 : COLOR 4, 1, 0: CLS
   b. SCREEN 1 : COLOR 0, 0: CLS

5. Describe the display of characters following the execution of a COLOR statement with a foreground color number of 20 in text mode.

6. Fill in the following:
   a. In medium- and high-resolution graphics modes, the intersection of a row and column is called a _____ or _____.
   b. If you plan to print a graphics display in DOS mode, enter the system command _____ before starting QBasic.
   c. If you enter WIDTH _____ in the medium-resolution graphics mode, the PC will switch to the high-resolution graphics mode.
   d. Use the _____ function to describe a tile pattern for the PAINT statement.
   e. To draw a wedge with the CIRCLE statement, add a _____ before the start and end parameters.
   f. The _____ and _____ statements are used in medium- and high-resolution graphics modes to produce high-quality computer animation.
   g. There are _____ bytes per element in an integer array; _____ bytes per element in a single-precision array; and _____ bytes per element in a double-precision array.

7. Consider the following valid program and answer these three questions:
   a. What is displayed if this program is executed?
   b. What are the foreground, background, and border colors that are due to line 3?
   c. What is the purpose of the second to the last line?

```
' Exercise 10.7
INPUT "Density (0 to 1) ===> ", Density
COLOR 4, 0, 0: CLS
WIDTH 40
RANDOMIZE TIMER
FOR Row% = 1 TO 24
   FOR Col% = 1 TO 40
      IF RND <= Density THEN
         LOCATE Row%, Col%
         PRINT CHR$(219);
      END IF
   NEXT Col%
NEXT Row%
LOCATE 25, 1
INPUT "Press the Enter key to quit...", Control$
COLOR 7, 0, 0: WIDTH 80
END
```

8. Write a program that draws the following three-dimensional box in the medium-resolution graphics mode, using the color brown. Color the background blue and activate palette 0. Paint the face of the figure red, the side brown, and the top green.

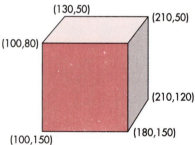

(130,50)   (210,50)
(100,80)
(210,120)
(100,150)   (180,150)

9. Evaluate each of the following. Assume that the statements are executed in the high-resolution graphics mode.

   a. `PSET (320, 100)`
   b. `GET (23, 46) - (75, 80), A%`
   c. `PUT (72, 96) - (125, 130), A%`
   d. `CIRCLE (50, 50), 15,, -3, -4`
   e. `CIRCLE (320, 160), 30,,,, 5/8`
   f. `LINE - (40, 30)`
   g. `LINE (0, 0) - (160, 100)`
   h. `DRAW "BM320,160 NR45 D45"`
   i. `SOUND 200, .03`
   j. `PLAY "XMUSIC$;"`

10. Use the PRINT statement, the CHR$ function, and ASCII code 219 to draw a box with the following characteristics in text mode. Assume that the screen is set to the 40 column display mode.
    a. Horizontal lines at rows 4 and 22.
    b. Vertical lines at columns 9 and 32.

11. Write a program that uses the WINDOW statement with coordinates (- 25, 25) - (25, - 25) in high-resolution graphics mode to establish the Cartesian coordinate system. Draw the x and y axes and the graph of the equation $y = 3x + 2$ between $x = 20$ and $x = -20$. Plot points, using the PSET statement every 0.01 units.

12. Identify each of the following PLAY commands:

    a. A-   b. L8   c. >C   d. "X" + VARPTR$(M$)   e. NO
    f. T100   g. P8   h. MS   i. ML   j. O3

13. Identify each of the following DRAW commands:

    a. BM 10, 20   b. M+3, +5   c. C1   d. F5   e. E20
    f. A3   g. U75   h. H5   i. L20   j. NL20

14. With respect to the PUT statement, define the action parameters PSET, AND, and XOR.

15. Write a program that constructs the following international logo of a child using a collection of simple overlapping primitives, such as circles and rectangles. For extra credit, also write programs to draw the international logos of a man and a woman.

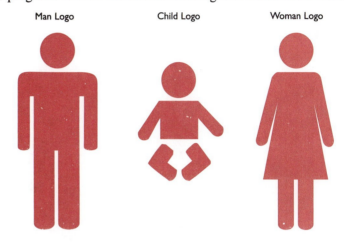

Man Logo   Child Logo   Woman Logo

16. Determine the required size for the integer array Animation% in the following GET statement. Assume that the statement is executed in high-resolution graphics mode.

    GET (20, 30) - (80, 100), Animation%

17. Write a program that displays the following Olympic flag with the five interlocking rings on a white background. The rings are blue, black, red, yellow, and green, respectively, in color. As an option, have the program play a few bars of the Olympic theme song.

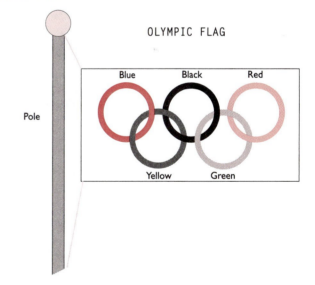

18. Sketch the actions of the following partial programs. Also specify the colors displayed.

    a.
```
KEY OFF
SCREEN 1, 0
COLOR 1, 0
CLS
PSET (0, 0)
FOR K = 0 TO 199
    PSET STEP(K, K)
NEXT K
```

    b.
```
RANDOMIZE TIMER
KEY OFF
SCREEN 1, 0
COLOR 1, 0
FOR K = 1 TO 100
    X = 319 * RND
    Y = 199 * RND
    Z = 3 * RND
    IF Z < 1 THEN
        Z = 1
    END IF
    PSET (X, Y), Z
NEXT K
```

19. Write a program that illustrates the additive effects of the primary colors of red (R), green (G), and blue (B). Initially, three circles are filled respectively with the three aforementioned colors. Via animation, move and superimpose the three circles in such a manner as to blend and display the colors of white (W), magenta (M), cyan (C), and yellow (Y) (or brown on some PC monitors).

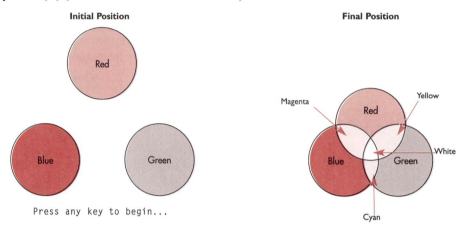

20. Sketch the display of following partial programs.

    a.
    ```
    SCREEN 1 : CLS
    WINDOW (0, 0) - (60, 60)
    CIRCLE (15, 50), 5
    ' ***************************
    VIEW (180, 60) - (250, 130), , 3
    CIRCLE (15, 50), 5
    ```

    b.
    ```
    SCREEN 1: CLS
    COLOR 1, 0
    WINDOW (60, 60) - (350, 200)
    LINE (60, 70) - (350, 200), , B
    GOSUB DRAW.CIRCLE
    VIEW (30, 30) - (150, 100), 1, 3
    GOSUB DRAW.CIRCLE
    VIEW (180, 130) - (280, 175), 1, 2
    GOSUB DRAW.CIRCLE
    END

    DRAW.CIRCLE:
        CIRCLE (250, 150), 40, 2, , , 5 / 18
        CIRCLE (250, 150), 40, 2, , , 1
    RETURN
    ```

21. Write a program using two nested For loops to create a grid of equally-spaced red dots on the screen in medium-resolution mode with a yellow background. Use a step value of 10 for each loop. Each row is to contain 32 dots and each column is to contain 20 dots.

22. **PC Hands-On Exercise:** Enter the partial program in Figure 10.7 on page 403. Display and execute the program. Change the PRINT USING statement in line 5 to a LPRINT USING statement. (See the printer's user guide regarding the proper switch settings for displaying the USA character set.) When the printer is ready, execute the modified version of the program.

23. **PC Hands-On Exercise:** Enter the partial program in Figure 10.22 on page 420. Delete lines 9 through 13. In line 6, change the initial value to 1 and the limit value to 1000. Replace line 7 with the following:

```
PSET(INT(319 * RND + 1), INT(199 * RND + 1))
```

Execute the program and see what happens.

24. **PC Hands-On Exercise:** Enter the partial program in Figure 10.23 on page 422. Change the background color to 0 and the palette to 0. Add the following line after line 7:

```
LINE -(100, 125) : LINE -(100, 75)
```

Execute the program and see what happens.

25. **PC Hands-On Exercise:** Enter the partial program in Figure 10.24(a) on page 422. Change the background color to blue and the active palette to 1. Delete the color parameters in lines 5 through 8. Execute the program and see what happens.

26. **PC Hands-On Exercise:** Enter the partial program in Figure 10.34 on page 438. Execute the program. Now modify the initial, terminal, and step values in line 8 and the duration parameter in line 9. See if you can get the program to cause the speaker to sound more like a police-car siren.

27. **PC Hands-On Exercise:** Enter the partial program in Figure 10.36 on page 439. Execute the program and listen to it play "Twinkle Twinkle Little Star." Double the parameter following each L command in lines 6 and 8. Execute the program and listen to the sound. Now triple the original values and execute the program again.

10.7 QBasic Programming Problems

1. Horizontal Bar Graph of Annual Sales for the Past Ten Years

Purpose: To become familiar with graphing in text mode.

Problem: A graph gives the user of a report a pictorial view of the information. Consider the following problem, which has as its defined output a horizontal bar graph. The Sales Analysis Department of the PUC Company requests from the Data Processing Department a report in the form of a horizontal bar graph representing the company's annual sales trend for the ten-year period 1993 through 2002. The annual sales are as follows:

Year	Sales (in millions)	Year	Sales (in millions)
1993	$22	1998	$43
1994	26	1999	40
1995	28	2000	45
1996	35	2001	50
1997	40	2002	48

Include the following characteristics in the graph:

1. Display the bar graph horizontally in the 80-column display mode.
2. Display vertically the column that represents the years.
3. Use a series of asterisks to represent the sales for each year.
4. Mark off the horizontal axis in increments of 5, beginning with 0 and ending with 55. Each unit represents a million dollars.

(**Hint:** See Program 10.2 on page 409.)

Input Data: Use the ten-year PUC Company data shown on the previous page. The data (year and sales) for each year is in the sequential data file EX101SAL. DAT on the Data Disk.

Output Results: Figure 10.37 presents the output results for Problem 1.

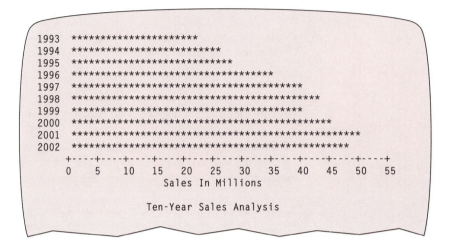

```
1993  **********************
1994  **************************
1995  ***************************
1996  **********************************
1997  *****************************************
1998  *********************************************
1999  *****************************************
2000  **************************************************
2001  ********************************************************
2002  *****************************************************
      +----+----+----+----+----+----+----+----+----+----+----+
      0    5    10   15   20   25   30   35   40   45   50   55
                       Sales In Millions

                     Ten-Year Sales Analysis
```

2. Graphing a Function

Purpose: To become familiar with using the PSET statement to graph a function on a world coordinate system in the high-resolution graphics mode.

Problem: Graph the function $y = 2x^3 + 6x^2 - 18x + 6$. Use a WINDOW statement with coordinates $(-6, 70) - (6, -70)$ to define the Cartesian coordinate system with its origin at the center of the screen. Graph the function between $x = -5$ and $x = 3$. Plot points every 1/100th of one unit. Label the axes as shown in the Output Results.

(**Hint:** See the partial program in Figure 10.32 on page 435 and choose your own colors for the axes, graph, and background.)

Input Data: None.

Output Results: Figure 10.38 presents the output results for Problem 2.

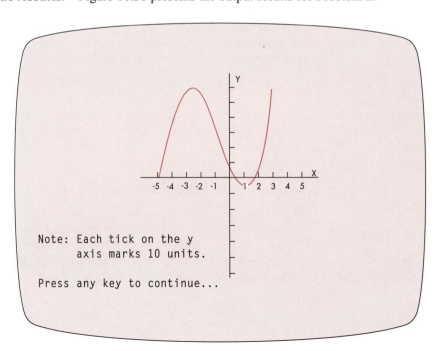

Note: Each tick on the y axis marks 10 units.

Press any key to continue...

3. Animating Push-ups

Purpose: To become familiar with simple animation through the use of the GET and PUT statements in medium-resolution graphics mode.

Problem: Draw an animation of the Mechanical Man doing push-ups. Phase 1 and Phase 2 of the animation are illustrated in Figure 10.39. Draw Phase 1 and use the GET statement to store it in an array. Do the same with Phase 2. Have the Mechanical Man do 50 push-ups by switching from one figure to another. Color the Mechanical Man's torso red and his head brown.

(**Hint:** See the partial program in Figure 10.33 on page 437.)

Extra Credit: Every time the Mechanical Man completes a push-up, display this value in a counter. As the Mechanical Man approaches 50 push-ups, make him slow down and *grunt*.

❙FIGURE 10.39
Positions of the Mechanical Man doing push-ups.

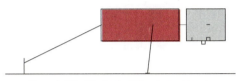

Phase 1: The Mechanical Man in position 1.

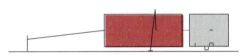

Phase 2: The Mechanical Man in position 2.

Input Data: None.

Output Results: The display of the Mechanical Man will switch between Phase 1 and Phase 2 fifty times as shown in Figure 10.39. Also, when the user presses a key, halt the display and *freeze* the screen.

4. Drawing a Design

Purpose: To become familiar with the LINE, CIRCLE, and PAINT statements.

Problem: Construct a top-down program that draws the design shown in the Output Results. Draw the design in medium-resolution graphics mode. Use the PAINT statement to color and tile the various sections of the design.

Input Data: None.

Output Results: Figure 10.40 on the next page presents the output results for Problem 4.

5. Playing the Musical Score "Yankee Doodle" on the PC

Purpose: To become familiar with the PLAY statement.

Problem: Obtain a song sheet of "Yankee Doodle." Use a For loop to play the song seven times, starting at octave 0 and ending at octave 6.

Input Data: None.

Output Results: The PC plays the song "Yankee Doodle" seven times, each time at a higher octave.

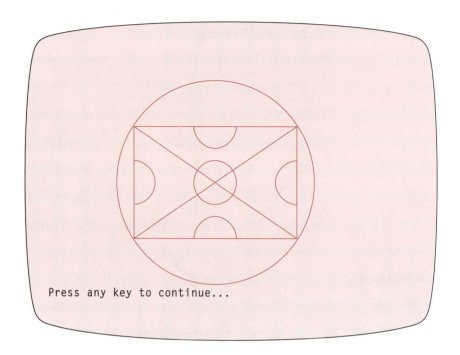

Press any key to continue...

6. The U.S.A. Flag and the National Anthem

Purpose: To illustrate graphical concepts with music.

Problem: Display the red-white-blue U.S.A. flag with the 50 stars. The flag is to be rigid and a few bars of the national anthem — "The Star-Spangled Banner" — should play in background mode. In addition, display the title UNITED STATES OF AMERICA above the flag. As an option, display below the flag the words of the national anthem as the music is played.

Extra Credit: Wave the flag gently (not flap).

Input Data: None.

Output Results: Figure 10.41 presents the output results for Problem 6.

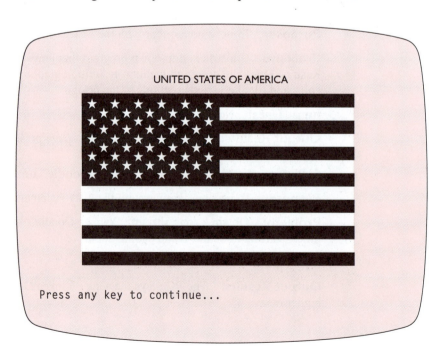

UNITED STATES OF AMERICA

Press any key to continue...

7. Animated Jumping Jacks

Purpose: To become familiar with simple animation through the use of the GET and PUT statements.

Problem: Draw an animation of the Woman Logo doing jumping jacks. Phase 1 and Phase 2 of the animation are illustrated under Output Results. Draw Phase 1 and use the GET statement to store it in an array. Do the same with Phase 2. Have the Woman do 50 jumping jacks by switching from one figure to another. Color the Woman's dress red and her face, arms, and legs accordingly.

Every time the Woman completes a jumping jack, display this value in a counter. As the Woman approaches 50 jumping jacks, make her slow down and *grunt* in a female tone.

Extra Credit: Add features to the Woman's face, such as eyes, nose, mouth, smile, frown, hair, and so on. Also, add the following self-explanatory options: (1) Pause: halt and freeze the display on the screen, (2) Continue: the animation and display, and (3) Abort: the animation and display.

Input Data: None.

Output Results: The display of the Woman will switch between Phase 1 and Phase 2 fifty times, as illustrated in Figure 10.42.

▌FIGURE 10.42
Phases 1 and 2 of the Woman Logo doing jumping jacks.

Phase 1: The Woman in Position 1

Phase 2: The Woman in Position 2

8. RGB Color Cube

Purpose: To display colors in a three-dimensional model.

Problem: Display the RGB color cube model and the text description for each of the points in their respective colors. Assume this: x-axis represents the color blue, y-axis represents the color red, and z-axis represents the color green. The point (0,0,0) corresponds to the color black, and the point (1, 1, 1) corresponds to the color white.

All definable colors should lie on the cube and should be derived from the primary colors of red, green, and blue in either an additive process or from the subdivision of the large cube into smaller units and the generation of colors in a definable spectrum. Also, display the words such as Green, White, Cyan and so forth. The word Black will not be displayed for obvious reasons.

(**Hint:** Insert the statement Screen 9 in your program.)

Extra Credit: Rotate the cube around the y-axis so the colors from the other faces are visible; or, remove the top, side, and front face of the cube to see the colors on the remaining faces.

Input Data: None.

Output Results: The results are displayed in Figure 10.43.

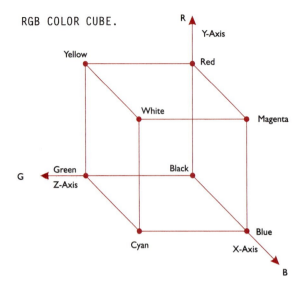

RGB COLOR CUBE.

9. Pouring a Liquid

Purpose: To illustrate two- and three-dimensional transformations.

Problem: An opaque container is filled partially with some kind of liquid as shown in Phase 1 of the Output Results. The container is lifted and rotated in order to pour the liquid into another container, which is transparent, as shown in Phase 2 of the Output Results. As the liquid is poured, the liquid will be seen rising in the receiving container.

Input Data: None.

Extra Credit: Use a menu to select the following variables:
1. The display of the liquid splashing in the receiving container versus no splashing.
2. The position from where the liquid is poured; for example, if the liquid is poured by the edge of the container, a vortex occurs; if the liquid is poured by the center of the container, splashing occurs.
3. Viscosity of the liquid; for example, water versus thick molasses versus a cryogenic liquid vs. a molten metal.
4. Shrinkage or expansion of the receiving container due to the temperature of the liquid.
5. Type of logo appearing on the opaque container.
6. Shape of the container; for example, cylindrical shape versus bottle shape versus carton shape.
7. Type of sounds made when liquid is poured; for example, splashing versus fizzing versus bubbling.

Output Results: Output for a variation of the problem is illustrated in Figure 10.44.

Phase 1:
Opaque Container

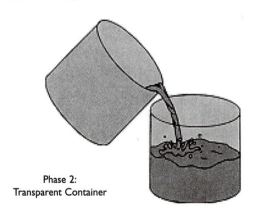

Phase 2:
Transparent Container

C H A P T E R

11

Subprograms, Functions, and Chaining

11.1 INTRODUCTION

A top-down program is easy to code, debug, and modify because it is written as a series of logical components. In previous chapters, the GOSUB and RETURN statements and the DEFFN and ENDDEF statements were used to implement the components of a program. We called these components subroutines and user-defined functions.

This chapter illustrates the use of subprograms and functions, rather than subroutines and user-defined functions, as a means to implement the top-down approach. Subprograms are more independent than subroutines and often are reusable by other programs. A function is called the same way a QBasic function such as SQR is called, by using its name in an expression.

Subprograms and functions collectively are called **procedures**. The code that calls the highest-level procedures is called the **Main Program**. The distinction between the Main Program and procedures will become more apparent later in this chapter.

This chapter also presents chaining. Unlike procedure calls, which take place in the same program, **chaining** involves linking different programs together through the CHAIN statement. When one program chains to another, the first program stops running; the second is loaded from auxiliary storage into main memory; and the second program starts running.

11.2 SUBPROGRAMS

A **subprogram** is a unit of code delimited by the SUB and END SUB statements and called (invoked) by the CALL statement. When the subprogram is finished executing, the END SUB statement transfers control back to the calling program.

Subroutines versus Subprograms

Figure 11.1 on the next page illustrates the similarity between the use of the GOSUB and RETURN statements and the CALL, SUB, and END SUB statements. Both partial programs call two lower-level components — A100.Accumulate.Totals and B200.Print.Record.

FIGURE 11.1
Subroutines versus subprograms.

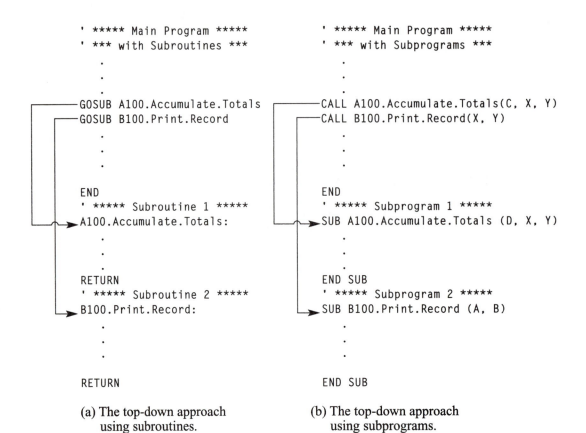

(a) The top-down approach using subroutines.

(b) The top-down approach using subprograms.

TABLE 11.1 - The SUB Statement	
General Form:	SUB subprogramname (p₁,...,pₙ) STATIC . . . END SUB where **subprogramname** is the name of the subprogram (up to 40 characters long); and **p₁ through pₙ** is an optional list of parameters (variables), separated by commas, that show the number and type of arguments to be passed to the subprogram from the CALL statement. If present, STATIC instructs the PC to retain the values of the local variables between calls. If STATIC is not present, then local variables are initialized to zeros or null strings each time the subprogram is called.
Purpose:	Defines a subprogram. The subprogram is called (invoked) by a CALL statement from the Main Program or from another subprogram.
Examples:	SUB statements without END SUB statements. See the corresponding CALL statements in Table 11.2. 1. SUB C100.Wrap.Up 2. SUB B300.Compute.Gross (Gross, Hours, Rate, Dependents) 3. SUB B320.Print.Detail (E.Name$, Age, Date.In$) STATIC 4. SUB B400.Accumulate (Gross.Total, Hours.Total) STATIC 5. SUB B510.Print.Message (Month, Message$) 6. SUB A110.Binary.Sort (Array())
Note:	The END SUB causes control to transfer from the subprogram back to the first executable statement immediately following the CALL statement that called (invoked) the subprogram.

The partial program in Figure 11.1(a) uses the GOSUB and RETURN statements to implement the top-down approach. Figure 11.1(b) implements the top-down approach using the CALL, SUB, and END SUB statements. Like the GOSUB statement, the CALL statement transfers control and retains the location of the next executable statement following the CALL. The END SUB statement carries out the same function as the RETURN statement in that it transfers control from the subprogram back to the first executable statement immediately following the CALL statement that called the subprogram.

The general forms of the SUB and CALL statements are given in Tables 11.1 and 11.2.

TABLE 11.2 – The CALL Statement	
General Form:	CALL subprogramname (a₁,..., aₙ)
	where **subprogramname** is the name of a subprogram; and
	a₁ through aₙ is an optional list of arguments (variables, constants, expressions, array elements, or entire arrays), separated by commas, that must agree in number and type with the parameter list in the corresponding SUB statement.
Purpose:	Causes control to transfer to a subprogram represented by subprogramname and the location of the next executable statement following the CALL to be retained. If an argument list is included, then the arguments are *passed* to the parameters in the order specified.
Examples:	These CALL statements reference the SUB statements in Table 11.1.
	1. CALL C100.Wrap.Up
	2. CALL B300.Compute.Gross(G, 46.5, Job * Class, D)
	3. CALL B320.Print.Detail(E.Name$, Age, Date.In$)
	4. CALL B400.Accumulate(Gr.Total, Hrs.Total)
	5. CALL B510.Print.Message(Month(1), "does not")
	6. CALL A110.Binary.Sort(Cost())
Note:	You can call a subprogram by using the name of the subprogram without the keyword CALL. For example, B400.Accumulate Gr.Total, Hrs.Total calls the subprogram B400.Accumulate the same as in Example 4. If the keyword CALL is not present, then do not surround the argument list with parentheses. This form of the CALL statement will not be used in this book.

Types of Subprograms

The two types of subprograms are: internal and external. An **internal subprogram,** also called an **associated subprogram,** is one that belongs to the same unit of code as the Main Program. When you save a program that has internal subprograms, they are all saved to disk under a given name. Furthermore, when you load a program into main memory, all internal subprograms also are loaded. How to enter and edit internal subprograms will be discussed in Section 11.3.

An **external subprogram** is independent from the calling program and resides in auxiliary storage in one of the following three forms:

1. A separate and distinct program
2. Part of another program
3. A QBasic library

With regards to external subprograms, we will cover only the first type, which requires the use of the CHAIN statement (see Section 11.5). For information on how to call subprograms located in another program or located in a QBasic library, see the QBasic user's manual or select *Modules and Procedures* under *Contents* in the Help menu.

Parameters and Arguments

The major difference between subroutines and subprograms is how variables are handled. With subroutines (Figure 11.1(a)), all variables defined in the program are **global variables,** that is, available to all modules throughout the program. With subprograms (Figure 11.1(b)), variables are by default **local variables,** that is, available only to the subprogram in question.

Values are passed to subprograms by assigning them to the arguments in the CALL statement. When the call is made, the arguments are assigned to the corresponding parameters in the SUB statement, where the first argument is passed to the first parameter, the second argument to the second parameter, and so on. With respect to the number of arguments in the CALL statement, the rule on the next page can be stated.

SUB RULE I

The number of arguments in the CALL *statement must agree exactly with the number of parameters in the* SUB *statement.*

This capability of *passing* only the required values to a subprogram is considered to be one of the major advantages over subroutines.

Whereas a **parameter** in a SUB statement must be a variable, an **argument** in a CALL statement can be a constant, variable, expression, array element, or entire array. Figure 11.2 illustrates the subprogram terminology and argument assignments.

FIGURE 11.2

The terminology used to describe the elements of a subprogram and argument assignment.

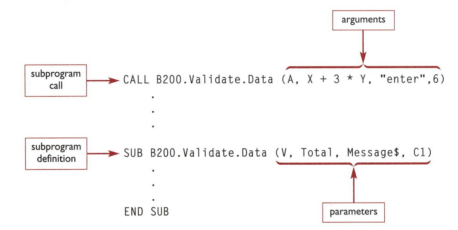

The remainder of this section is divided into subsections that illustrate the different ways that QBasic allows you to pass values between a calling program and a subprogram. As we shall see shortly, besides the argument-parameter-list technique, the COMMON and SHARED statements also can be used to pass values to a subprogram.

Passing No Values to a Subprogram

Not all subprograms require that the calling program pass values. For example, in Program 11.1 illustrated in Figure 11.3, the SUB statement in line 15 that defines the subprogram A100.Display.Message does not have a parameter list. Therefore, the CALL statement in line 5 does not have an argument list.

After the CALL statement transfers control to the subprogram A100.Display.Message, the PRINT statements are executed. Next, the END SUB statement returns control to line 6, the first executable statement below the CALL statement. The remaining lines in the Main Progam determine and display the hypotenuse of a right triangle with adjacent sides equal to 3 and 4.

Passing Constants and Expressions

Both constants and expressions can appear in the argument list of a CALL statement. Numeric constants and expressions can be passed only to numeric variables. Likewise, string constants and expressions can be passed only to string variables. If an attempt is made to pass a numeric value to a string variable, the PC displays a dialog box with the diagnostic message Type mismatch before terminating execution of the program.

Consider the argument list in line 5 and the parameter list in line 11 of Program 11.2 illustrated in Figure 11.4. The first argument, 4.67, is passed to the integer variable X%. Because the constant 4.67 is real and X% is an integer variable, the PC forces the constant to the type of X% and passes it as the value 5. The second argument is a numeric expression, and it is passed to the variable Y. When control transfers to the subprogram A100.Print.Detail.Line, Y is equal to 7.5. Finally, the string QBasic is passed to the string variable S$. In line 12 of subprogram A100.Print.Detail.Line, the PRINT statement displays the values of the three parameters X%, Y, and S$.

FIGURE 11.3

Program 11.1, passing no values to a subprogram.

```
 1   ' Program 11.1
 2   ' Passing No Values to a Subprogram
 3   ' *********************************
 4   CLS  ' Clear Screen
 5   CALL A100.Display.Message
 6   Side1 = 3
 7   Side2 = 4
 8   Hypotenuse = SQR(Side1 * Side1 + Side2 * Side2)
 9   PRINT "The Hypotenuse is"; Hypotenuse
10   END
11
12   ' *********************************
13   ' *          Display Message          *
14   ' *********************************
15   SUB A100.Display.Message
16      PRINT "This program displays the hypotenuse"
17      PRINT "of a right triangle with one side equal"
18      PRINT "to 3 and the other side equal to 4."
19      PRINT
20   END SUB
```

```
[run]

This program displays the hypotenuse
of a right triangle with one side equal
to 3 and the other side equal to 4.

The Hypotenuse is 5
```

The following rule summarizes the preceding discussion:

SUB RULE 2

Arguments in the CALL *statement must agree with the corresponding parameters in type. If an argument and a parameter are numeric, but do not agree in type, then the argument is forced to agree with the parameter.*

FIGURE 11.4

Program 11.2, passing constants and expressions.

```
 1   ' Program 11.2
 2   ' Passing Constants and Expressions
 3   ' *********************************
 4   CLS  ' Clear Screen
 5   CALL A100.Print.Detail.Line(4.67, (5 * 6) / 4, "QBasic")
 6   END
 7
 8   ' *********************************
 9   ' *          Print Detail Line          *
10   ' *********************************
11   SUB A100.Print.Detail.Line (X%, Y, S$)
12      PRINT X%, Y, S$
13   END SUB
```

```
[run]

5              7.5            QBasic
```

Passing Variables and Individual Array Elements

The values of simple variables and individual array elements can be passed to the parameters in a SUB statement the same as constants and expressions are passed. Lines 11 and 19 of Program 11.3 presented in Figure 11.5 illustrate this concept. The values of A(5), X, and Y$ are passed to the parameters D, G, and Message$ in the subprogram A100.Compute. As you can see, the variable names in the argument list *need not be the same* as the corresponding parameter names in the SUB statement.

FIGURE 11.5

Program 11.3, passing variables and array elements.

```
 1    ' Program 11.3
 2    ' Passing Variables and Array Elements
 3    ' *********************************
 4    CLS  ' Clear Screen
 5    DIM A(1 TO 10)
 6    A(5) = 2
 7    X = 150
 8    Y$ = "Change lead"
 9    PRINT
10    PRINT "Before CALL Statement ====> A(5) ="; A(5); " X ="; X; " Y$ = "; Y$
11    CALL A100.Compute(A(5), X, Y$)
12    PRINT
13    PRINT "After  CALL Statement ====> A(5) ="; A(5); " X ="; X; " Y$ = "; Y$
14    END
15
16    ' *********************************
17    ' *            Compute           *
18    ' *********************************
19    SUB A100.Compute (D, G, Message$)
20        D = D + 4
21        G = 3 * G
22        Message$ = "into gold"
23    END SUB

      [run]
```

> A(5) passes to D,
> X passes to G,
> Y$ passes to Message$

```
Before CALL Statement ====> A(5) = 2  X = 150  Y$ = Change lead

After  CALL Statement ====> A(5) = 6  X = 450  Y$ = into gold
```

Up to this point, we have talked only about passing values from the calling program to the subprogram. Unless specified, when the END SUB statement is executed, *all* values of the variables in the parameter list of a SUB statement are passed back to the variables in the argument list of a CALL statement. Thus, when you use variables as shown in Program 11.3, values are passed in both directions. This two-way street is called **pass-by-reference**.

When you pass-by-reference, the PC passes the *address* of the argument rather than the *value* of the argument to the corresponding parameter. The two PRINT statements in Program 11.3 illustrate the fact that the pass-by-reference technique is a two-way street. These two lines display the values of the argument list before and after the call. Note how the values of A(5), X, and Y$ have changed after control returns to the calling program from the subprogram.

An alternative to pass-by-reference is pass-by-value. **Pass-by-value** means that you are passing only the value of the argument, not the address of the argument. That is the case, for example, when you include a constant as an argument in a CALL statement. You can also pass-by-value a variable by enclosing it in *parentheses*. For example, assume we replace the CALL statement in Program 11.3 with the following:

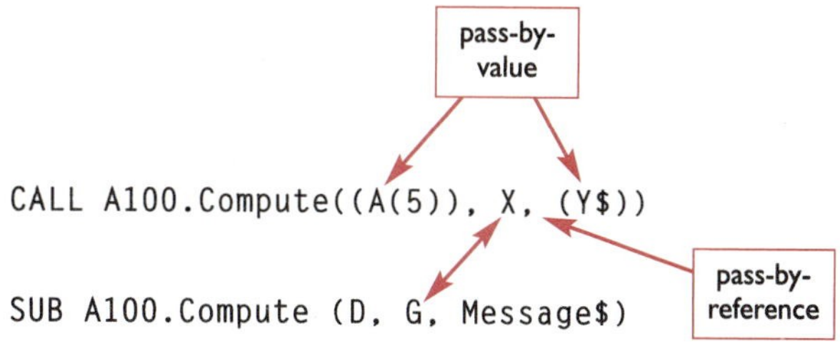

```
CALL A100.Compute((A(5)), X, (Y$))

SUB A100.Compute (D, G, Message$)
```

pass-by-value

pass-by-reference

When control returns to the calling program, A(5) and Y$ retain the values they had before the CALL statement was executed. However, because X is not enclosed in parentheses, its value changes to the value of G.

The following rule summarizes the preceding material.

SUB RULE 3

When you use the pass-by-reference method, values are passed in both directions between the calling program and the subprogram. When you use the pass-by-value method, values are passed only from the calling program to the subprogram.

Passing an Entire Array

You can pass all the elements of an array by including the array name followed immediately by open and close parentheses in the argument list of a CALL statement. The corresponding parameter in the SUB statement must also be a variable name followed immediately by open and close parentheses.

Program 11.4 presented in Figure 11.6 illustrates passing an entire array. After array Factor is dimensioned, the elements are assigned values by the For loop in lines 5 through 7. Line 8 calls the subprogram A100.Print.Array and passes array Factor to array Term. The For loop (lines 16 through 18) prints the values of the elements of array Term using the LBOUND and UBOUND functions.

Note that array Term is not dimensioned in the subprogram. You should only dimension the corresponding array (Factor) in the calling program. Like simple variables, arrays can be passed to a subprogram by using the pass-by-reference or pass-by-value methods.

FIGURE 11.6

Program 11.4, passing an entire array.

```
1   ' Program 11.4
2   ' Passing an Entire Array
3   ' ***********************
4   DIM Factor(1 TO 6)
5   FOR I% = 1 TO 6
6      Factor(I%) = I%
7   NEXT I%
8   CALL A100.Print.Array(Factor())
9   END
10
11  ' ***********************
12  ' *     Print Array     *
13  ' ***********************
14  SUB A100.Print.Array (Term())
15     CLS  ' Clear Screen
16     FOR I% = LBOUND(Term, 1) TO UBOUND(Term, 1)
17        PRINT Term(I%);
18     NEXT I%
19  END SUB


[run]

    1   2   3   4   5   6
```

Passing Values between Subprograms

As indicated in Table 11.1 on page 454, one subprogram may call another subprogram, which may call another, and so on. We pass values to a lower-level subprogram by using the argument-parameter-list technique described earlier and shown in the partial program presented in Figure 11.7. In Figure 11.7, the Main Program calls the subprogram B100.Print.Detail.Line. This subprogram in turn calls B200.Print.Headings whenever Line.Count is greater than or equal to Max.Lines.

FIGURE 11.7

Passing values between subprograms.

```
' *** Main Program ***
         .
         .
         .
CALL B100.Print.Detail.Line (Max.Lines, Emp.Number$, Age, Gender$, Seniority)
         .
         .
         .
END

'*** Print Detail Line ***
SUB B100.Print.Detail.Line (Max.Lines, Emp.Number$, Age, Gender$, Seniority)
    IF Line.Count >= Max.Lines THEN
           CALL B200.Print.Headings (Line.Count)
               .
               .
               .
END SUB

' *** Print Headings ***
SUB B200.Print.Headings (Line.Count)
      .
      .
      .
END SUB
```

Sharing Variables with Individual Subprograms

In addition to passing variables using the argument-parameter-list technique, the Main Program can share variables through the SHARED and COMMON statements. This section describes the use of the SHARED statement. The next section covers the COMMON statement.

A SHARED **statement** or a group of SHARED statements placed immediately after the SUB statement at the beginning of a subprogram can be used to declare a list of variables that you want to share in either direction between the Main Program and the subprogram. The general form of the SHARED statement is given in Table 11.3.

TABLE 11.3 - The SHARED Statement	
General Form:	SHARED v₁,...,vₙ where **v₁ through vₙ** is a list of variables to share between the Main Program and the subprogram in which the SHARED statement resides.
Purpose:	Shares the values of variables in both directions between a subprogram or function and the Main Program.
Examples:	SHARED A, B, C SHARED Factor()
Note:	The SHARED statement also can be used to define the type of variables in the list using the keyword AS. For example, SHARED K AS INTEGER, P AS DOUBLE declares K as an integer variable and P as a double-precision variable.

As an example of the use of the SHARED statement, consider Program 11.5 illustrated in Figure 11.8. This program is an alternative solution to Programming Case Study 3, Tailor's Calculations. Recall from Program 3.1 in Chapter 3 on page 56 that the customer's name, waist size, and weight are entered by the user. The PC then computes and displays the customer's neck size, hat size, and shoe size.

FIGURE 11.8

Program 11.5, sharing variables with individual subprograms.

```
1    ' Program 11.5
2    ' Sharing Variables between the Main Program
3    ' and Individual Subprograms
4    ' *****************************************
5    CALL A100.Accept.Measurements
6    Neck.Size = 3 * Weight / Waist
7    Hat.Size = 3 * Weight / (2.125 * Waist)
8    Shoe.Size = 50 * Waist / Weight
9    CALL B100.Print.Sizes(First.Name$)
10   END
11
12   ' *****************************************
13   ' *          Accept Measurements          *
14   ' *****************************************
15   SUB A100.Accept.Measurements
16      SHARED First.Name$, Waist, Weight
17      CLS  ' Clear Screen
18      INPUT "Customer's first name"; First.Name$
19      INPUT "Waistline"; Waist
20      INPUT "Weight"; Weight
21   END SUB
22
23   ' *****************************************
24   ' *              Print Sizes              *
25   ' *****************************************
26   SUB B100.Print.Sizes (First.Name$)   ◄─────
27      SHARED Neck.Size, Hat.Size, Shoe.Size
28      PRINT
29      PRINT First.Name$; "'s neck size is"; Neck.Size
30      PRINT First.Name$; "'s hat size is"; Hat.Size
31      PRINT First.Name$; "'s shoe size is"; Shoe.Size
32   END SUB
```

cannot include First.Name$ in the SHARED statement because it is not defined in this subprogram or in the Main Program

```
[run]


Customer's first name? Mike
Waistline? 35
Weight? 175

Mike's neck size is 15
Mike's hat size is 7.058824
Mike's shoe size is 10
```

In this alternative solution, the input data and output results are obtained through subprograms. The calculations are completed in the Main Program.

Line 5 in Program 11.5 calls the subprogram A100.Accept.Measurements. This subprogram accepts the data from the user via INPUT statements and passes the values back to the Main Program due to the SHARED statement in line 16.

After control returns to the Main Program, lines 6 through 8 determine the customer's neck, hat, and shoe size. Next, line 9 transfers control to the subprogram B100.Print.Sizes. The purpose of this subprogram is to display the output results — customer name, neck size, hat size, and shoe size. Because the string variable First.Name$ is not defined in the Main Program or subprogram B100.Print.Sizes, but rather is defined in line 18 of the subprogram A100.Accept.Measurements, we cannot pass First.Name$ in the SHARED statement. We must use the argument-parameter-list technique to pass this variable from the Main Program to the subprogram. This leads to the following rule:

SHARED RULE 1	*The* SHARED *statement can be used only to share variables defined in the Main Program or the subprogram in which the* SHARED *statement resides. The* SHARED *statement cannot be used to share variables between two subprograms.*

Sharing Variables with All Associated Subprograms

To share variables between the Main Program and all associated subprograms, you must use the COMMON **statement** with the attribute SHARED in the Main Program to list the variables that are available to all associated subprograms. Hence, through the COMMON statement, we identify the global variables, that is, variables shared with all associated subprograms.

Use the COMMON statement with the SHARED attribute when you have a large number of variables to share among the associated subprograms. The COMMON statement without the SHARED attribute also can be used to pass values to external subprograms. We will use this latter form of the COMMON statement in Section 11.5 when we discuss chaining.

The general form of the COMMON statement is given in Table 11.4.

TABLE 11.4 - The COMMON Statement	
General Form:	COMMON attribute $v_1, \ldots, v_n$
	where **attribute** is one of the following: SHARED, /blockname/, or null; and v_1 **through** v_n is the list of variables to share. If the attribute SHARED is included, then the COMMON statement declares that the variable list is to be shared with all associated subprograms. If the attribute is /blockname/ or null, then the variables that follow are identified as a group to be passed to an external subprogram that includes a similar COMMON statement.
Purpose:	Identifies variables that are to be shared globally between the Main Program and all associated subprograms, or between the Main Program and external programs.
Examples:	COMMON SHARED Sum, Count, Amount COMMON /AreaValues/Length, Width COMMON Rate(), Cost
Note:	1. The keyword SHARED may also be used in a DIM or REDIM statement to share variable sbetween a Main Program and subprograms. 2. If attribute is /blockname/, then the COMMON statement is called a **named** COMMON **block.** If attribute is null, then it is called a **blank** COMMON **block.**

Any number of COMMON statements may appear in a program. For example, the following statement

```
COMMON SHARED Gross, Tax, Dependents
```

is the same as the following list of statements:

```
COMMON SHARED Gross
COMMON SHARED Tax
COMMON SHARED Dependents
```

However, it is invalid to list the same variable name in more than one COMMON statement in the same program.

The COMMON statement must be located at the beginning of the Main Program as illustrated by Program 11.6 in Figure 11.9.

Program 11.6 is nearly identical to Program 11.5, except that all the variables have been made global by the COMMON SHARED statement in line 5. Note that in this new version, there are no argument lists in the CALL statements or parameter lists in the SUB statements. Furthermore, there are no COMMON statements in the subprograms. The output results due to the execution of Program 11.6 are the same as presented in Figure 11.8 (page 461) for Program 11.5.

▮FIGURE 11.9

Program 11.6, sharing variables between the Main Program and all associated subprograms.

```
1   ' Program 11.6
2   ' Sharing Variables between the Main Program
3   ' and All Associated Subprograms
4   ' ******************************************
5   COMMON SHARED First.Name$, Weight, Waist, Neck.Size, Hat.Size, Shoe.Size
6   CALL A100.Accept.Measurements
7   CALL B100.Compute.Measurements
8   CALL C100.Print.Sizes
9   END
10
11  ' ******************************************
12  ' *            Accept Measurements         *
13  ' ******************************************
14  SUB A100.Accept.Measurements
15     CLS  ' Clear Screen
16     INPUT "Customer's first name"; First.Name$
17     INPUT "Waistline"; Waist
18     INPUT "Weight"; Weight
19  END SUB
20
21  ' ******************************************
22  ' *            Compute Measurements        *
23  ' ******************************************
24  SUB B100.Compute.Measurements
25     Neck.Size = 3 * Weight / Waist
26     Hat.Size = 3 * Weight / (2.125 * Waist)
27     Shoe.Size = 50 * Waist / Weight
28  END SUB
29
30  ' ******************************************
31  ' *              Print Sizes               *
32  ' ******************************************
33  SUB C100.Print.Sizes
34     PRINT
35     PRINT First.Name$; "'s neck size is"; Neck.Size
36     PRINT First.Name$; "'s hat size is"; Hat.Size
37     PRINT First.Name$; "'s shoe size is"; Shoe.Size
38  END SUB

    [run]
```

these variables
are global

11.3 USING THE QBASIC EDITOR TO ENTER SUBPROGRAMS

The QBasic editor includes all the tools you need to enter, modify, and print subprograms. Program 11.6 will be used to illustrate the development of subprograms with the QBasic editor.

To initiate a subprogram, click Edit on the menu bar and then click New SUB as shown in Figure 11.10. QBasic displays the dialog box shown in Figure 11.11 requesting that you enter the subprogram name. After entering the subprogram name, A100.Accept.Measurements, click OK or press the Enter key. QBasic automatically includes the SUB and END SUB statements. You can press the Enter key to insert a blank line, thus making room for the subprogram code. Your screen will appear as shown in Figure 11.12.

FIGURE 11.10

The initiation of a new subprogram by selecting the command New SUB on the Edit menu.

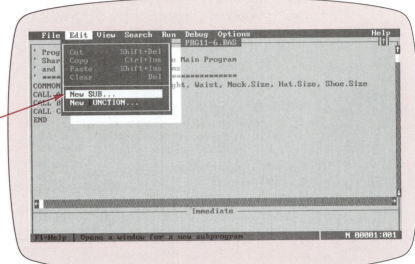

select this command to enter a new subprogram

FIGURE 11.11

Dialog box requesting the subprogram name.

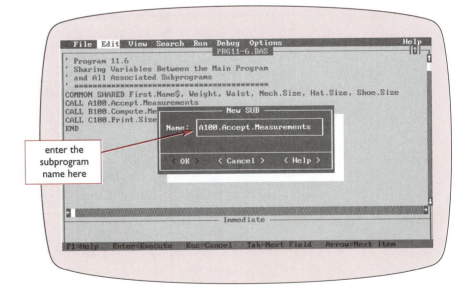

enter the subprogram name here

FIGURE 11.12

The display by QBasic of the
SUB *statement and* END
SUB *statement.*

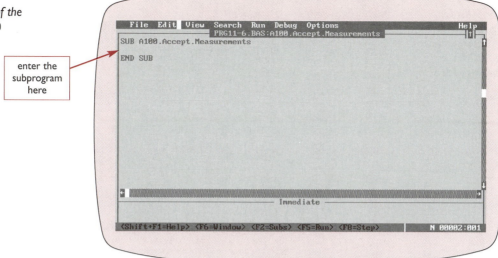

According to Program 11.6, we need to add a comment box above the first SUB statement. Use the Up Arrow key to move the cursor to the S in SUB. Press the Enter key. QBasic displays a dialog box cautioning you that only comments may be placed above a SUB statement. Click OK or press the Enter key and enter the comment box for the subprogram A100.Accept.Measurements (lines 11 to 13 of Program 11.6). Next, move the cursor back to the blank line between SUB and END SUB and enter the required statements in the subprogram.

To begin the second subprogram, click Edit on the menu bar and click New SUB again. QBasic again displays the screen shown in Figure 11.11. Enter the subprogram name, click OK, and make room to enter statements in the second subprogram.

Another way to initiate a new subprogram is to type the word SUB followed by the subprogram name after the END line in the Main Program or after END SUB in a subprogram. Pressing the Enter key then causes a screen like the one shown in Figure 11.12 to display.

Editing Subprograms

After entering the Main Program and the associated subprograms, the view window will display the last subprogram entered. At this point, you may want to review and correct entries in the Main Program and the associated subprograms. QBasic allows you to display and edit the different units of code (i.e., subprogram or function) in two ways:

1. Click View on the menu bar, click SUBs (Figure 11.13 on the next page), and then double-click the name of the unit you want to display.
2. Press Shift+F2 to display the next subprogram in alphabetical order by name. Press Ctrl+F2 to display the previous subprogram in reverse alphabetical order by name.

When you select the SUBs command on the View menu, QBasic displays the dialog box shown in Figure 11.14 on the next page. This dialog box has several features. First of all, it displays the names of the Main Program and associated subprograms. The subprogram names are indented below the Main Program name. In Figure 11.14, the name of the Main Program is PRG11-6 because we saved it under this name before entering the first SUB statement. The Main Program would be identified as <Untitled> if it had not been saved before displaying this screen.

FIGURE 11.13

Selection of the SUBs command in the View menu allows for the display and editing of the Main Program or any associated subprograms.

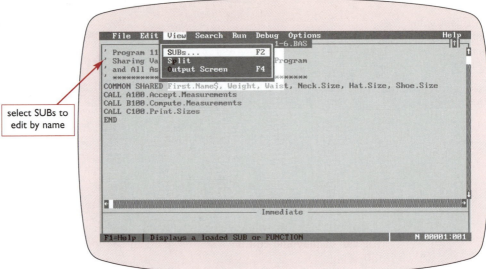

select SUBs to edit by name

FIGURE 11.14

The dialog box display of the names of the Main Program and associated subprograms.

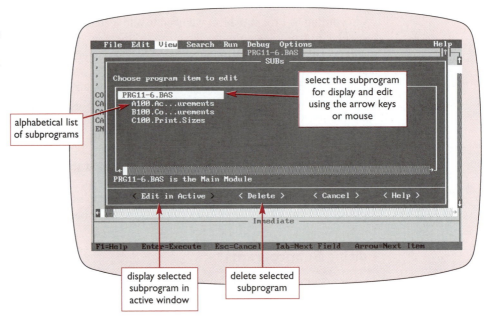

select the subprogram for display and edit using the arrow keys or mouse

alphabetical list of subprograms

display selected subprogram in active window

delete selected subprogram

To display the Main Program or any one of the associated subprograms, double-click the name. QBasic immediately displays the selected program in the view window.

Note in Figure 11.14 that there are buttons at the bottom of the dialog box. Table 11.5 summarizes the function of these buttons. To use them, click the program or subprogram name and then click the appropriate button. Edit in Active is the default button.

TABLE 11.5 - Function of the Buttons on the Dialog Box when the SUBs Command is Selected on the View Menu

BUTTON	FUNCTION
Edit in Active	Causes the highlighted program to replace the program in the active window. If the view window is split, the program in the inactive window remains where it is on the screen.
Delete	Causes the deletion of the highlighted subprogram.
Cancel	Cancels the dialog box and activates the view window.
Help	Displays a help window with information on using the SUBs dialog box.

Splitting the View Window

To split the view window horizontally into two view windows (Figure 11.15) so that you can display and edit the Main Program and a subprogram or two subprograms, do the following:

1. Click View on the menu bar and then click Split (Figure 11.13).
2. Position the mouse pointer in the lower window and then click.
3. Click View on the menu bar and then click SUBs (Figure 11.13). When the dialog box shown in Figure 11.14 displays, double-click the subprogram you want to display in the second window.

FIGURE 11.15

Split windows allow you to view and edit two subprograms or the Main Program and a subprogram at the same time.

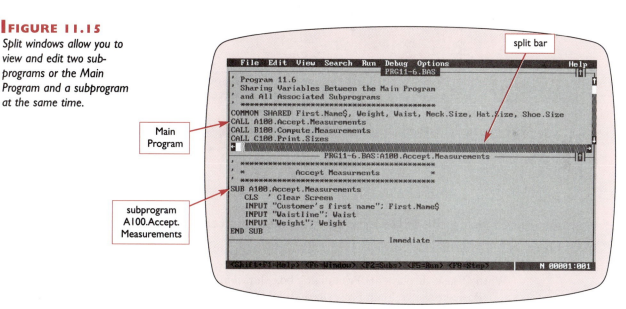

After the two programs display, click in the window you want to activate. To adjust the size of the active window, drag the split bar up or down with the mouse. To return to a single view window, activate the window you want to keep. Next, click View on the menu bar and then click Split. The Split command is like a toggle switch. Select it once, and the view window is divided into two view windows. Select it again, and the inactive window disappears.

Saving, Loading, and Executing the Main Program and Associated Subprograms

Use the Save command on the File menu to save the Main Program and associated subprograms. This command causes the Main Program and all associated subprograms to be saved under the same file name.

When you save a program that includes subprograms, QBasic automatically appends a DECLARE statement for each subprogram to the beginning of the Main Program. The DECLARE statements for Program 11.6 are shown in Figure 11.16. If you make changes to the parameter list in any subprogram, change the DECLARE statement for that subprogram so that its parameter list agrees with the parameter list in the SUB statement.

Use the Open command on the File menu to load the Main Program and associated subprograms from disk into main memory. Execute a program with subprograms like any other program. Execution begins with the first executable statement in the Main Program.

FIGURE 11.16

The display of the DECLARE *statements for Program 11.6, one for each subprogram.*

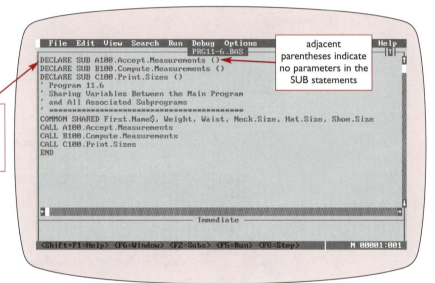

QBasic automatically inserts DECLARE statements at the beginning of the Main Program, one for each subprogram

adjacent parentheses indicate no parameters in the SUB statements

Printing the Main Program and Associated Subprograms

The Main Program and associated subprograms are printed the same way that you print a program without subprograms. That is, first select the Print command in the File menu. When QBasic displays the Print dialog box shown in Figure 11.17, select Entire Program.

QBasic prints the Main Program first, followed by the subprograms in alphabetical order by name. The use of a level number, such as A100 or B100, as part of the subprogram name should now be obvious to you. If you want to control the order in which the subprograms are printed, you must select appropriate names or print the Main Program and subprograms one at a time. To print the subprograms one at a time, do the following:

1. Load the subprogram into the view window.
2. Click File on the menu bar, click Print and then click Current Window in the Print dialog box (Figure 11.17).

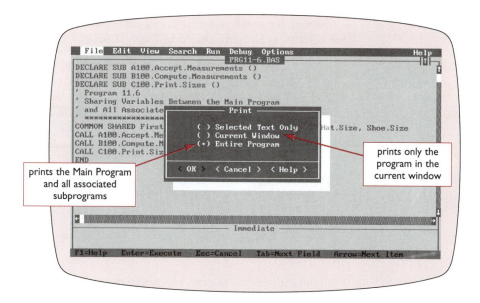

11.4 FUNCTIONS

The FUNCTION and END FUNCTION **statements** are similar to the DEF FN and END DEF statements in that they allow you to create user-defined functions. In both cases the functions are called by the function name in a LET, PRINT, LPRINT, or decision statement. If there are any arguments to pass to the function, they are passed in the same fashion as with subprograms. The arguments can be simple variables, expressions, constants, array elements, or entire arrays.

In the function definition, at least one statement must assign the function name a value. After the function is executed, the value assigned to the function name is returned to the statement that called the function.

Figure 11.18 illustrates the similarity between the use of the DEF FN and END DEF statements and the FUNCTION and END FUNCTION statements. Both partial programs call the function VOLUME. We use the style of capitalizing all letters in function names.

FIGURE 11.18
The DEF FN *statement versus the* FUNCTION *statement.*

```
' **** Function Volume ***
DEF FNVOLUME (L, W, H)
    FNVOLUME = L * W * H
END DEF

' ***** Main Program *****

READ L1, W1, H1
PRINT FNVOLUME(L1, W1, H1)
    .
    .
    .
END
```

```
' ***** Main Program *****
READ L1, W1, H1
PRINT VOLUME(L1, W1, H1)
    .
    .
    .
END

' **** Function VOLUME ****

FUNCTION VOLUME (L, W, H)
    VOLUME = L * W * H
END FUNCTION
```

(a) Using DEF FN and END DEF.

(b) Using FUNCTION and END FUNCTION.

Although the two forms of defining user-defined functions appear similar, some significant differences are summarized in Table 11.6.

TABLE 11.6 - Differences between using a DEF FN Statement and a FUNCTION Statement	
DEF FN ... END DEF	**FUNCTION ... END FUNCTION**
1. Must be defined in the Main Program before a statement can reference it.	1. Defined as a distinct unit of code in the same fashion as a subprogram.
2. Name must begin with FN	2. Name cannot begin with FN.
3. Variables are global.	3. Variables are local, unless shared.
4. Parameter list can only receive values using the pass-by-value method.	4. Parameter list can receive values using the pass-by-value or pass-by-reference method.
5. Cannot reference itself.	5. Can reference itself (recursive).
6. Single-line functions allowed.	6. Single-line functions not allowed.

All the methods for passing values discussed for subprograms in this chapter work the same way for functions defined with the FUNCTION statement. All the rules regarding the SUB statement and SHARED statement apply as well.

The general form for the FUNCTION statement is shown in Table 11.7.

TABLE 11.7 - The FUNCTION Statement	
General Form:	FUNCTION functionname ($p_1, \ldots, p_n$) STATIC . . . END FUNCTION where **functionname** is the name of the function (any QBasic variable name is valid except those that begin with FN) ; and $p_1, \ldots, p_n$ is an optional list of parameters, separated by commas, that shows the number and type of arguments to be passed to the function. If present, STATIC instructs the PC to retain the values of the local variables between calls. If STATIC is not present, then local variables are initialized to zeros or null strings each time the function is called.
Purpose:	Defines a function that is relevant to a particular application that can be called as frequently as needed.
Examples:	1. FUNCTION AREA (Side1, Side2) 2. FUNCTION FVALUE (P, I, C, N) 3. FUNCTION TABLESEARCH (Search.Argument, Table()) STATIC
Notes:	1. A function is called by using the name of the function in a QBasic statement. 2. The END FUNCTION causes control to transfer from the function back to the statement that called it. 3. To be consistent with the QBasic functions, capitalize all letters in the name of the function. 4. A function is declared integer, long integer, single precision, or double precision on the basis of the following:

Special Character Appended to Name	Type
Percent Sign (%)	Integer
Ampersand (&)	Long Integer
Exclamation Point (!) or no special character	Single precision
Number Sign (#)	Double precision

Consider Program 11.7 in Figure 11.19 which uses a user-defined function to determine the future value of a one-year investment. The function FUTUREVALUE is called in line 8 via a PRINT USING statement. The variables in the argument list are equal to 500, 0.0675, and 2. Thus, when control passes to the function FUTUREVALUE, the variables in the parameter list in line 14 are assigned the values 500, 0.0675, and 2. As with subprograms, the first argument is passed to the first parameter, the second argument to the second parameter, and so on.

The function name is assigned a value in line 15 of the function. When the END FUNCTION statement is executed, the value assigned to the function name (534.32) is returned to FUTUREVALUE(P, R, C) in line 8. Furthermore, the values of Principal, Rate, and Conversions are passed back to P, R, and C. In this function, however, the variables in the parameter list are not modified. Therefore, P, R, and C maintain their original values following the function call.

FIGURE 11.19

Program 11.7, using a function to compute the future value.

```
1    ' Program 11.7
2    ' Computing the Future Value
3    ' **************************
4    CLS  ' Clear Screen
5    P = 500
6    R = .0675
7    C = 2
8    PRINT USING "The future value is $###.##"; FUTUREVALUE(P, R, C)
9    END
10
11   ' ***********************************************
12   ' *           Compute Future Value             *
13   ' ***********************************************
14   FUNCTION FUTUREVALUE (Principal, Rate, Conversions)
15      FUTUREVALUE = Principal * (1 + Rate / Conversions) ^ Conversions
16   END FUNCTION

[run]

The future value is $534.32
```

An Example of a Recursive Function

The symbol n! is read *n factorial*. It is defined as the product of all the integers between 1 and n. Thus,

$$n! = n * (n - 1) * (n - 2) * \ldots * 2 * 1$$

For example,

$$5! = 5 * 4 * 3 * 2 * 1 = 120$$

n! can also be defined as n! = n * (n - 1)! This second representation of n! is called a **recursive definition**. For example,

5! = 5 * 4!	2! = 2 * 1!
4! = 4 * 3!	1! = 1 * 0!
3! = 3 * 2!	0! = 1 by definition

Recursive functions must have a condition that eventually stops the function from calling itself. With factorials, the function stops calling itself when 0! is evaluated. Program 11.8 in Figure 11.20 on the next page illustrates a recursive function that determines the factorial of any integer between 1 and 10.

FIGURE 11.20

Program 11.8, computing factorials using a recursive function.

```
 1    ' Program 11.8
 2    ' Computing Factorials Using a Recursive Function
 3    ' ***********************************************
 4    DO
 5       CLS  ' Clear Screen
 6       INPUT "Enter an Integer between 0 and 10 ===> ", Number%
 7       PRINT
 8       IF Number% >= 0 AND Number% <= 10 THEN
 9          PRINT USING "##_! = #,###,###"; Number%; FACTORIAL(Number%)
10       ELSE
11          PRINT USING "## is outside the range, please reenter"; Number%
12          PRINT
13          INPUT "Press Enter key to continue...", Halt$
14       END IF
15       PRINT
16       INPUT "Enter Y to determine another factorial, else N ==> ", Control$
17    LOOP UNTIL UCASE$(Control$) = "N"
18    END
19
20    ' ***********************************************
21    ' *              Factorial Function             *
22    ' ***********************************************
23    FUNCTION FACTORIAL (Number%)
24       IF Number% = 0 THEN
25          FACTORIAL = 1
26       ELSE
27          FACTORIAL = Number% * FACTORIAL(Number% - 1)
28       END IF
29    END FUNCTION
```

```
[run]

Enter an Integer between 0 and 10 ===> 8

8! =    40,320

Enter Y to determine another factorial, else N ==> N
```

When Program 11.8 is executed, line 6 requests the user to enter an integer between 0 and 10. Line 8 validates the Number%. If Number% is between 0 and 10, then line 9 references the function FACTORIAL. If Number% is outside the range 0 to 10, a diagnostic message displays, and the user is requested to press the Enter key to continue. Whether or not Number% is valid, line 16 requests the user to enter Y or N to continue or terminate the program.

Let us return to line 9 and discuss the function call. When the function is called, control transfers to line 23, the first executable statement in FACTORIAL. Next, line 24 tests the value of Number%. If Number% equals zero, then FACTORIAL is assigned the value 1. If Number% is not equal to zero, then control transfers to line 27 and FACTORIAL is assigned the product of Number% and FACTORIAL(Number% - 1). It is here in line 27 that the function calls itself.

Each time FACTORIAL calls itself, the value of the parameter is decremented by 1. Thus, with Number% equal to 8,

    FACTORIAL = 8 * 7 * 6 * 5 * 4 * 3 * 2 * 1 * 1

Hence, line 9 calls the function once, and line 27 calls itself eight times. Finally, line 27 returns the value of FACTORIAL to line 8.

To determine the factorial of integers greater than 10, change the function to double precision. For example, FUNCTION FACTORIAL# (Number%) returns a double-precision value with up to 15 digits of significance. When a function is declared by appending a special character to its name, any reference to the function must also include the special character. Note that upgrading the function to double precision would also require some minor changes to lines 23, 25 and 27.

Using the QBasic Editor to Enter Functions

A function is entered into the PC in a fashion similar to the way a subprogram is entered. You can initiate a new function by selecting the New FUNCTION command on the Edit menu (see Figure 11.10 on page 464). You can also enter a function by typing the keyword FUNCTION (instead of SUB) after the END statement in the Main Program or after END SUB in a subprogram.

To edit a function that is not active in the view window, use the same commands as described in this chapter for subprograms. That is, select a specific function by using the SUBs command on the View menu.

Like subprograms, functions are saved to disk with the Main Program under a single file name. When you save the program, QBasic appends a DECLARE statement at the beginning of the Main Program for each associated function. When the Main Program is loaded from disk into main memory, any associated functions and subprograms are also loaded into main memory.

To print the functions along with the Main Program, select Entire Program in the Print dialog box (see Figure 11.17 on page 469). The PC prints functions and subprograms in alphabetical order by name after printing the Main Program. To print a function by itself, load the function into the view window, and select Current Window in the Print dialog box.

PROGRAMMING CASE STUDY 4C – Finding the Single Discount Rate Using Subprograms and Functions

In Programming Case Study 4B, Finding the Single Discount Rate (on page 126), we solved the problem top-down using subroutines. In the following solution, we use subprograms and functions rather than subroutines. We have also included in this new solution validation of the rates entered by the user. The three rates must be between 0% and 100%.

The solution to Programming Case Study 4C, Program 11.9, is presented in Figure 11.21. A discussion of the solution also follows.

FIGURE 11.21

Program 11.9, the solution to Programming Case Study 4C.

```
 1  ' Program 11.9
 2  ' Finding the Single Discount Rate Using
 3  ' Subprograms and Functions
 4  ' *********************************************
 5  ' *              Main Program                 *
 6  ' *********************************************
 7  CALL A100.Initialization
 8  CALL B100.Process.Request
 9  CALL C100.Wrap.Up
10  END
11
12  ' *********************************************
13  ' *              Initialization               *
14  ' *********************************************
15  SUB A100.Initialization
16     CLS  ' Clear Screen
17     LOCATE 5, 25: PRINT "Single Discount Rate Information"
18     LOCATE 8, 25: PRINT "Enter in Percent Form (Valid Rates are 0% to 100%):"
19     LOCATE 10, 37: PRINT "First Discount ======> "
20     LOCATE 12, 37: PRINT "Second Discount ======> "
21     LOCATE 14, 37: PRINT "Third Discount ======> "
22     LOCATE 16, 25: PRINT "Single Discount in Percent ======>"
23     LOCATE 20, 25: PRINT "Enter Y to process another request, else N ==>"
24  END SUB
25
```

(continued)

FIGURE 11.21

(continued)

```
26   ' *************************************************
27   ' *                Process Request                *
28   ' *************************************************
29   SUB B100.Process.Request
30      DO
31         CALL B200.Accept.Rates(Rate1, Rate2, Rate3)
32         LOCATE 16, 59: PRINT USING " ##.##"; RATE(Rate1, Rate2, Rate3)
33         CALL B210.Refresh.Screen(Control$)
34      LOOP UNTIL UCASE$(Control$) = "N"
35   END SUB
36
37   ' *************************************************
38   ' *              Accept Discount Rates            *
39   ' *************************************************
40   SUB B200.Accept.Rates (Rate1, Rate2, Rate3)
41      LOCATE 10, 60: INPUT "", Rate1
42      DO WHILE VALIDATE(Rate1) = 0
43         Row = 10
44         CALL B300.Display.Error.Message(Row, Rate1)
45      LOOP
46      LOCATE 24, 25: PRINT SPC(45);
47      LOCATE 12, 60: INPUT "", Rate2
48      DO WHILE VALIDATE(Rate2) = 0
49         Row = 12
50         CALL B300.Display.Error.Message(Row, Rate2)
51      LOOP
52      LOCATE 24, 25: PRINT SPC(45);
53      LOCATE 14, 60: INPUT "", Rate3
54      DO WHILE VALIDATE(Rate3) = 0
55         Row = 12
56         CALL B300.Display.Error.Message(Row, Rate3)
57      LOOP
58   END SUB
59
60   ' *************************************************
61   ' *                 Refresh Screen                *
62   ' *************************************************
63   SUB B210.Refresh.Screen (Control$)
64      LOCATE 20, 72: INPUT "", Control$
65      LOCATE 10, 60: PRINT SPC(7);
66      LOCATE 12, 60: PRINT SPC(7);
67      LOCATE 14, 60: PRINT SPC(7);
68      LOCATE 16, 60: PRINT SPC(7);
69      LOCATE 20, 72: PRINT SPC(7);
70   END SUB
71
72   ' *************************************************
73   ' *              Display Error Message             *
74   ' *************************************************
75   SUB B300.Display.Error.Message (Row, Discount)
76      COLOR 31, 4
77      LOCATE 24, 25
78      PRINT "*** Discount "; Discount; "in error, please reenter ***";
79      COLOR 7, 0
80      LOCATE Row, 60: PRINT SPC(7);
81      LOCATE Row, 60: INPUT "", Discount
82   END SUB
83
84   ' *************************************************
85   ' *                    Wrap-Up                     *
86   ' *************************************************
87   SUB C100.Wrap.Up
```

```
88        CLS   ' Clear Screen
89        LOCATE 12, 25: PRINT "End of Program - Have a Nice Day"
90    END SUB
91
92    ' *********************************************
93    ' *                Rate Function              *
94    ' *********************************************
95    FUNCTION RATE (Rate1, Rate2, Rate3)
96        Factor1 = 1 - Rate1 / 100
97        Factor2 = 1 - Rate2 / 100
98        Factor3 = 1 - Rate3 / 100
99        RATE = (1 - Factor1 * Factor2 * Factor3) * 100
100   END FUNCTION
101
102   ' *********************************************
103   ' *                Validate Function          *
104   ' *********************************************
105   FUNCTION VALIDATE (Percent)
106       IF Percent < 0 OR Percent > 100 THEN
107           VALIDATE = 0
108       ELSE
109           VALIDATE = 1
110       END IF
111   END FUNCTION
112
113   ' ************** End of Program ***************

      [run]
```

Discussion of the Program Solution

Program 11.9 is similar to the previous program solutions in this book in that it uses the top-down approach. However, note that subprograms and functions are used rather than subroutines.

When Program 11.9 is executed, line 7 transfers control to the subprogram A100.Initialization (lines 15 through 24). This subprogram displays the screen shown in Figure 11.22 and then returns control to line 8 in the Main Program.

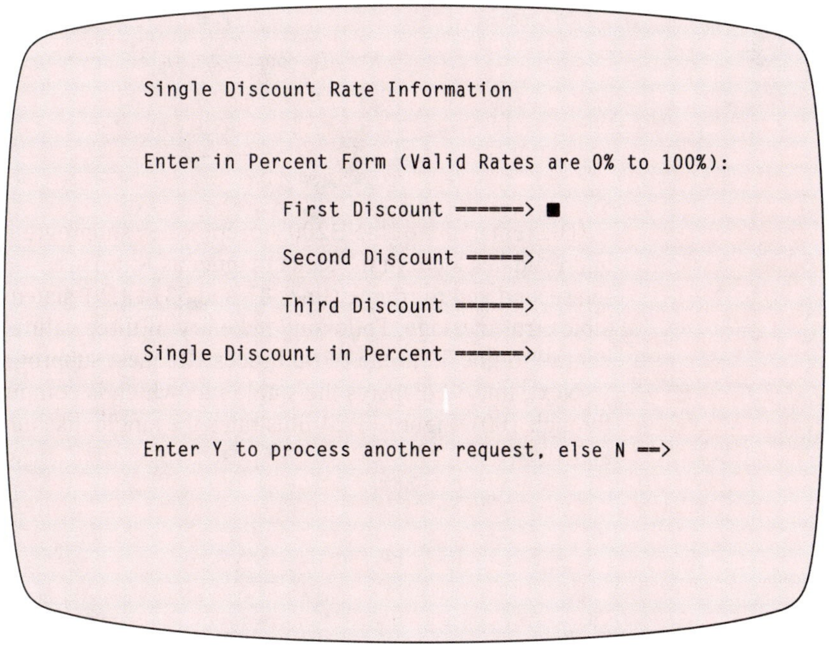

FIGURE 11.22

The display from Program 11.9 due to the execution of the subprogram A100.Initialization.

```
            Single Discount Rate Information


       Enter in Percent Form (Valid Rates are 0% to 100%):

                  First Discount ======> ■

                  Second Discount ======>

                   Third Discount ======>

       Single Discount in Percent ======>



       Enter Y to process another request, else N ==>
```

Line 8 calls the B100.Process.Request subprogram (lines 29 through 35). Control remains in this subprogram until Control$ is equal to the value N. The CALL statement in line 31 transfers control to subprogram B200.Accept.Rates (lines 40 through 58). Note that the argument list contains three variables — Rate1, Rate2, and Rate3. These arguments are used to pass to the calling program the three values entered by the user in response to the INPUT statements.

Line 41 in B200.Accept.Rates assigns the first value entered by the user to Rate1. The Do-While loop (lines 42 through 45) below the INPUT statement validates Rate1. The condition in the DO WHILE statement includes a call to the VALIDATE function (lines 105 through 111). In the call, the variable Rate1 is passed to the parameter Percent, which in turn is tested in line 106 to see if its value is between 0% and 100%. If the user enters a value outside the accepted range, then the VALIDATE function returns a 0 and the Do-While loop is executed. Otherwise, the Do-While loop is bypassed, and a value for Rate2 is requested in line 47.

When invalid data is entered for Rate1, the Do-While loop assigns Row the value 10 and calls the B300.Display.Error.Message subprogram (lines 75 through 82). This subprogram sets the color to a blinking, intense white on red. Next, a diagnostic message is displayed on line 78, and the color is set back to white on black as shown in Figure 11.23. The value of Row is used in lines 80 and 81 to clear the invalid entry from the screen and request a new value for Rate1.

FIGURE 11.23

The display from Program 11.9 due to entering an invalid discount rate (-10%).

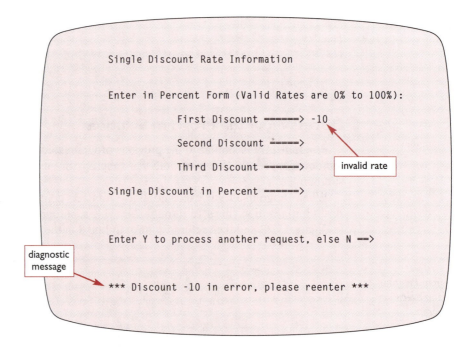

```
    Single Discount Rate Information


    Enter in Percent Form (Valid Rates are 0% to 100%):

              First Discount =======> -10

              Second Discount ======>

              Third Discount =======>           invalid rate

    Single Discount in Percent =======>



    Enter Y to process another request, else N ==>


    *** Discount -10 in error, please reenter ***
```

diagnostic message

The remainder of the B200.Accept.Rates subprogram accepts values for Rate2 and Rate3 and validates them in the same manner as Rate1 was validated. Note that prior to requesting the second and third rate (lines 47 and 53) PRINT statements clear output line 24 of any possible error message. Following the entry of three valid rates, the END SUB statement returns control to line 32 in the B100.Process.Request subprogram.

Next, line 32 displays the single rate which is computed by the RATE function (lines 95 through 100). Figure 11.24 illustrates the single discount rate for discounts of 40%, 20%, and 10%.

FIGURE 11.24
The display from Program 11.9 due to entering discount rates of 40%, 20%, and 10%.

```
                 Single Discount Rate Information


         Enter in Percent Form (Valid Rates are 0% to 100%):

                         First Discount =======> 40

                         Second Discount =====> 20

                         Third Discount ======> 10

                 Single Discount in Percent =======> 56.80



         Enter Y to process another request, else N ==> Y
```

11.5 CHAINING

Another technique that may be used to implement the top-down approach, especially when the programs are very large, involves writing external programs that are linked together by the CHAIN statement. The CHAIN **statement** may be used within a QBasic program to instruct your PC to stop executing the current program, load into main memory another program from auxiliary storage, and start executing the new program.

The COMMON **statement** is used together with the CHAIN statement to pass selected variables from the current program, also called the **chaining program**, to the new program, also called the **chained-to program**.

The general form of the CHAIN statement is shown in Table 11.8.

TABLE 11.8 - The CHAIN Statement	
General Form:	CHAIN "filespec" where **filespec** is the name of the program loaded from auxiliary storage and executed.
Purpose:	Instructs the PC to stop executing the current program, load into main memory another program from auxiliary storage, and start executing the new program.
Examples:	1. CHAIN "A:PROG2" 2. CHAIN "PROG3"
Note:	Do not use the *named* COMMON *block* form of the COMMON statement because *named* COMMON *blocks* are not preserved when chaining. Use a *blank* COMMON *statement* as shown in Programs 11.10 and 11.11.

In the first example in Table 11.8, the CHAIN statement terminates execution of the current program (the chaining program); loads PROG2 from the A drive; and begins execution of PROG2, which is the chained-to program.

Unless otherwise specified in a COMMON statement, none of the variables defined in the chaining program are available to PROG2, the chained-to program.

In the second example in Table 11.8, the CHAIN statement loads PROG3 from the default drive.

Care must be taken when using the READ and DATA statements in a chained-to program that may be called a number of times. Each time a chained-to program is executed, the pointer is moved back to the beginning of the data-sequence holding area. However, files that are opened in a chaining program remain opened, with the pointer at the same position in the file.

Figure 11.25 illustrates Programs 11.10 and 11.11. Assume that Program 11.10 is in main memory. Assume also that Program 11.11 is stored on the A-drive.

FIGURE 11.25

Program 11.10 chaining to Program 11.11.

```
1    ' Program 11.10
2    ' The Chaining Program
3    ' *******************
4    COMMON A, B, C
5    A = 3
6    B = 5
7    C = 10
8    CHAIN "A:PRG11-11"
9    END

     [run]


10   ' Program 11.11
11   ' The Chained-To Program
12   ' *********************
13   COMMON D, E, F
14   Total = D + E + F
15   CLS
16   PRINT "Value of D ===================>"; D
17   PRINT : PRINT "Value of E ==================>"; E
18   PRINT : PRINT "Value of F ==================>"; F
19   PRINT : PRINT "Value of Total ================>"; Total
20   END
```

When Program 11.10 is executed, the COMMON statement in line 4 establishes A, B, and C as common variables available to any program chained to a similar COMMON statement. Lines 5 through 7 assign the values 3, 5, and 10 to A, B, and C. Line 8 instructs the PC to stop executing Program 11.10, load Program 11.11 from auxiliary storage, and start executing it.

The COMMON statement in line 13 instructs the PC to assign the values of A, B, and C to D, E, and F. Line 14 assigns Total the sum of D, E, and F. Lines 16 through 19 display the values of D, E, F, and Total as shown in Figure 11.26. Note that the values of D, E, and F are identical to the values assigned to A, B, and C in Program 11.10.

FIGURE 11.26

The display due to Program 11.10 chaining to Program 11.11.

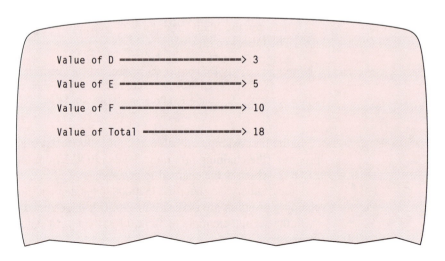

```
Value of D ==================> 3

Value of E ==================> 5

Value of F ==================> 10

Value of Total ==============> 18
```

In most beginning programming classes, programs seldom reach the size that would require the use of the CHAIN and COMMON statements and the chaining concept. However, in the real world of programming, programs that use the techniques described in Programs 11.10 and 11.11 are the rule rather than the exception.

11.6 What You Should Know

1. Subprograms and functions are collectively called procedures.
2. A subprogram is a unit of code delimited by the SUB and END SUB statements and called (invoked) by the CALL statement.
3. The CALL statement transfers control to a subprogram and retains the location of the next executable statement following the CALL statement.
4. The END SUB statement carries out the same function as the RETURN statement in that it transfers control from the subprogram back to the first executable statement immediately following the CALL statement.
5. There are two types of subprograms — internal and external. Internal means that it belongs to the same unit of code as the Main Program. External means that the subprogram is independent from the calling program. That is, it is stored on disk under another name.
6. We pass values to subprograms by assigning them to the **arguments** in the CALL statement. The arguments then are passed to the corresponding **parameters** in the SUB statement.
7. The arguments in the CALL statement or function reference must agree in type and number with the parameters in the SUB or FUNCTION statement.
8. A parameter in a SUB or FUNCTION statement must be a variable. An argument in a CALL statement or function reference may be a constant, variable, expression, array element, or an entire array.
9. Pass-by-reference means that values are passed in both directions between the calling program and the subprogram or function. Pass-by-value means that values are only passed from the calling program to the subprogram or function.
10. You can pass individual array elements or entire arrays to a subprogram or function.
11. A subprogram may call another subprogram, which may in turn call another, and so on.
12. The attribute STATIC in a SUB or FUNCTION statement instructs the PC to retain the values of the local variables between calls.
13. Function and subprogram names follow the same rules as for variable names.
14. The SHARED statement placed in a subprogram or function shares the values of variables in both directions between the subprogram or function and the Main Program.
15. The COMMON statement with the attribute SHARED identifies variables that are to be shared between the Main Program and all internal (associated) subprograms and functions or between the Main Program and external subprograms.
16. The QBasic editor includes all the tools you need to enter, modify, and print subprograms and functions.
17. The FUNCTION and END FUNCTION statements are similar to the DEF FN and END DEF statements in that they allow you to create user-defined functions.
18. Table 11.6 on page 470 describes the differences between defining a function using the FUNCTION and DEF FN statements.
19. All of the methods for passing values described in this chapter for subprograms work the same way for functions defined with the FUNCTION statement.
20. A function defined with the FUNCTION statement may call itself. This type of function is called a recursive function.
21. A recursive function must include a condition that eventually stops the function from calling itself.
22. A function is entered into the PC the same as a subprogram except that you use the New FUNCTION command in the Edit menu or type the keyword FUNCTION rather than SUB.

23. The CHAIN statement may be used within a QBasic program to instruct your PC to stop executing the current program, load the new program from auxiliary storage, and start executing the new program.

24. The COMMON statement is used in conjunction with the CHAIN statement to pass selected variables from the chaining program to the chained-to program.

11.7 Test Your QBasic Skills (Even-numbered answers are in Appendix E)

1. Consider the valid programs listed below. What is displayed if each is executed?

a.
```
' Exercise 11.1a
CLS ' CLear Screen
B = 20
CALL Compute(10, B, "Subprogram", C)
PRINT "The value of C ="; C
END

SUB Compute (X, Y, Term$, Z)
   Z = 3 * X ^ 2 + Y / 2 + LEN(Term$)
END SUB
```

b.
```
' Exercise 11.1b
CLS ' CLear Screen
Number = 12
PRINT "The square is"; SQUARE
END

FUNCTION SQUARE
   SHARED Number
   SQUARE = Number * Number
END FUNCTION
```

c. Assume Number, Place, and Operation$ are assigned the values 102.397, 2, and R.

```
' Exercise 11.1c
INPUT Number, Place, Operation$
IF Operation$ = "R" THEN
   PRINT "Rounded ====>"; ROUND(Number, Place)
ELSE
   PRINT "Truncated ===>"; TRUNCATE(Number, Place)
END IF
END

FUNCTION ROUND (N, E)
   ROUND = CINT(N * 10 ^ E)  / 10 ^ E
END FUNCTION

FUNCTION TRUNCATE (N, E)
   TRUNCATE = FIX(N * 10 ^ E) / 10 ^ E
END FUNCTION
```

2. Match each SUB statement to a CALL statement on the basis of type and number in the argument and parameter lists.

CALL Statements	SUB Statements
a. CALL SUBR (X, Y, Z)	1. SUB SUBR (A)
b. CALL SUBR	2. SUB SUBR (A, B, C$)
c. CALL SUBR(U, X, Y, "Z")	3. SUB SUBR (A, B, C, D)
d. CALL SUBR(X)	4. SUB SUBR (A$, B, C)
e. CALL SUBR("X", Y, Z)	5. SUB SUBR
f. CALL SUBR("X", "Y", 8)	6. SUB SUBR (A, B, C, D$)
g. CALL SUBR(3, 5, "Z")	7. SUB SUBR (A$, B$, C)
	8. None of the above.

3. What is wrong with the following SUB and FUNCTION statements?

a. SUB (A, C4, D, Male)
b. FUNCTION FNROUND (X, Y)
c. SUB Routine1 (A, 8 + 9, "Female")
d. FUNCTION COMPUTE (49, 81, B)

4. Fill in the missing word for each of the following:
   a. Subprograms and functions are collectively called _____.
   b. Use the _____ attribute in the SUB statement to instruct the PC to maintain the values of local variables between calls.
   c. External subprograms stored on disk as separate programs are called using the _____ statement.
   d. Pass-by-reference means that the PC passes the _____ of the argument to the corresponding parameter.
   e. A function that references itself is called a _____.

5. Rewrite the following program so that the input, computations, and output are done in separate subprograms.

```
' Exercise 11.5
' **************
CLS
INPUT "Gallons ===> ", Gallons
INPUT "Quarts ====> ", Quarts
INPUT "Pints =====> ", Pints
Ounces = 128 * Gallons + 32 * Quarts + 16 * Pints
PRINT : PRINT "Ounces ====>"; Ounces
END
```

6. Write a function using the FUNCTION statement that returns 1 if W is less than 10, 2 if W is between 10 and 100 inclusive, and 3 if W is greater than 100. Use the function name SWITCH.

7. A chaining program must pass the variables A, B, C, and D to U, X, Y, and Z in the chained-to program. First, write the statement for the chaining program to pass A, B, C, and D. Next, write the statement for the chained-to program, CHN-PRG, to receive the values for U, X, Y, and Z.

8. Explain how the SHARED statement is used to pass values between a Main Program and subprogram. Is this statement placed in the Main Program or subprogram?

9. Explain the difference between using DEF FN and FUNCTION to define a user-defined function.

10. Which menu option(s) are used to move from one subprogram to another in the QBasic editor?

11. **PC Hands-On Exercise**: Load Program 11.2 (PRG11-2) from the Data Disk. In line 5, change the argument list to (3.4, 12, "Book"). Execute the program and compare the results to those displayed by Program 11.2.

12. **PC Hands-On Exercise**: Load Program 11.5 (PRG11-5) from the Data Disk. Execute the program in the step mode by continuously pressing the F8 key. (See Appendix C for information on the step mode in QBasic.) When requested, enter the same data that was entered for Program 11.5. Consider how the CALL statement transfers control to a subprogram and the END SUB statement returns control to the calling program.

13. **PC Hands-On Exercise**: Load Program 11.8 (PRG11-8) from the Data Disk. First, execute the program for the following integers: −10, 5, 10, 0, 9. Next, execute the program for the integer 7 in the step mode. (See Appendix C for information on the step mode in QBasic.)

11.8 QBasic Programming Problems

1. Determining the Monthly Payment on a Loan Using Subprograms

Purpose: To become familiar with using subprograms to implement the top-down approach; the CALL, SUB, and END SUB statements; passing values through a parameter list; the hierarchy of operations; and a procedure for rounding a value.

Problem: Solve QBasic Programming Problem 3 on page 89 in Chapter 3 by writing a top-down program solution using subprograms rather than subroutines. Pass all values to the subprograms through a parameter list.

Input/Output: The input and output for this and the remaining programming problems is exactly the same as the original problems.

2. Determining the Eventual Cash Value of an Annuity Using Subprograms and Functions

Purpose: To become familiar with using subprograms to implement the top-down approach; the CALL, SUB, and END SUB statements; the FUNCTION and END FUNCTION statements; the LOCATE statement; passing values to subprograms through a parameter list validation; displaying diagnostic messages; and building a screen for data entry.

Problem: Solve QBasic Programming Problem 4 on page 138 in Chapter 4 by writing a top-down program solution using subprograms and functions rather than subroutines. Use a function to determine the eventual cash value.

Validate the payment per year (S) and number of installments (P) to ensure that they are greater than zero. Display a blinking, colored diagnostic message if either S or P are invalid.

(**Hint:** See Program 11.9 on pages 473 through 475.)

3. A Menu-Driven Program with Multifunctions Implemented Using Subprograms

Purpose: To become familiar with passing values to subprograms, data validation, the SELECT CASE statement, and the use of a menu.

Problem: Solve QBasic Programming Problem 8 on page 194 in Chapter 5 by writing a top-down program solution using subprograms rather than subroutines.

4. Sorting Customer Numbers Using Subprograms

Purpose: To become familiar with using subprograms to implement the top-down approach, passing arrays through a parameter list, the bubble sort algorithm, and the Shell sort algorithm.

Problem: Solve QBasic Programming Problem 6 on page 295 in Chapter 7 by writing a top-down program solution using subprograms rather than subroutines.

5. Determining the Mean, the Variance, and the Standard Deviation Using Subprograms

Purpose: To become familiar with passing values to subprograms using the COMMON SHARED statement and using subprograms to implement the top-down approach.

Problem: Solve QBasic Programming Problem 7 on page 297 in Chapter 7 by writing a top-down program solution using subprograms rather than subroutines. Write separate subprograms for the mean, variance, and standard deviation. Use the COMMON SHARED statement in the Main Program to make all variables global.

6. Payroll Problem X — Biweekly Payroll Computations with Time and a Half for Overtime

Purpose: To become familiar with using subprograms to implement the top-down approach.

Problem: Solve QBasic Programming Problem 10 on page 196 in Chapter 5 by writing a top-down program solution using subprograms rather than subroutines. Use COMMON SHARED to share variables with all subprograms.

12

An Introduction to Visual Basic

12.1 WHAT IS VISUAL BASIC?

Visual Basic is itself a Windows application. Its function, however, is to help you build your own special-purpose Windows applications. With Visual Basic, professional-looking applications that use the graphical user interface of Windows can be created by persons who have no previous training or experience in computer programming. Since its introduction in 1991, several million licenses for Visual Basic have been sold. The current release of Microsoft Visual Basic has four separate versions, each designed to meet differing programmer needs: Professional Edition, Enterprise Edition, Control Creation Edition, and Learning Edition.

Microsoft also has available an educational version of Visual Basic called the **Working Model Edition.** The Working Model Edition can be bundled with this textbook for a minimal charge. The major limitation of the Working Model Edition is the inability to convert Visual Basic programs to executable files that run outside of Visual Basic. The Working Model Edition, however, contains all the basic features and functionality necessary to achieve an introductory understanding of Visual Basic.

As you progress through this chapter, you will notice many similarities between the way QBasic programs were written in earlier chapters and the way applications are built with Visual Basic. The biggest difference between writing a QBasic program and building a Visual Basic application is that with QBasic you must create your own user interface. When you build a Windows application with Visual Basic, you can connect to the Windows GUI simply by assembling prebuilt graphical components.

12.2 THE THREE-STEP APPROACH TO BUILDING APPLICATIONS WITH VISUAL BASIC

In Visual Basic, the period of time during which applications are built is referred to as **design time**. This is in contrast to the time during which the completed application is actually functioning, called **run time**. Applications are built with Visual Basic by following a three-step method:

1. Create the interface
2. Set properties
3. Write code

Create the Interface

In this step, components of the graphical interface that will be used for getting input from the user and displaying output are assembled on one or more forms. A **form** is a container for different components of the interface. During run time, a form becomes a window on the desktop.

The graphical elements that make up the interface are called **objects** or **controls**. Controls can be added to a form during design time and during run time. Controls are added during design time by using the Toolbox to draw the controls on the form. The **Toolbox** (Figure 12.1) is a window in the Visual Basic environment that displays icons representing all of the controls that are available. Table 12.1 lists a description of the controls available in the Control Creation Edition.

FIGURE 12.1
The Visual Basic Toolbox.

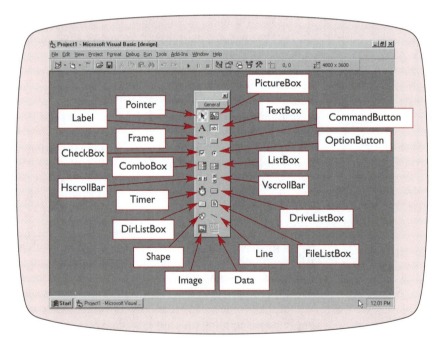

Additional controls are supplied with the Professional and Enterprise editions of Visual Basic. Third-party software vendors offer even more controls for purchase to add to your Toolbox.

CONTROL	DEFINITION
	The **Pointer** drags the border (resizes a control) or moves a control after it already has been added to a form.
	A **PictureBox** displays graphic images.
	A **Label** displays text that you do not want the user to be able to change during run time.
	A **TextBox** allows keyboard input during run time or displays text that the user can change during run time.
	A **Frame** groups controls. The frame is drawn first, and then the controls are drawn inside the frame.
	A **CommandButton** allows the user to initiate some event within the application during run time.
	A **CheckBox** creates an object that the user can check or uncheck by clicking it to indicate if something is true or false, or to indicate the user's acceptance or rejection of some option presented.
	OptionButtons in a group display a set of choices from which a single selection must be made.
	A **ComboBox** draws a combination list box and text box. The user can select either an item from the list or enter a value in the text box from the keyboard.
	A **ListBox** displays a list of items from which the user can select one item. If the list is longer than the size of the list box, a scroll bar is added automatically.
	An **HScrollBar**, or **horizontal scroll bar**, quickly moves left or right through a long list of items. It can indicate the current position on a scale or it can be used as an input device.
	A **VscrollBar**, or **vertical scroll bar**, performs the same functions as a horizontal scroll bar, but its orientation on the form is different, moving toward the top or bottom of the screen.
	A **Timer** initiates events at set intervals of time.
	A **DriveListBox** displays the drives that are available on the user's system.
	A **DirListBox**, or **directory list box**, displays a list of directories or folders in the user's system (usually from the selected drive).
	A **FileListBox** displays a list of files (usually from the selected directory).
	A **Shape** draws a variety of shapes, such as an oval or rectangle, on a form at design time.
	A **Line** draws lines of various widths and styles on a form at design time.
	An **Image** displays a graphic image from files with a .bmp, .ico, or .wmf file extension. Images displayed in an image control use fewer resources than a picture box.
	A **Data** allows access to data in a database.

TABLE 12.1 – Visual Basic Control Creation Edition Controls

Set Properties

Properties are characteristics or attributes of a control, such as color and size. Some properties also define aspects of the object's behavior, such as whether or not it will respond to a mouse click.

Because of Visual Basic's structure of objects and properties, it is sometimes referred to as an **object-oriented programming language (OOPL).** However, this is not really accurate because Visual Basic does not implement all of the features of true OOPL languages such as SmallTalk, C++, or Turbo Pascal for Windows.

Properties are set in the **Properties window** (Figure 12.2) at design time and are set during run time through code statements. The Properties window consists of three sections: the Object box, the properties list, and the description pane.

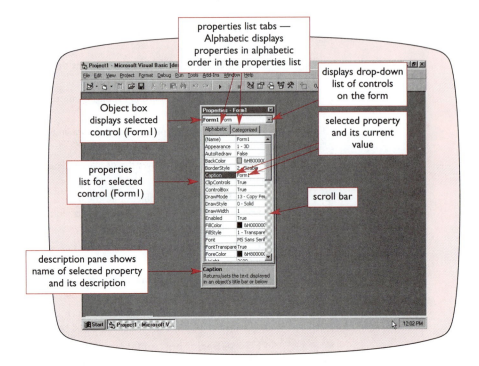

FIGURE 12.2

The Visual Basic Properties window.

1. **Object box** — shows the name of the control whose properties are being set (called the selected control).
2. **Properties list** — the set of properties that belong to the selected control and the current values of those properties. You can change a property value by selecting the property name and then typing the new setting or selecting the new setting from a drop-down list.
3. **Description pane** — lists the selected property name along with a short description of the property.

Different controls have various sets of properties. Because some controls' properties lists are very long, the properties list has a scroll bar to move through the list. It is not necessary to set every property of each control because Visual Basic assigns initial values for each of the properties. It is only necessary to change the properties that you want to be different from their initial, or **default**, values.

The form is also a control itself and has its own set of properties. Over 170 properties of the form and other controls are available in the Working Model Edition. Table 12.2 lists some of the more common properties.

Write Code

Visual Basic has a set of actions called **events** that can occur during run time. These include such actions as clicking the mouse or pressing a key on the keyboard.

Different Visual Basic objects are able to be associated with (or recognize) different events. There are over 30 different events in the Working Model Edition of Visual Basic. Table 12.3 lists some of these events.

TABLE 12.2 - Examples of Properties	
PROPERTY	**DEFINITION**
BackColor	Determines the background color of an object.
BorderStyle	Determines the type of border around a control.
Caption	Determines the text displayed in a form's title bar; determines the text displayed in or next to a control.
Enabled	Determines whether or not the form or control can respond to user-generated events, such as clicking.
Font	Determines the font, font style, and font size used to display text in a control or in a run-time drawing or printing operation.
Height	Determines the height of a control.
Left	Determines the distance between the internal left edge of an object and the left edge of its container.
(Name)	Determines the name used in code to identify a control.
Text	Determines the text contained in the edit area of a control.
Top	Determines the distance between the internal top edge of an object and the top edge of its container.
Width	Determines the width of a control.
Visible	Determines whether the control is visible or hidden during run time.

TABLE 12.3 - Examples of Events	
EVENT	**DESCRIPTION**
Click	Occurs when user clicks a control with the left mouse button.
DblClick	Occurs when user double-clicks a control with the left mouse button.
DragDrop	Occurs when a drag-and-drop operation is completed as a result of dragging a control over a form or control and releasing the mouse button.
DragOver	Occurs when a drag-and-drop operation is initiated.
GotFocus	In Windows, only one control at a time can receive mouse clicks or keyboard input; that control is said to have the focus. GotFocus occurs when an object receives the focus either by the user tabbing to or clicking the object, or by changing the focus in code using the SetFocus method.
MouseMove	Occurs when the user moves the mouse.

The combination of a specific control and a specific event is given a unique name consisting of the object's name, an underscore, and the event. For example, the event

```
Text1_Click
```

occurs whenever the user positions the pointer over the text box named Text1 and then clicks the left mouse button.

What happens or does not happen after an event occurs during run time is determined by a set of code statements associated with that event. These sets of code statements, called **procedures**, are subroutines similar to ones you have written in earlier chapters of this book. Unlike QBasic, which is a **procedural language**, nothing happens in a Visual Basic application until an event occurs. For this reason, Visual Basic is said to be **event driven**.

Events can be initiated by the user's actions, and they can also be initiated (called) by code statements in other event subroutines, in the same way that one QBasic subprogram can call another. The language and syntax for writing code in Visual Basic is very similar to that for QBasic. Many of the constructs and procedures, such as IF statements and loops, are directly applicable.

Many times, the actions that you want to happen within the application in response to events can be expressed as changes in the values of the properties of objects on the form. These are expressed as code statements with the syntax:

```
controlname.propertyname = propertyvalue
```

For example, the statement

```
Text1.Text = "Hello"
```

places the characters Hello in the text box named Text1. The value of the text property can be either numeric or string, where string data is enclosed in quotation marks. The statements

```
Command1.Top = 0
Command1.Left = 0
```

cause the control named Command1 to move to the upper left corner of its container.

You enter and edit code in the **Code window** (Figure 12.3) in a manner similar to the way you use the QBasic editor. An event subroutine (procedure) is displayed in the Code window by selecting an object from the drop-down Objects list and then selecting a procedure from the drop-down Procedures/Events list. The Code window has automatic formatting and syntax checking capabilities built in. If the syntax checker is turned on, Visual Basic displays a message when you enter code that has a syntax error.

FIGURE 12.3
Code window.

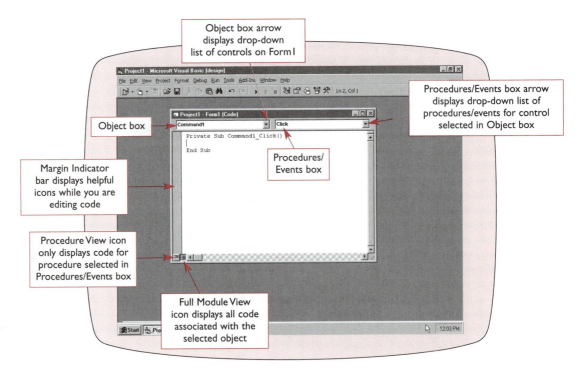

Methods

In Visual Basic, a **method** is a subroutine or a function that operates on an object. It is invoked through a code statement consisting of the control's name, a period, and the method. For example, the statement

```
Form1.Hide
```

applies the hide method to the control named Form1, and the statement

```
List1.AddItem "Gone With The Wind"
```

adds the name of a movie to the list of items in the control named List1.

Not all methods operate on all types of objects. Over 30 methods are available in the Working Model Edition. Table 12.4 lists a few of the methods.

TABLE 12.4 - Examples of Visual Basic Methods	
METHOD	**DESCRIPTION**
AddItem	Adds a new item to a list box or combo box, or adds a new row to a grid control at run time.
Hide	Makes a form not visible on the desktop.
Move	Moves a form or control.
SetFocus	Sets the focus to a form or control.
Show	Displays a form.

Functions

Similar to QBasic, Visual Basic supports functions that you create and also has a library of approximately 100 built-in functions.

For example, the Format function formats a number, date, time, or string according to instructions contained in a format expression. Its syntax is

```
Format(expression,fmt)
```

where **expression** is a numeric or string expression to be formatted; and

> **fmt** is a string of display-format characters that specify how the expression is to be displayed or the name of a commonly used format that has been predefined in Visual Basic such as *fixed* or *currency*.

A second example is the IsNumeric function, which evaluates whether a variable contains numeric data. The function

```
IsNumeric(Text1.Text)
```

returns a value of True if the Text property of the control Text1 contains numeric data; otherwise, it returns a value of False.

Many of these functions are identical in use and syntax to those you learned in QBasic.

12.3 THE VISUAL BASIC ENVIRONMENT

Perform the following steps to start Visual Basic:

1. Click the Start button on the taskbar.
2. Point to Programs on the Start menu.
3. Point to Visual Basic on the Programs menu.
4. Click Visual Basic on the Visual Basic submenu to start Visual Basic.

If the New Project dialog box displays (Figure 12.4 on the next page), click the New tab, click Standard EXE, and then click the Open button.

FIGURE 12.4
Visual Basic programming environment.

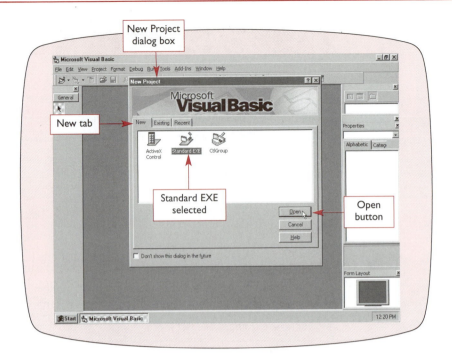

The desktop now displays six windows that make up the Visual Basic programming environment (Figure 12.5). If your PC did not display the New Project dialog box and your screen does not display a Form window, click the Add Standard EXE Project button on the Standard toolbar. If your PC does not display the Project Explorer window, the Properties window, the Form Layout window, or the Toolbox, click View on the menu bar and then click the appropriate window name.

FIGURE 12.5
Visual Basic programming environment.

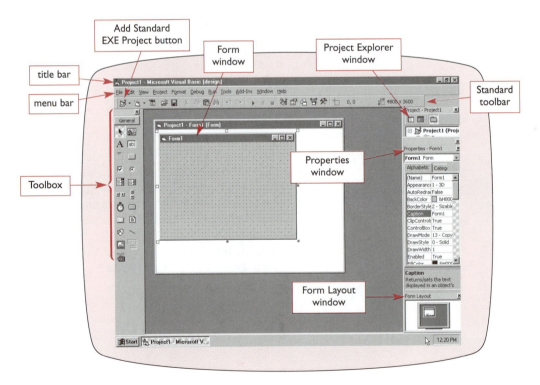

Some of the Visual Basic windows may overlap or display on top of each other. In order to work in any one of the Visual Basic windows, that window must be the active window. Visual Basic windows are made active in one of three ways:

1. Clicking the window if it is visible on the desktop.
2. Double-clicking its title bar if it is minimized.
3. Clicking Window on the menu bar and then clicking the window name if it is in the list.

You can arrange the Visual Basic windows on the desktop in many different ways without affecting Visual Basic's functions. As you become more experienced, you may find an arrangement that you prefer. For now, use the default sizes and arrangement of the windows shown in Figure 12.5.

12.4 BUILDING A CURRENCY CONVERSION APPLICATION

To illustrate the major features of Microsoft Visual Basic, the Currency Conversion application shown in Figure 12.6 will be built. In this application, the user enters a number in the text box labeled DOLLARS. When the user clicks one of the four buttons that are labeled with different currencies, the dollar amount is converted to the appropriate currency and displays in a box with the corresponding label. The Currency Conversion application has some of the common features of Windows applications. It occupies a window that the user can move on the desktop; it can be maximized or minimized; and it has a Control-menu box.

|FIGURE 12.6
Currency Conversion application.

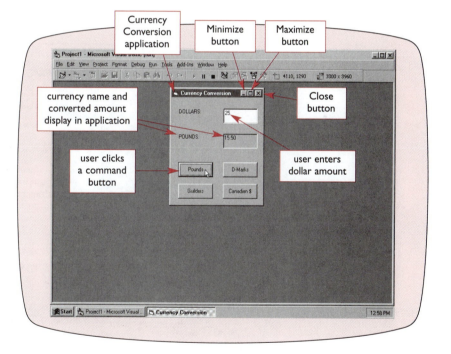

12.5 CREATING THE INTERFACE FOR THE CURRENCY APPLICATION

In Visual Basic, the applications that you build are called **projects.** A project usually begins with a form. At run time, a form becomes the window that the application occupies on the desktop. It is possible for one application to consist of more than one form.
Begin building the Currency Conversion application by specifying the size and position that you want the application's window to occupy on the desktop during run time.

You do this by adjusting the size and position of the form. Adjustments to the form's size and position can be made at any time during design time. The form also can be resized or repositioned during run time through code statements.

Setting the Size of a Form

Refer to Figure 12.7 to perform the following steps to set the size of the Currency Conversion form:

1. Point to the form's right middle sizing handle. The mouse pointer changes to a double arrow (↔).
2. Drag the form's right middle sizing handle toward the left side of the screen approximately one inch, so that the form's width looks similar to the form shown in Figure 12.7. As you drag the border, its new position appears as a shaded line. When you release the left mouse button, the form's right border moves to the position of the shaded line.
3. Drag the form's bottom middle sizing handle toward the bottom of the screen approximately one-quarter inch, so that the form's height looks similar to the form shown in Figure 12.7. As you drag the border, its new position appears as a shaded line. When you release the left mouse button, the form's bottom border moves to the position of the shaded line. The width and height of the form are shown as two numbers located to the right of the Standard toolbar.

FIGURE 12.7
Form resized.

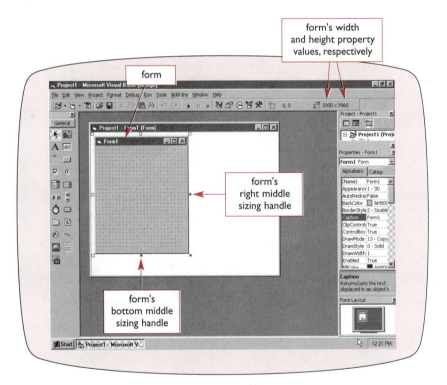

In the preceding steps, you set the form's width and height by dragging the form's right and bottom sizing handles. You can drag any of a form's sizing handles in either an inward or outward direction to change the size of the form. The form's width and height are measured in units called twips. The dimensions of the Form1 control display as 3300 × 3960 twips to the right of the Standard toolbar in Figure 12.7. It is not necessary for your form's dimensions to match exactly. A **twip** is a printer's measurement equal to 1/1440 inch. However, the width of a twip can vary slightly from one computer monitor to another.

Positioning a Form

The form's position on the desktop is set by dragging the form in the Form Layout window to the desired location. The form's position is given as two numbers. These numbers are the distance (in twips) between the left side of the desktop and the left border of the form and between the top of the desktop and the top border of the form.

The form's position can be changed as often as desired during design time. Sometimes it is useful to temporarily move the form in order to work more easily within the other Visual Basic windows. Refer to Figure 12.8 to perform the following steps to set the location on the desktop of the Currency Conversion window.

1. Point to the form in the Form Layout window. The mouse pointer changes to a four-headed arrow (⊕).
2. Drag the form down and to the right until the form is centered approximately on the picture of the desktop.
3. When the form is centered approximately on the picture of the desktop in the Form Layout window, release the left mouse button. The position of the form's upper left corner is shown as two numbers located to the right of the Standard toolbar. Your desktop should now look similar to the one shown in Figure 12.8. It is not necessary for your form's location and dimensions to match exactly the ones shown in Figure 12.8.

FIGURE 12.8
Form moved.

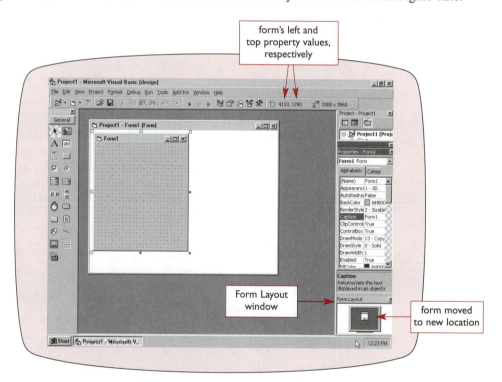

Adding and Removing Controls

Figure 12.1 on page 484 shows some of the graphical images, or objects, that are common to many Windows applications. In Visual Basic, these objects are also called controls. The Currency Conversion application contains three different types of controls as identified in Figure 12.9 on the next page. Refer back to Table 12.1 on page 485 to review the function of these controls.

Controls are added to a form by using the Visual Basic window called the Toolbox. In the following steps, you will add label, text box, and command button controls to the form.

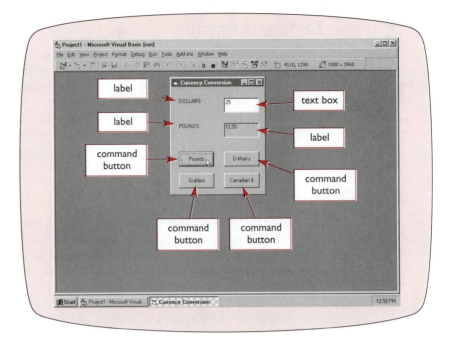

Perform the following steps to add the label controls to the Currency Conversion application:

1. Double-click the label button on the Toolbox. A label control named Label1 is added to the center of the form. Sizing handles display at each corner and in the middle of each side of the control.
2. Point to the center of the Label1 control and then drag and drop the Label1 control into the location shown in Figure 12.10. As you drag the control, a gray outline of the control moves with the mouse pointer. When you release the left mouse button, the control moves to the location of the gray outline.
3. Repeat step 1 and step 2 twice to add a second and third label control to the form as shown in Figure 12.10.

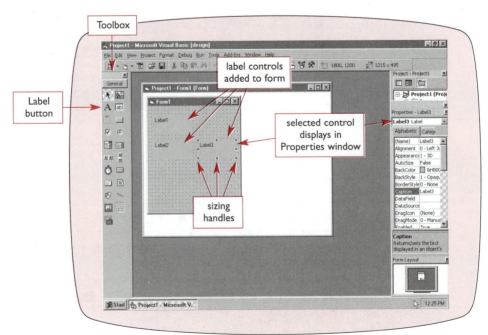

Controls can be made larger or smaller by dragging the sizing handles located around the control. Dragging a sizing handle located in the center of one of the borders of a control moves that one border. Dragging one of the handles located at the corner of a control simultaneously moves the two borders that form the corner.

If you choose the wrong control from the Toolbox or want to modify the project, controls can be removed from the form. This can be done at any time during design time. To remove a control, select the control to be removed by clicking it and then click Edit on the menu bar and click Cut, or press the Delete key.

You have now added three label controls to the form. Complete the following steps to add one text box control to the form:

1. Double-click the TextBox button on the Toolbox. A text box control named Text1 is added to the center of the form.
2. Point to the center of the Text1 control and then drag and drop the Text1 control into the location shown in Figure 12.11. As you drag the control, a gray outline of the control moves with the mouse pointer. When you release the left mouse button, the control moves to the location of the gray outline.

FIGURE 12.11
Text box control added to Currency Conversion application.

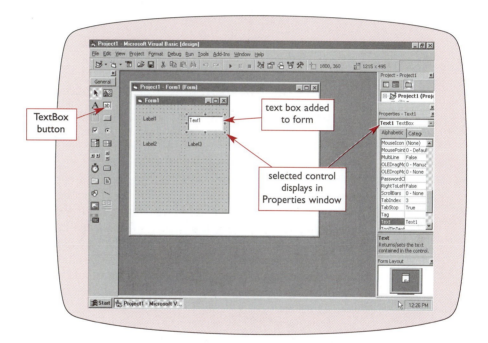

The text box was added to the form in the same way that the labels were added, by double-clicking the appropriate button on the Toolbox. This method can be used for adding any of the controls on the Toolbox to a form. Controls also can be added to a form by drawing them on the form. The following steps outline the process for drawing a control on a form:

1. Click the appropriate button on the Toolbox. The button becomes recessed on the Toolbox.
2. Move the mouse pointer to an area of the form where you want the control to appear. The mouse pointer changes from an arrow to a crosshair.
3. Drag the pointer down and to the right. A gray outline of the control appears.
4. When the control outline is the size that you want, release the left mouse button.

The next step is to add to your form the four command button controls identified in Figure 12.9. Use either the double-click method or the drawing method to add the controls, as shown in Figure 12.12 on the next page. If you use the double-click method, the size of your command buttons will match those shown in the figure. If you draw the command buttons, do not be concerned if the sizes do not match exactly.

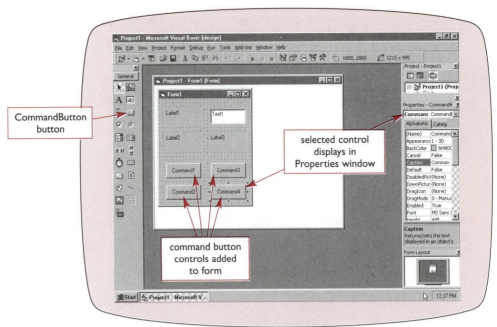

Changing the Location and Size of Controls

If you add a control to a form by double-clicking a button on the Toolbox, you will need to move the control from the center of the form, and frequently will want to change its size from its default. The location and size of any of the controls on a form can be changed at any time during design time.

The location given to a control by dragging and dropping it on a form during design time is the location that the control will have at the beginning of run time. However, a control does not have to remain in that location during run time. A control's location can be changed during run time by using code statements that change its Top and Left properties.

You should have noticed the similarity in the way that you set the location and size of the form on the desktop and the way that you set the locations and sizes of the labels, text boxes, and command buttons on the form. This should not be surprising though because a form is itself a type of control.

12.6 SETTING PROPERTIES FOR THE CURRENCY APPLICATION

Now that you have added controls to the form, the next step in Visual Basic application development is to set the controls' properties. Properties are characteristics or attributes of a control, such as its color or the text that appears on top of it.

The Caption Property

In the following steps, you will set the caption property of the Label1 control. The caption property of a control contains text that you want to appear on the control. Perform the following steps:

1. Select the Label1 label control by pointing to the control with the mouse and clicking the left mouse button. Sizing handles display around the control in the Form window. The object's name displays in the Object box of the Properties window. The currently selected property is highlighted in the properties list and its current value is shown to the right of the selected property.

2. Point to the Caption property in the properties list. If the property that you want to change is not visible in the properties list, you can use the scroll bar of the properties list to move the properties list within the Properties window.

3. Double-click the Caption property. The Caption property is highlighted in the properties list. The current value of the property, Label1, also is highlighted in the properties list.

4. Type

   ```
   DOLLARS:
   ```

   When you type the first character, the old value of the caption is replaced by that character. As you continue typing characters, they display in the properties list and on the label control on the form. If you make a mistake while typing, you can correct it by using the Backspace key or the Left Arrow and Delete keys.

5. Repeat steps 1 through 3 to select the Caption property of the second label control and then press the Delete key to make the caption blank. Do this again for the third label control.

6. Repeat steps 1 through 4 to change the captions of the command buttons as follows:

Control Name	Caption
Command1	Pounds
Command2	Guilders
Command3	D-Marks
Command4	Canadian$

7. Select the form control by pointing to an area of the form that does not contain any other controls and then clicking the left mouse button. Change the Form1 control's caption from Form1 to Currency Conversion.

In the preceding steps, you changed the Caption property of two different types of controls. The caption of a label appears as text on the form in the label control's location. This is a frequently used method to place text at different locations on a form. The Caption property of a form displays as text in the form's title bar.

An alternate method of selecting the control whose properties you want to change is to click the Object box arrow, and then click the control's name from the drop-down list of controls that displays. This list expands as you add more controls to a form.

The Text Property

The Text property of a text box is similar to the Caption property of a label. That is, whatever value you give to the Text property of a text box control will display in the text box at the beginning of run time.

The default value of a text box's Text property is the name of the control. In the Currency Conversion application, the text box should be empty when the application starts up, so you will set its Text property to be null, as described in the following steps:

1. Select the Text1 text box control by clicking at the Text1 control. The object's name displays in the Object box of the Properties window.

2. Point to the Text property in the properties list. If the property that you want to change is not visible in the properties list, you can use the scroll bar of the properties list to move the properties list within the Properties window.

3. Double-click the Text property. The Text property is highlighted in the properties list and the current value of the property, Text1, is highlighted in the properties list.

4. Change the value of the selected property to null by pressing the Delete key. The selected text box on the form no longer has any text inside it.

You should have noticed how similar the procedure for setting the Text property of the text boxes was to setting the Caption property of the labels. This same basic procedure is used for setting most of the properties of any type of control.

The BorderStyle Property

When a label control is added to a form, the default value of its BorderStyle property is 0 – None. That is, there is no border surrounding the control. Perform the following steps to add a border to the Label3 control:

1. Select the Label3 control by clicking it.
2. Select the BorderStyle property by clicking it in the properties list in the Properties window.
3. Display the possible values for the BorderStyle property by clicking the BorderStyle box arrow in the Properties window.
4. Click 1 - Fixed Single. A border displays around the Label3 control on the form. The application should appear similar to the one shown in Figure 12.13.

FIGURE 12.13

Caption, Text, and BorderStyle properties set in Currency Conversion application.

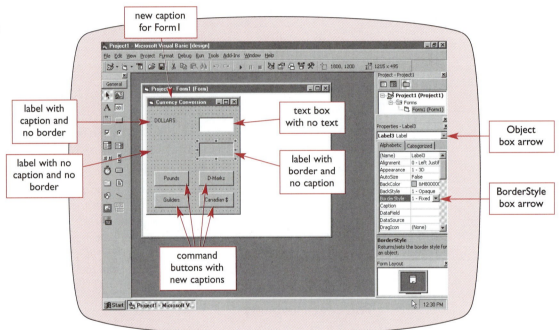

The Name Property

Visual Basic assigns unique default names to controls, such as Form1, Label1, Label2, Text1, and Command1. Although Visual Basic initially sets the Caption of some controls to be equal to the name of the control, the Name of a control and the Caption of a control are two different properties. For example, the Caption of the first command button in your application is Pounds; its Name is Command1.

Each control has its own unique name to distinguish it among a class of similar objects. Just as you use meaningful variable names in a program, you should use meaningful control names in your Visual Basic applications. Thus, you should change the default control names to meaningful control names. You change the name of a control by setting the Name property of the control. Perform the following steps to change the Name property of the Form1 control:

1. Point to an area of the form that does not contain any other control. This is so that you will select the form rather than one of the controls on the form. Select the Form1 control by clicking the left mouse button. The form becomes the selected control. The form's name displays in the Object box of the Properties window.
2. Scroll through the properties list to bring the (Name) property into view.
3. Double-click the (Name) property in the properties list to select it. The (Name) property is highlighted in the properties list, and the value of the property, Form1, also is highlighted in the properties list.
4. Type frmCurrency as the name. Press the Enter key on the keyboard. The value of the form's name changes to frmCurrency. Note that the form's Caption in the title bar is unchanged because this is a different property (Figure 12.14).

FIGURE 12.14

Name of Form1 changed to frmCurrency.

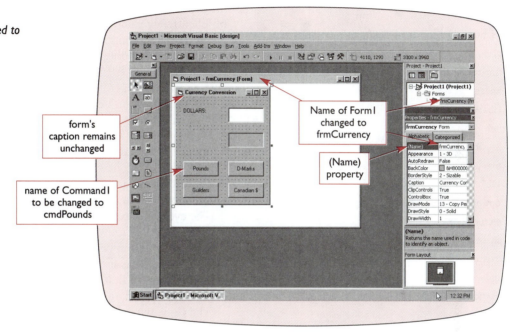

Visual Basic has a suggested standard for naming controls. A control's name should consist of a three-letter prefix that designates the type of control followed by a unique text description. Control types and name prefixes are listed in Table 12.5 on the next page.

Thus, the frm in frmCurrency indicates the control is a form. Perform the following steps to change the names of the remaining properties on the form.

1. Select the Label1 control by clicking it or clicking the Object box arrow and then clicking Label1 in the list.
2. Double-click the (Name) property in the Properties window.
3. Type lblDollars and then press the Enter key.

Repeat steps 1 through 3 to change the name of the remaining controls as follows:

Control Name	Name
Label2	lblCurrencyName
Label3	lblCurrencyAmount
Text1	txtDollars
Command1	cmdPounds
Command2	cmdGuilders
Command3	cmdDMarks
Command4	cmdCanadianDollars

TABLE 12.5 - Suggested Visual Basic Prefixes for Control Names

CONTROL	PREFIX
check box	chk
combo box	cbo
command button	cmd
data	dat
directory list box	dir
drive list box	drv
file list box	fil
form	frm
frame	fra
grid	grd
horizontal scroll bar	hsb
image	img
label	lbl
line	lin
list box	lst
menu	mnu
OLE	ole
option button	opt
picture box	pic
shape	shp
text box	txt
timer	tmr
vertical scroll bar	vsb

12.7 WRITING CODE FOR THE CURRENCY CONVERSION APPLICATION

You began the Currency Conversion application by building the user interface, consisting of a form and controls. You then set the properties of the controls. The remaining step in developing the application is to write the event procedures that will occur within the application.

When the user clicks one of the command buttons in the Currency Conversion application, the following occurs: If the data entered in the text box is numeric, then the caption of lblCurrencyName is set equal to the name of the currency on the command button that was clicked; and the caption of lblCurrencyAmount is set equal to the amount entered in the text box times the appropriate exchange rate. If the data entered by the user is not numeric, then the entry in the text box is erased and an insertion point displays in the text box.

As you probably have observed already, the code for this event uses the If-Then-Else structure presented in Chapter 5. There will be a similar event for each command button. The validity check is done with the IsNumeric function, and the output is formatted using the Format function. The insertion point is returned to the text box with the SetFocus method.

The event procedures in Visual Basic are written in subroutines. Each subroutine begins with a statement that includes the subroutine's name and ends with a statement that indicates there are no further instructions within that subroutine. These first and last statements are supplied by Visual Basic when you begin writing a new event subroutine.

The Code window functions as a text editor for writing your subroutines. You can add and change text within the Code window in the same ways that you use the QBasic editor. Refer to Figure 12.15 and the following steps to write the procedure for the cmdPounds_Click event.

FIGURE 12.15
Code Window.

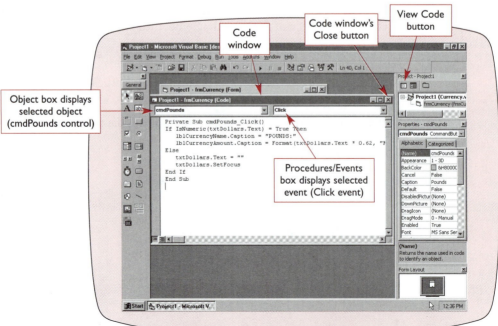

1. Open the Code window for the cmdPounds control by double-clicking the cmdPounds command button on the form (see Figure 12.15). Two lines of code display in the Code window and the insertion point displays at the beginning of a blank line between the two code statements.

2. Enter the code statements:

```
If IsNumeric(txtDollars.Text) = True Then
    lblCurrencyName.Caption = "POUNDS:"
    lblCurrencyAmount.Caption = Format(txtDollars.Text * 0.62, "Fixed")
Else
    txtDollars.Text = ""
    txtDollars.SetFocus
EndIf
```

3. Close the Code window by clicking the Code window's Close button.

If the Code window displays the wrong object, you can click the Object box arrow to display a list of all the objects on the form. Likewise, you can click the Procedures/Events box arrow to display a list of all events associated with the current object.

Repeat steps 1 through 3 for the three remaining command button click events using the following exchange rates: One dollar equals .9294 Guilders; 1.81 Marks; 1.39 Canadian Dollars.

You can simplify this step by copying and pasting code statements between event procedures the same way you copied and pasted code statements in the QBasic editor in previous chapters.

12.8 SAVING A VISUAL BASIC PROJECT

Before starting a new Visual Basic project or exiting Visual Basic, you will want to save your project. You also should save your project periodically while you are working on it and always before you run it for the first time.

Visual Basic projects are saved as a set of files. Forms are saved as files with a file name and an .frm extension. Visual Basic creates an additional file to save the project. This file has a file name and a .vbp extension. You will specify the path and file name for these files using the Save File As dialog box and the Save Project As dialog box. The Save File As and Save Project As dialog boxes are the same in many Windows applications. They are called **common dialog boxes**.

Figure 12.16 and the steps on the next page illustrate how to save the project to drive A. It is assumed that you have a formatted floppy disk in drive A.

FIGURE 12.16
Save File As dialog box.

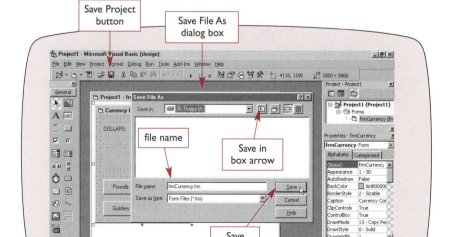

1. Click the Save Project button on the Standard toolbar. The Save File As dialog box opens. The current file name in the dialog box is the name that you assigned to the form earlier.
2. Click the Save in box arrow to display a list of drives.
3. Click 3½ Floppy (A:) in the drop-down list. The drop-down list closes, and drive A becomes the selected drive.
4. Click the Save button in the Save File As dialog box. The form is saved as the file FRMCURRENCY.FRM, and the Save Project As dialog box displays (Figure 12.17). The default project name, Project1, displays in the project name box.
5. Type Currency. The default name for the project is replaced in the File name box with the characters that you type. If you make an error while typing, you can use the Backspace key or the Left Arrow and Delete keys to erase the mistake and then continue typing.
6. Click the Save button in the Save Project As dialog box. The project is saved as CURRENCY.VBP and the dialog box closes.

FIGURE 12.17
Save Project As dialog box.

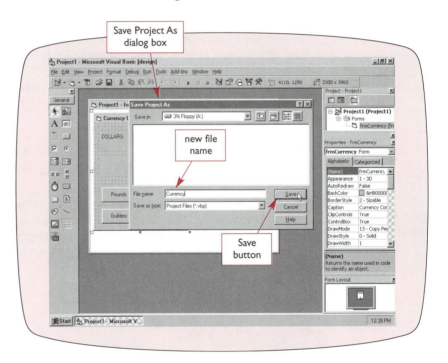

In the Save File As dialog box, you specified the drive to save the form file to, but you did not need to change the drive in the Save Project As dialog box. After you have changed a drive or folder in any of the common dialog boxes, it remains current in all the dialog boxes until you change it again.

Clicking the Save Project button on the Standard toolbar after you have saved a project will resave your work without opening the common dialog boxes. If you want to save your work with different file names, folders, or drives, you must click File on the menu bar and then click Save As.

12.9 STARTING, OPENING, AND RUNNING PROJECTS

In this section, you will learn how to start a new project, open an existing project, and run a project within the Visual Basic environment.

Starting a New Project

When you start Visual Basic, a new project opens automatically. No controls are on the form, no event procedures, and all properties have their default values. It is not necessary to restart Visual Basic each time you want to build a new application. Before beginning a new application, you should make sure that you have saved any work that you do not want to lose.

Because you already have saved the Currency Conversion application, you can start a new application by clicking File on the menu bar and then clicking New Project. The six Visual Basic windows display on the desktop with an empty form. The new form has the default form name, Form1, and the project has the default project name, Project1.

Each time you start Visual Basic, a new project is opened. If you attempt to open a new project before saving another project that you have been working with, Visual Basic displays a message box asking you if you want to save the previous work before proceeding to the new project.

Opening a Project

After a project has been saved, you can return to that project and make any necessary changes. You instruct Visual Basic which project you want to work with through the Open Project dialog box, similar to the way that you used the Save File As dialog box. Refer to Figure 12.18 and the following steps to open the project that you completed earlier.

FIGURE 12.18
Open Project dialog box.

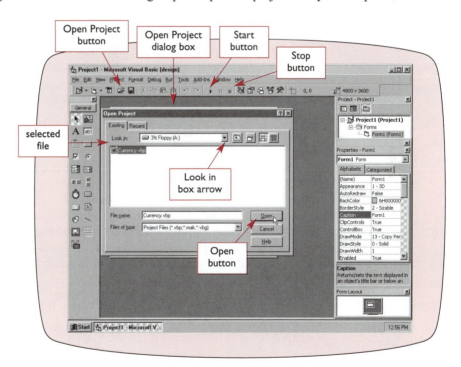

1. Click the Open Project button on the Standard toolbar. The Open Project dialog box displays. If drive A is not the selected drive, you can change it in the same way that you changed the selected drive when you saved the form file.
2. Click the project's name, Currency, in the file list. If the project's name is not visible in the file list, use the scroll bar to move the list until its name is visible.
3. Click the Open button in the Open Project dialog box. The files are read into memory and the Project window listing the all of the files associated with the project opens on the desktop. The Form window is reopened by clicking the View Form button in the Project window.

When you save a project, you must save the form file first and then save the project file. When you open a project, you only have to open the project file. Any other files associated with that project are opened automatically. All of these files are listed in the Project Explorer window.

Running an Application

In the following steps, you will run your application from within the Visual Basic environment.

1. Click the Start button on the Standard toolbar or click Run on the menu bar and then click Start. The word, design, in the Visual Basic title bar changes to run. The application's window displays on the desktop and an insertion point displays in the text box.
2. Type 25. The number displays in the text box. You can change or edit your entry using the Backspace key or the Left Arrow key and Delete key.
3. Click the command button with the Pounds caption. The number 15.50 displays in the label control (see Figure 12.9 on page 494).
4. Click the Stop button on the Standard toolbar. The application closes, and you return to the design environment.

Run your application again, trying different numbers for the dollar amounts and selecting different currencies. You do not need to start the application over each time you want to do another conversion. Click the text box to give it the focus, edit its contents, and then click a currency button. While the application is running, click the application's Minimize button. The application reduces to a program button on the taskbar, just like other Windows applications. Click the program button on the taskbar to continue working with the application. You can also close (stop) the application by clicking its Close button, as with other Windows applications.

12.10 EXITING VISUAL BASIC

Just like other Windows applications, Visual Basic can be minimized to allow you to work temporarily with another application such as a spreadsheet or word processor. You then can return by clicking the Visual Basic program button on the taskbar. When you have completed working with Visual Basic, you should exit the Visual Basic program to conserve memory space for other Windows applications.

Click the Close button at the right edge of the Visual Basic title bar. If you made changes to the project since the last time the project was saved, Visual Basic displays a dialog box. Choose the Yes button to resave your project and exit. Choose the No button to exit without saving the changes. Click the Cancel button to remove the dialog box and keep working with Visual Basic.

An alternative method of exiting Visual Basic is to click File on the menu bar and then click Exit.

12.11 What You Should Know

1. Visual Basic is a Windows application development system.
2. Applications are built with Visual Basic in a three-step process: design the interface, set properties, and write code.
3. Applications are built during design time; they are executed during run time.
4. The graphical elements in Visual Basic are called objects or controls.
5. A form is a control that serves as a container for other controls and displays as a window during run time.

6. Controls are added to a form by drawing them or by double-clicking the corresponding button on the Toolbox.
7. The characteristics of controls are called properties and are set during design time in the Properties window and are set during run time with code statements.
8. The actions that occur during run time are called events or procedures.
9. Methods are Visual Basic subroutines that operate on objects.
10. In addition to user-defined functions, Visual Basic has a library of over 100 built-in functions.
11. Event subroutines of QBasic-like code statements are written using the Code window.
12. Visual Basic applications are event-driven.
13. Visual Basic applications, called projects, are saved as a set of files. A project may have more than one Form file (with an .frm extension) and will have one project file (with a .vbp extension).

12.12 Visual Basic Application Problems

1. Determining a Salesperson's Commission

Create an application with a graphical user interface that will perform the calculation described in Programming Case Study 2 in Chapter 2 on page 22. The application should have four text boxes for the user to enter the rate, week 1 sales, week 2 sales, and returns. It should have one label for the output and one command button to initiate the calculation.

2. Tailor's Calculations

Create an application with a graphical user interface that will perform the tailor's calculations described in Programming Case Study 3 in Chapter 3 on page 55. The application should have two text boxes for the user to enter weight and waistline. It should use label controls to display the outputs and a command button to initiate the calculations.

3. Finding the Single Discount Rate

Create an application with a graphical user interface that will perform the calculation described in Programming Case Study 4A in Chapter 3 on page 63. How would you modify the application for a series of 4 or 5 rates? What about a user-supplied number of discount rates?

4. Deciphering a Coded Message

Create an application with a graphical user interface that will decipher messages described in Programming Case Study 13 in Chapter 8 on page 306. Use a text box for the user to enter the message.

(**Hint:** The Visual Basic application equivalent of Code$ in the case will be Text1.Text).p

Program Design Tools — Flowcharts, Pseudocode, Nassi-Schneiderman Charts, and Warnier-Orr Diagrams

The purpose of this appendix is to concentrate on preparing, using, and reading program flowcharts, pseudocode, Nassi-Schneiderman charts, and Warnier-Orr diagrams.

A.1 PROGRAM FLOWCHARTING

A **program flowchart** shows in graphic form the algorithm, or the method of solution, used in a program. By depicting a procedure for arriving at a solution, a program flowchart also shows how the application or job is to be accomplished. The term *flowchart* is used throughout this appendix to mean program flowchart.

Purpose of Flowcharting

A flowchart is used by programmers and analysts for the following purposes:

1. An aid in developing the logic of a program
2. An aid in breaking the program into smaller units when the top-down or modular approach is used
3. A verification that all possible conditions have been considered in a program
4. A means of communicating with others about the program
5. A guide in coding the program
6. A means of documenting the program

Flowchart Notation

Eight basic symbols are used commonly in flowcharting a program. They are given in Chapter 1, Table 1.5 on page 14, with their names and meanings and with some of the QBasic statements represented by them. In a flowchart, the process, input/output, decision, terminal, connector, and predefined process symbols are connected by solid lines. These solid lines, called **flowline symbols**, show the direction of flow. The annotation symbol, on the other hand, is connected by a broken line to any one of the other flowchart symbols, including any of the flowline symbols.

A fundamental rule to all flowcharts concerns direction. In constructing a flowchart, start at the top (or at the left-hand corner) of a page. The flow should be top to bottom or left to right. If the flow takes any other course, arrowheads must be used. No curved or diagonal flowline symbols are ever drawn. Although arrowheads are shown in Figure A.1 and in other flowcharts throughout this book, they need not be used in these cases, because their usage is optional when flow is both left to right and top to bottom.

FIGURE A.1

Flowcharts for Program A.1 (a) English-like, and (b) Basic-like.

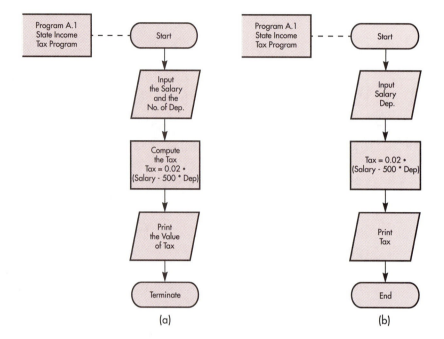

Inside each of the symbols, except the flowline symbols, write either English sentence-type notation, mathematical notation, or program language statements. These notations are arbitrary and their use depends on the kind of program being flowcharted, on the experience of the person constructing the flowchart, and on the standards that are used in the computer installation. One symbol or abbreviated description may represent more than one QBasic statement. The annotation symbol, with comments written inside it, is optional and is used whenever additional information is desired for the sake of clarity.

The first symbol in a flowchart usually is a terminal symbol with Start written inside it. This corresponds to no QBasic *statement* but is used solely to provide aid in finding the beginning point to a person who is unfamiliar with the flowchart.

Figure A.1 illustrates the logic of Program A.1, which calculates the state income tax. Two versions of the flowchart are given to show that the choice of the written contents inside each symbol is an arbitrary matter. Both versions have the same logic because the number, type, and arrangement of flowchart symbols are identical. The flowchart in Figure A.1(a) is more like English and would be used to communicate with a nonprogrammer, while the flowchart in Figure A.1(b) is more like QBasic and would be used to communicate with a programmer who is familiar with QBasic. A slight disadvantage in using English sentence-type notation is that ordinary English can become wordy and, at times, even unclear.

PROGRAM A.1

```
' Program A.1
' Computation of State Tax
' ************************
CLS  ' Clear Screen
INPUT "Please enter the salary ================> ", Salary
INPUT "Please enter the number of dependents ==> ", Dep
Tax = 0.02 * (Salary - 500 * Dep)
PRINT
PRINT "The State tax is =======================> $"; Tax
END

[run]

Please enter the salary ================> 19500
Please enter the number of dependents ==> 5

The state tax is =======================> $ 340
```

The advantage of using QBasic-like notation rather than English-like notation is that it permits the description of the operation to be presented in a compact and precise form. Table A.1 lists common notations, including mathematical ones, used in flowcharts.

TABLE A.1 – Common Notations Used in Flowcharts			
SYMBOL OR NOTATION	**EXPLANATION**	**SYMBOL OR NOTATION**	**EXPLANATION**
+	Addition or Positive Value	| |	Absolute Value
−	Subtraction or Negative Value	⌐ or !	Negation
* or x	Multiplication	EOF	End-of-File
/	Division	HI	High
\	Integer Division	LO	Low
^	Exponentiation	EQ	Equal
←	Is Replaced By or Is Assigned To	MOD	Modulo
=	Is Equal To	Yes or Y	
≠ or ⌐ = or ! =	Is Not Equal To	No or N	
:	Comparison	On	
>	Is Greater Than	Off	Self-Explanatory
≥	Is Greater Than or Equal To	True or T	
<	Is Less Than	False or F	
≤	Is Less Than or Equal To		

The advantage of using program-language statements in a flowchart is that this type of flowchart can improve communication among programmers who are familiar with the given language. This book, which favors a combination of English sentence-type, mathematical, and QBasic-type notation, will use whichever notation renders a given operation clear and unambiguous.

A.2 GUIDELINES FOR PREPARATION OF FLOWCHARTS

Before the flowchart can be drawn, a thorough analysis of the problem, the data, and the desired output results must be performed. The logic required to solve the problem also must be determined. On the basis of this analysis, a **general flowchart** of the main path of the logic can be sketched. This can be refined until the overall logic is fully determined. This general flowchart is used to make one or more **detailed flowcharts** of the various parts and levels in and exceptions to the main path of logic. After each detailed flowchart has been freed of logical errors and other undesirable features, such as unnecessary steps, the actual coding of the program in a computer language can be undertaken.

Straight-Line Flowcharts

Figure A.2 illustrates a general flowchart, that is straight-line. A **straight-line flowchart** is one in which the symbols are arranged sequentially, without any deviations or looping, until the terminal symbol that represents the end of the flowchart is reached. Once the operation indicated in any one symbol has been performed, that operation is never repeated.

Flowcharts with Looping

A general flowchart that illustrates an iterative, or repeating, process known as looping is shown in Figure A.3. The logic illustrated by this flowchart is in three major parts: initialization, process, and wrap-up. A flowline exits from the bottom symbol in Figure A.3 and enters above the diamond-shaped decision symbol that determines whether the loop is to be executed again. This flowline forms part of a loop inside which some operations are executed repeatedly until specified conditions are satisfied. This flowchart shows the input, process, and output pattern; it also uses a decision symbol that shows where the decision is made to continue or stop the looping process.

|FIGURE A.2
Basic pattern of a straight-line general flowchart.

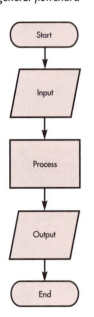

|FIGURE A.3
Basic pattern of a general flowchart with looping.

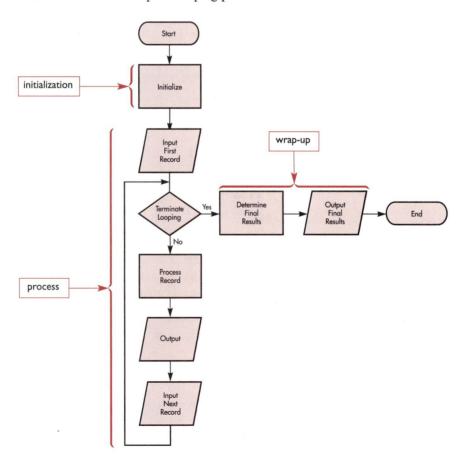

Figure A.3 also contains three braces that show initialization, process, and wrap-up operations. For example, setting the program counters to 0 may represent an initialization operation and displaying the values of counters may represent a wrap-up operation.

Like the straight-line flowchart, a flowchart with looping need not have all the symbols shown in Figure A.3, or a flowchart can have many more symbols. For example, the process symbol within the loop in Figure A.3, when applied to a particular problem, may expand to include branching forward to bypass a process or backward to redo a process. It is also possible that through the use of decision symbols, the process symbol in Figure A.3 could be shown expanded to several loops, some of which might be independent from each other and some of which might be within other loops.

The main point to remember is that the flowchart shows a process that is carried out. Flowcharts are flexible; they can show any process no matter how complex it may be, and they can show it in whatever detail is needed.

The two flowcharts illustrated in Figure A.4 represent the same program; that is, the program simply reads and then prints a record. Then the program loops back to the reading operation and repeats the sequence, reading and printing any number of records.

Although the flowcharts in Figure A.4 illustrate two ways a loop can be represented, the particular loop that is shown is an **endless**, or **infinite**, loop. This type of loop should be avoided in constructing business programs. In order to make a program finite, you must define it so it will terminate when specified conditions are satisfied. For example, if 15 aging accounts are to be processed, the program can be instructed to process no more than 15 accounts and then stop. Figure A.5 illustrates the use of a counter in terminating the looping process. Note that the counter is first set to 0 in the initialization step. After an account is read and a message of action is printed, the counter is incremented by 1 and tested to find whether it is now equal to 15. If the value of the counter is not 15, the looping process continues. If the value of the counter is 15, the looping process terminates.

For the flowchart used in Figure A.5, the exact number of accounts to be processed must be known beforehand. In practice, this will not always be the case because the number of accounts may vary from one run to the next.

A way to solve this type of problem is shown in Figure A.6 on the next page, which illustrates the use of an end-of-file test to terminate the looping process. The value -999999 has been chosen to be the last account number. This kind of value is sometimes known as the **sentinel value** because it *guards* against reading past the end-of-file. Also, the numeric item chosen for the last value cannot possibly be confused with a valid item because it is outside the range of the account numbers. Programs using an end-of-file test, such as the one shown in Figure A.6, are far more flexible and less limited than programs that do not, such as those illustrated in Figures A.4 and A.5.

I FIGURE A.4

Two methods of representing an endless loop in a flowchart.

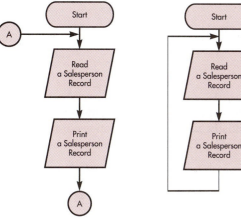

I FIGURE A.5

Termination of a loop by use of a counter.

FIGURE A.6

Termination of a loop by testing for the end-of-file.

FIGURE A.7

Flowchart with looping, illustrating the concept of counting the number of records in an inventory file.

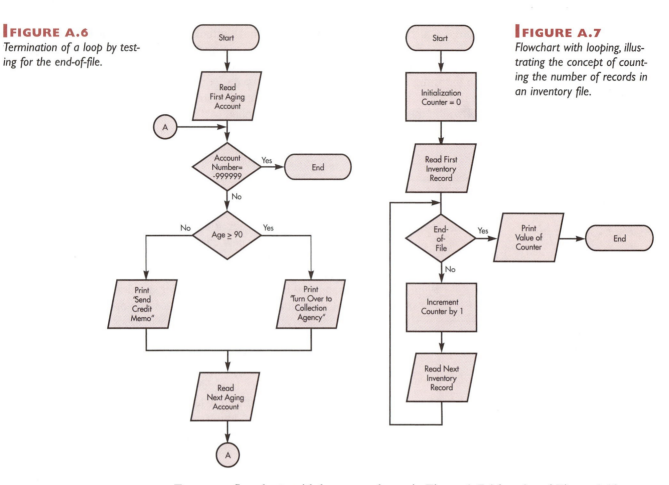

Two more flowcharts with loops are shown in Figure A.7 (above) and Figure 1.13 on page 15. Figure A.7 illustrates the concept of counting, and Figure 1.13 illustrates the computations required to compute the average commission paid to a company's sales personnel. Both flowcharts incorporate the end-of-file test.

The technique of flowcharting may not be very useful in simple computer programs such as Program A.1 on page 509. However, as programs become more complex with many different paths of execution, a flowchart is not only useful but usually is a prerequisite for successful analysis and coding of the program. Indeed, developing the problem solution by arranging and rearranging the flowchart symbols can lead to a more efficient computer program.

A.3 CONTROL STRUCTURES

Computer professionals agree that high-quality programs can be constructed from the following three basic logic structures:

1. Sequence
2. If-Then-Else or Selection
3. Do-While or Repetition

The following are two common extensions to these logic structures:

Do-Until or Repeat-Until
Case (an extension of the If-Then-Else logic structure)

The **Sequence structure** is used to show one action or one action followed by another, as illustrated in Figure A.8. Every flowchart in this text includes this control structure.

Sequence structure: (a) one action; (b) one action followed by another.

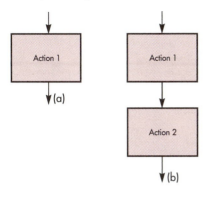

The **If-Then-Else** structure represents a two-way decision with action specified for each of the two alternatives. This logic structure is shown in Figure A.9. The flowcharts presented in Figures A.5 and A.6 include this logic structure. The action can be null for one alternative, as shown in Figure A.9(b).

The **Do-While structure** is the logic structure most commonly used to create a process that will repeat as long as the condition is true. The Do-While structure is illustrated in Figure A.10 and has been used earlier in Figures A.3, A.6, and A.7. Because the decision to perform the action within the structure is at the top of the loop, the action may not occur.

The **Do-Until structure** (Figure A.11) also is used for creating a process that will be repeated. The major differences between the Do-Until and the Do-While structures are that (1) the action within the structure of a Do-Until will always be executed at least once, (2) the decision to perform the action within the structure is at the bottom of the Do-Until loop, and (3) the Do-Until loop exits when the condition is true.

Figure A.11 illustrates the Do-Until structure, and the flowchart presented in Figure A.5 on page 511 includes a Do-Until structure.

FIGURE A.9

If-Then-Else structure: (a) action specified for each of the two alternatives (true or false); (b) additional action taken for one alternative.

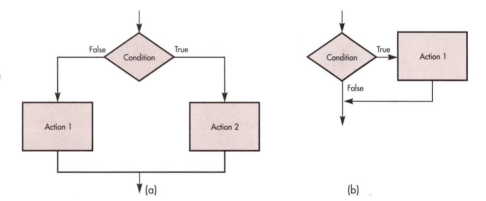

FIGURE A.10

Do-While structure.

FIGURE A.11

Do-Until structure.

The **Case structure** is similar to the If-Then-Else structure except that it provides more than two alternatives. Figure A.12 on the next page illustrates the Case structure.

A high-quality program can be developed through the use of just these five logic structures. The program will be easy to read, easy to modify, and reliable; most important of all, the program will do what it is intended to do!

FIGURE A.12

Case structure.

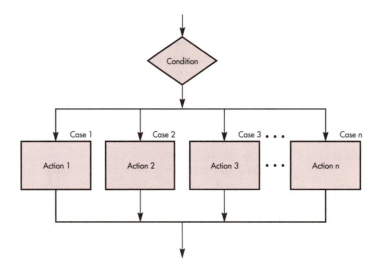

A.4 PROPER PROGRAMS

A **proper program** is one that has the following characteristics:

1. One entry point
2. One exit point
3. No unreachable code
4. No infinite loops

A program constructed with just the five logic structures will form the basis for a proper program. Figure A.13 illustrates the breaking up — the decomposition — of a program into some of the control structures presented in the previous section. On the other hand, Figure A.14 illustrates a flowchart that will result in an **improper program**.

This book stresses the construction of proper programs. However, you should be aware that in the real world the characteristics of a proper program may be relaxed or even intentionally violated, and these types of real-world programs are referred to as improper programs.

A.5 FLOWCHARTING TIPS

Shown on pages 515-516 are some flowchart suggestions. These suggestions assume that the input, processing, and output of the problem are defined properly.

1. Sketch a general flowchart and the necessary detail flowcharts before coding the problem. Repeat this step until you are satisfied with your flowcharts.
2. Use the control structures described in section A.3.
3. Put yourself in the position of the reader, keeping in mind that the purpose of the flowchart is to improve communications between one person and another concerning the method of solution for the problem.
4. Show the flow of processing from top to bottom and from left to right. When in doubt, use arrowheads as required to indicate the direction of flow.
5. Draw the flowchart so that it is neat and clear. Use the connector symbols to avoid excessively long flowlines.
6. Choose notation and wording that explain the function of each symbol in a clear and precise manner.

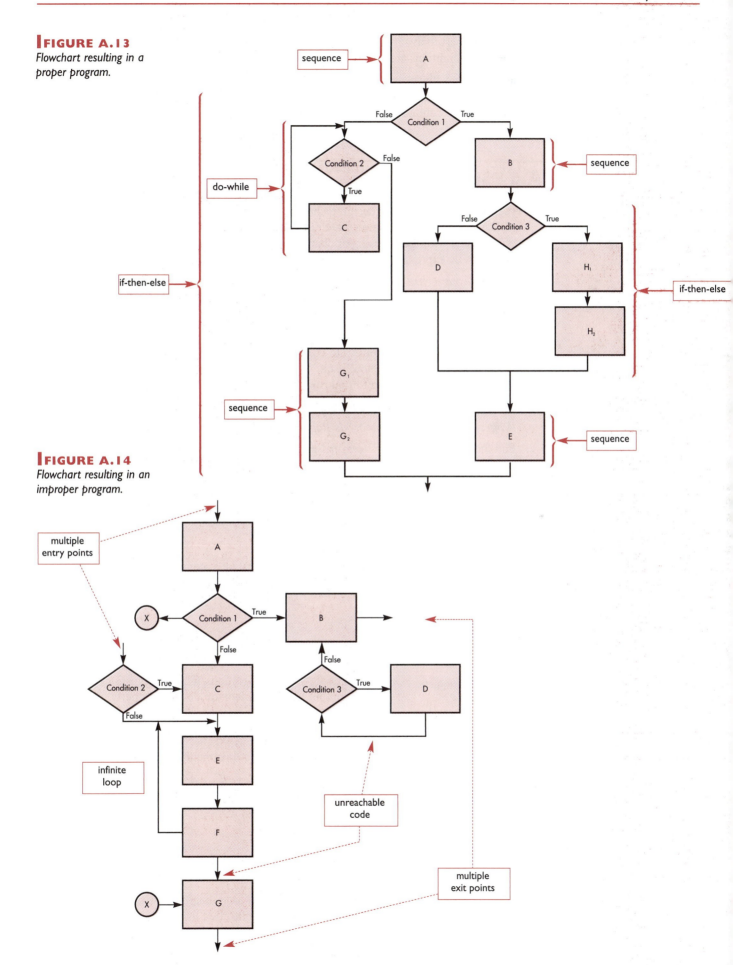

FIGURE A.13
Flowchart resulting in a proper program.

FIGURE A.14
Flowchart resulting in an improper program.

7. Do your best to avoid endless loops; construct loops so they will be terminated when specific conditions are satisfied.

The reason that flowcharts are so important is simple: the difficulties in programming lie mostly in the realm of logic, not in the syntax and semantics of the computer language. In other words, most computer errors are mistakes in logic, and a flowchart aids in detecting logic mistakes!

A.6 PSEUDOCODE

Pseudocode is a program design technique that uses natural English and resembles QBasic code. It is an intermediate notation that allows the logic of a program to be formulated without diagrams or charts. Pseudocode resembles QBasic in that specific operations can be expressed, as the following three examples demonstrate:

Read employee record
Add 1 to male counter
Display employee record

What makes pseudocode appealing to many programmers is that it has no formal syntactical rules, which allows programmers to concentrate on the design of the program rather than on the peculiarities of the logic tool itself.

Although pseudocode has no formal rules, the following are commonly accepted:

1. Begin the pseudocode with a program title statement.

   Program: Monthly Sales Analysis Report

2. End the pseudocode with a terminal program statement.

   End: Monthly Sales Analysis Report

3. Begin each statement on a new line. Use simple and short imperative sentences that contain a single transitive verb and a single object.

   Open employee file
   Subtract 10 from quantity

4. Express assignment as a formula or as an English-like statement.

   Withholding tax = 0. 20 × (gross pay – 38.46 × dependents)

   or

   Compute withholding tax

5. To implement the design, try to avoid using logic structures not available in the programming language being used.

6. For the If-Then-Else structure, use the following conventions:
   a. Indent the true and false tasks.
   b. Use *End If* as the structure terminator.
   c. Vertically align the If, Else, and End-if.

These conventions for the If-Then-Else structure are illustrated in Figures A.15 and A.16.

FIGURE A.15

```
If balance < 500 then
  Display credit ok
Else
  Display credit not ok
End if
```

7. For the Do-While structure, use the following conventions:

   a. If the structure represents a counter-controlled loop, begin the structure with *Do*.
   b. If the structure does not represent a counter-controlled loop, begin the structure with *Do While*.

   c. Specify the condition on the Do While or Do line.
   d. Use *End Do* as the last statement of the structure.
   e. Align the Do While or Do and the End Do vertically.
   f. Indent the statements within the loop.

FIGURE A.16

```
If gender code = male Then
  Add 1 to male count
  If age > 21 Then
    Add 1 to male adult count
  Else
    Add 1 to male minor count
  End if
Else
  Add 1 to female count
  If age > 21 Then
    Add 1 to female adult count
  Else
    Add 1 to female minor count
  End if
End if
```

The conventions for the Do-While structure are illustrated in Figures A.17 and A.18

FIGURE A.17

```
Program: Employee File List
Display report and column headings
Set employee count to 0
Read first employee record
Do While not end-of-file
    Add 1 to employee count
    Display employee record
    Read next employee record
End Do
Display employee count
Display end-of-job message
End: Employee File List
```

FIGURE A.18

```
Program: Sum first 100 Integers
Set sum to 0
Do integer = 1 to 100
    Add integer to sum
End Do
Display sum
Display end-of-job message
End: Sum first 100 Integers
```

8. For the Do-Until structure, use the following conventions:

   a. Begin the structure with *Do Until*.
   b. Specify the condition on the Do Until line.
   c. Use *End Do* as the last statement of the structure.
   d. Align the Do Until and the End Do vertically.
   e. Indent the statements within the loop.

The conventions for the Do-Until structure are illustrated in Figure A.19.

FIGURE A.19

```
Program: Sum first 100 Integers
Set sum to 0
Set integer to 1
Do Until integer >100
    Add integer to sum
    Add 1 to integer
End Do
Display sum
Display end-of-job message
End: Sum first 100 Integers
```

9. For the Case structure, use the following conventions:

   a. Begin the structure with *Start Case*, followed by the variable to be tested.
   b. Use *End Case* as the structure terminator.

c. Align *Start Case* and *End Case* vertically.

d. Indent each alternative.

e. Begin each alternative with *Case*, followed by the value of the variable that equates to the alternative.

f. Indent the action of each alternative.

These conventions are illustrated in Figure A.20.

FIGURE A.20

Start Case customer code
  Case 100
    Add 1 to high-risk customer count
  Case 200
    Add 1 to risk customer count
  Case 300
    Add 1 to regular customer count
  Case 400
    Add 1 to special customer count
End Case

For an additional example on using pseudocode, see Figure 1.14 in Chapter 1 on page 15 and Figure 1.15 on page 16.

A.7 NASSI-SCHNEIDERMAN CHARTS

Nassi-Schneiderman charts, also called **N-S charts**, are often referred to as structured flowcharts. Unlike program flowcharts, they contain no flowlines or flowchart symbols and thus have no provision to include a GOTO statement.

N-S charts are made up of a series of rectangles. The flow of control always runs top-to-bottom. The sequence structure in an N-S chart is illustrated in Figure A.21.

FIGURE A.21

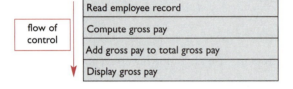

FIGURE A.22

	age ≥21	
False		True
Add 1 to minor count		Add 1 to adult count
Display "Minor"		Display "Adult"

The If-Then-Else structure is shown by three triangles within a rectangle and a vertical line separating the true and false tasks, as shown in Figure A.22. The N-S chart indicates a decision (age ≥ 21) and the actions to be taken for an adult and minor. If a person's age is greater than or equal to 21, then the actions specified for the true case are processed. If a person's age is less than 21, then the actions specified for the false case are processed. It is not possible for both the true and false tasks to be processed for the same person.

The Do-While structure (test at the top of the loop) is referred to by a rectangle within a rectangle, as shown in Figure A.23.

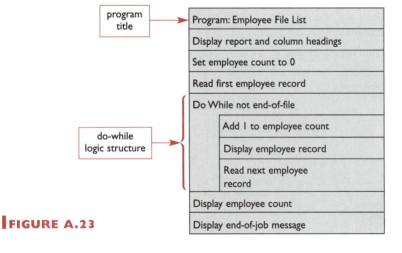

FIGURE A.23

The diagram indicates that the statements within the inner rectangle are to be processed in sequence as long as it is not end-of-file. When the end-of-file is sensed, control passes to the statement below the Do-While structure.

The Do-Until structure (test at the bottom of the loop) is similarly referred to by a rectangle within a rectangle, as shown in Figure A.24.

The Case structure is represented as shown in Figure A.25. As with the If-Then-Else structure, only one of the actions specified will be processed for each customer.

▌FIGURE A.24

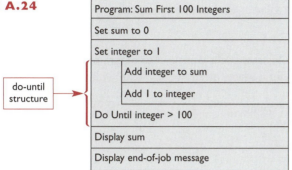

▌FIGURE A.25

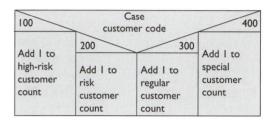

Those professionals who advocate the use of N-S charts claim they are effective in all phases of the program development cycle, especially for system and program documentation. Nassi and Schneiderman go even further. They write:

> Programmers who first learn to design programs with these symbols never develop the bad habits which other flowchart notation systems permit. . . . Since no more than fifteen or twenty symbols can be drawn on a single sheet of paper, the programmer must modularize his program into meaningful sections. The temptation to use off-page connectors, which lead only to confusion, is eliminated. Finally, the ease with which a structured flowchart can be translated into a structured program is pleasantly surprising. *

Other professionals argue that N-S charts are nothing more than pseudocode with lines and rectangles around it.

A.8 WARNIER-ORR DIAGRAMS

In some respects, a **Warnier-Orr diagram** is similar to a top-down chart laid on its side. Both place a heavy emphasis on the idea of hierarchies. Warnier-Orr diagrams, however, go one step further and place an equal emphasis on flow of control.

Chapter 3 illustrates that a top-down chart is used primarily to show functionality or *what* must be done to solve a problem. When a top-down chart is complete, an intermediate tool, such as a program flowchart, an N-S chart, or pseudocode must be used to show the flow of control, or *how* and *when* things are to be done in the framework of a solution. With Warnier-Orr diagrams, no such intermediate step is required.

As with N-S charts, solutions are constructed by means of the three basic logic structures: sequence, selection (If-Then-Else or Case), and repetition (Do While or Do Until).

A Warnier-Orr diagram is made up of a series of left braces, pseudocode-like statements, and a few special symbols, as shown in Table A.2 on the next page.

---

* I. Nassi and B. Schneiderman, "Flowchart Techniques for Structured Programming," SIGPLAN, Notices of the ACM, v.8, n. 8, August 1973: 12-16.

TABLE A.2 - Warnier-Orr Symbols and Their Meanings	
SYMBOL	MEANING
{	The brace is used to enclose logically related events.
(0, 1)	An event is done zero or one time. Notation for selection structure.
(0, n) or (n)	An event is done n times. Notation for Do-While structure.
(1, n)	An event is done one to n times. Notation for Do-Until structure.
blank or (1)	An event is done one time.
⊕	Exclusive OR. Used together with the notation (0, 1) to show a selection structure.

The Sequence structure is illustrated in a Warnier-Orr diagram by listing the sequence of events from top to bottom within a brace, as shown in Figure A.26.

FIGURE A.26

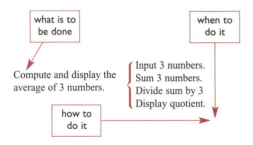

The left brace points to what is to be done. Within the brace is the list of events that show how to do it and, from top to bottom, when each event is to take place.

The If-Then-Else structure is shown by the use of the notation (0, 1) and the exclusive OR symbol. (See Figure A.27.) The Case structure is shown in a similar fashion. (See Figure A.28.)

FIGURE A.27

Increment male and female counters.
{
Male (0, 1) { Add 1 to male count.
⊕
Not Male (0,1) { Add 1 to female count.
}

FIGURE A.28

Evaluate customer code.
{
Code = 100 (0, 1) { Add 1 to high-risk customer count.
⊕
Code = 200 (0, 1) { Add 1 to risk customer count.
⊕
Code = 300 (0, 1) { Add 1 to regular customer count.
⊕
Code = 400 (0, 1) { Add 1 to special customer count.
}

The Warnier-Orr diagram in Figure A.29 shows a solution for reading an employee file and computing the gross pay for each employee. The solution includes a Do-While structure.

The event *Process file (0, records)* illustrates a Do-While structure. The *0* within parentheses means that the loop can be executed zero times if, for example, the employee file is empty. The term *records* within parentheses indicates the number of times the loop is to be executed. It is also valid to write the notation for the Do-While structure as *(records)*, rather than *(0, records)*.

The notation used to represent a Do-Until structure is similar to that of the Do-While structure except the notation below the event is written as (1, n) rather than (0, n), because the Do-Until structure is executed at least one time.

FIGURE A.29

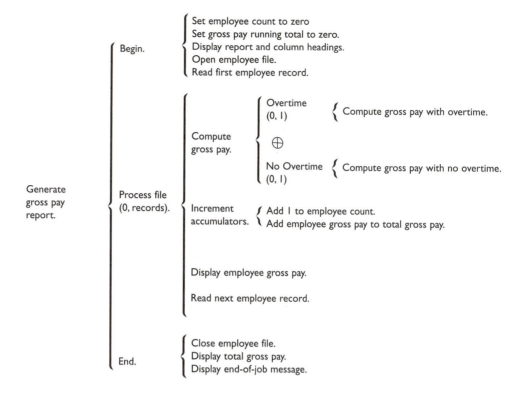

Generate gross pay report.

Begin.
- Set employee count to zero
- Set gross pay running total to zero.
- Display report and column headings.
- Open employee file.
- Read first employee record.

Process file (0, records).
- Compute gross pay.
  - Overtime (0, 1) — Compute gross pay with overtime.
  - ⊕
  - No Overtime (0, 1) — Compute gross pay with no overtime.
- Increment accumulators.
  - Add 1 to employee count.
  - Add employee gross pay to total gross pay.
- Display employee gross pay.
- Read next employee record.

End.
- Close employee file.
- Display total gross pay.
- Display end-of-job message.

A.9 Test Your QBasic Skills (Even-numbered answers are in Appendix E)

1. What is the first step in solving a problem that uses a computer?
2. Which of the flowchart symbols given in Chapter 1, Table 1.5 on page 14, are not required in that any program may be flowcharted without using them?
3. Can one flowchart symbol be used to simultaneously represent two or more QBasic statements?
4. In the flowchart in Figure A.30, what are the value of I and the value of J at the instant just after the statement J = J + 1 is executed for the fifth time? The value of I and J after the statement I = I + 2 is executed the 10th time? (A statement such as J = J + 1 is valid and is read as *the new value of J equals the old value of J plus one* or, equivalently, *the value of J is to be replaced by the value of J plus one*.)
5. Consider the flowchart portion in Figure A.31. It assumes that a relatively intelligent person is going to work. This individual usually has the car keys but occasionally forgets them. Does the flowchart portion in Figure A.31 incorporate the most efficient method of representing the actions to be taken? If not, redraw the flowchart portion given in Figure A.31.

FIGURE A.30

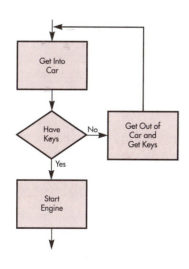

FIGURE A.31

FIGURE A.32

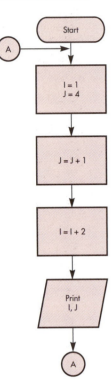

6. In Figure A.32, the flowchart of a valid though trivial program, what values of I and of J are printed when the output symbol is executed for the fiftieth time?

7. Two numbers U and V, located in main memory, are to be interchanged. Construct the flowchart (or N-S chart, or pseudocode or Warnier-Orr diagram) to represent this interchange.

8. Construct an efficient flowchart to solve for the roots of the following equation:

$$ax^2 + bx + c = 0 \text{ using the following formula: } x = \frac{-b \pm \sqrt{b^2 - 4ac}}{2a}$$

input three values containing the coefficients *a*, *b*, and *c*, respectively. Print the values of the two real roots. If complex roots exist ($b^2 - 4ac < 0$), print a message to that effect. If the roots are equal, print one root. (Assume that the coefficient *a* does not have a value of zero so that an attempted division by zero will not occur.)

Problems 9-12: An employee file contains the following data on each employee:

- Name
- Gender — M for male or F for female
- Age — a two-digit number between 18 and 65 inclusive
- Education — 1 for 11th grade education or less, 2 for high school diploma, 3 for bachelor's degree, or 4 for master's degree
- Race — 1 for Black, 2 for Caucasian, 3 for Hispanic, or 4 for Other
- Seniority — a two-digit number between 0 and 46

9. Construct the flowchart (or N-S chart, or pseudocode, or Warnier-Orr Diagram) to read the records in the employee file, print the number of males, the number of females, the total number of employees, and the percentage that are male and percentage female.

10. Construct the flowchart (or N-S chart, or pseudocode, or Warnier-Orr Diagram) to print the number of employees who are female Blacks or female Hispanics that have a bachelor's or master's degree.

11. Construct the flowchart (or N-S chart, or pseudocode, or Warnier-Orr Diagram) to print the name and age of all male employees greater than or equal to the age of 64.

FIGURE A.33

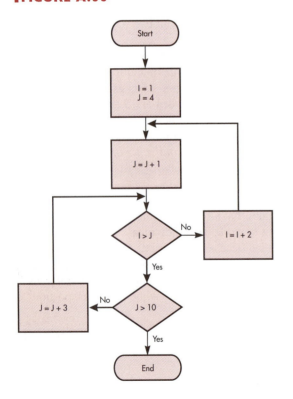

12. Construct the flowchart (or N-S chart, or pseudocode, or Warnier-Orr Diagram) to print the Name, Gender, Education, Race, and Seniority of those employees who are female, Hispanic or Other, have a high school diploma or less, and have more than 20 years seniority. Also print the number of employees that meets these requirements.

13. An opaque urn contains three diamonds, four rubies, and two pearls. Construct a flowchart that describes the following events: Draw a gem from the urn. If it is a diamond, lay it aside. If it is not a diamond, return it to the urn. Continue in this fashion until all the diamonds have been removed. After all the diamonds have been removed, repeat the same procedure until all the rubies have been removed. After all the rubies have been removed, continue in the same fashion until all the pearls have been removed.

14. In the flowchart represented by Figure A.33, what is the value of I and the value of J at the instant the terminal symbol with the word End is reached?

15. **Part I:** Draw one flowchart, and only one, that will cause the *mechanical mouse* to go through any of the four mazes shown in Figure A.34. At the beginning, a user will place the mouse on the entry side of the maze, in front of the entry point, facing *up* toward the maze. The instruction *Move to next cell* will put the mouse inside the maze. Each maze has four cells. After that, the job is to move from cell to cell until the mouse emerges on the exit side. If the mouse is instructed to *Move to next cell* when there is a wall in front of it, it will hit the wall and fall apart. Obviously, the mouse must be instructed to test whether it is *Facing a wall* before any *Move*. The mechanical mouse's instruction set is listed below Figure A.34.

FIGURE A.34

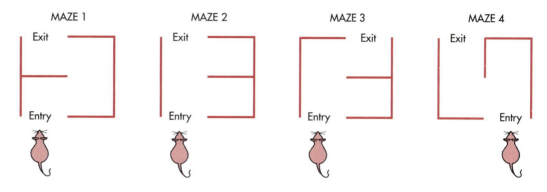

a. Physical movement:
   (1) Move to next cell. (The mouse will move in the direction it is facing.)
   (2) Turn right.
   (3) Turn left.
   (4) Turn around. (All turns are made in place, without moving to another cell.)
   (5) Halt.

b. Logic:
   (1) Facing a wall? (Through this test, the mouse determines whether there is a wall immediately in front of it, that is, on the border of the cell it is occupying and in the direction it is facing.)
   (2) Outside the maze?
   (3) On the entry side?
   (4) On the exit side?

Part II (Extra Credit): If your flowchart can cause the mechanical mouse to go through all of the mazes in Part I without falling apart, then try your flowchart for mazes 5, 6, and 7 in Figure A.35 on the next page. See whether you can produce one flowchart that will work for mazes 1 through 7.

FIGURE A.35

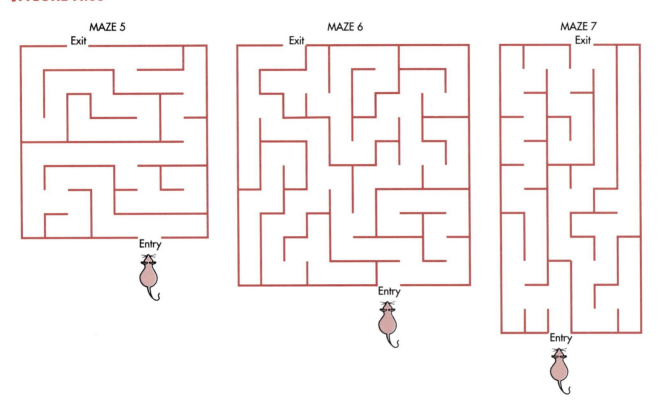

Menu Commands and Windows

This appendix describes the functions of the QBasic commands that are accessible through the menu bar at the top of the screen. This appendix also describes how to manipulate the windows on the screen to your advantage.

B.1 SELECTING COMMANDS

The menu bar is at the top of the screen (Figure B.1). To open the File menu (Figure B.2 on the next page), click the menu name. When the menu is open, click the desired command. To close the opened menu, click the view window or click another menu name on the menu bar. The term *click* means move the mouse pointer to the command or area and then press and release the left mouse button.

FIGURE B.1
The menu bar.

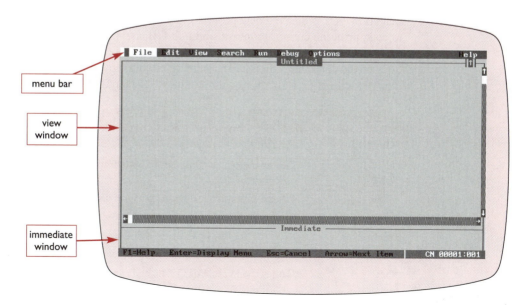

menu bar

view window

immediate window

525

FIGURE B.2

The File menu.

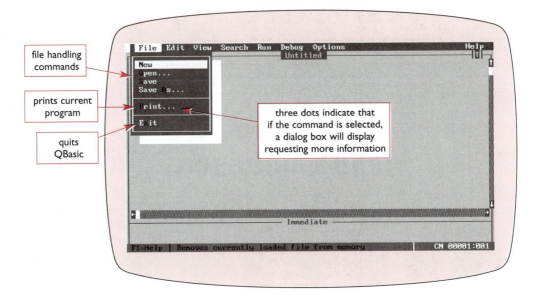

Certain menu commands can be executed directly from the view window by pressing the corresponding shortcut key. Shortcut keys reduce the number of keystrokes required to execute a command and thus save time. The shortcut keys and the commands they execute are described in the appropriate tables of this appendix.

B.2 THE QBASIC MENU BAR

The following sections describe the commands available in each menu of QBasic.

The File Menu

The File menu (Figure B.2) is used more than any other menu. It includes the commands that allow you to create a new program, load a program from disk, save the current program to disk, print the current program, and quit QBasic. (See Sections 2.7 and 2.8 in Chapter 2 for examples of the use of the commands on the File menu.) Table B.1 summarizes the functions of the commands on the File menu. Note that any command that ends with three dots means additional information will be requested via a dialog box.

TABLE B.1 - The File Menu	
COMMAND	**FUNCTION**
New	Causes the current program to be erased and indicates the beginning of a new program.
Open ...	Loads a previously stored program on disk into main memory.
Save	Saves the current program to disk under its previously assigned name.
Save As ...	Saves the current program to disk under a specified name.
Print ...	Prints all or part of the current program on the printer.
Exit	Causes the PC to exit QBasic and returns control to DOS or Windows.

The Edit Menu

The Edit menu (Figure B.3) primarily is used to delete, copy, and move blocks of code in the current program. (See Section 2.6 in Chapter 2 for additional editing techniques.)

FIGURE B.3
The Edit menu.

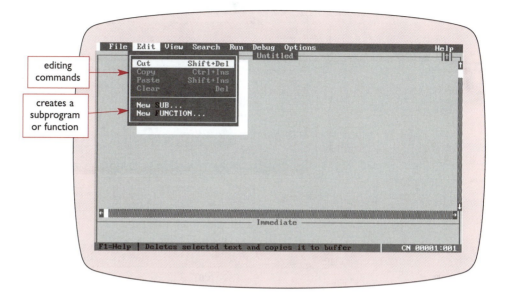

editing commands

creates a subprogram or function

Some of the Edit commands require you to select first the block of code in the current program. Drag the mouse pointer from the first character of the block to the last. Dragging the pointer highlights the block of code. Dragging is the process of moving the mouse while holding down the left mouse button.

Table B.2 describes the functions of the Edit commands and the shortcut keys. For example, the shortcut Shift+Delete means hold down the Shift key and then press the Delete key to delete the selected text and place it on the clipboard.

	TABLE B.2 - The Edit Menu	
COMMAND	**SHORTCUT KEYS**	**FUNCTION**
Cut	Shift+Delete	Cuts (deletes) the selected block of code from the current program and places it on the Clipboard.
Copy	Ctrl+Insert	Copies the selected block of code in the current program to the Clipboard.
Paste	Shift+Insert	Pastes (inserts) at the cursor location of the current program the block of code on the Clipboard.
Clear	Delete	Cuts (deletes) the selected block of code from the current program.
New SUB . . .		Opens a window for a new Subprogram.
New FUNCTION . . .		Opens a window for a new Function.

The View Menu

The View menu (Figure B.4 on the next page) includes commands that allow you to modify what is displayed on the screen. Table B.3 on the next page summarizes the View menu commands.

FIGURE B.4

The View menu.

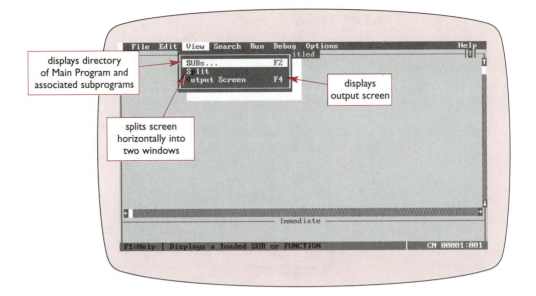

displays directory
of Main Program and
associated subprograms

displays
output screen

splits screen
horizontally into
two windows

TABLE B.3 - The View Menu		
COMMAND	**SHORTCUT KEYS**	**FUNCTION**
SUBs ...	F2	Displays a list of the names of the Main Program and associated subprograms and functions. (For additional information, see Section 11.3 in Chapter 11.)
Split		Toggles between a split-view window and a single-view window.
Output Screen	F4	Switches the display from the view window to the output screen.

The Search Menu

The Search menu (Figure B.5) is used to find strings as well as replace strings in the current program. Table B.4 describes the functions of the Search commands.

FIGURE B.5

The Search menu.

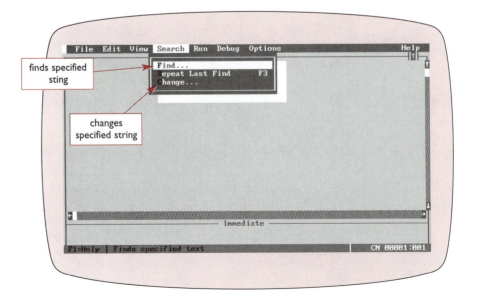

finds specified
sting

changes
specified string

TABLE B.4 - The Search Menu		
COMMAND	SHORTCUT KEYS	FUNCTION
Find ...		Finds specified string.
Repeat Last Find	F3	Finds next specified string.
Change ...		Changes specified string to another string.

The Run Menu

The Run menu (Figure B.6) includes commands that are used primarily to execute the current program. Table B.5 describes the functions of the Run commands.

FIGURE B.6

The Run menu.

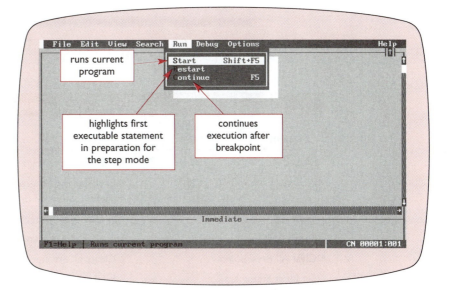

TABLE B.5 - The Run Menu		
COMMAND	SHORTCUT KEYS	FUNCTION
Start	Shift+F5	Runs the current program in the view window.
Restart		Restarts the current program from the beginning. Halts on the line with the first executable statement and highlights it in preparation for the step mode.
Continue	F5	Continues execution from the last statement executed if the current program was suspended, or executes the current program from the beginning.

The Debug Menu

The Debug menu (Figure B.7 on the next page) includes commands used to debug the current program. Table B.6 on the next page describes the functions of the Debug commands. (For additional information and examples on the use of the commands in the Debug menu, see Section C.1 in Appendix C.)

FIGURE B.7
The Debug menu.

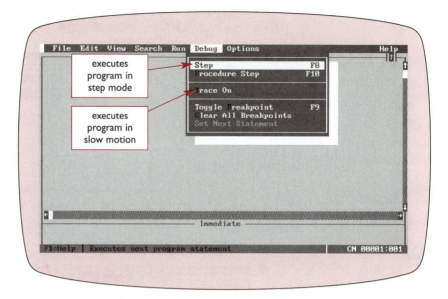

FIGURE B.7
The Debug menu.

TABLE B.6 - The Debug Menu		
COMMAND	**SHORTCUT KEYS**	**FUNCTION**
Step	F8	Executes the program one statement at a time.
Procedure Step	F10	Executes the program one statement at a time and bypasses any subprogram or function calls.
Trace On		Executes the program in slow motion.
Toggle Breakpoint	F9	Toggles the breakpoint on and off at the cursor location.
Clear All Breakpoints		Clears all breakpoints.
Set Next Statement		Establishes the next line to execute in a program that has been halted. Execution continues at the line to which the cursor was moved.

The Options Menu

The Options menu (Figure B.8) contains commands that control some of the special features of QBasic. Table B.7 describes the functions of the Options commands.

FIGURE B.8
The Options menu.

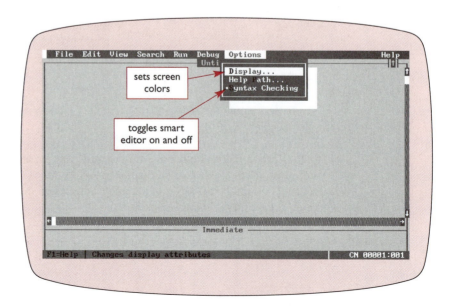

TABLE B.7 - The Options Menu	
COMMAND	**FUNCTION**
Display ...	Sets the display attributes (colors, scroll bars, tab stops).
Help Path ...	Sets the search paths for Help files.
Syntax Checking	Turns QBasic's smart editor on and off. The **smart editor** checks for **syntax errors**, formats lines, and translates the line to executable form if the syntax is correct.

The Help Menu

The Help menu (Figure B.9) offers on-line help through the QB Survival Guide. Table B.8 summarizes the five Help commands found in the Help menu. (For additional information on the QB Survival Guide, see Section 2.9 in Chapter 2.)

FIGURE B.9

The Help menu.

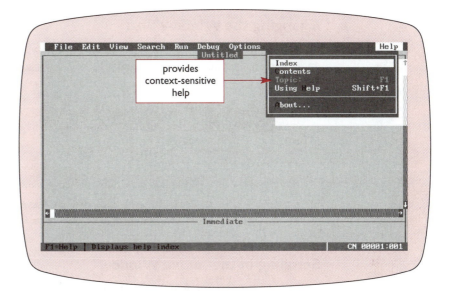

TABLE B.8 - The Help Menu		
COMMAND	**SHORTCUT KEYS**	**FUNCTION**
Index		Displays an alphabetical list of the QBasic keywords. Move the cursor to any keyword and right-click or press F1 for information on the keyword.
Contents		Displays a table of contents. Move the cursor to any subject and right-click or press F1.
Topic:	F1	Displays information on the syntax and usage of the QBasic variable, symbol, keyword, menu, command, or dialog box at or containing the cursor.
Using Help	Shift+F1	Displays information on how to use the mouse or keyboard to get help on an item displayed on the screen.
About ...		Displays a QBasic copyright message.

B.3 USING WINDOWS TO YOUR ADVANTAGE

When you start QBasic, two windows display on the screen — the view window and the immediate window, as shown in Figure 2.4 on page 33. Two other windows open up when certain commands are used. The help window opens at the top of the screen when you request context-sensitive help. In this section we describe how you can change the active window, change the window size, and scroll within the window.

Changing the Active Window

The window that contains the cursor is the active window. To make another window active, press F6 or Shift+F6. F6 cycles the cursor down through the windows. Shift+F6 cycles the cursor up through the windows.

To use your mouse, move the mouse pointer to the window you want to activate and click the left mouse button.

Changing the Window Size

You can increase or decrease the size of a window, or expand a window to encompass the entire screen. The keys used to change the window size are summarized in Table B.9.

TABLE B.9 - Changing the Window Size	
KEYS	FUNCTION
Alt+Plus key (+)	Increases the size of the active window by one line.
Alt+Minus key (–)	Decreases the size of the active window by one line.
Ctrl+F10	Toggles between expanding the active window to encompass the screen and returning the active window to its former size.

Scrolling in the Active Window

If the program is too wide or too long to fit in the view window, you can move the window up, down, right, or left one character at a time by using the arrow keys. Table B.10 summarizes the keys for moving the window more than one character at a time. Moving the window to view parts of the program that do not fit on the screen is called scrolling.

TABLE B.10 - Scrolling More Than One Character at a Time	
KEYS	FUNCTION
Home	Beginning of line.
End	End of line.
Page Up	Page up one full window.
Page Down	Page down one full window.
Ctrl+Page Up	Left one full window.
Ctrl+Page Down	Right one full window.
Ctrl+Home	Move window so beginning of program shows.
Ctrl+End	Move window so end of program shows.

With your mouse, you can move the window up, down, right, or left by dragging the mouse pointer along the scroll bars located at the bottom and right side of the view window. The scroll bars are shown in Figure 2.4 on page 33.

QBasic Debugging Techniques and Programming Tips

C.1 DEBUGGING TECHNIQUES

Although the top-down approach and structured programming techniques help minimize errors, they by no means guarantee error-free programs. Owing to carelessness or insufficient thought, programs can be constructed that do not work as anticipated and give erroneous results. When such problems occur, techniques are needed to isolate the errors and correct the erroneous program statements.

QBasic can detect many **grammatical errors** and display appropriate diagnostic messages. However, no programming language can detect all errors. Some of these errors can go undetected by QBasic until either an abnormal end occurs during execution or the program terminates with the results in error.

Several techniques are available for attempting to discover the portion of the program that is in error. These methods are called **debugging techniques**. The errors themselves are **bugs**, and the activity involved in their detection is **debugging**. QBasic has a fully integrated debugger that pinpoints errors by tracing, or highlighting, the QBasic source code. The QBasic debugging features include the following:

1. Examining values through the immediate window
2. Executing one statement at a time
3. Setting breakpoints
4. Tracing
5. Set next statement
6. Break on errors

Examining Values through the Immediate Window

Following the execution of a program, the program's variables remain equal to the latest values assigned. Through the immediate window, you can examine their values. This is an easy-to-use and yet powerful debugging tool.

To activate the immediate window, click anywhere in the window. You may then display the values of any variables in the program by using the PRINT statement and the names of the variables. When a statement is entered in the immediate window, it is executed immediately. After viewing the values, deactivate the immediate window and activate the view window by clicking anywhere in the view window.

Executing One Statement at a Time

Another debugging tool is the step mode shown on the Debug menu, Figure B.7 on page 530. In the **step mode**, the PC executes the program one statement at a time. To activate the step mode, click Step on the Debug menu or press F8. The first time you press F8, the PC displays and highlights the first executable statement in reverse video. Thereafter, each time you press the F8 key, the PC executes the statement in reverse video and displays the next executable statement in reverse video. Hence, the PC steps through the program one statement at a time as you press F8.

While the PC is in step mode and before you press the F8 key again, you can do any of the following to better understand what the program is doing:

1. Activate the immediate window and use the PRINT statement to display the values of variables.
2. Use the F4 key to toggle between displaying the program and the output screen.
3. Modify any statement in the program. If you modify the statement in reverse video, the reverse video disappears. However, it reappears as soon as you move the cursor off the line.

To exit step mode, press F5. The F5 key continues normal execution of the program. If you want to halt the program again, press Ctrl+Break. To continue execution after pressing Ctrl+Break, you can do one of the following:

1. Click Run and then click Continue (or press F5) to continue normal execution.
2. Click Run and then click Start (or press Shift+F5) to start execution from the beginning of the program.
3. Click Debug and then click Step (or press F8) to activate step mode.

Setting Breakpoints

A **breakpoint** is a line in the program where you want execution to halt. Breakpoints are established by moving the cursor to the line in question and then pressing F9 or selecting the Toggle Breakpoint command on the Debug menu (Figure B.7 on page 530). When you execute the program after setting one or more breakpoints, the PC halts execution at the next breakpoint and displays and highlights it in reverse video. When the program halts at a breakpoint, you can do one of the following:

1. Press F8 to enter step mode and execute one statement at a time to the next breakpoint.
2. Display the values of variables in the immediate window.
3. Edit the program.
4. Delete or add new breakpoints.
5. Click Run and then click Continue (or press F5) to continue execution of the program.

To toggle off a breakpoint, move the cursor to the breakpoint and press F9. An alternative method for clearing breakpoints is to select the command Clear All Breakpoints on the Debug menu. This latter method can be useful, especially when you have set a number of breakpoints and cannot remember where they are located in the program. A breakpoint displays only in reverse video when it halts execution of the program.

To save time, you should select breakpoints carefully. Commonly used breakpoints include lines immediately following input, calculations, and decision statements.

Tracing

The Trace On command on the Debug menu (Figure B.7 on page 530) causes the PC to trace the program. **Tracing** means that the program will execute in slow motion. As the program executes in slow motion, the PC highlights each statement as it executes it. With the Trace On command you can quickly get an idea of the flow of control in your program. This activity must be observed to be appreciated.

The Trace On command works like a toggle switch. Select it once and the PC will trace the flow of control. Select it again, and you turn tracing off. You know that tracing is on when a bullet displays in front of the command in the Debug menu.

Two QBasic statements that carry out the same function as the Trace On command are TRON and TROFF. The TRON statement turns on tracing for all future statements executed. The TROFF statement turns tracing off. Although most QBasic programmers use the Trace On command to trace a program, some find the TRON and TROFF statements useful for tracing small sections of a program.

Set Next Statement

The Set Next Statement command on the Debug menu allows you to establish with the cursor where execution will continue following a program halt. For example, assume that you have set a breakpoint in a program. When the PC halts execution at the statement, you can move the cursor to any line in the program and select the Set Next Statement command. When execution resumes, it will begin at the line where the cursor resides rather than at the statement in reverse video. The Set Next Statement command works much like the infamous GOTO statement. Use caution when evaluating the program results following the use of this command because skipping over code can produce unexpected results.

C.2 TRAPPING USER ERRORS (ON ERROR GOTO AND RESUME)

A thoroughly tested program cannot be guaranteed to be reliable once it is turned over to a user. Most abnormal terminations in a production environment are due to user errors and not programmer errors. This is especially true for programs that interact with the user. Good programmers will attempt to trap as many user errors as possible. User errors fall into two basic categories:

1. Erroneous data entered in response to INPUT statements
2. Failure to follow the instructions given

Errors that fall into the first category can be trapped by validating incoming data to ensure it is reasonable or within limits as shown in Chapter 5. The second category of user errors includes both soft errors and hard errors. A **soft error** is any error that causes the PC to display a diagnostic message followed by continued execution of the program. Entering string data in response to an INPUT statement with a numeric variable is an example of a soft error. The PC will display an error message and request the data be re-entered.

A **hard error** is any error that causes the PC to display a dialog box with a diagnostic message followed by termination of execution of the program. Examples of hard errors include the following:

1. Not placing a floppy disk in the disk drive
2. A defective disk
3. A floppy disk that has not been formatted

In some situations, it is preferable to handle both hard and soft errors within the program through the use of the ON ERROR GOTO and RESUME statements. The ON ERROR GOTO **statement** provides a common branch point for any error that occurs following its execution in a program. The branch point and the statements that follow it are an **error-handling routine**. In an error-handling routine, it is often desirable to resume execution of the program at a specified point. The RESUME **statement** is used for this purpose. The general forms of the ON ERROR GOTO and RESUME statements are shown in Tables C.1 and C.2.

TABLE C.1 - The ON ERROR GOTO Statement	
General Form:	ON ERROR GOTO label where **label** is equal to a line label or line number.
Purpose:	Activates error trapping and specifies the line label or line number of an error-handling routine to transfer control to when an error occurs. When label = 0, error trapping is deactivated, and a diagnostic message is displayed followed by termination of the program.
Examples:	ON ERROR GOTO X100.Special.Handler ON ERROR GOTO X200.Error.Routine ON ERROR GOTO 0
Note:	In the error-trapping routine, the special variables ERR and ERL may be tested where ERR represents the error code of the last error and ERL represents the line number of the statement that caused the error. ERL returns 0 if no line numbers are used in the program.

TABLE C.2 - The RESUME Statement	
General Form:	RESUME n where **n** is null, zero, label, or the keyword NEXT.
Purpose:	Continues execution of the program after an error-handling routine has been performed. RESUME or RESUME 0 resumes execution at the statement that caused the error. RESUME NEXT resumes execution at the statement immediately following the one that caused the error. RESUME label resumes execution at the specified line label or line number.
Examples:	RESUME RESUME 0 RESUME NEXT RESUME Around
Note:	This statement should not be executed unless the ON ERROR GOTO statement has been previously executed.

After the ON ERROR GOTO statement is inserted in a program, any error that normally terminates execution now causes the PC to transfer control to the error-handling routine. QBasic provides two functions, ERL and ERR, that return values before the ON ERROR GOTO statement transfers control to the error-handling routine. ERL is assigned the line number of the statement that caused the error. If line numbers are not used, then ERL returns a zero. ERR is assigned an error code as shown in Table C.3.

Table C.3 lists the error description and corresponding error code the ON ERROR GOTO statement traps. The table entries are alphabetized by error description.

Through the use of IF statements, a decision can be made in the error-handling routine to terminate execution or resume execution at some point in the program. The ON ERROR GOTO 0 statement directs the PC to disable error trapping, display a diagnostic message, and terminate execution. On the other hand, the RESUME statement may be used to transfer control to any point in the program to continue execution. If execution is to resume following an

TABLE C.3 – Error Descriptions and Their Corresponding Error Codes

ERROR DESCRIPTION	ERROR CODE	ERROR DESCRIPTION	ERROR CODE	ERROR DESCRIPTION	ERROR CODE
Advanced feature	73	Permission denied	70	Out of string space	14
Bad file mode	54	Division by zero	11	Overflow	6
Bad file name	64	Duplicate definition	10	Path/file access error	75
Bad file number	52	Field overflow	50	Path not found	76
Bad record number	63	FIELD statement		Rename across disks	74
Bad record length	59	active	56	RESUME without	
CASE ELSE expected	39	File already exists	58	error	20
Communication		File already open	55	RETURN without	
buffer overflow	69	File not found	53	GOSUB	3
Device fault	25	Illegal function call	5	String formula too	
Device I/0 error	57	Input past end	62	complex	16
Device timeout	24	Internal error	51	Subscript out of range	9
Device unavailable	68	No RESUME	19	Syntax error	2
Disk full	61	Out of data	4	Too many files	67
Disk media error	72	Out of memory	7	Type mismatch	13
Disk not ready	71	Out of paper	27	Variable required	40

error, an error recovery procedure, such as displaying a message or assigning a value to a variable, is performed before resuming execution outside the error-handling routine. The ON ERROR GOTO statement must be placed in a program in such a way that it is executed before the lines in which errors are to be trapped.

Program C.1 uses the ON ERROR GOTO statement to trap user errors. In the error-handling routine, the ERR function is compared to selected error codes. If ERR is equal to 25 (Device fault, such as printer not ready) or 27 (Out of paper), a recovery procedure is executed. If ERR equals any other code, then a message is displayed informing the user to record the program name and the error code, and transmit this information to someone in charge of resolving the error.

Use the letter X to identify error-catching subroutines. The letter X will cause these subroutines to reside at the very bottom of the program listing.

PROGRAM C.1

```
1    ' Program C.1
2    ' Illustrating the Use of
3    ' the ON ERROR GOTO Statement
4    ' ***************************
5    ON ERROR GOTO Handler
6    LPRINT "Number", "Amount"
7    LPRINT
8    READ Number$, Amount
9    DO WHILE Number$ <> "EOF"
10       LPRINT Number$, Amount
11       READ Number$, Amount
12    LOOP
13    LPRINT "Job Complete"
```

(continued)

PROGRAM C.1

(continued)

```
14    ' *******Data Follows********
15    DATA 123, 124.89, 126, 145.91, 134, 234.78
16    DATA 210, 567.34, 235, 435.12, 345, 192.45
17    DATA EOF, 0
18    END
19
20    ' **************************
21    ' *  Error-Handling Routine *
22    ' **************************
23    Handler:
24       CLS  ' Clear Screen
25       SELECT CASE ERR
26          CASE 25, 27
27             GOSUB X100.Printer.Error
28             RESUME
29          CASE ELSE
30             GOSUB X110.Irrecoverable.Error
31             END
32       END SELECT
33    RETURN
34
35    ' *************************
36    ' *      Printer Error      *
37    ' *************************
38    X100.Printer.Error:
39       PRINT "Please check the printer."
40       PRINT "It may be turned off, out of"
41       PRINT "paper or it is not properly"
42       PRINT "connected."
43       PRINT
44       INPUT "Press the Enter key when the printer is ready...", Control$
45    RETURN
46
47    ' *************************
48    ' *   Irrecoverable Error   *
49    ' *************************
50    X110.Irrecoverable.Error:
51       BEEP: BEEP: BEEP: BEEP
52       PRINT "An Irrecoverable error has occurred"
53       PRINT "Please copy down the following:"
54       PRINT "error code.  Transmit the error code"
55       PRINT "and the program name to the Data"
56       PRINT "Processing department."
57       PRINT
58       PRINT "Error code ========> "; ERR
59       PRINT : PRINT "Thank You"
60    RETURN
```

In Program C.1, line 5 activates QBasic's error-trapping feature. If an error occurs following line 5, then control transfers to line 23. In the SELECT CASE (lines 25 through 32), if the error code is equal to 25 or 27, then control passes to the subroutine X100.Printer.Error (lines 38 through 45) and an appropriate message is displayed. If the error code is not 25 or 27, then control transfers to the X100.Irrecoverable.Error subroutine (lines 50 through 60) and a message displays requesting the user to transmit the error code and the program name to someone in charge of resolving the error.

A second END statement is used in line 31 instead of a STOP statement or ON ERROR GOTO 0, so the output screen remains on the monitor to give the user the opportunity to copy the message. Both STOP and ON ERROR GOTO 0 cause the PC to immediately display the view window rather than the output screen.

C.3 PROGRAMMING TIPS

Many different ways are available to code a program using QBasic and still obtain the same results. This section presents some tips for coding a program to improve its performance, efficiency, structure, and clarity. Each tip is explained and applied accordingly. You are encouraged to add to the tips in this section.

Tip 1: Use Simple Arithmetic

Addition is performed faster than multiplication, which in turn is faster than division or exponentiation. For example, use the code on the left rather than on the right.

```
Area = Base * Height * .5          instead of:   Area = Base * Height / 2
Length = Side1 + Side1                            Length = 2 * Side1
Vol = Length * Length * Length                    Vol = Length ^ 3
```

Tip 2: Avoid Repetitive Evaluations of Expressions

If identical computations are performed in several statements, evaluate the common expression once and save the result in a variable for use in later statements. For example, use the code on the left rather than on the right.

```
Disc = SQR(B * B - 4 * A * C)    instead of:   Root1 = -B + SQR(B * B - 4 * A * C)
Root1 = -B + Disc                              Root2 = -B - SQR(B * B - 4 * A * C)
Root2 = -B - Disc
```

Tip 3: Avoid Recomputation of Constants within a Loop

Do not make unnecessary computations. Remove the unnecessary code from a loop including expressions and statements that do not affect the loop. Place such code outside and before the range of the loop. For example, use the code on the left rather than on the right.

```
Pi = 3.141598           instead of:   Pi = 3.141598
K = 4 * Pi                            FOR Rad = 1 TO 500
X = Y + 2                                PRINT 4 * Pi * Rad * Rad
FOR Rad = 1 TO 500                       X = Y + 2
   PRINT K * Rad * Rad               NEXT Rad
NEXT Rad
```

Regardless of the value of Rad, 4π is always constant. Instead of calculating 4π five hundred times, remove this expression from the loop and compute it once. It also is not necessary to compute the value of X each time through the loop because the loop never changes the value of X.

Tip 4: Use Integer Variables for Counters and Whole Number Running Totals

Integer arithmetic is many times faster than single-precision arithmetic. Hence, use integer variables for counters and whole number running totals in a program. For example, use the code on the next page.

```
Count% = Count% + 1
Enrollment% = Enrollment% + Division%
```

instead of:

```
Count = Count + 1
Enrollment = Enrollment + Division
```

If you wish to avoid writing the percent sign (%) after each variable name and still use the latter two statements as they are, you may precede these statements with:

```
DEFINT C-E
```

which declares all variables whose names begin with C through E as integer type.

Tip 5: Use Integer Variables As the Control Variables in For Loops

For the same reason indicated in Tip 4, use integer variables rather than single-precision variables for the loop variable in a FOR statement as shown by the partial programs in Figures 8.9 and 8.10 on page 324. For example, use the following code:

```
FOR Loop.Variable% = 1 TO 1000
```

instead of:

```
FOR Loop.Variable = 1 TO 1000
```

(Note that the code in Tip 3 can further be improved by applying Tip 5 to the variable named RAD.)

Tip 6: Use For Loops instead of Do Loops for Counter-Controlled Loops

For loops execute faster than Do loops. Thus, when the loop is controlled by a counter, use a For loop rather than a Do loop. For example, use the code on the left rather than on the right.

```
FOR I% = 1 TO 10          instead of:          I% = 1
     .                                          DO WHILE I% <= 10
     .                                               .
     .                                               .
NEXT I%                                              .
                                                I% = I% + 1
                                                LOOP
```

Tip 7: Use QBasic Functions

Use the QBasic functions wherever possible because in many cases they conserve main memory and execute faster than the same capability written in QBasic. For example, use the code on the left rather than on the right.

```
Disc = SQR(B * B - 4 * A * C)    instead of: Disc = (B * B - 4 * A * C) ^ (0.5)
```

Tip 8: Write Clearly and Avoid Clever or Tricky Code

Resist the temptation to write clever or tricky code that is difficult to understand. Later modification by someone else may take additional time and may be costly in the long run. For example, use the following code.

```
FOR Row% = 1 TO 10
   FOR Column% = 1 TO 10
      IF Row% = Column% THEN
         Array(Row%, Column%) = 1
      ELSE
         Array(Row%, Column%) = 0
      END IF
   NEXT Column%
NEXT Row%
```

instead of:

```
FOR Row = 1 TO 10
   FOR Column = 1 TO 10
      Array(Row, Column) = INT(Row / Column) * INT(Column / Row)
   NEXT Column
NEXT Row
```

This section of code generates an array called Array where ones are placed on the main diagonal and zeros everywhere else.

Tip 9: Avoid Needless IF Statements Whenever Possible

You can avoid the need for more IF statements and additional code if you use compound conditions in IF statements. For example, do the following:

```
IF I = J AND K = L THEN
   A = 99
END IF
```

instead of:

```
IF I = J THEN
   IF K = L THEN
      A = 99
   END IF
END IF
```

Tip 10: Use the SELECT CASE Rather Than IF Statements When More Than Two Paths are Involved

The SELECT CASE statement is easier for maintenance programmers to read and interpret than a series of nested IF statements. For an example, see page 170 in Chapter 5.

To make a SELECT CASE statement efficient, place the CASE statements with the most frequently occurring conditions first.

C.4 PROGRAM STYLE TIPS

Throughout this book we have offered tips on how to style your program. The following list summarizes these tips.

Tip 1:   A program should be easy for a person to read and understand.
Tip 2:   Use blank spaces to improve readability.
Tip 3:   Use one statement per line unless multiple statements improve readability.

Tip 4: At the beginning of the program, include comments to identify the author, date written, program name, and to describe what the program does. (See Chapter 2, page 50.) Depending on the complexity of the program, you may want to include comments pertaining to usage, I/O requirements, execution time, and special operating requirements.

Tip 5: Use a boxed-in comment at the beginning of each subroutine to identify it and clarify any ambiguities.

Tip 6: Begin a subroutine name with a letter. The letter should identify the leg to which the subroutine belongs in the top-down chart. Begin with the letter A in the left-most leg, followed by the letter B for the next leg, and so on.

Tip 7: Develop a method for naming special-type subroutines, such as those that have multiple superiors or are error-catching subroutines. For example, begin subroutine names that have multiple superiors with the letter M. Begin error-catching subroutines with the letter X.

Tip 8: Follow the letter in a subroutine name with a level number (for example, 100, 200, 310, etc.). The level number should correspond to the level of the corresponding module in the top-down chart.

Tip 9: Follow the letter and level number with a period (.) and a self-explanatory subroutine name.

Tip 10: Do not comment for the sake of commenting. Comments should add to the understanding of a section of code.

Tip 11: Be sure all variable names and label names are meaningful and self-explanatory.

Tip 12: Capitalize only the first letter in a variable name or label name. If two or more words make up the name, then separate the two words with a period and capitalize the first letter of each word. Capitalize all the letters in a FUNCTION name.

Tip 13: Use parentheses in complex expressions with arithmetic, relational, or logical operators to prevent errors and improve readability.

Tip 14: Use at most one variable per INPUT statement.

Tip 15: Place the DATA statements near the end of the program or below the subroutine that reads the data.

Tip 16: Include in each DATA statement the number of data items read each time the READ statement is executed.

Tip 17: Indent the statements within a subroutine by three spaces.

Tip 18: Indent the statements within any loop by three spaces.

Tip 19: Indent the statements in the true task and false task of an IF statement by three spaces.

Tip 20: Indent the statements in a CASE statement by three spaces.

Tip 21: End each subroutine with a blank line.

ASCII Character Set
and Personal Computer Literature
and Web Sites

This appendix presents the ASCII character set and a list of popular magazines, newspapers, and Web sites that relate to the personal computer.

D.1 ASCII CHARACTER CODES

Table D.1 on the next page lists all 256 ASCII decimal codes and their corresponding characters. Each time you press a key, the associated *decimal code* is transmitted to main memory and the *character* is displayed on the screen. Special characters may be displayed on the screen by using PRINT CHR$(n), where n is the corresponding decimal code. (See Figure 10.7 on page 403.)

ASCII decimal codes 126 to 255 represent the USA character set. However, foreign character sets may also be represented by these decimal codes. Note also the appearance of some of the mathematical and graphical characters by these decimal codes.

D.2 PERSONAL COMPUTER MAGAZINES, NEWSPAPERS, AND URLS

This section contains a select list of some of the popular magazines, newspapers, and Uniform Resource Locators (URLs) for personal computers. Many libraries have copies of these materials, and you are encouraged to look them over.

You can subscribe to the magazines and newspapers on page 545 by contacting the publishers.

TABLE D.1 - ASCII Character Set

DECIMAL CODE	CHARACTER	DECIMAL CODE	CHARACTER	DECIMAL CODE	CHARACTER	DECIMAL CODE	CHARACTER	DECIMAL CODE	CHARACTER
000	(null)	052	4	104	h	156	£	208	╨
001	☺	053	5	105	i	157	¥	209	╤
002	●	054	6	106	j	158	₧	210	╥
003	♥	055	7	107	k	159	ƒ	211	╙
004	♦	056	8	108	l	160	á	212	╘
005	♣	057	9	109	m	161	í	213	╒
006	♠	058	:	110	n	162	ó	214	╓
007	(beep)	059	;	111	o	163	ú	215	╫
008	◘	060	<	112	p	164	ñ	216	╪
009	(tap)	061	=	113	q	165	Ñ	217	┘
010	(line feed)	062	>	114	r	166	ª	218	┌
011	(home)	063	?	115	s	167	º	219	█
012	(form feed)	064	@	116	t	168	¿	220	▄
013	(carriage return)	065	A	117	u	169	⌐	221	▌
014	♫	066	B	118	v	170	¬	222	▐
015	☼	067	C	119	w	171	½	223	▀
016	►	068	D	120	x	172	¼	224	α
017	◄	069	E	121	y	173	¡	225	β
018	↕	070	F	122	z	174	«	226	Γ
019	‼	071	G	123	{	175	»	227	π
020	¶	072	H	124			176	░	228	Σ
021	§	073	I	125	}	177	▒	229	σ
022	▬	074	J	126	~	178	▓	230	µ
023	↨	075	K	127	⌂	179	│	231	τ
024	↑	076	L	128	Ç	180	┤	232	Φ
025	↓	077	M	129	ü	181	╡	233	θ
026	→	078	N	130	é	182	╢	234	Ω
027	←	079	O	131	â	183	╖	235	δ
028	(cursor right)	080	P	132	ä	184	╕	236	∞
029	(cursor left)	081	Q	133	à	185	╣	237	ø
030	(cursor up)	082	R	134	å	186	║	238	∈
031	(cursor down)	083	S	135	ç	187	╗	239	∩
032	(space)	084	T	136	ê	188	╝	240	≡
033	!	085	U	137	ë	189	╜	241	±
034	"	086	V	138	è	190	╛	242	≥
035	#	087	W	139	ï	191	┐	243	≤
036	$	088	X	140	î	192	└	244	⌠
037	%	089	Y	141	ì	193	┴	245	⌡
038	&	090	Z	142	Ä	194	┬	246	÷
039	'	091	[	143	Å	195	├	247	≈
040	(	092	\	144	É	196	─	248	°
041	)	093	]	145	æ	197	┼	249	●
042	*	094	^	146	Æ	198	╞	250	•
043	+	095	_	147	ô	199	╟	251	√
044	,	096	`	148	ö	200	╚	252	ⁿ
045	-	097	a	149	ò	201	╔	253	²
046	.	098	b	150	û	202	╩	254	■
047	/	099	c	151	ù	203	╦	255	(blank)
048	0	100	d	152	ÿ	204	╠		
049	1	101	e	153	Ö	205	═		
050	2	102	f	154	Ü	206	╬		
051	3	103	g	155	¢	207	╧		

Personal Computer Magazines

1. *Byte*, www.byte.com
2. *Family PC Magazine*, familypc.zdnet.com
3. *Macworld Magazine*, www.macworld.com
4. *PC Computing*, www.zdnet.com/pccomp
5. *PC Magazine*, www.zdnet.com/pcmag
6. *PC World*, www.pcworld.com
7. *Tech Web Buyer's Guide*, www.techweb.com
8. *Game Developer Magazine*, www.gdmag.com

Personal Computer Newspapers

A number of newspapers cover a variety of topics concerning personal computers. As with PC magazines, you can subscribe to these newspapers by contacting the publishers.

1. *Computerworld*, www.computerworld.com
2. *Info World*, www.infoworld.com
3. *Network World*, www.networld.com
4. *PC Week*, www.pcweek.com
5. *Inter@ctive Week*, www.interactive-week.com

URLs

The Internet is an excellent source of information on the latest developments dealing with PC hardware and software products. Table D.2 lists some interesting Uniform Resource Locators (URLs) regarding the latest news and products.

TABLE D.2 - Personal Computer Web Sites	
COMPANY	**URL**
Adobe Systems	www.adobe.com
Autodesk, Inc.	www.autodesk.com
Boston Computer Museum	www.mos.org/home.html
Carrera Computers, Inc.	www.carrera.com
Compaq Computer	www.compaq.com
Corel Corporation	www.corel.com
Gateway 2000	www.gw2k.com
Hewlett-Packard Company	www.hp.com
Intel Corporation	www.intel.com
International Business Machines	www.ibm.com
Macromedia, Inc.	www.macromedia.com
Meta Tools, Inc.	www.metatools.com
Microsoft Corporation	www.microsoft.com
Qualcomm	www.qualcomm.com
Sun Microsystems	www.sun.com
Tech Web Buyer's Guides	www.techweb.com
The Computer Museum History Center	www.computerhistory.org
World Wide Web Consortium	www.w3.org

A P P E N D I X

Answers to the Even-Numbered Test Your QBasic Skills Exercises

CHAPTER 1

2. The basic subsystems of a computer are input, main memory, central processing unit, auxiliary storage, and output.
   Input — a device that allows programs and data to enter into the computer system.
   Main Memory — a subsystem that allows for the storage of programs and data for the central processing unit to process at a given time.
   Central Processing Unit (CPU) — the unit that controls and supervises the entire computer system and performs the arithmetic and logical operations on data that is specified by the stored program.
   Auxiliary Storage — a subsystem that is used to store programs and data for immediate recall.
   Output — a device that allows the computer system to communicate the results of a program to the user.

4. A floppy disk unit and a hard disk unit both serve as input and output devices.

6. Hardware is the physical equipment of a computer system. The subsystems as described in number 2 above are hardware. Software refers to the programs, languages, written procedures, and documentation concerned with the operation of a computer system.

8. The different storage capacities of 3½ inch floppy disks are as follows:
   double density — 720K; high density — 1.44M; very-high density — 2.88M.

10. a. Male.Cnt = 2, Female.Cnt = 1, Sale.Cnt = 3, Commission Average = 700
    b. Male.Cnt = 1, Female.Cnt = 0, Sale.Cnt = 1, Commission Average = 500
    c. Male.Cnt = 0, Female.Cnt = 0, a diagnostic message displays when an attempt is made to compute Commission Average because the value of Sale.Cnt is zero and division by zero is not permitted.

12. **Word processing** — A program used to write, revise, and edit letters, reports, and manuscripts with efficiency and economy (MS Word or Corel WordPerfect).
Spreadsheets — A program used to organize data that can be defined in terms of rows and columns (MS Excel or Lotus 1-2-3).
Database — A program used to organize data into files and easily generate reports and access the data (MS Access).
Graphics — A program used to create line graphs, bar graphs, pie charts, and 3-D graphic images (MS PowerPoint).
Desktop Publishing — A program used to integrate words and pictures and generate typeset-quality documents quickly and economically (QuarkXPress).
Browser — A program used to access the World Wide Web and display information in the form of text, graphics, sound, music, video clips, and animation (MS Internet Explorer or Netscape Navigator).

14. Answer will vary depending on your system.

CHAPTER 2

2.

		Line	A	B	C	Displayed
1	A = 9	1	9	0	0	
2	B = 2	2	9	2	0	
3	C = 5	3	9	2	5	
4	C = C + 3	4	9	2	8	
5	A = C * B	5	16	2	8	
6	PRINT A	6	16	2	8	16
7	B = B + 2	7	16	4	8	
8	PRINT B	8	16	4	8	4
9	C = C - 4	9	16	4	4	
10	PRINT C	10	16	4	4	4
11	A = A - 10	11	6	4	4	
12	PRINT A	12	6	4	4	6
13	C = C / B	13	6	4	1	
14	PRINT C	14	6	4	1	1
15	END	15	6	4	1	

4. a. $T = 3$
   b. $X = T - 2$
   c. $P = T * X$
   d. $T = 3 * T$
   e. $A = P / X$
   f. $X = X + 1$
   g. $R = R \wedge 3$ or $R = R * R * R$

6. (1) Insert the data as constants in the LET statement used to calculate a result.
   (2) Assign each data item to a variable. Use these variables in the LET statement to calculate a result.
   (3) Use the INPUT statement to assign the data items to variables. Use these variables in the LET statement to calculate a result.

8. **Exit** — Causes the PC to exit QBasic and returns control to the operating system.
   New — Causes the current program to be erased and indicates the beginning of a new program.
   Open — Loads a previously stored program on disk into main memory.
   Print — Prints all or part of the current program to the printer.
   Save As — Saves the current program to disk under a specified name.
   Start — Runs the current program.

10. No. The PRINT statement must be coded after the LET statement that calculates the gross pay, not before it. As it stands, the program prints zero for the gross pay.

CHAPTER 3

2. 4.36E10

4. a. 7   b. 26   c. 40

6. c — INT is a reserved word (keyword).
   e — First character is not a letter.
   f — PRINT is a reserved word.
   g — First character is not a letter.
   h — No hyphens allowed.

8. The type can be specified by appending a special character (such as %, &, !, space, #) to the variable name.

10. a. 0   b. 16   c. 39   d. 16777216 e. 21   f. 8192

12. a. $Q = (D + E) ^ (1 / 3)$
    b. $D = (A ^ 2) ^ 3.2$
    c. $B = 20 / (6 - S)$
    d. $Y = A1 * X + A2 * X ^ 2 + A3 * X ^ 3 + A4 * X ^ 4$
    e. $H = X ^ (1/2) + X / (X - Y)$
    f. $S = (19.2 * X ^ 3) ^ (1/2)$
    g. $V = 100 - (2 / 3) ^ (100 - B)$
    h. $T = (76234 / (2.37 + D)) ^ (1 / 2)$
    i. $V = 1234.0005D-4 - (M ^ 3 / (M - N))$
    j. $Q = ((F - 1000 * M) ^ (2 * B)) / (4 * M) - 1 / E$

14. a, d, e, f, h, j

16. a. -1
    b. 7.4

18. Principal ===> 3000
    Rate in % ===> 12
    Amount ======> 3360

20. a. 3
    b. -4
    c. 20
    d. Illegal function call

CHAPTER 4

2. a.
```
' Exercise 4.2a
READ S, B
D = S - B
LOCATE 26, 14, 1: PRINT TAB(3); D
DATA 4, 6: ' Data for READ
END
```

b.
```
' Exercise 4.2b
DATA 1, 2, 5, 6, 8, 7, 1, 3, 2, 0, 0, 0
READ X, Y, Z
DO WHILE X > 0
   X1 = X * Y
   X1 = X1 * Z
   READ X, Y, Z
LOOP
PRINT X1
END
```

4.
```
LOCATE 2, 7: PRINT A2
LOCATE 5, 45: PRINT B5
```

6.
```
PRINT USING "The amount is **$####. ##+"; Amount
```

8.
```
CLS
LOCATE 8, 8: PRINT 8
```

10. The cursor is located in column 12 of line 14.

12.
```
   VVVVV
  X     X
 X  0 0  X
 X       X
 X   U   X
 X (   ) X
 X   -   X
  X     X
   XXXXX
```

14. a. `PRINT USING "!"; Last.Name$`
    b. `PRINT USING "&"; Last.Name$`
    c. `PRINT USING "\    \"; Last.Name$`
    d. `PRINT USING "\\"; Last.Name$`

16. Assume ƀ represents a blank character.
    a. ƀƀ5
    b. ƀƀƀ24.70
    c. ƀƀƀ$44.30-
    d. $ƀƀ213.45ƀ
    e. *****44.42
    f. 4,131.0
    g. ƀ1.53ƀ
    h. %-246.40
    i. ƀƀƀƀ24.323
    j. ƀ4.33E+02
    k. W
    l. WXYZ
    m. WXY
    n. WXYZ

CHAPTER 5

2. X = 0
   T = 10

   a. X = X + 1
      T = T + 1

   b. X = X + 7
      T = T + 7

   c. X = X + 2
      T = T + 2

   d. X = 2 * X
      T = 2 * T

   e. X = X - 1
      T = T - 1

4. a. Q value greater than 8 or Q value equal to 3.
   b. Q value greater than or equal to 0.
   c. Q value less than 27.
   d. Q may be equal to any value that is within the limits of the PC.

6. a.
```
IF X > 18 THEN
    A = A + 1
END IF
T = T + 1
```

   b.
```
IF G$ = "M" THEN
    M = M + 1
ELSE
    F = F + 1
END IF
```

8.

a.

b.

10. a.

```
A200.Accept.Value:
   INPUT "Percent (0 < Percent <= 25) =====> ", Percent
   DO WHILE Percent < 0 OR Percent > 25
      BEEP: BEEP: BEEP: BEEP
      PRINT "Percent"; Percent; "is in error, please re-enter"
      INPUT "Percent (0 < Percent <= 25) =====> ", Percent
   LOOP
RETURN
```

b.

```
A200.Accept.Value:
   INPUT "Balance ($550.99 <= Balance <= $765.50) =====> ", Balance
   DO WHILE Balance < 550.99 OR Balance > 765.50
      BEEP: BEEP: BEEP: BEEP
      PRINT "Balance"; Balance; "is in error, please re-enter"
      INPUT "Balance ($550.99 <= Balance <= $765.50) =====> ", Balance
   LOOP
RETURN
```

Also the DO WHILE statement can be written as follows:

```
DO WHILE NOT(Balance >= 550.99 AND Balance <= 765.50)
```

c.

```
A200.Accept.Value:
   INPUT "Code (A, D, E or F) =====> ", Code$
   DO WHILE NOT(Code$ = "A" OR Code$ = "D" OR Code$ = "E" OR Code$ = "F")
      BEEP: BEEP: BEEP: BEEP
      PRINT "Code "; Code$; " is in error, please re-enter"
      INPUT "Code (A, D, E or F) =====> ", Code$
   LOOP
RETURN
```

d.

```
A200.Accept.Value:
    INPUT "Customer =====> ", Customer$
    DO WHILE MID$(Customer$, 3, 1) <> "4"
        BEEP: BEEP: BEEP: BEEP
        PRINT "Customer"; Customer$; "is in error, please re-enter"
        INPUT "Customer =====> ", Customer$
    LOOP
RETURN
```

12.
```
' Exercise 5.12 Solution
Negative = 0
Zero = 0
Positive = 0
READ Number
DO WHILE Number <> -999
    IF Number < 0 THEN
        Negative = Negative + 1
    ELSE
        IF Number = 0 THEN
            Zero = Zero + 1
        ELSE
            Positive = Positive + 1
        END IF
    END IF
    READ Number
LOOP
PRINT Negative, Zero, Positive
DATA 4, 2, 3, -9, 0, 0, -4, -6, -8, 3, 2, 0, 0, 8, -3, 4
DATA -999
END
```

The nested IF can also be written as follows:

```
IF Number < 0 THEN Negative = Negative + 1
IF Number = 0 THEN Zero = Zero + 1
IF Number > 0 THEN Positive = Positive + 1
```

14.
```
' Exercise 5.14 Solution
CLS  ' Clear Screen
INPUT "Number of Fibonacci Numbers (3 < X <= 190) ===> ", X%
DO WHILE X% <=3 OR X% > 190
    PRINT "The number"; X%; "is out of range, please re-enter"
    INPUT "Number of Fibonacci Numbers ===> ", X%
LOOP
Fib1 = 1
Fib2 = 1
PRINT
PRINT Fib1;
PRINT Fib2;
Number% = 3
DO WHILE Number% <= X%
    Fib3 = Fib2 + Fib1
    PRINT Fib3;
    Fib1 = Fib2
    Fib2 = Fib3
    Number% = Number% + 1
LOOP
PRINT : PRINT : PRINT "Job Complete"
```

16.
```
' Exercise 5.16 Solution
IF U < V THEN
   IF U < W THEN
      Little = U
   ELSE
      Little = W
   END IF
ELSE
   IF V < W THEN
      Little = V
   ELSE
      Little = W
   END IF
END IF
```

18. a. A
    b. Count = 3; Sum = 9
    c. 5, including the End of Report message
    d. 39
    e. 9

20.
```
' Exercise 5.20 Solution
IF C = 0 AND D = 0 THEN
   A = -1
ELSE
   IF C <> 0 AND D <> 0 THEN
      A = -2
   ELSE
      IF C = 0 XOR D = 0 THEN
         A = -3
      END IF
   END IF
END IF
```

CHAPTER 6

2. a. OPEN, OUTPUT, APPEND
   b. OPEN, INPUT
   c. closed
   d. EOF(N)
   e. APPEND

4.
```
OPEN "A:SALES1.DAT" FOR INPUT AS #1
OPEN "A:SALES2.DAT" FOR INPUT AS #2
OPEN "A:SALES3.DAT" FOR INPUT AS #3
```

6. a — Filespec must precede the mode.
   e — Comma must immediately follow filenumber.
   g — Filenumber must not be preceded by a number sign.
   h — Comma at the end of the list is invalid.

8. a. Line.Count = Line.Count + 1
   b. Line.Count = Line.Count + 2
   c. Line.Count = Line.Count + 3

CHAPTER 7

2. a. L(2, 2) b. L(3, 3) or L(2, 4) c. L(3, 2) d. L(5, 2)
   e. L(3, 4) f. L(2, 1) g. L(1, 3) h. L(5, 1)

4. The partial program assigns the value of each element of array A to the corresponding element in array B and then displays the lower bound of the first dimension of the array A, the upper bound of the first dimension of array A, the lower bound of the second dimension of array B, and the upper bound of the second dimension of array B.

6. a. c b. c c. e d. a

8.
```
' Exercise 7.8 Solution
Low = 0
Mid = 0
High = 0
FOR I = 1 TO 50
   IF Number(I) >= 0 AND Number(I) <= 18 THEN
      Low = Low + 1
   END IF
   IF Number(I) >= 26 AND Number(I) <= 29 THEN
      Mid = Mid + 1
   END IF
   IF Number(I) >= 42 AND Number(I) <= 47 THEN
      High = High + 1
   END IF
NEXT I
END
```

10.
```
' Exercise 7.10 Solution
FOR I = 1 TO 100
   IF A(I) < B(I) THEN
      C(I) = -1
   ELSE
      IF A(I) = B(I) THEN
         C(I) = 0
      ELSE
         C(I) = 1
      END IF
   END IF
NEXT I
END
```

The nested IF statement also may be written as follows:

```
IF A(I) < B(I) THEN C(I) = -1
IF A(I) = B(I) THEN C(I) = 0
IF A(I) > B(I) THEN C(I) = 1
```

12.
```
'Exercise 7.12 Solution
OPTION BASE 1
SUM = 0
FOR J = 1 TO 20
    Sum = Sum + R(J, J) + S(J, J)
NEXT J
END
```

14. 1400

16.
```
' Exercise 7.16 Solution
DIM A(1 TO 50)

    .

    .

    .
Positive = 0
Zero = 0
Negative = 0
FOR I = 1 TO 50
    IF A(I) > 0 THEN
        Positive = Positive + 1
    ELSE
        IF A(I) = 0 THEN
            Zero = Zero + 1
        ELSE
            Negative = Negative + 1
        END IF
    END IF
NEXT I
```

You also may write the nested IF statement as follows:

```
IF A(I) > 0 THEN Positive = Positive + 1
IF A(I) = 0 THEN Zero = Zero + 1
IF A(I) < 0 THEN Negative = Negative + 1
```

18.
```
' Exercise 7.18 Solution
Greatest.Sales = Sales(1)
Salesperson$ = Person$(1)
FOR I = 2 TO 30
    IF Sales(I) > Greatest.Sales THEN
        Salesperson$ = Person$(I)
        Greatest.Sales = Sales(I)
    END IF
NEXT I
PRINT Salesperson$, Greatest.Sales
END
```

20.
```
' Exercise 7.20 Solution
DIM Item$(1 TO 100), Sales(1 TO 100)

    .

    .

    .
FOR I = 1 TO 100
    IF Sales(I) > 3000 THEN
        PRINT Item$(I), Sales(I)
    END IF
NEXT I
END
```

CHAPTER 8

2. a. 77
    b. The entire string
    c. If⊘I⊘ (where ⊘ indicates a blank character)
    d. ran
    e. 36.8
    f. 73
    g. G
    h. AAAAAAAAAAAAA
    i. "-13.691"
    j. 16
    k. The word giants is replaced by the word friends in the string assigned to Phr$.
    l. ⊘⊘⊘⊘ (where ⊘ indicates a blank character)

4. a. 99   b. 43   c. ?   d. "44.5"   e. 1
    f. XYZ   g. %   h. 58   i. 15   j. 64

6.
```
' Exercise 8.6 Solution
Number$ = "2587"
Number  = VAL(Number$)
D4   = INT(Number / 1000)
D3   = INT((Number - D4 * 1000) / 100)
D2   = INT((Number - D4 * 1000 - D3 * 100) / 10)
D1   = INT(Number - D4 * 1000 - D3 * 100 - D2 * 10)
Sum  = D4 + D3 + D2 + D1
PRINT "The Sum of the digits is"; Sum
```

Also, lines 3 to 7 may be written as shown below:

```
D1 = VAL(MID$(Number$, 1, 1))
D2 = VAL(MID$(Number$, 2, 1))
D3 = VAL(MID$(Number$, 3, 1))
D4 = VAL(MID$(Number$, 4, 1))
```

8. The program displays the prime numbers between 1 and 100. Any whole number greater than 1 that has no factors other than 1 and itself is called a **prime number**. In number theory, it can be proven that if a number has no factors between 2 and the square root of the number, then the number is prime. The program uses this method for finding the prime numbers between 1 and 100.

10. a. P = SQR(A * A + B * B)
    b. B = SQR(ABS(TAN(X) - .51))
    c. Q = 8 * (COS(X)) ^ 2 + 4 * SIN(X)
    d. Y = EXP(X) + LOG(1 + X)

12. a. Sign = SGN(2 * X ^ 3 + 3 * X + 5)
    b. Inte = INT(4 * X + 5)
    c. Rounded.2 = INT((X + .005) * 100) / 100
       Rounded.1 = INT((X + .05) * 10) / 10

14. POS — Returns the current column position of the cursor relative to the left edge of the display screen.

    CSRLIN — Equal to the current row position of the cursor relative to the top of the display screen.

    SCREEN — Returns the ASCII code for the character found at the specified location.

16.
```
' Exercise 8.16 Solution
RANDOMIZE TIMER
FOR R% = 1 TO 100
   PRINT INT(75 * RND + 1)
NEXT R%
END
```

18. `DEF FNDISCOUNT(Purchase) = .10 * (Purchase - 200)`

20. The program is valid and displays the value 44.

CHAPTER 9

2. a. record variable, `DIM`
   c. record variable

   b. `TYPE, DIM`
   d. `LOC(n)`

4. The label name is used in the `TYPE` statement to identify the group of fields in the random record. The record variable is assigned the same type as the label name in the `DIM` statement and reserves main memory for the random record.

6. a — The parameter `LEN` must be assigned the length of the record variable (`LEN(Sales)`) rather than the value of the record variable.
   d — A string variable as the second parameter in a `GET` statement is invalid.
   f — Period (.) is invalid in a label name.
   g — The `GET` requires a record variable to indicate where the record is to be placed in main memory.

8. The sequential data file contains the keys that are read into an array by the Initialization subprogram. The random data file contains the data records that are accessed by using the subscript of the element in the array that has the key as its value.

CHAPTER 10

2. a.
```
' Exercise 10.2a Solution
SCREEN 1: CLS
PSET (0, 50)
LINE -(200, 25)
LINE -(100, 125)
LINE -(0, 50)
END
```

   b.
```
' Exercise 10.2b Solution
SCREEN 1: CLS
LINE (0, 0) - (160, 100),, B
LINE -(0, 0)
LINE (160, 0) - (0, 100)
END
```

   c.
```
' Exercise 10.2c Solution
SCREEN 1: CLS
Pi = 3.141593
CIRCLE (70, 80), 45
PSET (70, 80)
CIRCLE (70, 80), 45,, Pi, 1/6
END
```

```
d. ' Exercise 10.2d Solution
   SCREEN 1: CLS
   Pi = 3.141593
   CIRCLE (75, 60), 70,, -Pi, -3 * Pi/2
   END
```

4. a. The screen has a blue background, a black border, and a red foreground.
   b. The screen has a black background and border and a brown foreground. The default color on palette 0.

6. a. point, pixel   b. GRAPHICS   c. 80
   d. CHR$ e. minus sign   f. GET, PUT
   g. 2, 4, 8

8.
```
' Exercise 10.8 Solution
SCREEN 1: CLS
COLOR 1, 0
LINE (100, 80) - (180, 150), 3, B
PAINT(140, 135), 2, 3
LINE (100, 80) - (130, 50), 3
LINE -(210, 50), 3
LINE -(180, 80), 3
PAINT (140, 65), 1, 3
LINE (210, 50) - (210, 120), 3
LINE -(180, 150), 3
PAINT (185, 135), 3, 3
END
```

10.
```
' Exercise 10.10 Solution
CLS: WIDTH 40
LOCATE 4, 9
FOR I% = 9 TO 32
   PRINT CHR$(219);
NEXT I%
LOCATE 22, 9
FOR I% = 9 TO 32
   PRINT CHR$(219);
NEXT I%
FOR I% = 4 TO 22
   LOCATE I%, 9: PRINT CHR$(219)
NEXT I%
FOR I% = 4 TO 22
   LOCATE I%, 32: PRINT CHR$(219)
NEXT I%
END
```

12. a. Causes the note A flat to be played.
    b. Sets all notes that follow to lengths of 1/8.
    c. Sets all notes that follow to the next octave and causes the C note to be played.
    d. Executes the subcommand M$, which contains additional commands.
    e. Rest.
    f. Sets the tempo to 100 quarter notes per minute.
    g. Pauses a length of 1/8.
    h. Music staccato — each note that follows plays 3/4 of the time specified by L.
    i. Music legato — each note that follows plays the full period set by L.
    j. Sets the octave to 3.

14. PSET — Puts the pixel array on the screen exactly as defined in the array named in the PUT statement.

AND — Within the specified area on the screen, turns *on* those pixels that are *on* in the array named in the PUT statement and *on* on the screen.

XOR — Within the specified area, turns *on* those pixels that are *on* in the array named in the PUT statement and *off* on the screen or *off* in the array named in the PUT statement and *on* on the screen.

16. `(4 + 60 * INT ((70 + 7) / 8)) /2 = 272 bytes`

18. a. The background will be blue with red dots as shown below:

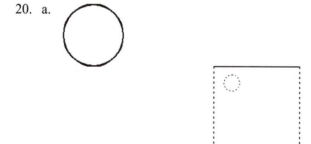

b. The background will be blue with a random pattern 100 colored dots.

20. a.

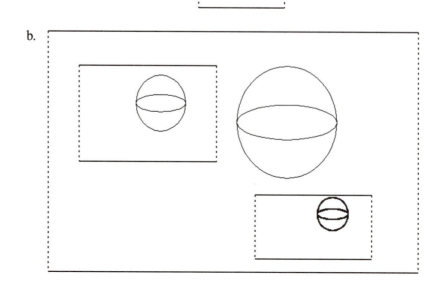

b.

CHAPTER 11

2. a. 8
    b. 5
    c. 6
    d. 1
    e. 4
    f. 7
    g. 2

4   a. procedures
    b. STATIC
    c. CHAIN
    d. address
    e. recursive

6.
```
FUNCTION SWITCH (W)
    IF W < 10 THEN
        SWITCH = 1
    END IF
    IF W >= 10 AND W <= 100
        SWITCH = 2
    END IF
    IF SWITCH > 100
        SWITCH = 3
    END IF
END FUNCTION
```

8. The SHARED statement declares variables to be global when used in conjuction with the COMMON statement. The SHARED statement must be located in the Main Module.

10. To move from one subprogram to another, use the SUBs command in the View menu.

APPENDIX A

2. The annotation, terminal, and connector symbols.

4. Part I: I = 9, J = 9
    Part II: I = 21, J = 14

6. I = 3, J = 5

8.

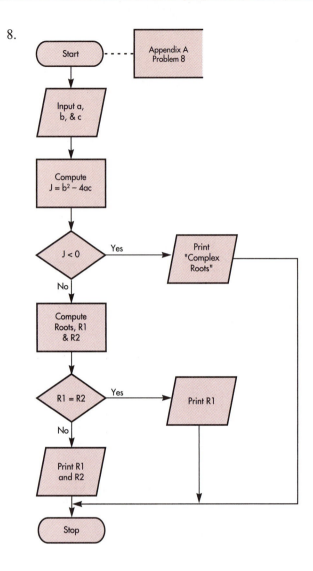

10.

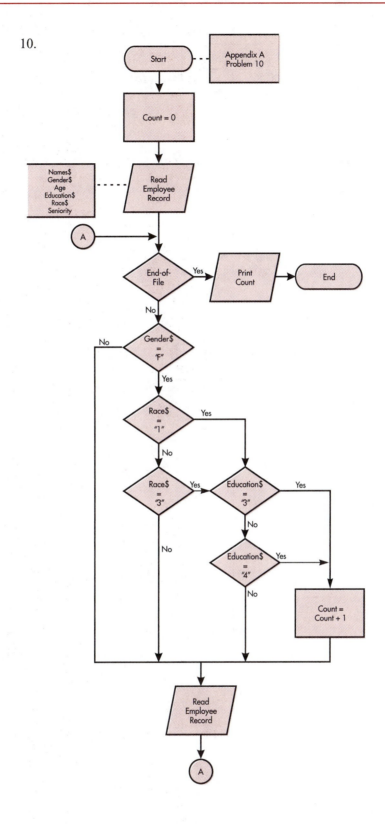

12.

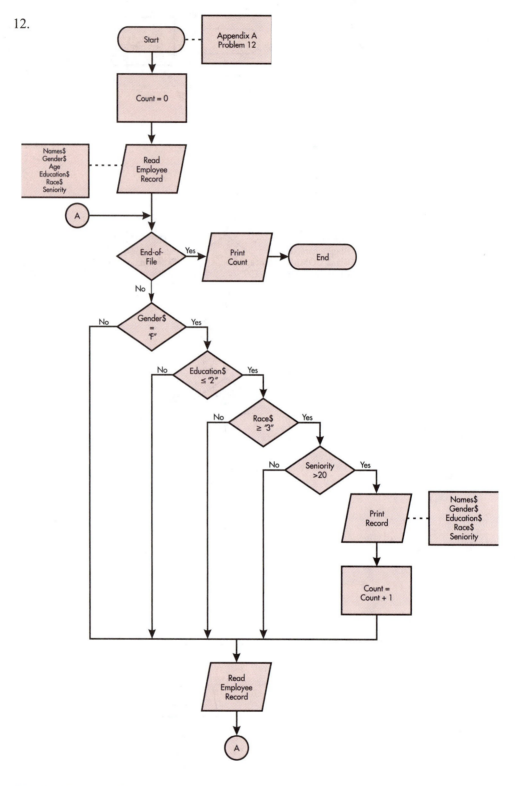

14. I = 17 and J = 16

I N D E X

ABS function, **317**
Accessing records, 372-374
Accumulators, **149**-154, 221
Active page, SCREEN statement, **402**
Active window, changing, 532
Adding
  controls, 493-495
  records, 349, 350-357
Addition (+), 22, 23, 65, 66, 539
Address, **3**
Algorithms, **13**
  performance of, 323
  sort, 267-272
Alignment
  decimal-point, 112
  PRINT USING statement and, 112
  string constant, 119-120
American Standard Code for Information Interchange (ASCII), **147**, 305, 403-404
  code set, 543-544
Ampersand (&), variable-length string field and, 119
AND logical operator, 145, **161**-162, 165
Angles, 322
Annotation symbol, 14, 507
Apostrophe ('), abbreviating REM using, 31
Append mode (APPEND), **200**
Applications, performance of, 323
Arcs, drawing, 423
Arguments, **70**
  CALL statement, 455-**456**, 458
  search, 276, 277
  TAB function and, 110
  table, 276, 277, 280-281
Argument-organized tables, **274**, 276-277, 280-281
Arithmetic functions, **317**
Arithmetic-logic section, of CPU, **4**
Arithmetic-logic unit (ALU), 148
Arithmetic operators, **22**, 65, 539
Arrays, **241**
  binary search, 282
  declaring, 254-257
  dynamic allocation of, 256
  initializing, 265
  integer, 436
  manipulating, 257-258
  multidimensional, 255, 264-266
  parallel, 259, 263, 277
  passing entire, to subprogram, 459
  passing individual elements to subprogram, 458-459
  simple variables versus, 253-254
  sorting data items in, 268-272
Array name, **253**, **255**, 257
  GET statement for graphics and, 435
  PUT statement for graphics and, 436
ASC function, **305**
Ascending sequence sort, **267**
ASCII, *see* American Standard Code for Information Interchange
Assignment statement, **22**
Associated subprogram **455**
Asterisk (*)
  format symbol, 118
  multiplication and, 22, **23**, 65
ATN function, **322**

Auxiliary storage
  data files in, 197, 198, 199, 201
  types of, 3, 7-8
Auxiliary storage unit, **3**

Background color, **411**, **419**
Backslash (\), integer division and, 23, 65
Backslashes (\\), displaying string value and, 119
Backspace key, **36**
Bar graphs, 398, 403, 407-410
BEEP statement, 166, 179, 437
Benchmarking, **323**
Binary search, **277**, 281-284
  formula for, 285
Blank character, **29**
Blank COMMON block, **462**
Blank lines, creating, 109
Blinking characters, 413
Block IF statement, 147
Border, **411**
BorderStyle property, 498
Boundary, PAINT statement and, **425**
Box
  LINE statement and, **421**
  volume of, **194**
Breakpoint, **534**
Bubble sort, **267**-272
Buffer, **199**, 201
Bugs, **533**. *See also* Debugging
Buttons, **35**
Bytes, **3**

C, 9
C++, 9
Calculations, PRINT statement and, 110
CALL statement, 454, **455**
  arguments in, 455-456, 458
Calling program, 455-460
Caption property, 496-497, 498-499
Caret symbol (^), exponentiation and, 23, 65
Cartesian coordinate system, 431
Case, **169**
  converting, 128, 306
CASE clause, 169, 172
Case control structure, **143**, 144, 169-180, **513**
  Nassi-Schneiderman charts and, 518
  pseudocode and, 517
  Warnier-Orr diagrams and, 520
CASE ELSE clause, 170-172
Case-sensitive, **61**
CD-ROM, 3
Cells, empty, 372
CGA (Color/Graphics Adaptor) hardware, 399-401
CHAIN statement, 453, 455, **477**-479
Chained-to program, **477**-478
Chaining, **453**, 477-479
Chaining program, **477**-478
Character(s)
  row/column intersection, 323
  blank, 309
  blinking, 413
  case conversion, 128, 306
  deleting, 36
  duplicating, 309
  graphics, 403-404

  pending, 315
  per line, 402
  trimming blank, 309
Character codes
  ASCII, 543-544
  converting, 305-306
Character position, **400**
Check digit, **139**
Check protection asterisks, **118**
CHR$ function, **305**, 308
  Form Feed character and, 214
  text-mode graphics and, 403, 406
  tile mask and, 426-427
CINT(N) function, **317**, 318
CIRCLE statement, **423**-425
Clearing
  screen, 29, 402, 406
  view window, 40, 42
Clipboard, **36**
CLOSE statement, **201**
  flowchart of, 206
  random files and, 364
  sequential files and, 201-202
Closing
  random files, 364
  sequential files, 201-202
CLS statement, **29**
COBOL (**CO**mmon **B**usiness **O**riented **L**anguage), **9**
Code
  currency application, 500-501
  pseudo-, 516-518
  reviewing, 13, 45
  Visual Basic, 486-488
Code check, **168**
Code window, **488**
Coded message, deciphering, 306-308
Coding, 13, 45
  form, **29**
  techniques, 29-30
Collating sequence, **147**
Colon (:)
  separating statements with, 32
  string containing, 60
Color
  characters, 403
  CIRCLE statement and, **424**
  LINE statement, **421**
Color monitor, 399-401, 412, 419
COLOR statement
  medium-resolution graphics mode, 419
  text mode, **411**-414
Color switch, SCREEN statement, **402**
Column
  cursor position, 322
  graphics coordinates, 419
  positioning cursor in, using LOCATE statement, **126**
  row intersection, 323, 400-401
  screen display, 402
Comma (,), 116
  numeric format and, 112
  separating items in PRINT statement, 108
  string containing, 60
  variable names separated by, 26
  WRITE #n statement and, 207
Comma separator, **108**
Command(s)
  menu, 525-531
  QBasic, 33

Command button controls, 495-496
Comment(s), **30**
Comment box, **79**, 465
COmmon **B**usiness **O**riented **L**anguage (COBOL), **9**
Common dialog boxes, **501**
COMMON statement, **462**-463
  CHAIN statement and, **477**-478
Compact disc drives, 3
Compiler, **12**
Complemented (reversed) truth value, in condition, **160**
Compound conditions, **160**-166
  effect of parentheses in evaluation of, 165-166
Compressed format, **109**
Computer, **1**
  advantages of, 1
  disadvantages of, 1
  hardware, **2**-8
  software, **8**-12
Concatenation operator (+), **65**, **72**, 300
  OPEN statement and, 201
Conditions, **97**, **101**
  combining using logical operators, 145, 160-166
  complemented (reversed) truth value, 160
  compound, 160-166
  DO statement and, **100**
  evaluation of, 148
  For loop and, 242, 244
  If-Then-Else control structure and, 144, 146-147, 156-159
  logical operators and, 160-166
  LOOP statement and, **101**
  numeric expressions, 147
  relational operators used in, 102
  string expressions, 147
Cone, volume of, **194**
Connector symbol, 14, 507
Constants, **22**-23, 25
  as arguments in CALL statement, 458
  avoiding recomputation of, 539
  passing to subprogram, 456
Context-sensitive help, **42**
Control(s), **484**
  adding, 493-495
  command button, 495-496
  events and, 486-487
  label, 494, 496-497
  location and size of, 495, 496
  names, 498-499
  properties, 485-486, 496-499
  removing, 493-495
Control break(s), **197**, 219, **220**-230
  single-level, 221-225
  two levels, 226-230
Control-break processing, 197, 219-230
Control field, **220**
Control section, of CPU, **4**
Control stack, **82**
Control structures, 512-514
  Case, 143, 144, 169-180, 513
  Do-Until, 143, 145, 155-156, 513
  Do-While, 143, 145, 155-156, 513
  If-Then-Else, 143, 144, 145-148, 156-166, 513
  logical operators and, 160-166
  selection, 143, 145, 513
  sequence, 143, 144, 512

Control variables, **220**-221
  in For loops, integer variables used as, 540
Coordinates, graphics, 419, 431, 432
Copying lines, 36
COS function, **322**
Cosecant, 322
Cosine, 322
Cotangent, 322
Counter(s)
  Do-While loop and, **149,** 151, 154, 156-159, 161, 242
  flowchart showing, 511
  For loop and, 242-243
  integer variables used for, 539
Counter-controlled loop, **242**-253, 540
CPU, 3-4, 6-7
Cryptogram, **306**
CSRLIN function, **322**
Currency conversion application, Visual Basic, 491-504
Current master file, **350,** 351, 352
Cursor, **28**
  location of, 34
  position of, 322
  positioning using LOCATE statement, **126**
  view window and, 34
Cursor control keys, ASCII values of, 404
Cut and paste text, **36**
Cut command (Edit menu), 36
Cylinder, volume of, **194**

Data, **3**
  sorting, 241, 267-273
  storage of, 3
  writing to sequential file, 206-207
Data files, entering data using, 197-213
Data-sequence holding area, **104**-105
DATA statement, 95, 99, 100, **103**
  chained-to program and, 478
  READ statement and, 104-105
Data types, modifying, 308
Data validation, **145, 166**-169, 178
Database system, **9**
DATE$ function, **310**
DATE$ statement, **314**
Debug/debugging, 10, **29, 111, 533**-538
  structured programming and, 143
  techniques, **533**
  top-down, 74
Debug menu, 529-530
Decimal argument, TAB function and, 110
Decimal fraction values, in FOR statement, 246
Decimal places, truncating number to, 318
Decimal-point alignment, 112
Decimal point (.) format symbol, 116
Decision
  flowchart representation, 14, 144, 507, 510
  IF statement and, 146
  logical operators and, 160-166
Decision making, **144**
Decision symbol, 14, 507, 510
Declaring arrays, 254-257
DEF FN statement, **329**-331, 469-470
Default values, **486**
DEFDBL (double precision), 62
DEFINT (integer), 62
DEFLNG (long integer), 62
DEFSNG (single precision), 62

DEFSTR (string), 62
Delete key (DEL), **36**
Deleting
  characters, 36
  lines, 36
  records, 349, 350, 358-363
Descending sequence sort, **267**
Description pane (Properties window), **486**
Descriptor field, 112, **113**
Design the program, *see* Program design
Design time, **484**
Desk checking, **45**
Desktop, **11**
Desktop publishing system, **9**
Detail line, **122**
  report, 213
Detailed flowcharts, **510,** 514
Device name, filespec and, 40
Diagnostic message, **79**
Dialog boxes, **35**
Digit check, **168**
DIM statement, **254**-255
  multidimensional arrays, 264-266
  record structure and, 366
  SHARED keyword used in, 462
  TO option in, 256
Dimension, array, **254**-255, 264
Dirs/Drives box (Save As dialog box), 41
Disk drives, 3
  filespec and, 40
Disk unit, **3**
Displaying records, 379-388
Division (/), 23, 65, 539
  see Integer division
  order of operations and, 66
Do loop, **97**
  EOF function and, 212-213
  pass through, 99
  selecting, 101
  testing for end-of-file in, 99-100
  ways to formulate, 101
DO statement, general form of, 100
DO UNTIL statement, 100, 101, 145, 155
DO WHILE statement, 97, 99, 100, 101, 145, 155, 242
Dollar sign ($)
  fixed, 112, 118
  floating, 112, 118
  variable name ending with, 61
Double precision (exponential form) numeric constant, 58
Double precision numeric constant, 58
Double precision numeric variable, 62
Do-Until control structure, 143, 145, **513**
  implementing, 155
  Nassi-Schneiderman charts and, 518
  pseudocode and, 517
  Warnier-Orr diagrams and, 520
Do-While control structure, **143, 145, 513**
  data validation and, 167-169
  EOF function and, 212-213, 218
  implementing, 155-156
  Nassi-Schneiderman charts and, 518
  pseudocode and, 516
  Warnier-Orr diagrams and, 520
Do-While loop, **143,** 145, 155-156
  binary search, 283
  For loop versus, 242
DRAW statement, **428**-430
Drawing object, defined by string expression, 428

Dummy variables, **330**
Duration, sound, **438**
DVD, 3
Dynamically-dimensioned array, **256**

Edit menu, 527
  Cut command, 36
  New SUB command, 464
  Paste command, 36
Editing, **35**-36
  465-467
Editor, 10. *See also* QBasic editor
Electronic spreadsheet program, **9**
Ellipses, drawing, 423
ELSE clause, 146, 156-159
  null, 157
ELSEIF keyword, SELECT CASE versus, 146, 169
Embedded For loop, **250**-252
Empty cells, **372**
Empty list, **29**
Empty string, **59**
End, CIRCLE statement and, **424**
END DEF statement, 329
END FUNCTION statement, **469,** 470
END IF statement, 146-147, 156-159
END SELECT, 169-171
END statement, **23,** 79
END SUB statement, 454, 456
Endless loop, **511**
End-of-file, testing for, 99-100
End-of-file mark, **212,** 218
End-of-file routine, **99**
Enhanced resolution graphics mode, **399**-400, 401
EOF value, 99
EOF(n) function, **212**-213
Equal sign (=), **22**
  LET statement and, 22, 25, 62, 63
  user-defined function and, 329
Equation, plotting, 398
EQV (equivalence) logical operator, **163**
Ergonomic keyboards, 5
Error(s), trapping user, 535-538
Error-handling routine, **536**
Evaluation of numeric expressions, 66-68
Event, Visual Basic, **486**-487
Event driven, **487**
Event trapping, 299, 335-336
Exclamation point (!), displaying string constant and, 119-120
Executing programs, 22, 37
  event trapping and, 335
  immediate window and, 34
  of LET statement, 63
  Main Program and associated subprograms, 468
  one statement at a time, 534
  suspending, 25, 26-27, 316, 414-418
  terminating, 99
  time, 323-324
Exit command (File menu), 35
EXIT FOR statement, serial search, 278
EXIT statement, **248**-249
EXP function, **319**
Expansion slots, 4
Exponential form numeric constant, **56, 57**-58
Exponential functions, **318**-319
Exponentiation (^), 23, 65, 66, 539
Expressions, 65-72
  passing to subprogram, 456
  tips for evaluation, 539
  Visual Basic, **489**
Extended ASCII character set, **403**

Extension, filespec and, 40
External subprogram, **455**

FACTORIAL function, 472
Field name, TYPE statement, **365, 366**
Field type, TYPE statement, **366**
Figure, zooming and panning, 431-432
File(s), **198**
  flushing, 353
  indexed, 349-350
  master, 233, 350, 351
  merging, 350-357
  random, 349
  relative, 349
  sequential, 199-213
  simulated-indexed, 375-388
  transaction, 239, 350
File folder, filespec and, 40
File maintenance, **349**-363
  random files, 349, 364-374
  sequential files, 350-363
File menu, 525, 526
  Exit command, 35
  New command, 40, 42
  Open command, 41
  Print command, 38
  Save As command, 40-41
  Save command, 40-41, 468
File names, filespec and, 40
File organization, **199**
  random, 349, 364-374
  sequential, 199-213
File processing
  random, 349, 364-374
  sequential, 199-213
File specification, **40.**
File-handling statements, **198,** 199
filenumber
  CLOSE statement, 202
  GET statement, **367**
  OPEN statement for random files, **364**
  OPEN statement for sequential files, **200,** 201
  PRINT #n statement and, 203
Files box, 41
filespec, **40**
  CHAIN statement, **477**
  OPEN statement for random files, **364**
  OPEN statement for sequential files, **200,** 201
Filler, **110**
FIX(N) function, **317,** 318
Fixed dollar sign ($), 112, **118**
Fixed plus sign, **117**
Fixed point numeric constant, **56**
Floating dollar sign ($), 112, **118**
Floating plus sign, **117**
Floppy disk, **7**
Floppy disk drives, 3
Flowcharts, **13,** 32, 75, **507**-516
  arrays, 260
  CLOSE statement, 206
  decision representation, 144
  detailed, 510, 514
  For loop, 244
  general, 510, 514
  guidelines for preparing, 510-512
  looping and, 510-512
  menu-driven program, 175
  notation, 14, 507-509
  OPEN statement, 206
  purpose of, 507
  simulated-indexed files, 375
  single-level control break, 222
  straight-line, 508
  structured, 518
  symbols, 14, 507

system, 350
tips, 514-516
Flowline symbol, 14, **507,** 510
Flushing the files, **353**
FNSWITCH$ function, 329
For loop, **242**-253
  Do-While loop versus, 242
  execution of, 242-244
  flowchart, 244
  integer variables used as control
    variables in, 540
  iterations in, 249
  nested, 250-252
  object motion and, 436
  premature exit, 248, 278
  range of, 244
  serial search, 278
  sorting and, 270
  time to execute, 323-324
  window size and, 432
FOR statement, counter-controlled
  loop, 242-253
Foreground color, **411,** 414
Form, **484,** 491
  adding controls to, 494
  positioning, 493
  size of, 492
Form Feed character, **214**
Formalize the solution, 13, 46
Format/formatted
  compressed, 109
  numeric output, 112-118
  output, 112-121
  packed, 109
  screen layout, 126
  string output, 119-120
Format field, 112, **113**
Format symbols, 113-114
FORmula **TRAN**slation
  (FORTRAN), **9**
FORTRAN (**FOR**mula
  TRANslation), **9**
Forward slash (/), division and, 23,
  65
Freeze Screen module, 174, 175
Frequency, sound, **438**
Function(s), 453, 469-476, 540
  arithmetic, 317
  exponential, 318-319
  numeric, 316-328
  QBasic editor used to enter, 473
  recursive, 471
  string, 299-316
  table, 274-276
  trigonometric, 322
  user-defined, 299, 329-335,
    469-471
  utility, 322-323
  Visual Basic, 488, 489
Function keys, 34
Function parameter, **329,** 330
Function references print items, 107
FUNCTION statement, 331,
  469-470
Functionality, top-down chart
  showing, 75
FUTUREVALUE function, 471

Garbage Doesn't Get In (GDGI),
  166
Garbage In Garbage Out (GIGO),
  166
GB (gigabyte), **7**
General flowchart, **510,** 514
GET statement, **367**
  for graphics, **435**-437
Gigabyte (GB), 7
Global, **331**
Global variables, **455**
GOSUB statement, **77**-82, 454
  event-trapping and, 335

Grammatical errors, **533**
Graphic standards, 6, 399-401
Graphical interface, 11
Graphical User Interface (GUI), **11**
Graphics, 397-437
  characters, 403-404
  coordinates, 419, 431, 432
  high resolution mode, 399, 401,
    418, 431
  medium resolution mode, 399, 401,
    402, 418-437
  modes, 399-437
  text-mode, 399, 400, 401, 403-418
  Windows applications, 493
Graphics program, 9
GUI, *see* Graphical User Interface

Hard copy output, **38**-39
Hard disk, 8
Hard disk drive, 3
Hard error, **535**
Heading lines, **122**
Help
  context-sensitive, 42
  online, 33, 42
Help menu, 531
Help window, 532
Hierarchy chart, **74**
Hierarchy of operations, 66, 164
High-level design, 74, **75**
High-level languages, **9**
High resolution graphics mode, **399,**
  401, 418, 431
Hit, table search, 277
Home position, **126**
Horizontal bar graph, 407-410

IBM personal computers and
  compatibles, 4-8
Icons, **11**
IF statement, 144, 145-148, 156-159
  Case structure and, 169
  logical operators and, 160-166
  needless, 541
  nested, 147, 541
  paging report and, 213
  serial search, 278
  string functions and, 299
  user-defined function and, 329
If-Then-Else control structure, **143,**
  156-166, **513**
  IF statement and, 144, 145-148
  implementing, 156-159
  Nassi-Schneiderman charts and,
    518
  nested forms of, 158-159
  pseudocode and, 516
  simple forms of, 156-158
  Warnier-Orr diagrams and, 520
Immediate window, **34,** 532
  activating, 111
  examining values through, 533-534
  size of, 111
IMP (implication) logical operator,
  163
Improper program, **514**
Increment value, FOR statement,
  243, 244, 247-248
Indexed files, **349**-350
  simulated, 375-388
Infinite loop, **511**
Initial value, FOR statement, **243,**
  244, 247-248
Initialization
  arrays, 265
  flowchart showing, 511
  loop variable, 243, 244, 246
  numeric variables, 149, 154
INKEY$ function, **315**-316, 404

Input
  data validation and, 166-169, 178
  flowchart showing, 510
  keyboard, 5
  mouse and, 11
  string, 314-316
INPUT$(N) function, **316**
INPUT #n statement, **211**-212
Input/Output (I/O) symbol, 14, 206,
  507
Input prompt, **25**
Input prompt message, **26**-27
INPUT statement, **25**-27
  data validation and, 166-169
  LINE INPUT statement versus,
    315
  numeric constants and, 57
  READ and DATA statements
    versus, 95
  string constants and, 59, 60
  variable names in, 26
  variables assigned value using, 60
Input unit, **3**
Insert key (INS), **36**
Insert mode, **36**
INSTR function, **303**-304
INT (integer) function, **70,** 317
  print items, 107
  RND function combined with, 325
Integer array, 436
Integer division (\), 23, 65, 66
Integer numeric constant, **56**
Integer variables
  using as control variables in For
    loops, 540
  using for counters, 539
Intel microprocessors, 6
Interconnected **net**works, *see*
  Internet
Interface, currency application,
  491-496
Internal subprogram, **455**
Internet (**inter**connected **net**works),
  10
Internet browser program, **9,** 10
Internet service provider, 10
Interpreter, **12**
Inventory retrieval and update, 375
Investment, determining time to
  double, 319-321
I/O symbol. *See* Input/Output
  symbol
IRGB color bits, **412**
Item
  print, **107**
  PRINT #n statement and, **203**
Iterations, For loop, **249**

Java, 9
Joins, **300**

KB (kilobyte), **7**
Key, 349-350, 375
Keyboard, **3, 5**
Keyword, **22**
Kilobyte (KB), 7

Label, **77**
  RESTORE statement, **106**
Label control, 494
  border, 498
  caption property, 496-497
Label name, TYPE statement, **365,**
  366
LAN, *see* Local area network
LBOUND function, 459
LCASE$ function, **306,** 308
Lead read, **99**
Leading asterisks, 118
Leading blank characters, 309

Leading minus sign, **28,** 108
Leading space, **28**
  numeric output, 108
  string containing, 60
Leading zeros, formatting, 116
LEFT$ function, 301
LEFT$ string function, 72, 168-169
Left-justify string values, **112**
LEN function, 167, 300-301, 308
LEN string function, 72
Length argument, string, 302
LET statement, **22,** 25
  general form of, 62-63
  string constants assigned to
    variables in, 59
  string functions and, 299
  variables assigned value using, 60
Level number, **75**
Limit value, FOR statement, **243,**
  244, 247-248
Line(s)
  adding new, 36
  blank, 109
  changing or replacing, 36
  copying, 36
  deleting, 36
  listing on printer, 38
  listing on screen, 39
Line counter, **213,** 218
LINE INPUT statement, **314**-315
  INPUT statement versus, 315
LINE statement, **421**-423
Linear search, **277**
List, **26**
  empty, 29
  null, 29
  PRINT #n, USING statement and,
    203
  PRINT USING statement and, **112**
Loading Main Program and
  associated subprograms, 468
LOC(n) function, **368**
Local area network (LAN), **8**
Local variables, **455**
LOCATE statement, 95, **126**-131
  reasonableness check and, 167
LOF(n) function, **368**
LOG function, **319**
Logical operators, **145,** 160-166
  AND, 145, 161-162, 165
  combining, 164-165
  EQV (equivalence), 163
  IMP (implication), 163
  NOT, 145, 160-161, 165
  OR, 145, 162-163, 165
  rules of precedence, 164
  XOR (exclusive OR), 163
Long integer numeric constant, 58
Long integer numeric variable, 62
Loop
  counter-controlled, 242-253, 540
  data validation and, 167-169
  Do, *see* Do loop
  Do-While, *see* Do-While loop
  endless, 511
  flowcharts and, 510-512
  For, *see* For loop
  infinite, 511
  pass through, 268, 270, 323
  terminating, 101, 103, 145, 155
  terminating early, 248
  time to pass through, 323
LOOP statement, 97, 99, 101, 145,
  155, 242
LOOP UNTIL statement, 101, 145,
  155
Loop variable, **243,** 244
  stepping, 245-246
LOOP WHILE statement, 101
Lower-bound value, of array, **254,**
  255, 256, 257, 266

Lowercase, 306
Low-level languages, **9**
LPRINT statement, 39, **111**
  printer characteristics and, 214
LPRINT USING statement, 121-122
LTRIM$ function, **309**

Machine language, 12
Magazines, personal computer, 543, 545
Magnetic tape drives, 3
Main memory, 3
  array in, 254
  buffer, 199, 201
  numeric constants stored in, 58
  stored program and, 8
  subprograms in, 455
Main memory unit, **3**, 6-7
Main module, **76**
  control returned to, 77
Main Program, **77, 453**
  printing, 468
  returning control to, 99
  saving, loading, and executing, 468
Maintain the program, *see* Program maintenance
Master file, **233, 350**
Matchexpression, **171**, 172
Matching records, 358-363
MB (megabyte), **7**
Medium resolution graphics mode, **399**, 401, 402, 418-437
Megabyte (MB), **7**
Megahertz (MHz), **7**
Memory
  main, *see* Main memory unit
  read-only, 7
Menu, **144**
Menu bar, **33**-34, 526-531
  deactivating, 34
Menu commands, 525-531
Menu-driven program, **144**, 173-180
Merging files, 350, **351**-357
Method, **488**-489
MHz (megahertz), 7
Microprocessor, **6**
Microsoft Corporation, 10
Microsoft Windows, 11
Microsoft Windows 98, 11
Microsoft Windows 2000 Professional, 11
Microsoft Windows NT Workstation, 11
MID$ function, 301, 308
MID$ statement, **304**-305
MID$ string function, 72
Minus sign (-)
  leading, 28
  subtraction and, 22, **23**, 65
Minus sign (-) format symbol, 117
MOD (modulo), 23, 65, 66
Mode
  OPEN statement and, **200**
  SCREEN statement, **402**
Modular approach to problem solving, 73-82
Module, **76**
  menu-driven program, 174
  multiple superior, 174
Modulo, *see* MOD
Modulo operator, **65**
Monitor, **3**, 5-6
  color, 399-401, 412, 419
  pixels, 5-6, 401, 427
  RGB, 412
  twips and, 492
Mother board, **6**
Motion, object, 435
Mouse, **3, 11**, 525
Moving text, 36
MS-DOS, **11**

Multidimensional arrays, 255, 264-266
Multimedia-enhancing (MMX) technology, 6
Multiplication (*), 22, 23, 65, 66, 539
Multitask, **11**
Music, 437-440
  defined by string expression, 439

n factorial (n!), 471
n! symbol (n factorial), 471
NAME statement, 351
Named COMMON block, **462**
Naperian base, **319**
Nassi-Schneiderman charts, **518**-519
Negative number, 108
Negative values, in FOR statement, 246
Nested For loop, 250-252
Nested IF statement, **147**
  SELECT CASE statement versus, 541
Nested IF-Then-Else structure, 158-159
Nested parentheses, **67**
Nested subroutines, 80-82
Network, **8**
New command (File menu), 40, 42
New master file, **350**
New SUB command (Edit menu), 464
Newspapers, personal computer, 543, 545
NEXT statement, counter-controlled loop, 242-253
NOT logical operator, 145, **160**-161, 165
N-S charts, **518**
Null list, **29**
  in PRINT statement, 109
Null string, **59**, 302
Number(s)
  negative, 108
  positive, 108
  pseudo-random, 324
  rounding, 70-71, 318
  truncating, 70-71, 318
Number function, random, 324-328
Number sign (#) format symbol, 113-115, 116
Numeric constants, **56**-57
  DATA statement and, 103
  exponential form, 56, 57-58
  forms of, 56
  type and range of, 58
Numeric expressions, **65**
  comparing in IF statement, 147
  error-free, 69
  evaluation of, 66-68
  formation of, 65-66
  in FOR statement, 246
  spacing and, 110
  TAB function and, 110
  Visual Basic, 489
Numeric functions, **70**, 316-328
  user-defined, 330
Numeric output, 108
  formatted, 112-118
Numeric value, string equivalent, 308
Numeric variables, **60**
  accumulators, 149
  declared, 62
  initialization of, 149, 154
  INPUT #n statement, 212

Object
  Visual Basic, **484**
  Windows applications, 493
Object box (Properties window), **486**

Object-oriented programming language (OOPL), 9, **485**
ON ERROR GOTO statement, **536**
ON TIMER statement, 335-336
Online help system, *see* Help system
Open architecture, of computers, 4
Open command (File menu), 41
OPEN statement
  flowchart of, 206
  random files, 364
  sequential files, **199**-201
Opening
  random files, 364
  sequential files, 199-201
  Visual Basic project, 503
Operating system, 10-11
OPTION BASE statement, 255, **256**
Options menu, 530-531
OR logical operator, 145, **162**-163, 165
Order of operations, 66, 164
Organization, top-down chart showing, 75
Output, 3
  flowchart showing, 510
  formatted, 112-121
  hard copy, 38-39
  monitor, 3, 4-5
  numeric, *see* Numeric output
  printer, 111, 213-218
  screen, 37, 39, 95, 107-111, 218-219
  sequential file, 200
  slowing down, 414
  string, *see* String output
Output screen, **29, 37**
Output Screen command (View menu), 37
Overtype mode, 36

Packed format, **109**
Page counter, 218
Paging the report, **213**-219
PAINT statement, **425**-426
Palette, **419**
Panning figure, 431
Parallel arrays, **259**, 263
  table search, 277
Parameters, **126**
  SUB statement, 455-**456**
Parentheses ()
  evaluating compound conditions and, 165-166
  function parameter and, 329
  evaluating numeric expressions and, 67-68
Pascal, 9
Pascal's triangle, **290**
Pass, **268**, 270
  time to make, 323
Pass, through Do loop, 99
Pass-by-reference, **458**
Pass-by-value, **458**
Paste command (Edit menu), 36
Pasting, **36**
Path, filespec and, 40
Pattern, tile, 426
Payment dates, validating, 310-313
PC-DOS, **11**
PCs, *see* Personal computers
Peer review group, **76**
Pentium III, 6
Performance testing, 323-324
Period (.), separating words in variable names using, 61
Personal computer(s), family of, 4-8
Personal computer magazines, newspapers, and URLs, 543, 545
Physical coordinate system, **431**, 432
Piano, converting PC into, 439

Picture element (pixel), **5**-6, 401, 427
Pie charts, 398
Pixel. See **Picture element**
PLAY statement, **439**-440
Plus sign (+)
  addition and, 22, **23**, 65
  concatenation and, 65, 72
  fixed, 117
  floating, 117
Plus sign (+) format symbol, 117
PMAP function, **432**-433
POINT function, **433**-434
Pointer, **104**, 199, **212**
POS function, **322**
Position, form, 493
Position argument, string, 302
Positionally-organized tables, **274**-276
Positive value, 317
Predefined process symbol, 14, **80**, 507
Premature exit from For loop, **248**, 278
PRESET (point reset) statement, **420**
Press any key to continue… message, 316
Primary read, **99**
PRINT #n statement, **202**-203
PRINT #n, USING statement, **203**
Print command (File menu), 38
Print headings, report, 213, 218
Print items, **107**
Print positions, **108**, 109
PRINT statement, 23, **107**-111
  calculations within, 110
  quotation marks in, 28
  screen output, 219
  string constants and, 59
  string functions and, 299
  text-mode graphics, 403
PRINT USING statement, **112**-121
Print zone, **108**
Printers, **3**
  characteristics of, 214
  listing program lines on, 38
  output to, 111
  report generated to, 213-218
  twips and, 492
Printer spacing chart, **122**, 154
Printing Main Program and associated subprograms, 468
Problem analysis, 13, 44, 74
Problem solving, 510
  control structures and, 144
  program and, 12-15
  top-down (modular) approach, 73-82
Procedural language, **487**
Procedures, **487**
  flowchart or pseudocode showing, 75
Process, flowchart showing, 510
Process symbol, 14, 507
Program(s), **3**, 8
  chained to, 477-478
  chaining, 453, 477-479
  compiled, 12
  entering, 13, 45
  guide to writing, 43-46
  improper, 514
  interpreted, 12
  loading from disk, 41-42
  Main. *See* Main Program
  menu-driven, 144, 173-180
  multifunction, 173
  problem solving and, 12-15
  proper, 514
  saving, 40-41
  starting new, 42
  stored, 3, 8

straight-line, 95
Program design, 13, 44
  detailed, 76
  high-level, 74-76
  testing, 13, 45
Program development life cycle, **12**-13
Program documentation, 30-32
Program flowcharts, *see* Flowcharts
Program maintenance, 13, 46
Program specifications, **43**
Program tasks, **44**
Program testing, 13, 46
Programming
  object-oriented, 9, 485
  structured, 143-169
  styles, 154
  tips, 539-541
  top-down, 74
Programming language
  high-level, 9
  low-level, 9
  procedural, 487
  QBasic, *see* QBasic
Projects, Visual Basic, **491**
  opening, 503
  saving, 501-502
  starting new, 503
Proper program, **514**
Properties, **485**-486
  currency application, 496-499
Properties list (Properties window), **486**
Properties window, **486**
PSET (point set) statement, **420**
Pseudocode, **13**, **14**-16, 75, **516**-518
Pseudo-random numbers, **324**
Pull-down menus, 10, 34
PUT statement, **367**-368
  for graphics, **435**-437
QBasic (**Q**uick **B**eginner's **A**ll-purpose **S**ymbolic **I**nstruction **C**ode), **9**
QBasic commands, 33
QBasic editor
  entering functions using, 473
  entering subprograms using, 463-468
QBasic language, 10
QBasic operating environment, 11, **21**, 32-35
QB Survival Guide, **33**, 42
QBasic program
  characteristics of, 21
  creating, 21-47
  editing, *see* Editing
QBasic screen, 33-35
QBasic session
  starting, 32-33
  terminating, 35
Question mark (?), input prompt and, **25**
Quick **B**eginner's **A**ll-purpose **S**ymbolic **I**nstruction **C**ode, *see* QBasic
QuickBASIC compiler, 12
Quitting QBasic session, 35
Quotation marks ("")
  in PRINT statement, 28
  strings and, 59, 60, 104
  surrounding input prompt message, 27
  WRITE #n statement, 207

R TRIM$ function, **309**
Radians, **322**
Radius, CIRCLE statement and, **424**
RAM (random-access memory), **6**-7
Random-access memory, *see* RAM
Random file, **349**
  creating, 369-372

file maintenance, 349, 364-374
  opening and closing, 364
  record structure for, 365-366
  sequential files used with, 375
Random file processing, 349, 364-374
Random number function, 324-328
RANDOMIZE statement, **326**-327
Range check, **167**-168
Range of For loop, **244**
Range of statements, **99**
Range of values, subscript assigned, **254**
Read
  lead, 99
  primary, 99
READ statement, 95, 99-100, **104**
  chained-to program and, 478
  DATA statement and, 104-105
Reading records, 367
Read-only memory, *see* ROM
Read/write memory, 6
Reasonableness check, **167**
recl, OPEN statement for random files, **364**
Record(s)
  accessing, 372-374
  adding, 349, 350-357
  changing or updating, 349, 350, 358-363, 379-388
  data items within, 198
  deleting, 349, 350, 358-363
  displaying, 379-388
  matching, 358-363
  reading and transferring, 367
  sentinel, 99
  trailer, 99, 100
  writing to file, 367
Record layout, **365**
Record length, **364**
Record number
  GET statement, 367
  LOC function, 368
Record structure, **365**-366
Record variable, **365**, **367**
Recursive definition, **471**
Recursive function, 471
REDIM statement, SHARED keyword used in, 462
Refresh screen, 130, 131
Relational expression, **160**
Relational operators, **101**-102
Relative file, **349**
REM statements, **30**-32
Removing controls, 493-495
RENAME command (DOS), 351
Repetition control structure, **143**
Reports
  paging, 213-219
  sorted data, 241, 267-273
  subtotals within, 197, 219-230
  writing to sequential file, 202-203
Reserved words, **22**, **61**
RESTORE statement, 106-107
RESUME statement, **536**
RETURN statement, **77**-82, 99
Review the code, *see* Code, reviewing
Rewind, **202**
RGB monitors, **412**
RIGHT$ function, 301
RIGHT$ string function, 72
Right-justify string values, **112**
RND function, 324-328, 332-333
  INT function combined with, 325
ROM (read-only memory), **7**
Rounding, 70-71, 318
  decimal fractional digits, 116
  PRINT USING statement and, 112, 116, 318
Routine, end-of-file, 99

Row
  column intersection, 323, 400
  cursor position, 322
  graphics coordinates, 419
  positioning cursor in using LOCATE statement, 126
Rules of precedence, 66, **164**
Run, **22**
Run menu, 529
  Start command, 37
Run time, **484**
Running totals, **149**, 151, 154
Running Visual Basic application, 504

Sale price, determining, 95-132
Salesperson's commission, determining, 22-47
Save As command (File menu), 40-41
Save command (File menu), 40-41, 468
Saving
  Main Program and associated subprograms, 468
  program, 40-41
  Visual Basic project, 501
Scientific notation, **57**
Screen, **3**
  clearing, 29, 402, 406
  output, *see* Output screen
  refreshing, 130, 131
  report paged to, 218-219
  tiling, 426-428
  time displayed on, 335
  viewport, 434
  writing information to, 95, 107-111
SCREEN function, **323**
Screen layout format, **126**
Screen mode, **400**, 401
  COLOR statement, 411, 419
SCREEN parameter, WINDOW statement and, 431
SCREEN statement, **401**-402
Scroll bars, 34
Scrolling, 34, 532
Search
  binary, 277, 281-284
  linear, 277
  sequential, 277
  serial, 277-281, 284
  string argument for substring, 303-304
  table, 276-277
  word, 303
Search argument, **276**
  binary search, 281, 283
  serial search, 277
Search menu, 528-529
Secant, 322
Seed, **326**
SELECT CASE statement, **169**-180
  ELSEIF versus, 146, 169
  nested IF statements versus, 541
Selection control structure, **143**, 145, **513**
Semicolon (;)
  cursor location and, 28
  print items separated by, 109
  separating message from variable, 27
Semicolon separator, **109**
Sentinel record, **99**
Sentinel value, **99**, 100, **511**
Sequence control structure, **143**, 144, **512**
Sequential file, **199**-213
  closing, 201-202
  file maintenance, 350-363
  opening, 199-201
  random file used with, 375

updating, 350
  writing data to, 206-207
  writing reports to, 202-203
Sequential file processing, 199-213
Sequential search, **277**
Serial search, **277**-281, 284
SGN(N) function, **317**
Shape, CIRCLE statement and, **424**
SHARED statement, **460**-462
Shell sort, **267**, 272-273
Short integer numeric constant, 58
Short integer numeric variable, 62
Sign status, displaying, 112
Silicon chip, **6**
Simple variables, **60**
Simulated-indexed files, 375-388
SIN function, **322**
Sine, 322
Single precision numeric constant, 58
Single precision (exponential form) numeric constant, 58
Single precision numeric variable, 62
Size
  controls, 495, 496
  DIM statement and, **255**
  form, 492
  window, 532
SLEEP statement, **414**-418
Soft error, **535**
Software, *see* Computer software
Sort/sorting, **241**, 267-273
  bubble, 267-272
  Shell, 267, 272-273
Sound, 437-440
SOUND statement, **438**
Space(s), **29**, 309
  displaying, 110
  formatting in numeric output, 113
  leading, 28
  trailing, 28
SPACE$ function, **309**
SPC function, **110**, 130-131, 309
Speakers, 3, 437
Sphere, volume of, **194**
Split command (View menu), 467
Splitting view window, 467
SQR function, **70**, **318**
  print items, 107
Start, CIRCLE statement and, **424**
Start command (Run menu), 37
Starting
  QBasic session, 32-33
  Visual Basic project, 503
Statement, **104**
Statements, 21
  executing one at a time, 534
  multiple, per line, 32
  nonexecutable, 30
  range of, 99
  relationships between, 23-24
Status line, **34**-35
STEP keyword, 243, 245-246, 249
Step mode, **534**
Stepping the loop variable, 243, **245**-246
Stereo speakers, **3**
Storage
  auxiliary, *see* Auxiliary storage
  numeric constants, 58
  types of, 6-7
Stored program, **8**
STR$ function, **308**
Straight-line flowcharts, **510**
Straight-line programs, **95**
String(s)
  case conversion, 128, 306
  concatenated, 72, 300
  duplicating, 309
  empty, 59

joins, 300
null, 59, 302
 numeric equivalent, 308
 sub-, *see* Substrings
String argument
 searching for substring, 303-304
 string function as, 302
String constants, **56**, 59-60, 71
 displaying, 119
 PRINT USING statement and, 113
String data, 299-316
 accepting, 314-316
 DATA statement and, 104
String expressions, **65**, 71-72
 and, **314**
 drawing object defined by, 428
 music defined by, 439
 PRINT #n, USING statement and, **203**
 PRINT USING statement and, **112**-113
 TIME$ statement and, **314**
 Visual Basic, 489
String field, variable-length, 119
String functions, **59**, 71, 299-316
STRING$ function, **309**
String output, formatted, 119-120
String variables, 59-**60**, 71
 declared, 62
 INPUT #n statement, 212
 output line assigned to, 154
 PRINT USING statement and, 113
 switch, 270
Structure, record, **365**-366
Structured flowcharts, 518
Structured programming, **143**-169
 top-down programming versus, 145
Structured walk-through, **76**
Stub, **82**
Style, LINE statement, **421**
SUB statement, **454**
 parameters in, 455-456
Subprograms, **453**-468
 associated, 455
 editing, 465-467
 entering using QBasic editor, 463-468
 external, 455
 internal, 455
 passing constants and expressions, 456
 passing entire array to, 459
 passing no values to, 456
 passing values between, 460
 passing variables and individual array elements, 458-459
 printing, 468
 saving, loading, and executing, 468
 sharing variables with, 460-462
 subroutines versus, 453-455
 types of, 455
Subroutine(s), **76**
 control transferred to, 77
 error-catching, 536-537
 nested, 80-82
 subprograms versus, 453-455
 Visual Basic, 488
Subroutine name, **77**
Subscript, array, 253, 254, 257, 264, 266
Subscripted variables, **60**
Substrings, 300, **301**
 replacement, 304-305
 searching string argument for, 303-304
Subtotals, report, 197, 219-230
Subtraction (-), 22, 23, 65, 66, 539
Super VGA standard, 6
SWAP statement, **269**
Swapping, **268**

Switch, **270**
Symbols
 flowchart, 14, 206, 507
 format, 113-114
System event trapping, **299**, 335-336
System flowchart, **350**

TAB function, **109**-110
Table, **241**
 argument- organized, 274, 276-277
 binary search, 277, 281-284
 positionally-organized, 274-276
 serial search, 277-281, 284
 two-dimensional array in form of, 264-265
Table argument, **276**
 binary search, 281
 serial search, 277, 280-281
Table functions, **274**
Table lookup, **276**
Table processing, 274-285
Table search, **276**-277
Tailor's Calculations, 55-84
TAN function, **322**
Tangent, 322
Terminal symbol, 14, 507, 508
Test data, **13**
Test the design, *see* Program design, testing
Test the program, *see* Program testing
Testexpression, **171**
Testing
 for end-of-file, 99-100
 performance, 323-324
 structured programming and, 143
 top-down, 74
Text
 copying, 36
 cutting, 36
 moving, 36
Text boxes, **35**
 added to form, 495
 Text property of, 497
Text graphics mode, **399**, 400, 401, 403-418
Text property, 497
THEN clause, 146, 156-159
 null, 158
Tile mask, **426**-427
Tiling, **426**-428
Time, on screen display, 335
TIME$ function, **310**
TIME$ statement, **314**
TIMER function, **323**-324
TIMER OFF statement, 336
TIMER ON statement, 335-336
TIMER STOP statement, 336
Title line, **34**
Toolbox, **484**, 485, 493
Top-down approach, **73**-82
Top-down chart, **74**-75
 arrays, 260
 horizontal bar graphs, 407
 menu-driven program, 174
 merging files, 352
 single-level control break, 222
Top-down design, **74**-76
Top-down programming, **74**
 structured programming versus, 145
Top-down testing and debugging, **74**
Total
 accumulators, 149-154, 221
 running, 149, 151, 154
Total line, **122**
Tracing, **535**
Trailer record, **99**, 100
Trailing blank characters, 309

Trailing space, **28**
 numeric output, 108
 string containing, 60
Trailing zeros, formatting, 116
Transaction file, **239**, **350**, 351, 352
Transferring records, 367
Trapping events, 299, 335-336
Trapping user errors, 535-538
Trigonometric functions, **322**
TROFF statement, 535
TRON statement, 535
Truncation, 70-71, 318
Truth tables, 164
Twip, **492**
TYPE statement, 365

UBOUND function, 459
UCASE$ function, 128, **306**
Underscore (-), displaying string constant and, 119
Uniform Resource Locator, 10
 personal computer information, 543, 545
Updating records, 349, 350, 358-363, 379-388
Upper-bound value, of array, **254**, 255, 256, 257, 266
Uppercase, 128, 306
URL, *see* Uniform Resource Locator
USA character set, **403**
User-defined functions, **299**, **329**-335, 469-471
User errors, trapping, 535-538
User interface
 QBasic, 483
 Visual Basic, 483, 484

VAL function, **308**
Value(s)
 examining through immediate window, 533-534
 incrementing, 242-243
 range check, 167-168
 seed, 326
 sentinel, 99, 100
Value check, **168**
Variable(s), **22**
 array and, 241
 graphic relationship between, 398
 loop, *see* Loop variable
 record, 365, 367
 sign of, 28
 arrays versus simple, 253-254
 assigning data items to, 103
 control, 220-221
 declaring types, 62
 displaying values of, 533-534
 dummy, 330
 FOR statement, 246-247
 global, 455
 INPUT statement, 26, 27
 list of, 26
 local, 455
 numeric. *See* Numeric variables
 passing to subprogram, 458-459
 passing using chaining, 477
 READ statement and, 104-106
 to right of equal sign in LET statement, 25
 sharing with subprograms, 460-462
 simple, 60
 string. *See* String variables
 subroutines versus subprograms, 455
 subscripted, 60, 255, 257
 SWAP statement, 269
 switch, 270
 user-defined function, 330-331

Variable names, **22**, **61**
 array and, 241, 253, 255
 capitalizing first letter of, 30
 INPUT statement, 26
 selection of, 61-62
 Variable1, SWAP statement, **269**
 Variable2, SWAP statement, **269**
Very-high resolution graphics mode, **399**-400, 401
VGA standard, 5
Video display device, **3**
View menu, 527-528
 Output Screen command, 37
 Split command, 467
VIEW statement, **434**-435
View window, **34**, 532
 activating, 34, 111
 clearing, 40, 42
 splitting, 467
Viewport, screen, 434
Visual Basic, 9, 483-505
 approach to building applications with, 484-489
 currency conversion application, 491-504
 exiting, 504
 running application, 504
 saving project, 501-502
Visual Basic environment, 489-491
Visual page, SCREEN statement, **402**
Visual Table of Contents (VTOC), **74**
Volume, formulas for, 194

Warnier-Orr diagrams, **519**-521
Web pages, 10
Wedges, drawing, 423
WEND statement, 156
WHILE statement, 156
WIDTH statement, **402**-403
Window
 active, 532
 immediate. *See* Immediate window
 size, 432, 532
 splitting, 467
 view. *See* View window
WINDOW statement, **431**-432
Word processing program, **9**
Words
 reserved, 22
 search for, 303
Working Model Edition, Visual Basic, **483**
World coordinate system, **431**, 432
World Wide Web (WWW), 10
WRITE #n statement, **206**-207
Writing data, to sequential file, 206-207
WWW, *see* World Wide Web

XGA standard, 6
XOR (exclusive OR) logical operator, **163**

Zeros
 leading, 116
 trailing, 116
Zooming figure, 431-432

MICROSOFT QBasic REFERENCE CARD

Legend: *Uppercase letters are required keywords. You must supply items within < >. You must select one of the entries within { }. Items within [ ] are optional. Three ellipsis points (...) indicate that an item may be repeated as many times as you wish. The symbol ƀ represents a blank character.*

A page number of QBS means that the seldom used statement or function is not covered in the text, but additional information is available through the QB Survival Guide (see page 42).

Summary of QBasic Statements

STATEMENT	PAGE
BEEP — Causes the speaker on the PC to beep for a fraction of a second.	166
CALL <name> [,(argumentlist)] — Transfers control to subprogram.	455
CHAIN "filespec" — Instructs the PC to stop executing the current program, load another program from auxiliary storage, and start executing it.	477
CHDIR <pathspecification> — Changes the current directory for the specified drive.	QBS
CIRCLE <(x, y)>,radius> [,color [,start,end [,shape]]] — Causes the PC to draw an ellipse, circle, arc, or wedge with center at (x, y).	424
CLEAR [,,stack] — Reinitializes all program variables, closes files, and sets the stack size.	QBS
CLOSE [#] [filenumber] [,[#] [filenumber]]... — Closes specified files.	202
CLS — Erases the information on the screen and places the cursor in the upper left corner of the screen.	29
COLOR [background] [,palette] — In medium-resolution mode, sets the color for the background and palette of colors.	419
COLOR [foreground] [,background] [,border] — In text mode, defines the color of the foreground characters, background, and border around the screen.	411
COM(n) {ON / OFF / STOP} — Enables or disables trapping of communications activity on adaptor n.	146
COMMON [SHARED] <variable> [,variable]... — Passes specified variables to a subprogram or chained program.	462
CONST <constantname> = <expression> [, constantname = expression]... — Declares symbolic constants that can be used in place of numeric or string expressions.	QBS

STATEMENT	PAGE
DATA <data item> [,data item]... — Provides for the creation of a sequence of data items for use by the READ statement.	103
DATE$ = mm {- / /} dd {- / /} yy/yy where mm = month, dd = day, yy = 2 digit year, yyyy = 4 digit year. Sets the system date.	314
DECLARE {FUNCTION / SUB} name [parameterlist] — Declares references to QBasic procedures and invokes argument-type checking.	468
DEF FN <name> [(variable, [,variable]...)] = <expression> — Defines and names a function that can be referenced in a program as often as needed. Multiline functions end with an END DEF statement.	330
DEFtype <letterrange> [,letterrange]... — Sets the data type for variables and functions.	62
DIM [SHARED] < arrayname(size)> [AS type], [arrayname(size) [AS type]]... — Reserves storage locations for arrays and declares array types.	255
DO — Causes the statements between DO and LOOP to be executed repeatedly. The loop is controlled by a condition in the corresponding LOOP statement.	100
DO UNTIL <condition> — Causes the statements between DO UNTIL and LOOP to be executed repeatedly until the condition is true.	100
DO WHILE <condition> — Causes the statements between DO WHILE and LOOP to be executed repeatedly while the condition is true.	100
DRAW <string expression> — Causes the PC to draw the object that is defined by the value of the string expression.	428
ENVIRON stringconstant — Modifies a parameter in the DOS Environment string table.	QBS
END {DEF / FUNCTION / IF / SELECT / SUB / TYPE} — Ends a QBasic program, procedure, or block of code.	146
ERASE <arrayname> [, arrayname]... — Eliminates previously-defined arrays.	QBS
ERROR <integerexpression> — Simulates the occurrence of a QBasic error or allows the user to define error codes.	QBS
EXIT <statement> — Exits statement, where statement is equal to FOR, DO, DEF, FUNCTION, or SUB.	249

STATEMENT	PAGE
FIELD <#filenumber, width AS string variable> [,width AS string variable] — Allocates space for variables in a random file buffer.	QBS
FILES [filespecificatons] — Lists the name of all program and data files in auxiliary storage on the default drive or the drive specified by file specification.	QBS
FOR <loopvariable> = <initial> TO <limit> [STEP increment] — Causes the statements between the FOR and NEXT statement to be executed until the value of loopvariable exceeds the value of the limit.	243
FUNCTION <name> [(parameterlist)] [STATIC] — Declares the name, the parameters, and initiates a function procedure that ends with an END FUNCTION.	470
GET <(X_1, Y_1) - (N_2, Y_2)>, arrayname> — Reads the colors of the points in the specified area on the screen into an array.	435
GET < [#] filenumber> [,record number] — Reads the specified record from a random file and transfers it to the buffer that is defined by the corresponding FIELD statement.	367
GOSUB {linelabel / linenumber} — Causes control to transfer to a subroutine beginning at the specified line. Also retains the location of the next statement following the GOSUB statement.	77
GOTO {linelabel / linenumber} — Transfers control to the specified line.	100
IF <condition> THEN [clause] [ELSE [clause]] — The single line IF statement causes execution of the THEN clause if the condition is true. If the ELSE clause is included, it causes execution of the ELSE clause if the condition is false.	146
IF <condition > THEN [statementblock₁] [ELSE [statementblock₂]] END IF — The block IF statement allows for multiple lines in the THEN and ELSE clauses. Causes execution of the THEN clause if the condition is true. Causes execution of the ELSE clause if the condition is false. The ELSE IF <condition> THEN clause may be used in place of the ELSE clause.	146
**INPUT [;][,]"prompt message" {; / ,}	<variable> [,variable]** — Provides for the assignment of values to variables from a source external to the program such as the keyboard.	27

(QBasic Statements continued on page R.2 in left column)

MICROSOFT QBasic REFERENCE CARD

Summary of QBasic Statements (continued)

STATEMENT	PAGE
INPUT <# filenumber, variable> [,variable]... Provides for the assignment of values to variables from a sequential file in auxiliary storage.	211
KEY { n, string value / ON / OFF / LIST } Assigns a string value to a function key. Also used to display the values and enable or disable the function key display line.	335
KEY(n) { ON / OFF / STOP } Activates or deactivates trapping of the specified key n.	335
KILL <filespecification> Deletes a file from disk.	QBS
[LET] <variable> = <expression> Causes the evaluation of the expression, followed by the assignment of the resulting value to the variable to the left of the equal sign.	63
LINE [(x₁, y₁)]-(x₂, y₂)[,color][,B[F]][,Style] Draws a line or a box on the screen.	421
LINE INPUT [;]["prompt message";] <string variable> or LINE INPUT [#filenumber,] <string variable> Provides for the assignment of a line of up to 255 characters from a source external to the program, such as the keyboard or sequential file.	315
LOCATE [row] [,column] [,cursor] [,start] [,stop] Positions the cursor on the screen. Can also be used to make the cursor visible or invisible, and to control the size of the cursor.	126
LOCK [#filenumber] , { record / [start] TO end } Locks all or some of the records in a file.	101
LOOP { WHILE / UNTIL } [condition] Identifies the end of a loop.	111
LPRINT [item] [{, / ; / b} item]... Provides for the generation of output to the printer.	121
LPRINT USING <string expression> <item> [{, / ; / b} item]... Provides for the generation of formatted output to the printer.	304
LSET <string variable> = <string expression> Moves string data left-justified into an area of a random file buffer that is defined by the string variable.	QBS
MID$ <(string var,start position [,number]>, <substring> Replaces a substring within a string.	QBS
MKDIR <pathname> Creates a new directory.	QBS

STATEMENT	PAGE
NAME <oldfilespecification> AS <newfilespecification> Renames a file on disk.	QBS
NEXT [numeric variable] [,numeric variable]... Identifies the end of the For loop(s).	243
ON COM(n) GOSUB { linelabel / linenumber } Causes control to transfer to the specified line when data is filling the communications buffer (n).	335
ON ERROR GOTO { linelabel / linenumber } Enables error trapping and specifies the first line of an error handling routine that the PC is to branch to in the event of an error. If linenumber is zero, error trapping is disabled.	536
ON <numeric expression> GOSUB { linelabel-list / linenumber-list } Causes control to transfer to the subroutine represented by the selected line. Also retains the location of the next statement following the ON-GOSUB statement.	QBS
ON <numeric expression> GOTO { linelabel-list / linenumber-list } Causes control to transfer to one of several lines according to the value of the numeric expression.	335
ON KEY(n) GOSUB { linelabel / linenumber } Causes control to transfer to the specified line when the function key or cursor control key (n) is pressed.	335
ON PEN GOSUB { linelabel / linenumber } Causes control to transfer to the specified line when the light pen is activated.	QBS
ON PLAY(n) GOSUB { linelabel / linenumber } Plays continuous background music. Transfers control to the specified line when a note (n) is sensed.	335
ON STRIG(n) GOSUB { linelabel / linenumber } Causes control to transfer to the specified line when one of the joystick buttons (n) is pressed.	335
ON TIMER(n) GOSUB { linelabel / linenumber } Causes control to transfer to the specified line when the specified period of time (n) in seconds has elapsed.	335
ON UEVENT GOSUB { linelabel / linenumber } Defines the event handler for a user-defined event.	QBS

STATEMENT	PAGE
OPEN <filespec> FOR <mode> AS <[#]filenumber> [LEN = recordlength] Allows a program to read or write records to a file. If record length is specified, then the file is opened as a random file. If the record length is not specified, then the file is opened as a sequential file.	200 and 364
OPTION BASE { 0 / 1 } Assigns a lower bound of 0 or 1 to all arrays declared with only an upper-bound value.	256
OUT <port>, <data> Sends a byte to a machine I/O port.	QBS
PAINT <(x, y)> [(,paint] [,boundary]] Paints an area on the screen with the selected color.	425
PALETTE [attribute, color] or PALETTE USING <arrayname> [(array index)] Changes one or more of the colors in the palette.	QBS
PCOPY <sourcepage> <destinationpage> Copies one screen page to another.	QBS
PEN(n) { ON / OFF / STOP } Enables or disables the PEN read function used to analyze light pen activity.	QBS
PLAY <string expression> Causes the PC to play music according to the value of the string expression.	439
PLAY { ON / OFF / STOP } Enables, disables, or suspends play event trapping.	QBS
POKE <address>, <byte> Writes a byte into a storage location.	QBS
PRESET <(x, y)>[,color] Draws a point in the color specified at (x, y). If no color is specified, it erases the point.	420
PRINT [item] [{, / ; / b} item]... Provides for the generation of output to the screen.	107
PRINT <#filenumber,> [item] [{, / ; / b} item]... Provides for the generation of output to a sequential file.	203
PRINT USING <string expression> <item> [{, / ; / b} item]... Provides for the generation of formatted output to the screen.	112 and 203

(QBasic Statements continued on page R.3 in left column)

MICROSOFT QBasic REFERENCE CARD

Summary of QBasic Statements (continued)

STATEMENT	PAGE
PRINT <#filenumber,> USING <string expression>> <item> [; ; b] item]... Provides for the generation of formatted output to a sequential file.	203
PSET <(x, y)> [,color] Draws a point in the color specified at (x, y).	420
PUT <(x₁, y₁), arrayname> [,action] Writes the colors of the points in the array onto an area of the screen.	436
PUT <[#filenumber] [,record number] Writes a record to a random file from a buffer defined by the corresponding FIELD statement.	368
RANDOMIZE [numeric expression] Reseeds a random number generator.	326
READ <variable> [,variable]... Provides for the assignment of values to variables from a sequence of data items created from DATA statements.	104
REDIM [SHARED] <arrayname(size)> [AS type] [arrayname(size)] [AS type]]... Changes the space allocated to an array declared $DYNAMIC.	QBS
{REM | '} [comment] Provides for the insertion of comments in a program.	31
RESET Closes all disk files.	QBS
RESTORE {linelabel | linenumber} Allows the data items in DATA statements to be reread.	106
RESUME {linelabel | NEXT | 0 | b} Continues program execution at the linelabel or the line following that which caused the error after an error-recovery procedure.	536
RETURN [linelabel | linenumber] Causes control to transfer from a subroutine back to the statement that follows the corresponding GOSUB or ON-GOSUB statement.	77
RMDIR <pathname> Removes a directory from disk after all files and subdirectories have been removed.	QBS
RSET <string variable> = <string expression> Moves string data right-justified into an area of a random file buffer that is defined by string variable.	QBS
RUN {linenumber | linelabel | b} Restarts the program in main memory.	QBS

STATEMENT	PAGE
SCREEN [model] [,color switch] [,active page] [,visual page] Sets the screen attributes for text mode, medium-resolution graphics, or high-resolution graphics.	402
SEEK <#filenumber> <position> Sets the position in a file for the next read or write.	QBS
SELECT CASE <testexpression> CASE <matchexpression> [range of statements₁] [CASE <matchexpression₂> [range of statements₂] . . . [range of statementsₙ] [CASE ELSE] END SELECT Causes execution of one of several ranges of statements depending on the value of testexpression.	171
SHARED <variable> [AS type] [,variable] [AS type]... Gives a SUB or FUNCTION procedure access to variables declared at the subprogram level without passing them as parameters.	460
SHELL [commandstring] Places the current QB session in a temporary wait state and returns control to operating system. Can also execute another program or operating system command as specified in commandstring.	QBS
SLEEP [seconds] Suspends execution of the calling program.	414
SOUND <frequency>, <duration> Causes the generation of sound through the PC's speaker.	438
STATIC <variablelist> Causes variables and arrays to be local to either a DEF FN, a FUNCTION, or a SUB, and maintains values between calls.	QBS
STOP Stops execution of a program. Unlike the END statement, files are left open.	QBS
STRIG [n] {ON|OFF|STOP} Enables or disables trapping of the joystick buttons.	QBS
SUB <globalname> [(parameterlist)] [STATIC] Establishes the beginning of a subprogram. The end of the subprogram is identified by the END SUB statement.	454
SWAP <variable₁>, <variable₂> Exchanges the values of two variables or two elements of an array.	269
SYSTEM Closes all open files and returns control to operating system.	QBS

STATEMENT	PAGE
TIME$ = hh[:mm[:ss]] Sets the system time, where hh = hours, mm = minutes, and ss = seconds.	314
TIMER {ON|OFF|STOP} Enables or disables trapping of timed events.	336
TROFF Disables statement tracing.	535
TRON Causes the PC to trace execution of program statements.	535
TYPE <labelname> <fieldname1> AS <fieldtype> . . . <fieldnamen> AS <fieldtype> END TYPE Creates user-defined data types containing one or more elements.	366
UEVENT {ON|OFF|STOP} Enables, disables, or suspends user-defined event trapping.	QBS
UNLOCK <#filenumber>, {record | [start] TO end} Unlocks records in a file.	QBS
VIEW [SCREEN] [(x₁, y₁) - (x₂, y₂) [,color] [,boundary] Defines a viewport.	434
VIEW PRINT [topline TO bottomline] Establishes boundaries for the screen text viewport.	QBS
WEND Identifies the end of a While loop.	156
WHILE <condition > Identifies the beginning of a While loop. Causes the statements between WHILE and WEND to be executed repeatedly while the condition is true.	156
WIDTH {40|80} Erases the information on the screen, sets the width of the line on the screen to 40 or 80 characters, and places the cursor in the upper left corner of the screen.	QBS
WIDTH LPRINT <width> Sets the printer column width.	403
WINDOW [SCREEN] [(x₁, y₁) - (x₂, y₂) Redefines the coordinates of a viewport. Allows you to draw objects in space and not be bounded by the limits of the screen.	403
WRITE [expression list] Writes data to the screen.	431

(QBasic Statements continued on page R.4 in left column)

MICROSOFT QBasic REFERENCE CARD

Summary of QBasic Statements (continued)

STATEMENT	PAGE
WRITE <#filenumber,> [item] [{;|,} item]... Writes data to a sequential file. Causes the PC to insert commas between the items written to the sequential file.	207

Summary of QBasic Functions

FUNCTION	PAGE
ABS(N) Returns the absolute value of n.	317
ASC(X$) Returns a two-digit numeric value that is equivalent in ASCII code to the first character of the string argument X$.	305
ATN(N) Returns the angle in radians whose tangent is the value of the argument N.	322
CDBL(N) Returns N converted to a double-precision value.	QBS
CHR$(N) Returns a single string character that is equivalent in ASCII code to the numeric argument N.	305
CINT(N) Converts n to an integer.	317
CLNG(N) Returns N converted to a long integer after rounding the fractional part of N.	QBS
COMMAND$ Returns the command line used to start the program.	QBS
COS(N) Returns the cosine of the argument N where N is in radians.	322
CSNG(N) Returns N converted to a single-precision value.	QBS
CSRLIN Returns the vertical (row) coordinate of the cursor.	322
CVI(X$), CVL(X$), CVS(X$), CVD(X$), Returns the integer, long integer, single-precision, or double-precision numeric value equivalent to the string X$. Used with random files.	QBS
DATE$ Returns the current date (mm-dd-yyyy).	310
EOF(filenumber) Returns -1 (true) if the end-of-file has been sensed on the sequential file associated with filenumber. Returns 0 (false) if the end-of-file has not been sensed.	212
ERDEV Returns an error code from the device that caused an error.	QBS
ERDEV$ Returns a string expression containing the name of the device that generated a vital error.	QBS
ERL Returns the line number preceding the line that caused the error. If no line numbers are used, then ERL returns a zero.	536
ERR Returns the error code for the last error that occurred.	536
EXP(N) Returns e(2.718281...) raised to the argument N.	318
FILEATTR Returns the file mode for an open file.	QBS
FIX(N) Returns the value of N truncated to an integer.	317
FRE(N) Returns the amount of available stack space (N = -2), string space (N not equal to -1 or -2), or size in bytes of the largest array you can create (N = -1).	QBS
FREEFILE Returns the next free QBasic file number.	317
HEX$(N) Returns the hexadecimal value of N.	QBS
INKEY$ Reads the last character entered from the keyboard.	QBS
INP(N) Returns the byte read from an I/O port N.	QBS
INPUT$(N) Suspends execution of the program until a string of N characters is received from the keyboard.	322
INPUT$(N,[#]filenumber) Returns a string of characters from the specified file.	QBS
INSTR(P, X$, S$) Returns the beginning position of the substring S$ in string X$. P indicates the position at which the search begins in the string X$.	322
INT(N) Returns the largest integer that is less than or equal to the argument N.	70
LBOUND(arrayname [,dimension]) Returns the lower-bound value for the specified dimension of arrayname.	303
LCASE$(X$) Returns X$ in all lowercase letters.	306
LEFT$(X$, N) Returns the left-most N characters of the string argument X$.	300
LEN(X$) Returns the length of the string argument X$.	72
LOC(#filenumber) With a random file, if returns the number of the last record read or written. With a sequential file, it returns the number of records read from or written to the file.	368
LOF(#filenumber) Returns the number of bytes allocated to a file.	368
LOG(N) Returns the natural log of the argument N where N is greater than 0.	318
LPOS(N) Returns the current position of the line printer's print head within the printer buffer where N is equal to 1 for LP1, 2 for LPT2, and so on.	QBS
LTRIM$(X$) Returns X$ with leading spaces removed.	309
MID$(X$, P, N) Returns N characters of the string argument X$ beginning at position P.	300
MKI$(N), MKL$(N), MKS$(N), MKD$(N) Returns the string equivalent of an integer, long integer, singleprecision, or double-precision value. Used with random files.	QBS
OCT$(N) Returns the octal equivalent of N.	QBS
PEEK(address) Returns the value at address.	QBS
PEN(N) Returns light pen coordinate information. The information is dependent on the value assigned to N.	QBS
PLAY(N) Returns the number of notes currently in the music background buffer.	QBS
PMAP(c, n) Returns the world coordinate of the physical coordinate c or vice versa. The parameter n varies between 0 and 3, and determines whether c is an x or y coordinate, and whether the coordinate is to be mapped from the physical to the world coordinate or vice versa.	432
POINT {(x, y)|(n)} With the argument (x, y), the PC returns the foreground color attribute of the point (x, y). With the argument n, the PC returns the physical or world x or y coordinate of the last point referenced. The parameter n varies in the range 0 to 3.	432

(QBasic Functions continued on page R.5 in left column)

MICROSOFT QBasic REFERENCE CARD

Summary of QBasic Functions (continued)

FUNCTION	PAGE	
POS(0)	322	Returns the current position of the cursor on the screen.
RIGHT$(X$, N)	300	Returns the right-most N characters of the string argument X$.
RND(N)	324	Returns a random number between 0 and 1.
RTRIM$(X$)	309	Returns X$ with trailing spaces removed.
SCREEN(row, column)	322	Returns the ASCII code for the character at the specified row (line) and column on the screen.
SEEK(filenumber)	QBS	Returns the current file position.
SGN(N)	317	Returns the sign of the argument N: -1 if the argument N is less than 0; 0 if the argument N is equal to 0; or +1 if the argument N is greater than 0.
SIN(N)	322	Returns the sine of the argument N where N is in radians.
SPACE$(N)	309	Returns a string of N spaces.
SPC(N)	110	Displays N spaces. Can be used only in an output statement such as PRINT or LPRINT.
SQR(N)	70	Returns the square root of the positive argument N.
STICK(N)	QBS	Returns the x and y coordinates of joystick N.
STR$(N)	308	Returns the string equivalent of the numeric argument N.
STRIG(n)	QBS	Returns the status of the joystick buttons.
STRING$(N, X$)	309	Returns N times the first character of X$.
TAB(N)	109	Causes the PC to tab over to position N on the output device. Can be used only in an output statement such as PRINT or LPRINT.
TAN(N)	322	Returns the tangent of the argument N where N is in radians.
TIMER	323	Returns a value that is equal to the number of seconds elapsed since midnight.

FUNCTION	PAGE	
TIME$	310	Returns the current time (hh:mm:ss).
UBOUND(arrayname [,dimension])	266	Returns the upper-bound value for the specified dimension of arrayname.
UCASE$(X$)	306	Returns X$ in all uppercase letters.
VAL(X$)	308	Returns the numeric value of string (X$).
VARPTR(variablename)	QBS	Returns the storage address of variablename.
VARPTR$(variablename)	428	Returns a string representation of the storage address of variablename for use in DRAW and PLAY statements.

Summary of All Operators

ORDER OF PRECEDENCE	OPERATOR	SYMBOL	PAGE
Highest	Arithmetic	^	
		+ or - (Unary + or - sign)	
		* or /	
		\	
		MOD	23
		+ or - (Binary + or - sign)	
	Concatenation	+	71
	Relational	=, >, >=, <, <=, or <>	102
	Logical	NOT	160
		AND	
		OR or XOR	
		EQV	
Lowest		IMP	

Summary of Command Line Options

For the desired effect, append one or more of the following to the QB command when you enter QBasic.

OPTION	FUNCTION	PAGE
/ah	Permits arrays to exceed 64 KB.	309
/b	Designates monochrome display.	
/csize	Sets the size of the communications port buffer.	
/cmd str	Passes the string str to the COMMAND$ function.	322
file	Loads and displays the QBasic program file.	323

OPTION	PAGE	FUNCTION
/g		Designates faster video output.
/h	310	Designates maximum resolution for the video device.
/l[lib]	266	Loads the specified library or QB QLB if lib is omitted.
/mbf	306	Causes conversion functions to treat IEEE format numbers as Microsoft binary format numbers.
/nohi	308	Allows monitor that does not support high intensity.
/run file	QBS	Loads and executes the QBasic program file before displaying it.

Limits to QBasic

Variable	MAXIMUM	MINIMUM
Variable name	40 characters	1 character
String length	32,767 characters	0 characters
Array dimensions	60	1
Array subscript value	32,767	-32,768
Integers	32,767	-32,768
Long integers	2,147,483,647	-2,147,483,648
Single precision (+)	3.402823E+38	1.401298E-45
Single precision (-)	-1.401298E-45	-3.402823E+38
Double precision (+)	1.797693134862315D+308	4.940656458412465D-324
Double precision (-)	4.940656458412465D-324	1.797693134862315D+308

Variable Type Definition

APPEND CHARACTER	DECLARATION
%	Integer variable
&	Long integer variable
!	Single-precision variable
#	Double-precision variable
$	String variable

QBasic Character Set

The QBasic character set consists of numeric characters, alphabetic characters, and special characters as described in Table D.1 of Appendix D on page 544.

MICROSOFT QBasic REFERENCE CARD

Cursor Movement Keys

KEYS	FUNCTION
←	Character left
→	Character right
↓	Down one line
↑	Up one line
Ctrl+←	Word left
Ctrl+→	Word right
Ctrl+End	End of program
Ctrl+Enter	Beginning of next line
Ctrl+Home	Beginning of program
Ctrl+Q+E	Top of window
Ctrl+Q+S	Beginning of current line
Ctrl+Q+N	Bottom of window
End	End of line
Home	First indent of current line
Tab	Tab to next tab setting

Scroll Keys

KEYS	FUNCTION	KEYS	FUNCTION
Ctrl+↓	Line down	Page Up	Page up
Ctrl+↑	Line up	Ctrl+Page Down	Left one full screen
Page Down	Page down	Ctrl+Page Up	Right one full screen

Execution and Debugging Keys

KEYS	FUNCTION
F5	Continues execution from current statement.
Shift+F5	Starts execution from beginning.
F7	Executes program to cursor.
F8	Executes next program statement.
Shift+F8	Traces execution history backward.
F9	Toggles the Debug menu Breakpoint command.
Shift+F9	Instant watch.
F10	Single step, tracing around a procedure call.
Shift+F10	Traces execution history forward.

View Keys

KEYS	FUNCTION
F2	Displays list of SUBs, modules, and files.
Shift+F2	Displays the next procedure.
Ctrl+F2	Displays previous procedure.
F4	Toggles between view window and output screen.
F6	Makes next window the active one.
Shift+F6	Makes previous window the active one.
Alt+Minus	Decreases size of window.
Alt+Plus	Increases size of window.

Help Keys

KEYS	FUNCTION
F1	Displays Help on the item in which the cursor is located.
Shift+F1	Displays help on Help.
Alt+F1	Displays previously requested Help topic.
Ctrl+F1	Displays next Help topic in Help file.
Shift+Ctrl+F1	Displays previous Help topic in Help file.
Alt+H	Displays help through Help menu commands.
Esc	Clears help from the screen.
Letter	Moves cursor to Help-topic title beginning with letter entered.
Shift+Letter	Moves cursor to previous Help-topic title beginning with letter entered.
Tab	Moves cursor to next Help-topic title in Help screen.
Shift+Tab	Moves cursor to previous Help-topic title in Help screen.

Insert and Copy Keys

KEYS	FUNCTION
Insert	Toggles insert or overtype.
Ctrl+Insert	Copies selection to Clipboard and keeps.
Shift+Insert	Inserts contents of Clipboard.
Shift+Delete	Copies selection to Clipboard and deletes.
Ctrl+Y	Copies current line to Clipboard and deletes.
Ctrl+Q+Y	Copies from cursor to end of line to Clipboard and deletes.

Search Keys

KEYS	FUNCTION
F3	Repeats the last find.
Ctrl+\	Searches for selected (highlighted) text.

Selection (Highlight) Keys

KEYS	FUNCTION
Shift+←	Character left
Shift+→	Character right
Shift+Ctrl+→	Word right
Shift+Ctrl+←	Word left
Shift+↓	Current line
Shift+↑	Line above
Shift+PgDn	Screen down
Shift+PgUp	Screen up
Shift+Ctrl+Home	To beginning of program
Shift+Ctrl+End	To end of program

Delete Keys

KEYS	FUNCTION
Backspace	Deletes character to left.
Ctrl+T	Deletes rest of word.
Delete	Deletes character at cursor or selected text.
Shift+Tab	Deletes leading spaces from selected lines.

Reserved Words

ABS	END	LPOS	SEEK
ACCESS	ENDIF	LPRINT	SEG
ALIAS	ENVIRON	LSET	SELECT
AND	ENVIRON$	LTRIM$	SETMEM
APPEND	EOF	MID$	SGN
AS	EQV	MKD$	SHARED
ASC	ERASE	MKDIR	SHELL
ATN	ERDEV	MKDMBF$	SIGNAL
BASE	ERDEV$	MKI$	SIN
BEEP	ERL	MKL$	SINGLE
BINARY	ERR	MKS$	SLEEP
BLOAD	ERROR	MKSMBF$	SOUND
BSAVE	EXIT	MOD	SPACE$
CALL	EXP	NAME	SPC
CALLS	FIELD	NEXT	SQR
CASE	FILEATTR	NOT	STATIC
CDBL	FILES	OCT$	STEP
CDECL	FIX	OFF	STICK
CHAIN	FOR	ON	STOP
CHDIR	FRE	OPEN	STR$
CHR$	FREEFILE	OPTION	STRIG
CINT	FUNCTION	OR	STRING
CIRCLE	GET	OUT	STRING$
CLEAR	GOSUB	OUTPUT	SUB
CLOSE	GOTO	PAINT	SWAP
CLS	HEX$	PALETTE	SYSTEM
COLOR	IF	PCOPY	TAB
COM	IMP	PEEK	TAN
COMMAND$	INKEY$	PEN	THEN
COMMON	INP	PLAY	TIMER
CONST	INPUT	PMAP	TIME$
COS	INPUT$	POINT	TO
CSNG	INSTR	POKE	TROFF
CSRLIN	INT	POS	TRON
CVD	INTEGER	PRESET	TYPE
CVDMBF	IOCTL	PRINT	UBOUND
CVI	IOCTL$	PRINT#	UCASE$
CVL	IS	PSET	UNLOCK
CVS	KEY	PUT	UNTIL
CVSMBF	KILL	RANDOM	USING
DATA	LBOUND	RANDOMIZE	VAL
DATE$	LCASE$	READ	VARPTR
DECLARE	LEFT$	REDIM	VARPTR$
DEF	LEN	REM	VARSEG
DEFDBL	LET	RESET	VIEW
DEFINT	LINE	RESTORE	WAIT
DEFLNG	LIST	RESUME	WEND
DEFSNG	LOC	RETURN	WHILE
DEFSTR	LOCAL	RIGHT$	WIDTH
DIM	LOCATE	RMDIR	WINDOW
DO	LOCK	RND	WRITE
DOUBLE	LOF	RSET	WRITE#
DRAW	LOG	RUN	XOR
ELSE	LONG	SADD	
ELSEIF	LOOP	SCREEN	